INSIDE THE JAVA VIRTUAL MACHINE

# McGRAW-HILL
# JAVA MASTERS TITLES

# Inside the Java Virtual Machine

**Bill Venners**

**McGraw-Hill**
New York • San Francisco • Washington, D.C. • Auckland
Bogotá • Caracas • Lisbon • London • Madrid • Mexico City
Milan • Montreal • New Delhi • San Juan • Singapore
Sydney • Tokyo • Toronto

**Library of Congress Cataloging-in-Publication Data**

Venners, Bill.
    Inside the Java virtual machine / Bill Venners
        p.    cm.—(Java masters series)
    Includes index.
    ISBN 0-07-913248-0
    1. Java (Computer program language)   2. Java virtual machine.
  I. Title.  II. Series.
  QA76.73.J38V46  1998
  005.6—dc21                              97-41801
                                          CIP

## McGraw-Hill

*A Division of The McGraw·Hill Companies*

PN 067482-5
PART OF ISBN 0-07-913248-0

*The sponsoring editor for this book was Judy Brief and the production supervisor was Pamela Pelton. It was set in Century Schoolbook by Douglas & Gayle, Limited.*

*Printed and bound by R. R. Donnelley & Sons Company.*

McGraw-Hill books are available at special quantity discounts to use as premiums and sales promotions, or for use in corporate training programs. For more information, please write to Director of Special Sales, McGraw-Hill, 11 West 19th Street, New York, NY 10011. Or contact your local bookstore.

 This book is printed on recycled, acid-free paper containing a minimum of 50% recycled de-inked fiber.

Portions of this book were derived from articles written by Bill Venners and first published in the column "Under the Hood" of JavaWorld, a division of Web Publishing, Inc., June 1996 through October 1997.

# DEDICATION

*To my parents*

# CONTENTS

# Contents

# Contents

# Contents

# PREFACE

My primary goal in writing this book was to explain the Java Virtual Machine (and the software technologies upon which it is based) to Java programmers. Although the Java Virtual Machine incorporates technologies that had been tried and proven in other programming languages, prior to Java many of these technologies had not yet entered into common use. As a consequence, many programmers will be encountering these technologies for the first time as they begin to program in Java. Garbage collection, multithreading, exception handling, dynamic extension—even the use of a virtual machine itself—may be new to many programmers. The aim of this book is to help programmers understand how all these things work and, in the process, to help them become more adept at Java programming.

Another goal I had in mind as I wrote this book was to experiment a bit with the changing nature of text. Web pages have three interesting characteristics that differentiate them from paper-based text: They're dynamic (they can evolve over time), they're interactive (especially if you embed Java applets in them), and they're interconnected (you can easily navigate from one to another). Besides the traditional text and figures, this book includes several Java applets (in a mini-Web site on the CD-ROM) that serve as "interactive illustrations" of the concepts presented in the text. In addition, I maintain a Web site on the Internet that serves as a launching point for readers to find more (and more current) information on the topics covered in the book. This book is composed of all these components: Text, figures, interactive illustrations, and constantly evolving links to further reading.

Bill Venners
Sunnyvale, California
August, 1997

# ACKNOWLEDGMENTS

I'd like to thank Michael O'Connell, the Editor-in-Chief of *JavaWorld*, for giving me the opportunity to write about Java. I'd also like to thank Jill Steinberg and the rest of the gang at *JavaWorld* for all their help with my column.

Thanks to my agent, Laura Belt of Adler & Robin, who, after reading one of my *JavaWorld* columns, e-mailed me inquiring about whether I'd like to write a book and then phoned me within five minutes of my pressing the reply button.

I'd like to thank Brad Schepp for pushing my proposal through at McGraw-Hill and for getting me started.

Thanks to my local reviewers: Siew Chuah, Terrin Eager, Peter Eldredge, Steve Engle, Matt Gerrans, Mark Johnson, Barbara Laird, Steve Schmidt, and Anil Somani—all of whom read partial drafts of the manuscript. Your feedback and moral support were invaluable. Also, a special thanks goes to the Coffee Society of Cupertino, who cheerily welcomed my reviewers and me on many a Wednesday night, even though none of us were young and few of us pierced.

I'd also like to thank Ron Johnston, who over the course of several years gave me many opportunities to write C++, and who, during the course of my writing this book, gave me the opportunity to create and present my first Java seminar.

I'd like to thank Tim Lindolm and Jeff Rice, both of whom navigated through the entire manuscript in search of technical bugs.

Thanks to those at Douglas & Gayle who helped form my manuscript into the book you're holding: Ray Robinson, project manager; Kelly Dobbs, production manager; and Claudia Bell and Dennis Clay Hager, layout technicians.

Finally, I'd like to thank Judy Brief, my editor at McGraw-Hill, for all her assistance and patience as I wrestled with this project.

# INTRODUCTION

This book describes the Java Virtual Machine, the abstract computer on which all Java programs run. Through a combination of tutorial explanations, working examples, reference material, and applets that interactively illustrate the concepts presented in the text, this book provides an in-depth, technical survey of Java as a technology.

The Java programming language seems poised to be the next popular language for mainstream commercial software development, the next step after C and C++. One of the fundamental reasons Java is a likely candidate for this role is that Java's architecture helps programmers deal with emerging hardware realities. Java has features that the shifting hardware environment is demanding, features that are made possible by the Java Virtual Machine.

The evolution of programming languages has to a great extent been driven by changes in the hardware being programmed. As hardware has grown faster, cheaper, and more powerful, software has become larger and more complex. The migration from assembly languages to procedural languages, such as C, and to object-oriented languages, such as C++, was largely driven by a need to manage ever greater complexity—complexity made possible by increasingly powerful hardware.

Today the progression toward cheaper, faster, and more powerful hardware continues, as does the need for managing increasing software complexity. Building on C and C++, Java helps programmers deal with complexity by rendering impossible certain kinds of bugs that frequently plague C and C++ programmers. Java's inherent memory safety—garbage collection, lack of pointer arithmetic, and runtime checks on the use of references—prevents most memory bugs from ever occurring in Java programs. Java's memory safety makes programmers more productive and helps them manage complexity.

In addition, besides the ongoing increase in the capabilities of hardware, another fundamental shift is taking place in the hardware environment—the network. As networks interconnect more and more computers and devices, new demands are being made on software. With the rise of the network, platform independence and security have become more important than they were in the past.

The Java Virtual Machine is responsible for the memory safety, platform independence, and security features of the Java programming language. Although virtual machines have been around for a long time, prior to Java they hadn't quite entered the mainstream. But given today's emerging hardware realities, software developers needed a programming language with a virtual machine, and Sun hit the market window with Java.

Thus, the Java Virtual Machine embodies the right software "stuff" for the coming years of computing. This book will help you get to know this virtual machine, and armed with this knowledge, you'll know how best to put the Java Virtual Machine to use in your programs.

# Who Should Read the Book

This book is aimed primarily at professional software developers and students who want to understand Java technology. I assume you are familiar, though not necessarily proficient, with the Java language. Reading this book should help you add depth to your knowledge of Java programming. If you are one of the elite few who are actually writing Java compilers or creating implementations of the Java Virtual Machine, this book can serve as a companion to the Java Virtual Machine specification. Where the specification specifies, this book explains.

# How to Use the Book

This book has five basic parts:

1. An introduction to Java's architecture (Chapters 1 through 4)
2. An in-depth, technical tutorial of Java internals (Chapters 5 through 20)
3. A class file and instruction set reference (Chapter 6, Appendices A through C)
4. Interactive illustrations, sample source code, and the JDK (on the CD-ROM)
5. The *Resources Web Site* (`http://www.artima.com/insidejvm`)

## An Introduction to Java's Architecture

Chapters 1 through 4 (Part One of this book) give an overview of Java's architecture, including the motivations behind—and the implications of —Java's architectural design. These chapters show how the Java Virtual

Machine relates to the other components of Java's architecture: The class file, API, and language. If you want a basic understanding of Java as a technology, consult these chapters. Here are some specific points of interest from this portion of the book:

- For an overview of Java's architecture and a discussion of its inherent trade-offs, see Chapter 1, "Introduction to Java's Architecture."

- For a discussion of what "platform independence" really means, how Java's architecture supports it, and seven steps to take to create a platform-independent Java program, see Chapter 2, "Platform Independence."

- For a description of the security model built into Java's core architecture, including a tutorial explaining how to write a security-minded class loader, see Chapter 3, "Security."

- For a discussion of the new paradigm of network-mobile software, see Chapter 4, "Network Mobility."

# A Tutorial of Java Internals

Chapters 5 through 20 (Part Two of this book) give an in-depth technical description of the inner workings of the Java Virtual Machine. These chapters will help you understand how Java programs actually work. All the material in Part Two is presented in a tutorial manner, with lots of examples. Here are some specific points of interest from this portion of the book:

- For a comprehensive overview of the inner workings of the Java Virtual Machine, see Chapter 5, "The Java Virtual Machine."

- If you are parsing, generating, or simply peering into Java class files, see Chapter 6, "The Java Class File," for a complete tutorial and reference on the class file format.

- For a discussion of the lifetime of a class inside the Java Virtual Machine, including the circumstances in which classes can be unloaded, see Chapter 7, "The Lifetime of a Class."

- For a thorough explanation of Java's linking model, including a tutorial and examples on writing your own class loaders, see Chapter 8, "The Linking Model."

- For a discussion of garbage collection and finalization, and suggestions on how to use finalizers, see Chapter 9, "Garbage Collection."

▦ For a tutorial on the Java Virtual Machine's instruction set, read Chapters 10 through 20.

▦ For an explanation of monitors and how you can use them to write thread-safe Java code, see Chapter 20, "Thread Synchronization."

## A Class File and Instruction Set Reference

In addition to being a tutorial on the Java class file, Chapter 6, "The Java Class File," serves as a complete reference of the class file format. Similarly, Chapters 10 through 20 form a tutorial of the Java Virtual Machine's instruction set, and Appendices A through C serve as a complete reference of the instruction set. If you need to look up something, check out these chapters and the appendices.

## Interactive Illustrations, Sample Source Code, and the JDK

For most of this book's chapters, material associated with the chapter—such as sample code or simulation applets—appears on the CD-ROM.

The **applets** directory of the CD-ROM contains a mini-Web site, called the *Interactive Illustrations Web Site*. It includes 15 Java applets that illustrate the concepts presented in the text. These "interactive illustrations" form an integral part of this book. Eleven of the applets simulate the Java Virtual Machine executing bytecodes. The other applets illustrate garbage collection, two's-complement and IEEE 754 floating-point numbers, and the loading of class files. The applets can be viewed on any platform by any Java-capable browser. The source code for the simulation applets is also included on the CD-ROM.

The copyright notice accompanying the HTML, .java, and .class files for the *Interactive Illustrations Web Site* enables you to post the Web site on any network, including the Internet, providing you adhere to a few simple rules. For example, you must post the Web site in its entirety, you can't make any changes to it, and you can't charge people to look at it. The full text of the copyright notice is given later in this introduction.

All the sample source code shown in this book appears on the CD-ROM in both source and compiled (class files) form. If some sample code in the text strikes you as interesting (or dubious), you can try it out for yourself.

Most of the sample code is illustrative and not likely to be of much practical use besides helping you to understand Java. Nevertheless, you are free to cut and paste from the sample code, use it in your own programs, and distribute it in binary (such as Java class file) form. The full text of the copyright notice for the sample source code is shown later in this introduction.

Besides the interactive illustrations and sample source code, the CD-ROM contains one last item: A full distribution of version 1.1.3 of Sun's JDK. It is contained in the CD-ROM's `jdk` directory.

## The Resources Web Site

To help you find more information and keep abreast of changes, I maintain a *Resources Web Site* with links to further reading about the material presented in this book. You will find at least one "resources page" for each chapter in the book. The main URL of the Resources Web Site is `http://www.artima.com/insidejvm/index.html`. The URL for each chapter's individual resources page is given at the end of each chapter in the "The Resources Page" section.

# Chapter-by-Chapter Summary

**CHAPTER 1: INTRODUCTION TO JAVA'S ARCHITECTURE**   This chapter gives an introduction to Java as a technology. It gives an overview of Java's architecture, describes the reasons that Java is important, and looks at Java's pros and cons.

**CHAPTER 2: PLATFORM INDEPENDENCE**   This chapter shows how Java's architecture enables programs to run on any platform, describes the factors that determine the true portability of Java programs, and looks at the relevant trade-offs.

**CHAPTER 3: SECURITY**   This chapter gives an overview of the security model built into Java's core architecture.

**CHAPTER 4: NETWORK MOBILITY**   This chapter examines the new paradigm of network-mobile software heralded by the arrival of Java and shows how Java's architecture makes it possible.

**CHAPTER 5: THE JAVA VIRTUAL MACHINE**   This chapter gives a detailed overview of the Java Virtual Machine's internal architecture.

Accompanying the chapter on the CD-ROM is an applet named *Eternal Math* that simulates the Java Virtual Machine executing a short sequence of bytecodes.

**CHAPTER 6: THE JAVA CLASS FILE**   This chapter describes the contents of the class file, including the structure and format of the constant pool, and it serves as both a tutorial and a complete reference of the Java class file format. Accompanying the chapter on the CD-ROM is an applet, named *Getting Loaded*, that simulates the Java Virtual Machine loading a Java class file.

**CHAPTER 7: THE LIFETIME OF A CLASS**   This chapter follows the lifetime of a type (class or interface) from the type's initial entrance into the virtual machine to its ultimate exit. It describes the processes of loading, linking, and initialization; object instantiation, garbage collection, and finalization; and type finalization and unloading.

**CHAPTER 8: THE LINKING MODEL**   This chapter takes an in-depth look at Java's linking model. It describes constant pool resolution and shows how to write class loaders to enable a Java application to dynamically extend itself at runtime.

**CHAPTER 9: GARBAGE COLLECTION**   This chapter describes various garbage collection techniques and explains how garbage collection works in Java Virtual Machines. Accompanying this chapter on the CD-ROM is an applet, named *Heap of Fish*, that simulates a compacting, mark-and-sweep garbage-collected heap.

**CHAPTER 10: STACK AND LOCAL VARIABLE OPERATIONS**
This chapter describes the Java Virtual Machine instructions that focus most exclusively on the operand stack—those that push constants onto the operand stack, perform generic stack operations, and transfer values back and forth between the operand stack and local variables. Accompanying this chapter on the CD-ROM is an applet named *Fibonacci Forever* that simulates the Java Virtual Machine executing a method that generates the Fibonacci sequence.

**CHAPTER 11: TYPE CONVERSION**   This chapter describes the instructions that convert values from one primitive type to another. Accompanying the chapter on the CD-ROM is an apple, named *Conversion*

*Diversion* that simulates the Java Virtual Machine executing a method that performs type conversion.

**CHAPTER 12: INTEGER ARITHMETIC**  This chapter describes integer arithmetic in the Java Virtual Machine. It explains two's-complement arithmetic and describes the instructions that perform integer arithmetic. Accompanying this chapter on the CD-ROM are two applets that interactively illustrate the material presented in the chapter. One applet, named *Inner Int*, allows you to view and manipulate a two's-complement number. The other applet, named *Prime Time*, simulates the Java Virtual Machine executing a method that generates prime numbers.

**CHAPTER 13: LOGIC**  This chapter describes the instructions that perform bitwise logical operations inside the Java Virtual Machine. These instructions include opcodes to perform shifting and Boolean operations on integers. Accompanying this chapter on the CD-ROM is an applet named *Logical Results* that simulates the Java Virtual Machine executing a method that uses several of the logic opcodes.

**CHAPTER 14: FLOATING-POINT ARITHMETIC**  This chapter describes the floating-point numbers and the instructions that perform floating-point arithmetic inside the Java Virtual Machine. Accompanying this chapter on the CD-ROM are two applets that interactively illustrate the material presented in the chapter. One applet, named *Inner Float*, allows you to view and manipulate the individual components that make up a floating-point number. The other applet, named *Circle of Squares*, simulates the Java Virtual Machine executing a method that uses several of the floating-point opcodes.

**CHAPTER 15: OBJECTS AND ARRAYS**  This chapter describes the Java Virtual Machine instructions that create and manipulate objects and arrays. Accompanying this chapter on the CD-ROM is an applet named *Three-Dimensional Array* that simulates the Java Virtual Machine executing a method that allocates and initializes a three-dimensional array.

**CHAPTER 16: CONTROL FLOW**  This chapter describes the instructions that cause the Java Virtual Machine to conditionally or unconditionally branch to a different location within the same method. Accompanying this chapter on the CD-ROM is an applet, named *Saying Tomato*, that simulates the Java Virtual Machine executing a method that includes bytecodes that perform table jumps (the compiled version of a Java `switch` statement).

**CHAPTER 17: EXCEPTIONS**    This chapter shows how exceptions are implemented in bytecodes. It describes the instruction for throwing an exception explicitly, explains exception tables, and shows how catch clauses work. Accompanying this chapter on the CD-ROM is an applet named *Play Ball!* that simulates the Java Virtual Machine executing a method that throws and catches exceptions.

**CHAPTER 18: Finally CLAUSES**    This chapter shows how **finally** clauses are implemented in bytecodes. It describes the relevant instructions and gives examples of their use. The chapter also describes some surprising behaviors exhibited by **finally** clauses in Java source code and explains this behavior at the bytecode level. Accompanying this chapter on the CD-ROM is an applet named *Hop Around* that simulates the Java Virtual Machine executing a method that includes **finally** clauses.

**CHAPTER 19: METHOD INVOCATION AND RETURN**    This chapter describes the four instructions that the Java Virtual Machine uses to invoke methods and the situations in which each instruction is used.

**CHAPTER 20: THREAD SYNCHRONIZATION**    This chapter describes monitors—the mechanism that Java uses to support synchronization—and shows how they are used by the Java Virtual Machine. It shows how one aspect of monitors, the locking and unlocking of data, is supported in the instruction set.

**APPENDIX A: INSTRUCTION SET BY OPCODE MNEMONIC**
This appendix lists the opcodes alphabetically by mnemonic. For each opcode, it gives the mnemonic, opcode byte value, instruction format (the operands, if any), a snapshot image of the stack before and after the instruction is executed, and a description of the execution of the instruction. Appendix A serves as the primary instruction set reference of the book.

**APPENDIX B: OPCODE MNEMONIC BY FUNCTION GROUP**
This appendix organizes the instructions by function group. The organization used in this appendix corresponds to the order the instructions are described in Chapters 10 through 20.

**APPENDIX C: OPCODE MNEMONIC BY OPCODE**    This appendix organizes the opcodes in numerical order. For each numerical value, this appendix gives the mnemonic.

**APPENDIX D: SLICES OF PI: A SIMULATION OF THE JAVA VIR-TUAL MACHINE**   This final appendix describes one final applet, *Slices of Pi*, that is part of the *Interactive Illustrations Web Site*. This applet simulates the Java Virtual Machine calculating pi.

# Copyright Notices

Here's the text of the copyright notice that appears in each of the sample source files (anything on the CD-ROM that isn't in either the `applets` or `jdk` directories):

The HTML pages (including the applets) and Java source files for the *Interactive Illustrations Web Site* (stored in the `applets` directory of the CD-ROM) all bear the following copyright notice:

a. All the Web pages and Java Applets (".html," ".gif," ".class," and ".java" files), including the source code, that are delivered in the **applets** directory of the CD-ROM that accompanies the book must be published together on the same Web site.

b. All the Web pages and Java Applets (".html," ".gif," ".class," and ".java" files) must be published "as is" and may not be altered in any way.

c. All use and access to this Web site must be free, and no fees can be charged to view these materials, unless express written permission is obtained from Bill Venners.

d. The Web pages and Java Applets may not be distributed on any media, other than a Web server on a network, and may not accompany any book or publication.

BILL VENNERS MAKES NO REPRESENTATIONS OR WARRANTIES ABOUT THE SUITABILITY OF THE SOFTWARE, EITHER EXPRESS OR IMPLIED, INCLUDING BUT NOT LIMITED TO THE IMPLIED WARRANTIES OF MERCHANTABILITY, FITNESS FOR PARTICULAR PURPOSE, OR NON-INFRINGEMENT. BILL VENNERS SHALL NOT BE LIABLE FOR ANY DAMAGES SUFFERED BY A LICENSEE AS A RESULT OF USING, MODIFYING OR DISTRIBUTING THIS SOFTWARE OR ITS DERIVATIVES.

# Some Terminology

In this book I've attempted to use terminology consistent with the Java Language and Java Virtual Machine specifications. In case you are not familiar with this terminology, I'd like to clarify a few terms up front.

First, in this book I have attempted to be meticulous about my use of the terms *type* and *class*. In Java jargon, variables and expressions have *type*. Objects and arrays have *class*. Every variable and expression in a Java program has a type that is known at compile-time, either a primitive type (**int**, **long**, **float**, **double**, and so on) or a reference type (a class, interface, or array). The type of a variable or expression determines the range and kind of values it can have, the operations it supports, and the meaning of those operations.

At runtime, every object and array has a class. Although an object is "an instance of" its class and all its superclasses, it "has" only one class. An object's class is either:

- the class mentioned in the class instance creation expression that created the object,

- the class represented by the **Class** object upon which **newInstance()** was invoked to create the object, or

- the class of the object upon which **clone()** was invoked to create the object.

Array classes have names like "**[D**" or "**[ [ [I**," which are not valid identifiers in the Java language. (Array class names are described in Chapter 6, "The Java Class File.") If at runtime a variable that has a reference type is not **null**, then that variable refers to an object whose *class* is compatible with the *type* of the variable.

To complicate the terminology situation a bit further, the specifications contain one other use of the term *type*. Because a variable can declare a class or interface as its type, classes and interfaces define new types for the program to use. (The ability to define new types is, of course, one of the fundamental concepts of object-oriented programming.) Throughout this book, I attempt to use the term *classes* to mean just classes (not classes and interfaces). Likewise, I use the term *interfaces* to mean just interfaces. When I want to refer to both, I sometimes say *classes and interfaces*, but often I just say *types*. For example, were I to say, "when the class loader loads a new *type* . . . ," I mean "when the class loader loads a new *class or interface* . . . ." In this sense, *type* does not refer to the compile-time notion of a variable's type, but to the new type that each class and interface definition represents.

The terms used by the Java specifications to describe the relationships between types (classes and interfaces) in an inheritance hierarchy are another set of terminology I'd like to clarify up front. Consider the inheritance hierarchy shown in Figure 0-1. In this figure, class **CockerSpaniel** extends class **Dog**, which extends class **Animal**, which extends class **Object**. In addition, interface **Friendly** extends interface **Happy**, and class **Dog** implements interface **Friendly**.

In Java terminology, classes above a class in an inheritance hierarchy are *superclasses*; classes below a class are *subclasses*. In Figure 0-1, **Dog**'s superclasses are **Animal** and **Object**, and **Dog** is a subclass of both **Animal** and **Object**. The superclass that is directly above a class in the inheritance hierarchy is the class's *direct superclass*. A subclass directly below a class is its *direct subclass*. For example, **Animal** is the direct superclass of **Dog**, and **CockerSpaniel** is a direct subclass of **Dog**.

This sub- and super- terminology can be applied to interfaces as well. For example, interfaces **Happy** and **Friendly** are *superinterfaces* of both

**Figure 0-1.**
*An inheritance hierarchy.*

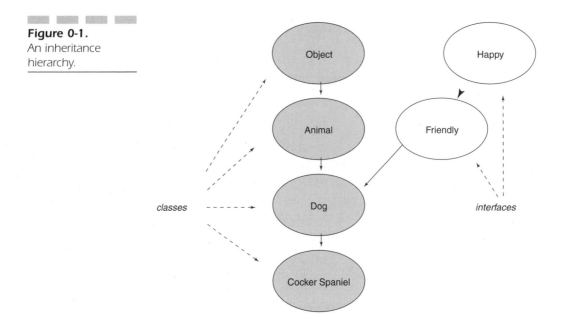

Dog and `CockerSpaniel`. Interface `Friendly` is a *direct superinterface* of `Dog` and a *direct subinterface* of `Happy`.

One last way to use the sub- and super- terminology is by grouping both classes and interfaces under the name *type*. In Figure 0-1, `Friendly`, `Dog`, and `CockerSpaniel` are *subtypes* of `Happy`. `Object`, `Animal`, `Happy`, `Friendly`, and `Dog` are all *supertypes* of `CockerSpaniel`.

# Font Conventions Used in this Book

Throughout this book, I use a fixed-width font for Java code and Java Virtual Machine opcode mnemonics. In the text, I use fixed-width font for Java language keywords only in certain cases, in an attempt to maximize readability. For example, I say public method instead of `public` method because in this case *public* is being used as a regular English adjective (in a sense of the word that is understood in Java circles), not necessarily as the Java keyword.

# Java Versions

The text of this book is current to JDK version 1.1, though little of the material covered by this book changed between 1.0 and 1.1. One change that occurred in JDK 1.0.2, a change of the semantics of the **invokespecial** instruction, is described in Chapter 19, "Method Invocation and Return," and in Appendix A, "Instruction Set by Opcode Mnemonic." Two attributes added to the class file format in 1.1 to support inner classes are described in Chapter 6, "The Java Class File." Also, the API of the **ClassLoader** class was extended in 1.1. Chapter 8, "The Linking Model," demonstrates the use of the 1.1 version of this API.

The bytecode examples shown throughout this book were generated by the **javac** compiler from various incarnations of Sun's JDK 1.1. Keep in mind that classes can be compiled in more than one way. Different compilers, even different versions of the same compiler, could generate different results.

The source code of the simulation applets (the interactive illustrations) adhere to Java version 1.0. As I discuss in Chapter 2, "Platform Independence," one of the realities of Java's platform independence promise is that you have to decide when a version of the Java Platform has been distributed widely enough to make it worthwhile to target that version. Although I had a 1.1 version of the Java Virtual Machine simulator applets working, when it came time to deliver the CD-ROM material to the publisher, I opted to drop the code back down to 1.0. At the time, neither Netscape Communicator nor Microsoft Internet Explorer fully supported 1.1. Because these applets are not sample source but are software products in their own right, I felt that releasing them in 1.1 didn't make sense. As a consequence, the applets will work in browsers that support either 1.0 or 1.1, and hopefully many versions into the future.

# Request for Comments

If you have a suggestion on how to improve this book or wish to report a bug or error, please visit **http://www.artima.com/insidejvm/feedback.html**. This page will give you instructions on how to submit your comments.

CHAPTER **1**

# Introduction to Java's Architecture

At the heart of Java technology lies the Java Virtual Machine—the abstract computer on which all Java programs run. Although the name *Java* is generally used to refer to the Java programming language, there is more to Java than the language. The Java Virtual Machine, Java API, and Java class file work together with the Java language to make the Java phenomenon possible.

The first four chapters of this book show how the Java Virtual Machine fits into the big picture. They show how the virtual machine relates to the other components of Java's architecture: the class file, API, and language. They describe the motivation behind—and the implications of —the overall design of Java technology.

This chapter gives an introduction to Java as a technology. It gives an overview of Java's architecture, describes the reasons that Java is important, and looks at Java's pros and cons.

# Why Java?

Over the ages people have used tools to help them accomplish tasks, but lately their tools have been getting smarter and interconnected. Microprocessors have appeared inside many commonly used items, and increasingly, they have been connected to networks. As the heart of personal computers and work stations, for example, microprocessors have been routinely connected to networks. They have also appeared inside devices with more specific functionality than the personal computer or the work station. Televisions, VCRs, audio components, fax machines, scanners, printers, cell phones, personal digital assistants, pagers, and wristwatches—all have been enhanced with microprocessors; most have been connected to networks.

Given the increasing capabilities and decreasing costs of information processing and data networking technologies, the network is rapidly extending its reach. The emerging infrastructure of smart devices and computers interconnected by networks represents a new environment for software—an environment that presents new challenges and offers new opportunities to software developers.

Java technology is a tool well suited to help you meet the challenges and seize the opportunities presented by the emerging computing environment. Java was designed for networks. Its suitability for networked environments is inherent in its architecture, which enables secure, robust, platform-independent programs to be delivered across networks and run on a great variety of computers and devices.

# The Challenges and Opportunities of Networks

One challenge presented to developers by a networked computing environment is the wide range of devices that networks interconnect. A typical network usually has many different kinds of attached devices, with diverse hardware architectures, operating systems, and purposes. Java addresses this challenge by enabling the creation of platform-independent programs. A single Java program can run unchanged on a wide range of computers and devices. Compared with programs compiled for a specific hardware and operating system, platform-independent programs written in Java can be easier and cheaper to develop, administer, and maintain.

Another challenge the network presents to software developers is security. In addition to their potential for good, networks represent an avenue for malicious programmers to steal or destroy information, steal computing resources, or simply be a nuisance. Virus writers, for example, can place their wares on the network for unsuspecting users to download. Java addresses the security challenge by providing an environment in which programs downloaded across a network can be run with customizable degrees of security. A downloaded program can do anything it wants inside the boundaries of the secure environment, but it can't read or write data outside those boundaries.

One aspect of security is simple program robustness. Java's architecture guarantees a certain level of program robustness by preventing certain types of pernicious bugs, such as memory corruption, from ever occurring in Java programs. This capability establishes trust that downloaded code will not inadvertently (or intentionally) crash, but it also has an important benefit unrelated to networks: it makes programmers more productive. Because Java prevents many types of bugs from ever occurring, Java programmers need not spend time trying to find and fix them.

One opportunity created by an omnipresent network is on-line software distribution. Java takes advantage of this opportunity by enabling the transmission of binary code in small pieces across networks. This capability can make Java programs easier and cheaper to deliver than programs that are not network-mobile. It can also simplify version control. Because the most recent version of a Java program can be delivered on-demand across a network, you needn't worry about what version your end users are running. They will always get the most recent version each time they use your program.

Platform independence, security, and network mobility—these three facets of Java's architecture work together to make Java suitable for the emerging networked computing environment. Because Java programs are platform independent, network delivery of software is more practical. The same version of a program can be delivered to all the computers and devices the network interconnects. Java's built-in security framework also helps make network delivery of software more practical. By reducing risk, the security framework helps to build trust in a new paradigm of network-mobile code.

# The Architecture

Java's architecture arises out of four distinct but interrelated technologies, each of which is defined by a separate specification from Sun Microsystems:

- the Java programming language
- the Java class file format
- the Java Application Programming Interface
- the Java Virtual Machine

When you write and run a Java program, you are tapping the power of these four technologies. You express the program in source files written in the Java programming language, compile the source to Java class files, and run the class files on a Java Virtual Machine. When you write your program, you access system resources (such as I/O, for example) by calling methods in the classes that implement the Java Application Programming Interface, or Java API. As your program runs, it fulfills your program's Java API calls by invoking methods in class files that implement the Java API. You can see the relationship among these four parts in Figure 1-1.

Together, the Java Virtual Machine and Java API form a "platform" for which all Java programs are compiled. In addition to being called the *Java runtime system*, the combination of the Java Virtual Machine and Java API is called the *Java Platform*. Java programs can run on many different kinds of computers because the Java Platform can itself be implemented in software. As you can see in Figure 1-2, a Java program can run anywhere the Java Platform is present.

## The Java Virtual Machine

At the heart of Java's network orientation is the Java Virtual Machine, which supports all three prongs of Java's network-oriented architecture: platform independence, security, and network mobility.

The Java Virtual Machine is an abstract computer. Its specification defines certain features every Java Virtual Machine must have but leaves many choices to the designers of each implementation. For example, although all Java Virtual Machines must be able to execute Java bytecodes, they can use any technique to execute them. Also, the specification is flexible enough to allow a Java Virtual Machine to be implemented either completely in software or to varying degrees in hardware. The flexible nature of the Java Virtual Machine's specification enables it to be implemented on a wide variety of computers and devices.

A Java Virtual Machine's main job is to load class files and execute the bytecodes they contain. As you can see in Figure 1-3, the Java Virtual Machine contains a *class loader*, which loads class files from both the

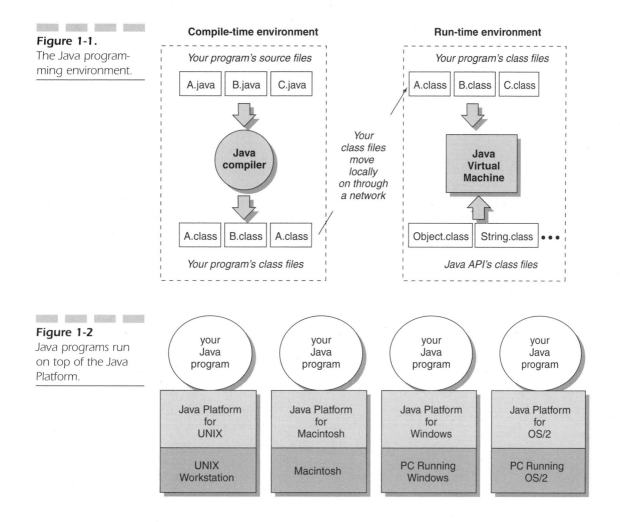

**Figure 1-1.**
The Java programming environment.

**Figure 1-2**
Java programs run on top of the Java Platform.

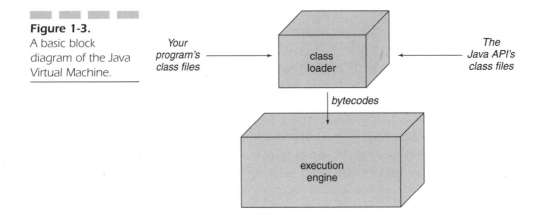

**Figure 1-3.**
A basic block
diagram of the Java
Virtual Machine.

program and the Java API. Only those class files from the Java API that are actually needed by a running program are loaded into the virtual machine. The bytecodes are executed in an *execution engine*, which is one part of the virtual machine that can vary in different implementations. On a Java Virtual Machine implemented in software, the simplest kind of execution engine just interprets the bytecodes one at a time. Another kind of execution engine, one that is faster but requires more memory, is a *just-in-time compiler*. In this scheme, the bytecodes of a method are compiled to native machine code the first time the method is invoked. The native machine code for the method is then cached, so it can be reused the next time that same method is invoked. On a Java Virtual Machine built on top of a chip that executes Java bytecodes natively, the execution engine is actually embedded in the chip.

Sometimes the Java Virtual Machine is called the *Java interpreter*; however, given the various ways in which bytecodes can be executed, this term can be misleading. Although "Java interpreter" is a reasonable name for a Java Virtual Machine that interprets bytecodes, virtual machines also use other techniques (such as just-in-time compiling) to execute bytecodes. Therefore, although all Java interpreters are Java Virtual Machines, not all Java Virtual Machines are Java interpreters.

When running on a Java Virtual Machine that is implemented in software on top of a host operating system, a Java program interacts with the host by invoking *native methods*. Java has two kinds of methods: Java and native. A Java method is written in the Java language, compiled to bytecodes, and stored in class files. A native method is written in some other language, such as C, C++, or assembly, and compiled to the native machine code of a particular processor. Native methods are stored in a dynamically linked library whose exact form is platform specific. Whereas

Java methods are platform independent, native methods are not. When a running Java program calls a native method, the virtual machine loads the dynamic library that contains the native method and invokes it. As you can see in Figure 1-4, native methods are the connection between a Java program and an underlying host operating system.

You can use native methods to give your Java programs direct access to the resources of the underlying operating system. Their use, however, will render your program platform specific because the dynamic libraries containing the native methods are platform specific. In addition, the use of native methods may render your program specific to a particular implementation of the Java Platform. One native method interface—*the Java Native Interface*, or *JNI*—enables native methods to work with any Java Platform implementation on a particular host computer. Vendors of the Java Platform, however, are not required to support JNI. They might provide their own proprietary native method interfaces in addition to (or in place of) JNI.

Java gives you a choice. If you want to access resources of a particular host that are unavailable through the Java API, you can write a platform-specific Java program that calls native methods. If you want to keep your program platform independent, however, you must call only Java methods and access the system resources of the underlying operating system through the Java API.

**Figure 1-4.**
A Java Virtual Machine implemented in software on top of a host operating system.

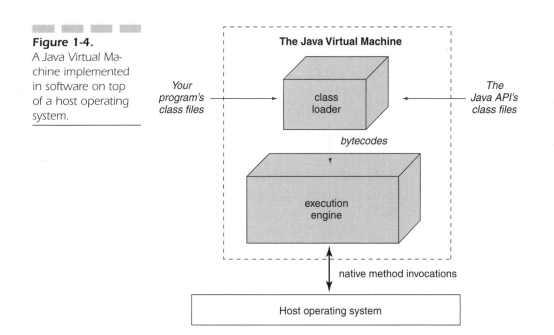

# The Class Loader Architecture

One aspect of the Java Virtual Machine that plays an important role in both security and network mobility is the class loader architecture. In the block diagrams of Figures 1-3 and 1-4, a single mysterious cube identifies itself as "the class loader," but in reality more than one class loader may be included inside a Java Virtual Machine. Thus, the class loader cube of the block diagram actually represents a subsystem that might involve many class loaders. The Java Virtual Machine has a flexible class loader architecture that allows a Java application to load classes in custom ways.

A Java application can use two types of class loaders: a "primordial" class loader and class loader objects. The primordial class loader is part of the Java Virtual Machine implementation. (Each implementation has only one primordial class loader.) For example, if a Java Virtual Machine is implemented as a C program on top of an existing operating system, then the primordial class loader will be part of that C program. The primordial class loader loads trusted classes, including the classes of the Java API, usually from the local disk.

At runtime, a Java application can install class loader objects that load classes in custom ways, such as by downloading class files across a network. The Java Virtual Machine considers any class it loads through the primordial class loader to be trusted, regardless of whether the class is part of the Java API. Classes it loads through class loader objects, however, it views with suspicion; by default, it considers them to be untrusted. Whereas the primordial class loader is an intrinsic part of the virtual machine implementation, class loader objects are not. Instead, class loader objects are written in Java, compiled to class files, loaded into the virtual machine, and instantiated just like any other object. They are really just another part of the executable code of a running Java application. You can see a graphical depiction of this architecture in Figure 1-5.

Because of class loader objects, you don't have to know at compile-time all the classes that may ultimately take part in a running Java application. They enable you to dynamically extend a Java application at runtime. As it runs, your application can determine what extra classes it needs and load them through one or more class loader objects. Because you write the class loader in Java, you can load classes in any manner. You can download them across a network, get them out of some kind of database, or even calculate them on the fly.

For each class it loads, the Java Virtual Machine keeps track of which class loader—whether primordial or object—loaded the class. When a loaded class first refers to another class, the virtual machine requests the refer-

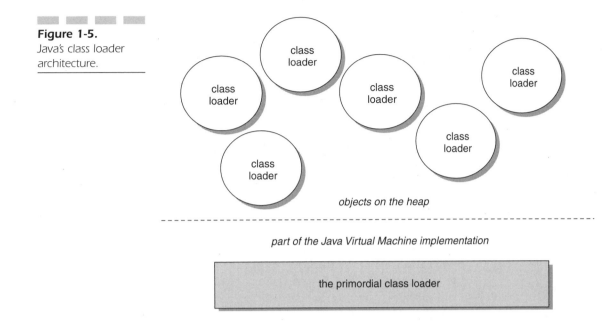

**Figure 1-5.**
Java's class loader architecture.

class loader

class loader

class loader

class loader

class loader

class loader

*objects on the heap*

*part of the Java Virtual Machine implementation*

the primordial class loader

enc*ed* class from the same class loader that originally loaded the referenc-*ing* class. For example, if the virtual machine loads class **Volcano** through a particular class loader, it will attempt to load any classes **Volcano** refers to through the same class loader. If **Volcano** refers to a class named **Lava**, perhaps by invoking a method in class **Lava**, the virtual machine will request **Lava** from the class loader object that loaded **Volcano**. The **Lava** class re-turned by the class loader is dynamically linked with class **Volcano**.

Because the Java Virtual Machine takes this approach to loading classes, classes can, by default, see only other classes that were loaded by the same class loader. This way, Java's architecture enables you to create multiple *name-spaces* inside a single Java application. Each class loader in your running Java program maintains its own name-space, which is populated by the names of all the classes it has loaded.

A Java application can instantiate multiple class loader objects either from the same class or from multiple classes. It can, therefore, create as many (and as many different kinds of) class loader objects as it needs. Classes loaded by different class loaders are in different name-spaces and cannot gain access to each other unless the application explicitly allows it. When you write a Java application, you can segregate classes loaded from different sources into dif-ferent name-spaces. In this way, you can use Java's class loader architecture to control any interaction between code loaded from different sources. You can prevent hostile code from gaining access to and subverting friendly code.

One example of dynamic extension is the web browser, which uses class loader objects to download the class files for an applet across a network. A web browser fires off a Java application that installs a class loader object—usually called *an applet class loader*—that knows how to request class files from an HTTP server. Applets are examples of dynamic extension, because the Java application doesn't know when it starts which class files the browser will ask it to download across the network. The class files to download are determined at runtime, as the browser encounters pages that contain Java applets.

The Java application started by the web browser usually creates a different applet class loader object for each location on the network from which it retrieves class files. As a result, class files from different sources are loaded by different class loader objects. They are placed into different name-spaces inside the host Java application. Because the class files for applets from different sources are placed in separate name-spaces, the code of a malicious applet is restricted from interfering directly with class files downloaded from any other source.

By allowing you to instantiate class loader objects that know how to download class files across a network, Java's class loader architecture supports network mobility. It supports security by allowing you to load class files from different sources through different class loader objects. This way, you can put the class files from different sources into different name-spaces, which allows you to restrict or prevent access between code loaded from different sources.

## The Java Class File

The Java class file helps make Java suitable for networks mainly in the areas of platform independence and network mobility. Its role in platform independence is serving as a binary form for Java programs that is expected by the Java Virtual Machine but independent of underlying host platforms. This approach breaks with the tradition followed by languages such as C or C++. Programs written in these languages are most often compiled and linked into a single binary executable file specific to a particular hardware platform and operating system. In general, a binary executable file for one platform won't work on another. The Java class file, by contrast, is a binary file that can be run on any hardware platform and operating system that hosts the Java Virtual Machine.

When you compile and link a C++ program, the executable binary file you get is specific to a particular target hardware platform and operating system because it contains machine language specific to the target processor. A Java compiler, by contrast, translates the instructions of the Java source files into bytecodes, the "machine language" of the Java Virtual Machine.

In addition to processor-specific machine language, another platform-dependent attribute of a traditional binary executable file is the byte order of integers. In executable binary files for the Intel X86 family of processors, for example, the byte order is *little-endian*, or lower order byte first. In executable files for the PowerPC chip, however, the byte order is *big-endian*, or higher order byte first. In a Java class file, byte order is big-endian irrespective of what platform generated the file and independent of whatever platforms may eventually use it.

In addition to its support for platform independence, the Java class file plays a critical role in Java's architectural support for network mobility. First, class files were designed to be compact, so they can more quickly move across a network. Also, because Java programs are dynamically linked and dynamically extensible, class files can be downloaded as needed. This feature helps a Java application manage the time it takes to download class files across a network, so the end user's wait time can be kept to a minimum.

## The Java API

The Java API helps make Java suitable for networks through its support for platform independence and security. The Java API is a set of runtime libraries that give you a standard way to access the system resources of a host computer. When you write a Java program, you assume the class files of the Java API will be available at any Java Virtual Machine that may ever have the privilege of running your program. This assumption is safe because the Java Virtual Machine and the class files for the Java API are the required components of any implementation of the Java Platform. When you run a Java program, the virtual machine loads the Java API class files that are referred to by your program's class files. The combination of all loaded class files (from your program and from the Java API) and any loaded dynamic libraries (containing native methods) constitutes the full program executed by the Java Virtual Machine.

The class files of the Java API are inherently specific to the host platform. The API's functionality must be implemented expressly for a particular platform before that platform can host Java programs. In a system in which bytecodes are executed directly in silicon (on a "Java chip"), the API will likely be implemented as part of a Java-based operating system. On a system in which the virtual machine is implemented in software on top of a non-Java operating system, the Java API will access the host resources through native methods. As you can see in Figure 1-6, the class files of the Java API invoke native methods so that your Java program doesn't have to. In this manner, the Java API's class files provide a Java program with a standard, platform-independent interface to the underlying host. To the Java program, the Java API looks the same and behaves predictably no matter what platform happens to be underneath. Precisely because the Java Virtual Machine and Java API are implemented specifically for each particular host platform, Java programs themselves can be platform independent.

The internal design of the Java API is also geared toward platform independence. For example, the graphical user interface library of the Java API, called the Abstract Windows Toolkit (or AWT), is designed to facilitate the creation of user interfaces that work on all platforms. Creating platform-independent user interfaces is inherently difficult, given that the native look and feel of user interfaces vary greatly from one platform to another. The AWT library's architecture does not coerce implementations of the Java API to give Java programs a user interface that looks exactly the same everywhere. Instead, it encourages implementations to adopt the look and feel of the underlying platform. Also, because the size of fonts, buttons, and other user interface components will vary from platform to platform, the AWT includes *layout managers* to position the ele-

**Figure 1-6.**
A platform-
independent Java
program.

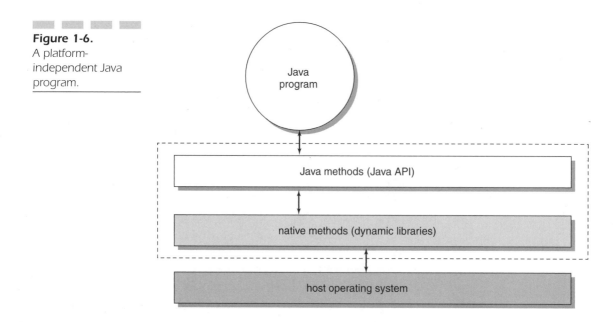

ments of a window or dialog box at runtime. Rather than force you to indicate exact $X$ and $Y$ coordinates for the various elements that constitute, say, a dialog box, the layout manager positions them when your dialog box is displayed. With the aim of making the dialog look its best on each platform, the layout manager will very likely position the dialog box elements slightly differently on different platforms. In these ways and others, the internal architecture of the Java API is aimed at facilitating the platform independence of the Java programs that use it.

In addition to facilitating platform independence, the Java API contributes to Java's security model. The methods of the Java API, before they perform any action that could potentially be harmful (such as writing to the local disk), check for permission from the *security manager*. The security manager, which is a special object that a Java application can instantiate, defines a custom security policy for the application. A security manager could, for example, forbid access to the local disk. If the application requested a local disk write by invoking a method from the Java API, that method would first check with the security manager. Upon learning from the security manager that disk access is forbidden, the Java API would refuse to perform the write. By enforcing the security policy established by the security manager, the Java API helps to establish a safe environment in which you can run potentially unsafe code.

## The Java Programming Language

Although Java was designed for the network, its utility is not restricted to networks. Platform independence, network mobility, and security are of prime importance in a networked computing environment, but you may not always find yourself facing network-oriented problems. As a result, you might not always want to write programs that are platform independent. You might not always want to deliver your programs across networks or limit their capabilities with security restrictions. Sometimes you may use Java technology primarily because you want to get the advantages of the Java programming language.

As a whole, Java technology leans heavily in the direction of networks, but the Java programming language is quite general purpose. The Java language allows you to write programs that take advantage of many software technologies:

- object-orientation
- multithreading

- structured error handling
- garbage collection
- dynamic linking
- dynamic extension

Instead of serving as a test bed for new and experimental software technologies, the Java language combines in a new way concepts and techniques that have already been tried and proven in other languages. These features make the Java programming language a powerful general-purpose tool that you can apply to a variety of situations, independent of whether they involve a network.

At the beginning of a new project, you may be faced with the question, "Should I use C++ (or some other language) for my next project, or should I use Java?" As an implementation language, Java has some advantages and some disadvantages over other languages. One of the most compelling reasons for using Java as a language is that it can enhance developer productivity. The main disadvantage is slower execution speed.

Java is, first and foremost, an object-oriented language. One promise of object orientation is that it promotes the reuse of code, resulting in better productivity for developers. This feature may make Java more attractive than a procedural language such as C, but it doesn't add much value to Java over C++, the object-oriented language that Java most closely resembles. Yet compared to C++, Java has some significant differences that can improve a developer's productivity. This productivity boost comes mostly from Java's restrictions on direct memory manipulation.

In Java, you cannot directly access memory by arbitrarily casting pointers to a different type or by using pointer arithmetic, as you can in C++. Java requires that you strictly obey rules of type when working with objects. If you have a *reference* (similar to a pointer in C++) to an object of type `Mountain`, you can manipulate it only as a `Mountain`. You can't cast the reference to type `Lava` and manipulate the memory as if it were a `Lava`. Neither can you simply add an arbitrary offset to the reference, as pointer arithmetic allows you to do in C++. You can, in Java, cast a reference to a different type, but only if the object really is of the new type. For example, if the `Mountain` reference actually referred to an instance of class `Volcano` (a specialized type of `Mountain`), you could cast the `Mountain` reference to a `Volcano` reference. Because Java enforces strict type rules at runtime, you cannot directly manipulate memory in ways that can accidentally corrupt it. As a result, you can't ever create certain kinds of bugs in Java programs that regularly harass C++ programmers and reduce their productivity.

Another way Java prevents you from inadvertently corrupting memory is through automatic garbage collection. Java has a **new** operator, just like C++, that you use to allocate memory on the heap for a new object. But unlike C++, Java has no corresponding **delete** operator, which C++ programmers use to free the memory for an object that is no longer needed by the program. In Java, you merely stop referencing an object, and at some later time, the garbage collector will reclaim the memory occupied by the object.

The garbage collector prevents Java programmers from needing to explicitly indicate which objects should be freed. As a C++ project grows in size and complexity, it often becomes increasingly difficult for programmers to determine when an object should be freed, or even whether an object has already been freed. This difficulty results in memory leaks, in which unused objects are never freed, and memory corruption, in which the same object is accidentally freed multiple times. Both kinds of memory troubles cause C++ programs to crash, but in ways that make tracking down the exact source of the problem difficult. You can be more productive in Java in part because you don't have to chase down memory corruption bugs. But perhaps more significantly, you can be more productive because when you no longer have to worry about explicitly freeing memory, program design becomes easier.

A third way Java protects the integrity of memory at runtime is array bounds checking. In C++, arrays are really shorthand for pointer arithmetic, which brings with it the potential for memory corruption. C++ allows you to declare an array of 10 items and then write to the 11th item, even though doing so tramples on memory. In Java, arrays are full-fledged objects, and array bounds are checked each time an array is used. If you create an array of 10 items in Java and try to write to the 11th, Java will throw an exception. Java won't let you corrupt memory by writing beyond the end of an array.

One final example of how Java ensures program robustness is by checking object references, each time they are used, to make sure they are not **null**. In C++, using a null pointer usually results in a program crash. In Java, using a null reference results in an exception being thrown.

The productivity boost you can get just by using the Java language results in quicker development cycles and lower development costs. You can realize further cost savings if you take advantage of the potential platform independence of Java programs. Even if you are not concerned about a network, you may still want to deliver a program on multiple platforms. Java can make support for multiple platforms easier and, therefore, cheaper.

As you might expect, however, all this good news about productivity, quick development cycles, and lower development costs does not come without a catch. The designers of Java made trade-offs. They designed an architecture that favors network-oriented features—such as platform independence, program robustness, security, and network mobility—over other concerns. The primary trade-off, and thus the primary hit you will take if you use Java, is execution speed.

Java's extra runtime housekeeping—array bounds checking, type-safe reference casting, checking for null references, and garbage collection—will cause your Java program to be slower than an equivalent C++ program. Yet often the trade-off in speed is made up for in productivity increases enjoyed by the developer and robustness enjoyed by the end user. And often, the Java program simply runs quickly *enough* to satisfy end users.

Another speed hit, and one that can be far more substantial, arises from the interpreted nature of Java programs. Whereas C++ programs are usually compiled to native machine code, which is stored in a monolithic executable file, Java programs are usually compiled to Java bytecodes, which are stored in class files. When the Java program runs, a virtual machine loads the class files and executes the bytecodes they contain. When running on a virtual machine that interprets bytecodes, a Java program may be 10 to 30 times slower than an equivalent C++ program compiled to native machine code.

This performance degradation is primarily a trade-off in exchange for platform independence. Instead of compiling a Java program to platform-specific native machine code, you compile it to platform-independent Java bytecodes. Native machine code can run fast, but only on the native platform. Java bytecodes (when interpreted) run slowly but can be executed on any platform that hosts the Java Virtual Machine.

Fortunately, other techniques can improve the performance of bytecode execution. For example, just-in-time compiling can speed up program execution 7 to 10 times over interpreting. Rather than merely interpret a method's bytecodes, a virtual machine can compile the bytecodes to native machine code the first time the method is invoked. (The method is compiled "just-in-time" for its first use by the virtual machine.) The native machine code version of the method is then cached by the virtual machine and reused the next time the method is invoked by the program. Execution techniques such as just-in-time compiling allow Java programs to be delivered as platform-independent class files and still, in many cases, run quickly enough to satisfy end users.

Raw execution speed is not always the most important factor determining an end user's perception of a program's performance. In some situations, programs spend much of their time waiting for data to come across a network or waiting for the user to press another key on the keyboard. In such cases, even executing the program via an interpreter may be adequate. For more demanding applications, a just-in-time compiler may be sufficient to satisfy the end user's need for speed.

The simulation applets incorporated into the later chapters of this book are examples of types of programs for which execution speed is not very critical. Most of time in these programs is spent waiting for the user to click a button. For many programs, however, execution speed is extremely important. For such programs, if you want to use the Java language, you may have to execute part or all of your program natively. One way to do so is to run the class files on a virtual machine built on top of a chip that executes bytecodes directly in silicon. If you (or your end users) don't have such a chip handy, another possibility is to identify time-critical portions of your program and implement them as native methods. Using native methods yields a program that is delivered as a combination of platform-independent class files and platform-specific dynamic libraries. The bytecodes from the class files are executed by interpreting or just-in-time compiling, but the time-critical code stored in the dynamic libraries is executed natively.

One final alternative is to compile the Java program to a platform-specific, monolithic native executable, as is usually done with C++ programs. Such a strategy bypasses class files entirely and generates a platform-specific binary. A monolithic native executable can be faster than the same program just-in-time compiled for several reasons. First, just-in-time compilers do not usually perform as much optimization as native compilers because of the time trade-off. When compiling a Java program to a monolithic native executable, you have plenty of time to spend performing optimization. When you are just-in-time compiling, however, time is more scarce. The whole point of just-in-time compiling is to speed up program execution on the fly, but at some stage the speedup gained by certain optimizations will not be worth the time spent doing the optimization. The just-in-time compiler also is slower than a native executable because the just-in-time compiled program will likely occupy a larger memory footprint. The larger footprint could require more paging (or swapping) on a virtual memory system.

So when you compile your Java program to a monolithic native executable, you give up binary platform independence in return for speed. In cases in which platform independence is not important to you, or speed is more important, compiling to a native executable can give you both fast execution and the productivity benefits of the Java language.

One way to get the best of both the platform-independence and speed-execution worlds is by install-time compiling. In this scheme, you deliver platform-independent class files, which are compiled at install time to a platform-specific, monolithic native executable. The binary form that you deliver (Java class files) is platform independent, but the binary form that the end user executes (a monolithic native executable) is platform specific. Because the translation from class files to native executable is done during installation on the end user's system, optimizations can be made for the user's particular system setup.

Java, therefore, gives you many options of program delivery and execution. Moreover, if you write your program in the Java language, you need not choose just one option. You can use several or all methods of program delivery and execution made possible by Java. You can deliver the same program to some users over a network, where they are executed via interpreting or just-in-time compiling. To other users, you can deliver class files that are install-time compiled. To still other users, you can deliver a monolithic native executable.

Although program speed is a concern when you use Java, you can address it in different ways. By appropriate use of the various techniques for developing, delivering, and executing Java programs, you can often satisfy end user's expectations for speed. As long as you can address the speed issue successfully, you can use the Java language and realize its benefits: productivity for the developer and program robustness for the end user.

## Architectural Trade-offs

Although Java's network-oriented features are desirable, especially in a networked environment, they did not come for free. They required trade-offs against other desirable features. Whenever a potential trade-off between desirable characteristics arose, the designers of Java made the architectural choice that made better sense in a networked world. Hence, Java is not the right tool for every job. It is suitable for solving problems that involve networks and has utility in many problems that don't involve networks, but its architectural trade-offs will disqualify it for certain types of jobs.

As mentioned before, one of the prime costs of Java's network-oriented features is the potential reduction in program execution speed compared to other technologies such as C++. Java programs can run slower than an equivalent C++ program for many reasons:

- Interpreting bytecodes is 10 to 30 times slower than native execution.
- Just-in-time compiling bytecodes can be 7 to 10 times faster than interpreting but still not quite as fast as native execution.
- Java programs are dynamically linked.
- The Java Virtual Machine may have to wait for class files to download across a network.
- Array bounds are checked on each array access.
- All objects are created on the heap (no objects are created on the stack).
- All uses of object references are checked at runtime for `null`.
- All reference casts are checked at runtime for type safety.
- The garbage collector is likely less efficient (though often more effective) at managing the heap than you could be if you managed it directly as in C++.
- Primitive types in Java are the same on every platform, rather than adjusting to the most efficient size on each platform as in C++.
- Strings in Java are always UNICODE. When you really need to manipulate just an ASCII string, a Java program will be slightly less efficient than an equivalent C++ program.

Although many of Java's speed hits are manageable through techniques such as just-in-time compiling, some—such as those that result from runtime checking—can't be eliminated even by compilation to a native executable. Still, you get something, such as platform independence or program robustness, for all the speed hits associated with Java programs. In many cases, the end user will not be able to perceive any speed deficit. In many other cases, the benefits of platform independence and improved program robustness will be worth the speed degradation. Sometimes, however, Java may be disqualified as a tool to help you solve a problem because that problem requires the utmost in speed, and Java can't deliver it.

Another trade-off is loss of control of memory management. Garbage collection can help make programs more robust and easier to design, but it adds a level of uncertainty to the runtime performance of the program. You can't always be sure when a garbage collector will decide to collect garbage nor how long it will take. This loss of control of memory management makes Java a questionable candidate for software problems that require a real-time response to events. Although you possibly can create a garbage collector that attempts to meet real-time requirements, for many real-time problems, robustness and platform independence are simply not important enough to justify using Java.

Still another trade-off arises from Java's goal of platform independence. One difficulty inherent in any API that attempts to provide cross-platform functionality is the lowest-common-denominator problem. Although a great deal of overlap exists between operating systems, each operating system usually has a handful of traits all its own. An API that aims to give programs access to the system services of any operating system has to decide which capabilities to support. If a feature exists on only one operating system, the designers of the API may decide not to include support for that feature. If a feature exists on most operating systems but not all, the designers may decide to support it anyway. This support will require an implementation of something similar in the API on operating systems that lack the feature. Both of these lowest-common-denominator kinds of choices may to some degree offend developers and end users on the affected operating systems.

What's worse, not only does the lowest-common-denominator problem afflict the designers of a platform-independent API, it also affects the designer of a program that uses that API. Consider a user interface, for example. The AWT attempts to give your program a user interface that adopts the native look on each platform. You might find it difficult, however, to design a user interface in which the components interact in a way that *feels* native on every platform, even though the individual components may have the native look. So on top of the lowest-common-denominator choices that were made when the AWT was designed, you might find yourself faced with your own lowest-common-denominator choices when you use the AWT.

One last trade-off stems from the dynamically linked nature of Java programs combined with the close relationship between Java class files and the Java programming language. Because Java programs are dynamically linked, the references from one class file to another are symbolic. In a statically linked executable, references between classes are direct pointers or offsets. Inside a Java class file, by contrast, a reference to another class spells out the name of the other class in a text string. If the reference is to a field, the field's name and *descriptor* (the field's type) are also specified. If the reference is to a method, the method's name and descriptor (the method's return type, number, and types of its arguments) are specified. Moreover, not only do Java class files contain symbolic references to the fields and methods of other classes, but they also contain symbolic references to their own fields and methods. Java class files also may contain optional debugging information that includes the names and types of local variables. A class file's symbolic information and the close relationship between the bytecode instruction set and the Java language make it quite easy to decompile Java class files back into Java source. This capability, in turn, makes it quite easy for your competitors to borrow heavily from your hard work.

Although it has always been possible for competitors to decompile a statically linked binary executable and glean insights into your program, by comparison decompilation is far easier with an intermediate (not yet linked) binary form such as Java class files. Decompilation of statically linked binary executables is more difficult not only because the symbolic information (the original class, field, method, and local variable names) is missing, but also because statically linked binaries are usually heavily optimized. The more optimized a statically linked binary is, the less it corresponds to the original source code. Still, if you have an algorithm buried in your binary executable, and it is worth the trouble to your competitors, they can peer into your binary executable and retrieve that algorithm.

Fortunately, you can combat the easy borrowing of your intellectual property: you can obfuscate your class files. Obfuscation alters your class files by changing the names of classes, fields, methods, and local variables, but without altering the operation of the program. Your program can still be decompiled but will no longer have the meaningful names you originally gave to all your classes, fields, methods, and local variables. For large programs, obfuscation can make the code that comes out of the decompiler so cryptic as to require nearly the same effort to steal your work as would be required by a statically linked executable.

## Future Trends

As Java matures, some of the trade-offs described in this chapter may change. One area in which you can expect improvement over time is in the execution speed of Java programs. Sun, for example, is currently working on a technology called "hot-spot compiling," which is a hybrid of interpreting and just-in-time compiling. The developers at Sun claim this technique will yield Java programs that run as fast as natively compiled C++. Although this claim seems rash, when you look at the approach, the fact that speeds very close to natively compiled C++ could be achievable makes sense.

As a programmer, you may sometimes be faced with the task of speeding up a program by looking through your code for ways to optimize. Often, programmers waste time optimizing code that is rarely executed when the program runs. The proper approach is usually to profile the program to discover exactly where the program spends most of its time. Programs often spend 80 or 90 percent of their time in 10 to 20 percent of the code. To be most effective, you should focus your optimization efforts on just the 10 to 20 percent of the code that really matters to execution speed.

In a sense, a Java Virtual Machine that does just-in-time compiling is like a programmer who spends time optimizing all the code in a program. Probably 80 to 90 percent of the time such a virtual machine spends just-in-time compiling is spent on code that runs only 10 to 20 percent of the time. Because all the code is just-in-time compiled, the memory footprint of the program grows much larger than that of an interpreted program, in which all the code remains in bytecode form. Also, because so much time is spent just-in-time compiling everything, the virtual machine doesn't have enough time left over to do a thorough job of optimization.

A Java Virtual Machine that does hot-spot compiling, by contrast, is like a programmer who profiles the code and optimizes only the code's time-critical portions. In this approach, the virtual machine begins by interpreting the program. As it interprets bytecodes, it analyzes the execution of the program to determine the program's "hot spot"—that part of the code where the program is spending most of its time. When it identifies the hot spot, the virtual machine just-in-time compiles only that part of the code that makes up the hot spot. As the program continues to run, the virtual machine continues to analyze it. If the hot spot moves, the virtual machine can just-in-time compile and optimize new areas as they move into the hot spot. Also, it can revert back to using bytecodes for areas that move out of the hot spot, to keep the memory footprint at a minimum.

Because only a small part of the program is just-in-time compiled, the memory footprint of the program remains small, and the virtual machine has more time to perform optimizations. On systems with virtual memory, a smaller memory footprint means less paging. On systems that lack virtual memory—such as many embedded devices—a smaller memory footprint may mean the difference between a program fitting or not fitting in memory at all. More time for optimizations yields hot-spot code that could potentially be optimized as much as natively compiled C++.

In the hot-spot compiling approach, the Java Virtual Machine loads platform-independent class files, just-in-time compiles and heavily optimizes only the most time-critical code and interprets the rest of the code. Such a program could spend 80 to 90 percent of its time executing native code that is optimized as heavily as natively compiled C++. At the same time, it could keep a memory footprint that is not much larger than a Java program that is 100 percent interpreted. It makes sense that a Java program running on such a virtual machine could achieve speeds very close to the speed of natively compiled C++.

If emerging technologies, such as hot-spot compiling, fulfill their promise, the speed trade-off of Java programs could eventually become much less significant. However, what execution speeds such technologies will actually be able to achieve remain to be seen. For links to the latest information about emerging virtual machine technologies, visit the resources page for this chapter.

Another area in which much work is being done is the user interface. One of the trade-offs listed in this chapter for writing platform-independent programs is the lowest-common-denominator problem. A major area in which this problem reveals itself is user interfaces. To provide a user-interface library that could map to native components on most platforms, Sun filled the AWT library in Java 1.0 and 1.1 with a lowest-common-denominator subset of components. The 1.0 AWT library included a button class, for example, because every platform had a native button. The library did not include more advanced components such as tab controls or spin controls, however, in part because of schedule constraints but also because these kinds of controls weren't native to enough platforms.

The Java programmer was faced with an AWT library that directly supported the creation of rather simple user interfaces. With work, however, the programmer could build a fancier user interface on top of the AWT primitives. Many third-party vendors built more advanced user interface libraries on top of AWT to help ease the programmer's burden. Microsoft's *Application Foundation Classes* (AFC) and Netscape's *Internet Foundation Classes* (IFC) are two good examples. These libraries add support for more advanced user-interface components and functionality to those directly supported by the AWT. They are, however, built on top of AWT, so programs that use them are still platform independent.

Sun has announced *Java Foundation Classes* (JFC), which is their approach to solving the lowest-common-denominator problem with the 1.0 and 1.1 AWT libraries. Rather than attempt to map more components to native counterparts, the Sun's strategy is to provide what they call "lightweight components." A lightweight component doesn't directly map to a native component. Instead, it is built out of the AWT primitives. So, for example, instead of providing a tab control that maps to a native tab control on each platform that supports one, JFC would provide a *Java Platform tab control*. When such a control is used on Windows 95, which supports tab controls natively, the control would not necessarily have the native Windows look and feel. It would have the Java Platform look and feel.

As Java user interface libraries evolve, they will reduce the pain of writing platform-independent user interfaces. Sun's lightweight component approach could enable the Java Platform to become more of a driving force in the evolution of user interfaces. Rather than just trying to catch up with the user interfaces available on native platforms, Sun can develop the user interface of the Java Platform. With lightweight components, they need not be restrained by lowest-common-denominator choices between native user interfaces.

To what extent users will accept a Java Platform look and feel over a native one is not clear, but the user interface does seem to be evolving toward more heterogeneity. Back in the 1980s, the Apple Macintosh established a principle that stated all Macintosh applications should adhere to certain user-interface guidelines. The theory was that software would be easier to use if all a user's applications were homogeneous: if they all used familiar metaphors and exhibited the same look and feel. Today, however, when Macintosh users browse the World Wide Web, they don't expect every web page to look like a Macintosh page. When they go to the IBM site, they expect it to look like IBM. When they go to the Disney site, they expect it to look like Disney. This approach is similar to the real world in that when you go to New York, you expect it to look and feel like New York. When you go to Paris, you expect it to look and feel like Paris. You don't expect all cities to have the same look and feel. As users are exposed to the web, they are becoming accustomed to working with more heterogeneous user interfaces than they might have encountered on an isolated personal computer.

As Java user-interface libraries evolve, the lowest-common-denominator problem inherent in platform-independent user interfaces may gradually become less painful. However, the extent to which users will accept interfaces that do not look and feel 100 percent native remains to be seen. For links to the latest information about the evolution of user interface technologies for Java, visit the resources page for this chapter.

# The Resources Page

For links to more information about the material presented in this chapter, visit the resources page at **http://www.artima.com/insidejvm/ intro.html**.

# 2

# Platform Independence

The first chapter showed how Java's architecture makes it a useful tool for developing software solutions in a networked environment. This chapter and the next two take a closer look at how Java's architecture accomplishes its suitability for networks. This chapter examines platform independence in detail. It shows how Java's architecture enables programs to run on any platform, describes the factors that determine the true portability of Java programs, and looks at the relevant trade-offs.

# Why Platform Independence?

One of the key reasons Java technology is useful in a networked environment is that Java enables you to create binary executables that will run unchanged on multiple platforms. This capability is important in a networked environment because networks usually interconnect many different kinds of computers and devices. An internal network at a medium-sized company might connect Macintoshes in the art department, UNIX work stations in engineering, and PCs running Windows everywhere else. Also, various kinds of embedded devices, such as printers, scanners, and fax machines, would typically be connected to the same network. Although this arrangement enables various kinds of computers and devices within the company to share data, it requires a great deal of administration. Such a network presents a system administrator with the task of keeping different platform-specific editions of programs up to date on many different kinds of computers. Programs that can run without change on any networked computer, regardless of the computer's type, make the system administrator's job simpler, especially if those programs can actually be delivered across the network.

On the developer's side, Java can reduce the cost and time required to develop and deploy applications on multiple platforms. Even though historically, many (or most) applications have been supported on only one platform, often the reason was that the cost involved in supporting multiple platforms wasn't worth the added return. Java can help make multiplatform support affordable for more types of programs.

For software developers, Java's platform independence can be both an advantage and a disadvantage. If you are developing and selling a software product, Java's support for platform independence can help you to compete in more markets. Instead of developing a product that runs only on Windows, for example, you can write one that runs on Windows, Macintosh, UNIX, and OS/2. With Java, you can have more potential customers. The trouble is, so can everyone else. Imagine, for example, that you have focused your efforts on writing great software for OS/2. Java enables others to more easily write software that competes in your chosen market niche. With Java, therefore, you might not only end up with more potential customers, but also with more potential competitors.

# Java's Architectural Support for Platform Independence

Java's architecture facilitates the creation of platform-independent software but also allows you to create software that is platform specific. When you write a Java program, platform independence is an *option*.

Support for platform independence, like support for security and network mobility, is spread throughout Java's architecture. All the components of the architecture—the language, the class file, the API, and the virtual machine—play a role in enabling platform independence.

## The Java Platform

Java's architecture supports the platform independence of Java programs in several ways, but primarily through the Java Platform itself. The Java Platform acts as a buffer between a running Java program and the underlying hardware and operating system. Java programs are compiled to run on a Java Virtual Machine, with the assumption that the class files of the Java API will be available at runtime. The virtual machine runs the program; the API gives the program access to the underlying computer's resources. No matter where a Java program goes, it need only interact with the Java Platform. It needn't worry about the underlying hardware and operating system. As a result, it can run on any computer that hosts a Java Platform.

## The Java Language

The Java programming language reflects Java's platform independence in one principal way: the ranges and behavior of its primitive types are defined by the language. In languages such as C or C++, the range of the primitive type `int` is determined by its size, and its size is determined by the target platform. The size of an `int` in C or C++ is generally chosen by the compiler to match the word size of the platform for which the program is compiled. Therefore, a C++ program might have different behavior when compiled for different platforms merely because the ranges of the primitive types are not consistent across the platforms. For example, no matter what underlying platform might be hosting the program, an **int** in Java behaves as a signed 32-bit two's complement number. A **float** adheres to the 32-bit IEEE 754 floating-point standard. This consistency is also reflected in the internals of the Java Virtual Machine, which has primitive data types that match those of the language, and in the class file, where the same primitive data types appear. By guaranteeing that primitive types behave the same on all platforms, the Java language itself promotes the platform independence of Java programs.

## The Java Class File

As mentioned in the preceding chapter, the class file defines a binary format that is specific to the Java Virtual Machine. Java class files can be generated on any platform. They can be loaded and run by a Java Virtual Machine that sits on top of any platform. Their format, including the big-endian order of multibyte values, is strictly defined and independent of any platform that hosts a Java Virtual Machine.

## Scaleability

One aspect of Java's support for platform independence is its scaleability. The Java Platform can be implemented on a wide range of hosts with varying levels of resources, from embedded devices to mainframe computers.

Even though Java first came to prominence by riding on top of a wave that was crashing through the desktop computer industry, the World Wide Web, Java was initially envisioned as a technology for embedded devices, not desktop computers. Part of the early reasoning behind the creation of Java was that although Microsoft and Intel had a dominant clutch on the desktop market, no such dominance existed in the embedded systems market. Microprocessors had been appearing in device after device for years—audio-video equipment, cell phones, printers, fax machines, copiers —and the coming trend was that, increasingly, embedded microprocessors would be connected to networks. An original design goal of Java, therefore, was to provide a way for software to be delivered across networks to any kind of embedded device—independent of its microprocessor and operating system.

To accomplish this goal, the Java runtime system (the Java Platform) had to be compact enough to be implemented in software using the resources available to a typical embedded system. Embedded microprocessors often have special constraints, such as small memory footprint, no hard disk, a nongraphical display, or no display.

Given the special requirements of embedded systems, several incarnations of the Java Platform exist just for embedded systems:

- the Java Embedded Platform
- the Java Personal Platform
- the Java Card Platform

These Java Platforms are composed of a Java Virtual Machine and a smaller shell of runtime libraries than are available in the Java Core Platform. The difference between the Core and the Embedded Platform, therefore, is that the Embedded Platform guarantees the availability of fewer Java API runtime libraries. The Personal Platform guarantees fewer APIs than the Embedded Platform; and the Card Platform, fewer than the Personal.

In addition to guaranteeing the smallest set of APIs, the Card Platform, which is targeted at SmartCards, uses only a subset of the full Java Virtual Machine instruction set. Only a subset of the features of the Java language is supported by this smaller instruction set. As a result, only Java programs that restrict themselves to features available on the Card Platform can run on a SmartCard.

Because the Java Platform is compact, it can be implemented on a wide variety of embedded systems. The compactness of the Java Platform, however, does not restrict implementation at the opposite end of the spectrum. The Java Platform also scales up to personal computers, work stations, and mainframes.

# Factors That Influence Platform Independence

When you write a Java program, its degree of platform independence depends on several factors. If you are a developer, some of these factors are beyond your control, but most are within your control. Primarily, the degree of platform independence of any Java program you write depends on how you write it.

## Java Platform Deployment

The most basic factor determining a Java program's platform independence is the extent to which the Java Platform has been deployed on multiple platforms. Java programs will run only on computers and devices that host a Java Platform. Thus, before one of your Java programs will run on a particular computer owned by, say, your friend Alicia, two things must happen. First, the Java Platform must be ported to Alicia's particular type of hardware and operating system. After the port has been done by some Java Platform vendor, that port must in some way get installed on Alicia's computer. So a critical factor determining the true extent of platform independence of Java programs—and one that is beyond the control of the average developer—is the availability of Java Platform implementations and their distribution.

Fortunately for the Java developer, the deployment of the Java Platform has proceeded with great momentum, starting with web browsers and then moving on to desktop, work station, and network operating systems. With the advent of chips optimized to execute Java bytecodes efficiently, the Java Platform will, to some extent, work its way into many different kinds of embedded devices. It is increasingly likely, therefore, that your friend Alicia will have a Java Platform implementation on her computer.

## The Java Platform Version and Edition

The deployment of the Java Platform is a bit more complicated, however, because not all standard runtime libraries are guaranteed to be available at every Java Platform. The basic set of libraries guaranteed to be available at a Java Platform is called the *Java Core API*. A Java Virtual Machine accompanied by the class files that constitute the Core API is called the *Java Core Platform*. This edition of the Java Platform has the minimum set of Java API libraries that you can assume will be available at network computers, desktop computers, and work stations. As mentioned earlier, three other editions of the Java Platform—the Embedded, Personal, and Card Platforms—provide subsets of the Core API for embedded systems. The standard runtime libraries not guaranteed to be available at the Core Platform are collectively called the *Java Standard Extension API*. These libraries include services such as telephony, commerce, and media such as audio, video, or 3D. If your program uses libraries from the Standard Extension API, it will run anywhere those standard extension API libraries are available, but not on a computer that implements only the basic Java Core Platform.

Another complicating factor is that, in a sense, the Java Platform is a moving target; it evolves over time. Although the Java Virtual Machine is likely to evolve very gradually, the Java API will probably change more frequently. Over time, features will be added to and removed from both the Core and Standard Extension APIs, and parts of the Standard Extension API may migrate into the Core API. The changes made to the Java Platform should, for the most part, be upward compatible, meaning they won't break existing Java programs, but some changes may not be. As obsolete features are removed in a new version of the Java Platform, existing Java programs that depend on those features won't run on the new version. Also, changes may not be downward compatible, meaning programs that are compiled for a new version of the Java Platform won't necessarily work on an old version. The dynamic nature of the Java Platform complicates things somewhat for the developer wishing to write a Java program that will run on any computer.

In theory, your program should run on all computers that host a Java Core Platform as long as you depend only on the runtime libraries in the Core API. In practice, however, new versions of the Core API will take time to percolate everywhere. When your program depends on newly added features of the latest version of the Java Core API, you might find that some hosts can't run it because they have an older version. This problem is not new to software developers; programs written for Windows 95, for example, don't work on the previous version of the operating system, Windows 3.1. However, because Java enables the network delivery of software, the problem becomes more acute. The promise of Java is not only that porting programs from one platform to another is easy, but that one version of a binary executable Java program placed on a server can be delivered across a network and run on all computers.

As a developer, you can't control the release cycles or deployment schedules of the Java Platform, but you can choose the Java Platform edition and version on which your programs depend. In practice, therefore, you will have to decide when a new version of the Java Platform has been distributed to a great enough extent to justify writing programs for that version.

# Native Methods

Besides the Java Platform version and edition your program depends on, the other major factor determining the extent of platform independence of your Java program is whether you call native methods. The most important rule to follow when you are writing a platform-independent Java program is: don't directly or indirectly invoke any native methods that aren't part of the Java API. As you can see in Figure 2-1, calling native methods outside the Java API renders your program platform specific.

Calling native methods directly is appropriate in situations in which you don't want platform independence. In general, native methods are useful in three cases:

- for accessing features of an underlying host platform that are not accessible through the Java API

- for accessing a legacy system or using an already existing library that isn't written in Java

- for speeding up the performance of a program by implementing time-critical code as native methods

If you need to use native methods and also need your program to run on several platforms, you'll have to port the native methods to all the re-

**Figure 2-1.**
A platform-specific
Java program.

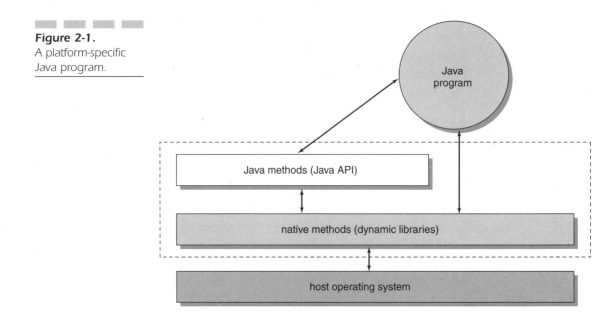

quired platforms. This porting must be done the old-fashioned way, and after you've done it, you'll have to figure out how to deliver the platform-specific native method libraries to the appropriate hosts. Because Java's architecture was designed to simplify multiplatform support, your initial goal in writing a platform-independent Java program should be to avoid native methods altogether and interact with the host only through the Java API.

# Nonstandard Runtime Libraries

Native methods aren't inherently incompatible with platform independence. What's important is whether the methods you invoke are implemented "everywhere." Implementations of the Java API on operating systems such as Windows or Solaris use native methods to access the host. When you call a method in the Java API, you are certain it will be available everywhere. It doesn't matter if in some places the method is implemented as a native method.

Java Platform implementations can come from a variety of vendors, and although every vendor must supply the standard runtime libraries of the Java API, individual vendors may also supply extra libraries. If you are interested in platform independence, you must remain aware of whether any nonstandard runtime libraries you use call native methods. Nonstandard libraries that don't call native methods don't degrade your program's platform independence. Using nonstandard libraries that do call native methods, however, yields the same result as calling native methods directly: it renders your program platform specific.

For example, Microsoft offers several sets of nonstandard runtime libraries with its Java Platform implementation. One set is the *Application Foundation Classes* (AFC). The AFC library is delivered along with the Java Platform implementation in Microsoft's Internet Explorer (version 4.0 and beyond) web browser. The AFC library extends the capabilities provided by the standard runtime libraries of the Java API but doesn't call native methods outside the Java API. The AFC library accesses the host only through the Java API. As a result, programs that use AFC should run on all implementations of the Java Platform.

One concern surrounding the use of a nonstandard class library (such as AFC) that doesn't call native methods is that you must deliver it to Java Platforms that don't support it directly. For example, imagine you write a Java program that uses AFC and make it available for downloading across a network. If you want the program to run on all platforms, you'll have to make the AFC classes available for downloading too. Compared to other browsers, the program might get started sooner at Microsoft's browser because it already has the AFC classes close at hand. Other browsers that don't store the AFC library locally would have to download the needed AFC classes across the network. Other than this potential difference in download time, using a nonstandard library that interacts with the host only through the Java API won't reduce the platform independence of a Java program. To keep your program platform independent, however, you must deliver the library along with your program.

One other Microsoft extension to the standard libraries of the Java Platform gives you a way to generate Java class files that grant access to *Component Object Model* (COM) objects. If you want to interact with a particular COM object, you use Microsoft's tool to generate a Java class file that gives your program a Java interface to the COM object. In effect, the generated class files form an extra runtime library that is available only at Microsoft's Java Platform implementation. Although this extra library offers more capabilities to Java programs, it reduces the platform independence of any Java program that takes advantage of it. Why? Because the extra libraries call native methods that are, initially at least, available only on Windows 95 and Windows NT. (In the future, Microsoft plans to port the Java/COM interface to non-Microsoft platforms.) Because the extra libraries provided by Microsoft use native methods that are specific to Microsoft operating systems, Java programs that use the extra libraries will work only on Microsoft operating systems.

Another potential ramification of using a vendor's nonstandard runtime library that calls native methods directly is that your program will work only on that vendor's Java Platform implementation. For example, the class files described previously that give your Java program access to COM objects use a special native method interface (the Java/COM interface) of Microsoft's Java Virtual Machine. Currently, this special native method interface is available only on Microsoft's virtual machine implementation on Windows 95 and Windows NT. Microsoft may port the Java/COM interface to other platforms, to increase the platform independence of programs that take advantage of it. But even if Microsoft is able to port it to every major platform, Java programs that use it will most likely work properly only when running on a Microsoft implementation of the Java Virtual Machine.

Because Java Platforms can come from different vendors, different Java Platform implementations from different vendors can be available for the same hardware and operating system. To run a Java program on Windows 95, for example, you could use a Java Platform from Sun, Microsoft, Borland, Symantec, or Asymetrix. The level of platform independence that a Java program has depends not only on how many different host computers it can run on, but also on how many different Java Platform implementations it can run on each host.

## Virtual Machine Dependencies

Two other rules to follow when writing a platform-independent Java program involve portions of the Java Virtual Machine that can be implemented differently by different vendors. The rules are

1. Don't depend on timely finalization for program correctness.
2. Don't depend on thread prioritization for program correctness.

These two rules address the variations allowed in the Java Virtual Machine specification for garbage collection and threads.

All Java Virtual Machines must have a garbage-collected heap, but different implementations can use different garbage-collection techniques. This flexibility in the Java Virtual Machine specification means that the objects of a particular Java program can be garbage collected at completely different times on different virtual machines. This capability, in turn, means that finalizers, which are run by the garbage collector before an object is freed, can run at different times on different virtual machines. If you use a finalizer to free finite memory resources, such as file handles, your program may run on some virtual machine implementations but not others. On some implementations, your program could run out of the finite resource before the garbage collector gets around to invoking the finalizers that free the resource.

Another variation allowed in different implementations of the Java Virtual Machine involves thread prioritization. The Java Virtual Machine specification guarantees that all runnable threads at the highest priority in your program will get some CPU time. The specification also guarantees that lower priority threads will run when higher priority threads are blocked. The specification does not, however, prohibit lower priority threads from running when higher priority threads aren't blocked. On some virtual machine implementations, therefore, lower priority threads may get some CPU time even when the higher priority threads aren't blocked. If your program depends for correctness on this behavior, however, it may work on some virtual machine implementations but not others. To keep your multithreaded Java program platform independent, you must rely on synchronization—not prioritization—to coordinate interactivity between threads.

## User Interface Dependencies

Another major variation between different Java Platform implementations is the user interface. The user interface is one of the more difficult issues in writing platform-independent Java programs. The AWT user interface library gives you a set of basic user interface components that map to native components on each platform. Libraries such as Microsoft's AFC, Netscape's IFC, and Sun's JFC give you advanced components that don't map directly to native components. From this raw material, you must build an interface that users on many different platforms will feel comfortable with. Doing so is not always an easy task.

Users on different platforms are accustomed to different ways of interacting with their computers. The metaphors are different. The components are different. The interaction between the components is different. Although the AWT library makes it fairly easy to create a user interface that runs on multiple platforms, this library doesn't necessarily make it easy to devise an interface that keeps users happy on multiple platforms.

## Bugs in Java Platform Implementations

One final source of variation among different implementations of the Java Platform is bugs. Although Sun has developed a comprehensive suite of tests that Java Platform implementations must pass, some implementations may still be distributed with bugs in them. The only way you can defend yourself against this possibility is through testing. If a bug exists, you can determine through testing whether the bug affects your program, and if so, you can attempt to find a workaround.

## Testing

Given the allowable differences among Java Platform implementations, the platform dependent ways you can potentially write a Java program, and the simple possibility of bugs in any particular Java Platform implementation, you should test your Java programs on all platforms you plan to claim it runs on. Java programs are not platform independent to a great enough extent that you need test them on only one platform. You still need to test a Java program on multiple platforms, and you should probably test it on the various Java Platform implementations that are likely to be found on each host computer you claim your program runs on. In practice, therefore, testing your Java program on the various host computers and Java Platform implementations that you plan to claim your program works on is a key factor in making your program platform independent.

# Seven Steps to Platform Independence

Java's architecture allows you to choose between platform independence and other concerns. You make your choice by the way in which you write your program. If your goal is to take advantage of platform-specific features not available through the Java API, to interact with a legacy system, to use an existing library written or not written in Java, or to maximize the execution speed of your program, you can use native methods to help you achieve that goal. In such cases, your programs will have reduced platform independence, and that will usually be acceptable. If, on the other hand, your goal is platform independence, then you should follow certain rules when writing your program. The following seven steps outline one path you can take to maximize your program's portability:

1. Choose a set of host computers on which you will claim your program runs (your *target hosts*).

2. Choose a version of the Java Platform that you feel is well enough distributed among your target hosts. Write your program to run on this version of the Java Platform.

3. For each target host, choose a set of Java Platform implementations on which you will claim your program runs (your *target runtimes*).

4. Write your program so that it accesses the host computer only through the standard runtime libraries of the Java API. (Don't invoke native methods or use vendor-specific libraries that invoke native methods.)

5. Write your program so that it doesn't depend for correctness on timely finalization by the garbage collector or on thread prioritization.

**6.** Strive to design a user interface that works well on all your target hosts.

**7.** Test your program on all your target runtimes and all your target hosts.

If you follow the preceding seven steps, your Java program will definitely run on all your target hosts. If your target hosts cover most major Java Platform vendors on most major host computers, you stand a very good chance that your program will run everywhere else as well.

If you wish, you can have your program certified as "100 Percent Pure Java." You might want to do so if you are writing a program that you intend to be platform independent. For example, if your program is certified 100 Percent Pure, you can brand it with the 100 Percent Pure Java coffee cup icon. You can also potentially participate in comarketing programs with Sun. You may, however, wish to go through the certification process simply as an added check of the platform independence of your program. In this case, you have the option of just running 100 Percent Pure verification tools you can download for free. These tools will report problems with your program's "purity" without requiring you to go through the full certification process.

The 100 Percent Pure certification is not quite a full measure of platform independence. Part of platform independence is that users' expectations are fulfilled on multiple platforms. The 100 Percent Pure testing process does not attempt to measure user fulfillment. It checks to make certain your program depends only on the Java Core Platform. You could write a Java program that passes the 100 Percent Pure tests but still doesn't work well on all platforms from the perspective of users. Nonetheless, running your code through the 100 Percent Pure testing process can be a worthwhile step on the road to creating a platform-independent Java program.

# The Politics of Platform Independence

As illustrated in Figure 2-2, Java Platform vendors are allowed to extend the standard components of the Java Platform in nonstandard and platform-specific ways, but they must always support the standard components. In the future, Sun Microsystems intends to prevent the standard components of the Java Platform from splitting into several competing,

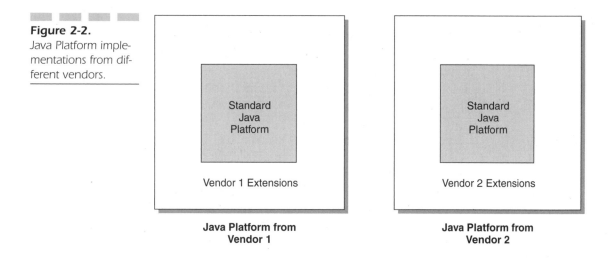

**Figure 2-2.**
Java Platform implementations from different vendors.

slightly incompatible systems, as happened, for example, with UNIX. The license that all Java Platform vendors must sign requires compatibility at the level of the Java Virtual Machine and the Java API but permits differentiation in the areas of performance and extensions. As mentioned previously, vendors are allowed some flexibility in the way they implement threads, garbage collection, and user interface look and feel. If things go as Sun plans, the core components of the Java Platform will remain a standard to which all vendors faithfully adhere, and the ubiquitous nature of the standard Java Platform will enable you to write programs that really are platform independent.

You can rely on the standard components of the Java Platform because every Java Platform vendor must support them. If you write a program that depends only on these components, it should "run anywhere" but may suffer to some extent from the lowest-common-denominator problem. Yet because vendors are allowed to extend the Java Platform, they can give you a way to write platform-specific programs that take full advantage of the features of the underlying host operating system. The presence of both required standard components and permitted vendor extensions at any Java Platform implementation gives developers a choice. This arrangement allows developers to balance platform independence with other concerns.

Currently, a marketing battle is raging for the hearts and minds of software developers over how they will write Java programs—in particular, whether they will choose to write platform-independent or platform-specific programs. The choice that Java graciously gives to developers also potentially threatens some vested interests in the software industry.

Java's support for platform independence threatens to weaken the "lock" enjoyed by operating system vendors. If all your software runs on only one operating system, then your next computer will also very likely run that same operating system. You are "locked in" to one operating system vendor because your investment in software depends on an API proprietary to that vendor. You are also likely locked into one hardware architecture because the binary form of your programs requires a particular kind of microprocessor. If, instead, much of your software is written to the Java API and stored as bytecodes in class files, you can more easily migrate to a different operating system vendor the next time you buy a computer. Because the Java Platform can be implemented in software on top of existing operating systems, you can switch operating systems and take all your old platform-independent Java-based software with you.

Microsoft dominates the desktop operating system market largely because most available software runs only on Microsoft operating systems. It is in Microsoft's strategic interest to continue this status quo, so Microsoft is encouraging developers to use Java as a language to write programs that run only on Microsoft platforms. It is in just about every other operating system vendor's strategic interest to weaken Microsoft's lock on the operating system market, so the other players are encouraging developers to write Java programs that are platform independent. Sun, Netscape, IBM, and many others have banded together to promote Sun's "100 Percent Pure Java initiative," through which they hope to educate and persuade developers to go the platform-independence route.

Microsoft's approach to Java is to make Windows the best platform on which to develop and run Java programs. It wants developers to use Microsoft's tools and libraries whether or not the developer chooses platform independence. Microsoft's AFC library, for example, enables Java developers to build advanced platform-independent user interfaces. Microsoft also provides the Java/COM native method interface, which allows developers to use Java to write full-fledged, platform-specific Windows programs. Still, in the "spin" Microsoft gives to Java in promotional material to developers, it strongly favors the platform-specific Windows path. Microsoft extols the virtues of using Java to write programs that take full advantage of the Windows platform.

Sun and the other operating system vendors behind the 100 Percent Pure Java initiative are attempting to counter Microsoft's spin with some of their own. The promotional material from these companies focuses on the benefits of writing platform-independent Java programs.

On one level, this battle is between two icons. If you write your Java program Microsoft's way, you get to brand your product with a Windows

95/NT icon that displays the famous four-paneled Windows logo. If you go the 100 Percent Pure Java route, you get to brand your product with a 100 Percent Pure Java icon that displays the famous steaming coffee cup logo.

If you are a developer, the politics and propaganda swirling around the software industry need not be a major factor when you decide how to write a particular Java program. For some programs you write, platform independence may be the right approach; for others, a platform-specific program may make more sense. In each individual case, you can make a decision based on what you feel your customers want and how you want to position yourself in the marketplace with respect to your competitors.

## The Resources Page

For links to more information about Java and platform independence, visit the resources page for this chapter: `http://www.artima.com/insidejvm/platindep.html`.

# Security

Aside from platform independence, discussed in the preceding chapter, the other major technical challenge a network-oriented software technology must deal with is security. Networks, because they allow computers to share data and distribute processing, can potentially serve as a way to break into a computer system, enabling someone to steal information, destroy information, or steal computing resources. As a consequence, connecting a computer to a network raises many security issues.

To address the security concerns raised by networks, Java's architecture comes with an extensive built-in security model. This chapter gives an overview of the security model built into Java's core architecture.

# Why Security?

Java's security model is one of the key architectural features that makes it an appropriate technology for networked environments. Security is important because networks represent a potential avenue of attack to any computer hooked to them. This concern becomes especially strong in an environment in which software is downloaded across the network and executed locally, as is done, for example, with Java applets. Because the class files for an applet are automatically downloaded when a user goes to the containing web page in a browser, the user is likely to encounter applets from untrusted sources. Without any security, this system would be a convenient way to spread viruses. Thus, Java's security mechanisms help make Java suitable for networks because they establish a needed trust in the safety of network-mobile code.

Java's security model is focused on protecting end users from hostile programs downloaded across a network from untrusted sources. To accomplish this goal, Java provides a customizable "sandbox" in which Java programs run. A Java program must play only inside its sandbox. It can do anything within the boundaries of its sandbox, but it can't take any action outside those boundaries. The sandbox for untrusted Java applets, for example, prohibits many activities, including

- reading or writing to the local disk
- making a network connection to any but the host from which the applet came
- creating a new process
- loading a new dynamic library and directly calling a native method

By making it impossible for downloaded code to perform certain actions, Java's security model protects the end user from the threat of hostile code.

# The Sandbox

Traditionally, you had to trust software before you ran it. You achieved security by being careful only to use software from trusted sources and by regularly scanning for viruses just to make sure. After some software got access to your system, it had full reign. If it was malicious, it could do a great deal of damage because no restrictions were placed on it by the runtime environment of your computer. So in the traditional security scheme, you tried to prevent malicious code from ever gaining access to your computer in the first place.

The sandbox security model makes it easier to work with software that comes from sources you don't fully trust. Instead of approaching security by requiring you to prevent any code you don't trust from ever making its way onto your computer, the sandbox model allows you to welcome code from any source. But as code from an untrusted source runs, the sandbox restricts code from untrusted sources from taking any actions that could possibly harm your system. You don't need to figure out what code you can and can't trust. You don't need to scan for viruses. The sandbox itself prevents any viruses or other malicious code you may invite into your computer from doing any damage.

If you have a properly skeptical mind, you'll need to be convinced a sandbox has no leaks before you trust it to protect you. To make sure the sandbox has no leaks, Java's security model involves every aspect of its architecture. If security were weak in some areas of Java's architecture, a malicious programmer (a "cracker") could potentially exploit those areas to "go around" the sandbox. To understand the sandbox, therefore, you must look at several different parts of Java's architecture and understand how they work together.

The fundamental components responsible for Java's sandbox are

- the class loader architecture
- the class file verifier
- safety features built into the Java Virtual Machine (and the language)
- the security manager and the Java API

One of the greatest strengths of Java's security model is that two of these components, the class loader and the security manager, are customizable. By customizing these components, you can create a customized security policy for a Java application. As a developer, you may never need to create your own customized sandbox. You can often make use of sandboxes created by others. When you write and run a Java applet, for example, you make use of a sandbox created by the developers of the web browser that hosts your applet.

# The Class Loader Architecture

In Java's sandbox, the class loader architecture is the first line of defense. It is the class loader, after all, that brings code into the Java Virtual Machine—code that could be hostile. The class loader architecture contributes to Java's sandbox in two ways:

1. It guards the borders of the trusted class libraries.
2. It prevents malicious code from interfering with benevolent code.

The class loader architecture guards the borders of the trusted class libraries by preventing any untrusted classes from pretending to be trusted. If a malicious class could successfully trick the Java Virtual Machine into believing it was a trusted class from the Java API, that malicious class could potentially break through the sandbox barrier. By preventing untrusted classes from impersonating trusted classes, the class loader architecture blocks one potential approach to compromising the security of the Java runtime.

The class loader architecture prevents malicious code from interfering with benevolent code by providing protected name-spaces for classes loaded by different class loaders. A *name-space* is a set of unique names for loaded classes; it is maintained by the Java Virtual Machine. After a Java Virtual Machine has loaded a class named **Volcano** into a particular name-space, for example, loading a different class named **Volcano** into that same name-space is impossible. You can load multiple **Volcano** classes into a Java Virtual Machine, however, because you can create multiple name-spaces inside a Java application by creating multiple class loaders. If you create three separate name-spaces (one for each of three class loaders) in a running Java application, then, by loading one **Volcano** class into each name-space, your program could load three different **Volcano** classes into your application.

Name-spaces contribute to security because you can place a shield between classes loaded into different name-spaces. Inside the Java Virtual Machine, classes in the same name-space can interact with one another directly. Classes in different name-spaces, however, can't even detect each other's presence unless you explicitly provide a mechanism that allows them to interact. If a malicious class, once loaded, had guaranteed access to every other class currently loaded by the virtual machine, that class could potentially learn things it shouldn't know or interfere with the proper execution of your program.

Often, a class loader object relies on other class loaders—at the very least, on the primordial class loader—to help it fulfill some of the class load requests that come its way. For example, imagine you write a Java application that installs a class loader whose particular manner of loading class files is by downloading them across a network. Assume that, during the course of running the Java application, a request is made of your class loader to load a class named `Volcano`. One way you could write the class loader is to have it first ask the primordial class loader to find and load the class from its trusted repository. In this case, because `Volcano` is not a part of the Java API, assume the primordial class loader can't find a class named `Volcano`. When the primordial class loader responds that it can't load the class, your class loader could then attempt to load the `Volcano` class in its custom manner, by downloading it across the network. Assuming your class loader was able to download class `Volcano`, that `Volcano` class could then play a role in the application's future course of execution.

To continue with the same example, assume that at some time later a method of class `Volcano` is invoked for the first time, and that method references class `String` from the Java API. Because it is the first time the reference was used by the running program, the virtual machine asks your class loader (the one that loaded `Volcano`) to load `String`. As before, your class loader first passes the request to the primordial class loader, but in this case, the primordial class loader can return a `String` class back to your class loader. (The primordial class loader most likely didn't have to actually load `String` at this point because, given that `String` is such a fundamental class in Java programs, it was almost certainly used before and therefore already loaded. Most likely, the primordial class loader just returned the `String` class that it had previously loaded from the trusted repository.) Because the primordial class loader could find the class, your class loader doesn't attempt to download it across the network; it merely passes to the virtual machine the `String` class returned by the primordial class loader. From that point forward, the virtual machine uses that `String` class whenever class `Volcano` references a class named `String`.

When you write a class loader, you create a new environment in which the loaded code runs. If you want the environment to be free of security holes, you must follow certain rules when you write your class loader. In general, you will want to write class loaders so that they protect the borders of trusted class libraries, such as those of the Java API.

Java allows classes in the same package to grant each other special access privileges that aren't granted to classes outside the package. So, if your class loader receives a request to load a class that by its name brazenly declares itself to be part of the Java API (for example, a class named `java.lang.Virus`), it could gain special access to the trusted classes of `java.lang` and could possibly use that special access for devious purposes. Consequently, you would normally write a class loader so that it simply refuses to load any class that claims to be part of the Java API (or any other trusted runtime library) but that doesn't exist in the local trusted repository. In other words, after your class loader passes a request to the primordial class loader, and the primordial class loader indicates it can't load the class, your class loader should check to make sure the class doesn't declare itself to be a member of a trusted package. If it does, your class loader, instead of trying to download the class across the network, should throw a security exception.

In addition, in the trusted repository you may have installed some packages that contain classes you want your application to be able to load through the primordial class loader but that you don't want to be accessible to classes loaded through your class loader. For example, assume you have created a package named `absolutepower` and installed it on the local repository accessible by the primordial class loader. Assume also that you don't want classes loaded by your class loader to be able to load any class from the `absolutepower` package. In this case, you would write your class loader so that the very first thing it does is make sure the requested class doesn't declare itself as a member of the `absolutepower` package. If such a class is requested, your class loader, rather than passing the class name to the primordial class loader, should throw a security exception.

The only way a class loader can know whether a class is from a restricted package, such as `java.lang`, or a forbidden package, such as `absolutepower`, is by the class's name. Thus, a class loader must be given a list of the names of restricted and forbidden packages. Because the name of class `java.lang.Virus` indicates it is from the `java.lang` package, and `java.lang` is on the list of restricted packages, your class loader should throw a security exception if the primordial class loader can't load it. Likewise, because the name of class `absolutepower.FancyClassLoader` indicates it is part of the `absolutepower` package, and the `absolutepower` package is on the list of forbidden packages, your class loader should throw a security exception absolutely.

A common way, therefore, to write a security-minded class loader is by using the following four steps:

1. If packages exist from which this class loader is not allowed to load classes, the class loader checks whether the requested class is in one of those forbidden packages. If so, it throws a security exception. Else, it continues on to step 2.

2. The class loader passes the request to the primordial class loader. If the primordial class loader successfully returns the class, the class loader returns that same class. Else, it continues on to step 3.

3. If trusted packages exist to which this class loader is not allowed to add classes, the class loader checks whether the requested class is in one of those restricted packages. If so, it throws a security exception. Else, it continues on to step 4.

4. Finally, the class loader attempts to load the class in the custom way, such as by downloading it across a network. If successful, it returns the class. Else, it throws a **no class definition found** error.

By performing steps 1 and 3 as outlined here, the class loader guards the borders of the trusted packages. With step 1, it prevents a class from a forbidden package to be loaded at all. With step 3, it doesn't allow an untrusted class to insert itself into a trusted package.

# The Class File Verifier

Working in conjunction with the class loader, the class file verifier ensures that loaded class files have a proper internal structure. If the class file verifier discovers a problem with a class file, it throws an exception. Although compliant Java compilers should not generate malformed class files, a Java Virtual Machine can't tell how a particular class file was created. Because a class file is just a sequence of binary data, a virtual machine can't know whether a particular class file was generated by a well-meaning Java compiler or by shady crackers bent on compromising the integrity of the virtual machine. As a consequence, all Java Virtual Machine implementations have class file verifiers that can be invoked on untrusted classes, to make sure the classes are safe to use.

One of the security goals that the class file verifier helps achieve is program robustness. If a buggy compiler or savvy cracker generated a class file that contained a method whose bytecodes included an instruction to jump beyond the end of the method, this method could, if it were invoked, cause the virtual machine to crash. Thus, for the sake of robustness, the virtual machine should verify the integrity of the bytecodes it imports. Although Java Virtual Machine designers can decide when their virtual machines will perform these checks, many implementations will do most checking just after a class is loaded. Such a virtual machine, rather than checking every time it encounters a jump instruction as it executes bytecodes, analyzes bytecodes (and verifies their integrity) once, before they are ever executed. As part of its verification of bytecodes, the Java Virtual Machine makes sure all jump instructions cause a jump to another valid instruction in the bytecode stream of the method. In most cases, checking all bytecodes once, before they are executed, is a more efficient way to guarantee robustness than checking every bytecode instruction every time it is executed.

A class file verifier that performs its checking as early as possible most likely operates in two distinct phases. During phase one, which takes place just after a class is loaded, the class file verifier checks the internal structure of the class file, including verifying the integrity of the bytecodes it contains. During phase two, which takes place as bytecodes are executed, the class file verifier confirms the existence of symbolically referenced classes, fields, and methods.

## Phase One: Internal Checks

During phase one, the class file verifier checks everything that's possible to check in a class file by looking at only the class file itself. In addition to verifying the integrity of the bytecodes during phase one, the verifier performs many checks for proper class file format and internal consistency. For example, every class file must start with the same four bytes, the magic number: **0xCAFEBABE**. The purpose of magic numbers is to enable file parsers to easily recognize a certain type of file. Thus, the first thing a class file verifier likely checks is that the imported file does indeed begin with **0xCAFEBABE**.

The class file verifier also checks to make sure the class file is neither truncated nor enhanced with extra trailing bytes. Although different class files can be different lengths, each individual component contained inside a class file indicates its length as well as its type. The verifier can use the component types and lengths to determine the correct total length for each individual class file. In this way, it can verify that the imported file has a length consistent with its internal contents.

The verifier also looks at individual components to make sure they are well-formed instances of their type of component. For example, a method descriptor (its return type and the number and types of its parameters) is stored in the class file as a string that must adhere to a certain context-free grammar. One check the verifier performs on individual components is to make sure each method descriptor is a well-formed string of the appropriate grammar.

In addition, the class file verifier checks that the class itself adheres to certain constraints placed on it by the specification of the Java programming language. For example, the verifier enforces the rule that all classes, except class **Object**, must have a superclass. Thus, the class file verifier checks at runtime some of the Java language rules that should have been enforced at compile-time. Because the verifier has no way of knowing if the class file was generated by a benevolent, bug-free compiler, it checks each class file to make sure the rules are followed.

After the class file verifier has successfully completed the checks for proper format and internal consistency, it turns its attention to the bytecodes. During this part of phase one, which is commonly called the "bytecode verifier," the Java Virtual Machine performs a data-flow analysis on the streams of bytecodes that represent the methods of the class. To understand the bytecode verifier, you need to understand a bit about bytecodes and frames.

The bytecode streams that represent Java methods are a series of one-byte instructions, called *opcodes*, each of which can be followed by one or more *operands*. The operands supply extra data needed by the Java Virtual Machine to execute the opcode instruction. The activity of executing bytecodes, one opcode after another, constitutes a thread of execution inside the Java Virtual Machine. Each thread is awarded its own *Java Stack*, which is made up of discrete *frames*. Each method invocation gets its own frame, a section of memory where it stores, among other things, local variables and intermediate results of computation. The part of the frame in which a method stores intermediate results is called the method's *operand stack*. An opcode and its (optional) operands may refer to the data stored on the operand stack or in the local variables of the method's frame. Thus, the virtual machine can use data on the operand stack, in the local variables, or both, in addition to any data stored as operands following an opcode when it executes the opcode.

The bytecode verifier does a great deal of checking. It checks to make sure that no matter what path of execution is taken to get to a certain opcode in the bytecode stream, the operand stack always contains the same number and types of items. It checks to make sure no local variable is accessed before it is known to contain a proper value. It checks that fields of the class are always assigned values of the proper type and that methods of the class are always invoked with the correct number and types of arguments. The bytecode verifier also checks to make sure that each opcode is valid, that each opcode has valid operands, and that for each opcode, values of the proper type are in the local variables and on the operand stack. These checks are just a few of the many checks performed by the bytecode verifier, which can, through all its checking, verify that a stream of bytecodes is safe for the Java Virtual Machine to execute.

Phase one of the class file verifier makes sure the imported class file is properly formed, internally consistent, adheres to the constraints of the Java programming language, and contains bytecodes that will be safe for the Java Virtual Machine to execute. If the class file verifier finds that any of these is not true, it throws an error, and the class file is never used by the program.

## Phase Two: Verification of Symbolic References

Although phase one happens immediately after the Java Virtual Machine loads a class file, phase two is delayed until the bytecodes contained in the class file are actually executed. During phase two, the Java Virtual Machine follows the references from the class file being verified to the referenced class files, to make sure the references are correct. Because phase two has to look at other classes external to the class file being checked, phase two may require that new classes be loaded. Most Java Virtual Machine implementations will likely delay loading classes until they are actually used by the program. If an implementation does load classes earlier, perhaps in an attempt to speed up the loading process, then it must still give the impression that it is loading classes as late as possible. If, for example, a Java Virtual Machine discovers during early loading that it can't find a certain referenced class, it doesn't throw a **class definition not found** error until (and unless) the referenced class is used for the first time by the running program. Therefore, phase two, the checking of symbolic references, is usually delayed until each symbolic reference is actually used for the first time during bytecode execution.

Phase two of class file verification is really just part of the process of dynamic linking. When a class file is loaded, it contains symbolic references to other classes and their fields and methods. A symbolic reference is a character string that gives the name and possibly other information about the referenced item—enough information to uniquely identify a class, field, or method. Thus, symbolic references to other classes give the full name of the class; symbolic references to the fields of other classes give the class name, field name, and field descriptor; symbolic references to the methods of other classes give the class name, method name, and method descriptor.

Dynamic linking is the process of *resolving* symbolic references into direct references. As the Java Virtual Machine executes bytecodes and encounters an opcode that, for the first time, uses a symbolic reference to another class, the virtual machine must resolve the symbolic reference. The virtual machine performs two basic tasks during resolution:

1. finds the class being referenced (loading it if necessary)
2. replaces the symbolic reference with a direct reference, such as a pointer or offset, to the class, field, or method

The virtual machine remembers the direct reference so that, if it encounters the same reference again later, it can immediately use the direct reference without needing to spend time resolving the symbolic reference again.

When the Java Virtual Machine resolves a symbolic reference, phase two of the class file verifier makes sure the reference is valid. If the reference is not valid—for example, if the class cannot be loaded or if the class exists but doesn't contain the referenced field or method—the class file verifier throws an error.

As an example, consider again the **Volcano** class. If a method of class **Volcano** invokes a method in a class named **Lava**, the name and descriptor of the method in **Lava** are included as part of the binary data in the class file for **Volcano**. So, during the course of execution when the **Volcano**'s method first invokes the **Lava**'s method, the Java Virtual Machine makes sure a method that has a name and descriptor that matches those expected by class **Volcano** exists in class **Lava**. If the symbolic reference (class name, method name, and descriptor) is correct, the virtual machine replaces it with a direct reference, such as a pointer, which it will use from then on. But if the symbolic reference from class **Volcano** doesn't match any method in class **Lava**, phase two verification fails, and the Java Virtual Machine throws a **NoSuchMethodError**.

## Binary Compatibility

Phase two of the class file verifier must look at classes that refer to one another to make sure they are compatible because Java programs are dynamically linked. Java compilers will often recompile classes that depend on a class you have changed, and in so doing, detect any incompatibility at compile-time. But sometimes your compiler doesn't recompile a dependent class. For example, if you are developing a large system, you will likely partition the various parts of the system into packages. If you compile each package separately, then a change to one class in a package would cause a recompilation of affected classes within that same package, but not necessarily in any other package. Moreover, if you are using someone else's packages, especially if your program downloads class files from someone else's package across a network as it runs, you might not be able to check for compatibility at compile-time. For that reason, phase two of the class file verifier must check for compatibility at runtime.

As an example of incompatible changes, imagine you compiled class **Volcano** (from the preceding example) with a Java compiler. Because a method in **Volcano** invokes a method in another class named **Lava**, the Java compiler would look for a class file or a source file for class **Lava** to make sure a method exists in **Lava** with the appropriate name, return type, and number and types of arguments. If the compiler couldn't find any **Lava** class, or if it encountered a **Lava** class that didn't contain the desired method, the compiler would generate an error and would not create a class file for **Volcano**. Otherwise, the Java compiler would produce for **Volcano** a class file that is compatible with the class file for **Lava**. In this case, the Java compiler refused to generate a class file for **Volcano** that wasn't already compatible with class **Lava**.

The converse, however, is not necessarily true. The Java compiler could conceivably generate for **Lava** a class file that isn't compatible with **Volcano**. If the **Lava** class doesn't refer to **Volcano**, you could potentially change the name of the method **Volcano** invokes from the **Lava** class and then recompile only the **Lava** class. If you tried to run your program using the new version of **Lava** but still using the old version of **Volcano** that wasn't recompiled since you made your change to **Lava**, the Java Virtual Machine would, as a result of phase two class file verification, throw a **NoSuchMethodError** when **Volcano** attempted to invoke the now nonexistent method in **Lava**.

In this case, the change to class **Lava** *broke binary compatibility* with the preexisting class file for **Volcano**. In practice, this situation may arise when you update a library you have been using, and your existing code isn't compatible with the new version of the library. To make it easier to alter the code for libraries, the Java programming language was designed to allow you to make many kinds of changes to a class that don't require recompilation of classes that depend on it. The changes you are allowed to make, which are listed in the Java Language Specification, are called the *rules of binary compatibility*. These rules clearly define what can be changed, added, or deleted in a class without breaking binary compatibility with preexisting class files that depend on the changed class. For example, adding a new method to a class is always a binary compatible change, but never deleting a method that other classes may be using. So ,in the case of **Lava**, you violated the rules of binary compatibility when you changed the name of the method used by **Volcano**, because you, in effect, deleted the old method and added a new. If you had, instead, added the new method and then rewritten the old method so it calls the new, that change would have been binary compatible with any preexisting class file that already used **Lava**, including **Volcano**.

# Safety Features Built into the Java Virtual Machine

After the Java Virtual Machine has loaded a class and performed phase one of class file verification, the bytecodes are ready to be executed. Besides the verification of symbolic references (phase two of class file verification), the Java Virtual Machine has several other built-in security mechanisms operating as bytecodes are executed. They are the same mechanisms listed in Chapter 1, "Introduction to Java's Architecture," as features of the Java programming language that make Java programs robust. They are, not surprisingly, also features of the Java Virtual Machine:

- type-safe reference casting
- structured memory access (no pointer arithmetic)
- automatic garbage collection (can't explicitly free allocated memory)
- array bounds checking
- checking references for **null**

By granting a Java program only safe, structured ways to access memory, the Java Virtual Machine makes Java programs more robust, but it also makes their execution more secure. Why? There are two reasons. First, a program that corrupts memory, crashes, and possibly causes other programs to crash represents one kind of security breach. If you are running a mission-critical server process, it is critical that the process doesn't crash. This level of robustness is also important in embedded systems, such as a cell phone, which people don't usually expect to have to reboot.

Second, unrestrained memory access is a security risk because a wily cracker could potentially use it to subvert the security system. If, for example, a cracker could learn where in memory a class loader is stored, it could assign a pointer to that memory and manipulate the class loader's data. By enforcing structured access to memory, the Java Virtual Machine yields programs that are robust but also frustrates crackers who dream of harnessing the internal memory of the Java Virtual Machine for their own devious plots.

Another safety feature built into the Java Virtual Machine—one that serves as a backup to structured memory access—is the unspecified manner in which the runtime data areas are laid out inside the Java Virtual Machine. The *runtime data areas* are the memory areas in which the Java Virtual Machine stores the data it needs to execute a Java application: Java stacks (one for each thread), a *method area*, where bytecodes are stored, and a *garbage-collected heap*, where the objects created by the running program are stored. If you peer into a class file, you won't find any memory addresses. When the Java Virtual Machine loads a class file, it decides where in its internal memory to put the bytecodes and other data it parses from the class file. When the Java Virtual Machine starts a thread, it decides where to put the Java stack it creates for the thread. When it creates a new object, it decides where in memory to put the object. Thus, a cracker cannot predict by looking at a class file where in memory the data representing that class, or objects instantiated from that class, will be kept. What's worse (for the cracker) is the cracker can't tell anything about memory layout by reading the Java Virtual Machine specification either. The manner in which a Java Virtual Machine lays out its internal data is not part of the specification. The designers of each Java Virtual Machine implementation decide which data structures their implementation will use to represent the runtime data areas and where in memory their implementation will place them. As a result, even if a cracker were somehow able to break through the Java Virtual Machine's memory access restrictions, they would next be faced with the difficult task of finding something to subvert by looking around.

The prohibition on unstructured memory access is not something the Java Virtual Machine must actively enforce on a running program; rather, it is intrinsic to the bytecode instruction set itself. Just as you cannot express an unstructured memory access in the Java programming language, you also cannot express it in bytecodes—even if you write the bytecodes by hand. Thus, the prohibition on unstructured memory access is a solid barrier against the malicious manipulation of memory.

The security barriers erected by the Java Virtual Machine can be penetrated, however. Although the bytecode instruction set doesn't give you an unsafe, unstructured way to access memory, you can go around bytecodes by using native methods. Basically, when you call a native method, Java's security sandbox becomes dust in the wind. First of all, the robustness guarantees don't hold for native methods. Although you can't corrupt memory from a Java method, you can from a native method. But most importantly, native methods don't go through the Java API (they are the way you go around the Java API), so the security manager isn't checked before a native method attempts to do something that could be potentially damaging. (This process is, of course, often how the Java API itself gets anything done. But the native methods used by the Java API are "trusted.") Thus, after a thread gets into a native method, no matter what security policy was established inside the Java Virtual Machine, it doesn't apply anymore to that thread as long as that thread continues to execute the native method. For this reason, the security manager includes a method that establishes whether a program can load dynamic libraries, which are necessary for invoking native methods. Applets, for example, aren't allowed to load a new dynamic library; therefore, they can't install their own new native methods. They can, however, call methods in the Java API, methods that may be native but that are always trusted. When a thread invokes a native method, that thread leaps outside the sandbox. The security model for native methods is, therefore, the same security model described earlier as the traditional approach to computer security: You have to trust a native method before you call it.

One final mechanism built into the Java Virtual Machine that contributes to security is structured error handling with exceptions. Because of its support for exceptions, the Java Virtual Machine has something structured to do when a security violation occurs. Instead of crashing, the Java Virtual Machine can throw an exception or an error, which may result in the death of the offending thread but shouldn't crash the system. Throwing an error (as opposed to throwing an exception) almost always results in the death of the thread in which the error was thrown. This end result is usually a major inconvenience to a running Java program but won't necessarily result in termination of the entire program. If the program has other threads doing useful things, those threads may be able to carry on without their recently departed colleague. Throwing an exception, on the other hand, may result in the death of the thread but is often just used as a way to transfer control from the point in the program where the exception condition arose to the point in the program where the exception condition is handled.

# The Security Manager and the Java API

By using class loaders, you can prevent code loaded by different class loaders from interfering with one another inside the Java Virtual Machine. To protect assets external to the Java Virtual Machine, though, you must use a security manager. The security manager defines the outer boundaries of the sandbox. Because it is customizable, the security manager allows you to establish a custom security policy for an application. The Java API enforces the custom security policy by asking the security manager for permission before it takes any action that is potentially unsafe. For each potentially unsafe action, the security manager has a method that defines whether that action is allowed by the sandbox. Each method's name starts with *check*, so for example, `checkRead()` defines whether a thread is allowed to read to a specified file, and `checkWrite()` defines whether a thread is allowed to write to a specified file. The implementation of these methods defines the custom security policy of the application.

Most of the activities that are regulated by a "check" method are as follows. The classes of the Java API check with the security manager before they

- accept a socket connection from a specified host and port number
- modify a thread (change its priority, stop it, and so on)
- open a socket connection to a specified host and port number
- create a new class loader
- delete a specified file
- create a new process
- cause the application to exit
- load a dynamic library that contains native methods
- wait for a connection on a specified local port number
- load a class from a specified package (used by class loaders)
- add a new class to a specified package (used by class loaders)
- access or modify system properties
- access a specified system property
- read from a specified file
- write to a specified file

Because the Java API always checks with the security manager before it performs any of the activities in the preceding list, the Java API will not perform any action forbidden under the security policy established by the security manager.

Two actions not present in the preceding list that could potentially be unsafe are allocation of memory and invocation of threads. Currently, a hostile applet can possibly crash the browser by

- allocating memory until it runs out
- firing off threads until everything slows to a crawl

These kinds of attacks are called *denial of service* because they deny the end users from using their own computers. The security manager does not allow you to enforce any kind of limit on allocated memory or thread creation. (The security manager class does not have `checkAllocateMemory()` or `checkCreateThread()` methods.) The difficulty in attempting to thwart this kind of hostile code is that it is hard to tell the difference, for example, between a hostile applet allocating a lot of memory and an image processing applet attempting to do useful work. Other kinds of hostile applets that are currently possible are

- applets that send unauthorized e-mail from the end user's computer
- applets that make annoying noises even after you leave the web page
- applets that display offensive images or animations

A security manager isn't enough to prevent every possible action that could possibly offend or inconvenience an end user. Other than the attacks listed here, however, the security manager attempts to provide a check method that allows you to control access to any potentially unsafe action.

When a Java application starts, it has no security manager, but the application can install one at its option. If it does not install a security manager, no restrictions are placed on any activities requested of the Java API; the Java API will do whatever it is asked. (For this reason, Java applications, by default, do not have any security restrictions such as those that limit the activities of untrusted applets.) If the application does install a security manager, then that security manager will be in charge for the entire remainder of the lifetime of that application. It can't be replaced, extended, or changed. From that point on, the Java API will fulfill only those requests that are sanctioned by the security manager.

In general, a "check" method of the security manager throws a security exception if the checked-on activity is forbidden and simply returns if the activity is permitted. Therefore, the procedure a Java API method generally follows when it is about to perform a potentially unsafe activity involves two steps. First, the Java API code checks whether a security manager has been installed. If not, it skips step 2 and goes ahead with the potentially unsafe action. Otherwise, as step 2, it calls the appropriate "check" method in the security manager. If the action is forbidden, the "check" method will throw a security exception, which will cause the Java API method to immediately abort. The potentially unsafe action will never be taken. If, on the other hand, the action is permitted, the "check" method will simply return. In this case, the Java API method carries on and performs the potentially unsafe action.

Although you can install only one security manager, you can write the security manager so that it establishes multiple security policies. In addition to the "check" methods, the security manager also offers methods that allow you to determine whether a request is being made either directly or indirectly from a class loaded by a class loader object, and if so, which class loader object. This capability enables you to implement a security policy that varies depending on which class loader loaded the classes making the request. You can also vary the security policy based on information about the class files loaded by the class loader, such as whether or not the class files were downloaded across a network or imported from the local disk. So even though an application can have only one security manager, that security manager can establish a flexible security policy that varies depending on the trustworthiness of the code requesting the potentially unsafe action.

## Authentication

The support for authentication introduced in Java 1.1 in the `java.security` package expands your ability to establish multiple security policies by enabling you to implement a sandbox that varies depending on who actually created the code. Authentication allows you to verify that a set of class files was blessed as trustworthy by some vendor and that the class files were not altered en route to your virtual machine. Thus, to the extent you trust the vendor, you can ease the restrictions placed on the code by the sandbox. You can establish different security policies for code that comes from different vendors.

For links to more information about authentication and `java.security`, visit the resources page for this chapter.

# Security Beyond the Architecture

Security is a trade-off between cost and risk: the lower the security risk, the higher the cost of security. The costs associated with any computer or network security strategy must be weighed against the costs that would be associated with the theft or destruction of the information or computing resources being protected. The nature of a computer or network security strategy should be shaped by the value of the assets being protected.

To be effective, a computer or network security strategy must be comprehensive. It cannot consist exclusively of a sandbox for running downloaded Java code. For example, it may not matter much that the Java applets you download from the Internet and run on your computer can't read the word processing file of your top-secret business plan if you

- routinely download untrusted native executables from the Internet and run them
- throw away extra printed copies of your business plan without shredding them
- leave your doors unlocked when you're gone
- hire someone to help you who is actually a spy for your arch-rival

In the context of a comprehensive security strategy, however, Java's security model can play a useful role.

The nice thing about Java's security model is that, after you set it up, it does most of the work for you. You don't have to worry about whether a particular program is trusted—the Java runtime will determine that information for you—and if it is untrusted, the Java runtime will protect your assets by encasing the untrusted code in a sandbox.

End users of Java software cannot rely only on the security mechanisms built into Java's architecture. They must have a comprehensive security policy appropriate to their actual security requirements.

Similarly, the security strategy of Java technology itself does not rely exclusively on the architectural security mechanisms described in this chapter. For example, one aspect of Java's security strategy is that anyone can sign a license agreement and get a copy of the source code of Sun's Java Platform implementation. Instead of keeping the internal implementation of Java's security architecture a secret "black box," it is open to anyone who wishes to look at it. This way, security experts seeking a good technical challenge are encouraged try to find security holes in the implementation. When security holes are discovered, they can be patched. Thus, the openness of Java's internal implementation is part of Java's overall security strategy.

Besides openness, several other aspects to Java's overall security strategy don't directly involve its architecture. You can find out more information about these aspects on the resources page for this chapter.

# The Resources Page

For more information about Java and security, see the resource page for this chapter: `http://www.artima.com/insidejvm/security.html`.

# 4

# Network Mobility

The preceding two chapters described how Java's architecture deals with the two major challenges presented to software developers by a networked computing environment. Platform independence deals with the challenge that many different kinds of computers and devices are usually connected to the same network. The sandbox security model deals with the challenge that networks represent a convenient way to transmit viruses and other forms of malicious code. This chapter describes not how Java's architecture deals with a challenge, but how it seizes an opportunity made possible by the network.

One of the fundamental reasons Java is a useful tool for networked software environments is that Java's architecture enables the network mobility of software. In fact, it was primarily this aspect of Java technology that was considered by many in the software industry to represent a paradigm shift. This chapter examines the nature of this new paradigm of network-mobile software and how Java's architecture makes it possible.

# Why Network Mobility?

Prior to the advent of the personal computer, the dominant computing model was the large mainframe computer serving multiple users. By time sharing, a mainframe computer divided its attention among several users, who logged onto the mainframe at dumb terminals. Software applications were stored on disks attached to the mainframe computer, allowing multiple users to share the same applications while they shared the same CPU. A drawback of this model was that if one user ran a CPU-intensive job, all other users would experience degraded performance.

The appearance of the microprocessor led to the proliferation of the personal computer. This change in the hardware status quo changed the software paradigm as well. Rather than share software applications stored at a mainframe computer, individual users had individual copies of software applications stored at each personal computer. Because each user ran software on a dedicated CPU, this new model of computing addressed the difficulties of dividing CPU time among many users attempting to share one mainframe CPU.

Initially, personal computers operated as unconnected islands of computing. The dominant software model was of isolated executables running on isolated personal computers. But soon, personal computers were connected to networks. Because a personal computer gave its user undivided attention, it addressed the CPU time-sharing difficulties of mainframes. But unless personal computers were connected to a network, they couldn't replicate the mainframe's ability to let multiple users view and manipulate a central repository of data.

As personal computers connected to networks became the norm, another software model began to increase in importance: client/server. The client/server model divided work between two processes running on two different computers: a client process ran on the end user's personal computer, and a server process ran on some other computer hooked to the same network. The client and server processes communicated with one another by sending data back and forth across the network. The server process often simply accepted data query commands from clients across the network, retrieved the requested data from a central database, and sent the retrieved data back across the network to the client. Upon receiving the data, the client processed, displayed, and allowed a user to manipulate the data. This model allowed users of personal computers to view and manipulate data stored at a central repository, while not forcing them to share a central CPU for all of the processing of that data. Users did share the CPU running the server process, but to the extent that data processing was performed by the clients, the burden on the central CPU hosting the server process was lessened.

The client/server architecture was soon extended to include more than two processes. The original client/server model began to be called *2-tier client/server*, to indicate two processes: one client and one server. More elaborate architectures were called *3-tier*, to indicate three processes; *4-tier*, to indicate four processes; *or N-tier*, to indicate people were getting tired of counting processes. Eventually, as more processes became involved, the distinction between client and server blurred, and people just started using the term *distributed processing* to encompass all these schemes.

The distributed processing model leveraged the network and the proliferation of processors by dividing processing work loads among many processors while allowing those processors to share data. Although this model had many advantages over the mainframe model, one notable disadvantage was apparent: distributed processing systems were more difficult to administer than mainframe systems. On mainframe systems, software applications were stored on a disk attached to the mainframe. Even though an application could serve many users, it had to be installed and maintained in only one place. When an application was upgraded, all users got the new version the next time they logged on and started the application. By contrast, the software executables for different components of a distributed processing system were usually stored on many different disks. In a client/server architecture, for example, each computer that hosted a client process usually had its own copy of the client software stored on its local disk. As a result, a system administrator had to install and maintain the various components of a distributed software system in many different places. When a software component was upgraded, the system administrator had to physically upgrade each copy of the component on each computer that hosted it. As a result, system administration was more difficult for the distributed processing model than for the mainframe model.

The arrival of Java, with an architecture that enabled the network mobility of software, heralded yet another model for computing. Building on the prevailing distributed processing model, the new model added the automatic delivery of software across networks to computers that ran the software. This model addressed the difficulties involved in system administration of distributed processing systems. For example, in a client/server system, client software could be stored at one central computer attached to the network. Whenever an end user needed to use the client software, the binary executable would be sent from the central computer across the network to the end user's computer, where the software would run.

Network mobility of software therefore represented another step in the evolution of the computing model. In particular, it addressed the difficulty of administering a distributed processing system. It simplified the job of distributing any software that was to be used on more than one CPU. It allowed data to be delivered together with the software that can manipulate or display the data. Because code was sent along with data, end users would always have the most up-to-date version of the code. Thus, because of network mobility, software can be administered from a central computer, reminiscent of the mainframe model, but processing can still be distributed among many CPUs.

# A New Software Paradigm

The shift away from the mainframe model toward the distributed processing model was a consequence of the personal computer revolution, which was made possible by the rapidly increasing capabilities and decreasing costs of processors. Similarly, lurking underneath the latest software paradigm shift toward distributed processing with network-mobile code is another hardware trend—the increasing capabilities and decreasing costs of network bandwidth. As *bandwidth* (the amount of information that can be carried by a network) increases, it becomes practical to send new kinds of information across a network; and with each new kind of information a network carries, the network takes on a new character. Thus, as bandwidth grows, simple text sent across a network can become enhanced with graphics, and the network begins to take on an appearance reminiscent of newspapers or magazines. After bandwidth expands enough to support live streams of audio data, the network begins to act like a radio, a CD player, or a telephone. With still more bandwidth, video becomes possible, resulting in a network that competes with TV and VCRs for the attention of couch potatoes. But one other kind of bandwidth-hungry content becomes increasingly practical as bandwidth improves: computer software. Because networks, by definition, interconnect processors, one processor can, given enough bandwidth, send code across a network for another processor to execute. Once networks begin to move software as well as data, the network begins to look like a computer in its own right.

As software begins to travel across networks, not only does the network begin to take on a new character, but so does the software itself. Network-mobile code makes it easier to ensure that an end user has the necessary software to view or manipulate some data sent across the network because the software can be sent along with the data. In the old model, software executables from a local disk were invoked to view data that came across the network; thus the software application was usually a distinct entity, easily discernible from the data. In the new model, because software and data are both sent across the network, the distinction between software and data is not as stark; software and data blur together to become *content*.

As the nature of software evolves, the end user's relationship to software evolves as well. Prior to network mobility, an end user had to think in terms of software applications and version numbers. Software was generally distributed on media such as tapes, floppy disks, or CD-ROMs. To use an application, an end user had to get the installation media, physically insert them into a drive or reader attached to the computer, and run an installation program that copied files from the installation media to the computer's hard disk. Moreover, the end user often did this process multiple times for each application because software applications were routinely replaced by new versions that fixed old bugs and added new features (and usually added new bugs too). When a new version was released, end users had to decide whether to upgrade. If an end user decided to upgrade, the installation process had to be repeated. Thus, end users had to think in terms of software applications and version numbers and take deliberate action to keep their software applications up to date.

In the new model, end users think less in terms of software applications with discrete versions and more in terms of self-evolving *content services*. Whereas installing a traditional software application or an upgrade was a deliberate act on the part of the end user, network mobility of software enables installation and upgrading that are more automatic. Network-delivered software need not have discrete version numbers that are known to the end user. The end user need not decide whether to upgrade and need not take any special action to upgrade. Network-delivered software can just evolve of its own accord. Instead of buying discrete versions of a software application, end users can subscribe to a content service—software that is delivered across a network along with relevant data—and watch as both the software and data evolve automatically over time.

Once you move away from delivering software in discrete versions toward delivering software as self-evolving streams of interactive content, your end-user loses some control. In the old model, if a new version that had serious bugs appeared, end users could simply opt not to upgrade. But in the new model, end users can't necessarily wait until the bugs are worked out of a new version before upgrading to the new version because they may have no control over the upgrading process.

For certain kinds of products, especially those that are large and full-featured, end users may prefer to retain control over whether and when to upgrade. Consequently, in some situations software vendors may publish discrete versions of a content service over the network. At the very least, a vendor can publish two branches of a service: a beta branch and a released branch. End users who want to stay on the bleeding edge can subscribe to the beta service, and the rest can subscribe to the released service that, although it may not have all the newest features, is likely more robust.

Yet for many content services, especially simple ones, most end users won't want to have to worry about versions because worrying about versions makes software harder to use. The end users must have knowledge about the differences between versions, make decisions about when and if to upgrade, and take deliberate action to cause an upgrade. Content services that are not chopped up into discrete versions are easier to use because they evolve automatically. Such a content service, because the end users don't have to maintain it but can just simply use it, takes on the feel of a "software appliance."

Many self-evolving content services will share two fundamental characteristics with common household appliances: a focused functionality and a simple user interface. Consider the toaster. A toaster's functionality is focused exclusively on the job of preparing toast, and it has a simple user interface. When you walk up to a toaster, you don't expect to have to read a manual. You expect to put the bread in at the top and push down a handle until it clicks. You expect to be able to peer in and see orange wires glowing and, after a moment, to hear that satisfying pop and see your bread transformed into toast. If the result is too light or too dark, you expect to be able to slide a knob to indicate to the toaster that the next time you want your toast a bit darker or lighter. That's the extent of the functionality and user interface of a toaster. Likewise, the functionality of many content services will be as focused, and the user interface will be as simple. If you want to order a movie through the network, for example, you don't want to worry about whether you have the correct version of movie-ordering software. You don't want to have to install it. You just want to switch on the movie-ordering content service and, through a simple user interface, order your movie. Then you can sit back and enjoy your network-delivered movie as you eat your toast.

A good example of a content service is a World Wide Web page. If you look at an HTML file, it looks like a source file for some kind of program. But if you see the browser as the program, the HTML file looks more like data. Thus, the distinction between code and data is blurred. Also, people who browse the World Wide Web expect web pages to evolve over time, without any deliberate action on their part. They don't expect to see discrete version numbers for web pages. They don't expect to have to do anything to upgrade to the latest version of a page besides simply revisiting the page in their browsers.

In the coming years, many of today's media may, to some extent, be assimilated by the network and transformed into content services. (As with the Borg from *Star Trek*, resistance is futile.) Broadcast radio, broadcast and cable TV, telephones, answering machines, faxes, video rental stores, newspapers, magazines, books, computer software—all will be affected by the proliferation of networks. But just as TV didn't supplant radio entirely, content services will not entirely supplant existing media. Instead, content services will likely take over some aspects of existing media, leaving the existing media to adjust accordingly, and create some new forms that didn't previously exist.

In the computer software domain, the content service model will not completely replace the old models either. Instead, it will likely take over certain aspects of the old models that fit better in the new model, add new forms that didn't exist before, and leave the old models to adjust their focus slightly in light of the newcomer.

This book is an example of how the network can affect existing media. The book was not entirely replaced by a content service counterpart, but instead of including resource pointers (sources where you can find further information on topics presented in the book) as part of the book, they were placed on a web page. Because resource pointers change so often, letting the network assimilate that part of the book made sense. Thus, the resource pointers portion of the book has become a content service.

The crux of the new software paradigm, therefore, is that software begins to act more like appliances. End users no longer have to worry about installation, version numbers, or upgrading. As code is sent along with data across the network, software delivery and updating become automatic. In this way, simply by making code mobile, Java unleashes a whole new way to think about software development, delivery, and use.

## Java's Architectural Support for Network Mobility

Java's architectural support for network mobility begins with its support for platform independence and security. Although they are not strictly required for network mobility, platform independence and security help make network mobility practical. Platform independence enables you to deliver a program across the network more easily because you don't have to maintain a separate version of the program for different platforms, and you don't have to figure out how to get the right version to each computer. One version of a program can serve all computers. Java's security features help promote network mobility because they give end users confidence to download class files from untrusted sources. In practice, therefore, Java's architectural support for platform independence and security facilitate the network mobility of its class files.

Beyond platform independence and security, Java's architectural support for network mobility is focused on managing the time it takes to move software across a network. If you store a program on a server and download it across a network when you need it, your program will likely take longer to start than if you had started the same program from a local disk. Thus, one of the primary issues of network-mobile software is the time it takes to send a program across a network. Java's architecture addresses this issue by rejecting the traditional monolithic binary executable in favor of small binary pieces: Java class files. Class files can travel across networks independently, and because Java programs are dynamically linked and dynamically extensible, end users needn't wait until all of a program's class files are downloaded before the program starts. The program starts when the first class file arrives. Class files themselves are designed to be compact so that they fly more quickly across networks. Therefore, the main way Java's architecture facilitates network mobility directly is by breaking up the monolithic binary executable into compact class files, which can be loaded as needed.

The execution of a Java application begins at a **main()** method of some class, and other classes are loaded and dynamically linked as they are needed by the application. If a class is never actually used during one session, that class won't ever be loaded during that session. For example, if you are using a word processor that has a spelling checker, but during one session you never invoke the spelling checker, the class files for the spelling checker will not be loaded during that session.

In addition to dynamic linking, Java's architecture also enables dynamic extension. Dynamic extension is another way the loading of class files (and the downloading of them across a network) can be delayed in a Java application. Using class loader objects, a Java program can load extra classes at runtime; they then become part of the running program. Therefore, dynamic linking and dynamic extension give Java programmers some flexibility in designing when class files for a program are loaded, and as a result, how much time end users must spend waiting for class files to come across the network.

Besides dynamic linking and dynamic extension, another way Java's architecture directly supports network mobility is through the class file format itself. To reduce the time it takes to send them across networks, class files are designed to be compact. In particular, the bytecode streams they contain are designed to be compact. They are called *bytecodes* because each instruction occupies only one byte. With only two exceptions, all opcodes and their ensuing operands are byte aligned to make the bytecode streams smaller. The two exceptions are opcodes that may have one to three bytes of padding after the opcode and before the start of the operands so that the operands are aligned on word boundaries. Other than the two opcodes that might have a small amount of padding, all data in a class file is byte aligned.

One of the implications of the compactness goal for class files is that Java compilers are not likely to do any local optimization. Because of binary compatibility rules, Java compilers can't perform global optimizations such as inlining the invocation of another class's method. (Inlining means replacing the method invocation with the code performed by the method, which saves the time required to invoke and return from the method as the code executes.) Binary compatibility requires that a method's implementation can be changed without breaking compatibility with preexisting class files that depend on the method. Inlining could be performed in some circumstances on methods within a single class, but in general that kind of optimization is not done by Java compilers, partly because it goes against the grain of class file compactness. Optimizations are often a trade-off between execution speed and code size. Therefore, Java compilers generally leave optimization up to the Java Virtual Machine, which can optimize code as it loads classes for interpreting or just-in-time compiling.

Beyond the architectural features of dynamic linking, dynamic extension, and class file compactness are some strategies that, although they are really not necessarily part of the architecture, help manage the time required to move class files across a network. Because HTTP protocols require that each class file of a Java applet be requested individually, often a large percentage of applet download time is the result not of the actual transmission of class files across the network, but of the network handshaking of each class file request. The overhead for a file request is multiplied by the number of class files being requested. To address this problem, Java 1.1 included support for JAR (Java ARchive) files. JAR files enable many class files to be sent in one network transaction, which greatly reduces the overhead time required to move class files across a network compared with sending one class file at a time. Moreover, the data inside a JAR file can be compressed, which results in an even shorter download time. Sometimes sending software across a network in one big chunk pays off. If a program definitely needs a set of classes before it can start, those class files can be more speedily transmitted if they are sent together in a JAR file.

One other strategy to minimize an end user's wait time is to not download class files on demand. Through various techniques, such as the subscription model used by Marimba Castanet, class files can be downloaded before they are needed, resulting in a program that starts faster. You can obtain more information about Castanet's model from the resource page for this chapter.

Therefore, other than platform independence and security, which help make network mobility practical, the main focus of Java's architectural support for network mobility is managing the time required to send class files across a network. Dynamic linking and dynamic extension allow Java programs to be designed in small functional units that are downloaded as needed by the end users. Class file compactness helps reduce the time required to move a Java program across the network. The JAR file enables compression and the sending of multiple class files across the network in a single network file-transfer transaction.

# The Applet: An Example of Network-Mobile Java

Java is a network-oriented technology that first appeared at a time when the network was looking increasingly like the next revolution in computing. Java was adopted so rapidly and so widely, however, not simply because it was a timely technology, but because it had timely marketing. Java was not the only network-oriented technology being developed in the early to mid-1990s. And although it was a good technology, it wasn't the necessarily the best technology—but it probably had the best marketing. Java was the one technology to hit a slim market window in early 1995, resulting in such a strong response that many companies developing similar technologies canceled their projects, including Microsoft, which canceled a project code-named Blackbird. Companies that carried on with their technologies, such as AT&T did with a network-oriented technology named Inferno, saw Java steal much of their potential thunder.

Several important factors in how Java was initially unleashed on the world contributed to its successful marketing. First, it had a cool name—one that could be appreciated by programmers and nonprogrammers alike. Second, it was, for all practical purposes, free—always a strong selling point among prospective buyers. The most critical factor contributing to the successful marketing of Java, however, was that Sun's engineers hooked Java technology to the World Wide Web at the precise moment Netscape was looking to transform its web browser from a graphical hypertext viewer to a full-fledged computing platform. As the World Wide Web swept through the software industry (and the global consciousness) like an ever-increasing tidal wave, Java rode with it. Therefore, in a sense, Java became a success because Java "surfed the web." It caught the wave at just the right time and kept riding it as, one by one, its potential competitors dropped uneventfully into the cold, dark sea. The way the engineers at Sun hooked Java technology to the World Wide Web—and therefore, the key way Java was successfully marketed—was by creating a special flavor of Java program that ran inside a web browser: the Java applet.

The Java applet showed off all of Java's network-oriented features: platform independence, network mobility, and security. Platform independence was one of the main tenets of the World Wide Web, and Java applets fit right in. Java applets can run on any platform as long as a Java-capable browser is available for that platform. Java applets also demonstrated Java's security capabilities because they run inside a strict sandbox. But most significantly, Java applets demonstrated the promise of network mobility. As shown in Figure 4-1, Java applets can be maintained on one server, from which they can travel across a network to many different kinds of computers. To update an applet, you need only to update the server. Users will automatically get the updated version the next time they use the applet. Thus, maintenance is localized, but processing is distributed.

Java-capable browsers fire off a Java application that hosts the applets the browsers display. To display a web page, a web browser requests an HTML file from an HTTP server. If the HTML file includes an applet, the browser will see an HTML tag such as this:

```
<applet CODE="HeapOfFish.class"
CODEBASE="gcsupport/classes"
WIDTH=525
HEIGHT=360></applet>
```

This "applet" tag provides enough information to enable the browser to display the applet. The **CODE** attribute indicates the name of the applet's

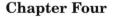

**Figure 4-1.**
The Java applet and
the network.

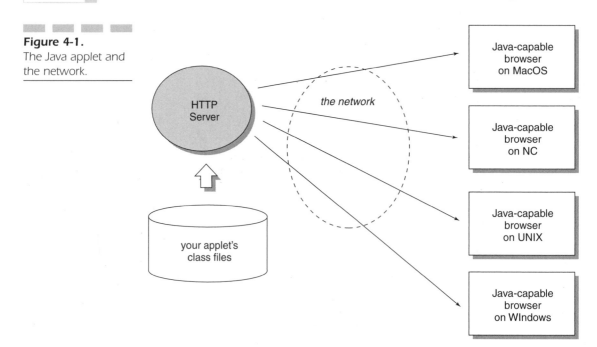

starting class file, in this case: **HeapOfFish.class**. The **CODEBASE** attribute
gives the location of the applet's class files relative to the base URL of the
web page. The **WIDTH** and **HEIGHT** attributes indicate the size in pixels of
the applet's panel, the visible portion of the applet that is displayed as
part of the web page.

When a browser encounters a web page that includes an applet tag, it
passes information from the tag to the running Java application. The Java
application either creates a new class loader object or reuses an existing
one to download the starting class file for the applet. It then initializes
the applet, by invoking the **init()** method of the applet's starting class.
The other class files for the applet are downloaded on an as-needed basis
by the normal process of dynamic linking. For example, when a new class
is first used by the applet's starting class, the symbolic reference to the
new class must be resolved. During resolution, if the class has not already
been loaded, the Java Virtual Machine will ask the same class loader object that loaded the applet's starting class to load the new class. If the
class loader object cannot load the class from the local trusted repository
through the primordial class loader, the class loader object will attempt
to download the class file across the network from the same location it retrieved the applet's starting class. After initialization of the applet is complete, the applet appears as part of the web page inside the browser.

Network-mobile Java can take other forms besides Java applets, but the framework that supports other network-mobile forms will likely look very similar to the framework for applets. Like applets, other forms of network-mobile Java code will, in general, be implemented as special flavors of Java program running in the context of a host Java application. Network-mobile class files will generally be loaded by class loader objects for two reasons. The first reason is simply that a class loader object can download class files across a network in custom ways that a primordial class loader can't. But the second reason involves security. Because network-mobile class files are not always known to be trustworthy, the separate name-spaces provided by class loader objects are needed to protect a malicious applet from interfering with applets loaded from other sources. Also because network-mobile class files can't always be trusted, generally a security manager will establish a sandbox for the network-mobile code.

# The Resources Page

For links to information about other examples of network-mobile Java, such as Marimba Castanet Channels, Jeeves Servlets, and Aglets (Java-based autonomous software agents), see the resource page for this chapter: `http://www.artima.com/insidejvm/mobility.html`.

# 5

# The Java Virtual Machine

The preceding four chapters of this book gave a broad overview of Java's architecture. They showed how the Java Virtual Machine fits into the overall architecture relative to other components such as the language and API. The remainder of this book will focus more narrowly on the Java Virtual Machine. This chapter gives an overview of the Java Virtual Machine's internal architecture.

The Java Virtual Machine is called *virtual* because it is an abstract computer defined by a specification. To run a Java program, you need a concrete implementation of the abstract specification. This chapter describes primarily the abstract specification of the Java Virtual Machine. To illustrate the abstract definition of certain features, however, this chapter also describes various ways in which those features could be implemented.

# What Is a Java Virtual Machine?

To understand the Java Virtual Machine, you must first be aware that you may be talking about any of three different things when you say "Java Virtual Machine." You may be speaking of

▪ the abstract specification,

▪ a concrete implementation, or

▪ a runtime instance.

The abstract specification is a concept, described in detail in the book *The Java Virtual Machine Specification*, by Tim Lindholm and Frank Yellin. Concrete implementations, which exist on many platforms and come from many vendors, are either all software or a combination of hardware and software. A runtime instance hosts a single running Java application.

Each Java application runs inside a runtime instance of some concrete implementation of the abstract specification of the Java Virtual Machine. In this book, the term *Java Virtual Machine* is used in all three of these senses. Where the intended sense is not clear from the context, one of the terms *specification*, *implementation*, or *instance* is added to the term *Java Virtual Machine*.

# The Lifetime of a Java Virtual Machine

A runtime instance of the Java Virtual Machine has a clear mission in life: to run one Java application. When a Java application starts, a runtime instance is born. When the application completes, the instance dies. If you start three Java applications at the same time, on the same computer, using the same concrete implementation, you'll get three Java Virtual Machine instances. Each Java application runs inside its own Java Virtual Machine.

A Java Virtual Machine instance starts running its solitary application by invoking the **main()** method of some initial class. The **main()** method must be public, static, return **void**, and accept one parameter: a **String** array. Any class with such a **main()** method can be used as the starting point for a Java application.

For example, consider an application that prints out its command-line arguments:

```
// On CD-ROM in file jvm/ex1/Echo.java
class Echo {

    public static void main(String[] args) {
        int len = args.length;
        for (int i = 0; i < len; ++i) {
            System.out.print(args[i] + " ");
        }
        System.out.println();
    }
}
```

You must in some implementation-dependent way give a Java Virtual Machine the name of the initial class that has the **main()** method that will start the entire application. One real-world example of a Java Virtual Machine implementation is the **java** program from Sun's JDK. If you wanted to run the **Echo** application using Sun's **java** on Windows 95, for example, you would type in a command such as

**java Echo Greetings, Planet.**

The first word in the command, **java**, indicates that the Java Virtual Machine from Sun's JDK should be run by the operating system. The second word, **Echo**, is the name of the initial class. **Echo** must have a public static method named **main()** that returns **void** and takes a **String** array as its only parameter. The subsequent words, **Greetings, Planet.**, are the command-line arguments for the application. They are passed to the **main()** method in the **String** array in the order in which they appear on the command line. So, for the preceding example, the contents of the **String** array passed to main in **Echo** are as follows:

**arg[0]** is **"Greetings,"**
**arg[1]** is **"Planet."**

The **main()** method of an application's initial class serves as the starting point for that application's initial thread. The initial thread can in turn fire off other threads.

Inside the Java Virtual Machine, threads come in two flavors: *daemon* and *nondaemon*. A daemon thread is ordinarily a thread used by the virtual machine itself, such as a thread that performs garbage collection. The application, however, can mark any threads it creates as daemon threads. The initial thread of an application—the one that begins at **main()**—is a non-daemon thread.

A Java application continues to execute (the virtual machine instance continues to live) as long as any non-daemon threads are still running. When all non-daemon threads of a Java application terminate, the virtual machine instance will exit. If permitted by the security manager, the application can also cause its own demise by invoking the `exit()` method of class `Runtime` or `System`.

In the preceding `Echo` application, the `main()` method doesn't invoke any other threads. After it prints out the command-line arguments, `main()` returns. This action terminates the application's only non-daemon thread, which causes the virtual machine instance to exit.

# The Architecture of the Java Virtual Machine

In the Java Virtual Machine specification, the behavior of a virtual machine instance is described in terms of subsystems, memory areas, data types, and instructions. These components describe an abstract inner architecture for the abstract Java Virtual Machine. The purpose of these components is not so much to dictate an inner architecture for implementations, but it is more to provide a way to strictly define the external behavior of implementations. The specification defines the required behavior of any Java Virtual Machine implementation in terms of these abstract components and their interactions.

Figure 5-1 shows a block diagram of the Java Virtual Machine that includes the major subsystems and memory areas described in the specification. As mentioned in previous chapters, each Java Virtual Machine has a *class loader subsystem*: a mechanism for loading types (classes and interfaces) given fully qualified names. Each Java Virtual Machine also has an *execution engine*: a mechanism responsible for executing the instructions contained in the methods of loaded classes.

When a Java Virtual Machine runs a program, it needs memory to store many things, including bytecodes and other information it extracts from loaded class files, objects the program instantiates, parameters to methods, return values, local variables, and intermediate results of computations. The Java Virtual Machine organizes the memory it needs to execute a program into several *runtime data areas*.

Although the same runtime data areas exist in some form in every Java Virtual Machine implementation, their specification is quite abstract.

**Figure 5-1.**

The internal
architecture of the
Java Virtual Machine.

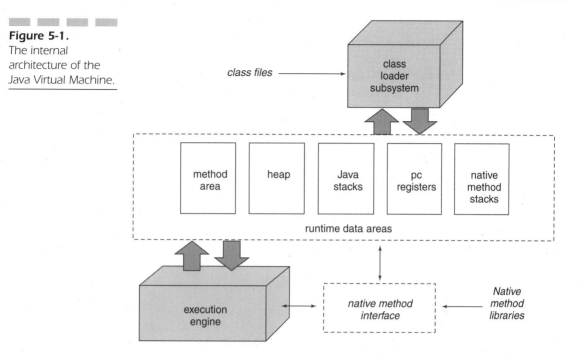

Many decisions about the structural details of the runtime data areas are left to the designers of individual implementations.

Different implementations of the virtual machine can have very different memory constraints. Some implementations may have a lot of memory in which to work, others may have very little. Some implementations may be able to take advantage of virtual memory, others may not. The abstract nature of the specification of the runtime data areas helps make it easier to implement the Java Virtual Machine on a wide variety of computers and devices.

Some runtime data areas are shared among all of an application's threads, and others are unique to individual threads. Each instance of the Java Virtual Machine has one *method area* and one *heap*. These areas are shared by all threads running inside the virtual machine. When the virtual machine loads a class file, it parses information about a type from the binary data contained in the class file. It places this type information into the method area. As the program runs, the virtual machine places all objects the program instantiates onto the heap. See Figure 5-2 for a graphical depiction of these memory areas.

As each new thread comes into existence, it gets its *own pc register* (program counter) and *Java stack*. If the thread is executing a Java

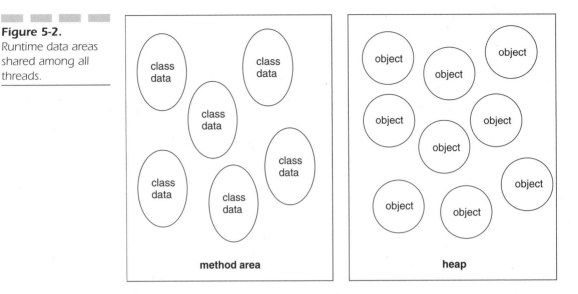

method (not a native method), the value of the pc register indicates the next instruction to execute. A thread's Java stack stores the state of Java (not native) method invocations for the thread. The state of a Java method invocation includes its local variables, the parameters with which it was invoked, its return value (if any), and intermediate calculations. The state of native method invocations is stored in an implementation-dependent way in *native method stacks*, as well as possibly in registers or other implementation-dependent memory areas.

The Java stack is composed of *stack frames* (or *frames*). A stack frame contains the state of one Java method invocation. When a thread invokes a method, the Java Virtual Machine pushes a new frame onto that thread's Java stack. When the method completes, the virtual machine pops and discards the frame for that method.

The Java Virtual Machine has no registers to hold intermediate data values. The instruction set uses the Java stack for storage of intermediate data values. This approach was taken by Java's designers to keep the Java Virtual Machine's instruction set compact and to facilitate implementation on architectures with few or irregular general-purpose registers.

See Figure 5-3 for a graphical depiction of the memory areas the Java Virtual Machine creates for each thread. These areas are private to the owning thread. No thread can access the pc register or Java stack of another thread.

Figure 5-3 shows a snapshot of a virtual machine instance in which three threads are executing. At the instant of the snapshot, threads one

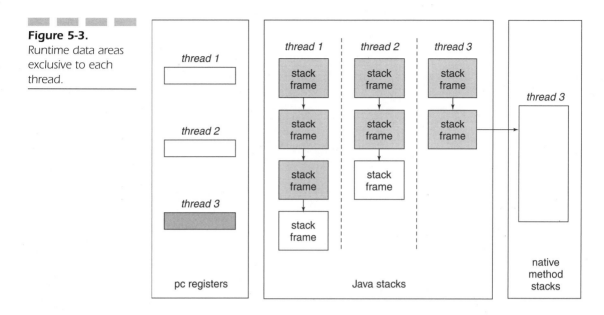

**Figure 5-3.**
Runtime data areas exclusive to each thread.

and two are executing Java methods. Thread three is executing a native method.

In Figure 5-3, as in all graphical depictions of the Java stack in this book, the stacks are shown growing downward. The "top" of each stack is shown at the bottom of the figure. Stack frames for currently executing methods are shown in a lighter shade. For threads that are currently executing a Java method, the pc register indicates the next instruction to execute. In Figure 5-3, such pc registers (the ones for threads one and two) are shown in a lighter shade. Because thread three is currently executing a native method, the contents of its pc register—the one shown in dark gray—are undefined.

# Data Types

The Java Virtual Machine computes by performing operations on certain types of data. Both the data types and operations are strictly defined by the Java Virtual Machine specification. The data types can be divided into a set of *primitive types* and a *reference type*. Variables of the primitive types hold *primitive values*, and variables of the reference type hold *reference values*. Reference values refer to objects but are not objects themselves. Primitive values, by contrast, do not refer to anything. They are the actual data themselves. You can see a graphical depiction of the Java Virtual Machine's families of data types in Figure 5-4.

All the primitive types of the Java programming language, except **boolean**, are primitive types of the Java Virtual Machine. When a compiler translates Java source code into bytecodes, it uses **int**s or **byte**s to represent **boolean**s. In the Java Virtual Machine, **false** is represented by integer zero and **true** by any nonzero integer. Operations involving **boolean** values use **int**s. Arrays of **boolean** are accessed as arrays of **byte**, though they can be represented on the heap as arrays of **byte** or as bit fields.

The primitive types of the Java programming language other than **boolean** form the *numeric types* of the Java Virtual Machine. The numeric types are divided between the *integral types*—**byte**, **short**, **int**, **long**, and **char**—and the *floating-point types*—**float** and **double**. As with the Java programming language, the primitive types of the Java Virtual Machine have the same range everywhere. A **long** in the Java Virtual Machine always acts like a 64-bit signed two's-complement number, independent of the underlying host platform.

The Java Virtual Machine works with one other primitive type that is unavailable to the Java programmer: the **returnValue** type. This primitive type is used to implement **finally** clauses of Java programs. The use of the **returnValue** type is described in detail in Chapter 18, "Finally Clauses."

**Figure 5-4.**
Data types of the Java Virtual Machine.

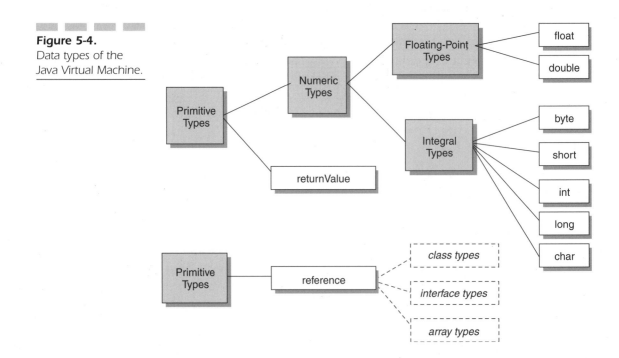

The reference type of the Java Virtual Machine is cleverly named **reference**. Values of type **reference** come in three flavors: the *class type*, the *interface type*, and the *array type*. All three types have values that are references to dynamically created objects. The class type's values are references to class instances. The array type's values are references to arrays, which are full-fledged objects in the Java Virtual Machine. The interface type's values are references to class instances that implement an interface. One other reference value is the **null** value, which indicates the **reference** variable doesn't refer to any object.

The Java Virtual Machine specification defines the range of values for each of the data types but does not define their sizes. The number of bits used to store each data type value is a decision of the designers of individual implementations. The ranges of the Java Virtual Machines data types are shown in Table 5-1. More information on the floating-point ranges is given in Chapter 14, "Floating-Point Arithmetic."

## Word Size

The basic unit of size for data values in the Java Virtual Machine is the *word*—a fixed size chosen by the designer of each Java Virtual Machine implementation. The word size must be large enough to hold a value of type **byte**, **short**, **int**, **char**, **float**, **returnValue**, or **reference**. Two words must be large enough to hold a value of type **long** or **double**. Implementation designers must therefore choose a word size that is at least 32 bits,

**Table 5-1.**

*Ranges of the Java Virtual Machine's data types*

| Type | Range |
|------|-------|
| **byte** | 8-bit signed two's-complement integer ($-2^7$ to $2^7 - 1$, inclusive) |
| **short** | 16-bit signed two's-complement integer ($-2^{15}$ to $2^{15} - 1$, inclusive) |
| **int** | 32-bit signed two's-complement integer ($-2^{31}$ to $2^{31} - 1$, inclusive) |
| **long** | 64-bit signed two's-complement integer ($-2^{63}$ to $2^{63} - 1$, inclusive) |
| **char** | 16-bit unsigned Unicode character (0 to $2^{16} - 1$, inclusive) |
| **float** | 32-bit IEEE 754 single-precision float |
| **double** | 64-bit IEEE 754 double-precision float |
| **returnValue** | address of an opcode within the same method |
| **reference** | reference to an object on the heap, or **null** |

but otherwise they can pick whatever word size will yield the most efficient implementation. The word size is often chosen to be the size of a native pointer on the host platform.

The specification of many of the Java Virtual Machine's runtime data areas is based on this abstract concept of a word. For example, two sections of a Java stack frame—the local variables and operand stack—are defined in terms of words. These areas can contain values of any of the virtual machine's data types. When placed into the local variables or operand stack, a value occupies either one or two words.

As they run, Java programs cannot determine the word size of their host virtual machine implementation. The word size does not affect the behavior of a program. It is only an internal attribute of a virtual machine implementation.

## The Class Loader Subsystem

The part of a Java Virtual Machine implementation that takes care of finding and loading types is the *class loader subsystem*. Chapter 1, "Introduction to Java's Architecture," gives an overview of this subsystem. Chapter 3, "Security," shows how the subsystem fits into Java's security model. This chapter describes the class loader subsystem in more detail and shows how it relates to the other components of the virtual machine's internal architecture.

As mentioned in Chapter 1, the Java Virtual Machine contains two kinds of class loaders: a *primordial class loader* and *class loader objects*. The primordial class loader is a part of the virtual machine implementation, and class loader objects are part of the running Java application. Classes loaded by different class loaders are placed into separate *namespaces* inside the Java Virtual Machine.

The class loader subsystem involves many other parts of the Java Virtual Machine and several classes from the `java.lang` library. For example, class loader objects are regular Java objects whose class descends from `java.lang.ClassLoader`. The methods of class `ClassLoader` allow Java applications to access the virtual machine's class loading machinery. Also, for every type a Java Virtual Machine loads, it creates an instance of class `java.lang.Class` to represent that type. Like all objects, class loader objects and instances of class `Class` reside on the heap. Data for loaded types resides in the method area.

**LOADING, LINKING, AND INITIALIZATION**  The class loader subsystem is responsible for more than just locating and importing the binary data for classes. It must also verify the correctness of imported classes, allocate and initialize memory for class variables, and assist in the resolution of symbolic references. These activities are performed in a strict order:

1. Loading: finding and importing the binary data for a type
2. Linking: performing verification, preparation, and (optionally) resolution
   a. Verification: ensuring the correctness of the imported type
   b. Preparation: allocating memory for class variables and initializing the memory to default values
   c. Resolution: transforming symbolic references from the type into direct references
3. Initialization: invoking Java code that initializes class variables to their proper starting values

The details of these processes are given in Chapter 7, "The Lifetime of a Class."

**THE PRIMORDIAL CLASS LOADER**  Java Virtual Machine implementations must be able to recognize and load classes and interfaces stored in binary files that conform to the Java class file format. An implementation is free to recognize other binary forms besides class files, but it must recognize class files. One example of an alternative binary format recognized by a particular Java Virtual Machine implementation is the CAB file. This file format, which is an archive of class files and other data files, is defined by Microsoft and recognized by Microsoft's implementation of the Java Virtual Machine.

Every Java Virtual Machine implementation has a primordial class loader, which knows how to load trusted classes, including the classes of the Java API. The Java Virtual Machine specification doesn't define how the primordial loader should locate classes. That is another decision the specification leaves to implementation designers.

Given a fully qualified type name, the primordial class loader must *in some way* attempt to locate a file with the type's simple name plus `.class`. One common approach is demonstrated by the Java Virtual Machine implementation in Sun's 1.1 JDK on Windows 95. This implementation searches a user-defined directory path stored in an environment variable named **CLASSPATH**. The primordial loader looks in each directory, in the order the directories appear in the **CLASSPATH**, until it finds a file with the appropriate name: the type's simple name plus **.class**. Unless the type is part of the unnamed package, the primordial loader expects the file to be in a subdirectory of one of the directories in the **CLASSPATH**. The path name of the subdirectory is built from the package name of the type. For example, if the primordial class loader is searching for class **java.lang.Object**, it will look for **Object.class** in the **java\lang** subdirectory of each **CLASSPATH** directory.

**CLASS LOADER OBJECTS**    Although class loader objects themselves are part of the Java application, three of the methods in class **ClassLoader** are gateways into the Java Virtual Machine:

```
// Three of the methods declared in class
//java.lang.ClassLoader:
protected final Class defineClass(byte data[], int offset,
    int length);
protected final Class findSystemClass(String name);
protected final void resolveClass(Class c);
```

Any Java Virtual Machine implementation must take care to connect these methods of class **ClassLoader** to the internal class loader subsystem.

The **defineClass()** method accepts a **byte** array, **data[]**, as input. Starting at position **offset** in the array and continuing for **length** bytes, class **ClassLoader** expects binary data conforming to the Java class file format—binary data that represents a new type for the running application. Every Java Virtual Machine implementation must make sure the **defineClass()** method of class **ClassLoader** can cause a new type to be imported into the method area.

The **findSystemClass()** method accepts a **String** representing a fully qualified name of a type. When a class loader object invokes this method, it is requesting that the virtual machine attempt to load the named type via its primordial class loader. If the primordial class loader has already loaded or successfully loads the type, it returns a reference to the **Class** object representing the type. If it can't locate the binary data for the type, it throws **ClassNotFoundException**. Every Java Virtual Machine implementation must make sure the **findSystemClass()** method can invoke the primordial class loader in this way.

The `resolveClass()` method accepts a reference to a `Class` instance. This method causes the type represented by the `Class` instance to be linked and initialized (if it hasn't already been linked and initialized). The `defineClass()` method, described earlier, takes care of loading only. (See the section "Loading, Linking, and Initialization" for definitions of these terms.) When `defineClass()` returns a `Class` instance, the binary file for the type has definitely been located and imported into the method area but not necessarily linked and initialized. Java Virtual Machine implementations make sure the `resolveClass()` method of class `ClassLoader` can cause the class loader subsystem to perform linking and initialization.

The details of how a Java Virtual Machine performs class loading, linking, and initialization with class loader objects are given in Chapter 8, "The Linking Model."

**NAME-SPACES**   As mentioned in Chapter 3, each class loader maintains its own name-space populated by the types it has loaded. Because each class loader has its own name-space, a single Java application can load multiple types with the same fully qualified name. A type's fully qualified name, therefore, is not always enough to uniquely identify it inside a Java Virtual Machine instance. If multiple types of that same name have been loaded into different name-spaces, the identity of the class loader that loaded the type (the identity of the name-space it is in) will also be needed to uniquely identify that type.

Name-spaces arise inside a Java Virtual Machine instance as a result of the process of resolution. As part of the data for each loaded type, the Java Virtual Machine keeps track of the class loader that imported the type. When the virtual machine needs to resolve a symbolic reference from one class to another, it requests the referenced class from the same class loader that loaded the referencing class. This process is described in detail in Chapter 8.

## The Method Area

Inside a Java Virtual Machine instance, information about loaded types is stored in a logical area of memory called the *method area*. When the Java Virtual Machine loads a type, it uses a class loader to locate the appropriate class file. The class loader reads in the class file—a linear stream of binary data—and passes it to the virtual machine. The virtual machine extracts information about the type from the binary data and stores the information in the method area. Memory for class (static) variables declared in the class is also taken from the method area.

The manner in which a Java Virtual Machine implementation represents type information internally is a decision of the implementation designer. For example, multibyte quantities in class files are stored in big-endian (most significant byte first) order. When the data is imported into the method area, however, a virtual machine can store the data in any manner. If an implementation sits on top of a little-endian processor, the designers may decide to store multibyte values in the method area in little-endian order.

The virtual machine will search through and use the type information stored in the method area as it executes the application it is hosting. Designers must attempt to devise data structures that will facilitate speedy execution of the Java application but must also think of compactness. If designing an implementation that will operate under low memory constraints, designers may decide to trade off some execution speed in favor of compactness. If designing an implementation that will run on a virtual memory system, on the other hand, designers may decide to store redundant information in the method area to facilitate execution speed. (If the underlying host doesn't offer virtual memory but does offer a hard disk, designers could create their own virtual memory system as part of their implementation.) Designers can choose whatever data structures and organization they feel optimize their implementations performance, in the context of its requirements.

All threads share the same method area, so access to the method area's data structures must be designed to be thread-safe. If two threads attempt to find a class named `Lava`, for example, and `Lava` has not yet been loaded, only one thread should be allowed to load it while the other one waits.

The size of the method area need not be fixed. As the Java application runs, the virtual machine can expand and contract the method area to fit the application's needs. Also, the memory of the method area need not be contiguous. It could be allocated on a heap—even on the virtual machine's own heap. Implementations may allow users or programmers to specify an initial size for the method area, as well as a maximum or minimum size.

The method area can also be garbage collected. Because Java programs can be dynamically extended via class loader objects, classes can become "unreferenced" by the application. If a class becomes unreferenced, a Java Virtual Machine can unload the class (garbage collect it) to keep the memory occupied by the method area at a minimum. The unloading of classes and the conditions under which a class can become "unreferenced" are described in Chapter 7.

**TYPE INFORMATION**  For each type it loads, a Java Virtual Machine must store the following kinds of information in the method area:

- The fully qualified name of the type
- The fully qualified name of the type's direct superclass (unless the type is an interface or class **java.lang.Object**, neither of which have a superclass)
- Whether the type is a class or an interface
- The type's modifiers ( some subset of **public**, **abstract**, **final**)
- An ordered list of the fully qualified names of any direct superinterfaces

Inside the Java class file and Java Virtual Machine, type names are always stored as *fully qualified names*. In Java source code, a fully qualified name is the name of a type's package, plus a dot, plus the type's *simple name*. For example, the fully qualified name of class **Object** in package **java.lang** is **java.lang.Object**. In class files, the dots are replaced by slashes, as in **java/lang/Object**. In the method area, fully qualified names can be represented in whatever form and data structures a designer chooses.

In addition to the basic type information in the preceding list, the virtual machine must also store the following for each loaded type:

- The constant pool for the type
- Field information
- Method information
- All class (static) variables declared in the type, except constants
- A reference to class **ClassLoader**
- A reference to class **Class**

This data is described in the following sections.

**THE CONSTANT POOL**  For each type it loads, a Java Virtual Machine must store a *constant pool*. A constant pool is an ordered set of constants used by the type, including literals (string, integer, and floating-point constants) and symbolic references to types, fields, and methods.

Entries in the constant pool are referenced by index, much like the elements of an array. Because it holds symbolic references to all types, fields, and methods used by a type, the constant pool plays a central role in the dynamic linking of Java programs. The constant pool is described in more detail later in this chapter and in Chapter 6, "The Java Class File."

**FIELD INFORMATION**  For each field declared in the type, the following information must be stored in the method area. In addition to the information for each field, the order in which the fields are declared by the class or interface must also be recorded. Here's the list for fields:

- The field's name
- The field's type
- The field's modifiers (some subset of `public`, `private`, `protected`, `static`, `final`, `volatile`, `transient`)

**METHOD INFORMATION**  For each method declared in the type, the following information must be stored in the method area. As with fields, the order in which the methods are declared by the class or interface must be recorded as well as the data. Here's the list:

- The method's name
- The method's return type (or *void*)
- The number and types (in order) of the method's parameters
- The method's modifiers (some subset of `public`, `private`, `protected`, `static`, `final`, `synchronized`, `native`, `abstract`)

In addition to the items in the preceding list, the following information must also be stored with each method that is not abstract or native:

- The method's bytecodes
- The sizes of the operand stack and local variables sections of the method's stack frame (described in a later section of this chapter)
- An exception table (described in Chapter 17, "Exceptions")

**CLASS VARIABLES**

Class variables are shared among all instances of a class and can be accessed even in the absence of any instance. These variables are associated with the class—not with instances of the class—so they are logically part of the class data in the method area. Before a Java Virtual Machine uses a class, it must allocate memory from the method area for each nonfinal class variable declared in the class.

Constants (class variables declared final) are not treated in the same way as nonfinal class variables. Every type that uses a final class variable gets a copy of the constant value in its own constant pool. As part of the constant pool, final class variables are stored in the method area—just like nonfinal class variables. But whereas nonfinal class variables are stored as part of the data for the type that *declares* them, final class variables are stored as part of the data for any type that *uses* them. This special treatment of constants is explained in more detail in Chapter 6.

**A REFERENCE TO CLASS ClassLoader** For each type it loads, a Java Virtual Machine must keep track of whether the type was loaded via the primordial class loader or a class loader object. For those types loaded via a class loader object, the virtual machine must store a reference to the class loader object that loaded the type. This information is stored as part of the type's data in the method area.

The virtual machine uses this information during dynamic linking. When one type refers to another type, the virtual machine requests the referenced type from the same class loader that loaded the referencing type. This process of dynamic linking is also central to the way the virtual machine forms separate name-spaces. So that it can properly perform dynamic linking and maintain multiple name-spaces, the virtual machine needs to know what class loader loaded each type in its method area. The details of dynamic linking and name-spaces are given in Chapter 8.

**A REFERENCE TO CLASS Class** An instance of class **java.lang. Class** is created by the Java Virtual Machine for every type it loads. The virtual machine must in some way associate a reference to the **Class** instance for a type with the type's data in the method area.

Your Java programs can obtain and use references to **Class** objects. One static method in class **Class** allows you to get a reference to the **Class** instance for any loaded class:

```
// A method declared in class java.lang.Class:
public static Class forName(String className);
```

If you invoke **forName("java.lang.Object")**, for example, you will get a reference to the **Class** object that represents **java.lang.Object**. If you invoke **forName("java.util.Enumeration")**, you will get a reference to the `Class` object that represents the `Enumeration` interface from the `java.util` package. You can use `forName()` to get a `Class` reference for any loaded type from any package as long as the type can be (or already has been) loaded into the current name-space. If the virtual machine cannot load the requested type into the current name-space, `forName()` will throw `ClassNotFoundException`.

An alternative way to get a `Class` reference is to invoke `getClass()` on any object reference. This method is inherited by every object from class `Object` itself:

```
// A method declared in class java.lang.Object:
public final Class getClass();
```

If you have a reference to an object of class `java.lang.Integer`, for example, you could get the `Class` object for `java.lang.Integer` simply by invoking `getClass()` on your reference to the `Integer` object.

Given a reference to a `Class` object, you can find out information about the type by invoking methods declared in class `Class`. If you look at these methods, you will quickly realize that class `Class` gives the running application access to the information stored in the method area. Here are some of the methods declared in class `Class`:

```
// Some of the methods declared in class java.lang.Class:
public String getName();
public Class getSuperClass();
public boolean isInterface();
public Class[] getInterfaces();
public ClassLoader getClassLoader()
```

These methods just return information about a loaded type. `getName()` returns the fully qualified name of the type. `getSuperClass()` returns the `Class` instance for the type's direct superclass. If the type is class `java.lang.Object` or an interface, none of which have a superclass, `getSuperClass()` returns `null`. `isInterface()` returns `true` if the `Class` object describes an interface, `false` if it describes a class. `getInterfaces()` returns an array of `Class` objects, one for each direct superinterface. The superinterfaces appear in the array in the order they are declared as superinterfaces by the type. If the type has no direct superinterfaces, `getInterfaces()` returns an array of length zero. `getClassLoader()` returns a reference to the `ClassLoader` object that loaded this type, or `null` if the type was loaded by the primordial class loader. All this information comes straight out of the method area.

**METHOD TABLES** The type information stored in the method area must be organized to be quickly accessible. In addition to the raw type information listed previously, implementations can include other data structures that speed up access to the raw data. One example of such a data structure is a *method table*. For each nonabstract class a Java Virtual Machine loads, it could generate a method table and include it as part of the class information it stores in the method area. A method table is an array of direct references to all the instance methods that may be invoked on a class instance, including instance methods inherited from superclasses. (A method table isn't helpful in the case of abstract classes or interfaces because the program will never instantiate them.) A method table allows a virtual machine to quickly locate an instance method invoked on an object. Method tables are described in detail in Chapter 8.

**AN EXAMPLE OF METHOD AREA USE** As an example of how the Java Virtual Machine uses the information it stores in the method area, consider these classes:

```
// On CD-ROM in file jvm/ex2/Lava.java
class Lava {

    private int speed = 5; // 5 kilometers per hour

    void flow() {
    }
}

// On CD-ROM in file jvm/ex2/Volcano.java
class Volcano {

    public static void main(String[] args) {
        Lava lava = new Lava();
        lava.flow();
    }
}
```

The following paragraphs describe how an implementation might execute the first instruction in the bytecodes for the **main()** method of the **Volcano** application. Different implementations of the Java Virtual Machine can operate in very different ways. The following description illustrates one way—but not the only way—a Java Virtual Machine could execute the first instruction of **Volcano**'s **main()** method.

To run the **Volcano** application, you give the name **Volcano** to a Java Virtual Machine in an implementation-dependent manner. Given the name **Volcano**, the virtual machine finds and reads in file **Volcano.class**. It extracts the definition of class **Volcano** from the binary data in the imported class file and places the information into the method area. The virtual machine then invokes the **main()** method by interpreting the bytecodes stored in the method area. As the virtual machine executes **main()**, it maintains a pointer to the constant pool (a data structure in the method area) for the current class (class **Volcano**).

Note that this Java Virtual Machine has already begun to execute the bytecodes for **main()** in class **Volcano** even though it hasn't yet loaded class **Lava**. Like many (probably most) implementations of the Java Virtual Machine, this implementation doesn't wait until all classes used by the application are loaded before it begins executing **main()**. It loads classes only as it needs them.

**main()**'s first instruction tells the Java Virtual Machine to allocate enough memory for the class listed in constant pool entry one. The virtual machine uses its pointer into **Volcano**'s constant pool to look up entry one and finds a symbolic reference to class **Lava**. It checks the method area to see whether **Lava** has already been loaded.

The symbolic reference is just a string giving the class's fully qualified name: **"Lava"**. Here you can see that the method area must be organized so that a class can be located—as quickly as possible—given only the class's fully qualified name. Implementation designers can choose whatever algorithm and data structures best fit their needs—a hash table, a search tree, anything. This same mechanism can be used by the static **forName()** method of class **Class**, which returns a **Class** reference given a fully qualified name.

When the virtual machine discovers that it hasn't yet loaded a class named **Lava**, it finds and reads in file **Lava.class**. It extracts the definition of class **Lava** from the imported binary data and places the information into the method area.

The Java Virtual Machine then replaces the symbolic reference in **Volcano**'s constant pool entry one, which is just the string **"Lava"**, with a pointer to the class data for **Lava**. If the virtual machine ever has to use **Volcano**'s constant pool entry one again, it won't have to go through the relatively slow process of searching through the method area for class **Lava** given only a symbolic reference, the string **"Lava"**. It can just use the pointer to more quickly access the class data for **Lava**. This process of replacing symbolic references with direct references (in this case, a native pointer) is called *constant pool resolution*. The symbolic reference is *resolved* into a direct reference by searching through the method area until the referenced entity is found, loading new classes if necessary.

Finally, the virtual machine is ready to actually allocate memory for a new **Lava** object. Once again, the virtual machine consults the information stored in the method area. It uses the pointer (which was just put into **Volcano**'s constant pool entry one) to the **Lava** data (which was just imported into the method area) to find out how much heap space is required by a **Lava** object.

A Java Virtual Machine can always determine the amount of memory required to represent an object by looking into the class data stored in the method area. The actual amount of heap space required by a particular object, however, is implementation dependent. The internal representation of objects inside a Java Virtual Machine is another decision made by implementation designers. Object representation is discussed in more detail later in this chapter.

After the Java Virtual Machine has determined the amount of heap space required by a **Lava** object, it allocates that space on the heap and initializes the instance variable **speed** to zero, its default initial value. If class **Lava**'s superclass, **Object**, has any instance variables, they are also initialized to default initial values. (The details of initialization of both classes and objects are given in Chapter 7.)

The first instruction of **main()** completes by pushing a reference to the new **Lava** object onto the stack. A later instruction will use the reference to invoke Java code that initializes the **speed** variable to its proper initial value, five. Another instruction will use the reference to invoke the **flow()** method on the referenced **Lava** object.

## The Heap

Whenever a class instance or array is created in a running Java application, the memory for the new object is allocated from a single heap. As only one heap exists inside a Java Virtual Machine instance, all threads share it. Because a Java application runs inside its "own" exclusive Java Virtual Machine instance, a separate heap exists for every individual running application. This way, two different Java applications cannot trample on each other's heap data. Two different threads of the same application, however, could trample on each other's heap data. For this reason, you must be concerned about proper synchronization of multithreaded access to objects (heap data) in your Java programs.

The Java Virtual Machine includes an instruction that allocates memory on the heap for a new object but includes no instruction for freeing that memory. Just as you can't explicitly free an object in Java source code, you can't explicitly free an object in Java bytecodes. The virtual machine itself is responsible for deciding whether and when to free memory occupied by objects that are no longer referenced by the running application. Usually, a Java Virtual Machine implementation uses a *garbage collector* to manage the heap.

**GARBAGE COLLECTION**   A garbage collector's primary function is to automatically reclaim the memory used by objects that are no longer referenced by the running application. It also can move objects as the application runs to reduce heap fragmentation.

A garbage collector is not strictly required by the Java Virtual Machine specification. The specification requires only that an implementation manage its own heap *in some manner*. For example, an implementation could simply have a fixed amount of heap space available and throw an `OutOfMemory` exception when that space fills up. Although this implementation may not win many prizes, it does qualify as a Java Virtual Machine. The Java Virtual Machine specification does not say how much memory an implementation must make available to running programs. It does not say how an implementation must manage its heap. It says to implementation designers only that the program will be allocating memory from the heap but not freeing it. Designers, therefore, must figure out how they want to deal with this fact.

No garbage-collection technique is dictated by the Java Virtual Machine specification. Designers can use whatever techniques seem most appropriate given their goals, constraints, and talents. Because references to objects can exist in many places—Java Stacks, the heap, the method area, native method stacks—the choice of garbage-collection technique heavily influences the design of an implementation's runtime data areas. Various garbage-collection techniques are described in Chapter 9, "Garbage Collection."

As with the method area, the memory that makes up the heap need not be contiguous, and can be expanded and contracted as the running program progresses. An implementation's method area could, in fact, be implemented on top of its heap. In other words, when a virtual machine needs memory for a freshly loaded class, it could take that memory from the same heap on which objects reside. The same garbage collector that frees memory occupied by unreferenced objects could take care of finding and freeing (unloading) unreferenced classes. Implementations may allow users or programmers to specify an initial size for the heap, as well as a maximum and minimum size.

**OBJECT REPRESENTATION**   The Java Virtual Machine specification is silent on how objects should be represented on the heap. Object representation—an integral aspect of the overall design of the heap and garbage collector—is a decision made by implementation designers.

The primary data that must in some way be represented for each object are the instance variables declared in the object's class and all its superclasses. Given an object reference, the virtual machine must be able to quickly locate the instance data for the object. In addition, there must be some way to access an object's class data (stored in the method area) given a reference to the object. For this reason, the memory allocated for an object usually includes some kind of pointer into the method area.

One possible heap design divides the heap into two parts: a handle pool and an object pool. An object reference is a native pointer to a handle pool entry. A handle pool entry has two components: a pointer to instance data in the object pool and a pointer to class data in the method area. The advantage of this scheme is that it enables the virtual machine to combat heap fragmentation easily. When the virtual machine moves an object in the object pool, it need only update one pointer with the object's new address: the relevant pointer in the handle pool. The disadvantage of this approach is that every access to an object's instance data requires dereferencing two pointers. This approach to object representation is shown graphically in Figure 5-5. This kind of heap is demonstrated interactively by the **HeapOfFish** applet, described in Chapter 9.

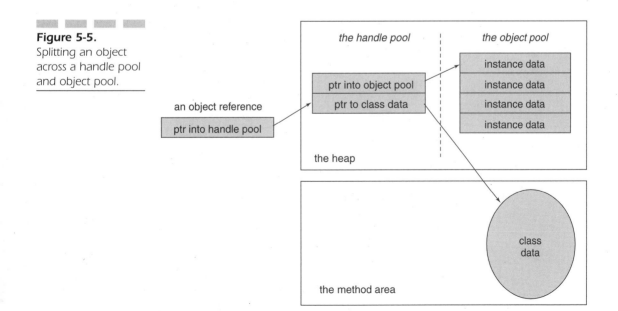

**Figure 5-5.**
Splitting an object across a handle pool and object pool.

Another design makes an object reference a native pointer to a bundle of data that contains the object's instance data and a pointer to the object's class data. This approach requires dereferencing only one pointer to access an object's instance data but makes moving objects more complicated. When the virtual machine moves an object to combat fragmentation of this kind of heap, it must update every reference to that object anywhere in the runtime data areas. This approach to object representation is shown graphically in Figure 5-6.

The virtual machine needs to get from an object reference to that object's class data for several reasons. When a running program attempts to cast an object reference to another type, the virtual machine must check to see whether the type being cast to is the actual class of the referenced object or one of its supertypes. It must perform the same kind of check when a program performs an **instanceof** operation. In either case, the virtual machine must look into the class data of the referenced object. When a program invokes an instance method, the virtual machine must perform dynamic binding: it must choose the method to invoke based not on the type of the reference, but on the class of the object. To do so, it must once again have access to the class data given only a reference to the object.

No matter what object representation an implementation uses, a method table is likely close at hand for each object. Method tables, because they speed up the invocation of instance methods, can play an im-

**Figure 5-6.**
Keeping object data all in one place.

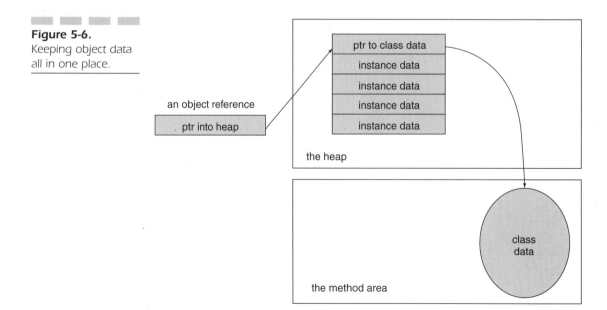

portant role in achieving good overall performance for a virtual machine implementation. Method tables are not required by the Java Virtual Machine specification and might not exist in all implementations. Implementations that have extremely low memory requirements, for example, may not be able to afford the extra memory space method tables occupy. If an implementation does use method tables, however, an object's method table will likely be quickly accessible given just a reference to the object.

One way an implementation could connect a method table to an object reference is shown graphically in Figure 5-7. This figure shows that the pointer kept with the instance data for each object points to a special structure. The special structure has two components:

- A pointer to the full class data for the object
- The method table for the object

The method table is an array of pointers to the data for each instance method that can be invoked on objects of that class. The method data pointed to by method table includes the following:

- The sizes of the operand stack and local variables sections of the method's stack
- The method's bytecodes
- An exception table

**Figure 5-7.**
Keeping the method
table close at hand.

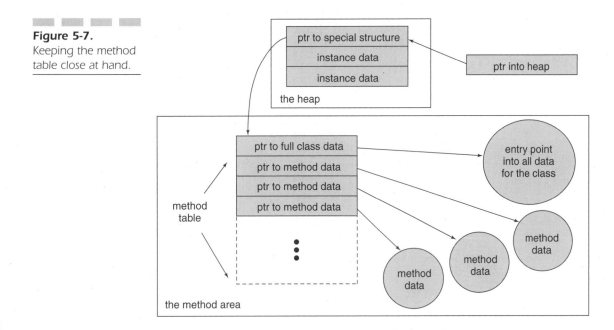

These items give the virtual machine enough information to invoke the method. The method table includes pointers to data for methods declared explicitly in the object's class or inherited from superclasses. In other words, the pointers in the method table can point to methods defined in the object's class or any of its superclasses. More information on method tables is given in Chapter 8.

If you are familiar with the inner workings of C++, you may recognize the method table as similar to the VTBL or virtual table of C++ objects. In C++, objects are represented by their instance data plus an array of pointers to any virtual functions that can be invoked on the object. This approach could also be taken by a Java Virtual Machine implementation. An implementation could include a copy of the method table for a class as part of the heap image for every instance of that class. This approach would consume more heap space than the approach shown in Figure 5-7 but might yield slightly better performance on a system that enjoys large quantities of available memory.

One other kind of data that is not shown in Figures 5-5 and 5-6 but is logically part of an object's data on the heap is the object's *lock*. Each object in a Java Virtual Machine is associated with a lock (or *mutex*) that a program can use to coordinate multithreaded access to the object. Only one thread at a time can "own" an object's lock. So long as a particular thread owns a particular object's lock, only that thread can access that object's instance variables. All other threads that attempt to access the object's variables have to wait until the owning thread releases the object's lock. If a thread requests a lock that is already owned by another thread, the requesting thread has to wait until the owning thread releases the lock. After a thread owns a lock, it can request the same lock again multiple times but then has to release the lock the same number of times before it is made available to other threads. If a thread requests a lock three times, for example, that thread will continue to own the lock until it has released the lock three times.

Many objects will go through their entire lifetimes without ever being locked by a thread. The data required to implement an object's lock is not needed unless the lock is actually requested by a thread. As a result, many implementations, such as the ones shown in Figures 5-5 and 5-6, may not include a pointer to "lock data" within the object itself. Such implementations must create the necessary data to represent a lock when the lock is requested for the first time. In this scheme, the virtual machine must associate the lock with the object in some indirect way, such as by placing the lock data into a search tree based on the object's address.

Along with data that implements a lock, every Java object is logically associated with data that implements a *wait set*. Whereas locks help threads to work independently on shared data without interfering with one another, wait sets help threads to cooperate with one another to work together toward a common goal.

Wait sets are used in conjunction with wait and notify methods. Every class inherits from `Object` three "wait methods" (overloaded forms of a method named `wait()`) and two "notify methods" (`notify()` and `notifyAll()`). When a thread invokes a wait method on an object, the Java Virtual Machine suspends that thread and adds it to that object's wait set. When a thread invokes a notify method on an object, the virtual machine will at some future time wake up one or more threads from that object's wait set. As with the data that implements an object's lock, the data that implements an object's wait set is not needed unless a wait or notify method is actually invoked on the object. As a result, many implementations of the Java Virtual Machine may keep the wait set data separate from the actual object data. Such implementations could allocate the data needed to represent an object's wait set when a wait or notify method is first invoked on that object by the running application. For more information about locks and wait sets, see Chapter 20, "Thread Synchronization."

One last example of a type of data that may be included as part of the image of an object on the heap is any data needed by the garbage collector. The garbage collector must in some way keep track of which objects are referenced by the program. This task invariably requires data to be kept for each object on the heap. The kind of data required depends on the garbage-collection technique being used. For example, if an implementation uses *a mark and sweep* algorithm, it must be able to mark an object as referenced or unreferenced. For each unreferenced object, it may also need to indicate whether the object's finalizer has been run. As with thread locks, this data may be kept separate from the object image. Some garbage-collection techniques require this extra data only while the garbage collector is actually running. A mark and sweep algorithm, for example, could potentially use a separate bitmap for marking referenced and unreferenced objects. More details on various garbage-collection techniques and the data required by each of them are given in Chapter 9.

In addition to data that a garbage collector uses to distinguish between referenced and unreferenced objects, a garbage collector needs data to keep track of the objects on which it has already executed a finalizer. Garbage collectors must run the finalizer of any object whose class declares one before it reclaims the memory occupied by that object. The Java language specification states that a garbage collector will execute an object's finalizer only once, but it allows that finalizer to "resurrect" the object: to make the object referenced again. When the object becomes unreferenced for a second time, the garbage collector must not finalize it again. Because most objects will likely not have a finalizer, and very few of them will resurrect their objects, this scenario of garbage collecting the same object twice will probably be extremely rare. As a result, the data used to keep track of objects that have already been finalized, though logically part of the data associated with an object, will likely not be part of the object representation on the heap. In most cases, garbage collectors will keep this information in a separate place. Chapter 9 gives more information about finalization.

**ARRAY REPRESENTATION**   In Java, arrays are full-fledged objects. Like objects, arrays are always stored on the heap. And as with objects, implementation designers can decide how they want to represent arrays on the heap.

Arrays have a **Class** instance associated with their class, just like any other object. All arrays of the same dimension and type have the same class. The length of an array (or the lengths of each dimension of a multidimensional array) does not play any role in establishing the array's class. For example, an array of 3 **int**s has the same class as an array of 300 **int**s. The length of an array is considered part of its instance data.

The name of an array's class has one open square bracket for each dimension plus a letter or string representing the array's type. For example, the class name for an array of **int**s is **"[I"**. The class name for a three-dimensional array of **byte**s is **"[[[B"**. The class name for a two-dimensional array of **Object**s is **"[[Ljava.lang.Object"**. The full details of this naming convention for array classes are given in Chapter 6.

Multidimensional arrays are represented as arrays of arrays. A two-dimensional array of **int**s, for example, would be represented by a one-dimensional array of references to several one-dimensional arrays of **int**s. This representation is shown graphically in Figure 5-8.

The data that must be kept on the heap for each array are the array's length, the array data, and some kind of reference to the array's class data. Given a reference to an array, the virtual machine must be able to determine the array's length, to get and set its elements by index (checking to make sure the array bounds are not exceeded), and to invoke any methods declared by **Object**, the direct superclass of all arrays.

# The Program Counter

Each thread of a running program has its own pc register, or program counter, which is created when the thread is started. The pc register is one word in size, so it can hold both a native pointer and a `returnValue`. As a thread executes a Java method, the pc register contains the address of the current instruction being executed by the thread. An *address* can be a native pointer or an offset from the beginning of a method's byte-codes. If a thread is executing a native method, the value of the pc register is undefined.

# The Java Stack

When a new thread is launched, the Java Virtual Machine creates a new Java stack for the thread. As mentioned earlier, a Java stack stores a thread's state in discrete frames. The Java Virtual Machine performs only two operations directly on Java Stacks: it pushes and pops frames.

The method that is currently being executed by a thread is the thread's *current method*. The stack frame for the current method is the *current frame*. The class in which the current method is defined is called the *cur-*

**Figure 5-8.**
One possible heap representation for arrays.

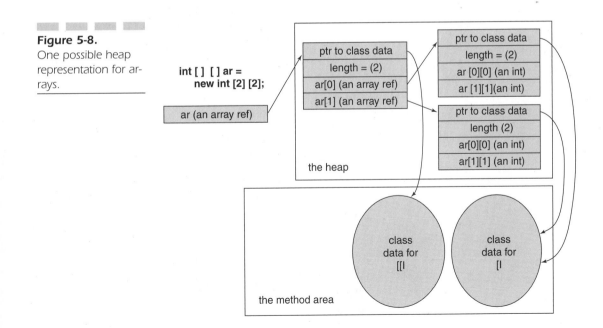

*rent class*, and the current class's constant pool is the *current constant pool*. As it executes a method, the Java Virtual Machine keeps track of the current class and current constant pool. When the virtual machine encounters instructions that operate on data stored in the stack frame, it performs those operations on the current frame.

When a thread invokes a Java method, the virtual machine creates and pushes a new frame onto the thread's Java stack. This new frame then becomes the current frame. As the method executes, it uses the frame to store parameters, local variables, intermediate computations, and other data.

A method can complete itself in either of two ways. If a method completes by returning, it is said to have *normal completion*. If it completes by throwing an exception, it is said to have *abrupt completion*. When a method completes, whether normally or abruptly, the Java Virtual Machine pops and discards the method's stack frame. The frame for the previous method then becomes the current frame.

All the data on a thread's Java stack is private to that thread. There is no way for a thread to access or alter the Java stack of another thread. Therefore, you need never worry about synchronizing multithreaded access to local variables in your Java programs. When a thread invokes a method, the method's local variables are stored in a frame on the invoking thread's Java stack. Only one thread can ever access those local variables: the thread that invoked the method.

Like the method area and heap, the Java stack and stack frames need not be contiguous in memory. Frames could be allocated on a contiguous stack, or they could be allocated on a heap, or some combination of both. The actual data structures used to represent the Java stack and stack frames must be decided by implementation designers. Implementations may allow users or programmers to specify an initial size for Java stacks, as well as a maximum or minimum size.

## The Stack Frame

The stack frame has three parts: local variables, operand stack, and frame data. The sizes of the local variables and operand stack, which are measured in words, depend on the needs of each individual method. These sizes are determined at compile-time and included in the class file data for each method. The size of the frame data is implementation dependent.

When the Java Virtual Machine invokes a Java method, it checks the class data to determine the number of words required by the method in the local variables and operand stack. It creates a stack frame of the proper size for the method and pushes it onto the Java stack.

**LOCAL VARIABLES**   The local variables section of the Java stack frame is organized as a zero-based array of words. Instructions that use a value from the local variables section provide an index into the zero-based array. Values of type **int**, **float**, **reference**, and **returnValue** occupy one entry in the local variables array. Values of type **byte**, **short**, and **char** are converted to **int** before being stored into the local variables. Values of type **long** and **double** occupy two consecutive entries in the array.

To refer to a long or double in the local variables, instructions provide the index of the first of the two consecutive entries occupied by the value. For example, if a **long** occupies array entries three and four, instructions would refer to that **long** by index three. All values in the local variables are word aligned. Dual-entry **long**s and **double**s can start at any index.

The local variables section contains a method's parameters and local variables. Compilers place the parameters into the local variable array first, in the order in which they are declared. Figure 5-9 shows the local variables section for the following two methods:

```
// On CD-ROM in file jvm/ex3/Example3a.java
class Example3a {

    public static int runClassMethod(int i, long l, float f,
        double d, Object o, byte b) {

        return 0;
    }

    public int runInstanceMethod(char c, double d, short s,
        boolean b) {
```

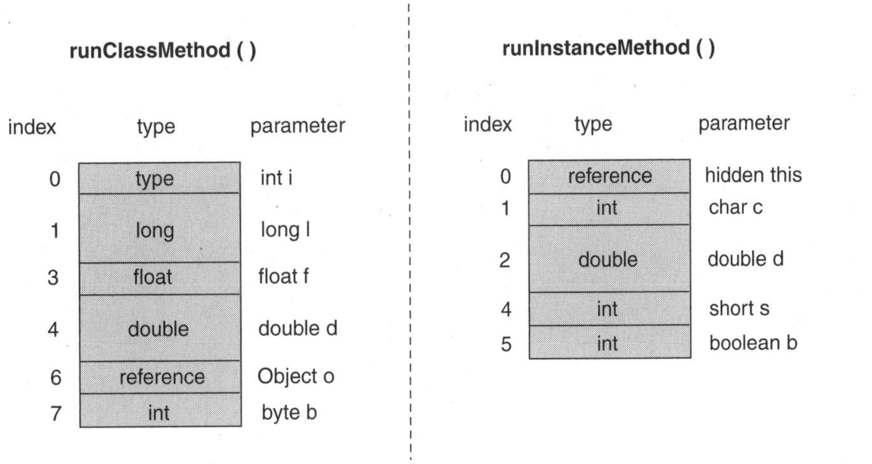

**Figure 5-9.**
Method parameters on the local variables section of a Java stack.

| runClassMethod ( ) | | |
|---|---|---|
| index | type | parameter |
| 0 | type | int i |
| 1 | long | long l |
| 3 | float | float f |
| 4 | double | double d |
| 6 | reference | Object o |
| 7 | int | byte b |

| runInstanceMethod ( ) | | |
|---|---|---|
| index | type | parameter |
| 0 | reference | hidden this |
| 1 | int | char c |
| 2 | double | double d |
| 4 | int | short s |
| 5 | int | boolean b |

```
        return 0;
    }
}
```

Figure 5-9 shows that the first parameter in the local variables section for `runInstanceMethod()` is of type `reference`, even though no such parameter appears in the source code. This reference is the hidden `this` passed to every instance method. Instance methods use this reference to access the instance data of the object upon which they were invoked. As you can see by looking at the local variables for `runClassMethod()` in Figure 5-9, class methods do not receive a hidden `this`. Class methods are not invoked on objects. You can't directly access a class's instance variables from a class method because no instance is associated with the method invocation.

Note also that types `byte`, `short`, `char`, and `boolean` in the source code become `int`s in the local variables. This is also true of the operand stack. As mentioned earlier, the `boolean` type is not supported directly by the Java Virtual Machine. The Java compiler always uses `int`s to represent `boolean` values in the local variables or operand stack. Data types `byte`, `short`, and `char`, however, are supported directly by the Java Virtual Machine. They can be stored on the heap as instance variables or array elements, or in the method area as class variables. When placed into local variables or the operand stack, however, values of type `byte`, `short`, and `char` are converted into `int`s. They are manipulated as `int`s while on the stack frame and then converted back into `byte`, `short`, or `char` when stored back into the heap or method area.

Also note that `Object o` is passed as a reference to `runClassMethod()`. In Java, all objects are passed by reference. As all objects are stored on the heap, you will never find an image of an object in the local variables or operand stack, only object references.

Aside from a method's parameters, which compilers must place into the local variables array first and in order of declaration, Java compilers can arrange the local variables array as they wish. Compilers can place the method's local variables into the array in any order, and they can use the same array entry for more than one local variable. For example, if two local variables have limited scopes that don't overlap, such as the `i` and `j` local variables in `Example3b`, which follows, compilers are free to use the same array entry for both variables. During the first half of the method, before `j` comes into scope, entry zero could be used for `i`. During the second half of the method, after `i` has gone out of scope, entry zero could be used for `j`.

```java
// On CD-ROM in file jvm/ex3/Example3b.java
class Example3b {

    public static void runtwoLoops() {

        for (int i = 0; i < 10; ++i) {
            System.out.println(i);
        }

        for (int j = 9; j >= 0; -j) {
            System.out.println(j);
        }
    }
}
```

As with all the other runtime memory areas, implementation designers can use whatever data structures they deem most appropriate to represent the local variables. The Java Virtual Machine specification does not indicate how **long**s and **double**s should be split across the two array entries they occupy. Implementations that use a word size of 64 bits could, for example, store the entire **long** or **double** in the lower of the two consecutive entries, leaving the higher entry unused.

**OPERAND STACK**  Like the local variables, the operand stack is organized as an array of words. But unlike the local variables, which are accessed via array indices, the operand stack is accessed by pushing and popping values. If an instruction pushes a value onto the operand stack, a later instruction can pop and use that value.

The virtual machine stores the same data types in the operand stack that it stores in the local variables: **int**, **long**, **float**, **double**, **reference**, and **returnType**. It converts values of type **byte**, **short**, and **char** to **int** before pushing them onto the operand stack.

Other than the program counter, which can't be directly accessed by instructions, the Java Virtual Machine has no registers. The Java Virtual Machine is stack-based rather than register-based because its instructions take their operands from the operand stack rather than from registers. Instructions can also take operands from other places, such as immediately following the opcode (the byte representing the instruction) in the bytecode stream, or from the constant pool. The Java Virtual Machine instruction set's main focus of attention, however, is the operand stack.

The Java Virtual Machine uses the operand stack as a work space. Many instructions pop values from the operand stack, operate on them, and push the result. For example, the **iadd** instruction adds two integers by popping two **int**s off the top of the operand stack, adding them, and pushing the **int** result. Here is how a Java Virtual Machine would add two local variables that contain **int**s and store the **int** result in a third local variable:

```
iload_0      // push the int in local variable
iload_1      // push the int in local variable 1
iadd         // pop two ints, add them, push result
istore_2     // pop int, store into local variable 2
```

In this sequence of bytecodes, the first two instructions, **iload_0** and **iload_1**, push the **int**s stored in local variable positions zero and one onto the operand stack. The **iadd** instruction pops those two **int** values, adds them, and pushes the **int** result back onto the operand stack. The fourth instruction, **istore_2**, pops the result of the add off the top of the operand stack and stores it into local variable position two. In Figure 5-10, you can see a graphical depiction of the state of the local variables and operand stack while executing the preceding instructions. In this figure, unused slots of the local variables and operand stack are left blank.

**FRAME DATA**   In addition to the local variables and operand stack, the Java stack frame includes data to support constant pool resolution, normal method return, and exception dispatch. This data is stored in the *frame data* portion of the Java stack frame.

Many instructions in the Java Virtual Machine's instruction set refer to entries in the constant pool. Some instructions merely push constant values of type **int**, **long**, **float**, **double**, or **String** from the constant pool onto the operand stack. Some instructions use constant pool entries to refer to classes or arrays to instantiate, fields to access, or methods to invoke. Other

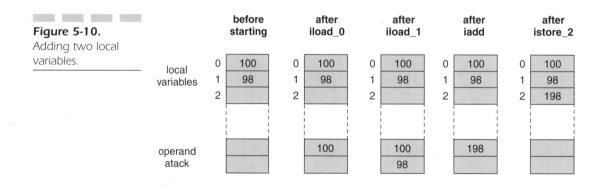

**Figure 5-10.**
Adding two local variables.

instructions determine whether a particular object is a descendant of a particular class or interface specified by a constant pool entry.

Whenever the Java Virtual Machine encounters any of the instructions that refer to an entry in the constant pool, it uses the frame data's pointer to the constant pool to access that information. As mentioned earlier, references to types, fields, and methods in the constant pool are initially symbolic. When the virtual machine looks up a constant pool entry that refers to a class, interface, field, or method, that reference may still be symbolic. If so, the virtual machine must resolve the reference at that time.

Aside from constant pool resolution, the frame data must assist the virtual machine in processing a normal or abrupt method completion. If a method completes normally (by returning), the virtual machine must restore the stack frame of the invoking method. It must set the pc register to point to the instruction in the invoking method that follows the instruction that invoked the completing method. If the completing method returns a value, the virtual machine must push that value onto the operand stack of the invoking method.

The frame data must also contain some kind of reference to the method's exception table, which the virtual machine uses to process any exceptions thrown during the course of execution of the method. An exception table, which is described in detail in Chapter 17, defines ranges within the bytecodes of a method that are protected by catch clauses. Each entry in an exception table gives a starting and ending position of the range protected by a catch clause, an index into the constant pool that gives the exception class being caught, and a starting position of the catch clause's code.

When a method throws an exception, the Java Virtual Machine uses the exception table referred to by the frame data to determine how to handle the exception. If the virtual machine finds a matching catch clause in the method's exception table, it transfers control to the beginning of that catch clause. If the virtual machine doesn't find a matching catch clause, the method completes abnormally. The virtual machine uses the information in the frame data to restore the invoking method's frame. It then rethrows the same exception in the context of the invoking method.

In addition to data to support constant pool resolution, normal method return, and exception dispatch, the stack frame may also include other information that is implementation dependent, such as data to support debugging.

**POSSIBLE IMPLEMENTATIONS OF THE JAVA STACK** Implementation designers can represent the Java stack in whatever way they wish. As mentioned earlier, one potential way to implement the stack is by allocating each frame separately from a heap. As an example of this approach, consider the following class:

```
// On CD-ROM in file jvm/ex3/Example3c.java
class Example3c {

    public static void addAndPrint() {
        double result = addTwoTypes(1, 88.88);
        System.out.println(result);
    }

    public static double addTwoTypes(int i, double d) {
        return i + d;
    }
}
```

Figure 5-11 shows three snapshots of the Java stack for a thread that invokes the **addAndPrint()** method. In the implementation of the Java Virtual Machine represented in this figure, each frame is allocated separately from a heap. To invoke the **addTwoTypes()** method, the **addAndPrint()** method first pushes an **int** one and **double** 88.88 onto its operand stack. It then invokes the **addTwoTypes()** method.

The instruction to invoke **addTwoTypes()** refers to a constant pool entry. The Java Virtual Machine looks up the entry and resolves it if necessary.

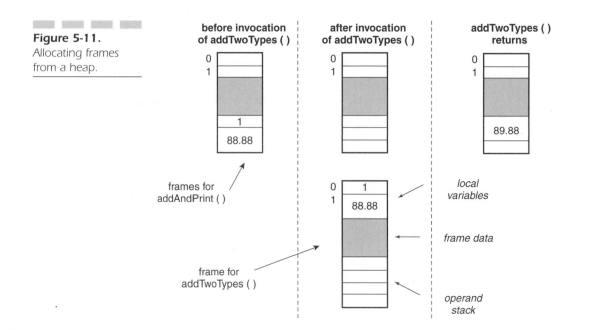

**Figure 5-11.**
Allocating frames from a heap.

Note that the **addAndPrint()** method uses the constant pool to identify the **addTwoTypes()** method, even though it is part of the same class. Like references to fields and methods of other classes, references to the fields and methods of the *same* class are initially symbolic and must be resolved before they are used.

The resolved constant pool entry points to information in the method area about the **addTwoTypes()** method. The virtual machine uses this information to determine the sizes required by **addTwoTypes()** for the local variables and operand stack. In the class file generated by Sun's **javac** compiler from the JDK 1.1, **addTwoTypes()** requires three words in the local variables and four words in the operand stack. (As mentioned earlier, the size of the frame data portion is implementation dependent.) The virtual machine allocates enough memory for the **addTwoTypes()** frame from a heap. It then pops the **double** and **int** parameters (88.88 and one) from **addAndPrint()**'s operand stack and places them into **addTwoType()**'s local variable slots one and zero.

When **addTwoTypes()** returns, it first pushes the **double** return value (in this case, 89.88) onto its operand stack. The virtual machine uses the information in the frame data to locate the stack frame of the invoking method, **addAndPrint()**. It pushes the **double** return value onto **addAndPrint()**'s operand stack and frees the memory occupied by **addTwoType()**'s frame. It makes **addAndPrint()**'s frame current and continues executing the **addAndPrint()** method at the first instruction past the **addTwoType()** method invocation.

Figure 5-12 shows snapshots of the Java stack of a different virtual machine implementation executing the same methods. Instead of allocating each frame separately from a heap, this implementation allocates frames from a contiguous stack. This approach allows the implementation to overlap the frames of adjacent methods. The portion of the invoking method's operand stack that contains the parameters to the invoked method becomes the base of the invoked method's local variables. In this example, **addAndPrint()**'s entire operand stack becomes **addTwoType()**'s entire local variables section.

This approach saves memory space because the same memory is used by the calling method to store the parameters as is used by the invoked method to access the parameters. It saves time because the Java Virtual Machine doesn't have to spend time copying the parameter values from one frame to another.

Note that the operand stack of the current frame is always at the "top" of the Java stack. Although this setup may be easier to visualize in the contiguous memory implementation of Figure 5-12, it is true no matter

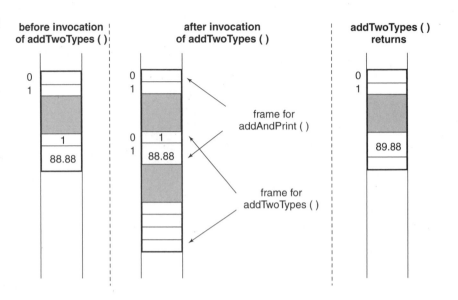

**Figure 5-12.**
Allocating frames
from a contiguous
stack.

how the Java stack is implemented. (As mentioned earlier, in all the graphical images of the stack shown in this book, the stack grows downward. The "top" of the stack is always shown at the bottom of the picture.) Instructions that push values onto (or pop values off) the operand stack always operate on the current frame. Thus, pushing a value onto the operand stack can be seen as pushing a value onto the top of the entire Java stack. In the remainder of this book, "pushing a value onto the stack" refers to pushing a value onto the operand stack of the current frame.

One other possible approach to implementing the Java stack is a hybrid of the two approaches shown in Figures 5-11 and 5-12. A Java Virtual Machine implementation can allocate a chunk of contiguous memory from a heap when a thread starts. In this memory, the virtual machine can use the overlapping frames approach shown in Figure 5-12. If the stack outgrows the contiguous memory, the virtual machine can allocate another chunk of contiguous memory from the heap. It can use the separate frames approach shown in Figure 5-11 to connect the invoking method's frame sitting in the old chunk with the invoked method's frame sitting in the new chunk. Within the new chunk, it can once again use the contiguous memory approach.

## Native Method Stacks

In addition to all the runtime data areas defined by the Java Virtual Machine specification and described previously, a running Java application can use other data areas created by or for native methods. When a thread invokes a native method, it enters a new world in which the structures and security restrictions of the Java Virtual Machine no longer hamper its freedom. A native method can likely access the runtime data areas of the virtual machine (depending on the native method interface), but can also do anything else it wants. It can use registers inside the native processor, allocate memory on any number of native heaps, or use any kind of stack.

Native methods are inherently implementation dependent. Implementation designers are free to decide what mechanisms they will use to enable a Java application running on their implementation to invoke native methods.

Any native method interface will use some kind of native method stack. When a thread invokes a Java method, the virtual machine creates a new frame and pushes it onto the Java stack. When a thread invokes a native method, however, that thread leaves the Java stack behind. Instead of pushing a new frame onto the thread's Java stack, the Java Virtual Machine will simply dynamically link to and directly invoke the native method. One way to think of this situation is that the Java Virtual Machine is dynamically extending itself with native code. It is as though the Java Virtual Machine implementation is just calling another (dynamically linked) method within itself at the behest of the running Java program.

If an implementation's native method interface uses a C-linkage model, then the native method stacks are C stacks. When a C program invokes a C function, the stack operates in a certain way. The arguments to the function are pushed onto the stack in a certain order. The return value is passed back to the invoking function in a certain way. This would be the behavior of the native method stacks in that implementation.

A native method interface will likely (once again, the designers must decide) be able to call back into the Java Virtual Machine and invoke a Java method. In this case, the thread leaves the native method stack and enters another Java stack.

Figure 5-13 shows a graphical depiction of a thread that invokes a native method that calls back into the virtual machine to invoke another Java method. This figure shows the full picture of what a thread can expect inside the Java Virtual Machine. A thread might spend its entire lifetime executing Java methods, working with frames on its Java stack. Or it might jump back and forth between the Java stack and native method stacks.

As depicted in Figure 5-13, a thread first invoked two Java methods, the second of which invoked a native method. This act caused the virtual machine to use a native method stack. In this figure, the native method stack is shown as a finite amount of contiguous memory space. Assume it

**Figure 5-13.**
The stack for a
thread that invokes
Java and native
methods.

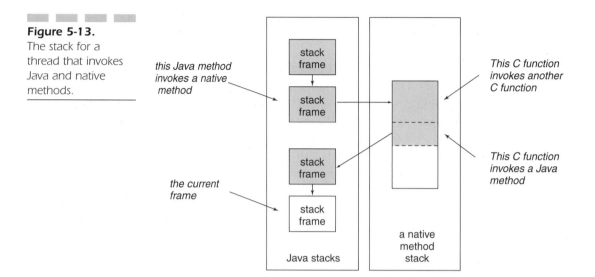

is a C stack. The stack area used by each C-linkage function is shown in gray and bounded by a dashed line. The first C-linkage function, which was invoked as a native method, invoked another C-linkage function. The second C-linkage function invoked a Java method through the native method interface. This Java method invoked another Java method, which is the current method shown in the figure.

As with the other runtime memory areas, the memory they occupied by native method stacks need not be of a fixed size. It can expand and contract as needed by the running application. Implementations may allow users or programmers to specify an initial size for the native method stacks, as well as a maximum or minimum size.

## Execution Engine

At the core of any Java Virtual Machine implementation is its execution engine. In the Java Virtual Machine specification, the behavior of the execution engine is defined in terms of an instruction set. For each instruction, the specification describes in detail *what* an implementation should do when it encounters the instruction as it executes bytecodes, but it says very little about *how*. As mentioned in previous chapters, implementation designers are free to decide how their implementations will execute bytecodes. Their implementations can interpret, just-in-time compile, execute natively in silicon, use a combination of these methods, or dream up some brand new technique.

Similar to the three senses of the term *Java Virtual Machine* described at the beginning of this chapter, the term *execution engine* can also be used in any of three senses: an abstract specification, a concrete implementation, or a runtime instance. The abstract specification defines the behavior of an execution engine in terms of the instruction set. Concrete implementations, which may use a variety of techniques, are either software, hardware, or a combination of both. A runtime instance of an execution engine is a thread.

Each thread of a running Java application is a distinct instance of the virtual machine's execution engine. From the beginning of its lifetime to the end, a thread is either executing bytecodes or native methods. A thread may execute bytecodes directly, by interpreting or executing natively in silicon, or indirectly, by just-in-time compiling and executing the resulting native code. A Java Virtual Machine implementation can use other threads invisible to the running application, such as a thread that performs garbage collection. Such threads need not be "instances" of the implementation's execution engine. All threads that belong to the running application, however, are execution engines in action.

**THE INSTRUCTION SET**    A method's bytecode stream is a sequence of instructions for the Java Virtual Machine. Each instruction consists of a one-byte *opcode* followed by zero or more *operands*. The opcode indicates the operation to be performed. Operands supply extra information needed by the Java Virtual Machine to perform the operation specified by the opcode. The opcode itself indicates whether it is followed by operands and the form the operands (if any) take. Many Java Virtual Machine instructions take no operands and therefore consist only of an opcode. Depending on the opcode, the virtual machine may refer to data stored in other areas in addition to (or instead of) operands that trail the opcode. When it executes an instruction, the virtual machine can use entries in the current constant pool, entries in the current frame's local variables, or values sitting on the top of the current frame's operand stack.

The abstract execution engine runs by executing bytecodes one instruction at a time. This process takes place for each thread (execution engine instance) of the application running in the Java Virtual Machine. An execution engine fetches an opcode and, if that opcode has operands, fetches the operands. It executes the action requested by the opcode and its operands and then fetches another opcode. Execution of bytecodes continues until a thread completes either by returning from its starting method or by not catching a thrown exception.

From time to time, the execution engine may encounter an instruction that requests a native method invocation. On such occasions, the execution engine will dutifully attempt to invoke that native method. When the native method returns (if it completes normally, not by throwing an exception), the execution engine will continue executing the next instruction in the bytecode stream.

One way to think of native methods, therefore, is as programmer-customized extensions to the Java Virtual Machine's instruction set. If an instruction requests an invocation of a native method, the execution engine invokes the native method. Running the native method is the way the Java Virtual Machine executes the instruction. When the native method returns, the virtual machine moves on to the next instruction. If the native method completes abnormally (by throwing an exception), the virtual machine follows the same steps to handle the exception as it does when any instruction throws an exception.

Part of the job of executing an instruction is determining the next instruction to execute. An execution engine determines the next opcode to fetch in one of three ways. For many instructions, the next opcode to execute directly follows the current opcode and its operands, if any, in the bytecode stream. For some instructions, such as `goto` or `return`, the execution engine determines the next opcode as part of its execution of the current instruction. If an instruction throws an exception, the execution engine determines the next opcode to fetch by searching for an appropriate catch clause.

Several instructions can throw exceptions. The `athrow` instruction, for example, throws an exception explicitly. This instruction is the compiled form of the `throw` statement in Java source code. Every time the `athrow` instruction is executed, it will throw an exception. Other instructions throw exceptions only when certain conditions are encountered. For example, if the Java Virtual Machine discovers, to its chagrin, that the program is attempting to perform an integer divide by zero, it will throw an `ArithmeticException`. This situation can occur while executing any of four instructions—`idiv`, `ldiv`, `irem`, and `lrem`—that perform divisions or calculate remainders on `int`s or `long`s.

Each type of opcode in the Java Virtual Machine's instruction set has a mnemonic. In the typical assembly language style, streams of Java bytecodes can be represented by their mnemonics followed by (optional) operand values.

For an example of a method's bytecode stream and mnemonics, consider the `doMathForever()` method of this class:

```
// On CD-ROM in file jvm/ex4/Act.java
class Act {

    public static void doMathForever() {
```

```
int i = 0;
for (;;) {
    i += 1;
    i *= 2;
}
        }
    }
```

The stream of bytecodes for **doMathForever()** can be disassembled into mnemonics as shown next. The Java Virtual Machine specification does not define any official syntax for representing the mnemonics of a method's bytecodes. The following code illustrates the manner in which streams of bytecode mnemonics will be represented in this book. The left-hand column shows the offset in bytes from the beginning of the method's bytecodes to the start of each instruction. The center column shows the instruction and any operands. The right-hand column contains comments, which are preceded with a double slash, just as in Java source code.

```
// Bytecode stream: 03 3b 84 00 01 1a 05 68 3b a7 ff f9
// Disassembly:
// Method void doMathForever()
// Left column: offset of instruction from start of method
// |    Center column: instruction mnemonic and any operands
// |    |                    Right column: comment
   0    iconst_0             // 03
   1    istore_0             // 3b
   2    iinc 0, 1            // 84 00 01
   5    iload_0              // 1a
   6    iconst_2             // 05
   7    imul                 // 68
   8    istore_0             // 3b
   9    goto 2               // a7 ff f9
```

This way of representing mnemonics is very similar to the output of the **javap** program of Sun's JDK. **javap** allows you to look at the bytecode mnemonics of the methods of any class file. Note that jump addresses are given as offsets from the beginning of the method. The **goto** instruction causes the virtual machine to jump to the instruction at offset two (an **iinc**). The actual operand in the stream is minus seven. To execute this instruction, the virtual machine adds the operand to the current contents of the pc register. The result is the address of the **iinc** instruction at offset two. To make the mnemonics easier to read, the operands for jump instructions are shown as though the addition has already taken place. Instead of saying "**goto -7**," the mnemonics say "**goto 2**."

The central focus of the Java Virtual Machine's instruction set is the operand stack. Values are generally pushed onto the operand stack before they are used. Although the Java Virtual Machine has no registers for storing arbitrary values, each method has a set of local variables. The instruction set treats the local variables, in effect, as a set of registers that are referred to by indexes. Nevertheless, other than the `iinc` instruction, which increments a local variable directly, values stored in the local variables must be moved to the operand stack before being used.

For example, to divide one local variable by another, the virtual machine must push both onto the stack, perform the division, and then store the result back into the local variables. To move the value of an array element or object field into a local variable, the virtual machine must first push the value onto the stack and then store it into the local variable. To set an array element or object field to a value stored in a local variable, the virtual machine must follow the reverse procedure. First, it must push the value of the local variable onto the stack and then pop it off the stack and into the array element or object field on the heap.

Several goals—some conflicting—guided the design of the Java Virtual Machine's instruction set. These goals are basically the same as those described in Part One of this book as the motivation behind Java's entire architecture: platform independence, network mobility, and security.

The platform independence goal was a major influence in the design of the instruction set. The instruction set's stack-centered approach, described previously, was chosen over a register-centered approach to facilitate efficient implementation on architectures with few or irregular registers, such as the Intel 80X86. This feature of the instruction set—the stack-centered design—makes it easier to implement the Java Virtual Machine on a wide variety of host architectures.

As mentioned in Chapter 4, "Network Mobility," one major design consideration was class file compactness. Compactness is important because it facilitates speedy transmission of class files across networks. In the bytecodes stored in class files, all instructions—except two that deal with table jumping—are aligned on byte boundaries. The total number of opcodes is small enough so that opcodes occupy only one byte. This design strategy favors class file compactness possibly at the cost of some performance when the program runs. In some Java Virtual Machine implementations, especially those executing bytecodes in silicon, the single-byte opcode may preclude certain optimizations that could improve performance. Also, better performance may have been possible on some implementations if the bytecode streams were word aligned instead of byte aligned. (An implementation could always realign bytecode streams or translate opcodes into a more efficient form as classes are loaded. Bytecodes are byte aligned in the class file and in the specification of the abstract method area and execution engine. Concrete implementations can store the loaded bytecode streams any way they wish.)

Another goal that guided the design of the instruction set was the ability to do bytecode verification, especially all at once by a data flow analyzer. The verification capability is needed as part of Java's security framework. The ability to use a data flow analyzer on the bytecodes when they are loaded, rather than verifying each instruction as it is executed, facilitates execution speed. One way this design goal manifests itself in the instruction set is that most opcodes indicate the type they operate on.

For example, instead of simply having one instruction that pops a word from the operand stack and stores it in a local variable, the Java Virtual Machine's instruction set has two. One instruction, **istore**, pops and stores an **int**. The other instruction, **fstore**, pops and stores a **float**. Both of these instructions perform the exact same function when executed: they pop a word and store it. Distinguishing between popping and storing an **int** versus a **float** is important only to the verification process.

For many instructions, the virtual machine needs to know the types being operated on to know how to perform the operation. For example, the Java Virtual Machine supports two ways of adding two words together, yielding a one-word result. One addition treats the words as **int**s; the other, as **float**s. The difference between these two instructions facilitates verification but also tells the virtual machine whether it should perform integer or floating-point arithmetic.

A few instructions operate on any type. The **dup** instruction, for example, duplicates the top word of a stack irrespective of its type. Some instructions, such as **goto**, don't operate on typed values. Most of the instructions, however, operate on a specific type. The mnemonics for most of these "typed" instructions indicate their type by a single-character prefix that starts their mnemonic. Table 5-2 shows the prefixes for the various types. A few instructions, such as **arraylength** or **instanceof**, don't include a prefix because their type is obvious. The **arraylength** opcode requires an array reference. The **instanceof** opcode requires an object reference.

Values on the operand stack must be used in a manner appropriate to their type. It is illegal, for example, to push four **int**s and then add them as if they were two **long**s. It is illegal to push a **float** value onto the operand stack from the local variables and then store it as an **int** in an array on the heap. It is illegal to push a **double** value from an object field on the heap and then store the topmost of its two words into the local variables as an value of type **reference**. The strict type rules that are enforced by Java compilers must also be enforced by Java Virtual Machine implementations.

**Table 5-2.**

Type prefixes
of bytecode
mnemonics

| Type | Code | Example | Description |
|------|------|---------|-------------|
| byte | b | baload | load **byte** from array |
| short | s | saload | load **short** from array |
| int | i | iaload | load **int** from array |
| long | l | laload | load **long** from array |
| char | c | caload | load **char** from array |
| float | f | faload | load **float** from array |
| double | d | daload | load **double** from array |
| reference | a | aaload | load **reference** from array |

Implementations must also observe rules when executing instructions that perform generic stack operations independent of type. As mentioned above, the **dup** instruction pushes a copy of the top word of the stack, irrespective of type. This instruction can be used on any value that occupies one word: an **int**, **float**, **reference**, or **returnValue**. Using **dup**, however, when the top of the stack contains either a **long** or **double**, the data types that occupy two consecutive operand stack locations, is illegal. A **long** or **double** sitting on the top of the operand stack can be duplicated in its entirety by the **dup2** instruction, which pushes a copy of the top two words onto the operand stack. The generic instructions cannot be used to split up dual-word values.

To keep the instruction set small enough to enable each opcode to be represented by a single byte, not all operations are supported on all types. Most operations are not supported for types **byte**, **short**, and **char**. These types are converted to **int** when moved from the heap or method area to the stack frame. They are operated on as **int**s and then converted back to **byte**, **short**, or **char** before being stored back into the heap or method area.

Table 5-3 shows the computation types that correspond to each storage type in the Java Virtual Machine. As used here, a *storage type* is the manner in which values of the type are represented on the heap. The storage type corresponds to the type of the variable in Java source code. A *computation type* is the manner in which the type is represented on the Java stack frame.

Implementations of the Java Virtual Machine must in some way ensure that values are operated on by instructions appropriate to their type. They can verify bytecodes up front as part of the class verification process, on

**Table 5-3.**

Storage and
computation types
inside the Java
Virtual Machine

| Storage Type | Minimum Bits in Heap or Method Area | Computation Type | Words in the Java Stack Frame |
|---|---|---|---|
| byte | 8 | int | 1 |
| short | 16 | int | 1 |
| int | 32 | int | 1 |
| long | 64 | long | 2 |
| char | 16 | int | 1 |
| float | 32 | float | 1 |
| double | 64 | double | 2 |
| reference | 32 | reference | 1 |

the fly as the program executes, or some combination of both. Bytecode verification is described in more detail in Chapter 7. The entire instruction set is covered in detail in Chapters 10 through 20.

**EXECUTION TECHNIQUES** Various execution techniques that can be used by an implementation—interpreting, just-in-time compiling, hotspot compiling, native execution in silicon—were described in Chapter 1. The main point to remember about execution techniques is that an implementation can use any technique to execute bytecodes as long as it adheres to the semantics of the Java Virtual Machine instruction set.

**THREADS** The Java Virtual Machine specification defines a threading model that aims to facilitate implementation on a wide variety of architectures. One goal of the Java threading model is to enable implementation designers, where possible and appropriate, to use native threads. Alternatively, designers can implement a thread mechanism as part of their virtual machine implementation. One advantage to using native threads on a multiprocessor host is that different threads of a Java application could run simultaneously on different processors.

One trade-off of Java's threading model is that the specification of priorities is lowest-common-denominator. A Java thread can run at any one of 10 priorities. Priority 1 is the lowest, and priority 10 is the highest. If designers use native threads, they can map the 10 Java priorities onto the native priorities however seems most appropriate. The Java Virtual Machine specification defines the behavior of threads at different priorities only by saying that all threads at the highest priority will get some CPU time. Threads at lower priorities are guaranteed to get CPU time only when all higher priority threads are blocked. Lower priority threads *may* get some CPU time when higher priority threads aren't blocked, but there are no guarantees.

The specification doesn't assume time-slicing between threads of different priorities because not all architecture's time-slice. (As used here, *time-slicing* means that all threads at all priorities will be guaranteed some CPU time, even when no threads are blocked.) Even among those architectures that do time-slice, the algorithms used to allot time slots to threads at various priorities can differ greatly.

As mentioned in Chapter 2, "Platform Independence," you must not rely on time-slicing for program correctness. You should use thread priorities only to give the Java Virtual Machine hints at what it should spend more time on. To coordinate the activities of multiple threads, you should use synchronization.

The thread implementation of any Java Virtual Machine must support two aspects of *synchronization*: object locking and thread wait and notify. Object locking helps keep threads from interfering with one another while working independently on shared data. Thread wait and notify helps threads to cooperate with one another while working together toward some common goal. Running applications access the Java Virtual Machine's locking capabilities via the instruction set, and its wait and notify capabilities via the `wait()`, `notify()`, and `notifyAll()` methods of class `Object`. For more details, see Chapter 20.

In the Java Virtual Machine Specification, the behavior of Java threads is defined in terms of *variables*, a *main memory*, and *working memories*. Each Java Virtual Machine instance has a main memory, which contains all the program's variables: instance variables of objects, components of arrays, and class variables. Each thread has a working memory, in which the thread stores "working copies" of variables it uses or assigns. Local variables and parameters, because they are private to individual threads, can be logically seen as part of either the working memory or main memory.

The Java Virtual Machine Specification defines many rules that govern the low-level interactions of threads with main memory. For example, one rule states that all operations on primitive types—except in some cases, `long`s and `double`s—are atomic. For example, if two threads compete to write two different values to an `int` variable, even in the absence of synchronization, the variable will end up with one value or the other. The variable will not contain a corrupted value. In other words, one thread will win the competition and write its value to the variable first.

The losing thread need not sulk, however, because it will write its value the variable second, overwriting the "winning" thread's value.

The exception to this rule is any **long** or **double** variable that is not declared **volatile**. Rather than being treated as a single atomic 64-bit value, such variables may be treated by some implementations as two atomic 32-bit values. Storing a non-volatile **long** to memory, for example, could involve two 32-bit write operations. This nonatomic treatment of **long**s and **double**s means that two threads competing to write two different values to a **long** or **double** variable can legally yield a corrupted result.

Although implementation designers are not required to treat operations involving nonvolatile **long**s and **double**s atomically, the Java Virtual Machine specification encourages them to do so anyway. This nonatomic treatment of **long**s and **double**s is an exception to the general rule that operations on primitive types are atomic. This exception is intended to facilitate efficient implementation of the threading model on processors that don't provide efficient ways to transfer 64-bit values to and from memory. In the future, this exception may be eliminated. For the time being, however, Java programmers must be sure to synchronize access to shared **long**s and **double**s.

Fundamentally, the rules governing low-level thread behavior specify when a thread can and when it must

1. copy values of variables from the main memory to its working memory, and
2. write values from its working memory back into the main memory.

For certain conditions, the rules specify a precise and predictable order of memory reads and writes. For other conditions, however, the rules do not specify any order. The rules are designed to enable Java programmers to build multithreaded programs that exhibit predictable behavior, while giving implementation designers some flexibility. This flexibility enables designers of Java Virtual Machine implementations to take advantage of standard hardware and software techniques that can improve the performance of multithreaded applications.

The fundamental high-level implication of all the low-level rules that govern the behavior of threads is this: If access to certain variables isn't synchronized, threads are allowed to update those variables in main memory in any order. Without synchronization, your multithreaded applications might exhibit surprising behavior on some Java Virtual Machine implementations. With proper use of synchronization, however, you can create multithreaded Java applications that behave in a predictable way on any implementation of the Java Virtual Machine.

## Native Method Interface

Java Virtual Machine implementations aren't required to support any particular native method interface. Some implementations may support no native method interfaces at all. Others may support several, each geared toward a different purpose.

Sun's Java Native Interface, or JNI, is geared toward portability. JNI is designed so that it can be supported by any implementation of the Java Virtual Machine, no matter what garbage-collection technique or object representation the implementation uses. This capability, in turn, enables developers to link the same (JNI compatible) native method binaries to any JNI-supporting virtual machine implementation on a particular host platform.

Implementation designers can choose to create proprietary native method interfaces in addition to, or instead of, JNI. To achieve its portability, the JNI uses a lot of indirection through pointers to pointers and pointers to functions. To obtain the ultimate in performance, designers of an implementation may decide to offer their own low-level native method interface that is tied closely to the structure of their particular implementations. Designers could also decide to offer a higher-level native method interface than JNI, such as one that brings Java objects into a component software model.

To do useful work, a native method must be able to interact to some degree with the internal state of the Java Virtual Machine instance. For example, a native method interface may allow native methods to do some or all of the following:

- Pass and return data
- Access instance variables or invoke methods in objects on the garbage-collected heap
- Access class variables or invoke class methods
- Access arrays
- Lock an object on the heap for exclusive use by the current thread
- Create new objects on the garbage-collected heap
- Load new classes
- Throw new exceptions

■ Catch exceptions thrown by Java methods that the native method invoked

■ Catch asynchronous exceptions thrown by the virtual machine

■ Indicate to the garbage collector that it no longer needs to use a particular object

Designing a native method interface that offers these services can be complicated. The design needs to ensure that the garbage collector doesn't free any objects that are being used by native methods. If an implementation's garbage collector moves objects to keep heap fragmentation at a minimum, the native method interface design must make sure that either

1. an object can be moved after its reference has been passed to a native method, or

2. any objects whose references have been passed to a native method are pinned until the native method returns or otherwise indicates it is done with the objects.

As you can see, native method interfaces are very intertwined with the inner workings of a Java Virtual Machine.

# The Real Machine

As mentioned at the beginning of this chapter, all the subsystems, runtime data areas, and internal behaviors defined by the Java Virtual Machine specification are abstract. Designers aren't required to organize their implementations around "real" components that map closely to the abstract components of the specification. The abstract internal components and behaviors are merely a vocabulary with which the specification defines the required external behavior of any Java Virtual Machine implementation.

In other words, an implementation can be anything on the inside as long as it behaves like a Java Virtual Machine on the outside. Implementations must be able to recognize Java class files and must adhere to the semantics of the Java code the class files contain. But otherwise, anything goes. How bytecodes are executed, how the runtime data areas are organized, how garbage collection is accomplished, how threads are implemented, how the primordial class loader finds classes, what native method interfaces are supported—these decisions, like many others, are left to implementation designers.

The flexibility of the specification gives designers the freedom to tailor their implementations to fit their circumstances. In some implementations, minimizing usage of resources may be critical. In other implementations, where resources are plentiful, maximizing performance may be the one and only goal.

By clearly marking the line between the external behavior and the internal implementation of a Java Virtual Machine, the specification preserves compatibility among all implementations while promoting innovation. Designers are encouraged to apply their talents and creativity toward building ever-better Java Virtual Machines.

# Eternal Math: A Simulation

The CD-ROM contains several simulation applets that serve as interactive illustrations for the material presented in this book. The applet shown in Figure 5-14 simulates a Java Virtual Machine executing a few bytecodes. You can run this applet by loading **applets/EternalMath.html**

**Figure 5-14.**
The **Eternal Math** applet.

| Applet Viewer: EternalMath.class |
|---|
| Applet |

**ETERNAL MATH**

| Local Variables | | | | pc | 7 | The Method | | |
|---|---|---|---|---|---|---|---|---|
| *index* | *hex value* | *value* | | | | *offset* | *bytecode* | *mnemonic* |
| | | | | | | 0 | 03 | iconst_0 |
| | | | | | | 1 | 3b | istore_0 |
| 0 | 00000003 | 3 | | | | 2 | 84 | iinc 0 1 |
| | | | | | | 3 | 00 | |
| | | | | | | 4 | 01 | |
| | | | | | | 5 | 1a | iload_0 |
| *optop* | 2 | Operand Stack | | | | 6 | 05 | iconst_2 |
| | *offset* | *hex value* | *value* | pc > | | 7 | 68 | imul |
| | 0 | 00000003 | 3 | | | 8 | 3b | istore_0 |
| | 1 | 00000002 | 2 | | | 9 | a7 | goto 2 |
| | | | | | | 10 | ff | |
| *optop* > | | | | | | 11 | f9 | |

| Step | Run |
|---|---|
| Reset | Stop |

*imul will pop two integers, multiply them, and push the result.*

from the CD-ROM into any Java-enabled web browser or applet viewer that supports JDK 1.1.

The instructions in the simulation represent the body of the **doMathForever()** method of class **Act**, shown in "The Instruction Set" section of this chapter. This simulation shows the local variables and operand stack of the current frame, the pc register, and the bytecodes in the method area. It also shows an optop register, which you can think of as part of the frame data of this particular implementation of the Java Virtual Machine. The optop register always points to one word beyond the top of the operand stack.

The applet has four buttons: Step, Reset, Run, and Stop. Each time you click the Step button, the Java Virtual Machine simulator will execute the instruction pointed to by the pc register. Initially, the pc register points to an **iconst_0** instruction. The first time you click the Step button, therefore, the virtual machine will execute **iconst_0**. It will push a zero onto the stack and set the pc register to point to the next instruction to execute. Subsequent clicks of the Step button will execute subsequent instructions, and the pc register will lead the way. If you click the Run button, the simulation will continue with no further coaxing on your part until you click the Stop button. To start the simulation over, click the Reset button.

The value of each register (pc and optop) is shown two ways. The contents of each register, an integer offset from the beginning of either the method's bytecodes or the operand stack, are shown in an edit box. Also, a small arrow (either "pc>" or "optop>") indicates the location contained in the register.

In the simulation the operand stack is shown growing down the panel (up in memory offsets) as words are pushed onto it. The top of the stack recedes back up the panel as words are popped from it.

The **doMathForever()** method has only one local variable, **i**, which sits at array position zero. The first two instructions, **iconst_0** and **istore_0**, initialize the local variable to zero. The next instruction, **iinc**, increments **i** by one. This instruction implements **the i += 1** statement from **doMathForever()**. The next instruction, **iload_0**, pushes the value of the local variable onto the operand stack. **iconst_2** pushes an **int** 2 onto the operand stack. **imul** pops the top two **int**s from the operand stack, multiplies them, and pushes the result. The **istore_0** instruction pops the result of the multiply operation and puts it into the local variable. The previous four instructions implement the **i *= 2** statement from **doMathForever()**. The last instruction, **goto**, sends the program counter back to the **iinc** instruction. The **goto** implements the **for (;;)** loop of **doMathForever()**.

With enough patience and clicks of the Step button (or a long enough run of the Run button), you can get an arithmetic overflow. When the Java Virtual Machine encounters such a condition, it just truncates, as is shown by this simulation. It does not throw any exceptions.

For each step of the simulation, a panel at the bottom of the applet contains an explanation of what the next instruction will do. Happy clicking.

## On the CD-ROM

The CD-ROM contains the source code examples from this chapter in the `jvm` directory. The *Eternal Math* applet is contained in a web page on the CD-ROM in the file `applets/EternalMath.html`. The source code for this applet is found alongside its class files, in the `applets/JVMSimulators` and `applets/JVMSimulators/COM/artima/jvmsim` directories.

## The Resources Page

For links to more information about the Java Virtual Machine, visit the resources page for this chapter: `http://www.artima.com/insidejvm/jvm.html`.

# 6

# The Java
# Class File

The preceding chapter gave an overview of the Java Virtual Machine. The next four chapters will focus on different aspects of the Java Virtual Machine. This chapter takes a look at the Java class file. It describes the contents of the class file, including the structure and format of the constant pool. This chapter serves as a complete reference to the Java class file format.

Accompanying this chapter on the CD-ROM is an applet that interactively illustrates the material presented in the chapter. The applet, named *Getting Loaded*, simulates the Java Virtual Machine loading a Java class file. At the end of this chapter, you will find a description of this applet and instructions on how to use it.

# What Is a Java Class File?

The Java class file is a precisely defined binary file format for Java programs. Each Java class file represents a complete description of one Java class or interface. You cannot put more than one class or interface into a single class file. The precise definition of the class file format ensures that any Java class file can be loaded and correctly interpreted by any Java Virtual Machine, no matter what system produced the class file or what system hosts the virtual machine.

Although the class file is related to the Java language architecturally, it is not inextricably linked to the Java language. As shown in Figure 6-1, you could write programs in other languages and compile them to class files, or you could compile your Java programs to a different binary file format. Nevertheless, most Java programmers will likely use the class file as the primary vehicle for delivering their programs to Java Virtual Machines.

As mentioned in earlier chapters, the Java class file is a binary stream of 8-bit bytes. Data items are stored sequentially in the class file with no

**Figure 6-1.**

The nonexclusive relationship of the Java language and class file.

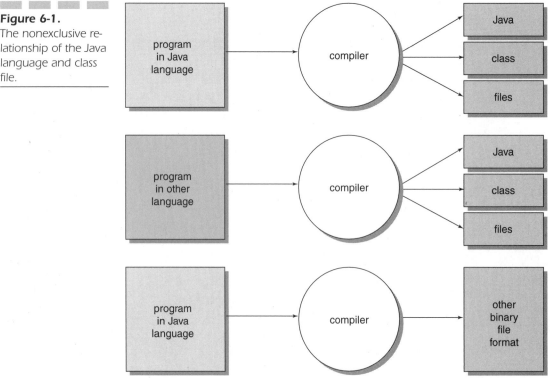

padding between adjacent items. The lack of padding helps keep class files compact. Items that occupy more than one byte are split up into several consecutive bytes that appear in *big-endian* (higher bytes first) order.

Just as your Java classes can contain varying numbers of fields, methods, method parameters, local variables, and so on, the Java class file can contain many items that vary in size or number from one class file to another. In the class file, the size or length of a variable-length item precedes the actual data for the item. This arrangement allows class file streams to be parsed from beginning to end, reading in the size of an item first, followed by the item data.

# What Is in a Class File?

The Java class file contains everything a Java Virtual Machine needs to know about one Java class or interface. The remainder of this chapter describes the class file format using tables. Each table has a name and shows an ordered list of items that can appear in a class file. Items appear in the table in the order in which they appear in the class file. Each item has a type, a name, and a count. The type is either a table name or one of the "primitive types" shown in Table 6-1. All values stored in items of type **u2**, **u4**, and **u8** appear in the class file in big-endian order.

The major components of the class file, in their order of appearance in the class file, are shown in Table 6-2. Each of these components is described in more detail in the following sections.

### magic

The first four bytes of every Java class file are its *magic number*, 0xCAFEBABE. The magic number makes non-Java class files easier to

**Table 6-1.**

Class file "primitive types"

| Type | Description |
| --- | --- |
| **u1** | a single unsigned byte |
| **u2** | two unsigned bytes |
| **u4** | four unsigned bytes |
| **u8** | eight unsigned bytes |

**Table 6-2.**

Format of a
**ClassFile** Table

| Type | Name | Count |
|------|------|-------|
| u4 | magic | 1 |
| u2 | minor_version | 1 |
| u2 | major_version | 1 |
| u2 | constant_pool_count | 1 |
| cp_info | constant_pool | constant_pool_count - 1 |
| u2 | access_flags | 1 |
| u2 | this_class | 1 |
| u2 | super_class | 1 |
| u2 | interfaces_count | 1 |
| u2 | interfaces | interfaces_count |
| u2 | fields_count | 1 |
| field_info | fields | fields_count |
| u2 | methods_count | 1 |
| method_info | methods | methods_count |
| u2 | attributes_count | 1 |
| attribute_info | attributes | attributes_count |

identify. If a file doesn't start with 0xCAFEBABE, it definitely isn't a Java class file. A file format's designers can choose a magic number to be any arbitrary number that isn't already in widespread use. The magic number for the Java class file was chosen back in the days when "Java" was called "Oak." According to Patrick Naughton, a key member of the original Java team, the magic number was chosen "long before the name Java was ever uttered in reference to this language. We were looking for something fun, unique, and easy to remember. It is only a coincidence that 0xCAFEBABE, an oblique reference to the cute baristas at Peet's Coffee, was foreshadowing for the name Java."

## minor_version **and** major_version

The second four bytes of the class file contain the minor and major version numbers. As Java technology evolves, new features may occasionally be added to the Java class file format. Each time the class file format changes, the version numbers will change as well. To the Java Virtual Machine, the version numbers identify the format to which a particular class file adheres. Java Virtual Machines generally can load class files with a given major version number and a range of minor version numbers. Java Virtual Machines must reject class files with version numbers outside their valid range.

For class files generated by 1.0 or 1.1 compilers, the major version number is 45. The minor version number is 3.

## constant_pool_count and constant_pool

Following the magic and version numbers in the class file is the *constant pool*. As mentioned in Chapter 5, "The Java Virtual Machine," the constant pool contains the constants associated with the class or interface defined by the file. Constants such as literal strings, final variable values, class names, and method names are stored in the constant pool. The constant pool is organized as a list of entries. A count of the number of entries in the list, `constant_pool_count`, precedes the actual list, `constant_pool`.

Many entries in the constant pool refer to other entries in the constant pool, and many items that follow the constant pool in the class file refer back to entries in the constant pool. Throughout the class file, constant pool entries are referred to by the integer index that indicates their position in the `constant_pool` list. The first entry in the list has an index of one, the second has an index of two, and so on. Although no entry in the `constant_pool` list has an index of zero, the missing zeroth entry is included in the `constant_pool_count`. For example, if a `constant_pool` list includes 14 entries (with indexes one through fourteen), the `constant_pool_count` would be 15.

Each constant pool entry starts with a one-byte tag that indicates the type of constant making its home at that position in the list. After a Java Virtual Machine grabs and interprets this tag, it knows what to expect after the tag. Table 6-3 shows the names and values of the constant pool tags.

Each tag shown in Table 6-3 has a corresponding table. The name of the table is formed by appending `_info` to the tag name. For example, the table that corresponds to the `CONSTANT_Class` tag is called `CONSTANT_Class_info`. The `CONSTANT_Utf8_info` table stores a compressed form of Unicode strings. The tables for the various kinds of constant pool entries are described in detail later in this chapter.

**Table 6-3.**

Constant pool tags

| Entry Type | Tag Value | Description |
|---|---|---|
| CONSTANT_Utf8 | 1 | A UTF-8 encoded Unicode string |
| CONSTANT_Integer | 3 | An **int** literal value |
| CONSTANT_Float | 4 | A **float** literal value |
| CONSTANT_Long | 5 | A **long** literal value |
| CONSTANT_Double | 6 | A **double** literal value |
| CONSTANT_Class | 7 | A symbolic reference to a class or interface |
| CONSTANT_String | 8 | A **String** literal value |
| CONSTANT_Fieldref | 9 | A symbolic reference to a field |
| CONSTANT_Methodref | 10 | A symbolic reference to a method declared in a class |
| CONSTANT_InterfaceMethodref | 11 | A symbolic reference to a method declared in an interface |
| CONSTANT_NameAndType | 12 | Part of a symbolic reference to a field or method |

The constant pool plays an important role in the dynamic linking of Java programs. In addition to literal constant values, the constant pool contains the following kinds of symbolic references:

- Fully qualified names of classes and interfaces
- Field names and descriptors
- Method names and descriptors

A *field* is an instance or class variable of the class or interface. A *field descriptor* is a string that indicates the field's type. A *method descriptor* is a string that indicates the method's return type and the number, order, and types of its parameters. The constant pool's fully qualified names and method and field descriptors are used at runtime to link code in this class or interface with code and data in other classes and interfaces. The class file contains no information about the eventual memory layout of its components; therefore, classes, fields, and methods cannot be referenced directly by the bytecodes in the class file. The Java Virtual Machine resolves the actual address of any referenced item at runtime given a symbolic reference from the constant pool. For example, bytecode instructions that invoke a method give a constant pool index of a symbolic reference to the method to invoke. This process of using the symbolic references in the constant pool is described in more detail in Chapter 8, "The Linking Model."

### access_flags

The first two bytes after the constant pool, the *access flags*, reveal several pieces of information about the class or interface defined in the file. To start with, the access flags indicate whether the file defines a class or an interface. The access flags also indicate what modifiers were used in the declaration of the class or interface. Classes and interfaces can be public or abstract. Classes can be final, though final classes cannot be abstract. Interfaces can't be final. The bits used for the various flags are shown in Table 6-4.

The **ACC_SUPER** flag is used for backward compatibility with Sun's older Java compilers. In Sun's older Java Virtual Machines, the **invokespecial** instruction had more relaxed semantics. All new compilers should set the **ACC_SUPER** flag. All new implementations of the Java Virtual Machine should implement the newer, stricter **invokespecial** semantics. (See the **invokespecial** instruction in Appendix A, "Instruction Set by Opcode Mnemonic," for a description of these semantics.) Sun's older compilers generate class files with the **ACC_SUPER** flag set to zero. Sun's older Java Virtual Machines ignore the flag if it is set.

All unused bits in **access_flags** must be set to zero and ignored by Java Virtual Machine implementations.

**Table 6-4.**

Flag bits in the **access_flags** item of **ClassFile** tables

| Flag Name | Value | Meaning If Set | Set By |
|-----------|-------|----------------|--------|
| ACC_PUBLIC | 0x0001 | Type is public | Classes and interfaces |
| ACC_FINAL | 0x0010 | Class is final | Classes only |
| ACC_SUPER | 0x0020 | Use new **invokespecial** semantics | Classes and interfaces |
| ACC_INTERFACE | 0x0200 | Type is an interface, not a class | All interfaces, no classes |
| ACC_ABSTRACT | 0x0400 | Type is abstract | All interfaces, some classes |

## this_class

The next two bytes are the **this_class** item, an index into the constant pool. The constant pool entry at position **this_class** must be a **CONSTANT_Class_info** table, which has two parts: a **tag** and a **name_index**. The tag will have the value **CONSTANT_Class**. The constant pool entry at position **name_index** will be a **CONSTANT_Utf8_info** table containing the fully qualified name of the class or interface.

The **this_class** item provides a glimpse of how the constant pool is used. By itself, the **this_class** item is just an index into the constant pool. When a Java Virtual Machine looks up the constant pool entry at position **this_class**, it will find an entry that identifies itself via its **tag** as a **CONSTANT_Class_info**. The Java Virtual Machine knows **CONSTANT_Class_info** entries always have an index into the constant pool, called **name_index**, following their **tag**. So the virtual machine looks up the constant pool entry at position **name_index**, where it should find a **CONSTANT_Utf8_info** entry that contains the fully qualified name of the class or interface. See Figure 6-2 for a graphical depiction of this process.

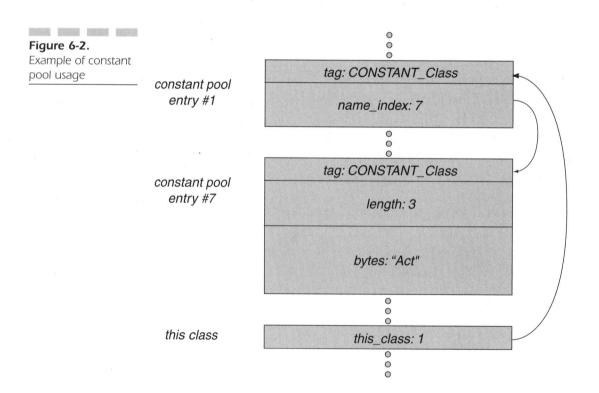

**Figure 6-2.**
Example of constant pool usage

## super_class

Following **this_class** in the class file is the **super_class** item, another two-byte index into the constant pool. The constant pool entry at position **super_class** will be a **CONSTANT_Class_info** entry that refers to the fully qualified name of this class's superclass. Because the base class of every object in Java programs is the **java.lang.Object** class, the **super_class** constant pool index will be valid for every class except **Object**. For **Object**, **super_class** is a zero. For interfaces, the constant pool entry at position **super_class** is **java.lang.Object**.

## interfaces_count and interfaces

The component that follows **super_class** starts with **interfaces_count**, a count of the number of superinterfaces directly implemented by the class or interface defined in this file. Immediately following the count is **interfaces**, an array that contains one index into the constant pool for each superinterface directly implemented by this class or interface. Each superinterface is represented by a **CONSTANT_Class_info** entry in the constant pool that refers to the fully qualified name of the interface. Only direct superinterfaces, those that appear in the **implements** clause of the class or the **extends** clause of the interface declaration, appear in this array. The superinterfaces appear in the array in the order in which they appear (left to right) in the **implements** or **extends** clause.

## fields_count and fields

Following the interfaces component in the class file is a description of the fields declared by this class or interface. This component starts with **fields_count**, a count of the number of fields, including both class and instance variables. Following the count is a list of variable-length **field_info** tables, one for each field. (The **fields_count** indicates the number of **field_info** tables in the list.) The only fields that appear in the **fields** list are those that were declared by the class or interface defined in the file. No fields inherited from superclasses or superinterfaces appear in the **fields** list.

Each **field_info** table reveals information about one field. The table contains the field's name, descriptor, and modifiers. If the field is declared as final, the `field_info` table also reveals the field's constant value. Some of this information is contained in the `field_info` table itself, and some is contained in constant pool locations referred to by the table. The `field_info` table is described in more detail later in this chapter.

## `methods_count` and `methods`

Following the fields in the class file is a description of the methods declared by the class or interface. This component starts with `methods_count`, a two-byte count of the number of methods in the class or interface. The count includes only those methods that are explicitly defined by this class or interface. (It does not include any methods inherited from superclasses or superinterfaces.) Following the method count are the methods themselves, described in a list of `method_info` tables. (The `methods_count` indicates the number of `method_info` tables in the list.)

The `method_info` table contains several pieces of information about the method, including the method's name and descriptor (its return type and argument types). If the method is not abstract, the `method_info` table includes the number of stack words required for the method's local variables, the maximum number of stack words required for the method's operand stack, a table of exceptions caught by the method, the bytecode sequence, and optional line number and local variable tables. If the method can throw any checked exceptions, the `method_info` table includes a list of those checked exceptions. The `method_info` table is described in detail later in this chapter.

## `attributes_count` and `attributes`

The last component in the class file is the attributes, which give general information about the particular class or interface defined by the file. The attributes component starts with `attributes_count`, a count of the number of `attribute_info` tables appearing in the subsequent `attributes` list. The first item in each `attribute_info` table is an index into the constant pool of a `CONSTANT_Utf8_info` table that gives the attribute's name.

Attributes come in many varieties. Several varieties are defined by the Java Virtual Machine specification, but anyone can create varieties of attributes (following certain rules) and place them into class files. Java Virtual Machine implementations must silently ignore any attributes they don't recognize. The rules surrounding the creation of new varieties of attributes are described later in this chapter.

Attributes appear in several places in the class file, not just in the **attributes** item of the top-level **ClassFile** table. The attributes that appear in the **ClassFile** table give more information about the class or interface defined by the file. Attributes that give more information about a field can be included as part of **field_info** table. Attributes that give more information about a method can be included as part of a **method_info** table.

The Java Virtual Machine specification defines two kinds of attributes that can appear in the attributes list of the **ClassFile** table: **SourceCode** and **InnerClasses**. These two attributes are described in detail later in this chapter.

# Special Strings

The symbolic references contained in the constant pool involve three special kinds of strings: fully qualified names, simple names, and descriptors. Each symbolic reference includes the fully qualified name of a class or interface. A symbolic reference to a field includes a simple field name and field descriptor in addition to a fully qualified type name. A symbolic reference to a method includes a simple method name and method descriptor in addition to a fully qualified name.

The same special strings are used to describe the class or interface that is defined by the class file. The class or interface name, the superclass name (if any), and the names of any superinterfaces are all given as fully qualified names. For each field declared by the class or interface, the constant pool contains a simple name and field descriptor. For each method declared by the class or interface, the constant pool contains a simple name and method descriptor.

## Fully Qualified Names

Whenever constant pool entries refer to classes and interfaces, they give the fully qualified names of the classes or interfaces. In the class file, the dots in fully qualified names are replaced with slashes. For example, the representation of the fully qualified name of **java.lang.Object** in the class file is **java/lang/Object**. The fully qualified name of **java.util.Hashtable** in the class file is **java/util/Hashtable**.

## Simple Names

The names of fields and methods appear in constant pool entries as simple (not fully qualified) names. For example, a constant pool entry that refers to the `String toString()` method of class `java.lang.Object` would give its method name as `"toString"`. A constant pool entry that refers to the `java.io.PrintStream out` field of class `java.lang.System` would specify the field name simply as `"out"`.

## Descriptors

Symbolic references to fields and methods include descriptor strings in addition to fully qualified class or interface names and simple field or method names. A field descriptor gives the field's type. A method descriptor gives the method's return type and the number and types of the method's parameters.

Field and method descriptors are defined by the context-free grammar shown in the following example. Nonterminals of this grammar, such as *FieldType*, are shown in italic font. Terminals, such as `B` or `V`, are shown in fixed-width font. The asterisk character (*) stands for zero or more occurrences of the item that precedes it placed side by side (with no intervening white space).

*FieldDescriptor:*

    *FieldType*

*ComponentType:*

    *FieldType*

*FieldType:*

    `BaseType`

    *ObjectType*

    *ArrayType*

*BaseType:*

    `B`

    `C`

    `D`

    `F`

    **I**

    **J**

    **S**

    <cc>>Z

*ObjectType:*

    **L<classname>;**

    *ArrayType:*

    **[** *ComponentType*

*ParameterDescriptor:*

    *FieldType*

*MethodDescriptor:*

    **(** *ParameterDescriptor\** **)** *ReturnDescriptor*

*ReturnDescriptor:*

    *FieldType*

    **V**

The meaning of each of the *BaseType* terminals is shown in Table 6-5. The **v** terminal represents methods that return **void**.

Some examples of field descriptors are shown in Table 6-6.

Some examples of method descriptors are shown in Table 6-7. Note that method descriptors don't include the hidden **this** parameter passed as the first argument to all instance methods.

**Table 6-5.**

BaseType
terminals

| Terminal | Type |
| --- | --- |
| B | byte |
| C | char |
| D | double |
| F | float |
| I | int |
| J | long |
| S | short |
| Z | boolean |

**Table 6-6.**

Examples of field descriptors

| Descriptor | Field Declaration |
|---|---|
| I | int i; |
| [[J | long[][] windingRoad; |
| [Ljava/lang/Object; | java.lang.Object[] stuff; |
| Ljava/util/Hashtable; | java.util.Hashtable ht; |
| [[[Z | boolean[][][] isReady; |

**Table 6-7.**

Examples of method descriptors

| Descriptor | Method Declaration |
|---|---|
| ()I | int getSize(); |
| ()Ljava/lang/String; | String toString(); |
| ([Ljava/lang/String;)V | void main(String[] args); |
| ()V | void wait() |
| (JI)V | void wait(long timeout, int nanos) |
| (ZILjava/lang/String;II)Z | boolean regionMatches(boolean ignoreCase, int toOffset, String other, int ooffset, int len); |
| ([BII)I | int read(byte[] b, int off, int len); |

# The Constant Pool

The constant pool is an ordered list of **cp_info** tables, each of which follows the general form shown in Table 6-8. The **tag** item of a **cp_info** table, an unsigned byte, indicates the table's variety and format. **cp_info** tables come in 11 varieties, each of which is described in detail in the following sections.

**Table 6-8.**

General form of a **cp_info** table

| Type | Name | Count |
|---|---|---|
| u1 | tag | 1 |
| u1 | info | depends on tag value |

## The CONSTANT_Utf8_info Table

A **CONSTANT_Utf8_info** table stores one constant string value in a modified UTF-8 format. This table is used to store many different kinds of strings, including

- string literals that get instantiated as **String** objects
- the fully qualified name of the class or interface being defined
- the fully qualified name of the superclass (if any) of the class being defined
- the fully qualified names of any superinterfaces of the class or interface being defined
- the simple names and descriptors of any fields declared by the class or interface
- the simple names and descriptors of any methods declared by the class or interface
- fully qualified names of any referenced classes and interfaces
- simple names and descriptors of any referenced fields
- simple names and descriptors of any referenced methods
- strings associated with attributes

As you can see from the preceding list, four basic kinds of information are stored in **CONSTANT_Utf8_info** tables: string literals, descriptions of the class or interface being defined, symbolic references to other classes and interfaces, and strings associated with attributes. Some examples of strings associated with attributes are the name of the attribute, the name of the source file from which the class file was generated, and the names and descriptors of local variables.

The UTF-8 encoding scheme allows all two-byte Unicode characters to be represented in a string but enables ASCII characters to be represented by just one byte. Table 6-9 shows the format of a **CONSTANT_Utf8_info** table.

**Table 6-9.**

Format of a **CONSTANT_Utf8_info** table

| Type | Name | Count |
|------|------|-------|
| u1 | tag | 1 |
| u2 | length | 1 |
| u1 | bytes | length |

**tag**   The **tag** item has the value **CONSTANT_Utf8** (1).

**length**   The **length** item gives the length in bytes of the subsequent **bytes** item.

**bytes**   The **bytes** item contains the characters of the string stored in a modified UTF-8 format. Characters in the range '**\u0001**' through '**\u007f**' (all the ASCII characters except the null character) are represented by one byte:

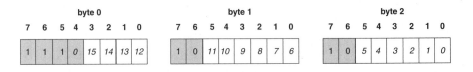

The **null** character, '**\u0000**', and the characters in the range '**\u0080**' through '**\u07ff**' are represented by two bytes:

Characters in the range '**\u0800**' through '**\uffff**' are represented by three bytes:

The encoding of UTF-8 strings in the **bytes** item of **CONSTANT_Utf8_info** tables differs from the standard UTF-8 format in two ways. First, in the standard UTF-8 encoding scheme, the **null** character is represented by one byte. In a **CONSTANT_Utf8_info** table, **null** characters are represented by two bytes. This two-byte encoding of **null**s means that the **bytes** item never contains any byte equal to zero. The second way the **bytes** item of a **CONSTANT_Utf8_info** departs from the standard UTF-8 encoding is that only one-, two-, and three-byte encodings are used in the **bytes** item. The standard UTF-8 includes longer formats that aren't used in **CONSTANT_Utf8_info** tables.

## The **CONSTANT_Integer_info** Table

The **CONSTANT_Integer_info** table stores a constant **int** value. This table is used only to store **int** literals; it is not used in symbolic references. Table 6-10 shows the format of a **CONSTANT_Integer_info** table.

**tag**   The **tag** item has the value **CONSTANT_Integer** (3).

**bytes**   The **bytes** item contains the **int** value stored in big-endian order.

## The **CONSTANT_Float_info** Table

The **CONSTANT_Float_info** table stores a constant **float** value. This table is used only to store **float** literals; it is not used in symbolic references. Table 6-11 shows the format of a **CONSTANT_Float_info** table.

**tag**   The **tag** item has the value **CONSTANT_Float** (4).

**bytes**   The **bytes** item contains the **float** value stored in big-endian order. For the details of the representation of **float** in the Java class file, see Chapter 14, "Floating-Point Arithmetic."

**Table 6-10.**

Format of a
**CONSTANT_
Integer_info**
table

| Type | Name | Count |
|------|------|-------|
| u1 | tag | 1 |
| u4 | bytes | 1 |

**Table 6-11.**

Format of a
**CONSTANT_Float_
info** table

| Type | Name | Count |
|------|------|-------|
| u1 | tag | 1 |
| u4 | bytes | 1 |

## The CONSTANT_Long_info **Table**

The CONSTANT_Long_info table stores a constant **long** value. This table is used only to store **long** literals; it is not used in symbolic references. Table 6-12 shows the format of a CONSTANT_Long_info table.

As noted previously, a **long** occupies two slots in the constant pool table. In the class file, a **long** entry is just followed by the next entry, but the index of the next entry is two more than that of the **long** entry.

**tag**  The **tag** item has the value CONSTANT_Long (5).

**bytes**  The **bytes** item contains the **long** value stored in big-endian order.

## The CONSTANT_Double_info **Table**

The CONSTANT_Double_info table stores a constant **double** value. This table is used only to store **double** literals; it is not used in symbolic references. Table 6-13 shows the format of a CONSTANT_Double_info table.

As noted previously, a **double** occupies two slots in the constant pool table. In the class file, a **double** entry is just followed by the next entry, but the index of the next entry is two more than that of the **double** entry.

**tag**  The **tag** item has the value CONSTANT_Double (6).

**Table 6-12.**

Format of a
CONSTANT_Long_
**info** table

| Type | Name | Count |
|------|------|-------|
| u1 | tag | 1 |
| u8 | bytes | 1 |

**Table 6-13.**

Format of a
CONSTANT_
Double_info table

| Type | Name | Count |
|------|------|-------|
| u1 | tag | 1 |
| u8 | bytes | 1 |

**bytes** The **bytes** item contains the **double** value stored in big-endian order. For the details of the representation of **double** in the Java class file, see Chapter 14.

## The CONSTANT_Class_info **Table**

The **CONSTANT_Class_info** table represents a class or interface in symbolic references. All symbolic references, whether they refer to a class, interface, field, or method, include a **CONSTANT_Class_info** table. Table 6-14 shows the format of a **CONSTANT_Class_info** table.

**tag** The **tag** item has the value **CONSTANT_Class** (7).

**name_index** The **name_index** item gives the index of a **CONSTANT_Utf8_info** table that contains a fully qualified name of a class or interface.

## The CONSTANT_String_info **Table**

A **CONSTANT_String_info** represents a literal string value, which will be represented as an instance of class **java.lang.String**. This table is used only to represent literal strings; it is not used in symbolic references. Table 6-15 shows the format of a **CONSTANT_String_info** table.

**tag** The **tag** item has the value **CONSTANT_String** (8).

**Table 6-14.**

Format of a
**CONSTANT_Class_
info** table

| Type | Name | Count |
|------|------|-------|
| u1 | tag | 1 |
| u2 | name_index | 1 |

**Table 6-15.**

Format of a
**CONSTANT_String
_info** table

| Type | Name | Count |
|------|------|-------|
| u1 | tag | 1 |
| u2 | string_index | 1 |

**string_index** The **string_index** item gives the index of a **CONSTANT_Utf8_info** entry that contains the value of the literal string.

## The **CONSTANT_Fieldref_info** Table

The **CONSTANT_Fieldref_info** table represents a symbolic reference to a field. Table 6-16 shows the format of a **CONSTANT_Fieldref_info** table.

**tag** The **tag** item has the value **CONSTANT_Fieldref** (9).

**class_index** The **class_index** gives the index of the **CONSTANT_Class_info** entry for the class that declares the referenced field.

Note that the **CONSTANT_Class_info** specified by **class_index** must represent a class, not an interface. Although interfaces can declare fields, those fields are by definition public, static, and final. As mentioned in earlier chapters, class files do not contain symbolic references to static final fields of other classes. Instead, class files contain a copy of the constant value of any static final fields it uses. For example, if a class uses a static final field of type **float** that is declared in an interface, the class would have a **CONSTANT_Float_info** table in its own constant pool that stores the **float** value. For more information about this special treatment of static final fields, see Chapter 8.

**name_and_type_index** The **name_and_type_index** gives the index of a **CONSTANT_NameAndType_info** entry that gives the field's simple name and descriptor.

## The **CONSTANT_Methodref_info** Table

The **CONSTANT_Methodref_info** table represents a symbolic reference to a method declared in a class, not in an interface. Table 6-17 shows the format of a **CONSTANT_Methodref_info** table.

**Table 6-16.**

Format of a **CONSTANT_ Fieldref_info** table

| Type | Name | Count |
|------|------|-------|
| u1 | tag | 1 |
| u2 | class_index | 1 |
| u2 | name_and_type_index | 1 |

**Table 6-17.**

Format of a
**CONSTANT_**
**Methodref_info**
table

| Type | Name | Count |
|------|------|-------|
| u1 | tag | 1 |
| u2 | class_index | 1 |
| u2 | name_and_type_index | 1 |

**Table 6-18.**

Format of a
**CONSTANT_**
**Interface-**
**Methodref_info**
table

| Type | Name | Count |
|------|------|-------|
| u1 | tag | 1 |
| u2 | class_index | 1 |
| u2 | name_and_type_index | 1 |

**tag**   The **tag** item has the value **CONSTANT_Methodref** (10).

**class_index**   The **class_index** gives the index of a **CONSTANT_Class_info**
entry for the class that declares the referenced method. The
**CONSTANT_Class_info** table specified by **class_index** must be a class, not
an interface. Symbolic references to methods declared in interfaces use
**CONSTANT_InterfaceMethodref**.

**name_and_type_index**   The **name_and_type_index** gives the index of a
**CONSTANT_NameAndType_info** entry that gives the method's simple name
and descriptor.

## The **CONSTANT_InterfaceMethodref_info** Table

The **CONSTANT_InterfaceMethodref_info** table represents a symbolic reference to a method declared in an interface, not in a class. Table 6-18
shows the format of a **CONSTANT_InterfaceMethodref_info** table.

**tag**   The **tag** item has the value **CONSTANT_InterfaceMethodref** (11).

**class_index**   The **class_index** gives the index of a **CONSTANT_Class_info**
entry for the interface that declares the referenced method. The
**CONSTANT_Class_info** table specified by **class_index** must be an interface, not a class. Symbolic references to methods declared in classes use
**CONSTANT_Methodref**.

**name_and_type_index**  The **name_and_type_index** gives the index of a **CONSTANT_NameAndType_info** entry that gives the method's simple name and descriptor.

### The CONSTANT_NameAndType_info Table

The **CONSTANT_NameAndType_info** table forms part of a symbolic reference to a field or method. This table gives constant pool entries of the simple name and the descriptor of the referenced field or method. Table 6-19 shows the format of a **CONSTANT_NameAndType_info** table.

**tag**  The **tag** item has the value **CONSTANT_NameAndType** (12).

**name_index**  The **name_index** gives the index of a **CONSTANT_Utf8_info** entry that gives the name of the field or method.

**descriptor_index**  The **descriptor_index** gives the index of a **CONSTANT_Utf8_info** entry that gives the descriptor of the field or method.

# Fields

Each field (class variable and instance variable) declared in a class or interface is described by a **field_info** table in the class file. The format of the **field_info** table is shown in Table 6-20.

### access_flags

The modifiers used in declaring the field are placed into the field's **access_flags** item. Table 6-21 shows the bits used by each flag.

**Table 6-19.**

Format of a
**CONSTANT_
NameAndType_
info** table

| Type | Name | Count |
|------|------|-------|
| u1 | tag | 1 |
| u2 | name_index | 1 |
| u2 | descriptor_index | 1 |

**Table 6-20.**

Format of a
**field_info** table

| Type | Name | Count |
|------|------|-------|
| u2 | access_flags | 1 |
| u2 | name_index | 1 |
| u2 | descriptor_index | 1 |
| u2 | attributes_count | 1 |
| attribute_info | attributes | attributes_count |

**Table 6-21.**

Flags in the
**access_flags**
item of
**field_info** tables

| Flag Name | Value | Meaning If Set | Set By |
|-----------|-------|----------------|--------|
| ACC_PUBLIC | 0x0001 | Field is public | Classes and interfaces |
| ACC_PRIVATE | 0x0002 | Field is private | Classes only |
| ACC_PROTECTED | 0x0004 | Field is protected | Classes only |
| ACC_STATIC | 0x0008 | Field is static | Classes and interfaces |
| ACC_FINAL | 0x0010 | Field is final | Classes and interfaces |
| ACC_VOLATILE | 0x0040 | Field is volatile | Classes only |
| ACC_TRANSIENT | 0x0080 | Field is transient | Classes only |

For fields declared in a class (not an interface), at most one of
**ACC_PUBLIC**, **ACC_PRIVATE**, and **ACC_PROTECTED** may be set. **ACC_FINAL** and
**ACC_VOLATILE** must not both be set. All fields declared in interfaces must
have the **ACC_PUBLIC**, **ACC_STATIC**, and **ACC_FINAL** flags set.

All unused bits in **access_flags** must be set to zero and ignored by
Java Virtual Machine implementations.

## name_index

The **name_index** gives the index of a **CONSTANT_Utf8_info** entry that gives
the simple (not fully qualified) name of the field.

## descriptor_index

The **descriptor_index** gives the index of a **CONSTANT_Utf8_info** entry
that gives the descriptor of the field.

### attributes_count and attributes

The **attributes** item is a list of **attribute_info** tables. The **attributes_count** indicates the number of **attribute_info** tables in the list. Two kinds of attributes defined by the Java Virtual Machine specification that may appear in this item are **ConstantValue** and **Synthetic**. These two attributes are described in detail later in this chapter.

# Methods

Each method declared in a class or interface or generated by the compiler is described in the class file by a **method_info** table. The two types of compiler-generated methods that can appear in class files are instance initialization methods (named **<init>**) and class initialization methods (named **<clinit>**). For more information on the compiler-generated methods, see Chapter 7, "The Lifetime of a Class." The format of the **method_info** table is shown in Table 6-22.

### access_flags

The modifiers used in declaring the method are placed into the method's **access_flags** item. Table 6-23 shows the bits used by each flag.

For methods declared in a class (not an interface), at most one of **ACC_PUBLIC**, **ACC_PRIVATE**, and **ACC_PROTECTED** may be set. If a method's **ACC_FINAL** flag is set, then its **ACC_SYNCHRONIZED**, **ACC_NATIVE**, and **ACC_ABSTRACT** flags must not be set. If a method's **ACC_PRIVATE** or **ACC_STATIC** flag is set, then its **ACC_ABSTRACT** flag must not be set. All methods declared in interfaces must have their **ACC_PUBLIC** and **ACC_ABSTRACT** flags set.

**Table 6-22.**

Format of a **method_info** table

| Type | Name | Count |
|------|------|-------|
| u2 | access_flags | 1 |
| u2 | name_index | 1 |
| u2 | descriptor_index | 1 |
| u2 | attributes_count | 1 |
| attribute_info | attributes | attributes_count |

**Table 6-23.**

Flags in the
**access_flags**
item of
**method_info**
tables

| Flag Name | Value | Meaning If Set | Set By |
|---|---|---|---|
| ACC_PUBLIC | 0x0001 | Method is public | Classes and all methods of interfaces |
| ACC_PRIVATE | 0x0002 | Method is private | Classes only |
| ACC_PROTECTED | 0x0004 | Method is protected | Classes only |
| ACC_STATIC | 0x0008 | Method is static | Classes only |
| ACC_FINAL | 0x0010 | Method is final | Classes only |
| ACC_SYNCHRONIZED | 0x0020 | Method is synchronized | Classes only |
| ACC_NATIVE | 0x0100 | Method is native | Classes only |
| ACC_ABSTRACT | 0x0400 | Method is abstract | Classes and all methods of interfaces |

Instance initialization (**<init>**) methods can only use flags **ACC_PUBLIC**, **ACC_PRIVATE**, and **ACC_PROTECTED**. Because class initialization (**<clinit>**) methods are invoked by the Java Virtual Machine, never directly by Java bytecodes, the **access_flags** for **<clinit>** methods are ignored.

All unused bits in **access_flags** must be set to zero and ignored by Java Virtual Machine implementations.

### name_index

The **name_index** gives the index of a **CONSTANT_Utf8_info** entry that gives the simple (not fully qualified) name of the method.

### descriptor_index

The **descriptor_index** gives the index of a **CONSTANT_Utf8_info** entry that gives the descriptor of the method.

### attributes_count **and** attributes

The **attributes** item is a list of **attribute_info** tables. The **attributes_count** indicates the number of **attribute_info** tables in the list. Three kinds of attributes that are defined by the Java Virtual Machine specification that can appear in this item are **Code**, **Exceptions**, and

**Synthetic**. These three attributes are described in detail later in this chapter.

# Attributes

As mentioned previously, attributes appear in several places inside a Java class file. They can appear in the **ClassFile**, **field_info**, **method_info**, and **Code_attribute** tables. The **Code_attribute** table, an attribute itself, is described later in this section.

Every attribute follows the same general format of the **attribute_info** table, shown in Table 6-24. The first two bytes of an attribute, the **attribute_name_index**, form an index into the constant pool of a **CONSTANT_Utf8_info** table that contains the string name of the attribute. Each **attribute_info**, therefore, identifies its "type" by the first item in its table much like **cp_info** tables identify their type by the initial **tag** byte. The difference is that whereas the type of a **cp_info** table is indicated by an unsigned byte value, such as 3 (**CONSTANT_Integer_info**), the type of an **attribute_info** table is indicated by a string.

Following the **attribute_name_index** is a four-byte **attribute_length** item, which gives the length of the entire **attribute_info** table minus the initial six bytes. This length is necessary because anyone, following certain rules (outlined below), can add attributes to a Java class file. Java Virtual Machine implementations are allowed to recognize new attributes. Implementations must ignore any attributes they don't recognize. The **attribute_length** allows virtual machines to skip unrecognized attributes as they parse the class file.

Anyone who wishes to add a new attribute to a Java class file must follow these two rules:

1. Any attribute that is not predefined by the specification must not affect the semantics of class or interface types. New attributes can only add more information to the class file, such as information used during debugging.

**Table 6-24.**

Format of an **attribute_info** table

| Type | Name | Count |
|------|------|-------|
| u2 | attribute_name_index | 1 |
| u4 | attribute_length | 1 |
| u1 | info | attribute_length |

**2.** The attribute must be named using the reverse Internet domain name scheme that is defined for package naming in the Java Language Specification. For example, if your Internet domain name were **artima.com** and you wished to create a new attribute named **CompilerVersion**, you would name the attribute: **COM.artima.CompilerVersion**.

**attribute_name_index**   The **attribute_name_index** gives the index in the constant pool of a **CONSTANT_Utf8_info** entry that contains the name of the attribute.

**attribute_length**   The **attribute_length** item indicates the length in bytes of the attribute data excluding the initial six bytes that contain the **attribute_name_index** and **attribute_length**.

**info**   The **info** item contains the attribute data.

The Java Virtual Machine specification defines eight types of attributes, which are shown in Table 6-25. All Java Virtual Machine implementations must recognize three of these attributes: **Code**, **ConstantValue**, and **Exceptions**. Implementations can choose whether to recognize or ignore the other predefined attributes. (The **InnerClasses** and **Synthetic** at-

**Table 6-25.**

Types of **attribute_info** tables defined by the specification

| Name | Used By | Description |
| --- | --- | --- |
| Code | method_info | The bytecodes and other data for one method |
| ConstantValue | field_info | The value of a final variable |
| Exceptions | method_info | The checked exceptions that a method may throw |
| InnerClasses | ClassFile | A description of the inner classes defined inside a class |
| LineNumberTable | Code_attribute | A mapping of line numbers to bytecodes for one method |
| LocalVariableTable | Code_attribute | A description of the local variables for one method |
| SourceFile | ClassFile | The name of the source file |
| Synthetic | field_info, method_info | An indicator that a field or method was generated by the compiler |

tributes were added in Java 1.1). All these predefined attributes are described in detail later in this chapter.

## The `Code` Attribute

One `Code_attribute` table appears in the `method_info` table of every method that is not abstract or native. The format of a `Code_attribute` table is shown in Table 6-26.

`attribute_name_index`   The `attribute_name_index` gives the index in the constant pool of a `CONSTANT_Utf8_info` entry that contains the string `"Code"`.

`attribute_length`   The `attribute_length` item gives the length in bytes of the `Code` attribute excluding the initial six bytes that contain the `attribute_name_index` and `attribute_length` items.

`max_stack`   The `max_stack` item gives the maximum number of words that will appear on the operand stack of this method at any point during its execution.

`max_locals`   The `max_locals` item gives the number of words in the local variables that are required by this method.

**Table 6-26.**

Format of a
`Code_attribute`
table

| Type | Name | Count |
|------|------|-------|
| u2 | attribute_name_index | 1 |
| u4 | attribute_length | 1 |
| u2 | max_stack | 1 |
| u2 | max_locals | 1 |
| u4 | code_length | 1 |
| u1 | code | code_length |
| u2 | exception_table_length | 1 |
| exception_info | exception_table | exception_table_length |
| u2 | attributes_count | 1 |
| attribute_info | attributes | attributes_count |

**code_length and code** The **code_length** item gives the length in bytes of the bytecode stream for this method. The bytecodes themselves appear in the **code** item.

**exception_table_length and exception_table** The **exception_table** item is a list of **exception_info** tables. Each **exception_info** table describes one exception table entry. The **exception_table_length** item gives the number of **exception_info** tables that appear in the **exception_table** list. The order in which the **exception_info** tables appear in the list is the order in which the Java Virtual Machine will check for a matching exception handler (catch clause) if an exception is thrown while this method executes. The format of an **exception_info** table is shown in Table 6-27. For more information about exception tables, see Chapter 17, "Exceptions."

**start_pc** The **start_pc** item gives the offset from the beginning of the code array for the beginning of the range covered by this exception handler.

**end_pc** The **end_pc** item gives the offset from the beginning of the code array for one byte past the end of the range covered by this exception handler.

**handler_pc** The **handler_pc** item gives the offset from the beginning of the code array for the instruction to jump to (the first instruction of the exception handler) if a thrown exception is caught by this entry.

**catch_type** The **catch_type** item gives the constant pool index of a **CONSTANT_Class_info** entry for the type of exception caught by this exception handler. The **CONSTANT_Class_info** entry must represent class **java.lang.Throwable** or one of its subclasses.

If the value of **catch_type** is zero (which isn't a valid index into the constant pool because the constant pool starts at index one), the exception handler handles all exceptions. A **catch_type** of zero is used to implement

**Table 6-27.**

Format of an **exception_info** table

| Type | Name | Count |
|------|------|-------|
| u2 | start_pc | 1 |
| u2 | end_pc | 1 |
| u2 | handler_pc | 1 |
| u2 | catch_type | 1 |

finally clauses. See Chapter 18, "Finally Clauses," for more information about how finally clauses are implemented.

**attributes_count and attributes**  The **attributes** item is a list of **attribute_info** tables. The **attributes_count** indicates the number of **attribute_info** tables in the list. The two kinds of attributes defined by the Java Virtual Machine specification that can appear in this item are **LineNumberTable** and **LocalVariableTable**. These two attributes are described in detail later in this chapter.

## The ConstantValue Attribute

The **ConstantValue** attribute appears in **field_info** tables for fields that have a constant value. In the **access_flags** of a **field_info** table that includes a **ConstantValue** attribute, the **ACC_STATIC** flag must be set. The **ACC_FINAL** flag can also be set, though it is not required. When the virtual machine initializes a field that has a **ConstantValue** attribute, it assigns the constant value to the field. The format of a **ConstantValue_attribute** table is shown in Table 6-28.

**attribute_name_index**  The **attribute_name_index** gives the index in the constant pool of a **CONSTANT_Utf8_info** entry that contains the string **"ConstantValue"**.

**attribute_length**  The **attribute_length** item of a **ConstantValue_attribute** is always 2.

**constantvalue_index**  The **constantvalue_index** item gives the index in the constant pool of an entry that gives a constant value. Table 6-29 shows the type of entry for each type of field.

**Table 6-28.**

Format of a
**ConstantValue_
attribute** table

| Type | Name | Count |
|------|------|-------|
| u2 | attribute_name_index | 1 |
| u4 | attribute_length | 1 |
| u2 | constantvalue_index | 1 |

# The Exceptions Attribute

The **Exceptions** attribute lists the checked exceptions that a method can throw. One **Exceptions_attribute** table appears in the **method_info** table of every method that can throw checked exceptions. The format of an **Exceptions_attribute** table is shown in Table 6-30.

**attribute_name_index**   The **attribute_name_index** gives the index in the constant pool of a **CONSTANT_Utf8_info** entry that contains the string **"Exceptions"**.

**attribute_length**   The **attribute_length** item gives the length in bytes of the **Exceptions_attribute** excluding the initial six bytes that contain the **attribute_name_index** and **attribute_length** items.

**number_of_exceptions** and **exception_index_table**   The **exception_index_table** is an array of indexes into the constant pool of **CONSTANT_Class_info** entries for the exceptions declared in this method's **throws** clause. In other words, the **exception_index_table** lists all the checked exceptions that this method can throw. The **number_of_exceptions** item indicates the number of indexes in the array.

**Table 6-29.**

Constant pool entry types for constant value attributes

| | |
|---|---|
| byte, short, char, int, boolean | CONSTANT_Integer_info |
| long | CONSTANT_Long_info |
| float | CONSTANT_Float_info |
| double | CONSTANT_Double_info |
| java.lang.String | CONSTANT_String_info |

**Table 6-30.**

Format of an **Exceptions_attribute** table

| Type | Name | Count |
|---|---|---|
| u2 | attribute_name_index | 1 |
| u4 | attribute_length | 1 |
| u2 | number_of_exceptions | 1 |
| u2 | exception_index_table | number_of_exceptions |

# The InnerClasses Attribute

The InnerClasses attribute lists any inner classes declared in a class. The InnerClasses_attribute table appears in the attributes of the ClassFile table for those classes that have inner classes. The format of an InnerClasses_attribute table is shown in Table 6-31.

attribute_name_index   The attribute_name_index gives the index in the constant pool of a CONSTANT_Utf8_info entry that contains the string "InnerClasses".

attribute_length   The attribute_length item gives the length in bytes of the Exceptions_attribute excluding the initial six bytes that contain the attribute_name_index and attribute_length items.

number_of_classes **and** classes   The classes item is an array of inner_class_info tables. The number_of_classes item gives the number of inner_class_info tables that appear in the classes array. The format of the inner_class_info table is shown in Table 6-32.

inner_class_info_index   The inner_class_info_index gives an index into the constant pool for a CONSTANT_Class_info entry for an inner class.

**Table 6-31.**

Format of an
**InnerClasses_
attribute** table

| Type | Name | Count |
|------|------|-------|
| u2 | attribute_name_index | 1 |
| u4 | attribute_length | 1 |
| u2 | number_of_classes | 1 |
| classes_info | classes | number_of_classes |

**Table 6-32.**

Format of an
**inner_class_
info** table

| Type | Name | Count |
|------|------|-------|
| u2 | inner_class_info_index | 1 |
| u2 | outer_class_info_index | 1 |
| u2 | inner_name_index | 1 |
| u2 | inner_class_access_flags | 1 |

**outer_class_info_index**   The **outer_class_info_index** gives an index into the constant pool for a **CONSTANT_Class_info** entry for the class in which the inner class described by this **inner_class_info** table is defined. If the inner class is not a member, the **outer_class_info_index** is zero.

**inner_name_index**   The **inner_name_index** gives an index in the constant pool for a **CONSTANT_Utf8_info** entry that gives the simple name of the inner class. If the inner class is anonymous, the **inner_name_index** is zero.

**inner_class_access_flags**   The **inner_class_access_flags** item gives the access flags for the inner class. The flags used in this item are the same as the ones shown in Table 6-4 for top-level classes.

## The **LineNumberTable** Attribute

The **LineNumberTable** attribute maps offsets in a method's bytecode stream to line numbers in the source file. One **LineNumberTable_attribute** table can appear (it is optional) in the attributes component of **Code_attribute** tables. The format of a **LineNumberTable_attribute** table is shown in Table 6-33.

**attribute_name_index**   The **attribute_name_index** gives the index in the constant pool of a **CONSTANT_Utf8_info** entry that contains the string **"LineNumberTable"**.

**attribute_length**   The **attribute_length** item gives the length in bytes of the **LineNumberTable_attribute** excluding the initial six bytes that contain the **attribute_name_index** and **attribute_length** items.

**Table 6-33.**

Format of a **Line NumberTable_ attribute** table

| Type | Name | Count |
|---|---|---|
| u2 | attribute_name_index | 1 |
| u4 | attribute_length | 1 |
| u2 | line_number_table_length | 1 |
| line_number_info | line_number_table | line_number_table_length |

**line_number_table_length** **and** **line_number_table** The **line_number_table** item is an array of **line_number_info** tables. The **line_number_table_length** gives the number of **line_number_info** tables that appear in the **line_number_table** array. The tables in this array can appear in any order, and you can have more than one table for the same line number. The format of a **line_number_info** table is shown in Table 6-34.

**start_pc** The **start_pc** item gives an offset from the beginning of the code array where a new line begins.

**line_number** The **line_number** item gives the line number of the line that begins at **start_pc**.

## The **LocalVariableTable** Attribute

The **LocalVariableTable** attribute maps words in the local variables portion of the method's stack frame to names and descriptors of local variables in the source code. One **LocalVariableTable_attribute** table can appear (it is optional) in the attributes component of **Code_attribute** tables. The format of a **LocalVariableTable_attribute** table is shown in Table 6-35.

**attribute_name_index** The **attribute_name_index** gives the index in the constant pool of a **CONSTANT_Utf8_info** entry that contains the string **"LocalVariableTable"**.

**Table 6-34.**

Format of a **line_number_info** table

| Type | Name | Count |
|------|------|-------|
| u2 | start_pc | 1 |
| u2 | line_number | 1 |

**Table 6-35.**

Format of a **LocalVariableTable_attribute** table

| Type | Name | Count |
|------|------|-------|
| u2 | attribute_name_index | 1 |
| u4 | attribute_length | 1 |
| u2 | local_variable_table_length | 1 |
| local_variable_info | local_variable_table | local_variable_table_length |

**attribute_length**  The **attribute_length** item gives the length in bytes of the **LocalVariableTable_attribute** excluding the initial six bytes that contain the **attribute_name_index** and **attribute_length** items.

**local_variable_table_length and local_variable_table**  The **local_variable_table** item is an array of **local_variable_info** tables. The **local_variable_table_length** gives the number of **local_variable_info** tables that appear in the **local_variable_table** array. The format of a **local_variable_info** table is shown in Table 6-36.

**start_pc and length**  The **start_pc** item gives an offset in the code array of the start of an instruction. The length item gives the length of the range of code that starts with **start_pc** for which a local variable is valid. The byte at offset **start_pc + length** from the beginning of the code array must either be the first byte of an instruction or the first byte past the end of the code array.

**name_index**  The **name_index** item gives an index in the constant pool of a **CONSTANT_Utf8_info** entry for the name of the local variable.

**descriptor_index**  The **descriptor_index** item gives an index in the constant pool of a **CONSTANT_Utf8_info** entry that contains the descriptor for this local variable. (A local variable descriptor adheres to the same grammar as a field descriptor.)

**index**  The **index** item gives the index in the local variable portion of this method's stack frame where the data for this local variable is kept as the method executes. If the local variable is of type **long** or **double**, the data occupies two words at positions **index** and **index + 1**. Otherwise the data occupies one word at position **index**.

**Table 6-36.**

Format of a **local_variable_info** table

| Type | Name | Count |
|------|------|-------|
| u2 | start_pc | 1 |
| u2 | length | 1 |
| u2 | name_index | 1 |
| u2 | descriptor_index | 1 |
| u2 | index | 1 |

## The `SourceFile` Attribute

The optional **SourceFile** attribute, which can appear in the attributes component of a **ClassFile** table, gives the name of the source file from which the class file was generated. The format of a **SourceFile_ attribute** table is shown in Table 6-37.

**attribute_name_index**   The **attribute_name_index** gives the index in the constant pool of a **CONSTANT_Utf8_info** entry that contains the string **"SourceFile"**.

**attribute_length**   The **attribute_length** item of a **SourceFile_ attribute** is always 2.

**sourcefile_index**   The **sourcefile_index** item gives the index in the constant pool of a **CONSTANT_Utf8_info** entry that contains the name of the source file. The source file name never includes a directory path.

## The `Synthetic` Attribute

The **Synthetic** attribute, which can optionally appear in the attributes components of **field_info** and **method_info** tables, indicates that a field or method was generated by the compiler. The **Synthetic** attribute was added in Java 1.1 to support inner classes. The format of a **Synthetic_ attribute** is shown in Table 6-38.

**Table 6-37.**

Format of a
**SourceFile_
attribute** table

| Type | Name | Count |
|------|------|-------|
| u2 | attribute_name_index | 1 |
| u4 | attribute_length | 1 |
| u2 | sourcefile_index | 1 |

**Table 6-38.**

Format of a
**Synthetic_
attribute** table

| Type | Name | Count |
|------|------|-------|
| u2 | attribute_name_index | 1 |
| u4 | attribute_length | 1 |

**attribute_name_index**  The **attribute_name_index** gives the index in the constant pool of a **CONSTANT_Utf8_info** entry that contains the string **"Synthetic"**.

**attribute_length**  The **attribute_length** must be zero.

# Getting Loaded: A Simulation

The *Getting Loaded* applet, shown in Figure 6-3, simulates a Java Virtual Machine loading a class file. The class file being loaded in the simulation was generated by the 1.1 **javac** compiler from the following Java source code. Although the snippet of code used in the simulation may not be very useful in the real world, it does compile to a real class file and provides a reasonably simple example of the class file format. This class is the same one used in the *Eternal Math* simulation applet described in Chapter 5.

```
// On CD-ROM in file classfile/ex1/Act.java
class Act {
```

**Figure 6-3.**
The **Getting Loaded** applet.

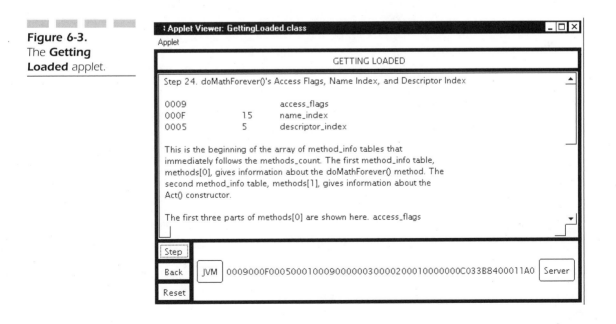

```
public static void doMathForever() {
    int i = 0;
    for (;;) {
        i += 1;
        i *= 2;
    }
}
}
```

The *Getting Loaded* applet allows you to drive the class load simulation one step at a time. For each step along the way, you can read about the next chunk of bytes that is about to be consumed and interpreted by the Java Virtual Machine. Just click the Step button to cause the Java Virtual Machine to consume the next chunk. Clicking Back will undo the previous step, and clicking Reset will return the simulation to its original state, allowing you to start over from the beginning.

The Java Virtual Machine is shown at the bottom left consuming the stream of bytes that makes up the class file **Act.class**. The bytes are shown in hex streaming out of a server on the bottom right. The bytes travel right to left, between the server and the Java Virtual Machine, one chunk at a time. The chunk of bytes to be consumed by the Java Virtual Machine on the next Step button click are shown in red. These highlighted bytes are described in the large text area above the Java Virtual Machine. Any remaining bytes beyond the next chunk are shown in black.

As mentioned in previous sections, many items in the class file refer to constant pool entries. So that you can more easily look up constant pool entries as you step through the simulation, a list of the contents of **Act**'s constant pool is shown in Table 6-39.

Each chunk of bytes is fully explained in the text area. Because a lot of detail appears in the text area, you may wish to skim through all the steps first to get the general idea and then look back for more details. Happy clicking.

# On the CD-ROM

The CD-ROM contains the source code examples from this chapter in the **classfile** directory. The *Getting Loaded* applet is contained in a web page on the CD-ROM in the file **applets/GettingLoaded.html**. The source code for this applet is found alongside its class files, in the **applets/GettingLoaded** directory.

**Table 6-39.**

Class **Act's**
constant pool

| Index | Type | Value |
|-------|------|-------|
| 1 | CONSTANT_Class_info | 7 |
| 2 | CONSTANT_Class_info | 16 |
| 3 | CONSTANT_Methodref_info | 2, 4 |
| 4 | CONSTANT_NameAndType_info | 6, 5 |
| 5 | CONSTANT_Utf8_info | "()V" |
| 6 | CONSTANT_Utf8_info | "<init>" |
| 7 | CONSTANT_Utf8_info | "Act" |
| 8 | CONSTANT_Utf8_info | "Act.java" |
| 9 | CONSTANT_Utf8_info | "Code" |
| 10 | CONSTANT_Utf8_info | "ConstantValue" |
| 11 | CONSTANT_Utf8_info | "Exceptions" |
| 12 | CONSTANT_Utf8_info | "LineNumberTable" |
| 13 | CONSTANT_Utf8_info | "LocalVariables" |
| 14 | CONSTANT_Utf8_info | "SourceFile" |
| 15 | CONSTANT_Utf8_info | "doMathForever" |
| 16 | CONSTANT_Utf8_info | "java/lang/Object" |

# The Resources Page

For more information about class files, visit the resources page for this chapter: **http://www.artima.com/insidejvm/classfile.html**.

# 7

# The Lifetime of a Class

The preceding chapter described in detail the format of the Java class file, the standard binary form for representing Java types. This chapter looks at what happens when binary type data is imported into a Java Virtual Machine. The chapter follows the lifetime of a type (class or interface) from the type's initial entrance into the virtual machine to its ultimate exit. It describes the processes of loading, linking, and initialization that occur at the beginning of a class's lifetime; the processes of object instantiation, garbage collection, and finalization that can occur in the prime of a class's lifetime; and the finalization and unloading of types that can occur at the end of a class's lifetime.

# Class Loading, Linking, and Initialization

The Java Virtual Machine makes types available to the running program through a process of *loading*, *linking*, and *initialization*. Loading is the process of bringing a binary form for a type into the Java Virtual Machine. Linking is the process of incorporating the binary type data into the runtime state of the virtual machine. Linking is divided into three substeps: *verification*, *preparation*, and *resolution*. Verification ensures the type is properly formed and fit for use by the Java Virtual Machine. Preparation involves allocating memory needed by the type, such as memory for any class variables. Resolution is the process of transforming symbolic references in the constant pool into direct references. Implementations can delay the resolution step until each symbolic reference is actually used by the running program. After verification, preparation, and (optionally) resolution are completed, the type is ready for initialization. During initialization, the class variables are given their proper initial values. See Figure 7-1 for a graphical depiction of this process.

As you can see from Figure 7-1, the processes of (1) loading, (2) linking, and (3) initialization must take place in this order. The only excep-

**Figure 7-1.**
The beginning of a
class' lifetime.

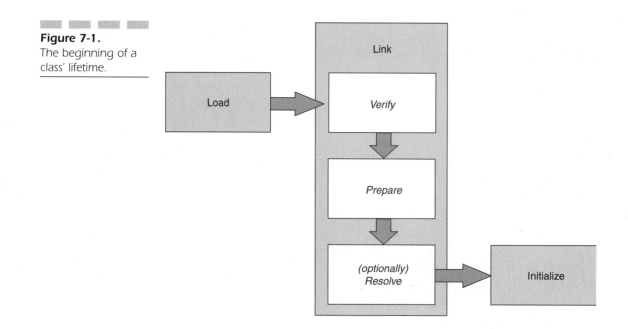

tion to this required ordering is the third phase of linking, resolution, which optionally can take place after initialization.

The Java Virtual Machine specification gives implementations flexibility in the timing of class and interface loading and linking but strictly defines the timing of initialization. All implementations must initialize each class and interface on its first *active use*. An active use of a class is

- the invocation of a constructor on a new instance of the class
- the creation of an array that has the class as its element type
- the invocation of a method declared by the class (not inherited from a superclass)
- the use or assignment of a field declared by the class (not inherited from a superclass or superinterface), except for fields that are both **static** and **final**, and are initialized by a compile-time constant expression

An active use of an interface is

- the use or assignment of a field declared by the interface (not inherited from a superinterface), except for fields that are initialized by a compile-time constant expression

All other uses of a type besides the five listed here are *passive uses* of the type. Several examples illustrating the differences between active and passive uses are given later in this chapter.

Aside from a class's own initial active use, one other situation will cause the initialization of a class: the initial active use of one of its subclasses. Initialization of a class requires prior initialization of all its superclasses.

The same is not true of interfaces, however. An interface is initialized only because a nonconstant field declared by the interface is used, never because a subinterface or class that implements the interface needs to be initialized. Thus, initialization of a class requires prior initialization of all its superclasses but not its superinterfaces. Initialization of an interface does not require initialization of its superinterfaces.

The "initialize on first active use" rule drives the mechanism that loads, links, and initializes classes. On its first active use, a type must be initialized. Before it can be initialized, however, it must be linked. And before it can be linked, it must be loaded. At their option, implementations can load and link types early. They need not wait until the type's first active use to load and link the type. If a type hasn't been loaded and linked before its first active use, however, it must be loaded and linked at that time so that it can be initialized.

# Loading

The loading process consists of three basic activities. To load a type, the Java Virtual Machine must

- produce a stream of binary data that represents the type
- parse the stream of binary data into internal data structures in the method area
- create an instance of class `java.lang.Class` that represents the type

The stream of binary data can adhere to the Java class file format but could alternatively follow some other format. As mentioned in previous chapters, all Java Virtual Machine implementations must recognize the Java class file format, but individual implementations can also recognize other binary formats.

The Java Virtual Machine specification does not say how the binary data for a type must be produced. Some potential ways to produce binary data for a type are to

- load a Java class file from the local file system
- download a Java class file across a network
- extract a Java class file from a ZIP, JAR, CAB, or other archive file
- extract a Java class file from a proprietary database
- compile a Java source file on the fly into the class file format
- compute the class file data for a type on the fly
- use any of the preceding methods but use a binary file format other than the Java class file

Given the binary data for a type, the Java Virtual Machine must process that data to a great enough extent that it can create an instance of class `java.lang.Class`. The virtual machine must parse the binary data into implementation-dependent internal data structures. (See Chapter 5, "The Java Virtual Machine," for a discussion of potential internal data structures for storing class data.) The `Class` instance, the end product of the loading step, serves as an interface between the program and the internal data structures. To access information about a type that is stored in the internal data structures, the program invokes methods on the `Class` instance for that type.

As described in previous chapters, types are loaded either through the primordial class loader or through class loader objects. The primordial class loader, a part of the virtual machine implementation, loads types (including the classes and interfaces of the Java API) in an implementation-dependent way. Class loader objects, instances of subclasses of **java.lang.ClassLoader**, load classes in custom ways. The inner workings of class loader objects are described in more detail in Chapter 8, "The Linking Model."

Class loaders (primordial or object) need not wait until a type's first active use before they load the type. Class loaders are allowed to cache binary representations of types, load types early in anticipation of eventual use, or load types together in related groups. If a class loader encounters a problem during early loading, however, it must report that problem (by throwing a subclass of **LinkageError**) only upon the type's first active use. In other words, if a class loader encounters a missing or malformed class file during early loading, it must wait to report that error until the class's first active use by the program. If the class is never actively used by the program, the class loader will never report the error.

## Verification

After a type is loaded, it is ready to be linked. The first step of the linking process is verification—ensuring that the type obeys the semantics of the Java language and that it won't violate the integrity of the virtual machine.

Verification is another area in which implementations of the Java Virtual Machine have some flexibility. Implementation designers can decide how and when to verify types. The Java Virtual Machine specification lists all the exceptions that a virtual machine can throw and under what circumstances it must throw them. No matter what kind of trouble a Java Virtual Machine might encounter, it is supposed to throw an exception or error. The specification says what exception or error should be thrown in each situation. In some cases, the specification says exactly when the exception or error should be thrown but usually doesn't dictate precisely how or when the error condition should be detected.

Nevertheless, certain kinds of checks are very likely to take place at certain times in most Java Virtual Machine implementations. For example, during the loading process, the virtual machine must parse the stream of binary data that represents the type and build internal data structures. At this point, certain checks must be done just to ensure the initial act of parsing the binary data won't crash the virtual machine. During this parsing, implementations will likely check the binary data to make sure it has the expected overall format. Parsers of the Java class file format might check the magic number, make sure each component is in the right place and of the proper length, verify that the file isn't too short or too long, and so on. Although these checks take place during loading, before the official verification phase of linking, they are still logically part of the verification phase. The entire process of detecting any kind of problem with loaded types is placed under the category of verification.

Another check that likely occurs during loading is making sure that every class except **Object** has a superclass. This process can be done during loading because, when the virtual machine loads a class, it must also make sure all the class's superclasses are loaded. The only way a virtual machine can know the name of a given class's superclass is by peering into the binary data for the class. Because the virtual machine is looking at every class's superclass data during loading anyway, it may as well make this check during the loading phase.

Another check—one that likely occurs after the official verification phase in most implementations—is the verification of symbolic references. As described in earlier chapters, the process of dynamic linking involves locating classes, interfaces, fields, and methods referred to by symbolic references stored in the constant pool, and replacing the symbolic references with direct references. When the virtual machine searches for a symbolically referenced entity (type, field, or method), it must first make sure the entity exists. If the virtual machine finds that the entity exists, it must further check that the referencing type has permission to access the entity, given the entity's access permissions. These checks for existence and access permission are logically a part of verification, the first phase of linking, but most likely happen during resolution, the third phase of linking. Resolution itself can be delayed until each symbolic reference is first used by the program, so these checks can even take place after initialization.

So what gets checked during the official verification phase? Anything that hasn't already been checked before the official verification phase and that won't get checked after it. Following are two lists of some of the things that are good candidates for checking during the official verification phase. This first list is composed of checks that ensure classes are binary compatible with each other:

- checking that final classes are not subclassed
- checking that final methods are not overridden
- if the type being checked is a nonabstract class, checking that all the methods declared in any interfaces implemented by the class are indeed implemented by the class

- making sure no incompatible method declarations (such as two methods that have the same name, the same number, order, and types of parameters, but different return types) appear between the type and its supertypes

Note that although these checks require looking at other types, they require looking only at supertypes. Superclasses need to be initialized before subclasses, so these classes are likely already loaded. Superinterfaces do not need to be initialized when a class that implements them is initialized. However, this verification step will require their loading. (They won't be initialized, just loaded and possibly linked at the option of the virtual machine implementation.) All a class's supertypes will have to be loaded to make sure they are all still binary compatible.

- checking that all constant pool entries are consistent with each other (For example, the **string_index** item of a **CONSTANT_String_info** entry must be the index of a **CONSTANT_Utf8_info** entry.)
- checking that all special strings contained in the constant pool (class names, field and method names, field and method descriptors) are well formed
- verifying the integrity of the bytecodes

The most complicated task in the preceding list is the last one: bytecode verification. All Java Virtual Machines must in some way verify the integrity of the bytecodes for every method they execute. For example, implementations are not allowed to crash because a jump instruction sends the virtual machine beyond the end of a method. They must detect that the jump instruction is invalid through some process of bytecode verification and then throw an error.

Java Virtual Machine implementations are not required to verify bytecodes during the official verification phase of linking. Implementations are free, for example, to verify individual instructions as each instruction is executed. One of the design goals of the Java Virtual Machine instruction set, however, was that it yield bytecode streams that can be verified all at once by a data flow analyzer. The ability to verify bytecode streams all at once during linking, rather than on the fly as the program runs, gives a big boost to the potential execution speed of Java programs.

When verifying bytecodes via a data flow analyzer, the virtual machine might have to load other classes to ensure that the semantics of the Java language are being followed. For example, imagine a class contained a method that assigned a reference to an instance of **java.lang.Float** to a field of type **java.lang.Number**. In this case, the virtual machine would have to load class **Float** during bytecode verification to make sure it was a subclass of class **Number**. It would have to load **Number** to make sure it wasn't declared final. The virtual machine must not initialize class **Float** at this time, just load it. **Float** will be initialized only upon its first active use.

For more information on the class verification process, see Chapter 3, "Security."

## Preparation

After a Java Virtual Machine has loaded a class and performed whatever verification it chooses to do up front, the class is ready for preparation. During the preparation phase, the Java Virtual Machine allocates memory for the class variables and sets them to default initial values. The class variables are not initialized to their proper initial values until the initialization phase. (No Java code is executed during the preparation step.) During preparation, the Java Virtual Machine sets the newly allocated memory for the class variables to a default value determined by the type of the variable. The default values for the various types are shown in Table 7-1.

No **boolean** is listed in Table 7-1 because **boolean** is not a primitive type in the Java Virtual Machine. Internally, **boolean** is implemented as an **int**, which gets set to zero (boolean **false**) by default. Therefore, **boolean** class variables are, in effect, initialized to boolean **false**.

**Table 7-1.**

Default initial values for the primitive types

| | |
|---|---|
| int | 0 |
| long | 0L |
| short | (short) 0 |
| char | '\u0000' |
| byte | (byte) 0 |
| reference | null |
| float | 0.0f |
| double | 0.0d |

During the preparation phase, Java Virtual Machine implementations can also allocate memory for data structures that are intended to improve the performance of the running program. An example of such a data structure is a method table, which contains a pointer to the data for every method in a class, including those inherited from its superclasses. A method table enables an inherited method to be invoked on an object without a search of superclasses at the point of invocation. Method tables are described in more detail in Chapter 8.

## Resolution

After a type has been through the first two phases of linking—verification and preparation—it is ready for the third and final phase of linking: resolution. Resolution is the process of locating classes, interfaces, fields, and methods referenced symbolically from a type's constant pool, and replacing those symbolic references with direct references. As mentioned earlier, this phase of linking is optional until (and unless) each symbolic reference is first used by the program. Constant pool resolution is described in detail in Chapter 8.

## Initialization

The final step required to ready a class or interface for its first active use is initialization, the process of setting class variables to their proper initial values. As used here, a "proper" initial value is the programmer's desired starting value for a class variable. A proper initial value contrasts with the default initial value given to class variables during preparation. As described previously, the virtual machine assigns default values based only on each variable's type. Proper initial values, by contrast, are based on some master plan known only to the programmer.

In Java code, a proper initial value is specified via a class variable initializer or static initializer. A class variable initializer is an equal sign and expression next to a class variable declaration, as in

```
// On CD-ROM in file classlife/ex1/Example1a.java
class Example1a {

    // "= 3 * (int) (Math.random() * 5.0)" is the class
    // variable initializer
    static int size = 3 * (int) (Math.random() * 5.0);
}
```

A static initializer is a block of code introduced by the **static** keyword, as in

```
// On CD-ROM in file classlife/ex1/Example1b.java
class Example1b {

    static int size;

    // This is the static initializer
    static {

        size = 3 * (int) (Math.random() * 5.0);
    }
}
```

All the class variable initializers and static initializers of a class are collected by the Java compiler and placed into one special method, the *class initialization method*. In the Java class file, the class initialization method is named "**<clinit>**". Regular methods of a Java application cannot invoke a class initialization method. This kind of method can be invoked only by the Java Virtual Machine, which invokes it to set a class's static variables to their proper initial values.

Initialization of a class consists of two steps:

1. Initializing the class's direct superclass (if any), if the direct superclass hasn't already been initialized

2. Executing the class's class initialization method, if it has one

When initializing a class's direct superclass, these same two steps must be followed. As a result, the first class that will be initialized will always be **Object**, then all the classes on down the inheritance hierarchy to the class being actively used. Superclasses will be initialized before subclasses.

Initialization of an interface does not require initialization of its superinterfaces. Initialization of an interface consists of only one step:

■ Executing the interface's class initialization method, if it has one

The code of a **<clinit>()** method does not explicitly invoke a superclass's **<clinit>()** method. Before a Java Virtual Machine invokes the **<clinit>()** method of a class, therefore, it must make certain the **<clinit>()** methods of superclasses have been executed.

Java Virtual Machines must also make sure the initialization process is properly synchronized. If multiple threads need to initialize a class, only one thread should be allowed to perform the initialization while the other threads wait. After the active thread completes the initialization process, it must notify any waiting threads. See Chapter 20, "Thread Synchronization," for information about synchronization, wait, and notify.

**THE CLASS INITIALIZATION METHOD**  As mentioned previously, Java compilers place the code for class variable initializers and static initializers into the `<clinit>()` method of the class file in the order in which they appear in the class declaration. For example, given this class

```
// On CD-ROM in file classlife/ex1/Example1c.java
class Example1c {

    static int width;
    static int height = (int) (Math.random() * 2.0);

    // This is the static initializer
    static {

        width = 3 * (int) (Math.random() * 5.0);
    }
}
```

The Java compiler generates the following `<clinit>()` method:

```
// The code for height's class variable initializer begins
// here
                              // Invoke Math.random(), which
                              // will push a double return
                              // value
  0 invokestatic #6 <Method double random()>
  3 ldc2_w #8 <Double 2.0>   // Push double constant 2.0
                              // Pop two doubles, multiply,
  6 dmul                      // push result
                              // Pop double, convert to
  7 d2i                       // int, push int
                              // Pop int, store into class
                              // variable height
  8 putstatic #5 <Field int height>

// The code for the static initializer begins here
 11 iconst_3                  // Push int constant 3
                              // Invoke Math.random(), which
                              // will push a double return
                              // value
 12 invokestatic #6 <Method double random()>
 15 ldc2_w #10 <Double 5.0>  // Push double constant 5.0
                              // Pop two doubles, multiply,
 18 dmul                      // push result
                              // Pop double, convert to int,
 19 d2i                       // push int
                              // Pop two ints, multiply, push
 20 imul                      // int result
```

```
                                          // Pop int, store into class
                                          // variable width
   21 putstatic #7 <Field int width>
                                          // Return void from <clinit>
   24 return                              // method
```

This `<clinit>()` method first executes the code for **Example1c**'s only class variable initializer, which initializes **height**, and then executes the code for the static initializer, which initializes **width**. The initialization is done in this order because the class variable initializer appears textually before the static initializer in the source code of the **Example1c** class.

Not all classes will necessarily have a `<clinit>()` method in their class file. If a class declares no class variables, it won't have a `<clinit>()` method. If a class declares class variables but doesn't explicitly initialize them with class variable initializers or static initializers, it won't have a `<clinit>()` method. If a class contains only class variable initializers for static final variables, and those class variable initializers use compile-time constant expressions, that class won't have a `<clinit>()` method. Only those classes that actually require Java code to be executed to initialize class variables to proper initial values will have a class initialization method.

Here's an example of a class that won't be awarded a `<clinit>()` method by the Java compiler:

```
// On CD-ROM in file classlife/ex1/Example1d.java
class Example1d {

    static final int angle = 35;
    static final int length = angle * 2;
}
```

Class **Example1d** declares two constants, **angle** and **length**, and initializes them with expressions that are compile-time constants. The compiler knows that **angle** represents the value 35 and **length** represents the value 70. When the **Example1d** class is loaded by a Java Virtual Machine, **angle** and **length** are not stored as class variables in the method area. As a result, no `<clinit>()` method is needed to initialize them. The **angle** and **length** fields are not class variables; they are constants, which are treated specially by the Java compiler.

Instead of treating **Example1d**'s **angle** and **length** fields as class variables, the Java compiler places the constant **int** values they represent into the constant pool or bytecode streams of any class that uses them. For example, if a class uses **Example1d**'s **angle** field, that class will not have in its constant pool a symbolic reference to the **angle** field of class

**Example1d**. Instead, the class will have operands embedded in its bytecode streams that have the value 35. If the constant value of **angle** were outside the range of a **short** (–32,768 to 32,767), say 35,000, the class would have a **CONSTANT_Integer_info** entry in its constant pool with the value of 35,000.

Here's a class that uses both a constant and a class variable from other classes:

```
// On CD-ROM in file classlife/ex1/Example1e.java
class Example1e {

    // The class variable initializer for symbolicRef uses
    // a symbolic reference to the size class variable of
    // class Example1a
    static int symbolicRef = Example1a.size;

    // The class variable initializer for localConst
    // doesn't use a symbolic reference to the length field
    // of class Example1d. Instead, it just uses a copy of
    //  the constant value 70.
    static int localConst = Example1d.length *
        (int) (Math.random() * 3.0);
}
```

The Java compiler generates the following <clinit>() method for class **Example1e**:

```
// The code for symbolicRef's class variable initializer
//    begins here:
                            // Push int value from
                            // Example1a.size. This
                            // getstatic instruction refers
                            // to a symbolic reference to
                            // Example1a.size.
  0 getstatic #9 <Field int size>
                            // Pop int, store into class
                            // variable symbolicRef
  3 putstatic #10 <Field int symbolicRef>

// The code for localConst's class variable initializer
//    begins here:
                            // Expand byte operand to int,
                            // push int result. This is the
                            // local copy of Example1d's
  6 bipush 70               // length constant, 70.
                            // Invoke Math.random(), which
                            // will push a double return
                            // value
  8 invokestatic #8 <Method double random()>
 11 ldc2_w #11 <Double 3.0> // Push double constant 3.0
```

```
                                    // Pop two doubles, multiply,
 14 dmul                            // push result
                                    // Pop double, convert to int,
 15 d2i                             // push int
                                    // Pop two ints, multiply, push
 16 imul                            // int result
                                    // Pop int, store into class
                                    // variable localConst
 17 putstatic #7 <Field int localConst>
                                    // Return void from <clinit>
 20 return                          // method
```

The **getstatic** instruction at offset zero uses a symbolic reference (in constant pool entry nine) to the **size** field of class **Example1a**. The **bipush** instruction at offset six is followed by a byte that contains the constant value represented by **Example1d.length**. **Example1e**'s constant pool contains no symbolic reference to anything in class **Example1d**.

Interfaces may also be awarded a **<clinit>()** method in the class file. All fields declared in an interface are implicitly public, static, and final and must be initialized with a field initializer. If an interface has any field initializers that don't resolve at compile-time to a constant, that interface will have a **<clinit>()** method. Here's an example:

```
// On CD-ROM in file classlife/ex1/Example1f.java
interface Example1f {

    int ketchup = 5;
    int mustard = (int) (Math.random() * 5.0);
}
```

The Java compiler generates the following **<clinit>()** method for interface **Example1f**:

```
// The code for mustard's class variable initializer begins
//here
                                    // Invoke Math.random(), which
                                    // will push a double return
                                    // value
  0 invokestatic #6 <Method double random()>
  3 ldc2_w #7 <Double 5.0> // Push double constant 2.0
                                    // Pop two doubles, multiply,
  6 dmul                            // push result
                                    // Pop double, convert to int,
  7 d2i                             // push int
                                    // Pop int, store into class
                                    // variable mustard
  8 putstatic #5 <Field int mustard>
                                    // Return void from <clinit>
 11 return                          // method
```

Note that only the `mustard` field is initialized by this `<clinit>()` method. Because the `ketchup` field is initialized to a compile-time constant, it is treated specially by the compiler. Although types that use `Example1f.mustard` will contain a symbolic reference to the field, types that use `Example1f.ketchup` will contain a local copy of `ketchup`'s constant value, 5.

**ACTIVE VERSUS PASSIVE USE**   As mentioned previously, the Java Virtual Machine initializes types on their first active use or, in the case of classes, upon the first active use of a subclass. Only four activities constitute an active use: invoking a class initialization method on a new instance of a class, creating an array whose element type is the class, invoking a method declared in a class, and accessing a nonconstant field declared in a class or interface.

A use of a nonconstant field is an active use of only the class or interface that actually declares the field. For example, a field declared in a class may be referred to via a subclass. A field declared in an interface may be referred to via a subinterface or class that implements the interface. These are passive uses of the subclass, subinterface, or class implement the interface—uses that won't trigger their initialization. They are an active use only of the class or interface in which the field is actually declared. Here's an example that illustrates this principle:

```java
// On CD-ROM in file classlife/ex2/NewParent.java
class NewParent {

    static int hoursOfSleep = (int) (Math.random() * 3.0);

    static {
        System.out.println("NewParent was initialized.");
    }
}
```

```java
// On CD-ROM in file classlife/ex2/NewbornBaby.java
class NewbornBaby extends NewParent {

    static int hoursOfCrying = 6 + (int) (Math.random() *
        2.0);

    static {
        System.out.println("NewbornBaby was initialized.");
    }
}
```

```java
// On CD-ROM in file classlife/ex2/Example2.java
class Example2 {

    // Invoking main() is an active use of Example2
```

```
    public static void main(String[] args) {

        // Using hoursOfSleep is an active use of Parent,
        // but a passive use of NewbornBaby
        int hours = NewbornBaby.hoursOfSleep;
        System.out.println(hours);
    }

    static {
        System.out.println("Example2 was initialized.");
    }
}
```

In the preceding example, executing **main()** of **Example2** causes only **Example2** and **Parent** to be initialized. **NewbornBaby** is not initialized and need not be loaded. The following text is printed to the standard output:

```
Example2 was initialized.
NewParent was initialized.
2
```

A use of a field that is both **static** and **final** and initialized by a compile-time constant expression is not an active use of the type that declares the field. As mentioned earlier, the Java compiler resolves references to such fields to a local copy of the constant value that resides either in the referring classes constant pool, in its bytecode streams, or both. Here's an example that illustrates this special treatment of static final fields:

```
// On CD-ROM in file classlife/ex3/Angry.java
interface Angry {

    String greeting = "Grrrr!";

    int angerLevel = Dog.getAngerLevel();
}

// On CD-ROM in file classlife/ex3/Dog.java
class Dog {

    static final String greeting = "Woof, woof, world!";

    static {
        System.out.println("Dog was initialized.");
    }

    static int getAngerLevel() {

        System.out.println("Anger was initialized");
```

```
            return 1;
        }
    }

// On CD-ROM in file classlife/ex3/Example3.java
class Example3 {

    // Invoking main() is an active use of Example4
    public static void main(String[] args) {

        // Using Angry.greeting is a passive use of Angry
        System.out.println(Angry.greeting);


        // Using Dog.greeting is a passive use of Dog
        System.out.println(Dog.greeting);
    }

    static {
        System.out.println("Example3 was initialized.");
    }
}
```

Running the **Example4** application yields the following output:

```
Example3 was initialized.
Grrrr!
Woof, woof, world!
```

Had **Angry** been initialized, the string **"Angry was initialized."** would have been written to the standard output. Likewise, had **Dog** been initialized, the string **"Dog was initialized."** would have been written to the standard output. As you can see from the preceding output, neither interface **Angry** or class **Dog** were ever initialized during the execution of the **Example3** application.

For more information about this special treatment of static final variables, see Chapter 8.

## The Lifetime of an Object

After a class has been loaded, linked, and initialized, it is ready for use. The program can access its static fields, invoke its static methods, or create instances of it. This section describes class instantiation and initialization, activities that take place at the beginning of an object's lifetime, and garbage collection and finalization, activities that mark the end of an object's lifetime.

# Class Instantiation

In Java programs, classes can be instantiated explicitly or implicitly. The three ways a class can be instantiated explicitly are with the **new** operator, by invoking **newInstance()** on a **Class** object, or by invoking **clone()** on any existing object. Here is an example showing each way to create a new class instance:

```
// On CD-ROM in file classlife/ex4/Example4.java
class Example4 implements Cloneable {

    Example4() {
        System.out.println(
            "Created by invoking newInstance()");
    }

    Example4(String msg) {
        System.out.println(msg);
    }

    public static void main(String[] args)
        throws ClassNotFoundException,
            InstantiationException, IllegalAccessException,
            CloneNotSupportedException {

        // Create a new Example4 object with the new
        // operator
        Example4 obj1 = new Example4("Created with new.");

        // Get a reference to the Class instance for
        // Example4, then invoke newInstance() on it to
        // create a new Example4 object
        Class myClass = Class.forName("Example4");
        Example4 obj2 = (Example4) myClass.newInstance();

        // Make an identical copy of the second
        // Example4 object
        Example4 obj3 = (Example4) obj2.clone();
    }
}
```

When executed, the **Example4** application prints this output:

```
Created with new.
Created by invoking newInstance()
```

Besides the preceding three ways to explicitly instantiate objects in Java source code, in several situations objects will be instantiated implicitly—without an explicit **new**, **newInstance()**, or **clone()** appearing in the source.

Possibly the first implicitly instantiated objects of any Java application are the **String** objects that hold the command-line arguments. References to these objects, one for each command-line argument, are delivered in the **String** array passed as the sole parameter to the **main()** method of every application.

Two other ways a class can be instantiated implicitly involve the process of class loading. First, for every type a Java Virtual Machine loads, it implicitly instantiates a new **Class** object to represent that type. Second, when the Java Virtual Machine loads a class that contains **CONSTANT_String_info** entries in its constant pool, it can instantiate new **String** objects to represent those constant string literals. The process of transforming a **CONSTANT_String_info** entry in the method area to a **String** instance on the heap is part of the process of constant pool resolution. This process is described in detail in Chapter 8.

Another way objects can be created implicitly is through the process of evaluating an expression that involves the string concatenation operator. If such an expression is not a compile-time constant, intermediate **String** and **StringBuffer** objects will be created in the process of evaluating the expression. Here's an example:

```
// On CD-ROM in file classlife/ex5/Example5.java
class Example5 {

    public static void main(String[] args) {

        if (args.length < 2) {
            System.out.println(
                "Must enter any two args.");
            return;
        }

        System.out.println(args[0] + args[1]);
    }
}
```

**javac** generates these bytecodes for **Example5**'s **main()** method:

```
0 aload_0       // Push the objref from loc var 0 (args)
1 arraylength   // Pop arrayref, calc array length,
                // push int length
2 iconst_2      // Push int constant 2
                // Pop 2 ints, compare, branch if
3 if_icmpge 15  // (length > 2) to offset 15.
                // Push objref from System.out
6 getstatic #11 <Field java.io.PrintStream out>
                // Push objref of string literal
9 ldc #1 <String "Must enter any two args.">
```

```
                          // Pop objref to String param, objref to
                          // System.out,
                          // invoke println()
11 invokevirtual #12
   <Method void println(java.lang.String)>
14 return          // Return void from main()
                          // Push objref from System.out
15 getstatic #11 <Field java.io.PrintStream out>

// The string concatenation operation begins here
                          // Allocate mem for new StringBuffer
                          // object, and initialize mem to default
                          // initial values, push objref to new
                          // object
18 new #6 <Class java.lang.StringBuffer>
21 dup             // Duplicate objref to StringBuffer object
22 aload_0         // Push ref from loc var 0 (args)
23 iconst_0        // Push int constant 0
                          // Pop int, arrayref, push String at
24 aaload          // arrayref[int], which is args[0]
                          // Pop objref, invoke String's class method
                          // valueOf(), passing it the objref to the
                          // args[0] String object. valueOf() calls
                          // toString() on the ref, and returns (and
                          // pushes) the result, which happens to be
                          // the original args[0] String. In this
                          // case, the stack will look precisely the
                          // same before and after this instruction
                          // is executed. Thus here, the 1.1 javac
                          // compiler has over-enthusiastically
                          // generated an unnecessary instruction.
25 invokestatic #14 <Method java.lang.String valueOf(
       java.lang.Object)>
                          // Pop objref to args[0] String, objref of
                          // the StringBuffer object, invoke
                          // <init>() method on the StringBuffer
                          // object passing the args[0] objref as
                          // the only parameter.
28 invokespecial #9
   <Method java.lang.StringBuffer(java.lang.String)>
31 aload_0         // Push objref from loc var 0 (args)
32 iconst_1        // Push int constant 1
                          // Pop int, arrayref, push String at
33 aaload          // arrayref[int], which is args[1]
                          // Pop objref to args[1] String, objref of
                          // the StringBuffer object (there's still
                          // another objref to this same object on
                          // the stack because of the dup instruction
                          // above), invoke append() method on
                          // StringBuffer object, passing args[1] as
                          // the only parameter. append() will
                          // return an objref to this StringBuffer
                          // object, which will be pushed back onto
```

```
                                      // the stack.
  34 invokevirtual #10 <Method java.lang.StringBuffer
     append(java.lang.String)>
                              // Pop objref to StringBuffer (pushed by
                              // append()), invoke toString() on it,
                              // which returns the value of the
                              // StringBuffer as a String object. Push
                              // objref of String object.
  37 invokevirtual #13 <Method java.lang.String toString()>
  // The string concatenation operation is now complete

                              // Pop objref of concatenated String,
                              // objref of System.out that was pushed by
                              // the getstatic instruction at offset 15.
                              // Invoke println() on System.out, passing
                              // the concatenated String as the only
                              // parameter.
  40 invokevirtual #12
     <Method void println(java.lang.String)>
  43 return          // Return void from main()
```

The bytecodes for **Example5**'s **main()** method contain three implicitly generated **string** objects and one implicitly generated **StringBuffer** object. References to two of the **string** objects appear as arguments passed to **main()** in the **args** array; they are pushed onto the stack by the **aaload** instructions at offset 23 and 33. The **StringBuffer** is created with the **new** instruction at offset 18 and initialized with the **invokespecial** instruction at offset 28. The final **string**, which represents the concatenation of **args[0]** and **args[1]**, is created by calling **toString()** on the **StringBuffer** object via the **invokevirtual** instruction at offset 37.

When the Java Virtual Machine creates a new instance of a class, either implicitly or explicitly, it first allocates memory on the heap to hold the object's instance variables. Memory is allocated for all variables declared in the object's class and in all its superclasses, including instance variables that are hidden. As described in Chapter 5, memory for other implementation-dependent components of an object's image on the heap, such as a pointer to class data in the method area, are also likely allocated at this point. As soon as the virtual machine has set aside the heap memory for a new object, it immediately initializes the instance variables to default initial values. They are the same values shown in Table 7-1 as default initial values for class variables.

After the virtual machine has allocated memory for the new object and initialized the instance variables to default values, it is ready to give the instance variables their proper initial values. The Java Virtual Machine uses two techniques to do so, depending on whether the object is being created because of a **clone()** invocation. If the object is being created because of a `clone()`, the virtual machine copies the values of the instance variables of the object being cloned into the new object. Otherwise, the virtual machine invokes *an instance initialization method* on the object. The instance initialization method initializes the object's instance variables to their proper initial values.

The Java compiler generates at least one instance initialization method for every class it compiles. In the Java class file, the instance initialization method is named `<init>`. For each constructor in the source code of a class, the Java compiler generates one `<init>()` method. If the class declares no constructors explicitly, the compiler generates a default no-arg constructor that just invokes the superclass's no-arg constructor. As with any other constructor, the compiler creates an `<init>()` method in the class file that corresponds to this default constructor.

An `<init>()` method can contain three kinds of code: an invocation of another `<init>()` method, code that implements any instance variable initializers, and code for the body of the constructor. If a constructor begins with an explicit invocation of another constructor in the same class (a `this()` invocation), its corresponding `<init>()` method will be composed of two parts:

- an invocation of the same-class `<init>()` method
- the bytecodes that implement the body of the corresponding constructor

If a constructor does not begin with a `this()` invocation and the class is not `Object`, the `<init>()` method will have three components:

- an invocation of a superclass `<init>()` method
- the bytecodes for any instance variable initializers
- the bytecodes that implement the body of the corresponding constructor

If a constructor does not begin with a `this()` invocation and the class *is* `Object`, the first component in the preceding list is missing. Because `Object` has no superclass, its `<init>()` method's cannot begin with a superclass `<init>()` method invocation.

If a constructor begins with an explicit invocation of a superclass constructor (a `super()` invocation), its `<init>()` method will invoke the corresponding superclass `<init>()` method. For example, if a constructor begins with an explicit invocation of the "`super(int, String)` constructor," the corresponding `<init>()` method will begin by invoking the superclass's "`<init>(int, String)`" method. If a constructor does not begin with an explicit **this()** or **super()** invocation, the corresponding **<init>()** method will invoke the superclass's no-arg **<init>()** method by default.

Here's an example with three constructors, numbered one through three:

```java
// On CD-ROM in file classlife/ex6/Example6.java
class Example6 {

    private int width = 3;

    // Constructor one:
    // This constructor begins with a this() constructor
    // invocation, which gets compiled to a same-class
    // <init>() method invocation.
    Example6() {
        this(1);
        System.out.println("Example6(), width = "
            + width);
    }

    // Constructor two:
    // This constructor begins with no explicit invocation
    // of another constructor, so it will get compiled to
    // an <init>() method that begins with an invocation
    // of the superclass's no-arg <init>() method.
    Example6(int width) {
        this.width = width;
        System.out.println("Example6(int), width = "
            + width);
    }

    // Constructor three:
    // This constructor begins with super(), an explicit
    // invocation of the superclass's no-arg constructor.
    // Its <init>() method will begin with an invocation
    // of the superclass's no-arg <init>() method.
    Example6(String msg) {
        super();
        System.out.println("Example6(String), width = "
            + width);
        System.out.println(msg);
    }

    public static void main(String[] args) {
        String msg
            = "The Agapanthus is also known as Lilly of"
            + " the Nile.";
        Example6 one = new Example6();
        Example6 two = new Example6(2);
        Example6 three = new Example6(msg);
    }
}
```

When executed, the **Example6** application prints this output:

```
Example6(int), width = 1
Example6(), width = 1
Example6(int), width = 2
Example6(String), width = 3
The Agapanthus is also known as Lilly of the Nile.
```

The bytecodes for **Example6**'s no-arg <init>() method (the <init>() method that corresponds to constructor one) are

```
// The first component, the same-class <init>() invocation,
// begins here:
 0 aload_0        // Push the objref from loc var 0 (this)
 1 iconst_1       // Push int constant 1
                  // Pop int and objref, invoke <init>()
                  // method on objref (this), passing
                  // the int (a 1) as the only parameter.
 2 invokespecial #12 <Method Example6(int)>

// The second component, the body of the constructor,
// begins here:
                  // Push objref from System.out
 5 getstatic #16 <Field java.io.PrintStream out>
                  // Allocate mem for new StringBuffer
                  // object, and initialize mem to default
                  // initial values, push objref to new
                  // object
 8 new #8 <Class java.lang.StringBuffer>
11 dup            // Duplicate objref to StringBuffer object
                  // Push objref to String literal from
                  // constant pool
12 ldc #1 <String "Example6(), width = ">
                  // Pop objref to literal String, pop
                  // objref of the StringBuffer object,
                  // invoke <init>() method on the
                  // StringBuffer object passing the args[0]
                  // objref as the only parameter.
14 invokespecial #14
   <Method java.lang.StringBuffer(java.lang.String)>
17 aload_0        // Push objref from loc var 0 (this)
                  // Pop this reference, Push int value of
                  // width field
18 getfield #19 <Field int width>
                  // Pop int (width), pop objref
                  // (StringBuffer object), invoke append()
                  // on StringBuffer object passing the
                  // width int as the only parameter.
                  // append() will add the string
                  // representation of the int to the end of
                  // the buffer, and return an objref to
                  // the same StringBuffer object.
```

```
21 invokevirtual #15
   <Method java.lang.StringBuffer append(int)>
                    // Pop objref to StringBuffer (pushed by
                    // append()),invoke toString() on it,
                    // which returns the value of the
                    // StringBuffer as a String object. Push
                    // objref of String object.
24 invokevirtual #18 <Method java.lang.String toString()>
                    // Pop objref of String, pop objref of
                    // System.out that was pushed by the
                    // getstatic instruction at offset 5.
                    // Invoke println() on System.out, passing
                    // the String as the only parameter:
                    // System.out.println(
                    // "Example6(), width = " + width);
27 invokevirtual #17
   <Method void println(java.lang.String)>
30 return          // Return void from <init>()
```

Note that the `<init>()` method for constructor one begins with an invocation of a same-class `<init>()` method and then executes the body of the corresponding constructor. Because the constructor begins with a `this()` invocation, its corresponding `<init>()` method doesn't contain bytecodes for the instance variable initializer.

The bytecodes for `Example6`'s `<init>()` method that takes an `int` parameter (the `<init>()` method that corresponds to constructor two) are

```
// The first component, the superclass <init>() invocation,
// begins here:
 0 aload_0        // Push the objref from loc var 0 (this)
                  // Pop objref (this), invoke the
                  // superclass's no-arg<init>() method on
                  // objref.
 1 invokespecial #11 <Method java.lang.Object()>

// The second component, the instance variable
// initializers, begins here:
 4 aload_0        // Push the objref from loc var 0 (this)
 5 iconst_3       // Push int constant 3
                  // Pop int (3), pop objref (this), store
                  // 3 into width instance variable of this
                  // object
 6 putfield #19 <Field int width>

// The third component, the body of the constructor, begins
// here:
 9 aload_0        // Push the objref from loc var 0 (this)
                  // Push int from loc var 1 (int param
10 iload_1        // width)
                  // Pop int (param width), pop objref
                  // (this), store int param value into
```

```
                      // width field of this object:
                      // this.width = width
   11 putfield #19 <Field int width>
                      // Push objref from System.out
   14 getstatic #16 <Field java.io.PrintStream out>
                      // Allocate mem for new StringBuffer
                      // object, and initialize mem to default
                      // initial values, push objref to new object
   17 new #8 <Class java.lang.StringBuffer>
   20 dup            // Duplicate objref to StringBuffer object
                      // Push objref to String literal from
                      // constant pool
   21 ldc #3 <String "Example6(int), width = ">
                      // Pop objref to literal String, pop
                      // objref of the StringBuffer object,
                      // invoke <init>() method on the
                      // StringBuffer object passing the args[0]
                      // objref as the only parameter.
   23 invokespecial #14
      <Method java.lang.StringBuffer(java.lang.String)>
   26 iload_1        // Push int from loc var 1 (int param width)
                      // Pop int (width), pop objref
                      // (StringBuffer object), invoke append()
                      // on StringBuffer object passing the
                      // width int as the only parameter.
                      // append() will add the string
                      // representation of the int to the end of
                      // the buffer, and return an objref to the
                      // same StringBuffer object.
   27 invokevirtual #15
      <Method java.lang.StringBuffer append(int)>
                      // Pop objref to StringBuffer (pushed by
                      // append()), invoke toString() on it,
                      // which returns the value of the
                      // StringBuffer as a String object. Push
                      // objref of String object.
   30 invokevirtual #18 <Method java.lang.String toString()>
                      // Pop objref of String, pop objref of
                      // System.out that was pushed by the
                      // getstatic instruction at offset 14.
                      // Invoke println() on System.out, passing
                      // the String as the only parameter:
                      // System.out.println(
                      // "Example6(int), width = " + width);
   33 invokevirtual #17
      <Method void println(java.lang.String)>
   36 return         // Return void from <init>()
```

The <init>() method for constructor two has three components. First,
it has an invocation of the superclass's (Object's) no-arg <init>()
method. The compiler generated this invocation by default, because no
explicit super() invocation appears as the first statement in the body

of constructor two. Following the superclass `<init>()` invocation is the second component: the bytecodes for width's instance variable initializer. Third, the `<init>()` method contains the bytecodes for the body of constructor two.

The bytecodes for **Example6**'s `<init>()` method that takes a **String** parameter (the `<init>()` method that corresponds to constructor three) are

```
// The first component, the superclass <init>() invocation,
// begins here:
 0 aload_0         // Push the objref from loc var 0 (this)
                   // Pop objref (this), invoke the
                   // superclass's no-arg<init>() method on
                   // objref.
 1 invokespecial #11 <Method java.lang.Object()>

// The second component, the instance variable
// initializers, begins here:
 4 aload_0         // Push the objref from loc var 0 (this)
 5 iconst_3        // Push int constant 3
                   // Pop int (3), pop objref (this), store 3
                   // into width instance variable of this
                   // object
 6 putfield #19 <Field int width>

// The third component, the body of the constructor, begins
// here:
                   // Push objref from System.out
 9 getstatic #16 <Field java.io.PrintStream out>
                   // Allocate mem for new StringBuffer
                   // object, and initialize mem to default
                   // initial values, push objref to new
                   // object
12 new #8 <Class java.lang.StringBuffer>
15 dup             // Duplicate objref to StringBuffer object
                   // Push objref to String literal from
                   // constant pool
16 ldc #2 <String "Example6(String), width = ">
                   // Pop objref to literal String, pop
                   // objref of the StringBuffer object,
                   // invoke <init>() method on the
                   // StringBuffer object passing the args[0]
                   // objref as the only parameter.
18 invokespecial #14
     <Method java.lang.StringBuffer(java.lang.String)>
21 aload_0         // Push objref from loc var 0 (this)
                   // Pop this reference, Push int value of
                   // width field
22 getfield #19 <Field int width>
                   // Pop int (width), pop objref
                   // (StringBuffer object), invoke append()
                   // on StringBuffer object passing the
                   // width int as the only parameter.
```

```
                       // append() will add the string
                       // representation of the int to the end of
                       // the buffer, and return an objref to the
                       // same StringBuffer object.
   25 invokevirtual #15
      <Method java.lang.StringBuffer append(int)>
                       // Pop objref to StringBuffer (pushed by
                       // append()), invoke toString() on it,
                       // which returns the value of the
                       // StringBuffer as a String object. Push
                       // objref of String object.
   28 invokevirtual #18 <Method java.lang.String toString()>
                       // Pop objref of String, pop objref of
                       // System.out that was pushed by the
                       // getstatic instruction at offset 9.
                       // Invoke println() on System.out, passing
                       // the String as the only parameter:
                       // System.out.println(
                       // "Example6(String), width = " + width);
   31 invokevirtual #17 <Method void println(java.lang.String)>
                       // Push objref from System.out
   34 getstatic #16 <Field java.io.PrintStream out>
   37 aload_1         // Push objref from loc var 1 (param msg)
                       // Pop objref of String, pop objref of
                       // System.out that was pushed by the
                       // getstatic instruction at offset 37.
                       // Invoke println() on System.out, passing
                       // the String as the only parameter:
                       // System.out.println(msg);
   38 invokevirtual #17
      <Method void println(java.lang.String)>
   41 return          // Return void from <init>()
```

The `<init>()` method for constructor three has the same three components as the `<init>()` method for constructor two: a superclass `<init>()` invocation, the bytecodes for width's initializer, and the bytecodes for the constructor body. One difference between constructor two and three is that constructor two does not begin with an explicit **this**() or **super**() invocation. As a result, the compiler places an invocation of the superclass's no-arg `<init>()` method in constructor two's `<init>()` method. By contrast, constructor three begins with an explicit **super**() invocation, which the compiler converts into the corresponding superclass `<init>()` invocation in constructor three's `<init>()` method.

For every class except **Object**, an `<init>()` method must begin with an invocation of another `<init>()` method belonging either to the same class or to the direct superclass. `<init>()` methods are not allowed to catch exceptions thrown by the `<init>()` method they invoke. If a subclass `<init>()` method invokes a superclass `<init>()` method that completes abnormally, for example, the subclass `<init>()` method must also complete abnormally.

## Garbage Collection and Finalization of Objects

As mentioned in earlier chapters, implementations of the Java Virtual Machine must have some kind of automatic storage management strategy for the heap, most likely a garbage collector. Applications can allocate memory for objects via the explicit and implicit ways described earlier in this chapter but cannot explicitly free that memory. When an object becomes unreferenced by the application, the virtual machine can reclaim (garbage collect) that memory. Implementations can decide when to garbage collect unreferenced objects—even whether to garbage collect them at all. Java Virtual Machine implementations are not required to free memory occupied by unreferenced objects.

If a class declares a method named **finalize()** that returns **void**, the garbage collector will execute that method (called a "finalizer") once on an instance of that class, before it frees the memory space occupied by that instance. Here's an example of a class that declares a finalizer:

```
// On CD-ROM in file classlife/ex7/Finale.java
class Finale {
    protected void finalize() {
        System.out.println(
            "A Finale object was finalized.");
        //...
    }
    //...
}
```

Because a finalizer is a regular Java method, it can be invoked directly by the application. Such a direct invocation will not affect the automatic invocation of the finalizer by the garbage collector. The garbage collector can invoke an object's finalizer at most once, sometime after the object becomes unreferenced and before the memory it occupies is reused. If the object becomes referenced again (resurrected) as a result of executing the finalizer code and then becomes unreferenced again later, the garbage collector must not automatically invoke the finalizer a second time.

Any exceptions thrown by the **finalize()** method during its automatic invocation by the garbage collector are ignored. The garbage collector can invoke `finalize()` methods in any order, using any thread, or even concurrently via multiple threads. Finalization is described in more detail in Chapter 9, "Garbage Collection."

# Unloading and Finalization of Classes

In many ways, the lifetime of a class in the Java Virtual Machine is similar to the lifetime of an object. The virtual machine creates and initializes objects, allows the program to use the objects, and optionally garbage collects the objects after they are no longer referenced by the program. Similarly, the virtual machine loads, links, and initializes classes, allows the program to use the classes, and optionally unloads the classes after they are no longer referenced by the program. Just as the Java Virtual Machine will run an object's `finalize()` method (if its class declares one) before it garbage collects the object, the Java Virtual Machine will run a class's `classFinalize()` method (if the class declares one) before it unloads the class.

Garbage collection and unloading of classes are important in the Java Virtual Machine because Java programs can be dynamically extended at runtime by loading types through class loader objects. All loaded types occupy memory space in the method area. If a Java application continuously loads types through class loader objects, the memory footprint of the method area will continuously grow. If some of the dynamically loaded types are needed only temporarily, the memory space occupied by those types can be freed by unloading the types after they are no longer needed.

The way in which a Java Virtual Machine can tell whether a dynamically loaded type is still needed by the application is similar to the way it tells whether an object is still needed by the program. If the application has no references to the type, then the type can't affect the future course of computation. The type is unreachable and can be garbage collected.

Types loaded through the primordial class loader will always be reachable and never be unloaded. Only dynamically loaded types—those loaded through class loader objects—can become unreachable and be unloaded by the virtual machine. A dynamically loaded type is unreachable if its `Class` instance is found to be unreachable through the normal process of garbage collecting the heap.

A `Class` instance of a dynamically loaded type can be reachable through the normal process of garbage collection in two ways. First and most obviously, a `Class` instance will be reachable if the application holds an explicit reference to it. Second, a **Class** instance will be reachable if there is a reachable object on the heap whose type data in the method area refers to the **Class** instance. As mentioned in Chapter 5, implementations must be able to locate the type data in the method for an object's class, given only a reference to the object. For this reason, the image of an object on the heap likely includes some kind of pointer to its type data in the method area. From the type data, the virtual machine must be able to locate the **Class** instances for the object's class, all its superclasses, and all its superinterfaces. See Figure 7-2 for a graphical depiction of this way of "reaching" **Class** instances.

Figure 7-2 shows the paths a garbage collector must traverse from a reachable object of class **MyThread** through the type data in the method area to find reachable **Class** instances. In this figure, objects on the heap are shown as light gray circles; type data in the method are shown as dark gray rectangles. The **MyThread** class has the following declaration:

```
// On CD-ROM in file classlife/ex8/MyThread.java
class MyThread extends Thread implements Cloneable {
}
```

From the reachable **MyThread** object (shown in the bottom right corner of the figure), the garbage collector follows a pointer to **MyThread**'s type data, where it finds

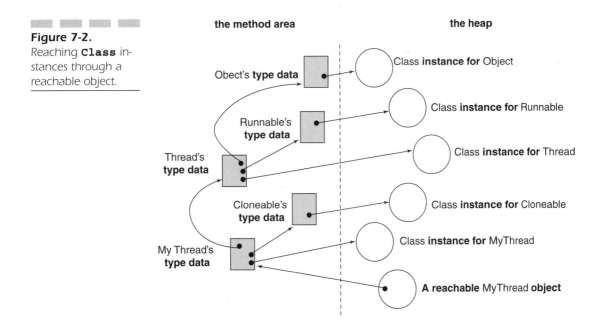

**Figure 7-2.**
Reaching **Class** instances through a reachable object.

the method area     the heap

Obect's **type data** → Class **instance for** Object

Runnable's **type data** → Class **instance for** Runnable

Thread's **type data** → Class **instance for** Thread

Cloneable's **type data** → Class **instance for** Cloneable

My Thread's **type data** → Class **instance for** MyThread

**A reachable** MyThread **object**

▨ a reference to **MyThread**'s **Class** instance on the heap

▨ a pointer to the type data for **MyThread**'s direct superinterface, **Cloneable**

▨ a pointer to the type data for **MyThread**'s direct superclass, **Thread**

From the type data for **Cloneable**, the garbage collector finds

▨ a reference to **Cloneable**'s **Class** instance on the heap

From the type data for **Thread**, the garbage collector finds

▨ a reference to **Thread**'s **Class** instance on the heap

▨ a pointer to the type data for **Thread**'s direct superinterface, **Runnable**

▨ a pointer to the type data for **Thread**'s direct superclass, **Object**

From the type data for **Runnable**, the garbage collector finds

▨ a reference to **Runnable**'s **Class** instance on the heap

From the type data for **Object**, the garbage collector finds

▨ a reference to **Objects**'s **Class** instance on the heap

Thus, given only a reference to a reachable instance of class **MyThread**, the garbage collector can "reach" the **Class** instances for **MyThread** and all its supertypes: **Cloneable**, **Thread**, **Runnable**, and **Object**.

If a class declares a method named **classFinalize()** that is static, takes no parameters, and returns **void**, the Java Virtual Machine will execute that method (called a "class finalizer") before it unloads the class. The class finalizer can have any access permission. Here's an example:

```
// On CD-ROM in file classlife/ex7/GrandFinale.java
class GrandFinale {
    static void classFinalize() {
        System.out.println(
            "Class GrandFinale was finally finalized.");
        //...
    }
    //...
}
```

Similar to the **finalize()** method, the **classFinalize()** method will be called only once by the Java Virtual Machine. If a class's **classFinalize()** method resurrects the class (makes it reachable again), the next time the class is unloaded, its **classFinalize()** method won't be invoked.

An example of dynamically loaded classes becoming unreachable and available for unloading is given at the end of Chapter 8.

## On the CD-ROM

The CD-ROM contains the source code examples from this chapter in the **classlife** directory.

## The Resources Page

For more information about the material presented in this chapter, visit the resources page: **http://www.artima.com/insidejvm/classlife.html**.

# 8

# The Linking Model

From the programmer's perspective, one of the most important aspects of Java's architecture to understand is the linking model. As mentioned in earlier chapters, Java's linking model allows you to design class loader objects that extend your application in custom ways at runtime. Through class loader objects, your application can load and dynamically link to classes and interfaces that were unknown or did not even exist when your application was compiled.

The engine that drives Java's linking model is the process of resolution. The preceding chapter described in detail all the various stages in the lifetime of a class, except for resolution. This chapter looks at resolution in depth and shows how the process of resolution fits in with dynamic extension. It gives an overview of the linking model, explains constant pool resolution, describes method tables, shows how to write and use class loaders, and gives several examples.

# Dynamic Linking and Resolution

When you compile a Java program, you get a separate class file for each class or interface in your program. Although the individual class files may appear to be independent, they actually harbor symbolic connections to one another and to the class files of the Java API. When you run your program, the Java Virtual Machine loads your program's classes and interfaces and hooks them together in a process of *dynamic linking*. As your program runs, the Java Virtual Machine builds an internal web of interconnected classes and interfaces.

A class file keeps all its symbolic references in one place, the constant pool. Each class file has a constant pool, and each class or interface loaded by the Java Virtual Machine has an internal version of its constant pool. The internal constant pool is an implementation-specific data structure that maps to the constant pool in the class file. Thus, after a type is initially loaded, all the symbolic references from the type reside in the type's internal constant pool.

At some point during the running of a program, if a particular symbolic reference is to be used, it must be *resolved*. Resolution is the process of finding the entity identified by the symbolic reference and replacing the symbolic reference with a direct reference. Because all symbolic references reside in the constant pool, this process is often called *constant pool resolution*.

As described in Chapter 6, "The Java Class File," the constant pool is organized as a sequence of items. Each item has a unique index, much like an array element. A symbolic reference is one kind of item that can appear in the constant pool. Java Virtual Machine instructions that use a symbolic reference specify the index in the constant pool where the symbolic reference resides. For example, the **getstatic** opcode, which pushes the value of a static field onto the stack, is followed in the bytecode stream by an index into the constant pool. The constant pool entry at the specified index, a **CONSTANT_Fieldref_info** entry, reveals the fully qualified name of the class in which the field resides, and the name and type of the field.

Keep in mind that the Java Virtual Machine contains a separate internal constant pool for each class and interface it loads. When an instruction refers to the fifth item in the constant pool, it is referring to the fifth item in the constant pool for the current class, the class that defined the method the Java Virtual Machine is currently executing.

Several instructions, from the same or different methods, can refer to the same constant pool entry, but each constant pool entry is resolved only once. After a symbolic reference has been resolved for one instruction, subsequent attempts to resolve it by other instructions take advantage of the hard work already done and therefore use the same direct reference resulting from the original resolution.

Linking involves not only the replacement of symbolic references with direct ones, it also involves checking for correctness and permission. As mentioned in Chapter 7, "The Lifetime of a Class," the checking of symbolic references for existence and access permission (one aspect of the full verification phase) is likely performed during resolution. For example, when a Java Virtual Machine resolves a `getstatic` instruction to a field of another class, the Java Virtual Machine checks to make sure that

- the other class exists
- this class has permission to access the other class
- the named field exists in the other class
- the field has the expected type (symbolic references to fields include the field type)
- this class has permission to access the field
- the field is really static—a class variable and not an instance variable

If any of these checks fail, an error is thrown and resolution fails. Otherwise, the symbolic reference is replaced by the direct reference and resolution succeeds.

As described in Chapter 7, different implementations of the Java Virtual Machine are permitted to perform resolution at different times during the execution of a program. An implementation can choose to link everything up front by following all symbolic references from the initial class and then all symbolic references from subsequent classes until every symbolic reference has been resolved. In this case, the application would be completely linked before its `main()` method was ever invoked. This approach is called *early resolution*. Alternatively, an implementation can choose to wait until the very last minute to resolve each symbolic reference. In this case, the Java Virtual Machine would resolve a symbolic reference only when it is first used by the running program. This approach is called *late resolution*. Other implementations could choose a resolution strategy in between these two extremes.

Although a Java Virtual Machine implementation has some freedom in choosing when to resolve symbolic references, every Java Virtual Machine must give the outward impression that it uses late resolution. No matter when a particular Java Virtual Machine performs its linking, it will always throw any error that results from attempting to resolve a symbolic reference at the point in the execution of the program where the symbolic reference was actually used for the first time. In this way, it will always appear to the user as if the linking were late. If a Java Virtual Machine does early linking, and during early linking discovers that a class file is missing, it won't report the class file missing by throwing the appropriate error until later in the program when something in that class file is actually used. If the class is never used by the program, the error will never be thrown.

# Resolution and Dynamic Extension

In addition to simply linking types at runtime, Java applications can decide at runtime which types to link. Java's architecture allows Java programs to be *dynamically extended*, the process of deciding at runtime other types to use, loading them, and using them. You can dynamically extend a Java application by creating a class loader object and using it to load types that are not part of your original application but are determined by your running application. An example of dynamic extension is a Java-capable web browser loading class files for applets from across a network. When the browser starts, it doesn't know what class files it will be loading across the network.

To dynamically extend a Java application, you must include a class loader as part of your application. To create your own class loader, you write a subclass of **java.lang.ClassLoader** and implement the **loadClass()** method. When the **loadClass()** method of a class loader successfully loads a type, it returns a **java.lang.Class** object to represent the newly loaded (and optionally, verified, prepared, resolved, and initialized) type. Here's the declaration of the **loadClass()** method:

```
// A method declared in class java.lang.ClassLoader:
protected abstract Class loadClass(String name, boolean
resolve)
    throws ClassNotFoundException;
```

The class loader takes care of loading, linking, and initializing types. Admittedly, the name **ClassLoader** might lead you to believe it is responsible only for loading, and not linking or initialization, but the name **ClassLoaderLinkerAndInitializer** is a bit unwieldy. Also, the purpose of creating your own class loader is to customize the load phase while still using the primordial link and initialization mechanisms. Class loaders differ not in how they link or initialize types, but in how they load types.

In other words, class loaders distinguish themselves by the manner in which they produce a binary form for a type given a fully qualified name.

The `loadClass()` method encompasses all three steps of loading, linking, and initialization of a new type. You pass the fully qualified name of the requested type to `loadClass()` in the parameter `name`. If you want linking and initialization to be performed at this time, you pass `true` in the parameter `resolve`. If `loadClass()` is invoked with `resolve` set to `false`, it will load but not link and initialize the type. From your programs, you will likely invoke `loadClass()` with the `resolve` parameter always set to `true`. Normally, the `loadClass()` method is invoked with the `resolve` parameter set to `false` only by the virtual machine itself. (More details on this subject are given later in this chapter.)

As mentioned in earlier chapters, each class loader—primordial or object—is awarded its own name-space, which is populated by the names of the types it has loaded. Dynamic extension and name-spaces are both supported by one aspect of the process of resolution: the way a virtual machine chooses a class loader when it resolves a symbolic reference to a type.

When the resolution of a constant pool entry requires loading a type, the virtual machine uses the same class loader that loaded the referencing type to load the referenced type. For example, imagine a `Cat` class refers via a symbolic reference in its constant pool to a type named `Mouse`. Assume `Cat` was loaded by a class loader object. When the virtual machine resolves the reference to `Mouse`, it checks to see whether `Mouse` has been loaded into the name-space to which `Cat` belongs. (It checks to see whether the class loader that loaded `Cat` has previously loaded a type named `Mouse`.) If not, the virtual machine requests `Mouse` from the same class loader that loaded `Cat`. This is true even if a class named `Mouse` had previously been loaded into a different name-space. When a symbolic reference from a type loaded by the primordial class loader is resolved, the Java Virtual Machine uses the primordial class loader to load the referenced type. When a symbolic reference from a type loaded by a class loader object is resolved, the Java Virtual Machine uses the same class loader object to load the referenced type.

# Constant Pool Resolution

This section describes the details of resolving each type of constant pool entry, including the errors that may be thrown during resolution. If an error is thrown during resolution, the error is seen as being thrown by the instruction that refers to the constant pool entry being resolved. Besides the errors described here, individual instructions that trigger the resolution of a constant pool entry may cause other errors to be thrown. For example, **getstatic** causes a **CONSTANT_Fieldref_info** entry to be resolved. If the entry is resolved successfully, the virtual machine performs one additional check: it makes sure the field is actually static (a class variable and not an instance variable). If the field is not static, the virtual machine throws an error. Any extra errors that may be thrown during resolution besides those described in this section are described for each individual instruction in Appendix A, "Instruction Set by Opcode Mnemonic."

## Resolution of CONSTANT_Class_info Entries

Of all the types of constant pool entries, the most complicated to resolve is **CONSTANT_Class_info**. This type of entry is used to represent symbolic references to classes (including array classes) and interfaces. Several instructions, such as **new** and **anewarray**, refer directly to the **CONSTANT_Class_info** entries. Other instructions, such as **putfield** or **invokevirtual**, refer indirectly to **CONSTANT_Class_info** entries through other types of entry. For example, the **putfield** instruction refers to a **CONSTANT_Fieldref_info** entry. The **class_index** item of a **CONSTANT_Fieldref_info** gives the constant pool index of a **CONSTANT_Class_info** entry.

The details of resolving a **CONSTANT_Class_info** entry vary depending on whether the type is an array and whether the referencing type (the one that contains in its constant pool the **CONSTANT_Class_info** entry being resolved) was loaded via the primordial class loader or a class loader object.

**ARRAY CLASSES** A **CONSTANT_Class_info** entry refers to an array class if its **name_index** refers to a **CONSTANT_Utf8_info** string that begins with a left bracket, as in **[I**. As described in Chapter 6, internal array names contain one left bracket for each dimension, followed by an element type. If the element type begins with an **L**, as in **Ljava.lang.Integer;**, the array is an array of references. Otherwise, the element type is a primitive type, such as **I** for **int** or **D** for **double**, and the array is an array of primitive types.

In the case of an array of references, the virtual machine resolves the element type. For example, if resolving an array class with the name **[[Ljava.lang.Integer;**, the virtual machine would make certain class **java.lang.Integer** is loaded, linked, and initialized.

The end product of the resolution of a symbolic reference to an array class is a **Class** instance that represents the array class. If a **Class** instance has already been created for the array type being resolved, that same **Class** instance is used. Otherwise, the virtual machine creates a new **Class** instance to represent the newly resolved array type.

**NONARRAY CLASSES AND INTERFACES** A **CONSTANT_Class_info** entry whose **name_index** refers to a **CONSTANT_Utf8_info** string that doesn't begin with a left bracket is a symbolic reference to nonarray class or an interface. Resolution of this kind of symbolic reference is a multiple step process.

The Java Virtual Machine performs the same basic steps, described in the following sections as Steps 1 through 2e, to resolve any symbolic reference (any **CONSTANT_Class_info** entry) to a nonarray class or interface. In Step 1, the type is loaded. In Steps 2a through 2e, the type is linked and initialized. The precise way in which the virtual machine performs these steps depends on whether the referencing type was loaded via the primordial class loader or a class loader object.

**STEP 1. LOAD THE TYPE AND ANY SUPERCLASSES** Resolution of a nonarray class or interface begins by making sure the type is loaded into the current name-space. If the virtual machine determines that the referenced type hasn't yet been loaded into the current name-space, it passes the fully qualified name of the type to a class loader. The class loader loads the type, parses the binary data into internal data structures, and creates a **Class** instance.

After the referenced type is loaded in, the virtual machine can peer into its binary data. If the type is a class and not **java.lang.Object**, the virtual machine determines from the class's data the fully qualified name of the class's direct superclass. The virtual machine then checks to see whether the superclass has been loaded into the current name-space. If not, it loads the superclass. After that class comes in, the virtual machine can again peer into its binary data to find its superclass. This process repeats all the way up to **Object**.

Through Step 1, the Java Virtual Machine makes sure a type is loaded, and if the type is a class, that all its superclasses are loaded. During this step, these types are not linked and initialized—just loaded.

If the referencing type (the one that contains in its constant pool the **CONSTANT_Class_info** entry being resolved) was loaded through the primordial class loader, the virtual machine uses the primordial class loader to load the referenced type (and its superclasses, if any). Otherwise, the referencing type was loaded through a class loader object, and the virtual machine uses the same class loader object to load the referenced type.

The Java Virtual Machine maintains a list of the names of all the types already loaded by each class loader. Each of these lists forms a name-space inside the Java Virtual Machine. The virtual machine uses this list during resolution to determine whether a class has already been loaded by a particular class loader. If, during resolution, the Java Virtual Machine encounters a symbolic reference to a class that was not previously loaded by the appropriate class loader, that class loader will be asked to load the class. If the appropriate class loader is a class loader object, the Java Virtual Machine will make the load request by invoking the class loader object's `loadClass()` method. On the other hand, if the Java Virtual Machine encounters a symbolic reference to a class previously loaded by the same class loader object, the class loader object will not be asked to load it again. Instead, the class previously loaded will automatically be used again. This process helps ensure that only one class with a given name is loaded by a particular class loader.

If the referencing type was loaded via the primordial class loader, the virtual machine will check the primordial class loader's name-space to see whether the class was already loaded. If not, the virtual machine will use the primordial class loader to load the referenced type in an implementation-dependent way. If the referenced type is a class, the virtual machine will make sure all the class's superclasses are loaded as well. If any of these classes haven't yet been loaded into the primordial loader's name-space, the virtual machine will use the primordial class loader to load those classes.

If the referencing type was loaded via a class loader object, the virtual machine invokes `loadClass()` on the class loader object that loaded the referencing type, passing in parameter `name` the fully qualified name of the referenced type and setting the `resolve` flag to `true`. When `loadClass()` returns, it will have performed both Step 1 (loading) and Steps 2a through 2e (linking and initialization). (It will perform Steps 2a through 2e because the `resolve` flag is set to `true`.) Nonetheless, the `loadClass()` method will perform Step 1 completely before embarking on Steps 2a through 2e.

When a class loader object's `loadClass()` method is invoked, it has two ways to do its job. One way is to use the primordial class loader by invoking `findSystemClass()`. In this case, the primordial loader will load, link, and initialize the requested type. Alternatively, `loadClass()` can produce the binary data in its own custom way, then call `defineClass()`, and —if `true` was passed in `loadClass()`'s `resolve` parameter—call `resolveClass()`. In this case, the class loader object would produce the binary form for the requested type in its own custom way and then use the primordial class loader's standard mechanism to link and initialize the type. Here are the declarations for `findSystemClass()`, `defineClass()`, and `resolveClass()`:

```
// Three methods declared in class java.lang.ClassLoader:
protected final Class findSystemClass(String name)
    throws ClassNotFoundException;
protected final Class defineClass(String name, byte data[],
    int offset, int length);
protected final void resolveClass(Class c);
```

If the `loadClass()` method invokes `findSystemClass()`, the class loader object is in effect asking the virtual machine to use the primordial loader to resolve the reference completely. The `findSystemClass()` method accepts the fully qualified name of the type to resolve in its **name** parameter. If the primordial class loader can successfully resolve the reference, it returns a reference to a `Class` instance that represents the referenced type. The `loadClass()` method would then just return a reference to the same `Class` instance. If the primordial class loader is unsuccessful, however, `findSystemClass()` will complete abnormally by throwing a `ClassNotFoundException`. In this case, the `loadClass()` method can either throw `ClassNotFoundException` itself or attempt to load the type in its custom way.

Types brought in through the primordial class loader via `findSystemClass()` are marked as having no class loader object. Any types they refer to will be requested directly from the primordial loader.

If the `loadClass()` method produces the stream of binary data for the type in its own custom way (such as if it downloads the type's class file across a network), it must invoke `defineClass()`, passing a reference to a **byte** array containing the type's binary data in the Java class file format.

Invoking `defineClass()` will cause the virtual machine to do two things. First, the virtual machine will parse the binary data into internal data structures and create a `Class` instance to represent the type. Second, if the type is a class and not `java.lang.Object`, the virtual machine will retrieve the name of the class's direct superclass. It will then check to see whether the direct superclass has been previously loaded by this class loader object (the one whose `loadClass()` method just invoked `defineClass()`). This check determines whether the direct superclass already resides in the current name-space. If the direct superclass has already been loaded by this class loader object, the `defineClass()` method returns the `Class` instance for the freshly loaded type. Otherwise, the virtual machine invokes `loadClass()` on the same class loader object, passing the fully qualified name of the direct superclass in the **name** parameter and setting the **resolve** flag to **false**. Because the **resolve** flag is **false**, the direct superclass (and recursively, all its superclasses) will be loaded but not linked or initialized.

The resolve flag is set to false when **loadClass()** is invoked by **defineClass()** because this is Step 1: loading of the type and any superclasses. Linking and initialization, which would occur if **resolve** were set to **true**, is saved for Step 2.

When **defineClass()** has made certain the type and all its superclasses, if any, have been loaded into the current name-space, it returns the new **Class** instance that represents the type. Step 1 is then complete.

During Step 1, the virtual machine may throw the following errors:

- If the binary data can't be produced (for example, if a class file of the appropriate name can't be found), the virtual machine throws **NoClassDefFoundError**.

- If the binary data is produced but isn't of the proper structure or a recognized version (such as if the minor or major version number of a Java class file is too high), the virtual machine throws **NoClassDefFoundError**.

- If the binary data is produced and well formed but doesn't contain the sought-after class or interface (such as if file **CuteKitty.class** is discovered to contain class **HungryTiger** instead of **CuteKitty**), the virtual machine throws **NoClassDefFoundError**.

- If the class doesn't contain a superclass and isn't class **Object** itself, the virtual machine throws a **ClassFormatError**. (Note that this check has to be done here, during the loading step, because that one piece of information—the symbolic reference to the superclass—is needed by the virtual machine during this step. During Step 1, the virtual machine must load in all the superclasses recursively.)

- If a class appears as its own superclass, the virtual machine throws **ClassCircularityError**.

**STEP 2. LINK AND INITIALIZE THE TYPE AND ANY SUPERCLASSES** At this point, the type being referred to by the **CONSTANT_Class_info** entry being resolved has been loaded but not linked or initialized. In addition, if the type being resolved is a class, all its superclasses have been loaded but not necessarily linked or initialized. Some of the superclasses might be initialized at this point because they may have been initialized during earlier resolutions.

As described in Chapter 7, superclasses must be initialized before subclasses. If the virtual machine is resolving a reference to a class (not an interface), it must make sure that the superclasses have been initialized, starting with **Object** and proceeding down the inheritance hierarchy to the referenced class. (Note that they were loaded in the opposite order in Step 1.) If a type hasn't yet been linked, it must be linked before it is initialized.

**Step 2a. Verify the Type**  Step 2 begins with the official verification phase of linking, described in Chapter 7. As mentioned in that chapter, the process of verification may require that the virtual machine load new types. For example, when verifying a type, the Java Virtual Machine must check all a type's superclasses and superinterfaces to make sure they are all binary compatible with the type. If the type being verified has superinterfaces, they might not yet be loaded. During Step 1, the virtual machine makes sure all the type's superclasses are loaded, but not its superinterfaces. Thus, verification may require that a type's superinterfaces be loaded. At this point, the virtual machine would load and possibly link the superinterfaces, but definitely not initialize them.

In addition, when verifying bytecodes, the Java Virtual Machine may need to load types to ensure the bytecodes are adhering to the semantics of the Java language. For example, if a reference to an instance of a particular class is assigned to a variable with a declared type of a different class, the virtual machine would have to load both types to make sure one is a subclass of the other. As with the superinterfaces described above, the virtual machine would at this point load and possibly link these classes, but definitely not initialize them.

If, during the verification process, the Java Virtual Machine uncovers trouble, it throws **VerifyError**.

**Step 2b. Prepare the Type**  After the official verification phase is complete, the type must be prepared. As described in Chapter 7, during preparation the virtual machine allocates memory for class variables and implementation-dependent data structures such as method tables. If the virtual machine discovers during this step that a class that is not declared abstract contains an abstract method, the virtual machine throws **AbstractMethodError**.

**Optional Step 2c. Resolve the Type**  At this point, the type has been loaded, verified, and prepared. As described in Chapter 7, a Java Virtual Machine implementation can optionally resolve the type at this point. Keep in mind that at this stage in the resolution process, Steps 1, 2a, and 2b have been performed on a referenced type to resolve a `CONSTANT_Class_info` entry in the constant pool of a referencing type. Step 2c is the resolution of symbolic references contained in the referenced type, not the referencing type.

For example, if the virtual machine is resolving a symbolic reference from class **Cat** to class **Mouse**, the virtual machine performs Steps 1, 2a, and 2b on class **Mouse**. At this stage of resolving the symbolic reference to **Mouse** contained in the constant pool of **Cat**, the virtual machine could optionally (as Step 2c) resolve all the symbolic references contained in the constant pool for **Mouse**. If **Mouse**'s constant pool contains a symbolic reference to class **Cheese**, for example, the virtual machine could load and optionally link (but not initialize) **Cheese** at this time. The virtual machine must not attempt to initialize **Cheese** here because **Cheese** is not being actively used. (Of course, **Cheese** may in fact have already been actively used elsewhere, so it have would been already loaded into this name-space, linked, and initialized.)

As mentioned earlier in this chapter, if an implementation does perform Step 2c at this point in the resolution process (early resolution), it must not report any errors until the symbolic references are actually used by the running program. For example, if, during the resolution of **Mouse**'s constant pool, the virtual machine can't find class **Cheese**, it won't throw a **NoClassDefFound** error until (and unless) **Cheese** is actually used by the program.

**Step 2d. Initialize the Type**   At this point, the type has been loaded, verified, prepared, and optionally resolved. At long last, the type is ready for initialization. As defined in Chapter 7, initialization consists of two steps. The initialization of the type's superclasses in top-down order, if the type has any superclasses, and the execution of the type's class initialization method, if it has one. Step 2d just consists of executing the class initialization method, if one exists. Because Steps 2a through 2e are performed for all the referenced type's superclasses, from the top down, Step 2d will occur for superclasses before it occurs for subclasses.

If the class initialization method completes abruptly by throwing some exception that isn't a subclass of **Error**, the virtual machine throws **ExceptionInInitializerError** with the thrown exception as a parameter to the constructor. Otherwise, if the thrown exception is already a subclass of **Error**, that error is thrown. If the virtual machine can't create a new **ExceptionInInitializerError** because not enough memory is available, it throws an **OutOfMemoryError**.

**Step 2e. Check Access Permission**   Lastly, after loading, linking, and initialization are complete, the virtual machine checks for access permission. If the referencing type does not have permission to access the referenced type, the virtual machine throws an **IllegalAccessError**. Step 2e is another activity that is logically part of verification, but that step is performed at some other time than the official verification phase of Step 2a. In this case, the check for access permission is delayed to just after initialization. (Actually, the error can be detected at some other time, such as in Step 2a. But regardless of when or how it is detected, an access violation must be reported only after the Steps 1 and 2a through 2d have been successfully completed. As mentioned in Chapter 7, the Java Virtual Machine specification says when errors should be thrown but doesn't dictate exactly when they should be detected.) After this check is complete, Step 2e—and the entire process of resolving the **CONSTANT_Class_info** entry—is complete.

If an error occurred in any of Steps 1 through 2e, the resolution of the type fails. But if all went well up until the access permission check of Step 2e, the type is still usable in general, just not usable by the referencing type. If an error occurred before the access permission check, however, the type is unusable and must be marked as such or discarded.

A class loader object's **loadClass()** method accomplishes Steps 2a through 2e by invoking **resolveClass()**, passing the reference to the **Class** instance returned by **defineClass()**. Invoking this method causes all of Steps 2a through 2e to be performed on the type and all its superclasses, starting from the furthest up superclass that hasn't yet been linked and initialized and proceeding down the inheritance hierarchy.

Remember that when **defineClass()** was invoked, the virtual machine brought in the type's superclasses by calling **loadClass()** with the **resolve** flag set to **false**. So those superclasses were only loaded; they weren't linked or initialized. Only if the superclasses were already linked and initialized before **defineClass()** was invoked would they be already linked and initialized before **resolveClass()** is invoked.

Note that the **loadClass()** method should invoke **resolveClass()** only on types it imported via calling **defineClass()**, which loads a type but doesn't link or initialize it. (In addition, **loadClass()** should invoke **resolveClass()** only if the resolve parameter is **true**.) As mentioned earlier, **findSystemClass()** takes care of linking and initialization as well as loading. You needn't invoke **resolveClass()** on types returned by **findSystemClass()**.

## Resolution of `CONSTANT_Fieldref_info` Entries

To resolve a constant pool entry of type `CONSTANT_Fieldref_info`, the virtual machine must first resolve the `CONSTANT_Class_info` entry specified in the `class_index` item. Therefore, any error that can be thrown because of the resolution of a `CONSTANT_Class_info` can be thrown during the resolution of a `CONSTANT_Fieldref_info`. If resolution of the `CONSTANT_Class_info` entry succeeds, the virtual machine checks to make sure the field exists and that the current class has permission to access it.

If the virtual machine discovers no field with the proper name and type exists in the referenced class, the virtual machine throws `NoSuchFieldError`. Otherwise, if the field exists, but the current class doesn't have permission to access the field, the virtual machine throws `IllegalAccessError`.

The virtual machine marks the entry as resolved and places a direct reference to the field in the data for the constant pool entry.

## Resolution of `CONSTANT_Methodref_info` Entries

To resolve a constant pool entry of type `CONSTANT_Methodref_info`, the virtual machine must first resolve the `CONSTANT_Class_info` entry specified in the `class_index` item. Therefore, any error that can be thrown because of the resolution of a `CONSTANT_Class_info` can be thrown during the resolution of a `CONSTANT_Methodref_info`. If the resolution of the `CONSTANT_Class_info` entry succeeds, the virtual machine checks to make sure the method exists and that the current class has permission to access it.

If the virtual machine discovers no method with the proper name, return type, and number and types of parameters exists in the referenced class, the virtual machine throws `NoSuchMethodError`. Otherwise, if the method exists, but the current class doesn't have permission to access the method, the virtual machine throws `IllegalAccessError`.

The virtual machine marks the entry as resolved and places a direct reference to the method in the data for the constant pool entry.

## Resolution of `CONSTANT_InterfaceMethodref_info` Entries

To resolve a constant pool entry of type `CONSTANT_InterfaceMethodref_info`, the virtual machine must first resolve the `CONSTANT_Class_info` entry specified in the `class_index` item. Therefore, any error that can be thrown because of the resolution of a `CONSTANT_Class_info` can be thrown during the resolution of a `CONSTANT_InterfaceMethodref_info`. If the resolution of the `CONSTANT_Class_info` entry succeeds, the virtual machine checks to make sure the method exists. (The virtual machine need not check to make sure the current class has permission to access the method because all methods declared in interfaces are implicitly public.)

If the virtual machine discovers no method with the proper name, return type, and number and types of parameters exists in the referenced interface, the virtual machine throws `NoSuchMethodError`.

The virtual machine marks the entry as resolved and places a direct reference to the method in the data for the constant pool entry.

## Resolution of `CONSTANT_String_info` Entries

To resolve an entry of type `CONSTANT_String_info`, the virtual machine must place a reference to an *interned* `String` object in the data for the constant pool entry being resolved. The `String` object (an instance of class `java.lang.String`) must have the character sequence specified by the `CONSTANT_Utf8_info` entry identified by the `string_index` item of the `CONSTANT_String_info`.

Each Java Virtual Machine must maintain an internal list of references to `String` objects that have been "interned" during the course of running the application. Basically, a `String` object is said to be interned simply if it appears in the virtual machine's internal list of interned `String` objects. The point of maintaining this list is that any particular sequence of characters is guaranteed to appear in the list no more than once.

To intern a sequence of characters represented by a `CONSTANT_String_info` entry, the virtual machine checks to see whether the sequence of characters is already in the list of interned strings. If so, the virtual machine uses the reference to the existing, previously interned `String` object. Otherwise, the virtual machine creates a new `String` object with the proper character sequence and adds a reference to that

String object to the list. To complete the resolution process for a CONSTANT_String_info entry, the virtual machine places the reference to the interned String object in the data of the constant pool entry being resolved.

In your Java programs, you can intern a string by invoking the intern() method of class String. All literal strings are interned via the process of resolving CONSTANT_String_info entries. If a string with the same sequence of Unicode characters has been previously interned, the intern() method returns a reference to the matching already-interned String object. If the intern() method is invoked on a String object that contains a sequence of characters that has not yet been interned, that object itself will be interned. The intern() method will return a reference to the same String object upon which it was invoked.

Here's an example:

```
// On CD-ROM in file linking/ex1/Example1.java
class Example1 {

    // Assume this application is invoked with one
    // command-line argument, the string "Hi!".
    public static void main(String[] args) {

        // argZero, because it is assigned a String from
        // the command line, does not reference a string
        // literal. This string is not interned.
        String argZero = args[0];

        // literalString, however, does reference a string
        // literal. It will be assigned a reference to a
        // String with the value "Hi!" by an instruction
        // that references a CONSTANT_String_info entry in
        // the constant pool. The "Hi!" string will be
        // interned by this process.
        String literalString = "Hi!";

        // At this point, there are two String objects on
        // the heap that have the value "Hi!". The one
        // from arg[0], which isn't interned, and the one
        // from the literal, which is interned.
        System.out.print("Before interning argZero: ");
        if (argZero == literalString) {
            System.out.println(
                "they're the same string object!");
        }
        else {
            System.out.println(
                "they're different string objects.");
        }

        // argZero.intern() returns the reference to the
```

```
        // literal string "Hi!" that is already interned.
        // Now both argZero and literalString have the
        // same value. The non-interned version of "Hi!"
        // is now available for garbage collection.
        argZero = argZero.intern();
        System.out.print("After interning argZero: ");
        if (argZero == literalString) {
            System.out.println(
                "they're the same string object!");
        }
        else {
            System.out.println(
                "they're different string objects.");
        }
    }
}
```

When executed with the string `"Hi!"` as the first command-line argument, the `Example1` application prints the following:

```
Before interning argZero: they're different string objects.
After interning argZero: they're the same string object!
```

## Resolution of Other Types of Entries

The **CONSTANT_Integer_info**, **CONSTANT_Long_info**, **CONSTANT_Float_info**, and **CONSTANT_Double_info** entries contain the constant values they represent within the entry itself. Resolving them is straightforward. To resolve this kind of entry, many virtual machine implementations might not have to do anything but use the value as is. Other implementations, however, might choose to do some processing on it. For example, a virtual machine on a little-endian machine could choose to swap the byte order of the value at resolve time.

Entries of type **CONSTANT_Utf8_info** and **CONSTANT_NameAndType_info** are never referred to directly by instructions. They are referred to only via other types of entries and resolved when those referring entries are resolved.

# Compile-Time Resolution of Constants

As mentioned in Chapter 7, references to static final variables initialized to a compile-time constant are resolved at compile-time to a local copy of the constant value. This is true for constants of all the primitive types and of type `java.lang.String`.

This special treatment of constants facilitates two features of the Java language. First, local copies of constant values enable static final variables to be used as `case` expressions in `switch` statements. The two virtual machine instructions that implement `switch` statements in bytecodes, `tableswitch` and `lookupswitch`, require the `case` values in-line in the bytecode stream. These instructions do not support runtime resolution of `case` values. See Chapter 16, "Control Flow," for more information about these instructions.

The other motivation behind the special treatment of constants is conditional compilation. Java supports conditional compilation via `if` statements whose expressions resolve to a compile-time constant. Here's an example:

```
// On CD-ROM in file linking/ex2/AntHill.java
class AntHill {

    static final boolean debug = true;
}

// On CD-ROM in file linking/ex2/Example2.java
class Example2 {

    public static void main(String[] args) {
        if (AntHill.debug) {
            System.out.println("Debug is true!");
        }
    }
}
```

Because of the special treatment of primitive constants, the Java compiler can decide whether to include the body of the `if` statement in `Example2.main()` depending on the value of `AntHill.debug`. Because `AntHill.debug` is `true` in this case, `javac` generates bytecodes for `Example2`'s `main()` method that include the body of the `if` statement but not a check of `AntHill.debug`'s value. The constant pool of `Example2` has no symbolic reference to class `AntHill`. Here are the bytecodes for `main()`:

```
                    // Push objref from System.out
  0 getstatic #8 <Field java.io.PrintStream out>
                    // Push objref to literal string
                    // "Debug is true!"
  3 ldc #1 <String "Debug is true!">
                    // Pop objref (to a String), pop objref(to
```

```
                    // System.out), invoke println() on
                    // System.out passing the string as the
                    // only parameter:
                    // System.out.println("Debug is true!");
  5 invokevirtual #9 <Method void println(java.lang.String)>
  8 return         // return void
```

If the reference to **AntHill.debug** were resolved at runtime, the compiler would always need to include a check of **AntHill.debug**'s value and the body of the **if** statement just in case the value of **AntHill.debug** ever changed. The value of **AntHill.debug** can't change after it is compiled, of course, because it is declared as final. Still, you could change the source code of **AntHill** and recompile **AntHill** but not recompile **Example2**.

Because the reference to **AntHill.debug** is resolved at compile-time, the compiler can conditionally compile out the body of the **if** statement if **AntHill.debug** is discovered to be **false**. Note that you therefore can't change the behavior of the **Example2** application just by setting **AntHill** to **false** and recompiling only **AntHill**. You have to recompile **Example2** as well.

**Example3**, which follows, is basically **Example2** with its name changed to **Example3** and compiled with an **AntHill** that has **debug** set to **false**:

```java
// On CD-ROM in file linking/ex3/AntHill.java
class AntHill {

    static final boolean debug = false;
}

// On CD-ROM in file linking/ex3/Example3.java
class Example3 {

    public static void main(String[] args) {
        if (AntHill.debug) {
            System.out.println("Debug is true!");
        }
    }
}
```

Here are the bytecodes generated by **javac** for **Example3**'s **main()** method:

```
  0 return         // return void
```

As you can see, the Java compiler has brazenly eliminated the entire **if** statement found in **Example3.main()**. Not even a hint of the **println()** invocation exists in this very short bytecode sequence.

# Direct References

The ultimate goal of constant pool resolution is to replace a symbolic reference with a direct reference. The forms of symbolic references are well defined in Chapter 6, but what forms do direct references take? As you might expect, the forms of direct references are yet another decision made by the designers of individual Java Virtual Machine implementations. Nevertheless, some characteristics are likely to be common among most implementations.

Direct references to types, class variables, and class methods are likely native pointers into the method area. A direct reference to a type can simply point to the implementation-specific data structure in the method area that holds the type data. A direct reference to a class variable can point to the class variable's value stored in the method area. A direct reference to a class method can point to a data structure in the method area that contains the data needed to invoke the method. For example, the data structure for a class method could include information such as whether the method is native. If the method is native, the data structure could include a function pointer to the dynamically linked native method implementation. If the method is not native, the data structure could include the method's bytecodes, max_stack, max_locals, and so on. If a just-in-time-compiled version of the method exists, the data structure could include a pointer to that just-in-time-compiled native code.

Direct references to instance variables and instance methods are offsets. A direct reference to an instance variable is likely the offset from the start of the object's image to the location of the instance variable. A direct reference to an instance method is likely an offset into a method table.

Using offsets to represent direct references to instance variables and instance methods depends on a predictable ordering of the fields in a class's object image and the methods in a class's method table. Although implementation designers can choose any way of placing instance variables into an object image or methods into a method table, they will almost certainly use the same way for all types. Therefore, in any one implementation, the ordering of fields in an object and methods in a method table is defined and predictable.

As an example, consider this hierarchy of three classes and one interface:

```
// On CD-ROM in file linking/ex4/Friendly.java
interface Friendly {

    void sayHello();
    void sayGoodbye();
```

```java
    }

// On CD-ROM in file linking/ex4/Dog.java
class Dog {

    // How many times this dog wags its tail when
    // saying hello.
    private int wagCount = ((int) (Math.random() * 5.0))
        + 1;

    void sayHello() {

        System.out.print("Wag");
        for (int i = 0; i < wagCount; ++i) {
            System.out.print(", wag");
        }
        System.out.println(".");
    }

    public String toString() {

        return "Woof!";
    }
}

// On CD-ROM in file linking/ex4/CockerSpaniel.java
class CockerSpaniel extends Dog implements Friendly {

    // How many times this Cocker Spaniel woofs when
    // saying hello.
    private int woofCount = ((int) (Math.random() * 4.0))
        + 1;

    // How many times this Cocker Spaniel wimpers when
    // saying goodbye.
    private int wimperCount =
        ((int) (Math.random() * 3.0)) + 1;

    public void sayHello() {

        // Wag that tail a few times.
        super.sayHello();

        System.out.print("Woof");
        for (int i = 0; i < woofCount; ++i) {
            System.out.print(", woof");
        }
        System.out.println("!");
    }

    public void sayGoodbye() {

        System.out.print("Wimper");
        for (int i = 0; i < wimperCount; ++i) {
            System.out.print(", wimper");
```

```
        }
        System.out.println(".");
    }
}

// On CD-ROM in file linking/ex4/Cat.java
class Cat implements Friendly {

    public void eat() {

        System.out.println("Chomp, chomp, chomp.");
    }

    public void sayHello() {

        System.out.println("Rub, rub, rub.");
    }

    public void sayGoodbye() {

        System.out.println("Scamper.");
    }

    protected void finalize() {

        System.out.println("Meow!");
    }
}
```

Assume these types are loaded into a Java Virtual Machine that organizes objects by placing the instance variables declared in superclasses into the object image before those declared in subclasses, and by placing the instance variables for each individual class in their order of appearance in the class file. Assuming no instance variables exist in class `Object`, the object images for `Dog`, `CockerSpaniel`, and `Cat` would appear as shown in Figure 8-1.

In this figure, the object image for `CockerSpaniel` best illustrates this particular virtual machine's approach to laying out objects. The instance variable for `Dog`, the superclass, appears before the instance variables for `CockerSpaniel`, the subclass. The instance variables of `CockerSpaniel` appear in order of declaration: `woofCount` first and then `wimperCount`.

Note that the `wagCount` instance variable appears at offset one in both `Dog` and `CockerSpaniel`. In this implementation of the Java Virtual Machine, a symbolic reference to the `wagCount` field of class `Dog` would be resolved to direct reference that is an offset of one. Regardless of whether the actual object being referred to was a `Dog`, a `CockerSpaniel`, or any other subclass of `Dog`, the `wagCount` instance variable would always appear at offset one in the object image.

**Figure 8-1.**
*Some object images.*

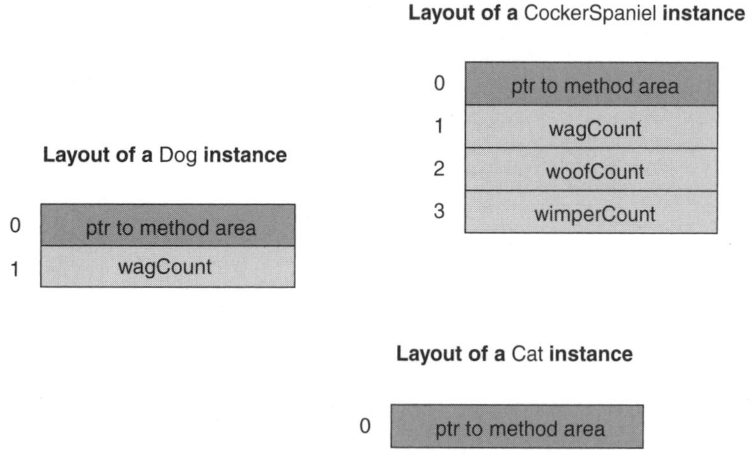

**Layout of a** CockerSpaniel **instance**

| | |
|---|---|
| 0 | ptr to method area |
| 1 | wagCount |
| 2 | woofCount |
| 3 | wimperCount |

**Layout of a** Dog **instance**

| | |
|---|---|
| 0 | ptr to method area |
| 1 | wagCount |

**Layout of a** Cat **instance**

| | |
|---|---|
| 0 | ptr to method area |

A similar pattern emerges in method tables. A method table entry is associated in some way with data structures in the method area that contain sufficient data to enable the virtual machine to invoke the method. Assume that in the Java Virtual Machine implementation being described here, method tables are arrays of native pointers into the method area. The data structures that the method table entries point to are similar to the data structures described earlier for class methods. Assume that the particular Java Virtual Machine implementation that loads these types organizes its method tables by placing methods for superclasses into the method table before those for subclasses and by placing pointers for each class in the order the methods appear in the class file. The exception to the ordering is that methods that methods overridden by a subclass appear in the slot where the overridden method first appears in a superclass.

The way this virtual machine would organize the method table for class **Dog** is shown in Figure 8-2. In this figure, the method table entries that point to methods defined in class **Object** are shown in dark gray. Entries that point to methods defined in **Dog** are shown in light gray.

Note that only nonprivate instance methods appear in this method table. Class methods, which are invoked via the **invokestatic** instruction, need not appear here because they are statically bound and don't need the extra indirection of a method table. Private methods and instance initialization methods need not appear here because they are invoked via the **invokespecial** instruction and are therefore statically bound. Only methods that are invoked with **invokevirtual** or **invokeinterface** appear in this method table. See Chapter 19, "Method Invocation and Return," for a discussion of the different invocation instructions.

**Figure 8-2.**

The method table for class **Dog**.

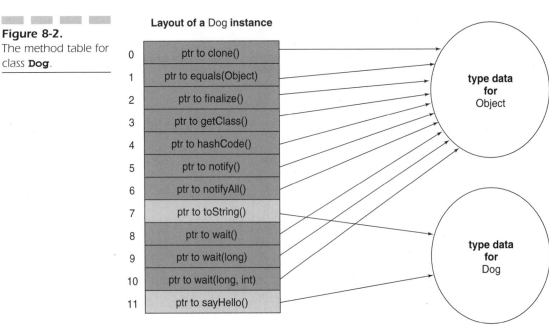

By looking at the source code, you can see that **Dog** overrides the **toString()** method defined in class **Object**. In **Dog**'s method table, the **toString()** method appears only once, in the same slot (offset seven) in which it appears in the method table for **Object**. The pointer residing at offset seven in **Dog**'s method table points to the data for **Dog**'s implementation of **toString()**. In this implementation of the Java Virtual Machine, the pointer to the method data for **toString()** will appear at offset seven for every method table of every class. (Actually, you could write your own version of java.lang.Object and load it in through a class loader object. In this manner you could create a name space in which the pointer to **toString()** occupies a method table offset other than seven in the same Java Virtual Machine implementation.)

Below the methods declared in **Object**, which appear first in this method table, come the methods declared in **Dog** that don't override any method in **Object**. Only one such method, **sayHello()**, has the method table offset 11. All of **Dog**'s subclasses will either inherit or override this implementation of **sayHello()**, and some version of **sayHello()** will always appear at offset 11 of any subclass of **Dog**.

Figure 8-3 shows the method table for **CockerSpaniel**. Note that because **CockerSpaniel** declares **sayHello()** and **sayGoodbye()**, the pointers for

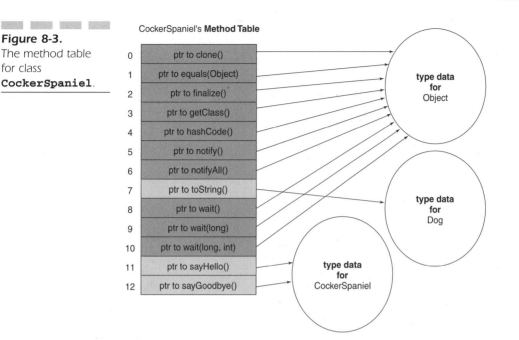

**Figure 8-3.**
The method table for class **CockerSpaniel**.

those methods point to the data for **CockerSpaniel**'s implementation of those methods. Because **CockerSpaniel** inherits **Dog**'s implementation of **toString()**, the pointer for that method (which is still at offset seven) points to the data for **Dog**'s implementation of that method. **CockerSpaniel** inherits all other methods from **Object**, so the pointers for those methods point directly into **Object**'s type data. Note also that **sayHello()** is sitting at offset 11, the same offset it has in **Dog**'s method table.

When the virtual machine resolves a symbolic reference (a **CONSTANT_Methodref_info** entry) to the **toString()** method of any class, the direct reference is method table offset seven. When the virtual machine resolves a symbolic reference to the **sayHello()** method of **Dog** or any of its subclasses, the direct reference is method table offset 11. When the virtual machine resolves a symbolic reference to the **sayGoodbye()** method of **CockerSpaniel** or any of its subclasses, the direct reference is the method table offset 12.

After a symbolic reference to an instance method is resolved to a method table offset, the virtual machine must still actually invoke the method. To invoke an instance method, the virtual machine goes through the object to get at the method table for the object's class. As mentioned in Chapter 5, "The Java Virtual Machine," given a reference to an object, every virtual machine implementation must have some way to get at the type data for that object's class. In addition, given a reference to an object, the method table (a part of the type data for the object's class) is usually very quickly accessible. (One potential scheme is shown in Figure 5-7.) After the virtual machine has the method table for the object's class, it uses the offset to find the actual method to invoke. Voila!

The virtual machine can always depend on method table offsets when it has a reference of a class type (a **CONSTANT_Methodref_info** entry). If the **sayHello()** method appears in offset seven in class **Dog**, it will appear in offset seven in any subclass of **Dog**. The same is not true, however, if the reference is of an interface type (a **CONSTANT_InterfaceMethodref_info** entry). With direct references to instance methods accessed through an interface reference, no method table offset is guaranteed. Consider the method table for class **Cat**, shown in Figure 8-4.

Note that both **Cat** and **CockerSpaniel** implement the **Friendly** interface. A variable of type **Friendly** could hold a reference to a **Cat** object or a **CockerSpaniel** object. With that reference, your program could invoke **sayHello()** or **sayGoodbye()** on a **Cat**, a **CockerSpaniel**, or any other ob-

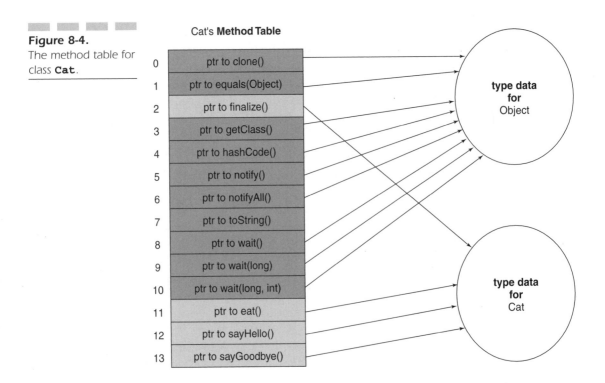

**Figure 8-4.**
The method table for class **Cat**.

Cat's **Method Table**

| | |
|---|---|
| 0 | ptr to clone() |
| 1 | ptr to equals(Object) |
| 2 | ptr to finalize() |
| 3 | ptr to getClass() |
| 4 | ptr to hashCode() |
| 5 | ptr to notify() |
| 6 | ptr to notifyAll() |
| 7 | ptr to toString() |
| 8 | ptr to wait() |
| 9 | ptr to wait(long) |
| 10 | ptr to wait(long, int) |
| 11 | ptr to eat() |
| 12 | ptr to sayHello() |
| 13 | ptr to sayGoodbye() |

type data for Object

type data for Cat

ject whose class implements the **Friendly** interface. The **Example4** application demonstrates this:

```
// On CD-ROM in file linking/ex4/Example4.java
class Example4 {

    public static void main(String[] args) {

        Dog dog = new CockerSpaniel();

        dog.sayHello();

        Friendly fr = (Friendly) dog;

        // Invoke sayGoodbye() on a CockerSpaniel object
        // through a reference of type Friendly.
        fr.sayGoodbye();

        fr = new Cat();

        // Invoke sayGoodbye() on a Cat object through a
        // reference of type Friendly.
        fr.sayGoodbye();
    }
}
```

In **Example4**, local variable **fr** invokes **sayGoodbye()** on both a **CockerSpaniel** object and a **Cat** object. The same constant pool entry, a **CONSTANT_InterfaceMethodref_info** entry, is used to invoke this method on both objects. But when the virtual machine resolves the symbolic reference to **sayHello()**, it can't just save a method table offset and expect that offset to always work in future uses of the constant pool entry.

The trouble is that classes that implement the **Friendly** interface aren't guaranteed to have a common superclass that also implements **Friendly**. As a result, the methods declared in **Friendly** aren't guaranteed to be in the same place in all method tables. If you compare the method table for **CockerSpaniel** against the method table for **Cat**, for example, you'll see that in **CockerSpaniel**, **sayHello()**'s pointer occupies offset 11. But in **Cat**, **sayHello()** occupies offset 12. Likewise, **CockerSpaniel**'s **sayGoodbye()** method pointer resides in offset 12, but **Cat**'s **sayGoodbye()** method pointer resides at offset 13.

Thus, whenever the Java Virtual Machine invokes a method from an interface reference, it must search the method table of the object's class until it finds the appropriate method. For this reason, invoking instance methods on interface references can be significantly slower than invoking instance methods on class references. Virtual machine implementations can attempt to be smart, of course, about how they search through a method table. For example, an implementation could save the last index at which it found the method and try there first the next time. Or during preparation an implementation could build data structures that help it search through method tables given an interface reference. Nevertheless, invoking a method given an interface reference will almost certainly be to some extent slower than invoking a method given a class reference.

# _quick **Instructions**

The Java Virtual Machine specification describes a technique used by Sun's Java Virtual Machine implementation to speed up the interpretation of bytecodes. This technique is likely common to many Java Virtual Machine implementations because many implementations are based on Sun's code. In this scheme, opcodes that refer to constant pool entries are replaced by a _quick opcode when the constant pool entry is resolved. When the virtual machine encounters a _quick instruction, it knows the constant pool entry is already resolved and can therefore execute the instruction faster.

The core instruction set of the Java Virtual Machine consists of 200 single-byte opcodes, all of which are described in Appendix A. These 200 opcodes are the only opcodes you will ever see in class files. Sun's virtual machine implementation uses another 25 single-byte opcodes internally, the _quick opcodes.

For example, when Sun's virtual machine resolves a constant pool entry referred to by an **ldc** instruction (opcode value 0x12), it replaces the **ldc** opcode byte in the bytecode stream with an **ldc_quick** instruction (opcode value 0xcb). This technique is part of the process of replacing a symbolic reference with a direct reference in Sun's virtual machine.

For some instructions, in addition to overwriting the normal opcode with a _quick opcode, the virtual machine overwrites the operands of the instruction with data that represents the direct reference. For example, in addition to replacing an **invokevirtual** opcode with an **invokevirtual_quick**, the virtual machine also puts the method table offset and the number of arguments into the two operand bytes that follow every **invokevirtual** instruction. Placing the method table offset in the bytecode stream following the **invokevirtual_quick** opcode saves the virtual machine the time it would take to look up the offset in the resolved constant pool entry.

# Example: The Linking of the Salutation Application

As an example of Java's linking model, consider the **Salutation** application shown here:

```java
// On CD-ROM in file linking/ex5/Salutation.java
class Salutation {

    private static final String hello = "Hello, world!";
    private static final String greeting =
        "Greetings, planet!";
    private static final String salutation =
        "Salutations, orb!";

    private static int choice = (int) (Math.random()
        * 2.99);

    public static void main(String[] args) {

        String s = hello;
        if (choice == 1) {
            s = greeting;
        }
        else if (choice == 2) {
            s = salutation;
        }

        System.out.println(s);
    }
}
```

Assume that you have asked a Java Virtual Machine to run **Salutation**. When the virtual machine starts, it attempts to invoke the **main()** method of **Salutation**. It quickly realizes, however, that it can't invoke **main()**. The invocation of a method declared in a class is an active use of that class, which is not allowed until the class is initialized. Thus, before the virtual machine can invoke **main()**, it must initialize **Salutation**. And before it can initialize **Salutation**, it must load and link **Salutation**. So, the virtual machine hands the fully qualified name of **Salutation** to the primordial class loader, which retrieves the binary form of the class, parses the binary data into internal data structures, and creates an instance of **java.lang.Class**. The constant pool for **Salutation** is shown in Table 8-1.

As part of the loading process for **Salutation**, the Java Virtual Machine must make sure that all **Salutation**'s superclasses have been loaded. To start this process, the virtual machine looks into **Salutation**'s

**Table 8-1.**

Class **Salutation's**
constant pool

| Index | Type | Value |
|-------|------|-------|
| 1 | CONSTANT_String_info | 30 |
| 2 | CONSTANT_String_info | 31 |
| 3 | CONSTANT_String_info | 39 |
| 4 | CONSTANT_Class_info | 37 |
| 5 | CONSTANT_Class_info | 44 |
| 6 | CONSTANT_Class_info | 45 |
| 7 | CONSTANT_Class_info | 46 |
| 8 | CONSTANT_Class_info | 47 |
| 9 | CONSTANT_Methodref_info | 7, 16 |
| 10 | CONSTANT_Fieldref_info | 4, 17 |
| 11 | CONSTANT_Fieldref_info | 8, 18 |
| 12 | CONSTANT_Methodref_info | 5, 19 |
| 13 | CONSTANT_Methodref_info | 6, 20 |
| 14 | CONSTANT_Double_info | 2.99 |
| 16 | CONSTANT_NameAndType_info | 26, 22 |
| 17 | CONSTANT_NameAndType_info | 41, 32 |
| 18 | CONSTANT_NameAndType_info | 49, 34 |
| 19 | CONSTANT_NameAndType_info | 50, 23 |
| 20 | CONSTANT_NameAndType_info | 51, 21 |
| 21 | CONSTANT_Utf8_info | "()D" |
| 22 | CONSTANT_Utf8_info | "()V" |
| 23 | CONSTANT_Utf8_info | "(Ljava/lang/String;)V" |
| 24 | CONSTANT_Utf8_info | "([Ljava/lang/String;)V" |
| 25 | CONSTANT_Utf8_info | "<clinit>" |
| 26 | CONSTANT_Utf8_info | "<init>" |
| 27 | CONSTANT_Utf8_info | "Code" |
| 28 | CONSTANT_Utf8_info | "ConstantValue" |
| 29 | CONSTANT_Utf8_info | "Exceptions" |

**Table 8-1.**

Continued.

| Index | Type | Value |
|-------|------|-------|
| 30 | CONSTANT_Utf8_info | "Greetings, planet!" |
| 31 | CONSTANT_Utf8_info | "Hello, world!" |
| 32 | CONSTANT_Utf8_info | "I" |
| 33 | CONSTANT_Utf8_info | "LineNumberTable" |
| 34 | CONSTANT_Utf8_info | "Ljava/io/PrintStream;" |
| 35 | CONSTANT_Utf8_info | "Ljava/lang/String;" |
| 36 | CONSTANT_Utf8_info | "LocalVariables" |
| 37 | CONSTANT_Utf8_info | "Salutation" |
| 38 | CONSTANT_Utf8_info | "Salutation.java" |
| 39 | CONSTANT_Utf8_info | "Salutations, orb!" |
| 40 | CONSTANT_Utf8_info | "SourceFile" |
| 41 | CONSTANT_Utf8_info | "choice" |
| 42 | CONSTANT_Utf8_info | "greeting" |
| 43 | CONSTANT_Utf8_info | "hello" |
| 44 | CONSTANT_Utf8_info | "java/io/PrintStream" |
| 45 | CONSTANT_Utf8_info | "java/lang/Math" |
| 46 | CONSTANT_Utf8_info | "java/lang/Object" |
| 47 | CONSTANT_Utf8_info | "java/lang/System" |
| 48 | CONSTANT_Utf8_info | "main" |
| 49 | CONSTANT_Utf8_info | "out" |
| 50 | CONSTANT_Utf8_info | "println" |
| 51 | CONSTANT_Utf8_info | "random" |
| 52 | CONSTANT_Utf8_info | "salutation" |

type data at the **super_class** item, which is a seven. The virtual machine looks up entry seven in the constant pool and finds a **CONSTANT_Class_info** entry that serves as a symbolic reference to class **java.lang.Object**. See Figure 8-5 for a graphical depiction of this symbolic reference. The virtual machine resolves this symbolic reference,

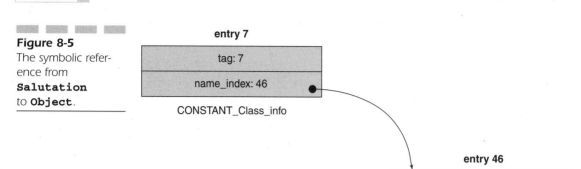

**Figure 8-5**
The symbolic refer-
ence from
**Salutation**
to **Object**.

which causes it to load class **Object**. Because **Object** is the top of **Salutation**'s inheritance hierarchy, the virtual machine links and initializes **Object** as well.

Now that the Java Virtual Machine has loaded the **Salutation** class and loaded, linked, and initialized all its superclasses, the virtual machine is ready to link **Salutation**. As the first step in the linking process, the virtual machine verifies the integrity of the binary representation of class **Salutation**. Assume this implementation of the Java Virtual Machine performs all verification up front, except for the verification of symbolic references. So by the time this official verification phase of linking is completed, the virtual machine will have verified

**1.** that **Salutation**'s binary data is structurally correct

**2.** that **Salutation** correctly implements the semantics of the Java language

**3.** that **Salutation**'s bytecodes won't crash the virtual machine

After the Java Virtual Machine has verified **Salutation**, it must prepare for **Salutation**'s use by allocating any memory needed by the class. At this stage, the virtual machine allocates memory for **Salutation**'s class variable, **choice**, and gives it a default initial value. Because the **choice** class variable is an **int**, it receives the default initial value of zero.

The three literal **string**s—**hello**, **greeting**, and **salutation**—are constants, not class variables. They do not occupy memory space as class variables in the method area. They don't receive default initial values. Because they are declared static and final, they appear as **CONSTANT_String_info** entries in **Salutation**'s constant pool. The constant pool for **Salutation** that was generated by **javac** is shown in Table 8-1. The entries that represent **Salutation**'s constant strings are for **greeting**, entry one; for **hello**, entry two; and for **salutation**, entry three.

After the processes of verification and preparation have successfully completed, the class is ready for resolution. As mentioned previously, different implementations of the Java Virtual Machine can perform the resolution phase of linking at different times. Resolution of **Salutation** is optional at this point in its lifetime. Java Virtual Machines are not required to perform resolution until each symbolic reference is actually used by the program. If a symbolic reference is never actually used by a program, the virtual machine is not required to resolve it.

A Java Virtual Machine implementation could perform the recursive resolution process, described earlier for **Salutation**, at this point in the lifetime of a program. If so, the program would be completely linked before **main()** is ever invoked. A different Java Virtual Machine implementation could perform none of the resolution process at this point. Instead, it could resolve each symbolic reference the first time it is actually used by the running program. Other implementations could choose a resolution strategy between these two extremes. Although different implementations can perform resolution at different times, all implementations will ensure that a type is loaded, verified, prepared, and initialized before it is used.

Assume this implementation of the Java Virtual Machine uses late resolution. As each symbolic reference is used for the first time by the program, it will be checked for accuracy and converted into a direct reference. Assume also that this implementation uses the technique of replacing the opcode that refers to the constant pool with **_quick** equivalents.

After this Java Virtual Machine implementation has loaded, verified, and prepared **Salutation**, the virtual machine is ready to initialize it. As mentioned earlier, the Java Virtual Machine must initialize all superclasses of a class before it can initialize the class. In this case, the virtual machine has already initialized **Object**, the superclass of **Salutation**.

After the virtual machine has made sure all of **Salutation**'s superclasses have been initialized (in this case, just class **Object**), it is ready to invoke **Salutation**'s **<clinit>()** method. Because **Salutation** contains a class variable, **width**, that has an initializer that doesn't resolve at compile-time to a constant, the compiler does place a **<clinit>()** method into **Salutation**'s class file.

Here's the `<clinit>()` method for `Salutation`:

```
                 // Invoke class method Math.random(), passing
                 // no parameters. Push double result.
  0 invokestatic #13 <Method double random()>
                 // Push double constant 2.99 from constant
                 // pool.
  3 ldc2_w #14 <Double 2.99>
                 // Pop two doubles, multiple, push double result.
  6 dmul         // result.
                 // Pop double, convert to int, push int
  7 d2i          // result.
                 // Pop int, store int Salutation.choice
  8 putstatic #10 <Field int choice>
 11 return       // Return void from <clinit>()
```

The Java Virtual Machine executes `Salutation`'s `<clinit>()` method to set the `choice` field to its proper initial value. Before executing `<clinit>()`, `choice` has its default initial value of zero. After executing `<clinit>()`, it has one of three values chosen pseudo-randomly: zero, one, or two.

The first instruction of the `<clinit>()` method, `invokestatic #13`, refers to constant pool entry 13, a `CONSTANT_Methodref_info` that represents a symbolic reference to the `random()` method of class `java.lang.Math`. You can see a graphical depiction of this symbolic reference in Figure 8-6. The Java Virtual Machine resolves this symbolic reference, which causes it to load, link, and initialize class

**Figure 8-6.**
The symbolic reference from **Salutation** to **Math.random()**.

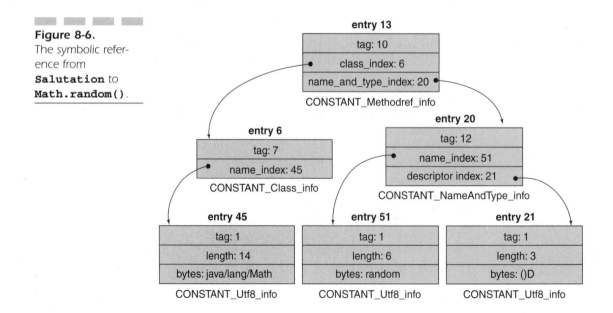

java.lang.Math. It places a direct reference to the random() method into constant pool entry 13, marks the entry as resolved, and replaces the invokestatic opcode with invokestatic_quick.

Having completed the resolution process for constant pool entry 13, the Java Virtual Machine is ready to invoke the method. When the virtual machine actually invokes the random() method, it will load, link, and initialize any types referenced symbolically from Math's constant pool and random()'s code. When this method returns, the virtual machine will push the returned double value onto the main() method's operand stack.

To execute the next instruction, ldc2_w #14, the virtual machine looks into constant pool entry 14 and finds an unresolved CONSTANT_Double_info entry. The virtual machine resolves this entry to the double value 2.99, marks the entry as resolved, and replaces the ldc2_w opcode with ldc2_w_quick. After the virtual machine has resolved constant pool entry 14, it pushes the constant double value, 2.99, onto the operand stack.

Note that this entry, a CONSTANT_Double_info, does not refer to any other constant pool entry or item outside this class. The eight bytes of the double value 2.99 are specified within the entry itself.

Note also that this constant pool does not have any entry with an index of 15. As mentioned in Chapter 6, entries of type CONSTANT_Double_info and CONSTANT_Long_info occupy two slots in the constant pool. Thus, the CONSTANT_Double_info at index 14 is considered to occupy both indices 14 and 15.

To execute the next instruction, dmul, the virtual machine pops two doubles, multiplies them, and pushes the double result. For the next instruction, the virtual machine pops the double, converts it to int, and pushes the int result. Assume that for this particular execution of Salutation, the result of this operation is the int value two.

The next instruction, putstatic #10, uses another symbolic reference from the constant pool, this one to the choice variable of Salutation itself. This instruction illustrates that a class's bytecodes use symbolic references to refer not only to fields and methods of other types, but also to its own fields and methods. When the virtual machine executes this instruction, it looks up constant pool entry 10 and finds an as-yet-unresolved CONSTANT_Fieldref_info item. See Figure 8-7 for a graphical depiction of this symbolic reference. The virtual machine resolves the reference by locating the choice class variable in Salutation's type data in the method area and placing a pointer to the actual variable data in constant pool entry 10. It marks the entry as resolved and replaces the putstatic opcode with putstatic_quick.

**Figure 8-7.**
The symbolic
reference from
**Salutation** to its
own **choice** field.

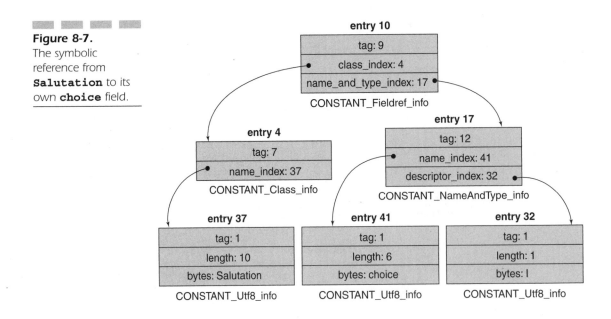

After it has resolved the **CONSTANT_Fieldref_info** entry for **choice**, the virtual machine pops an **int** (in this case a two) from the operand stack and places it into the **choice** variable. The execution of the **putstatic** instruction is now complete.

Lastly, the virtual machine executes the return instruction, which signals to the virtual machine that the **<clinit>()** method, and hence the initialization of class **Salutation**, is complete.

Now that class **Salutation** has been initialized, it is finally ready for use. The Java Virtual Machine invokes **main()**, and the program begins. Here's the bytecode sequence for **Salutation**'s **main()** method:

```
                // Push objref to literal string from
                // constant pool entry 2
0 ldc #2 <String "Hello, world!">
                // Pop objref into loc var 1:
2 astore_1      // String s = hello;
                // Push int from static field
                // Salutation.choice. Note that by this
                // time, choice has definitely been given
                // its proper initial value.
3 getstatic #10 <Field int choice>
6 iconst_1      // Push int constant 1
                // Pop two ints, compare, if not equal
                // branch to 16:
7 if_icmpne 16 // if (choice == 1) {
                // Here, choice does equal 1. Push objref
                // to string literal from constant pool:
```

```
10 ldc #1 <String "Greetings, planet!">
                    // Pop objref into loc var 1:
12 astore_1        // s = greeting;
13 goto 26         // Branch unconditionally to offset 26
                    // Push int from static field
                    // Salutation.choice
16 getstatic #10 <Field int choice>
19 iconst_2        // Push int constant 2
                    // Pop two ints, compare, if not equal
20 if_icmpne 26 // branch to 26: if (choice == 2) {
                    // Here, choice does equal 2. Push objref
                    // to string literal from constant pool:
23 ldc #3 <String "Salutations, orb!">
                    // Pop objref into loc var 1:
25 astore_1        // String s = salutation;
                    // Push objref from System.out
26 getstatic #11 <Field java.io.PrintStream out>
                    // Push objref (to a String) from loc
29 aload_1         // var 1
                    // Pop objref (to a String), pop objref(to
                    // System.out), invoke println() on
                    // System.out passing the string as the
                    // only parameter: System.out.println(s);
30 invokevirtual #12
    <Method void println(java.lang.String)>
33 return          // Return void from main()
```

The first instruction in **main()**, **ldc #2**, uses a symbolic reference to the string literal **"Hello, world!"**. When the virtual machine executes this instruction, it looks up constant pool entry two and finds a **CONSTANT_String_info** item that hasn't yet been resolved. See Figure 8-8 for a graphical depiction of the symbolic reference to this string literal.

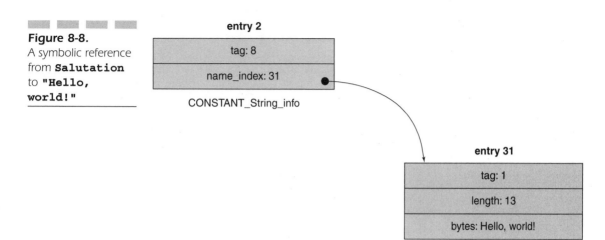

**Figure 8-8.**
A symbolic reference from **Salutation** to **"Hello, world!"**

entry 2

| tag: 8 |
| name_index: 31 |

CONSTANT_String_info

entry 31

| tag: 1 |
| length: 13 |
| bytes: Hello, world! |

CONSTANT_Utf8_info

As part of executing the **ldc** instruction, the virtual machine resolves the constant pool entry. It creates and interns a new **String** object with the value **"Hello, world!"**, places a reference to the string object in the constant pool entry, marks the entry as resolved, and replaces the **ldc** opcode with an **ldc_quick**.

Now that the virtual machine has resolved the **"Hello, world!"** string literal, it pushes the reference to that **String** object onto the stack. The next instruction, **astore_1**, pops the reference and stores it into local variable position one, the **s** variable.

To execute the next instruction, **getstatic #10**, the virtual machine looks up constant pool entry 10 and discovers a **CONSTANT_Fieldref_info** entry that has already been resolved. This entry, a symbolic reference to **Salutation**'s own **choice** field, was resolved by the **putstatic #10** instruction in the **<clinit>()** method. The virtual machine simply replaces the **getstatic** opcode with **getstatic_quick** and pushes the **int** value of **choice** onto the stack.

To execute **main()**'s next instruction, **iconst_1**, the virtual machine simply pushes **int** one onto the operand stack. For the next instruction, **ificmpne 16**, the virtual machine pops the top two **int**s and subtracts one from the other. In this case, because the value of **choice** was set by the **<clinit>()** method to be two, the result of the subtraction is not zero. As a consequence, the virtual machine takes the branch. It updates the pc register so that the next instruction it executes is the **getstatic** instruction at offset 16.

The **getstatic** instruction at offset 16 refers to the same constant pool entry referred to by the **getstatic** instruction at offset three: constant pool entry 10. When the virtual machine executes the **getstatic** at off-set 16, it looks up constant pool entry 10 and finds a **CONSTANT_Fieldref_info** entry that is already resolved. It replaces the **getstatic** opcode with **getstatic_quick** and pushes the **int** value of **Salutation**'s **choice** class variable (a two) onto the operand stack.

To execute the next instruction, **iconst_2**, the virtual machine pushes an **int** two onto the stack. For the next instruction, another **ificmpne 26**, the virtual machine again pops two **int**s and subtracts one from the other. This time, however, both **int**s equal two, so the result of the subtraction is zero. As a consequence, the virtual machine does not take the branch and continues on to execute the next instruction in the bytecode array, another **ldc**.

The **ldc** instruction at offset 23 refers to constant pool entry three, a **CONSTANT_String_info** entry that serves as a symbolic reference to the string literal **"Salutations, orb!"**. The virtual machine looks up this entry in the constant pool and discovers it is as yet unresolved. To resolve the entry, the virtual machine creates and interns a new **String** object with the value **"Salutations, orb!"**, places a reference to the new object in the data for constant pool entry three, and replaces the **ldc** opcode with **ldc_quick**. Having resolved the string literal, the virtual machine pushes the reference to the **String** object onto the stack.

To execute the next instruction, **astore_1**, the virtual machine pops the object reference to the **"Salutations, orb!"** string literal off the stack and stores it into local variable slot one, overwriting the reference to **"Hello, world!"** written there by the **astore_1** instruction at offset two.

The next instruction, **getstatic #11**, uses a symbolic reference to a public static class variable of **java.lang.System** with the name **out** and the type **java.io.PrintStream**. This symbolic reference occupies the **CONSTANT_Fieldref_info** entry at index 11 in the constant pool. See Figure 8-9 for a graphical depiction of this symbolic reference.

To resolve the reference to **System.out**, the Java Virtual Machine must load, link, and initialize **java.lang.System** to make sure it has a public static field, named **out**, of type **java.io.PrintStream**. Then the virtual machine will replace the symbolic reference with a direct reference, such as a native pointer, so that any future uses of **System.out** by **Saluation** won't require resolution and will be faster. Lastly, the virtual machine will replace the **getstatic** opcode with **getstatic_quick**.

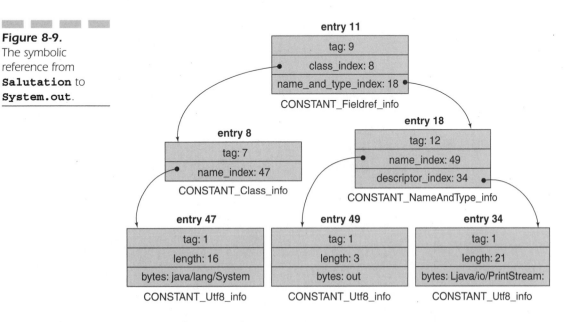

**Figure 8-9.**
The symbolic reference from **Salutation** to **System.out**.

After the virtual machine has successfully resolved the symbolic reference, it will push the reference to **System.out** onto the stack. To execute the next instruction, **aload_1**, the virtual machine simply pushes onto the stack the object reference from local variable one, which is the reference to the **"Salutations, orb!"** string literal.

To execute the next instruction, **invokevirtual #12**, the Java Virtual Machine looks up constant pool entry 12 and finds an unresolved **CONSTANT_Methodref_info** entry, a symbolic reference to the **println()** method of **java.io.PrintStream**. See Figure 8-10 for a graphical depiction of this symbolic reference. The virtual machine loads, links, and initializes **java.io.PrintStream**, and makes sure it has a **println()** method that is **public**, returns **void**, and takes a **String** argument. It marks the entry as resolved and puts a direct reference (an index into **PrintStream**'s method table) into the data for the resolved constant pool entry. Lastly, the virtual machine replaces the **invokevirtual** opcode with **invokevirtual_quick** and places the method table index and the number of arguments accepted by the method as operands to the **invokevirtual_quick** opcode.

When the virtual machine actually invokes the **println()** method, it will load, link, and initialize any types referenced symbolically from **PrintStream**'s constant pool and **println()**'s code.

The next instruction is the last instruction of the **main()** method: **return**. Because **main()** was being executed by the only non-deamon

**Figure 8-10.**
The symbolic reference from **Salutation** to **PrintStream. println()**.

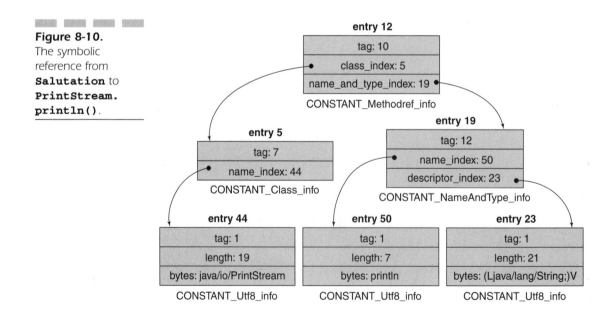

thread running in the **Salutation** application, executing the **return** instruction will cause the virtual machine to exit. Note that constant pool entry one, which contained a symbolic reference to the **"Greetings, planet!"** string literal, was never resolved during this execution of the **Salutation** application. Because **choice** happened to be initialized with a value of two, the instruction that referred to constant pool entry one, the **ldc #1** instruction at offset 10, was never executed. As a result, the virtual machine never created a **String** object with the value **"Greetings, planet!"**.

# Example: The Dynamic Extension of the Greet Application

As an example of an application that performs dynamic extension through class loader objects, consider the following class:

```
// On CD-ROM in file linking/ex6/Greet.java
import COM.artima.greeter.*;

public class Greet {

    // Arguments to this application:
    //      args[0] - path name of directory in which class
    //                  files for greeters are stored
    //      args[1], args[2], ... - class names of greeters
    //                  to load and invoke the greet() method
    //                  on.
    //
    // All greeters must implement the
    // COM.artima.greeter.Greeter interface.
    //
    static public void main(String[] args) {

        if (args.length <= 1) {
            System.out.println(
                "Enter base path and greeter class names"
                + " as args.");
            return;
        }

        GreeterClassLoader gcl =
            new GreeterClassLoader(args[0]);

        for (int i = 1; i < args.length; ++i) {
            try {
```

```
            // Load the greeter specified on the
            // command line
            Class c = gcl.loadClass(args[i], true);

            // Instantiate it into a greeter object
            Object o = c.newInstance();

            // Cast the Object ref to the Greeter
            // interface type so greet() can be
            // invoked on it
            Greeter greeter = (Greeter) o;

            // Greet the world in this greeter's
            // special way
            greeter.greet();
        }
        catch (Exception e) {
            e.printStackTrace();
        }
    }
}
}
```

The `Greet` application is a fancy incarnation of the typical "Hello, world!" program. `Greet` uses a class loader object to dynamically extend itself with classes—called "greeters"—that do the actual work of telling the world hello.

A greeter is any class that implements the `COM.artima.greeter.Greeter` interface:

```
// On CD-ROM in file
linking/ex6/COM/artima/greeter/Greeter.java
package COM.artima.greeter;

public interface Greeter {

    void greet();
}
```

As you can see from the preceding code, the `Greeter` interface declares only one method: `greet()`. When a greeter object's `greet()` method is invoked, the object should say hello to the world in its own unique way. Here are a few examples of greeters:

```
// On CD-ROM in file linking/ex6/greeters/Hello.java
import COM.artima.greeter.Greeter;

public class Hello implements Greeter {

    public void greet() {
```

```
            System.out.println("Hello, world!");
        }
    }

    // On CD-ROM in file linking/ex6/greeters/Greetings.java
    import COM.artima.greeter.Greeter;

    public class Greetings implements Greeter {

        public void greet() {
            System.out.println("Greetings, planet!");
        }
    }

    // On CD-ROM in file linking/ex6/greeters/Salutations.java
    import COM.artima.greeter.Greeter;

    public class Salutations implements Greeter {

        public void greet() {
            System.out.println("Salutations, orb!");
        }
    }

    // On CD-ROM in file linking/ex6/greeters/HowDoYouDo.java
    import COM.artima.greeter.Greeter;

    public class HowDoYouDo implements Greeter {

        public void greet() {
            System.out.println("How do you do, globe!");
        }
    }
```

Greeters can be more complex than the preceding four examples. Here's an example of a greeter that chooses a greeting based on the time of day:

```
    // On CD-ROM in file linking/ex6/greeters/HiTime.java
    import COM.artima.greeter.Greeter;
    import java.util.Date;

    public class HiTime implements Greeter {

        public void greet() {

            // Date's no-arg constructor initializes itself to
            // the current date and time
            Date date = new Date();
            int hours = date.getHours();

            // Some hours: midnight, 0; noon, 12; 11PM, 23;
```

```
if (hours >= 4 && hours <= 11) {
    System.out.println("Good morning, world!");
}
else if (hours >= 12 && hours <= 16) {
    System.out.println("Good afternoon, world!");
}
else if (hours >= 17 && hours <= 21) {
    System.out.println("Good evening, world!");
}
else if (hours >= 22 || hours <= 3) {
    System.out.println("Good night, world!");
}
else {
    // This should never happen.
    System.out.println(
        "Oh oh, the clock is broken, world!");
}
    }
}
```

The **Greet** application doesn't know at compile-time what greeter classes it will load and where those classes will be stored. At runtime, it takes a directory path as its first command-line argument and greeter class names as subsequent arguments. It attempts to load the greeters using the path name as a base directory.

For example, imagine you invoke the **Greet** application with the following command line:

**java Greet greeters Hello**

In this command line, **java** is the name of the Java Virtual Machine executable. **Greet** is the class name of the **Greet** application. **greeters** is the name of a directory relative to the current directory in which the **Greet** application should look for greeters. **Hello** is the name of the greeter.

When the **Greet** application is invoked with the preceding command line, it attempts to load **greeters/Hello.class** and invoke **Hello**'s **greet()** method. If the **Hello.class** file is indeed sitting in a directory named **greeters**, the application will print the following:

**Hello, world!**

The **Greet** application can handle more than one greeter. If you invoke it with the command line

**java Greet greeters Hello Greetings Salutations HowDoYouDo**

the **Greet** application will load each of the four greeters listed and invoke their **greet()** methods, yielding the following output:

```
Hello, world!
Greetings, planet!
Salutations, orb!
How do you do, globe!
```

The **Greet** application works by first checking to make sure that at least two command-line arguments exist: a directory path and at least one greeter class name. It then instantiates a new **GreeterClassLoader** object, which will be responsible for loading the greeters. (The inner workings of class **GreeterClassLoader**, a subclass of **java.lang.ClassLoader**, will be described later in this section.) The constructor for **GreeterClassLoader** accepts a **String** that it uses as a directory path in which to look for greeters.

After it has created the **GreeterClassLoader** object, the **Greet** application invokes its **loadClass()** method for each greeter name that appears on the command line. When it invokes **loadClass()**, it passes the greeter class name in **name** and sets the **resolve** flag to **true**:

```
// Load the greeter specified on the command line
Class c = gcl.loadClass(args[i], true);
```

If the **loadClass()** method is unsuccessful, it throws an exception or error. If the **loadClass()** method is successful, it returns the **Class** instance for the newly loaded, linked, and initialized type.

After **loadClass()** has returned a **Class** instance, the **Greet** application's **main()** method instantiates a new instance of the greeter by calling **newInstance()** on the **Class** instance:

```
// Instantiate it into a greeter object
Object o = c.newInstance();
```

When the **newInstance()** method is invoked on a **Class** object, the virtual machine creates and initializes a new instance of the class represented by the **Class** object. To initialize the new instance, the virtual machine invokes its no-arg constructor.

The **Greet** application then casts the **Object** reference that points to the greeter object to a **Greeter** reference:

```
// Cast the Object ref to the Greeter interface type
// so greet() can be invoked on it
Greeter greeter = (Greeter) o;
```

Finally, armed with a **Greeter** reference, the **main()** method invokes the **greet()** method on the greeter object:

```
// Greet the world in this greeter's special way
greeter.greet();
```

Here's the code for `GreeterClassLoader`:

```
// On CD-ROM in file

// linking/ex6/COM/artima/greeter/GreeterClassLoader.java
package COM.artima.greeter;

import java.io.*;
import java.util.Hashtable;

public class GreeterClassLoader extends ClassLoader {

    // types is this class loader object's private
    // cache of type names it has loaded. For each type
    // name, the Hashtable stores a reference to the
    // Class instance for that type
    private Hashtable types = new Hashtable();

    // basePath gives the path to which this class
    // loader appends "/<typename>.class" to get the
    // full path name of the class file to load
    private String basePath;

    public GreeterClassLoader(String basePath) {

        this.basePath = basePath;
    }

    public synchronized Class loadClass(String className,
        boolean resolveIt) throws ClassNotFoundException {

        Class result;
        byte classData[];

        // Check the local cache
        result = (Class) types.get(className);
        if (result != null) {
            // Return a cached class
            return result;
        }

        // Check with the primordial class loader
        try {
            result = super.findSystemClass(className);
            // Return a system class
            return result;
        }
        catch (ClassNotFoundException e) {
        }

        // Don't attempt to load a system file except
```

```
        // through the primordial class loader
        if (className.startsWith("java.")) {
            throw new ClassNotFoundException();
        }

        // Try to load it from the basePath directory.
        classData = getTypeFromBasePath(className);
        if (classData == null) {
            System.out.println("GCL - Can't load class: "
                + className);
            throw new ClassNotFoundException();
        }

        // Parse it
        result = defineClass(className, classData, 0,
            classData.length);
        if (result == null) {
            System.out.println("GCL - Class format error: "
                + className);
            throw new ClassFormatError();
        }

        if (resolveIt) {
            resolveClass(result);
        }

        // Add newly loaded type to private name cache
        types.put(className, result);

        // Return class from basePath directory
        return result;
    }

    private byte[] getTypeFromBasePath(String className) {

        InputStream in = null;
        String fileName = basePath + "/" + className
            + ".class";

        try {
            in = new FileInputStream(fileName);
        } catch (FileNotFoundException e) {
            return null;
        }

        ByteArrayOutputStream out =
            new ByteArrayOutputStream();

        try {
            int c = in.read();
            while (c != -1) {
                out.write(c);
```

```
                    c = in.read();
                }
            }
        catch (IOException e) {
            System.out.println(
                "GCL: Error reading bytes of:"
                + className);
            e.printStackTrace();
            return null;
        }

        return out.toByteArray();
    }
}
```

The **GreeterClassLoader** declares two instance variables, **classes** and **basePath**. The **classes** variable, a **Hashtable**, is used to store for each type this class loader object loads the type's name and a reference to its **Class** instance. The **basePath** variable, a **String**, is used to store the directory path (passed to **GreetingClassLoader**'s constructor) in which the **loadClass()** method should look for the class file of the type it has been requested to load.

The **loadClass()** method begins by checking to see whether the requested type has already been loaded by this class loader. It does so by looking up the type name passed in parameter **name** in the **Hashtable**. If the name exists in the **Hashtable**, **loadClass()** retrieves and returns the **Class** instance for that name:

```
// Check the local cache
result = (Class) classes.get(className);
if (result != null) {
    // Return a cached class
    return result;
}
```

Why does **GreeterClassLoader** maintain a list of the types it has loaded? As mentioned earlier in this chapter, the virtual machine maintains its own list of type names that have already been requested of each class loader. When loading superclasses in step 1 of resolution, the virtual machine always checks its own internal list before automatically invoking **loadClass()**. As a result, the virtual machine will never automatically invoke **loadClass()** on a class loader object with the name of a type already loaded by that class loader object. Nevertheless, **GreeterClassLoader** maintains its own list of the names of the types it has already loaded. Why? Because even though the virtual machine will never ask a class loader object to load the same type twice, the application just might.

As an example, imagine the **Greet** application were invoked with this command line:

```
java Greet greeters Hello Hello Hello Hello Hello
```

Given this command line, the **Greet** application would invoke **loadClass()** with the name **Hello** five times on the same **GreeterClassLoader** object. The first time, the **GreeterClassLoader** would load the class and add its name and **Class** instance to the **Hashtable**. The next four times, however, the **GreeterClassLoader** would simply extract the **Class** instance for **Hello** from its **Hashtable** and return that. It would load class **Hello** only once.

If the **loadClass()** method determines that the requested type has not been loaded into its name-space, it next passes the name of the requested type to **findSystemClass()**:

```
// Check with the primordial class loader
try {
    result = super.findSystemClass(className);
    // Return a system class
    return result;
}
catch (ClassNotFoundException e) {
}
```

When the **findSystemClass()** method is invoked, the primordial class loader attempts to load the type. If it successfully loads the type, the primordial class loader also links and initializes the type. (As mentioned earlier in this chapter, if the type is a class, the primordial class loader makes sure all the class's superclasses are loaded, linked, and initialized as well.) **findSystemClass()** returns the **Class** instance created by the primordial class loader when it successfully loaded the type, and **loadClass()** returns that same **Class** instance. Note that classes loaded via **findSystemClass()** are marked as having been loaded by the primordial class loader. The **loadClass()** method of **GreeterClassLoader** does not add the name of such types to its **Hashtable**.

If the primordial class loader cannot load the type, **findSystemClass()** throws **ClassNotFoundError**. In this case, the **loadClass()** method next checks to make sure the requested class is not part of the **java** package:

```
// Don't attempt to load a system file except through
// the primordial class loader
if (className.startsWith("java.")) {
    throw new ClassNotFoundException();
}
```

This check prevents members of the standard `java` packages (`java.lang`, `java.io`, and so on) from being loaded by anything but the primordial class loader. As mentioned in Chapter 3, "Security," class loader objects should not attempt to custom load types that declare themselves to be part of the Java API (or any other "restricted" packages) but that can't be loaded by the primordial class loader.

If the type name doesn't begin with `java`, the `loadClass()` method next invokes `getTypeFromBasePath()`, which attempts to import the binary data in the class loader object's custom way:

```
// Try to load it from the basePath directory.
classData = getTypeFromBasePath(className);
if (classData == null) {
    System.out.println("GCL - Can't load class: "
        + className);
    throw new ClassNotFoundException();
}
```

The `getTypeFromBasePath()` method looks for a file with the type name plus a `.class` extension in the base directory passed to the `GreeterClassLoader`'s constructor. If the `getTypeFromBasePath()` method cannot find the file, it returns a `null` result, and the `loadClass()` method throws `ClassNotFoundException`. Otherwise, `loadClass()` invokes `defineClass()`, passing the `byte` array returned by `getTypeFromBasePath()`:

```
// Parse it
result = defineClass(className, classData, 0,
    classData.length);
if (result == null) {
    System.out.println("GCL - Class format error: "
        + className);
    throw new ClassFormatError();
}
```

The `defineClass()` method uses the primordial class loader to complete the loading process: to parse the binary data into internal data structures and create a `Class` instance. The `defineClass()` method does not link and initialize the type. (As mentioned earlier in this chapter, if the type is a class, the `defineClass()` method also makes sure all the class's superclasses are loaded. It does so by invoking `loadClass()` on this class loader object for each superclass in the hierarchy that hasn't yet been loaded by this class loader, with the `resolve` flag set to `false`.)

If **defineClass()** is successful, it returns the newly created **Class** instance. The **loadClass()** method checks to see whether **resolve** is set to **true**. If so, it invokes **resolveClass()**, passing the **Class** instance returned by **defineClass()**. The **resolveClass()** method links and initializes the class. (As mentioned earlier in this chapter, **resolveClass()** also makes sure that, if the type is a class, all its superclasses are linked and initialized as well.)

```
if (resolveIt) {
    resolveClass(result);
}
```

Finally, the **loadClass()** method adds the name and **Class** instance for the newly loaded type into the class loader's **Hashtable** and returns the **Class** instance:

```
// Add newly loaded type to private name cache
classes.put(className, result);

// Return class from basePath directory
return result;
```

The **Greet** application demonstrates the flexibility inherent in Java's linking model. The **Greet** application does not know at compile-time what greeters it will be loading and dynamically linking to at runtime. In the preceding examples, class **Greet** invokes the **greet()** method in classes **Hello**, **Greetings**, **Salutations**, and **HowDoYouDo**. But if you look at **Greet**'s constant pool, it has no symbolic reference to any of these classes. It has only a symbolic reference to their shared superinterface, **COM.artima.greeter.Greeter**. Greeters themselves, as long as they implement the **COM.artima.greeter.Greeter** interface, can be anything and can be written and compiled anytime, even after the **Greet** application itself is compiled.

# Example: Unloading Unreachable Greeters

As an example of dynamically loaded types becoming unreachable and getting unloaded by the virtual machine, consider the following application:

```
// On CD-ROM in file linking/ex6/GreetAndForget.java
import COM.artima.greeter.*;

public class GreetAndForget {

    // Arguments to this application:
    //      args[0] - path name of directory in which class
    //                files for greeters are stored
    //      args[1], args[2], ... - class names of greeters
    //                to load and invoke the greet() method
    //                on.
    //
    // All greeters must implement the
    // COM.artima.greeter.Greeter interface.
    //
    static public void main(String[] args) {

        if (args.length <= 1) {
            System.out.println(
                "Enter base path and greeter class names"
                + "as args.");
            return;
        }

        for (int i = 1; i < args.length; ++i) {
            try {

                GreeterClassLoader gcl =
                    new GreeterClassLoader(args[0]);

                // Load the greeter specified on the
                // command line
                Class c = gcl.loadClass(args[i], true);

                // Instantiate it into a greeter object
                Object o = c.newInstance();

                // Cast the Object ref to the Greeter
                // interface type so greet() can be
                // invoked on it
                Greeter greeter = (Greeter) o;

                // Greet the world in this greeter's
                // special way
                greeter.greet();

                // Forget the class loader object, Class
                // instance, and greeter object
                gcl = null;
                c = null;
                o = null;
                greeter = null;
```

```
        // At this point, the types loaded through
        // the GreeterClassLoader object created
        // at the top of this for loop are
        // unreferenced and can be unloaded by the
        // virtual machine.
    }
    catch (Exception e) {
        e.printStackTrace();
    }
    }
    }
}
```

The **GreetAndForget** application accepts the same command-line arguments as the **Greet** application of the previous example. The first argument is a base directory path name where the **GreetAndForget** application will look for greeters. Subsequent arguments are greeter names. To understand this example, you should be familiar with the **Greet** application of the previous example.

Imagine you invoke the **GreetAndForget** application with the following command line:

```
java GreetAndForget greeters Surprise HiTime Surprise
```

The code for the **HiTime** greeter, which selects a different greeting based on the time of day, was shown previously in this chapter. The code for the **Surprise** greeter, which pseudo-randomly selects one of four helper greeters—**Hello**, **Greetings**, **Salutations**, or **HowDoYouDo**—and invokes its **greet()** method, is shown here:

```
// On CD-ROM in file linking/ex6/greeters/Surprise.java
import COM.artima.greeter.Greeter;

public class Surprise implements Greeter {

    public void greet() {

        // Choose one of four greeters pseudo-randomly and
        // invoke its greet() method.
        int choice = (int) (Math.random() * 3.99);

        Greeter g;

        switch(choice) {

        case 0:
```

```
            g = new Hello();
            g.greet();
            break;

        case 1:
            g = new Greetings();
            g.greet();
            break;

        case 2:
            g = new Salutations();
            g.greet();
            break;

        case 3:
            g = new HowDoYouDo();
            g.greet();
            break;
        }
    }
}
```

Given the preceding command line, the **GreetAndForget** application invokes the **greet()** method of the **Surprise** greeter first, then the **HiTime** greeter, and then the **Surprise** greeter again. **GreetAndForget**'s actual output would vary depending on the time of day and **Surprise**'s pseudo-random mood. For the purposes of this example, assume that you typed in the preceding command, pressed Return, and got the following output:

```
How do you do, globe!
Good afternoon, world!
Greetings, planet!
```

This output indicates **Surprise** chose to execute **HowDoYouDo**'s **greet()** method the first time around and **Greetings**'s **greet()** method the second time around.

For the first pass through **GreetAndForget**'s for loop, the virtual machine loads the **Surprise** class and invokes its **greet()** method. The constant pool for **Surprise** includes a symbolic reference to each of the four helper greeters that it can choose: **Hello**, **Greetings**, **Salutations**, and **HowDoYouDo**. Assuming the Java Virtual Machine that you used to run the **GreetAndForget** application uses late resolution, only one of these four symbolic references will be resolved during the first pass of **GreetAndForget**'s for loop: the symbolic reference to **HowDoYouDo**. The virtual machine resolves this symbolic reference when it executes the bytecodes that correspond to the following statement in **Surprise**'s **greet()** method:

```
g = new HowDoYouDo();
```

To resolve the symbolic reference from **Surprise**'s constant pool to **HowDoYouDo**, the virtual machine invokes the **GreeterClassLoader** object's **loadClass()** method, passing the string **"HowDoYouDo"** in the **name** parameter and setting the **resolve** flag to **true**. The virtual machine uses the **GreeterClassLoader** object to load **HowDoYouDo** because **Surprise** was loaded through the **GreeterClassLoader** object. As mentioned earlier in this chapter, when the Java Virtual Machine resolves a symbolic reference, it uses the same class loader that loaded the referencing type (in this case, **Surprise**) to load the referenced type (in this case, **HowDoYouDo**).

After **Surprise**'s **greet()** method has created a new **HowDoYouDo** instance, it invokes its **greet()** method:

```
g.greet();
```

As the virtual machine executes **HowDoYouDo**'s **greet()** method, it must resolve two symbolic references from **HowDoYouDo**'s constant pool—one to class **java.lang.System** and another to class **java.io.PrintStream**. To resolve these symbolic references, the virtual machine invokes the **GreeterClassLoader** object's **loadClass()** method, once with the name **java.lang.System** and once with the name **java.io.PrintStream**. As before, the virtual machine uses the **GreeterClassLoader** object to load these classes because the referencing class—in this case, **HowDoYouDo**— was loaded through the **GreeterClassLoader** object. But these two classes, both members of the Java API, will end up being loaded by the primordial class loader anyway.

Remember that before the **loadClass()** method of **GreeterClassLoader** attempts to look for a requested type in the base directory (in this case, directory **greeters**), it invokes **findSystemClass()**. Because **findSystemClass()**, which uses the primordial class loader to try to load the requested type, can load both **java.lang.System** and **java.io.PrintStream**, the **loadClass()** method will simply return the **Class** instance returned by **findSystemClass()**. These classes will be marked not as having been loaded by the **GreeterClassLoader** object, but as having been loaded by the primordial class loader. To resolve any references from **java.lang.System** or **java.io.PrintStream**, the virtual machine will not invoke the **loadClass()** method of the **GreeterClassLoader** object. It will just use the primordial class loader directly.

As a result, after **Surprise**'s **greet()** method has returned, two types will be marked as having been loaded by the **GreeterClassLoader** object: class **Surprise** and class **HowDoYouDo**. These two types will be in the virtual machine's internal list of the types loaded by the **GreeterClassLoader** object and will appear in the **Hashtable** pointed to by the **GreeterClassLoader** object's **classes** instance variable.

Just after **Surprise**'s **greet()** method returns, the **Class** instances for **Surprise** and **HowDoYouDo** can be reached by the application. The garbage collector will not reclaim the space occupied by these **Class** instances because the application's code can access and use them. See Figure 8-11 for a graphical depiction of the reachability of these two **Class** instances.

The **Class** instance for **Surprise** can be reached in three ways. First, it can be reached directly from local variable **c** of **GreetAndForget**'s **main()** method. Second, it can be reached from local variables **o** and **greeter**, which both point to the same **Surprise** object. From the **Surprise** object, the virtual machine can get at **Surprise**'s type data, which includes a reference to **Surprise**'s **Class** object. The third way the **Class** instance for **Surprise** can be reached is through the **gcl** local variable of **GreetAndForget**'s **main()** method. This local variable points to the **GreeterClassLoader** object, which includes a reference to a **HashTable** object in which a reference to **Surprise**'s **Class** instance is stored.

The **Class** instance for **HowDoYouDo** can be reached in two ways. One way is identical to the one of the paths to the **Class** instance for **Surprise**: the **gcl** local variable of **GreetAndForget**'s **main()** method points to the

**Figure 8-11.**
The reachability of the **Class** instances for **Surprise** and **HowDoYouDo**.

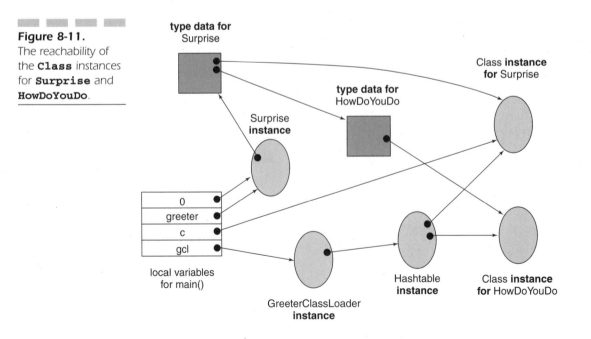

type data for
Surprise

Class **instance**
**for** Surprise

type data for
HowDoYouDo

Surprise
**instance**

0
greeter
c
gcl

local variables
for main()

Hashtable
**instance**

Class **instance**
**for** HowDoYouDo

GreeterClassLoader
**instance**

GreeterClassLoader object, which includes a reference to a HashTable object. The Hashtable contains a reference to HowDoYouDo's Class instance. The other way to reach HowDoYouDo's class instance is through Surprise's constant pool.

When the virtual machine resolved the symbolic reference from Surprise's constant pool to HowDoYouDo, it replaced the symbolic reference with a direct reference. The direct reference points to HowDoYouDo's type data, which includes a reference to HowDoYouDo's Class instance.

Thus, starting from Surprise's constant pool, the Class instance to HowDoYouDo is reachable. But why would the garbage collector look at direct references emanating from Surprise's constant pool in the first place? Because Surprise's Class instance can be reached. When the garbage collector finds that it can reach Surprise's Class instance, it makes sure it marks the Class instances for any types that are directly referenced from Surprise's constant pool as reachable. If Surprise is still live, the virtual machine can't unload any types Surprise might need to use.

Of the three ways that Surprise's Class instance can be reached, none of them involve a constant pool of another type. Surprise does not appear as a symbolic reference in the constant pool for GreetAndForget. Class GreetAndForget did not know about Surprise at compile-time. Instead, the GreetAndForget application decided at runtime to load and link to class Surprise. Thus, the Class instance for class Surprise can be reached only by starting from the local variables of GreetAndForget's main() method. Unfortunately for Surprise (and ultimately for HowDoYouDo), this approach does not constitute a very firm grasp on life.

The next four statements in GreetAndForget's main() method will change the reachability situation completely:

```
// Forget the class loader object, Class
// instance, and greeter object
gcl = null;
c = null;
o = null;
greeter = null;
```

These statements null out all four starting places from which Surprise's Class instance can be reached. As a result, after these statements have been executed, the Class instance for Surprise can no longer be reached. These statements also render unreachable the Class instance for HowDoYouDo, the Surprise instance that was formerly pointed to by the o and greeter variables, the GreeterClassLoader instance that was formerly pointed to by the gcl variable, and the Hashtable instance that was pointed to by the classes variable of the GreeterClassLoader object. All five of these objects are now available for garbage collection.

When (and if) the garbage collector gets around to freeing the unreferenced **Class** instances for **Surprise** and **HowDoYouDo**, it can also free up all the associated type data in the method area for **Surprise** and **HowDoYouDo**. Because these class's **Class** instances are unreachable, the types themselves are unreachable and can be unloaded by the virtual machine.

Note that two iterations of the for loop later (given the command line shown earlier), the **GreetAndForget** application will again load class **Surprise**. Keep in mind that the virtual machine will not reuse the type data for **Surprise** that was loaded during the first pass of the for loop. Granted, that type data became available for unloading at the end of the first pass. But even if the **Class** instance for **Surprise** hadn't become unreferenced at the end of the first pass, the type data from the first pass wouldn't be reused during the third pass.

With each pass of the for loop, the **main()** method of **GreetAndForget** creates a new **GreeterClassLoader** object. Thus, every greeter that **GreetAndForget** loads is loaded through a different class loader object. For example, if you invoke the **GreetAndForget** application with the **Hello** greeter listed five times on the command line, the application will create five instances of class **GreeterClassLoader**. The **Hello** greeter will be loaded five times by five different class loader objects. The method area will contain five different copies of the type data for **Hello**. The heap will contain five **Class** instances that represent the **Hello** class—one for each name-space into which **Hello** is loaded. When one of the **Class** instances for **Hello** becomes unreferenced, only the **Hello** type data associated with that particular **Class** instance would be available for unloading.

# On the CD-ROM

The CD-ROM contains the source code examples from this chapter in the **linking** directory.

# The Resources Page

For more information about the material presented in this chapter, visit the resources page at: **http://www.artima.com/insidejvm/linking.html**.

# 9

# Garbage Collection

The Java Virtual Machine's heap stores all objects created by a running Java application. Objects are created by the **new**, **newarray**, **anewarray**, and **multianewarray** instructions but never freed explicitly by the code. Garbage collection is the process of automatically freeing objects that are no longer referenced by the program.

This chapter does not describe an official Java garbage-collected heap because none exists. As mentioned in earlier chapters, the Java Virtual Machine specification does not require any particular garbage-collection technique. It doesn't even require garbage collection at all. But until infinite memory is invented, most Java Virtual Machine implementations will likely come with garbage-collected heaps. This chapter describes various garbage-collection techniques and explains how garbage collection works in Java Virtual Machines.

Accompanying this chapter on the CD-ROM is an applet that interactively illustrates the material presented in the chapter. The applet, named *Heap of Fish*, simulates a garbage-collected heap in a Java Virtual Machine. The simulation—which demonstrates a compacting, mark-and-sweep collector—allows you to interact with the heap as if you were a Java program: you can allocate objects and assign references to variables. The simulation also allows you to interact with the heap as if you were the Java Virtual Machine: you can drive the processes of garbage collection and heap compaction. At the end of this chapter, you will find a description of this applet and instructions on how to use it.

# Why Garbage Collection?

The name *garbage collection* implies that objects no longer needed by the program are "garbage" and can be thrown away. A more accurate and up-to-date metaphor might be *memory recycling*. When an object is no longer referenced by the program, the heap space it occupies can be recycled so that the space is made available for subsequent new objects. The garbage collector must somehow determine which objects are no longer referenced by the program and make available the heap space occupied by such unreferenced objects. In the process of freeing unreferenced objects, the garbage collector must run any finalizers of objects being freed.

In addition to freeing unreferenced objects, a garbage collector also can combat heap fragmentation. Heap fragmentation occurs through the course of normal program execution. New objects are allocated, and unreferenced objects are freed such that free portions of heap memory are left in between portions occupied by live objects. Requests to allocate new objects may have to be filled by extending the size of the heap even though enough total unused space is available in the existing heap. This situation will happen if there is not enough contiguous free heap space available into which the new object will fit. On a virtual memory system, the extra paging (or swapping) required to service an ever-growing heap can degrade the performance of the executing program. On an embedded system with low memory, fragmentation could cause the virtual machine to "run out of memory" unnecessarily.

Garbage collection relieves you from the burden of freeing allocated memory. Knowing when to explicitly free allocated memory can be very tricky. Giving this job to the Java Virtual Machine has several advantages. First, it can make you more productive. When programming in non-garbage-collected languages, you can spend many late hours (or days or weeks) chasing down an elusive memory problem. When programming in Java, you can use that time more advantageously by getting ahead of schedule or simply going home to have a life.

A second advantage of garbage collection is that it helps ensure program integrity. Garbage collection is an important part of Java's security strategy. Java programmers cannot accidentally (or purposely) crash the Java Virtual Machine by incorrectly freeing memory.

A potential disadvantage of a garbage-collected heap is that it adds an overhead that can affect program performance. The Java Virtual Machine has to keep track of which objects are being referenced by the executing program, and finalize and free unreferenced objects on the fly. This activity will likely require more CPU time than would have been required if the program explicitly freed unnecessary memory. In addition, programmers in a garbage-collected environment have less control over the scheduling of CPU time devoted to freeing objects that are no longer needed.

# Garbage-Collection Algorithms

Any garbage-collection algorithm must do two basic things. First, it must detect garbage objects. Second, it must reclaim the heap space used by the garbage objects and make the space available again to the program.

Garbage detection is ordinarily accomplished by defining a set of roots and determining *reachability* from the roots. An object is reachable if there is some path of references from the roots by which the executing program can access the object. The roots are always accessible to the program. Any objects that are reachable from the roots are considered "live." Objects that are not reachable are considered garbage because they can no longer affect the future course of program execution.

The root set in a Java Virtual Machine is implementation dependent but would always include any object references in the local variables and operand stack of any stack frame and any object references in any class variables. Other sources of roots are any object references, such as strings, in the constant pool of loaded classes. The constant pool of a loaded class can refer to strings stored on the heap, such as the class name, superclass name, superinterface names, field names, field signatures, method names, and method signatures. Another source of roots can be any object references that were passed to native methods that haven't been "released" by the native method. (Depending on the native method interface, a native method might be able to release references by simply returning, by explicitly invoking a call back that releases passed references, or some combination of both.) Another potential source of roots is any part of the Java

Virtual Machine's runtime data areas that are allocated from the garbage-collected heap. For example, the class data in the method area itself could be placed on the garbage-collected heap in some implementations, allowing the same garbage-collection algorithm that frees objects to detect and unload unreferenced classes.

Any object referred to by a root is reachable and is therefore a live object. Additionally, any objects referred to by a live object are also reachable. The program can access any reachable objects, so these objects must remain on the heap. Any objects that are not reachable can be garbage collected because the program has no way of accessing them.

The Java Virtual Machine can be implemented such that the garbage collector knows the difference between a genuine object reference and a primitive type (for example, an `int`) that appears to be a valid object reference. (One example is an `int` that, if it were interpreted as a native pinter, would point to an object on the heap.) Some garbage collectors, however, may choose not to distinguish between genuine object references and look-alikes. Such garbage collectors are called *conservative* because they may not always free every unreferenced object. Sometimes a garbage object will be wrongly considered to be live by a conservative collector because an object reference look-alike referred to it. Conservative collectors trade off an increase in garbage-collection speed for occasionally not freeing some actual garbage.

Two basic approaches to distinguishing live objects from garbage are *reference counting* and *tracing*. Reference-counting garbage collectors distinguish live objects from garbage objects by keeping a count for each object on the heap. The count keeps track of the number of references to that object. Tracing garbage collectors actually trace out the graph of references starting with the root nodes. Objects that are encountered during the trace are marked in some way. After the trace is complete, unmarked objects are known to be unreachable and can be garbage collected.

# Reference-Counting Collectors

Reference counting was an early garbage-collection strategy. In this approach, a reference count is maintained for each object on the heap. When an object is first created and a reference to it is assigned to a variable, the object's reference count is set to one. When any other variable is assigned a reference to that object, the object's count is incremented. When a reference to an object goes out of scope or is assigned a new value, the object's count is decremented. Any object with a reference count of zero can be garbage collected. When an object is garbage collected, any objects that it refers to have their reference counts decremented. In this way, the garbage collection of one object can lead to the subsequent garbage collection of other objects.

An advantage of this approach is that a reference-counting collector can run in small chunks of time closely interwoven with the execution of the program. This characteristic makes it particularly suitable for real-time environments in which the program can't be interrupted for very long. A disadvantage is that reference counting does not detect *cycles*: two or more objects that refer to one another. An example of a cycle is a parent object that has a reference to a child object that has a reference back to the parent. These objects will never have a reference count of zero even though they may be unreachable by the roots of the executing program. Another disadvantage of reference counting is the overhead of incrementing and decrementing the reference count each time.

Because of the disadvantages inherent in the reference counting approach, this technique is currently out of favor. It is more likely that the Java Virtual Machines you encounter in the real world will use a tracing algorithm in their garbage-collected heaps.

## Tracing Collectors

Tracing garbage collectors trace out the graph of object references starting with the root nodes. Objects that are encountered during the trace are marked in some way. Marking is generally done by either setting flags in the objects themselves or by setting flags in a separate bitmap. After the trace is complete, unmarked objects are known to be unreachable and can be garbage collected.

The basic tracing algorithm is called *mark and sweep*. This name refers to the two phases of the garbage-collection process. In the mark phase, the garbage collector traverses the tree of references and marks each object it encounters. In the sweep phase, unmarked objects are freed, and the resulting memory is made available to the executing program. In the Java Virtual Machine, the sweep phase must include finalization of objects.

# Compacting Collectors

Garbage collectors of Java Virtual Machines will likely have a strategy to combat heap fragmentation. Two strategies commonly used by mark-and-sweep collectors are compacting and copying. Both of these approaches move objects on the fly to reduce heap fragmentation. Compacting collectors slide live objects over free memory space toward one end of the heap. In the process, the other end of the heap becomes one large, contiguous free area. All references to the moved objects are updated to refer to the new location.

Updating references to moved objects is sometimes made simpler by adding a level of indirection to object references. Instead of referring directly to objects on the heap, object references refer to a table of object handles. The object handles refer to the actual objects on the heap. When an object is moved, only the object handle must be updated with the new location. All references to the object in the executing program will still refer to the updated handle, which did not move. Although this approach simplifies the job of heap defragmentation, it adds a performance overhead to every object access.

# Copying Collectors

Copying garbage collectors move all live objects to a new area. As the objects are moved to the new area, they are placed side by side, thus eliminating any free space that may have separated them in the old area. The old area is then known to be all free space. The advantage of this approach is that objects can be copied as they are discovered by the traversal from the root nodes. No separate mark-and-sweep phases are made. Objects are copied to the new area on the fly, and forwarding pointers are left in their old locations. The forwarding pointers allow the garbage collector to detect references to objects that have already been moved. The garbage collector can then assign the value of the forwarding pointer to the references so they point to the object's new location.

A common copying collector algorithm is called *stop and copy*. In this scheme, the heap is divided into two regions. Only one of the two regions is used at any time. Objects are allocated from one of the regions until all the space in that region has been exhausted. At that point, program execution is stopped, and the heap is traversed. Live objects are copied to the other region as they are encountered by the traversal. When the stop-and-copy procedure is finished, program execution resumes. Memory will be allocated from the new heap region until it too runs out of space. At that point, the program will once again be stopped. The heap will be traversed, and live objects will be copied back to the original region. The cost associated with this approach is that twice as much memory is needed for a given amount of heap space because only half of the available memory is used at any time.

You can see a graphical depiction of a garbage-collected heap that uses a stop-and-copy algorithm in Figure 9-1. This figure shows nine snapshots of the heap over time. In the first snapshot, the lower half of the heap is unused space. The upper half of the heap is partially filled by objects. The portion of the heap that contains objects is painted with diagonal gray lines. The second snapshot shows that the top half of the heap is gradually being filled up with objects until it becomes full, as shown in the third snapshot.

At that point, the garbage collector stops the program and traces out the graph of live objects starting with the root nodes. It copies each live object it encounters down to the bottom half of the heap, placing each object next to the previously copied object. This process is shown in snapshot four.

Snapshot five shows the heap after the garbage collection has finished. Now the top half of the heap is unused, and the bottom half is partially filled with live objects. The sixth snapshot shows the bottom half is now

**Figure 9-1.**
A stop-and-copy garbage-collected heap.

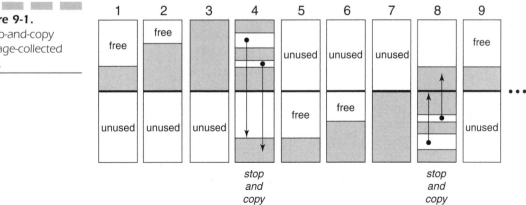

becoming gradually filled with objects, until it too becomes full in snapshot seven.

Once again, the garbage collector stops the program and traces out the graph of live objects. This time, it copies each live object it encounters up to the top half of the heap, as shown in snapshot eight. Snapshot nine shows the result of the garbage collection: the bottom half is once again unused space, and the top half is partially filled with objects. This process repeats again and again as the program executes.

# Generational Collectors

One disadvantage of simple stop-and-copy collectors is that *all* live objects must be copied at every collection. This facet of copying algorithms can be improved upon by taking into account two facts that have been empirically observed in most programs in a variety of languages:

1. Most objects created by most programs have very short lives.
2. Most programs create some objects that have very long lifetimes.

A major source of inefficiency in simple copying collectors is that they spend much of their time copying the same long-lived objects again and again.

Generational collectors address this inefficiency by grouping objects by age and garbage collecting younger objects more often than older objects. In this approach, the heap is divided into two or more subheaps, each of which serves one "generation" of objects. The youngest generation is garbage collected most often. As most objects are short-lived, only a small percentage of young objects are likely to survive their first collection. After an object has survived a few garbage collections as a member of the youngest generation, the object is promoted to the next generation: it is moved to another subheap. Each progressively older generation is garbage collected less often than the next younger generation. As objects "mature" (survive multiple garbage collections) in their current generation, they are moved to the next older generation.

The generational collection technique can be applied to mark-and-sweep algorithms as well as copying algorithms. In either case, dividing the heap into generations of objects can help improve the efficiency of the basic underlying garbage-collection algorithm.

# Adaptive Collectors

An adaptive garbage-collection algorithm takes advantage of the fact that some garbage-collection algorithms work better in some situations; whereas others work better in other situations. An adaptive algorithm monitors the current situation on the heap and adjusts its garbage-collection technique accordingly. It might tweak the parameters of a single garbage-collection algorithm as the program runs. It might switch from one algorithm to another on the fly. Or it might divide the heap into sub-heaps and use different algorithms on different subheaps simultaneously.

With an adaptive approach, designers of Java Virtual Machine implementations need not choose just one garbage-collection technique. They can employ many techniques, giving each algorithm work for which it is best suited.

# Finalization

In Java, an object can have a finalizer: a method that the garbage collector must run on the object prior to freeing the object. The potential existence of finalizers complicates the job of any garbage collector in a Java Virtual Machine.

To add a finalizer to a class, you simply declare a method in that class as follows:

```
// On CD-ROM in file gc/ex2/Example2.java
class Example2 {

    protected void finalize() throws Throwable {
        //...
        super.finalize();
    }
    //...
}
```

A garbage collector must examine all objects it has discovered to be unreferenced to see whether any include a `finalize()` method.

Because of finalizers, a garbage collector in the Java Virtual Machine must perform some extra steps each time it garbage collects. First, the garbage collector must in some way detect unreferenced objects (call this Pass I). Then it must examine the unreferenced objects it has detected to see whether any declare a finalizer. If it has enough time, it can at this point in the garbage-collection process finalize all unreference objects that declare finalizers.

After executing all finalizers, the garbage collector must once again detect unreferenced objects starting with the root nodes (call this Pass II). This step is needed because finalizers can "resurrect" unreferenced objects and make them referenced again. Finally, the garbage collector can free all objects that were found to be unreferenced in both Passes I and II.

To reduce the time required to free some memory, a garbage collector can optionally insert a step between the detection of unreferenced objects that have finalizers and the running of those finalizers. After the garbage collector has performed Pass I and found the unreferenced objects that need to be finalized, it can run a miniature trace starting not with the root nodes, but with the objects waiting to be finalized. Any objects that are (1) not reachable from the root nodes (those detected during Pass I) and (2) not reachable from the objects waiting to be finalized cannot be resurrected by any finalizer. These objects can be freed immediately.

If an object with a finalizer becomes unreferenced, and its finalizer is run, the garbage collector must in some way ensure that it never runs the finalizer on that object again. If that object is resurrected by its own finalizer or some other object's finalizer and later becomes unreferenced again, the garbage collector must treat it as an object that has no finalizer.

As you program in Java, you must keep in mind that the garbage collector runs finalizers on objects. Because you generally cannot predict exactly when unreferenced objects will be garbage collected, you cannot predict when object finalizers will be run. As mentioned in Chapter 2, "Platform Independence," you should avoid writing programs for which correctness depends on the timely finalization of objects. For example, if a finalizer of an unreferenced object releases a resource that is needed again later by the program, the resource will not be made available until after the garbage collector has run the object finalizer. If the program needs the resource before the garbage collector gets around to finalizing the unreferenced object, the program is out of luck.

# Heap of Fish: A Simulation

The *Heap of Fish* applet, shown in Figures 9-2 through 9-5, demonstrates a compacting, mark-and-sweep, garbage-collected heap. To facilitate compaction, this heap uses indirect handles to objects instead of direct references. It is called *Heap of Fish* because the only type of objects stored on the heap for this demonstration are fish objects, defined as follows:

```
// On CD-ROM in file gc/ex1/YellowFish.java
class YellowFish {

    YellowFish myFriend;
}

// On CD-ROM in file gc/ex1/BlueFish.java
class BlueFish {

    BlueFish myFriend;
    YellowFish myLunch;
}

// On CD-ROM in file gc/ex1/RedFish.java
class RedFish {

    RedFish myFriend;
    BlueFish myLunch;
    YellowFish mySnack;
}
```

As you can see, this applet has three classes of fish: red, yellow, and blue. The red fish is the largest because it has three instance variables. The yellow fish, with only one instance variable, is the smallest fish. The blue fish, which has two instance variables, is therefore medium-sized.

The instance variables of fish objects are references to other fish objects. **BlueFish.myLunch**, for example, is a reference to a **YellowFish** object. In this implementation of a garbage-collected heap, a reference to an object occupies 4 bytes. Therefore, the size of the instance data of a **RedFish** object is 12 bytes, a **BlueFish** object is 8 bytes, and a **YellowFish** object is 4 bytes.

*Heap of Fish* has five modes, which can be selected via radio buttons at the bottom left of the applet. When the applet starts, it is in swim mode. Swim mode is just a gratuitous animation, vaguely reminiscent of the familiar image of a big fish about to eat a medium-sized fish, which is about to eat a small fish. The other four modes—allocate fish, assign references, garbage collect, and compact heap—allow you to interact with the heap. In the allocate fish mode, you can instantiate new fish objects. In the assign references mode, you can build a network of local variables and fish that refer to other fish. In garbage collect mode, a mark-and-sweep operation will free any unreferenced fish. The compact heap mode allows you to slide heap objects so that they are side by side at one end of the heap, leaving all free memory as one large contiguous block at the other end of the heap.

**Figure 9-2.**
The allocate fish
mode of the **Heap
of Fish** applet.

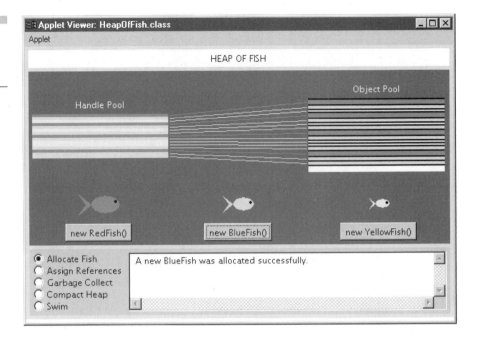

## Allocate Fish

The allocate fish mode, shown in Figure 9-2, allows you to allocate new fish objects on the heap. In this mode, you can see the two parts that make up the heap: the object pool and handle pool. The object pool is a contiguous block of memory from which space is taken for new objects. It is structured as a series of memory blocks. Each memory block has a four-byte header that indicates the length of the memory block and whether it is free. The headers are shown in the applet as black horizontal lines in the object pool.

The object pool in *Heap of Fish* is implemented as an array of **int**s. The first header is always at **objectPool[0]**. The object pool's series of memory blocks can be traversed by hopping from header to header. Each header gives the length of its memory block, which also reveals where the next header is going to be. The header of the next memory block will be the first **int** immediately following the current memory block.

When a new object is allocated, the object pool is traversed until a memory block is encountered with enough space to accommodate the new object. Allocated objects in the object pool are shown as colored bars. **YellowFish** objects are shown in yellow, **BlueFish** in blue, and **RedFish** in red. Free memory blocks, those that currently contain no fish, are shown in white.

The handle pool in *Heap of Fish* is implemented as an array of objects of a class named **ObjectHandle**. An **ObjectHandle** contains information about an object, including the vital index into the object pool array. The object pool index functions as a reference to the object's instance data in the object pool. The **ObjectHandle** also reveals information about the class of the fish object. As mentioned in Chapter 5, "The Java Virtual Machine," every object on the heap must in some way be associated with its class information stored in the method area. In *Heap of Fish*, the **ObjectHandle** associates each allocated object with information such as its class—whether it is a **RedFish**, **BlueFish**, or **YellowFish**—and some data used in displaying the fish in the applet user interface.

The handle pool exists to make it easier to defragment the object pool through compaction. References to objects, which can be stored in local variables of a stack or the instance variables of other objects, are not direct indexes into the object pool array. They are instead indexes into the handle pool array. When objects in the object pool are moved for compaction, only the corresponding **ObjectHandle** must be updated with the object's new object pool array index.

Each handle in the handle pool that refers to a fish object is shown as a horizontal bar painted the same color as the fish to which it refers. A line connects each handle to its fish instance variables in the object pool. Those handles that are not currently in use are drawn in white.

## Assign References

The assign references mode, shown in Figure 9-3, allows you to build a network of references between local variables and allocated fish objects. A reference is merely a local or instance variable that contains a valid object reference. Three local variables serve as the roots of garbage collection, one for each class of fish. If you do not link any fish to local variables, then all fish will be considered unreachable and freed by the garbage collector.

The assign references mode has three submodes: move fish, link fish, and unlink fish. You can select the submode via radio buttons at the bottom of the canvas upon which the fish appear. In move fish mode, you can click on a fish and drag it to a new position. You might want to do so to make your links more visible or just because you feel like rearranging fish in the sea.

In link fish mode, you can click on a fish or local variable and drag a link to another fish. The fish or local variable you initially drag from will be assigned a reference to the fish you ultimately drop upon. A line will

**Figure 9-3.**
The assign references
mode of the **Heap
of Fish** applet.

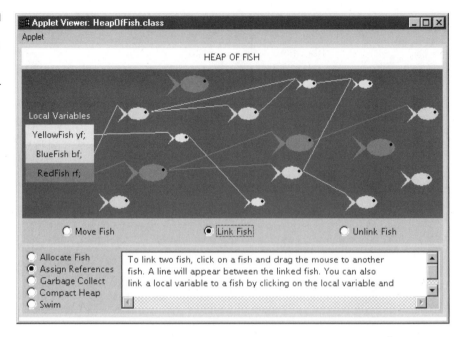

be shown connecting the two items. A line connecting two fish will be drawn between the nose of the fish with the reference to the tail of the referenced fish.

Class **YellowFish** has only one instance variable, **myFriend**, which is a reference to a **YellowFish** object. Therefore, a yellow fish can be linked to only one other yellow fish. When you link two yellow fish, the **myFriend** variable of the "dragged from" fish will be assigned the reference to the "dropped upon" fish. If this action were implemented in Java code, it might look like the following:

```
// Fish are allocated somewhere
YellowFish draggedFromFish = new YellowFish();
YellowFish droppedUponFish = new YellowFish();

// Sometime later the assignment takes place
draggedFromFish.myFriend = droppedUponFish;
```

Class **BlueFish** has two instance variables, **BlueFish myFriend** and **YellowFish myLunch**. Therefore, a blue fish can be linked to one blue fish and one yellow fish. Class **RedFish** has three instance variables, **RedFish myFriend**, **BlueFish myLunch**, and **YellowFish mySnack**. Red fish can therefore link to one instance of each class of fish.

In unlink fish mode, you can disconnect fish by moving the cursor over the line connecting two fish. When the cursor is over the line, the line will turn black. If you click a black line, the reference will be set to null and the line will disappear.

## Garbage Collect

The garbage collect mode, shown in Figure 9-4, allows you to drive the mark-and-sweep algorithm. The Step button at the bottom of the canvas takes you through the garbage-collection process one step at a time. You can reset the garbage collector at any time by clicking the Reset button. However, after the garbage collector has swept, the freed fish are gone forever. No manner of frantic clicking of the Reset button will bring them back.

The garbage-collection process is divided into a mark phase and a sweep phase. During the mark phase, the fish objects on the heap are traversed depth-first starting from the local variables. During the sweep phase, all unmarked fish objects are freed.

At the start of the mark phase, all local variables, fish, and links are shown in white. Each click of the Step button advances the depth-first traversal one more node. The current node of the traversal, either a local variable or a fish, is shown in magenta. As the garbage collector traverses down a branch, fish along the branch are changed from white to gray.

**Figure 9-4.**
The garbage collect mode of the **Heap of Fish** applet.

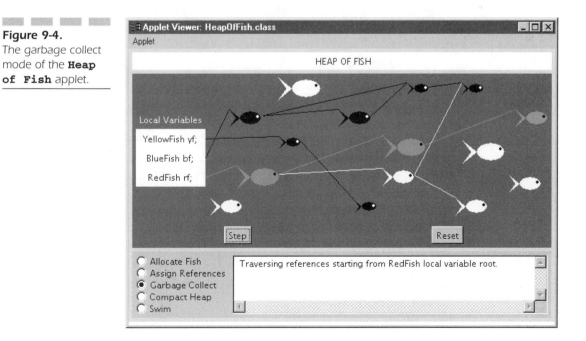

Gray indicates the fish has been reached by the traversal, but fish that have not been reached may yet be further down the branch. After the terminal node of a branch is reached, the color of the terminal fish is changed to black, and the traversal retreats back up the branch. After all links below a fish have been marked black, that fish is marked black, and the traversal returns back the way it came.

At the end of the mark phase, all reachable fish are colored black, and any unreachable fish are colored white. The sweep phase then frees the memory occupied by the white fish.

## Compact Heap

The compact heap mode, shown in Figure 9-5, allows you to move one object at a time to one end of the object pool. Each click of the Slide button will move one object. You can see that only the object instance data in the object pool moves; the handle in the handle pool does not move.

The *Heap of Fish* applet allows you to allocate new fish objects, link fish, garbage collect, and compact the heap. You can perform these activities in any order as much as you please. By playing around with this applet, you should be able to get a good idea how a mark-and-sweep garbage-

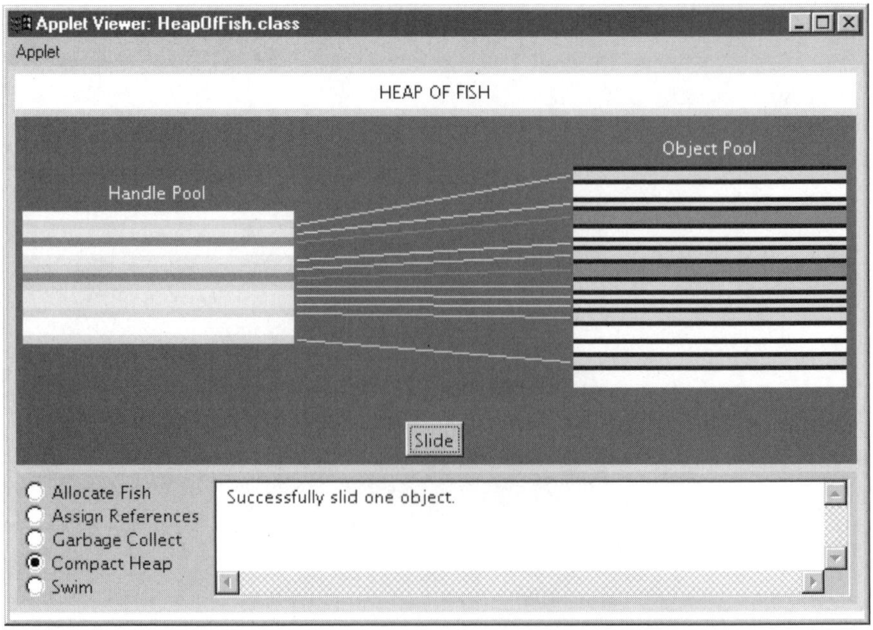

**Figure 9-5.**
The compact heap mode of the **Heap of Fish** applet.

collected heap works. Text at the bottom of the applet should help you as you go along. Happy clicking.

## On the CD-ROM

The CD-ROM contains the source code examples from this chapter in the **gc** directory. The *Heap of Fish* applet is contained in a web page on the CD-ROM in the file **applets/HeapOfFish.html**. The source code for this applet is found alongside its class files, in the **applets/HeapOfFish** directory.

## The Resources Page

For more information about the material presented in this chapter, visit the resources page: **http://www.artima.com/insidejvm/gc.html**.

# 10

# Stack and Local Variable Operations

As mentioned in Chapter 5, "The Java Virtual Machine," the abstract specification of the execution engine is defined in terms of an instruction set. The remaining chapters of this book (Chapters 10 through 20) are a tutorial of that instruction set. They describe the instructions in functional groups and give relevant background information for each group.

This chapter covers instructions that deal with the operand stack and local variables. As the Java Virtual Machine is a stack-based machine, almost all its instructions involve the operand stack in some way. Most instructions push values, pop values, or both as they perform their functions. This chapter describes the instructions that focus most exclusively on the operand stack—those that push constants onto the operand stack, perform generic stack operations, and transfer values back and forth between the operand stack and local variables.

Accompanying this chapter on the CD-ROM is an applet that interactively illustrates the material presented in the chapter. The applet, named *Fibonacci Forever*, simulates the Java Virtual Machine executing a method that generates the Fibonacci sequence. In the process, it demonstrates how the virtual machine pushes constants, pops values to local variables, and pushes values from local variables. At the end of this chapter, you will find a description of this applet and the bytecodes it executes.

# Pushing Constants onto the Stack

Many opcodes push constants onto the stack. Opcodes indicate the constant value to push in three different ways. The constant value is either implicit in the opcode itself, follows the opcode in the bytecode stream as an operand, or is taken from the constant pool.

Some opcodes by themselves indicate a type and constant value to push. For example, the `iconst_1` opcode tells the Java Virtual Machine to push integer value one. Such opcodes are defined for some commonly pushed numbers of various types. All these instructions are redundant to the instructions that take operands from the bytecode stream or refer to the constant pool, but these instructions are more efficient. Because these instructions occupy only one byte in the bytecode stream, they increase the efficiency of bytecode execution and reduce the size of bytecode streams. The opcodes that push `int`s and `float`s are shown in Table 10-1.

The opcodes shown in the Table 10-1 push `int`s and `float`s, which are single-word values. Each slot on the Java stack is one word in size (at least 32 bits wide). Therefore, each time an `int` or `float` is pushed onto the stack, it occupies one slot.

The opcodes shown in Table 10-2 push `long`s and `double`s. `long` and `double` values occupy 64 bits. Each time a `long` or `double` is pushed onto the stack, its value occupies two slots on the stack.

**Table 10-1.**

*Pushing single-word constants onto the stack*

| Opcode | Operand(s) | Description |
|---|---|---|
| **iconst_m1** | (none) | pushes **int** −1 onto the stack |
| **iconst_0** | (none) | pushes **int** 0 onto the stack |
| **iconst_1** | (none) | pushes **int** 1 onto the stack |
| **iconst_2** | (none) | pushes **int** 2 onto the stack |
| **iconst_3** | (none) | pushes **int** 3 onto the stack |
| **iconst_4** | (none) | pushes **int** 4 onto the stack |
| **iconst_5** | (none) | pushes **int** 5 onto the stack |
| **fconst_0** | (none) | pushes **float** 0 onto the stack |
| **fconst_1** | (none) | pushes **float** 1 onto the stack |
| **fconst_2** | (none) | pushes **float** 2 onto the stack |

**Table 10-2.**

*Pushing dual-word constants onto the stack*

| Opcode | Operand(s) | Description |
|---|---|---|
| **lconst_0** | (none) | pushes **long** 0 onto the stack |
| **lconst_1** | (none) | pushes **long** 1 onto the stack |
| **dconst_0** | (none) | pushes **double** 0 onto the stack |
| **dconst_1** | (none) | pushes **double** 1 onto the stack |

**Table 10-3.**

*Pushing a **null** reference onto the stack*

| Opcode | Operand(s) | Description |
|---|---|---|
| **aconst_null** | (none) | pushes a null object reference onto the stack |

One other opcode pushes an implicit constant value onto the stack. The **aconst_null** opcode, shown in Table 10-3, pushes a **null** object reference onto the stack.

As mentioned in earlier chapters, the format of an object reference depends on the Java Virtual Machine implementation. An object reference will somehow refer to a Java object on the garbage-collected heap. A **null** object reference indicates an object reference variable that does not currently refer to any valid object. The **aconst_null** opcode is used in the process of assigning **null** to an object reference variable.

Two opcodes indicate the constant to push with an operand that immediately follows the opcode. These opcodes, shown in Table 10-4, are used to push integer constants that are within the valid range for **byte** or **short** types. The **byte** or **short** that follows the opcode is expanded to an **int** before it is pushed onto the stack. Operations on **bytes** and **shorts** that have been pushed onto the stack are actually done on their **int** equivalents.

Three opcodes push constants from the constant pool. These opcodes take operands that specify a constant pool index. The Java Virtual Machine looks up the constant pool entry given the index, determines the constant's type and value, and pushes it onto the stack.

The constant pool index is an unsigned value that immediately follows the opcode in the bytecode stream. Opcodes **ldc** and **ldc_w** push a single-word item onto the stack, either an **int**, **float**, or an object reference to a **String**. The difference between **ldc** and **ldc_w** is that **ldc** can refer only to constant pool locations 1 through 255 because its index is just 1 byte. (Constant pool location zero is unused.) **ldc_w** has a 2-byte index, so it can refer to any constant pool location. **lcd2_w** also has a 2-byte index, and it is used to refer to any constant pool location containing a **long** or **double**, which occupies two words. The opcodes that push constants from the constant pool are shown in Table 10-5.

**Table 10-4.**

Pushing **byte** and **short** constants onto the stack

| Opcode | Operand(s) | Description |
|---|---|---|
| **bipush** | byte1 | expands byte1 (a **byte** type) to an **int** and pushes it onto the stack |
| **sipush** | byte1, byte2 | expands byte1, byte2 (a **short** type) to an **int** and pushes it onto the stack |

**Table 10-5.**

Pushing constant pool entries onto the stack

| Opcode | Operand(s) | Description |
|---|---|---|
| **ldc** | indexbyte1 | pushes single-word value from constant pool entry specified by indexbyte1 onto the stack |
| **ldc_w** | indexbyte1, indexbyte2 | pushes single-word value from constant pool entry specified by indexbyte1, indexbyte2 onto the stack |
| **ldc2_w** | indexbyte1, indexbyte2 | pushes dual-word value from constant pool entry specified by indexbyte1, indexbyte2 onto the stack |

All string literals from Java source code end up as entries in a constant pool. If multiple classes of the same application use the same string literal, that string literal will appear in the class file of every class that uses it. For example, if three classes use the string literal **"Harumph!"**, that string will appear in the constant pool of each of three class files. Methods of these classes can use the **ldc** or **ldc_w** instructions to push onto the operand stack a reference to a **String** object that has the value **"Harumph!"**.

As mentioned in Chapter 8, "The Linking Model," the Java Virtual Machine resolves all string literals that have the same sequence of characters into the same **String** object. In other words, if multiple classes use the same literal string, say **"Harumph!"**, the Java Virtual Machine will create only one **String** object with the value **"Harumph!"** to represent all those string literals.

When the virtual machine resolves the constant pool entry for a literal string, it "interns" the string. First, it checks to see whether the string's sequence of characters has already been interned. If so, it just uses the same reference as the already-interned string. Otherwise, it creates a new **String** object, adds a reference to the new **String** object to its set of interned strings, and uses the reference to the newly interned string.

## Generic Stack Operations

Although most instructions in the Java Virtual Machine's instruction set operate on a particular type, some instructions manipulate the stack independent of type. As mentioned in Chapter 5, these generic (typeless) instructions cannot be used to break up dual-word values. These instructions are shown in Table 10-6.

The last four instructions shown in Table 10-6 can be a bit difficult to understand. Consult the description of these instructions in Appendix A, "Instruction Set by Opcode Mnemonic," for a picture of the stack before and after these instructions have been executed.

## Pushing Local Variables onto the Stack

Several opcodes that push **int** and **float** local variables onto the operand stack exist. Some opcodes that implicitly refer to a commonly used local

**Table 10-6.**

Stack manipulation

| Opcode | Operand(s) | Description |
|---|---|---|
| nop | (none) | do nothing |
| pop | (none) | pop the top word from the operand stack |
| pop2 | (none) | pop the top two words from the operand stack |
| swap | (none) | swap the top operand stack two words |
| dup | (none) | duplicate top operand stack word |
| dup2 | (none) | duplicate top two operand stack words |
| dup_x1 | (none) | duplicate top operand stack word and put two down |
| dup_x2 | (none) | duplicate top operand stack word and put three down |
| dup2_x1 | (none) | duplicate top two operand stack words and put three down |
| dup2_x2 | (none) | duplicate top two operand stack words and put four down |

variable position are defined. For example, **iload_0** loads the **int** local variable at position zero. Other local variables are pushed onto the stack by an opcode that takes the local variable index from the first byte following the opcode. The **iload** instruction is an example of this type of opcode. The first byte following **iload** is interpreted as an unsigned 8-bit index that refers to a local variable.

The opcodes that push **int** and **float** local variables onto the stack are shown in Table 10-7.

Table 10-8 shows the instructions that push local variables of type **long** and **double** onto the stack. These instructions move two words from the local variable section of the stack frame to the operand stack section.

The final group of opcodes that push local variables move object references (which occupy one word) from the local variables section of the stack frame to the operand section. These opcodes are shown in Table 10-9.

# Popping to Local Variables

For each opcode that pushes a local variable onto the stack, a corresponding opcode exists that pops the top of the stack back into the local variable. The mnemonics of the pop opcodes can be formed from the mnemonics of the push opcodes by replacing "load" with "store." The opcodes that pop **int**s and **float**s from the top of the operand stack to a lo-

**Table 10-7.**

*Pushing single-word local variables onto the stack*

| Opcode | Operand(s) | Description |
|---|---|---|
| iload | vindex | pushes **int** from local variable position vindex |
| iload_0 | (none) | pushes **int** from local variable position zero |
| iload_1 | (none) | pushes **int** from local variable position one |
| iload_2 | (none) | pushes **int** from local variable position two |
| iload_3 | (none) | pushes **int** from local variable position three |
| fload | vindex | pushes **float** from local variable position vindex |
| fload_0 | (none) | pushes **float** from local variable position zero |
| fload_1 | (none) | pushes **float** from local variable position one |
| fload_2 | (none) | pushes **float** from local variable position two |
| fload_3 | (none) | pushes **float** from local variable position three |

**Table 10-8.**

*Pushing dual-word local variables onto the stack*

| Opcode | Operand(s) | Description |
|---|---|---|
| lload | vindex | pushes **long** from local variable positions vindex and (vindex + 1) |
| lload_0 | (none) | pushes **long** from local variable positions zero and one |
| lload_1 | (none) | pushes **long** from local variable positions one and two |
| lload_2 | (none) | pushes **long** from local variable positions two and three |
| lload_3 | (none) | pushes **long** from local variable positions three and four |
| dload | vindex | pushes **double** from local variable positions vindex and (vindex + 1) |
| dload_0 | (none) | pushes **double** from local variable positions zero and one |
| dload_1 | (none) | pushes **double** from local variable positions one and two |
| dload_2 | (none) | pushes **double** from local variable positions two and three |
| dload_3 | (none) | pushes **double** from local variable positions three and four |

cal variable are listed in Table 10-10. Each of these opcodes moves one single-word value from the top of the stack to a local variable.

Table 10-11 shows the instructions that pop values of type **long** and **double** into a local variable. These instructions move a dual-word value from the top of the operand stack to a local variable.

**Table 10-9.**

Pushing object reference local variables onto the stack

| Opcode | Operand(s) | Description |
|--------|-----------|-------------|
| **aload** | vindex | pushes object reference from local variable position vindex |
| **aload_0** | (none) | pushes object reference from local variable position zero |
| **aload_1** | (none) | pushes object reference from local variable position one |
| **aload_2** | (none) | pushes object reference from local variable position two |
| **aload_3** | (none) | pushes object reference from local variable position three |

**Table 10-10.**

Popping single-word values into local variables

| Opcode | Operand(s) | Description |
|--------|-----------|-------------|
| **istore** | vindex | pops **int** to local variable position vindex |
| **istore_0** | (none) | pops **int** to local variable position zero |
| **istore_1** | (none) | pops **int** to local variable position one |
| **istore_2** | (none) | pops **int** to local variable position two |
| **istore_3** | (none) | pops **int** to local variable position three |
| **fstore** | vindex | pops **float** to local variable position vindex |
| **fstore_0** | (none) | pops **float** to local variable position zero |
| **fstore_1** | (none) | pops **float** to local variable position one |
| **fstore_2** | (none) | pops **float** to local variable position two |
| **fstore_3** | (none) | pops **float** to local variable position three |

The final group of opcodes that pops to local variables are shown in Table 10-12. These opcodes pop an object reference from the top of the operand stack to a local variable.

# The wide Instruction

Unsigned 8-bit local variable indexes, such as the one that follows the **iload** instruction, limit the number of local variables in a method to 256. A separate instruction, **wide**, can extend an 8-bit index by another 8 bits, which raises the local variable limit to 65,536. The **wide** opcode modifies other opcodes. **wide** can precede an instruction, such as **iload**, that takes an 8-bit unsigned local variable index. Two bytes that form a 16-bit un-

**Table 10-11.**

Popping dual-word
values into local
variables

| Opcode | Operand(s) | Description |
|---|---|---|
| **lstore** | vindex | pops **long** to local variable positions vindex and (vindex + 1) |
| **lstore_0** | (none) | pops **long** to local variable positions zero and one |
| **lstore_1** | (none) | pops **long** to local variable positions one and two |
| **lstore_2** | (none) | pops **long** to local variable positions two and three |
| **lstore_3** | (none) | pops **long** to local variable positions three and four |
| **dstore** | vindex | pops **double** to local variable positions vindex and (vindex + 1) |
| **dstore_0** | (none) | pops **double** to local variable positions zero and one |
| **dstore_1** | (none) | pops **double** to local variable positions one and two |
| **dstore_2** | (none) | pops **double** to local variable positions two and three |
| **dstore_3** | (none) | pops **double** to local variable positions three and four |

**Table 10-12.**

Popping object
references into
local variables

| Opcode | Operand(s) | Description |
|---|---|---|
| **astore** | vindex | pops object reference to local variable position vindex |
| **astore_0** | (none) | pops object reference to local variable position zero |
| **astore_1** | (none) | pops object reference to local variable position one |
| **astore_2** | (none) | pops object reference to local variable position two |
| **astore_3** | (none) | pops object reference to local variable position three |

signed index into the local variables follow the **wide** opcode and the modified opcode.

Table 10-13 lists all but two of the opcodes that can be modified by **wide**. The other two opcodes, **iinc** and **ret**, are described in later chapters. The **iinc** instruction and its **wide** variant are described in Chapter 12, "Integer Arithmetic." The **ret** instruction and its **wide** variant are described in Chapter 18, "Finally Clauses."

When verifying bytecode sequences that include **wide** instructions, the opcode modified by **wide** is seen as an operand to **wide**. Jump instructions are not allowed to jump directly to an opcode modified by **wide**. For example, if a bytecode sequence includes the instruction

```
wide iload 257
```

**Table 10-13.**

Popping object references into local variables

| Opcode | Operand(s) | Description |
|--------|------------|-------------|
| `wide` | `iload`, indexbyte1, indexbyte2 | pushes **int** from local variable position index |
| `wide` | `lload`, indexbyte1, indexbyte2 | pushes **long** from local variable position index |
| `wide` | `fload`, indexbyte1, indexbyte2 | pushes **float** from local variable position index |
| `wide` | `dload`, indexbyte1, indexbyte2 | pushes **double** from local variable position index |
| `wide` | `aload`, indexbyte1, indexbyte2 | pushes object reference from local variable position index |
| `wide` | `istore`, indexbyte1, indexbyte2 | pops **int** to local variable position vindex |
| `wide` | `lstore`, indexbyte1, indexbyte2 | pops **long** to local variable position index |
| `wide` | `fstore`, indexbyte1, indexbyte2 | pops **float** to local variable position index |
| `wide` | `dstore`, indexbyte1, indexbyte2 | pops **double** to local variable position index |
| `wide` | `astore`, indexbyte1, indexbyte2 | pops object reference to local variable position index |

No other opcode of that method's bytecode sequence would be allowed to jump directly to the `iload` opcode. In this case, the `iload` opcode must always be executed as an operand to the `wide` opcode.

# Fibonacci Forever: A Simulation

The *Fibonacci Forever* applet, shown in Figure 10-1, demonstrates a Java Virtual Machine executing a sequence of bytecodes that generate the Fibonacci series. The applet is embedded in a web page on the CD-ROM in the file `applets/FibonacciForever.html`. The bytecode sequence in the simulation was generated by the `javac` compiler for the `calcSequence()` method of the following class:

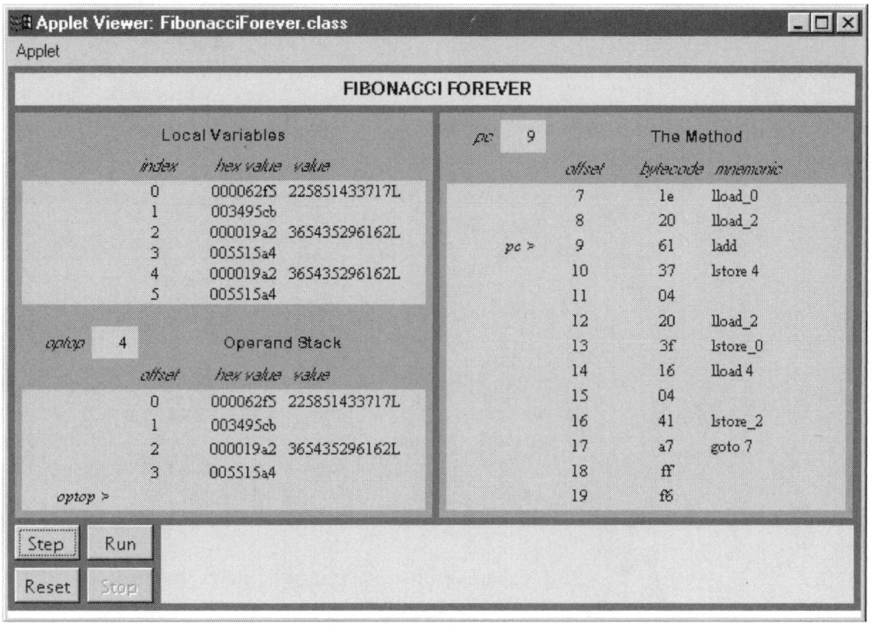

**Figure 10-1.**
The **Fibonacci**
**Forever** applet.

The **calcSequence()** method produces the Fibonacci series and places each Fibonacci number successively in the **fiboNum** variable. The first two numbers of the Fibonacci series are both ones. Each subsequent number is calculated by summing the previous two numbers, as in 1, 1, 2, 3, 5, 8, 13, 21, 34, 55, and so on.

The bytecodes generated by **javac** for the **calcSequence()** method are as follow:

```
// On CD-ROM in file stackops/ex1/Fibonacci.java
class Fibonacci {

    static void calcSequence() {
        long fiboNum = 1;
        long a = 1;
        long b = 1;

        for (;;) {
            fiboNum = a + b;
            a = b;
            b = fiboNum;
        }
    }
}
```

```
 0 lconst_1   // Push long constant 1
             // Pop long into local vars 0 & 1:
 1 lstore_0   // long a = 1;
 2 lconst_1   // Push long constant 1
             // Pop long into local vars 2 & 3:
 3 lstore_2   // long b = 1;
 4 lconst_1   // Push long constant 1
             // Pop long into local vars 4 & 5:
 5 lstore 4   // long fiboNum = 1;
 7 lload_0    // Push long from local vars 0 & 1
 8 lload_2    // Push long from local vars 2 & 3
 9 ladd       // Pop two longs, add them, push result
             // Pop long into local vars 4 & 5:
10 lstore 4   // fiboNum = a + b;
12 lload_2    // Push long from local vars 2 & 3
13 lstore_0   // Pop long into local vars 0 & 1: a = b;
14 lload 4    // Push long from local vars 4 & 5
             // Pop long into local vars 2 & 3:
16 lstore_2   // b = fiboNum;
17 goto 7     // Jump back to offset 7: for (;;) {}
```

The **javac** compiler placed local variable **a** from the source into local variable slots 0 and 1 on the stack frame. It put **b** into slots 2 and 3 and **fiboNum** into slots 4 and 5. As this method calculates each successive Fibonacci number, it places the number into the **fiboNum** variable. As you run the simulation, therefore, you will see the Fibonacci series appear in the **long** value stored in local variable slots 4 and 5.

You may notice that long values are split across the two words they occupy in the local variables by placing the lower half (bits 0 through 31) in the first slot and the upper half (bits 32 through 63) in the second slot. For example, the lower half of the **fiboNum** variable is stored in local variable slot 4. The upper half of **fiboNum** is stored in local variable slot 5. On the operand stack, a similar representation is used. When a **long** value is pushed onto the operand stack, the lower half of the word is pushed and then the upper half.

Keep in mind that this manner of representing **long** values in the local variables and on the operand stack is an artifact of this particular (simulated) implementation of the Java Virtual Machine. As mentioned in Chapter 5, the specification does not dictate any particular way to lay out **long**s and **double**s across the two words they occupy on the stack frame.

Although, according to the best mathematical minds, the Fibonacci series does indeed go on forever, the **calcSequence()** method can generate Fibonacci numbers only for a while. Unfortunately for **calcSequence()**, the **long** type has a finite range. The highest Fibonacci number this simulation can calculate, therefore, is the highest Fibonacci number that can be represented in a long: 7540113804746346429L. After the simulation arrives at this point in the Fibonacci series, the next addition will overflow.

To drive the *Fibonacci Forever* simulation, use the Step, Reset, Run, and Stop buttons. Each time you click the Step button, the simulator will execute the instruction pointed to by the pc register. If you click the Run button, the simulation will continue with no further coaxing on your part until you click the Stop button. To start the simulation over, click the Reset button. For each step of the simulation, a panel at the bottom of the applet contains an explanation of what the next instruction will do. Happy clicking.

## On the CD-ROM

The CD-ROM contains the source code examples from this chapter in the `stackops` directory. The *Fibonacci Forever* applet is contained in a web page on the CD-ROM in file `applets/FibonacciForever.html`. The source code for this applet is found alongside its class files, in the `applets/JVMSimulators` and `applets/JVMSimulators`.

## The Resources Page

For more information about the material presented in this chapter, visit the resources page: `http://www.artima.com/insidejvm/stackops.html`.

# 11

# Type Conversion

This chapter describes the instructions that convert values from one primitive type to another inside the Java Virtual Machine. It also looks at some of the idiosyncrasies of type conversion that arise from the virtual machine's limited support of **byte**s, **short**s, and **char**s.

Accompanying this chapter on the CD-ROM is an applet that interactively illustrates the material presented in the chapter. The applet, named *Conversion Diversion*, simulates the Java Virtual Machine executing a method that performs type conversion. At the end of this chapter, you will find a description of this applet and the bytecodes it executes.

# The Conversion Opcodes

The Java Virtual Machine includes many opcodes that convert from one primitive type to another. No operands follow the conversion opcodes in the bytecode stream. The value to convert is taken from the top of the stack. The Java Virtual Machine pops the value at the top of the stack, converts it, and pushes the result back onto the stack. Opcodes that convert between **int**, **long**, **float**, and **double** are shown in Table 11-1. An opcode is available for each possible from-to combination of these four types.

Opcodes that convert from an **int** to a type smaller than **int** are shown in Table 11-2. These opcodes pop one **int** off the operand stack; convert it to an **int** value that fits into a **byte**, **short**, or **char**; and push

**Table 11-1.**

Converting **ints, longs, floats,** and **doubles**

| Opcode | Operand(s) | Description |
|---|---|---|
| i2l | (none) | converts **int** to **long** |
| i2f | (none) | converts **int** to **float** |
| i2d | (none) | converts **int** to **double** |
| l2i | (none) | converts **long** to **int** |
| l2f | (none) | converts **long** to **float** |
| l2d | (none) | converts **long** to **double** |
| f2i | (none) | converts **float** to **int** |
| f2l | (none) | converts **float** to **long** |
| f2d | (none) | converts **float** to **double** |
| d2i | (none) | converts **double** to **int** |
| d2l | (none) | converts **double** to **long** |
| d2f | (none) | converts **double** to **float** |

**Table 11-2.**

Converting **ints, bytes, chars,** and **shorts.**

| Opcode | Operand(s) | Description |
|---|---|---|
| i2b | (none) | converts **int** to **byte** |
| i2c | (none) | converts **int** to **char** |
| i2s | (none) | converts **int** to **short** |

the resulting **int** back onto the operand stack. The **i2b** instruction truncates the popped **int** value to a **byte** and then sign-extends back out to an **int**. The **i2s** instruction truncates the popped **int** value to a **short** and then sign-extends back out to an **int**. The **i2c** instruction truncates the popped **int** value to a **char** and then zero-extends back out to an **int**.

No opcodes that convert directly from a **long**, **float**, or **double** to the types smaller than **int** exist. Therefore, converting from a **float** to a **byte**, for example, requires two steps. First, the **float** must be converted to an **int** with **f2i** and then the resulting **int** can be converted to a **byte** with **i2b**.

Although opcodes that convert an **int** to primitive types smaller than **int** (**byte**, **short**, and **char**) exist, no opcodes that convert in the opposite direction exist because any **byte**s, **short**s, or **char**s are effectively converted to **int** before being pushed onto the stack. The instructions that retrieve **byte**, **short**, and **char** values from arrays or objects on the heap and push them onto the stack convert the values to **int**. These instructions are described in Chapter 15, "Objects and Arrays."

Arithmetic operations on **byte**s, **short**s, and **char**s are done by first converting the values to **int**, performing the arithmetic operations on the **int**s, and being happy with an **int** result. If you add 2 **byte**s, therefore, you get an **int**, and if you want a **byte** result, you must explicitly convert the **int** result back to a **byte**. For example, the following code won't compile:

```
// On the CD-ROM in file opcodes/ex1/BadArithmetic.java
class BadArithmetic {

    static byte addOneAndOne() {
        byte a = 1;
        byte b = 1;
        byte c = a + b;
        return c;
    }
}
```

When presented with the preceding code, **javac** objects with the following remark:

```
BadArithmetic.java(7): Incompatible type for declaration.
Explicit cast needed to convert int to byte.
        byte c = a + b;
               ^
```

To remedy the situation, you must explicitly convert the **int** result of the addition of **a + b** back to a **byte**, as in the following code:

```
// On the CD-ROM in file opcodes/ex1/GoodArithmetic.java
class GoodArithmetic {

    static byte addOneAndOne() {
        byte a = 1;
        byte b = 1;
        byte c = (byte) (a + b);
        return c;
    }
}
```

This operation makes **javac** so happy that it drops a **GoodArithmetic.class** file, which contains the following bytecode sequence for the **addOneAndOne()** method:

```
 0 iconst_1      // Push int constant 1.
 1 istore_0      // Pop into local variable 0, which is a:
               // byte a = 1;
 2 iconst_1      // Push int constant 1 again.
 3 istore_1      // Pop into local variable 1, which is b:
               // byte b = 1;
 4 iload_0       // Push a (a is already stored as an int in
               // local
               // variable 0).
 5 iload_1       // Push b (b is already stored as an int in
               // local
               // variable 1).
 6 iadd          // Perform addition. Top of stack is
               // now (a + b), an int.
 7 i2b           // Convert int result to byte (result still
               // occupies 32 bits).
 8 istore_2      // Pop into local variable 3, which is
               // byte c: byte c = (byte) (a + b);
 9 iload_2       // Push the value of c so it can be
               // returned.
10 ireturn       // Proudly return the result of the
               // addition: return c;
```

# Conversion Diversion: A Simulation

The *Conversion Diversion* applet, shown in Figure 11-1, demonstrates a Java Virtual Machine executing a sequence of bytecodes. The applet is embedded in a web page on the CD-ROM in the file **applets/ ConversionDiversion.html**. The bytecode sequence in the simulation was generated by **javac** for the **Convert()** method of the following class:

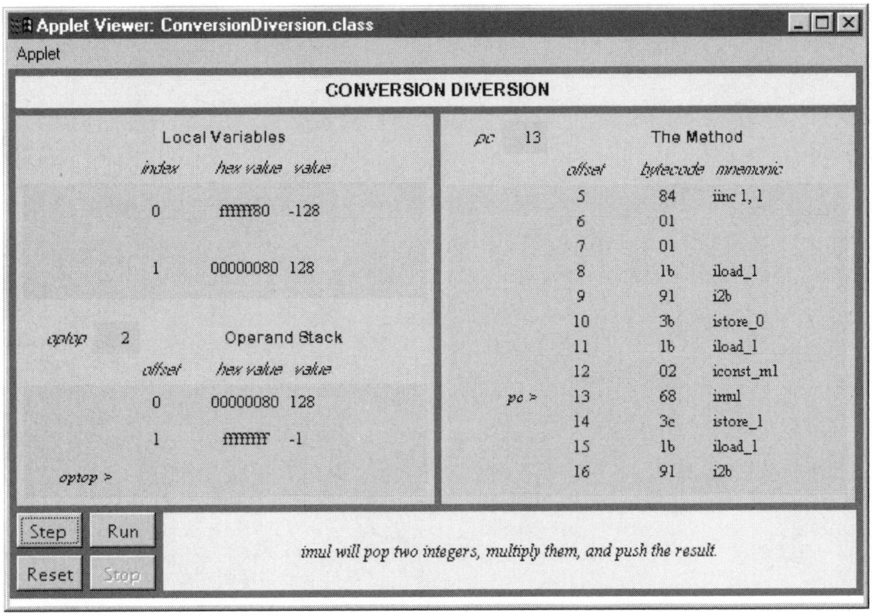

Figure 11-1.
The **Conversion Diversion** applet.

**Figure 11-1.**
The **Conversion Diversion** applet.

```
// On CD-ROM in file opcodes/ex1/Diversion.java
class Diversion {

    static void Convert() {

        byte imByte = 0;
        int imInt = 125;

        for (;;) {
            ++imInt;
            imByte = (byte) imInt;

            imInt *= -1;
            imByte = (byte) imInt;
            imInt *= -1;
        }
    }
}
```

The bytecodes generated by **javac** for **Convert()** are as follow:

```
0 iconst_0      // Push int constant 0.
               // Pop to local variable 0, which is
1 istore_0      // imByte: byte imByte = 0;
2 bipush 125    // Expand byte constant 125 to int and push.
               // Pop to local variable 1, which
4 istore_1      // is imInt: int imInt = 125;
               // Increment local variable 1 (imInt) by 1:
```

```
 5 iinc 1 1      // ++imInt;
 8 iload_1       // Push local variable 1 (imInt).
                 // Truncate and sign extend top of stack so
 9 i2b           // it has a valid byte value.
                 // Pop to local variable 0 (imByte):
10 istore_0      // imByte = (byte) imInt;
11 iload_1       // Push local variable 1 (imInt) again.
12 iconst_m1     // Push integer -1.
13 imul          // Pop top two ints, multiply, push result.
                 // Pop result of multiply to local variable
14 istore_1      // 1 (imInt): imInt *= -1;
15 iload_1       // Push local variable 1 (imInt).
                 // Truncate and sign extend top of stack
16 i2b           // so it has a valid byte value.
                 // Pop to local variable 0 (imByte):
17 istore_0      // imByte = (byte) imInt;
18 iload_1       // Push local variable 1 (imInt) again.
19 iconst_m1     // Push integer -1.
20 imul          // Pop top two ints, multiply, push result.
                 // Pop result of multiply to local variable
21 istore_1      // 1 (imInt): imInt *= -1;
                 // Jump back to the iinc instruction:
22 goto 5        // for (;;) {}
```

The `Convert()` method demonstrates the manner in which the Java Virtual Machine converts from **int** to **byte**. **imInt** starts out as 125. For each pass through the while loop, it is incremented and converted to a **byte**. Then it is multiplied by –1 and again converted to a **byte**. The simulation quickly shows what happens at the edges of the valid range for the **byte** type.

The maximum value for a **byte** is 127. The minimum value is –128. Values of type **int** that are within this range convert directly to **byte**. As soon as the **int** gets beyond the valid range for **byte**, however, things get interesting.

The Java Virtual Machine converts an **int** to a **byte** by truncating and sign extending. The highest order bit, the "sign bit," of **long**s, **int**s, **short**s, and **byte**s indicate whether the integer value is positive or negative. If the sign bit is zero, the value is positive. If the sign bit is one, the value is negative. Bit 7 of a **byte** value is its sign bit. To convert an **int** to a **byte**, bit 7 of the **int** is copied to bits 8 through 31. This action produces an **int** that has the same numerical value that the **int**'s lowest order byte would have if it were interpreted as a **byte** type. After the truncation and sign extension, the **int** will contain a valid **byte** value.

The simulation applet shows what happens when an **int** that is just beyond the valid range for **byte** types gets converted to a **byte**. For example, when the **imInt** variable has a value of 128 (0x00000080) and is converted to **byte**, the resulting **byte** value is –128 (0xffffff80). Later, when the **imInt** variable has a value of –129 (0xffffff7f) and is converted to **byte**, the resulting **byte** value is 127 (0x0000007f).

To drive the *Conversion Diversion* simulation, use the Step, Reset, Run, and Stop buttons. Each time you click the Step button, the simulator will execute the instruction pointed to by the pc register. If you click the Run button, the simulation will continue with no further coaxing on your part until you click the Stop button. To start the simulation over, click the Reset button. For each step of the simulation, a panel at the bottom of the applet contains an explanation of what the next instruction will do. Happy clicking.

# On the CD-ROM

The CD-ROM contains the source code examples from this chapter in the **opcodes** directory. The *Conversion Diversion* applet is contained in a web page on the CD-ROM in the file **applets/ConversionDiversion.html**. The source code for this applet is found alongside its class files, in the **applets/JVMSimulators** and **applets/JVMSimulators/COM/artima/ jvmsim** directories.

# The Resources Page

For more information about the material presented in this chapter, visit the resources page: **http://www.artima.com/insidejvm/typeconv.html**.

# 12

# Integer Arithmetic

This chapter describes integer arithmetic in the Java Virtual Machine. It explains two's-complement arithmetic (the mechanism used by the Java Virtual Machine to perform integer arithmetic) and describes the instructions that perform integer arithmetic.

Accompanying this chapter on the CD-ROM are two applets that interactively illustrate the material presented in the chapter. One applet, named Inner Int, allows you to view and manipulate the individual components that make up a two's-complement number. The other applet, named Prime Time, simulates the Java Virtual Machine executing a method that generates prime numbers. At the end of this chapter, you will find a description of this applet and the bytecodes it executes.

# Two's-Complement Arithmetic

All integer types supported by the Java Virtual Machine—**byte**s, **short**s, **int**s, and **long**s—are signed two's-complement numbers. The two's-complement scheme allows both positive and negative integers to be represented. The most significant bit of a two's-complement number is its sign bit. The sign bit is one for negative numbers and zero for positive numbers and for the number zero.

The number of unique values that can be represented by the two's-complement scheme is two raised to the power of the total number of bits. For example, the **short** type in Java is a 16-bit signed two's-complement integer. The number of unique integers that can be represented by this scheme is $2^{16}$, or 65,536. Half of the **short** type's range of values are used to represent zero and positive numbers; the other half of the **short** type's range are used to represent negative numbers. The range of negative values for a 16-bit two's-complement number is −32,768 (0x8000) to −1 (0xffff). Zero is 0x0000. The range of positive values is one (0x0001) to 32,767 (0x7fff).

Positive numbers are intuitive in that they are merely the base two representation of the number. Negative numbers can be calculated by adding the negative number to two raised to the power of the total number of bits. For example, the total number of bits in a **short** is 16, so the two's-complement representation of a negative number in the valid range for a **short** (−32,768 to −1) can be calculated by adding the negative number to $2^{16}$, or 65,536. The two's-complement representation for −1 is 65,536 + (−1) or 65,535 (0xffff). The two's-complement representation for −2 is 65,536 + (−2) or 65,534 (0xfffe).

Addition is performed on two's-complement signed numbers in the same way it would be performed on unsigned binary numbers. The two numbers are added, overflow is ignored, and the result is interpreted as a signed two's-complement number. This procedure will work as long as the result is actually within the range of valid values for the type. For example, to add 4 + (−2), just add 0x00000004 and 0xfffffffe. The result is actually 0x100000002, but because an **int** has only 32 bits, the overflow is ignored and the result becomes 0x00000002.

Overflow in integer operations does not throw any exception in the Java Virtual Machine. The result is merely truncated to fit into the result type (either **int** or **long**). For example, adding **int**s 0x7fffffff and 1 yields 0x80000000. Therefore, the Java Virtual Machine will report that 2,147,483,647 + 1 = −2,147,483,648 if the types of the values being added are **int**s, not **long**s. As you program in Java, you must keep in mind that overflow can happen. You must make sure you choose the appropriate type, **int** or **long**, in each situation. Integer division by zero does throw an **ArithmeticException**, so you should also keep in mind that this exception could be thrown and catch it if necessary.

If you encounter a situation in which **long** just isn't long enough, you can use the **BigInteger** class of the **java.math** package. Instances of this class are arbitrary-length integers. The **BigInteger** class supports all arithmetic operations on arbitrary-length integers that are provided for the primitive types by the Java Virtual Machine and the **java.lang.Math** package.

# Inner Int: A Java int Reveals Its Inner Nature

The *Inner Int* applet, shown in Figure 12-1, lets you play around with the two's-complement format of integers in the Java Virtual Machine. The Max and Min buttons will give you the maximum and minimum values of the **int** type. By clicking Max followed by ++, you can increment beyond the maximum integer and see what happens. Clicking Min followed by − − lets you decrement beyond the minimum integer. Both of these operations result in overflow, but no exceptions are thrown by the Java Virtual Machine. The applet is embedded in a web page on the CD-ROM in the file **applets/InnerInt.html**.

# Arithmetic Opcodes

The Java Virtual Machine offers several opcodes that perform integer arithmetic operations on **int**s and **long**s. As mentioned in earlier chap-

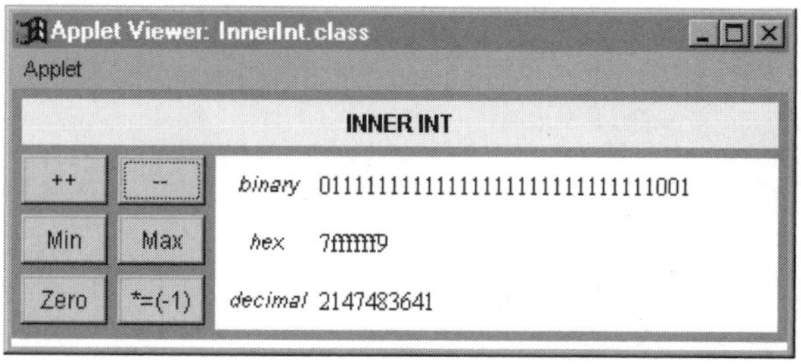

**Figure 12-1.**
The **Inner Int**
applet.

ters, values of type **byte, short**, and **char** are converted to **int** before they take part in arithmetic operations. For each opcode that performs arithmetic on **int**s, you will find a corresponding opcode that performs the same operation on **long**s.

Integer addition can be performed on **int**s and **long**s. Table 12-1 shows the opcodes that pop the top two values on the stack, add them, and push the resulting sum. The values to be added must have been pushed onto the stack by previous instructions. The type of the values is indicated by the opcode itself, and the result always has the same type as the numbers being added. No exceptions are thrown for any of these opcodes. Overflow is just ignored.

Table 12-2 shows the exception to the rule that arithmetic opcodes take their operands from the stack. The **iinc** opcode performs an addition on a local variable of type **int**. The local variable to increment is specified by the first byte that follows the **iinc** instruction in the bytecode stream. The amount to add to the local variable is taken from the second byte following the **iinc** instruction. The second byte is interpreted as an 8-bit signed two's-complement number. The local variable and 8-bit signed value are added, and the result is written back to the local variable. This opcode can be used to change a local variable value by any number between and including –128 through 127. This opcode makes for more efficient incrementing and decrementing of variables that are used to control execution of loops, such as for or while. As with the add instruction, no exceptions are thrown. Overflow is ignored.

The second row in Table 12-2 shows the **wide** variant of the **iinc** instruction. As mentioned in Chapter 10, "Stack and Local Variable Operations," the **wide** instruction is used to extend unsigned local variable in-

**Table 12-1.**

Integer addition

| Opcode | Operand(s) | Description |
|--------|------------|-------------|
| **iadd** | (none) | pops two **int**s, adds them, and pushes the **int** result |
| **ladd** | (none) | pops two **long**s, adds them, and pushes the **long** result |

**Table 12-2.**

Increment a local variable by a constant

| Opcode | Operand(s) | Description |
|--------|------------|-------------|
| **iinc** | vindex, const | adds const to an **int** at local variable position vindex |
| **wide** | **iinc**, indexbyte1, indexbyte2, constbyte1, constbyte2 | adds const to an **int** at local variable position index |

dexes from 8 bits to 16. Using 16 bits allows instructions to address up to 65,536 local variable slots. In the **iinc** case, the **wide** instruction also extends the size of the signed increment value from eight bits to sixteen. Therefore, the **wide** variant of the **iinc** opcode can be used to change a local variable value by any number between and including –32,768 through 32,767.

Integer subtraction is performed on **int**s and **long**s via the opcodes shown in Table 12-3. Each opcode causes the top two values of the appropriate type to be popped off the stack. The topmost value is subtracted from the value just beneath it. The result is pushed back onto the stack. No exceptions are thrown by these opcodes.

Integer multiplication of **int**s and **long**s is accomplished via the opcodes shown in Table 12-4. Each opcode causes two values of the same type to be popped off the stack and multiplied. The result, of the same type as the numbers being multiplied, is pushed back onto the stack. No exceptions are thrown.

The opcodes that perform division on **int**s and **long**s are shown in Table 12-5. The division opcodes cause the top two values of the appropriate type to be popped off the stack. The value just beneath the topmost value is divided by the topmost value. (In other words, the first value pushed onto the stack is used as the dividend or numerator. The second value pushed—the

**Table 12-3.**

Integer subtraction

| Opcode | Operand(s) | Description |
| --- | --- | --- |
| isub | (none) | pops two **int**s, subtracts them, and pushes the **int** result |
| lsub | (none) | pops two **long**s, subtracts them, and pushes the **long** result |

**Table 12-4.**

Integer multiplication

| Opcode | Operand(s) | Description |
| --- | --- | --- |
| imul | (none) | pops two **int**s, multiplies them, and pushes the **int** result |
| lmul | (none) | pops two **long**s, multiplies them, and pushes the **long** result |

**Table 12-5.**

Integer division

| Opcode | Operand(s) | Description |
| --- | --- | --- |
| idiv | (none) | pops two **int**s, divides them, and pushes the **int** result |
| ldiv | (none) | pops two **long**s, divides them, and pushes the **long** result |

top of the stack—is used as the divisor or denominator.) The result of the division is pushed back onto the stack. Integer division yields a result that is truncated down to the nearest integer value between it and zero. Integer division by zero throws an **ArithmeticException**.

The remainder operation is performed on **int**s and **long**s via the opcodes shown in Table 12-6. These opcodes cause the top two values to be popped from the stack. The value just beneath the topmost value is divided by the topmost value, and the remainder of that division is pushed back onto the stack. As with the division opcodes, integer remainder by zero throws an **ArithmeticException**.

The opcodes shown in Table 12-7 perform arithmetic negation on **int**s and **long**s. The negation opcodes pop the top value from the stack, negate it, and push the result.

# Prime Time: A Simulation

The *Prime Time* applet, shown in Figure 12-2, demonstrates a Java Virtual Machine executing a sequence of bytecodes that generates prime numbers. The applet is embedded in a web page on the CD-ROM in the file **applets/PrimeTime.html**. The bytecode sequence in the simulation

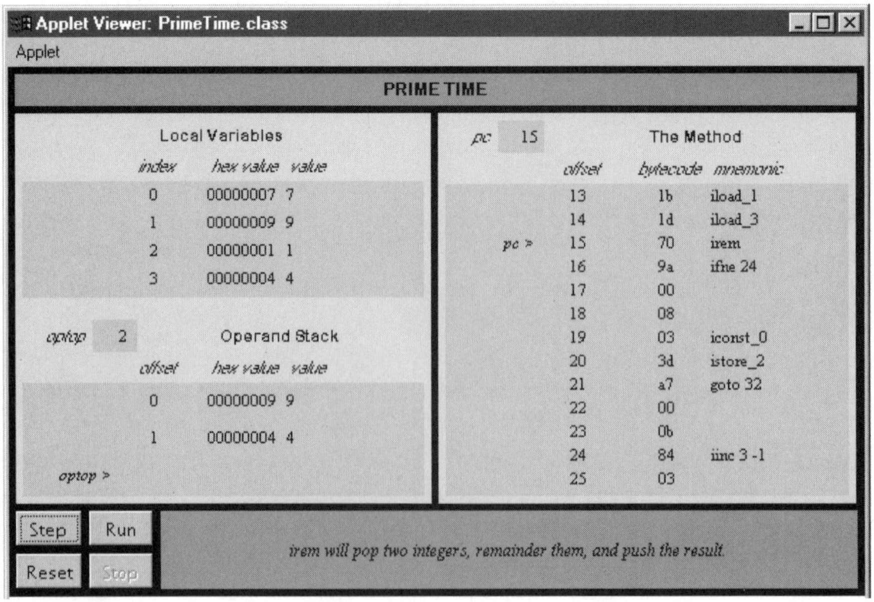

**Figure 12-2.**
The **Prime Time**
applet.

**Table 12-6.**

*Integer remainder*

| Opcode | Operand(s) | Description |
|--------|-----------|-------------|
| `irem` | (none) | pops two `int`s, divides them, and pushes the `int` remainder |
| `lrem` | (none) | pops two `long`s, divides them, and pushes the `long` remainder |

**Table 12-7.**

*Integer negation*

| Opcode | Operand(s) | Description |
|--------|-----------|-------------|
| `ineg` | (none) | pops an `int`, negates it, and pushes the result |
| `lneg` | (none) | pops a `long`, negates it, and pushes the result |

was generated by the `javac` compiler for the `findPrimes()` method of the following class:

```java
// On CD-ROM in file integer/ex1/PrimeFinder.java
class PrimeFinder {

    static void findPrimes() {

        int primeNum = 1;
        int numToCheck = 2;

        for (;;) {

            boolean foundPrime = true;

            for (int divisor = numToCheck / 2;
                 divisor > 1; -divisor) {

                if (numToCheck % divisor == 0) {
                    foundPrime = false;
                    break;
                }
            }

            if (foundPrime) {
                primeNum = numToCheck;
            }

            ++numToCheck;
        }
    }
}
```

The `findPrimes()` method places prime numbers, one at a time and in increasing numerical order, into the `primeNum` variable. To find the primes, it checks each positive integer in increasing numerical order starting with integer value two. It keeps the current number it is checking in the **numToCheck** variable. The outer for loop, a "forever" loop, keeps this process going indefinitely. To check a number, it divides the number by smaller integers looking for a zero remainder. If it encounters a zero remainder, then the number has integral factors other than one and itself and therefore isn't prime.

For each number to check, the **findPrimes()** method divides the number by two. The result of this integer division is the first value checked as a possible integral divisor for the number.

In the inner for loop, the **findPrimes()** method tries each number as a divisor between the result of the division by two and the divisor two. If the remainder of any of these divisions is zero, it breaks out of the inner for loop and skips to the next number to check. If it reaches divisor two and has found no divisor that yields a zero remainder, it has found the next prime number. It exits the inner for loop and sets **primeNum** equal to the number to check.

For example, when **numToCheck** is 10, **findPrimes()** first divides 10 by 2 to get the first divisor, 5. It then performs the remainder operation on 10 and 5 and discovers a zero remainder. So it breaks out of the inner for loop and sets **numToCheck** to 11. (It doesn't ever set **primeNum** to 10.) It divides 11 by 2 to get the first divisor to check, once again 5. It performs the remainder operation on 11 and integers 5, 4, 3, and 2, none of which yield a zero remainder. It completes the inner for loop, sets **primeNum** equal to 11, and continues on to check 12.

The bytecodes generated by **javac** for the **findPrimes()** method are as follow:

```
  0 iconst_1      // Push int constant 1
                  // Pop into local var 0:
  1 istore_0      // int primeNum = 1;
  2 iconst_2      // Push int constant 2
                  // Pop into local var 1:
  3 istore_1      // int numToCheck = 2;

// The outer for loop (the "forever" loop) begins here:
  4 iconst_1      // Push int constant 1
                  // Pop into local var 2:
  5 istore_2      // boolean foundPrime = true;

// The inner for loop begins here. First, initialize
// divisor.
  6 iload_1       // Push int in local var 1 (numToCheck)
  7 iconst_2      // Push int constant 2
                  // Pop two ints, divide them, push int
```

```
 8 idiv           // result
                  // Pop int into local var 3:
 9 istore_3       // int divisor = numToCheck / 2;

// Next, test the inner for loop's termination condition.
10 goto 27        // Jump to for loop condition check

// The body of the inner for loop begins here.
                  // Push the int in local var 1
13 iload_1        // (numToCheck)
14 iload_3        // Push the int in local var 3 (divisor)
                  // Pop two ints, remainder them, push
15 irem           // result
                  // Pop int, jump if equal to zero:
16 ifne 24        // if (numToCheck % divisor == 0)
19 iconst_0       // Push int constant 0
                  // Pop into local var 2:
20 istore_2       // foundPrime = false;
21 goto 32        // Jump out of inner for loop

// At this point, the body of the inner for loop is done.
// Now just perform the third statement of the for
// expression: decrement divisor.
24 iinc 3 -1      // Increment local var 3 by -1: -divisor

// The test for the inner for loop's termination condition
// begins here. This loop will keep on looping while
// (divisor > 1).
27 iload_3        // Push int from local var 3 (divisor)
28 iconst_1       // Push int constant 1
29 if_icmpgt 13   // Pop top two ints, jump if greater than

// At this point, the inner for loop has completed. Next
// check to see if a prime number was found.
32 iload_2        // Push int from local var 2 (foundPrime)
                  // Pop top int, jump if zero:
33 ifeq 38        // if (foundPrime) {
36 iload_1        // Push int from local var 1 (numToCheck)
                  // Pop into local var 0:
37 istore_0       // primeNum = numToCheck;
                  // Increment local var 1 by 1:
38 iinc 1 1       // ++numToCheck;
41 goto 4         // Jump back to top of outer for loop.
```

The **javac** compiler placed local variable **primeNum** from the source into local variable slots 0 on the stack frame. It put **numToCheck** into slot 1, **foundPrime** into slot 2, and **divisor** into slot 3. As mentioned earlier, as this method finds each successive prime number, it places the number into the **primeNum** variable. As you run the simulation, therefore, you will see the prime numbers appear sequentially in the **int** value stored in local variable slot 0.

One point to note about this bytecode sequence is that it demonstrates the way in which **boolean**s from Java source code are treated on the stack frame by Java bytecodes. The value stored in local variable slot 2, which represents the **boolean foundPrime** variable from the source, is an **int**. It is set to **true** or **false** by instructions that push a constant **int** zero or one. Its **boolean** value is checked by instructions that compare an **int** against zero.

Another point to note about this simulation is that eventually the **numToCheck** value will overflow. When it does, the virtual machine will throw no exceptions. It will just continue executing the **findPrimes()** method with **int** values that no longer hold any relationship to the prime numbers.

To drive the *Prime Time* simulation, use the Step, Reset, Run, and Stop buttons. Each time you click the Step button, the simulator will execute the instruction pointed to by the pc register. If you click the Run button, the simulation will continue with no further coaxing on your part until you click the Stop button. To start the simulation over, click the Reset button. For each step of the simulation, a panel at the bottom of the applet contains an explanation of what the next instruction will do. Happy clicking.

# On the CD-ROM

The CD-ROM contains the source code examples from this chapter in the **integer** directory. The *Prime Time* applet is contained in a web page on the CD-ROM in file **applets/PrimeTime.html**. The source code for this applet is found alongside its class files, in the **applets/JVMSimulators** and **applets/JVMSimulators**.

# The Resources Page

For more information about the material presented in this chapter, visit the resources page: **http://www.artima.com/insidejvm/integer.html**.

# 13

# Logic

This chapter describes the instructions that perform bit-wise logical operations inside the Java Virtual Machine. These instructions include opcodes to perform shifting and boolean operations on integers. The boolean operations are performed on individual bits of integer values.

Accompanying this chapter on the CD-ROM is an applet that interactively illustrates the material presented in the chapter. The applet, named *Logical Results*, simulates the Java Virtual Machine executing a method that uses several of the logic opcodes. At the end of this chapter, you will find a description of this applet and the byte-codes it executes.

# The Logic Opcodes

The Java Virtual Machine's logic capabilities operate on **ints** and **longs**. These operations treat **ints** and **longs** not so much as signed two's-complement numbers, necessarily, but as generic bit patterns. Integer shifting is accomplished via the **ishl**, **ishr**, and **iushr** opcodes. Java's **<<** operator is implemented by **ishl**. The **>>** operator is implemented by **ishr**, and the **>>>** operator is implemented by **iushl**. The difference between **ishr** and **iushr** is that only **ishr** does sign extension. Table 13-1 shows the instructions that shift **ints** left and right.

Table 13-2 shows the instructions that shift **longs** left and right.

The opcodes shown in Table 13-3 perform bitwise logical operations on **ints**. The opcodes implement Java's **&**, **|**, and **^** operators.

Table 13-4 shows the opcodes that perform bitwise logical operations on **longs**.

As mentioned in previous chapters, no native **boolean** type exists in the Java Virtual Machine. The Java Virtual Machine uses **ints** to represent

**Table 13-1.**

Shifting **ints**

| Opcode | Operand(s) | Description |
|--------|-----------|-------------|
| ishl | (none) | shifts **int** left |
| ishr | (none) | arithmetic shifts **int** right |
| iushr | (none) | logical shifts **int** right |

**Table 13-2.**

Shifting **longs**

| Opcode | Operand(s) | Description |
|--------|-----------|-------------|
| lshl | (none) | shifts **long** left |
| lshr | (none) | arithmetic shifts **long** right |
| lushr | (none) | logical shifts **long** right |

**Table 13-3.**

Bitwise logical operations on **ints**

| Opcode | Operand(s) | Description |
|--------|-----------|-------------|
| iand | (none) | boolean ANDs two **ints** |
| ior | (none) | boolean ORs two **ints** |
| ixor | (none) | boolean XORs two **ints** |

**Table 13-4.**

Bitwise logical operations on **longs**

| Opcode | Operand(s) | Description |
|--------|-----------|-------------|
| **land** | (none) | boolean ANDs two **long**s |
| **lor** | (none) | boolean ORs two **long**s |
| **lxor** | (none) | boolean XORs two **long**s |

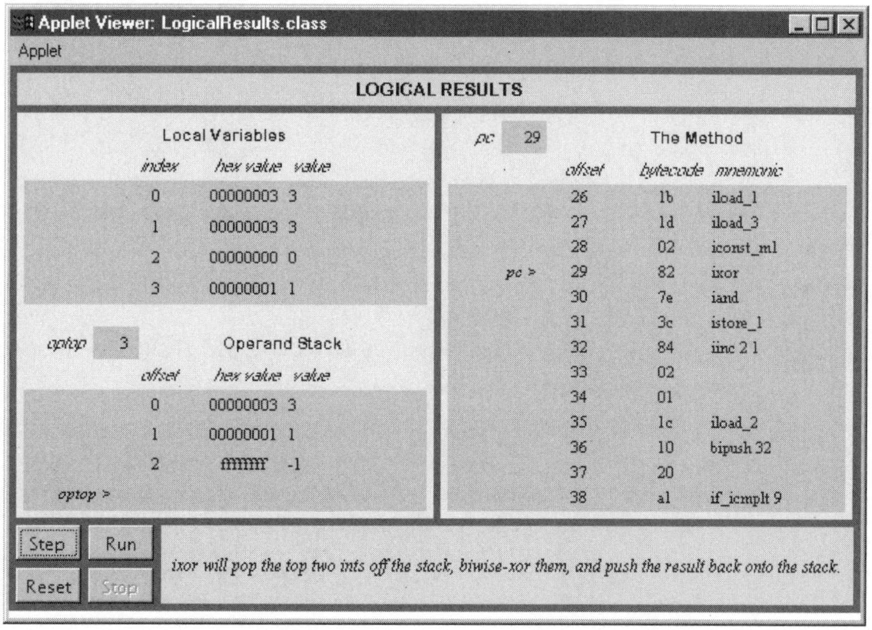

**Figure 13-1.**
The **Logical Results** applet.

Figure 13-1. The Logical Results applet.

**boolean**s. The instruction set includes many instructions that decide whether to jump based on an **int** value interpreted as a **boolean**. These instructions are covered in Chapter 16, "Control Flow."

# Logical Results: A Simulation

The *Logical Results* applet, shown in Figure 13-1, demonstrates a Java Virtual Machine executing a sequence of bytecodes. This applet is in a web page on the CD-ROM in the file **applets/LogicalResults.html**. The bytecode sequence in the simulation was generated by **javac** for the **incrementLogically()** method of the **VulcanCounter** class:

```
// On CD-ROM in file opcodes/ex1/VulcanCounter.java
class VulcanCounter {

    static void incrementLogically() {
        int spock = 0;
        for (;;) {
            int tempSpock = spock;
            for (int i = 0; i < 32; ++i) {
                int mask = 0x1 << i;
                if ((tempSpock & mask) == 0) {
                    tempSpock |= mask;   // Change 0 to 1
                    break;
                }
                else {
                    tempSpock &= ~mask; // Change 1 to 0
                }
            }
            spock = tempSpock;
        }
    }
}
```

The bytecodes generated by **javac** for **incrementLogically()** are as follow:

```
 0 iconst_0      // Push int constant 0.
 1 istore_0      // Pop to local variable 0: int spock = 0;
 2 iload_0       // Push local variable 0 (spock).
               // Pop to local variable 1:
 3 istore_1      // int tempSpock = spock;
 4 iconst_0      // Push int constant 0.
 5 istore_2      // Pop to local variable 2: int i = 0;
 6 goto 35       // Jump unconditionally ()
 9 iconst_1      // Push int constant 1.
10 iload_2       // Push local variable 2 (i).
               // Arithmetic shift left top int (i) by
11 ishl          // next to top int (1).
               // Pop to local variable 3:
12 istore_3      // int mask = i << 0x1;
13 iload_1       // Push local variable 1 (tempSpock).
14 iload_3       // Push local variable 3 (mask).
               // Bitwise AND top two ints:
15 iand          // (spock & mask)
               // Jump if top of stack is not equal to
16 ifne 26       // zero: if ((spock & mask) == 0) {
19 iload_1       // Push local variable 1 (tempSpock).
20 iload_3       // Push local variable 3 (mask).
               // Bitwise OR top two ints
21 ior           // (tempSpock | mask)
               // Pop to local variable 1:
22 istore_1      // tempSpock |= mask;
               // Jump unconditionally (to just after
23 goto 41       // inner for): break;
```

```
26 iload_1       // Push local variable 1 (tempSpock).
27 iload_3       // Push local variable 3 (mask).
28 iconst_m1     // Push -1.
                 // Bitwise EXCLUSIVE-OR top two ints:
29 ixor          // ~mask
                 // Bitwise AND top two ints:
30 iand          // tempSpock & (~mask)
31 istore_1      // Pop to local variable 1: tempSpock &= ~mask;
32 iinc 2 1      // Increment local variable 2 by 1: ++i
35 iload_2       // Push local variable 2 (i).
36 bipush 32     // Push integer constant 32.
                 // Jump (to top of inner for) if "next to
                 // top" integer is less than "top"
38 if_icmplt 9   // integer: i < 32
41 iload_1       // Push local variable 1 (tempSpock)
                 // Pop to local variable 0:
42 istore_0      // spock = tempSpock;
                 // Jump unconditionally (to top of outer
43 goto 2        // for).
```

The **incrementLogically()** method repeatedly increments an **int** without using the **+** or **++** operators. It uses only the logical operators: **&**, **|**, and **~**. An increment is accomplished by searching through the bits of the current **int**, starting with the lowest order bit, and turning ones to zeros. As soon as a one is encountered in the current **int**, it is changed to zero and the search stops. The resultant **int** now represents the old **int** incremented by one. The process is started again on the new **int**. Each incremented number is stored in the **spock** variable. **spock** is local variable zero in the compiled bytecodes, so you can watch local variable zero count 0, 1, 2, 3, and so on.

To drive the *Logical Results* simulation, use the Step, Reset, Run, and Stop buttons. Each time you click the Step button, the simulator will execute the instruction pointed to by the pc register. If you click the Run button, the simulation will continue with no further coaxing on your part until you click the Stop button. To start the simulation over, click the Reset button. For each step of the simulation, a panel at the bottom of the applet contains an explanation of what the next instruction will do. Happy clicking.

# On the CD-ROM

The CD-ROM contains the source code examples from this chapter in the **opcodes** directory. The *Logical Results* applet is in a web page on the CD-ROM in the file **applets/LogicalResults.html**. The source code for this applet is found alongside its class files, in the **applets/JVMSimulators** and **applets/JVMSimulators/COM/artima/jvmsim** directories.

# The Resources Page

For more information about the material presented in this chapter, visit the resources page: `http://www.artima.com/insidejvm/logic.html`.

# 14

# Floating-Point Arithmetic

This chapter describes the floating-point numbers and the instructions that perform floating-point arithmetic inside the Java Virtual Machine. The floating-point numbers described here conform to the IEEE 754 floating-point standard, which is the standard to which all Java Virtual Machine implementations must adhere.

Accompanying this chapter on the CD-ROM are two applets that interactively illustrate the material presented in the chapter. One applet, named *Inner Float*, allows you to view and manipulate the individual components that make up a floating-point number. The other applet, named *Circle of Squares*, simulates the Java Virtual Machine executing a method that uses several of the floating-point opcodes. Within this chapter, you will find descriptions of both of these applets.

# Floating-Point Numbers

The Java Virtual Machine's floating-point support adheres to the IEEE 754 1985 floating-point standard. This standard defines the format of 32-bit and 64-bit floating-point numbers and defines the operations on those numbers. In the Java Virtual Machine, floating-point arithmetic is performed on 32-bit **float**s and 64-bit **double**s. For each opcode that performs arithmetic on **float**s is a corresponding opcode that performs the same operation on **double**s.

A floating-point number has four parts: a sign, a mantissa, a radix, and an exponent. The sign is either a 1 or –1. The mantissa, always a positive number, holds the significant digits of the floating-point number. The exponent indicates the positive or negative power of the radix by which the mantissa and sign should be multiplied. The four components are combined as follows to get the floating-point value:

$$sign * mantissa * radix^{exponent}$$

Floating-point numbers have multiple representations because you can always multiply the mantissa of any floating-point number by some power of the radix and change the exponent to get the original number. For example, as shown in Table 14-1, the number –5 can be represented equally by any of the following forms in radix 10.

For each floating-point number, one representation is said to be normalized. A floating-point number is normalized if its mantissa is within the range defined by the following relation:

$$1/radix <= mantissa < 1$$

A normalized radix 10 floating-point number has its decimal point just to the left of the first nonzero digit in the mantissa. The normalized floating-point representation of –5 is $-1 * 0.5 * 10^1$. In other words, a normalized floating-point number's mantissa has no nonzero digits to the left of

**Table 14-1.**

**Forms of –5**

| Sign | Mantissa | Radix$^{exponent}$ |
|------|----------|-------------------|
| –1 | 50 | $10^{-1}$ |
| –1 | 5 | $10^0$ |
| –1 | 0.5 | $10^1$ |
| –1 | 0.05 | $10^2$ |

the decimal point and a nonzero digit just to the right of the decimal point. Any floating-point number that doesn't fit into this category is said to be denormalized. Note that the number zero has no normalized representation because it has no nonzero digit to put just to the right of the decimal point. "Why be normalized?" is a common exclamation among zeros.

Floating-point numbers in the Java Virtual Machine use a radix of two, so they have the following form:

sign * mantissa * $2^{exponent}$

The mantissa of a floating-point number in the Java Virtual Machine is expressed as a binary number. A normalized mantissa has its binary point (the base-two equivalent of a decimal point) just to the left of the most significant nonzero digit. Because the binary number system has just two digits—zero and one—the most significant digit of a normalized mantissa is always a one.

The most significant bit of a **float** or **double** is its sign bit. The mantissa occupies the 23 least significant bits of a **float** and the 52 least significant bits of a **double**. The exponent, 8 bits in a **float** and 11 bits in a **double**, sits between the sign and mantissa. Here, the format of a **float** is shown with the sign bit represented by an $s$, the exponent bits by $e$'s, and the mantissa bits by $m$'s:

s eeeeeeee mmmmmmmmmmmmmmmmmmmmmmm

A sign bit of zero indicates a positive number, and a sign bit of one indicates a negative number. The mantissa is always interpreted as a positive base-two number. It is not a two's-complement number. If the sign bit is one, the floating-point value is negative, but the mantissa is still interpreted as a positive number that must be multiplied by –1.

The exponent field is interpreted in one of three ways. An exponent of all ones indicates the floating-point number has one of the special values of plus or minus infinity, or "not a number" (NaN). NaN is the result of certain operations, such as the division of zero by zero. An exponent of all zeros indicates a denormalized floating-point number. Any other exponent indicates a normalized floating-point number.

The mantissa contains one extra bit of precision beyond those that appear in the mantissa bits. The mantissa of a **float**, which occupies only 23 bits, has 24 bits of precision. The mantissa of a **double**, which occupies 52 bits, has 53 bits of precision. The most significant mantissa bit is predictable and is therefore not included because the exponent of floating-point numbers in the Java Virtual Machine indicates whether the number is normalized. If the exponent is all zeros, the floating-point number is denormalized, and the most significant bit of the mantissa is known to be a zero. Otherwise, the floating-point number is normalized, and the most significant bit of the mantissa is known to be one.

The Java Virtual Machine throws no exceptions as a result of any floating-point operations. Special values, such as positive and negative infinity or NaN, are returned as the result of suspicious operations such as division by zero. An exponent of all ones indicates a special floating-point value. An exponent of all ones with a mantissa whose bits are all zero indicates an infinity. The sign of the infinity is indicated by the sign bit. An exponent of all ones with any other mantissa is interpreted to mean "not a number" (NaN). The Java Virtual Machine always produces the same mantissa for NaN, which is all zeros except for the most significant mantissa bit that appears in the number. These values are shown for a **float** in Table 14-2.

Exponents that are neither all ones nor all zeros indicate the power of two by which to multiply the normalized mantissa. The power of two can be determined by interpreting the exponent bits as a positive number and then subtracting a bias from the positive number. For a **float**, the bias is 126. For a **double**, the bias is 1023. For example, an exponent field in a **float** of 00000001 yields a power of two by subtracting the bias (126) from the exponent field interpreted as a positive integer (1). The power of two, therefore, is (1 – 126), which is –125. It is the smallest possible power of two for a **float**. At the other extreme, an exponent field of 11111110 yields a power of two of (254 – 126) or 128. The number 128 is the largest power of two available to a **float**. Several examples of normalized **float**s are shown in Table 14-3.

An exponent of all zeros indicates the mantissa is denormalized, which means the unstated leading bit is a zero instead of a one. The power of two in this case is the same as the lowest power of two available to a normalized mantissa. For the **float**, this number is –125. Therefore, normalized mantissas multiplied by two raised to the power of –125 have an exponent field of 00000001, whereas denormalized mantissas multiplied by two raised to the power of –125 have an exponent field of 00000000.

**Table 14-2.**

Special **float**

| Value | float Bits (Sign Exponent Mantissa) |
| --- | --- |
| +Infinity | 0 11111111 00000000000000000000000 |
| –Infinity | 1 11111111 00000000000000000000000 |
| NaN | 1 11111111 10000000000000000000000 |

**Table 14-3.**

Normalized **float** values

| Value | float Bits (Sign Exponent Mantissa) | Unbiased Exponent |
|---|---|---|
| Largest positive (finite) **float** | 0 11111110 11111111111111111111111 | 128 |
| Largest negative (finite) **float** | 1 11111110 11111111111111111111111 | 128 |
| Smallest normalized **float** | 1 00000001 00000000000000000000000 | −125 |
| Pi | 0 10000000 10010010000111111011011 | 2 |

**Table 14-4.**

Denormalized **float** values

| Value | float Bits (Sign Exponent Mantissa) |
|---|---|
| Smallest positive (nonzero) **float** | 0 00000000 00000000000000000000001 |
| Smallest negative (nonzero) **float** | 1 00000000 00000000000000000000001 |
| Largest denormalized **float** | 1 00000000 11111111111111111111111 |
| Positive zero | 0 00000000 00000000000000000000000 |
| Negative zero | 1 00000000 00000000000000000000000 |

The allowance for denormalized numbers at the bottom end of the range of exponents supports gradual underflow. If the lowest exponent was instead used to represent a normalized number, underflow to zero would occur for larger numbers. In other words, leaving the lowest exponent for denormalized numbers allows smaller numbers to be represented. The smaller denormalized numbers have fewer bits of precision than normalized numbers, but this is preferable to underflowing to zero as soon as the exponent reaches its minimum normalized value. Table 14-4 shows several denormalized floating-point values.

# Inner Float: A Java float Reveals Its Inner Nature

The *Inner Float* applet, shown in Figure 14-1, lets you play around with the floating-point format. The value of a **float** is displayed in several formats. The radix two scientific notation format shows the mantissa and exponent in base ten. Before being displayed, the actual mantissa is

**Figure 14-1.**
The **Inner Float**
applet.

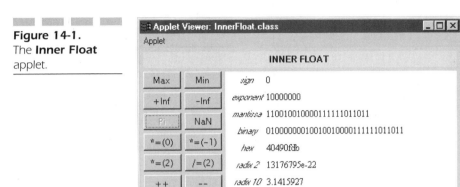

multiplied by $2^{24}$, which yields an integral number, and the unbiased exponent is decremented by 24. Both the integral mantissa and exponent are then easily converted to base ten and displayed. The applet is embedded in a web page on the CD-ROM in the file **applets/ InnerFloat.html**. The text of the web page includes several button-press sequences that demonstrate various properties of floating-point numbers.

# The Floating-Point Opcodes

Table 14-5 shows the opcodes that pop two floating-point values from the top of the stack, add them, and push the result. The type of the values is indicated by the opcode itself, and the result always has the same type as the numbers being added. No exceptions are thrown by these opcodes. Overflow results in a positive or negative infinity, and underflow results in a positive or negative zero.

Subtraction is performed on **float**s and **double**s via the opcodes shown in Table 14-6. Each opcode causes the top two values of the appropriate type to be popped off the stack. The topmost value is subtracted from the value just beneath the topmost value. The result is pushed back onto the stack. No exceptions are thrown by either of these opcodes.

Multiplication of **float**s and **double**s is accomplished via the opcodes shown in Table 14-7. Each opcode causes two values of the same type to be popped off the stack and multiplied. The result, of the same type as the numbers being multiplied, is pushed back onto the stack. No exceptions are thrown.

Division is performed on **float**s and **double**s by the opcodes shown in Table 14-8. The division opcodes cause the top two values of the appro-

**Table 14-5.**

*Floating-point addition*

| Opcode | Operand(s) | Description |
|--------|-----------|-------------|
| fadd | (none) | pops two **float**s, adds them, and pushes the **float** result |
| dadd | (none) | pops two **double**s, adds them, and pushes the **double** result |

**Table 14-6.**

*Floating-point subtraction*

| Opcode | Operand(s) | Description |
|--------|-----------|-------------|
| fsub | (none) | pops two **float**s, subtracts them, and pushes the **float** result |
| dsub | (none) | pops two **double**s, subtracts them, and pushes the **double** result |

**Table 14-7.**

*Floating-point multiplication*

| Opcode | Operand(s) | Description |
|--------|-----------|-------------|
| fmul | (none) | pops two **float**s, multiplies them, and pushes the **float** result |
| dmul | (none) | pops two **double**s, multiplies them, and pushes the **double** result |

**Table 14-8.**

*Floating-point division*

| Opcode | Operand(s) | Description |
|--------|-----------|-------------|
| fdiv | (none) | pops two **float**s, divides them, and pushes the **float** result |
| ddiv | (none) | pops two **double**s, divides them, and pushes the **double** result |

priate type to be popped off the stack. The value immediately beneath the topmost value is divided by the topmost value. (In other words, the value pushed first is the dividend or numerator. The value pushed second—the top of the stack—is the divisor or denominator.) The result of the division is pushed back onto the stack.

No exception is thrown as a result of any floating-point division. Floating-point division of a finite value by zero yields a positive or negative infinity. Floating-point division of zero by zero yields NaN. A summary of the result of dividing various combinations of infinity, zero, NaN, and finite values is given in Table 14-10.

The remainder operation is performed on **float**s and **double**s via the opcodes shown in Table 14-9. The following opcodes cause the top two values

**Table 14-9.**

Floating-point
remainder

| Opcode | Operand(s) | Description |
|--------|------------|-------------|
| frem | (none) | pops two **float**s, divides them, and pushes the **float** remainder |
| drem | (none) | pops two **double**s, divides them, and pushes the **double** remainder |

**Table 14-10.**

Results of various
floating-point
divisions

| a | b | a/b | a%b |
|---|---|-----|-----|
| Finite | +–0.0 | +–Infinity | NaN |
| Finite | +–Infinity | +–0.0 | a |
| +–0.0 | +–0.0 | NaN | NaN |
| +–Infinity | Finite | +–Infinity | NaN |
| +–Infinity | +Infinity | NaN | NaN |

to be popped from the stack. The value just beneath the topmost value is divided by the topmost value, and the remainder of that division is pushed back onto the stack.

No exception is thrown as a result of any floating-point remainder operation. Floating-point remainder of any value divided by zero yields a NaN result. A summary of the result of computing the remainder various combinations of infinity, zero, NaN, and finite values is given in Table 14-10.

The remainder operation provided by **frem** and **drem** follows the same rule as the integer remainder operation provided by **irem** and **lrem**:

```
(a/b)*b + a%b == a
```

In the floating-point case, the division **(a/b)** must be converted to an **int** or **long** to remove the fraction, as follows:

```
((long)(a/b))*b + a%b == a
```

This remainder does not follow the IEEE 754 standard. To obtain a floating-point remainder as defined by IEEE 754, use the **IEEEremainder()** method of **java.lang.Math**.

The opcodes shown in Table 14-11 perform arithmetic negation on **float**s and **double**s. Negation opcodes pop the top value from the stack, negate it, and push the result.

**Table 14-11.**

Floating-point
negation

| Opcode | Operand(s) | Description |
|--------|-----------|-------------|
| **fneg** | (none) | pops a **float**, negates it, and pushes the result |
| **dneg** | (none) | pops a **double**, negates it, and pushes the result |

# Circle of Squares: A Simulation

The *Circle of Squares* applet, shown in Figure 14-2, demonstrates a Java Virtual Machine executing a sequence of bytecodes that perform floating-point arithmetic. This applet is part of a web page on the CD-ROM in the file **applets/CircleOfSquares.html**. The bytecode sequence in the simulation was generated by **javac** for the **squareItForever()** method of the following class:

```
// On CD-ROM in file opcodes/ex1/SquareCircle.java
class SquareCircle {

    static void squareItForever() {
        float f = 2;
        for (;;) {
            f *= f;
```

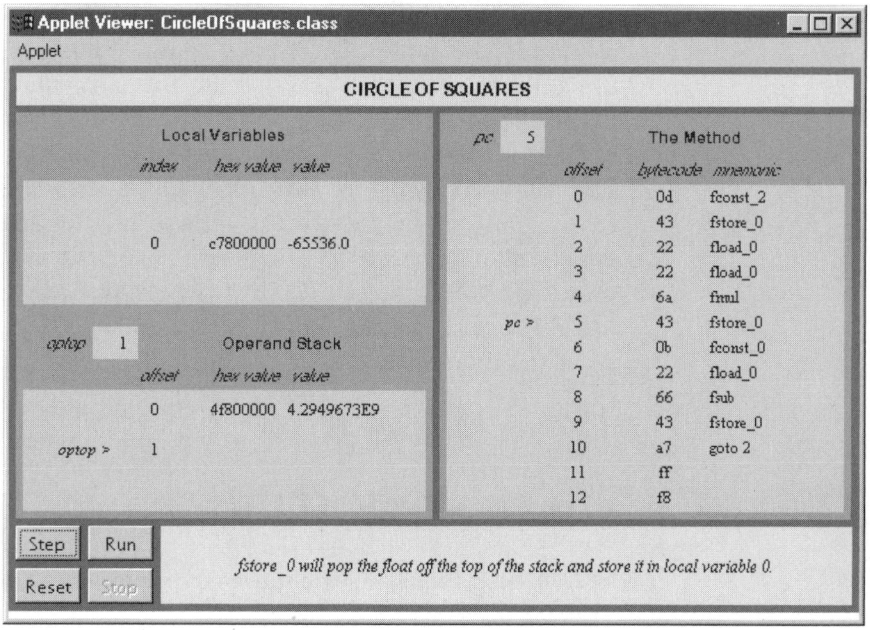

**Figure 14-2.**
The **Circle of Squares** applet.

```
                        f = 0 - f;
                }
        }
}
```

The bytecodes generated by `javac` for `squareItForever()` are as follow:

```
 0 fconst_2    // Push float constant 2.
             // Pop to local variable 0 (float f):
 1 fstore_0    // float f = 2;
 2 fload_0     // Push local variable 0 (float f).
 3 fload_0     // Push local variable 0 (float f).
             // Pop top two floats, multiply, push float
 4 fmul        // result.
 5 fstore_0    // Pop to local variable 0 (float f): f *= f;
 6 fconst_0    // Push float constant 0.
 7 fload_0     // Push local variable 0 (float f).
 8 fsub        // Subtract top float from next to top float:
             // imByte = (byte) imInt;
             // Pop result to local variable 0 (float f):
 9 fstore_0    // f = 0 - f;
             // Jump back to the first fload_0
10 goto 2     // instruction: for (;;) {}
```

The `squareItForever()` method repeatedly squares a `float` value until it hits infinity. Each time the `float` is squared, it is also negated. The `float` starts out as 2. It takes only seven iterations before infinity is reached, which isn't nearly as long as it takes in real life. The hex representation of the bits that make up the `float` are shown in the "hex value" column in the applet. The "value" column shows the number as humans are used to seeing it. This human-friendly value is generated by the `Float.toString()` method.

To drive the *Circle of Squares* simulation, use the Step, Reset, Run, and Stop buttons. Each time you click the Step button, the simulator will execute the instruction pointed to by the pc register. If you click the Run button, the simulation will continue with no further coaxing on your part until you click the Stop button. To start the simulation over, click the Reset button. For each step of the simulation, a panel at the bottom of the applet contains an explanation of what the next instruction will do. Happy clicking.

# On the CD-ROM

The CD-ROM contains the source code examples from this chapter in the **opcodes** directory.

The *Inner Float* applet is embedded in a web page on the CD-ROM in the file **applets/InnerFloat.html**. The text of the web page includes several button-press sequences that demonstrate various properties of floating-point numbers. The source code for this applet is found alongside its class files in the **applets/InnerFloat** directory.

The *Circle of Squares* applet is in a web page on the CD-ROM in the file **applets/CircleOfSquares.html**. The source code for this applet is found alongside its class files, in the **applets/JVMSimulators** and **applets/JVMSimulators/COM/artima/jvmsim** directories.

# The Resources Page

For more information about the material presented in this chapter, visit the resources page: **http://www.artima.com/insidejvm/float.html**.

# 15

# Objects
# and Arrays

This chapter describes the instructions that create and manipulate objects and arrays inside the Java Virtual Machine. All these instructions involve the heap. Most of them refer to entries in the constant pool.

Accompanying this chapter on the CD-ROM is an applet that interactively illustrates the material presented in the chapter. The applet, named *Three-Dimensional Array*, simulates the Java Virtual Machine executing a method that allocates and initializes a three-dimensional array. At the end of this chapter, you will find a description of this applet and the bytecodes it executes.

# A Refresher on Objects and Arrays

As mentioned in earlier chapters, in the Java Virtual Machine, memory is allocated on the garbage-collected heap only as objects. You cannot allocate memory for a primitive type on the heap, except as part of an object. If you want to use a primitive type where an **Object** reference is needed, you can allocate a wrapper object for the type from the **java.lang** package. For example, an **Integer** class wraps an **int** type with an object. Only object references and primitive types can reside on the Java stack as local variables. Objects can never reside on the Java stack.

The architectural separation of objects and primitive types in the Java Virtual Machine is reflected in the Java programming language, in which objects cannot be declared as local variables—only object references and primitive types. Upon declaration, an object reference refers to nothing. Only after the reference has been explicitly initialized—either with a reference to an existing object or with a call to **new**—does the reference refer to an actual object.

In the Java Virtual Machine instruction set, all objects are instantiated and accessed with the same set of opcodes, except for arrays. As mentioned in earlier chapters, arrays in Java are full-fledged objects. Like any other Java object, arrays are created dynamically. Array references can be used anywhere a reference to type **Object** is called for, and any method of **Object** can be invoked on an array. Still, in the Java Virtual Machine, array operations are handled by special bytecodes.

As with any other object, arrays cannot be declared as local variables; only array references can. Array objects themselves always contain either an array of primitive types or an array of object references. If you declare an array of objects, you get an array of object references. The objects themselves must be explicitly created with **new** and assigned to the elements of the array.

# Opcodes for Objects

Instantiation of new objects is accomplished via the **new** opcode, shown in Table 15-1. Two one-byte operands follow the **new** opcode. These two bytes are combined to form an unsigned 16-bit index into the constant pool. The constant pool entry at the specified offset gives information about the class of the new object. If it hasn't already, the virtual machine resolves the constant pool entry. It creates a new instance of the object on the heap,

**Table 15-1.**

Object creation

| Opcode | Operand(s) | Description |
| --- | --- | --- |
| new | indexbyte1, indexbyte2 | creates a new object on the heap, pushes reference |

**Table 15-2.**

Accessing instance variables

| Opcode | Operand(s) | Description |
| --- | --- | --- |
| putfield | indexbyte1, indexbyte2 | set field, indicated by index, of object to value (both taken from stack) |
| getfield | indexbyte1, indexbyte2 | pushes field, indicated by index, of object (taken from stack) |

**Table 15-3.**

Accessing class variables

| Opcode | Operand(s) | Description |
| --- | --- | --- |
| putstatic | indexbyte1, indexbyte2 | set field, indicated by index, of object to value (both taken from stack) |
| getstatic | indexbyte1, indexbyte2 | pushes field, indicated by index, of object (taken from stack) |

initializes the object's instance variables to default initial values, and pushes the reference to the new object onto the stack.

Table 15-2 shows the opcodes that put and get object fields. These opcodes, **putfield** and **getfield**, operate only on fields that are instance variables. Static variables are accessed by **putstatic** and **getstatic**, which are described later. The **putfield** and **getfield** instructions each take two one-byte operands, which are combined to form an unsigned 16-bit index into the constant pool. The constant pool entry at that index contains information about the type, size, and offset of the field. If it hasn't already, the virtual machine resolves the constant pool entry. The object reference is taken from the stack in both the **putfield** and **getfield** instructions. The **putfield** instruction takes the instance variable value from the stack, and the **getfield** instruction pushes the retrieved instance variable value onto the stack.

Class variables are accessed via the **getstatic** and **putstatic** opcodes, as shown in Table 15-3. Both **getstatic** and **putstatic** take two one-byte operands, which are combined by the Java Virtual Machine to form a 16-bit unsigned offset into the constant pool. The constant pool item at that location gives information about one static field of a class. If it hasn't already, the virtual machine resolves the constant pool entry. Because no particular object is associated with a static field, no object reference is used by either **getstatic** or **putstatic**. The **putstatic** instruction takes the value to assign from the stack. The **getstatic** instruction pushes the retrieved value onto the stack.

The following opcodes check to see whether the object reference on the top of the stack refers to an instance of the class or interface indexed by the operands following the opcode. In both cases, the virtual machine forms an unsigned 16-bit index into the constant pool from the two bytes that follow the opcode. If it hasn't already, the virtual machine resolves the constant pool entry.

The **checkcast** instruction throws **CheckCastException** if the object is not an instance of the specified class or interface. Otherwise, **checkcast** does nothing. The object reference remains on the stack, and execution is continued at the next instruction. This instruction ensures that casts are safe at runtime and forms part of the Java Virtual Machine's security blanket.

The **instanceof** instruction, shown in Table 15-4, pops the object reference from the top of the stack and pushes true or false. If the object is indeed an instance of the specified class or interface, true is pushed onto the stack; otherwise, false is pushed onto the stack. The **instanceof** instruction is used to implement the **instanceof** keyword of the Java language, which allows you to test whether an object is an instance of a particular class or interface.

# Opcodes for Arrays

Instantiation of new arrays is accomplished via the **newarray**, **anewarray**, and **multianewarray** opcodes, shown in Table 15-6. The **newarray** opcode is used to create arrays of primitive types other than object references. The particular primitive type is specified by a single one-byte operand, the "atype," following the **newarray** opcode. The **newarray** instruction can create arrays for **byte**, **short**, **char**, **int**, **long**, **float**, **double**, or **boolean**. Table 15-5 shows the legal values for atype and the corresponding array types.

**Table 15-4.**

Type checking

| Opcode | Operand(s) | Description |
|---|---|---|
| **checkcast** | indexbyte1, indexbyte2 | Throws **ClassCastException** if objectref on stack cannot be cast to class at index |
| **instanceof** | indexbyte1, indexbyte2 | Pushes true if objectref on stack is an instance of class at index, else pushes false |

**Table 15-5.**

Values for atype

| Array Type | atype |
|------------|-------|
| T_BOOLEAN  | 4     |
| T_CHAR     | 5     |
| T_FLOAT    | 6     |
| T_DOUBLE   | 7     |
| T_BYTE     | 8     |
| T_SHORT    | 9     |
| T_INT      | 10    |
| T_LONG     | 11    |

Note that the instructions that create arrays is one place in the Java Virtual Machine where **boolean** values are referred to explicitly. This capability enables implementations, especially those that must operate under constrained memory requirements, to compress arrays of **boolean** values into bitmaps. In such a representation, each **boolean** element of an array would be represented by one bit. On implementations that have more memory available, **boolean** arrays may instead be implemented as arrays of **byte**s. This representation would likely yield better performance than a bitmap approach, though it would consume more memory. No matter what internal implementation a particular virtual machine uses for **boolean** arrays, the elements of a **boolean** array are accessed with the same opcodes used to access **byte** arrays. These opcodes are described later in this chapter.

The **anewarray** instruction creates an array of object references. Two one-byte operands follow the **anewarray** opcode and are combined to form an unsigned 16-bit index into the constant pool. A description of the class of object for which the array is to be created is found in the constant pool at the specified index. If it hasn't already, the virtual machine resolves the constant pool entry. This instruction allocates space for the array of object references and initializes the references to null.

The **multianewarray** instruction is used to allocate multidimensional arrays, which are simply arrays of arrays. A multidimensional array could alternatively be allocated with repeated use of the **anewarray** and **newarray** instructions. The **multianewarray** instruction simply compresses the bytecodes needed to create multidimensional arrays into one instruction. Two one-byte operands follow the **multianewarray** opcode and are combined to form an unsigned 16-bit index into the constant pool. A description of the class of object for which the array is to be created is found in the constant pool at the specified index. If it hasn't already, the virtual machine resolves the symbolic reference. Immediately following the two one-byte operands that form the constant pool index is an unsigned one-byte operand that specifies the number of dimensions in this multidimensional array. The sizes for each dimension are popped off the stack. This instruction allocates space for all arrays that are needed to implement the multidimensional arrays.

The constant pool entry referred to by a **multianewarray** instruction contains a **Constant_CLASS** entry with an array class name. For example, the constant pool entry for a four-dimensional array of float would have the name "**[[[F**". The class name in the constant pool entry can have more (but not fewer) left brackets than indicated by the dimensions byte. The virtual machine always creates the number of dimensions specified by the dimensions byte.

Table 15-7 shows the **arraylength** instruction, which pops an array reference off the top of the stack and pushes the length of that array.

The opcodes shown in Table 15-8 retrieve an element from an array. The array index and array reference are popped from the stack, and the value at the specified index of the specified array is pushed back onto the stack. The **baload** opcode converts the **byte** or **boolean** value to **int** by sign-extending and then pushes the **int**. Likewise, the **saload** opcode con-

**Table 15-6.**

Creating new arrays

| Opcode | Operand(s) | Description |
|---|---|---|
| **newarray** | atype | pops length, allocates new array of primitive types of type indicated by atype, pushes objectref of new array |
| **anewarray** | indexbyte1, indexbyte2 | pops length, allocates a new array of objects of class indicated by indexbyte1 and indexbyte2, pushes objectref of new array |
| **multianewarray** | indexbyte1, indexbyte2, dimensions | pops dimensions number of array lengths, allocates a new multidimensional array of class indicated by indexbyte1 and indexbyte2, pushes objectref of new array |

**Table 15-7.**

Getting an array

| Opcode | Operand(s) | Description |
|---|---|---|
| **arraylength** | (none) | pops objectref of an array, pushes length of that array |

**Table 15-8.**

*Retrieving an array element*

| Opcode | Operand(s) | Description |
|--------|-----------|-------------|
| baload | (none) | pops index and arrayref of an array of **byte**s or **boolean**s, pushes arrayref[index] |
| caload | (none) | pops index and arrayref of an array of **char**s, pushes arrayref[index] |
| saload | (none) | pops index and arrayref of an array of **short**s, pushes arrayref[index] |
| iaload | (none) | pops index and arrayref of an array of **int**s, pushes arrayref[index] |
| laload | (none) | pops index and arrayref of an array of **long**s, pushes arrayref[index] |
| faload | (none) | pops index and arrayref of an array of **float**s, pushes arrayref[index] |
| daload | (none) | pops index and arrayref of an array of **double**s, pushes arrayref[index] |
| aaload | (none) | pops index and arrayref of an array of **objectref**s, pushes arrayref[index] |

verts the short value to **int** by sign-extending and then pushes the **int**. The **caload** instruction converts the **char** to an **int** by zero-extending and then pushes the **int**.

Table 15-9 shows the opcodes that store a value into an array element. The value, index, and array reference are popped from the top of the stack. The **bastore** instruction stores just the lower eight bits of the popped **int** value. The **sastore** and **castore** instructions just store the lower 16 bits of the popped **int** value.

# Three-Dimensional Array: A Simulation

The *Three-Dimensional Array* applet, shown in Figure 15-1, demonstrates a Java Virtual Machine executing a sequence of bytecodes. This applet is embedded in a web page on the CD-ROM in the file **applets/ ThreeDArray.html**.

The bytecode sequence in the simulation was generated by **javac** for the **initAnArray()** method of the following class:

**Table 15-9.**

Storing to an
array element

| Opcode | Operand(s) | Description |
| --- | --- | --- |
| **bastore** | (none) | pops value, index, and arrayref of an array of **byte**s or **boolean**s, assigns arrayref[index] = value |
| **castore** | (none) | pops value, index, and arrayref of an array of **char**s, assigns arrayref[index] = value |
| **sastore** | (none) | pops value, index, and arrayref of an array of **short**s, assigns arrayref[index] = value |
| **iastore** | (none) | pops value, index, and arrayref of an array of **int**s, assigns arrayref[index] = value |
| **lastore** | (none) | pops value, index, and arrayref of an array of **long**s, assigns arrayref[index] = value |
| **fastore** | (none) | pops value, index, and arrayref of an array of **float**s, assigns arrayref[index] = value |
| **dastore** | (none) | pops value, index, and arrayref of an array of **double**s, assigns arrayref[index] = value |
| **aastore** | (none) | pops value, index, and arrayref of an array of **objectref**s, assigns arrayref[index] = value |

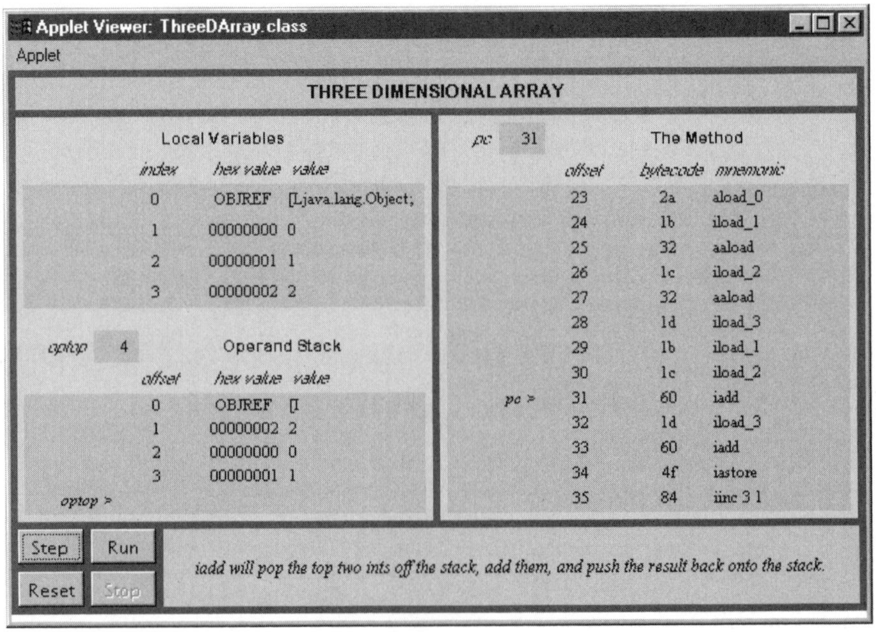

**Figure 15-1.**
The **Three-
Dimensional
Array** applet.

```
// On CD-ROM in file opcodes/ex1/ThreeDTree.java
class ThreeDTree {

    static void initAnArray() {

        int[][][] threeD = new int[5][4][3];

        for (int i = 0; i < 5; ++i) {
            for (int j = 0; j < 4; ++j) {
                for (int k = 0; k < 3; ++k) {
                    threeD[i][j][k] = i + j + k;
                }
            }
        }
    }
}
```

The bytecodes generated by **javac** for **initAnArray()** are as follow:

```
 0 iconst_5          // Push constant int 5.
 1 iconst_4          // Push constant int 4.
 2 iconst_3          // Push constant int 3.
                     // Create a new multi-dimensional array
                     // using constant pool entry #2 as the
                     // class (which is [[[I, an 3D array of
                     // ints) with a dimension of 3.
 3 multianewarray #2 dim #3 <Class [[[I>
                     // Pop object ref into local variable 0:
 7 astore_0          // int threeD[][][] = new int[5][4][3];
 8 iconst_0          // Push constant int 0.
                     // Pop int into local variable 1:
 9 istore_1          // int i = 0;
                     // Go to section of code that tests
10 goto 54           // outer loop.
13 iconst_0          // Push constant int 0.
                     // Pop int into local variable 2:
14 istore_2          // int j = 0;
                     // Go to section of code that tests
15 goto 46           // middle loop.
18 iconst_0          // Push constant int 0.
                     // Pop int into local variable 3:
19 istore_3          // int k = 0;
                     // Go to section of code that tests
20 goto 38           // inner loop.
23 aload_0           // Push object ref from local variable 0.
24 iload_1           // Push int from local variable 1 (i).
                     // Pop index and arrayref, push object
                     // ref at arrayref[index] (gets
25 aaload            // threeD[i]).
26 iload_2           // Push int from local variable 2 (j).
                     // Pop index and arrayref, push object
                     // ref at arrayref[index] (gets
```

```
27 aaload          // threeD[i][j]).
28 iload_3         // Push int from local variable 3 (k).
                   // Now calculate the int that will be
                   // assigned to threeD[i][j][k]
29 iload_1         // Push int from local variable 1 (i).
30 iload_2         // Push int from local variable 2 (j).
                   // Pop two ints, add them, push int
31 iadd            // result (i + j).
32 iload_3         // Push int from local variable 3 (k).
                   // Pop two ints, add them, push int
33 iadd            // result (i + j + k).
                   // Pop value, index, and arrayref; assign
                   // arrayref[index] = value:
34 iastore         // threeD[i][j][k] = i + j + k;
                   // Increment by 1 the int in local
35 iinc 3 1        // variable 3: ++k;
38 iload_3         // Push int from local variable 3 (k).
39 iconst_3        // Push constant int 3.
                   // Pop right and left ints, jump if
40 if_icmplt 23    // left < right: for (...; k < 3;...)
                   // Increment by 1 the int in local
43 iinc 2 1        // variable 2: ++j;
46 iload_2         // Push int from local variable 2 (j).
47 iconst_4        // Push constant int 4.
                   // Pop right and left ints, jump if
48 if_icmplt 18    // left < right: for (...; j < 4;...)
                   // Increment by 1 the int in local
51 iinc 1 1        // variable 1: ++i;
54 iload_1         // Push int from local variable 1 (i).
55 iconst_5        // Push constant int 5.
56 if_icmplt 13    // Pop right and left ints, jump if
                   // left < right: for (...; i < 5;...)
59 return
```

The `initAnArray()` method merely allocates and initializes a three-dimensional array. This simulation demonstrates how the Java Virtual Machine handles multidimensional arrays. In response to the `multianewarray` instruction, which in this example requests the allocation of a three-dimensional array, the Java Virtual Machine creates a tree of one-dimensional arrays. The reference returned by the `multianewarray` instruction refers to the base one-dimensional array in the tree. In the `initAnArray()` method, the base array has five components—`threeD[0]` through `threeD[4]`. Each component of the base array is itself a reference to a one-dimensional array of four components, accessed by `threeD[0][0]` through `threeD[4][3]`. The components of these five arrays are also references to arrays, each of which has three components. These components are `int`s, the elements of this multidimensional array, and they are accessed by `threeD[0][0][0]` through `threeD[4][3][2]`.

In response to the **multianewarray** instruction in the **initAnArray()** method, the Java Virtual Machine creates 1 five-dimensional array of arrays, 5 four-dimensional arrays of arrays, and 20 three-dimensional arrays of **ints**. The Java Virtual Machine allocates these 26 arrays on the heap, initializes their components so that they form a tree, and returns the reference to the base array.

To assign an **int** value to an element of the three-dimensional array, the Java Virtual Machine uses **aaload** to get a component of the base array. Then the Java Virtual Machine uses **aaload** again on this component—which is itself an array of arrays—to get a component of the branch array. This component is a reference to a leaf array of **ints**. Finally, the Java Virtual Machine uses **iastore** to assign an **int** value to the element of the leaf array. The Java Virtual Machine uses multiple one-dimensional array accesses to accomplish operations on multidimensional arrays.

To drive the *Three-Dimensional Array* simulation, use the Step, Reset, Run, and Stop buttons. Each time you click the Step button, the simulator will execute the instruction pointed to by the pc register. If you click the Run button, the simulation will continue with no further coaxing on your part until you click the Stop button. To start the simulation over, click the Reset button. For each step of the simulation, a panel at the bottom of the applet contains an explanation of what the next instruction will do. Happy clicking.

# On the CD-ROM

The CD-ROM contains the source code examples from this chapter in the **opcodes** directory. The *Three-Dimensional Array* applet is part of a web page on the CD-ROM in the file **applets/ThreeDArray.html**. The source code for this applet is found alongside its class files, in the **applets/JVMSimulators** and **applets/JVMSimulators/COM/artima/jvmsim** directories.

# The Resources Page

For more information about the material presented in this chapter, visit the resources page: **http://www.artima.com/insidejvm/objects.html**.

# 16

# Control Flow

This chapter describes the instructions that cause the Java Virtual Machine to conditionally or unconditionally branch to a different location within the same method. This chapter includes the instructions that implement the **if**, **if-else**, **while**, **do-while**, **for**, and **switch** statements of Java source code.

Accompanying this chapter on the CD-ROM is an applet that interactively illustrates the material presented in the chapter. The applet, named *Saying Tomato*, simulates the Java Virtual Machine executing a method that includes bytecodes that perform table jumps (the compiled version of a **switch** statement in Java source code). At the end of this chapter, you will find a description of this applet and the bytecodes it executes.

# Conditional Branching

In Java source code, you specify basic control flow within a method by using **if**, **if-else**, **while**, **do-while**, **for**, and **switch** statements. With the exception of **switch**, Java compilers draw from the same set of opcodes when translating all these source code constructs to bytecodes. For example, the simplest control flow construct Java offers is the **if** statement. When a Java program is compiled, the **if** statement can be translated to any one of a variety of opcodes, depending on the nature of the **if**'s expression. Each opcode either pops one or two values from the top of the stack and does a comparison. The opcodes that pop only one value compare that value with zero. The opcodes that pop two values compare one with the other. If the comparison succeeds (success is defined differently by each individual opcode), the Java Virtual Machine branches—or jumps—to the offset given as an operand to the comparison opcode.

For each of the conditional branch opcodes, the Java Virtual Machine follows the same procedure to determine the next instruction to execute. The virtual machine first performs the comparison specified by the opcode. If the comparison fails, the virtual machine continues execution with the instruction that immediately follows the conditional branch instruction. If the comparison succeeds, the virtual machine forms a signed 16-bit offset from two operand bytes that trail the opcode. It adds the offset to the contents of the current pc register (the address of the conditional branch opcode) to get the target address. The target address must point to an opcode of an instruction in the same method. Execution continues as the target address.

**Table 16-1.**

Conditional
branch: integer
comparison with
zero

| Opcode | Operand(s) | Description |
|--------|-----------|-------------|
| **ifeq** | branchbyte1, branchbyte2 | pop **int** value; if value == 0, branch to offset |
| **ifne** | branchbyte1, branchbyte2 | pop **int** value; if value != 0, branch to offset |
| **iflt** | branchbyte1, branchbyte2 | pop **int** value; if value < 0, branch to offset |
| **ifle** | branchbyte1, branchbyte2 | pop **int** value; if value <= 0, branch to offset |
| **ifgt** | branchbyte1, branchbyte2 | pop **int** value; if value > 0, branch to offset |
| **ifge** | branchbyte1, branchbyte2 | pop **int** value; if value >= 0, branch to offset |

One family of **if** opcodes, shown in Table 16-1, performs integer comparisons against zero. When the Java Virtual Machine encounters one of these opcodes, it pops one **int** off the stack and compares it with zero.

Another family of **if** opcodes, shown in Table 16-2, pops two integers off the top of the stack and compares them against one another. The virtual machine branches if the comparison succeeds. Just before these opcodes are executed, value2 is on the top of the stack; value1 is just beneath value2.

The opcodes shown in Table 16-2 operate on **ints**. These opcodes also are used for comparisons of types **short**, **byte**, and **char**; the Java Virtual Machine always manipulates types smaller than **int** by first converting them to **ints** and then manipulating the **ints**.

A third family of opcodes, shown in Table 16-3, takes care of comparisons of the other primitive types: **long**, **float**, and **double**. These opcodes

**Table 16-2.**

Conditional branch: comparison of two integers

| Opcode | Operand(s) | Description |
|---|---|---|
| if_icmpeq | branchbyte1, branchbyte2 | pop **int** value2 and value1; if value1 == value2, branch to offset |
| if_icmpne | branchbyte1, branchbyte2 | pop **int** value2 and value1; if value1 != value2, branch to offset |
| if_icmplt | branchbyte1, branchbyte2 | pop **int** value2 and value1; if value1 < value2, branch to offset |
| if_icmple | branchbyte1, branchbyte2 | pop **int** value2 and value1; if value1 <= value2, branch to offset |
| if_icmpgt | branchbyte1, branchbyte2 | pop **int** value2 and value1; if value1 > value2, branch to offset |
| if_icmpge | branchbyte1, branchbyte2 | pop **int** value2 and value1; if value1 >= value2, branch to offset |

**Table 16-3.**

Comparison of **longs, floats,** and **doubles**

| Opcode | Operand(s) | Description |
|---|---|---|
| lcmp | (none) | pop **long** value2 and value1, compare, push **int** result |
| fcmpg | (none) | pop **float** value2 and value1, compare, push **int** result |
| fcmpl | (none) | pop **float** value2 and value1, compare, push **int** result |
| dcmpg | (none) | pop **double** value2 and value1, compare, push **int** result |
| dcmpl | (none) | pop **double** value2 and value1, compare, push **int** result |

don't cause a branch by themselves. Instead, they push the **int** value that represents the result of the comparison—0 for equal to, 1 for greater than, and –1 for less than—and then use one of the **int** compare opcodes introduced above to force the actual branch.

The two opcodes for **float** comparisons (**fcmpg** and **fcmpl**) differ only in how they handle NaN ("not a number"). In the Java Virtual Machine, comparisons of floating-point numbers always fail if one of the values being compared is NaN. If neither value being compared is NaN, both **fcmpg** and **fcmpl** instructions push a 0 if the values are equal, a 1 if value1 is greater than value2, and a –1 if value1 is less than value2. But if one or both of the values are NaN, the **fcmpg** instruction pushes a 1, whereas the **fcmpl** instruction pushes a –1. Because both of these operands are available, any comparison between two **float** values can push the same result onto the stack independent of whether the comparison failed because of a NaN. This is also true for the two opcodes that compare **double** values: **dcmpg** and **dcmpl**.

A fourth family of **if** opcodes, shown in Table 16-4, pops one object reference off the top of the stack and compares it with **null**. If the comparison succeeds, the Java Virtual Machine branches.

The last family of **if** opcodes, which is shown in Table 16-5, pops two object references off the stack and compares them with each other. In this case, only two comparisons make sense: "equals" and "not equals." If the references are equal, then they refer to the exact same object on the heap. If not, they refer to two different objects. As with all the other **if** opcodes, if the comparison succeeds, the Java Virtual Machine branches.

**Table 16-4.**

Conditional branch: object reference comparison with **null**

| Opcode | Operand(s) | Description |
|---|---|---|
| ifnull | branchbyte1, branchbyte2 | pop reference value; if value == null, branches to offset |
| ifnonnull | branchbyte1, branchbyte2 | pop reference value; if value != null, branches to offset |

**Table 16-5.**

Conditional branch: comparison of two object references

| Opcode | Operand(s) | Description |
|---|---|---|
| if_acmpeq | branchbyte1, branchbyte2 | pop reference value2 and value1; if value1 == value2, branch to offset |
| if_acmpne | branchbyte1, branchbyte2 | pop reference value2 and value1; if value1 != value2, branch to offset |

# Unconditional Branching

The preceding section describes all the opcodes that cause the Java Virtual Machine to branch conditionally. One other family of opcodes, however, causes the virtual machine to branch unconditionally. Not surprisingly, these opcodes, shown in Table 16-6, are called **goto**. To execute a **goto** instruction, the virtual machine forms a signed 16-bit offset from two operand bytes that follow the **goto** opcode. (To execute a **goto_w** instruction, the virtual machine forms a signed 32-bit offset from four operand bytes that follow the **goto_w** opcode.) The virtual machine adds this offset to the current contents of the pc register. The resulting address must contain an opcode of an instruction in the current method. The virtual machine continues execution at this instruction.

The opcodes shown in Tables 16-1 through 16-6 are sufficient to express in the bytecodes any control flow specified in Java source code with an **if**, **if-else**, **while**, **do-while**, or **for** statement. The preceding opcodes also could be used to express a **switch** statement, but the Java Virtual Machine's instruction set includes two opcodes specially designed for the **switch** statement: **tableswitch** and **lookupswitch**.

# Conditional Branching with Tables

The **tableswitch** and **lookupswitch** instructions, shown in Table 16-7, both include one default branch offset and a variable-length set of **case** value/branch offset pairs. Both instructions pop the key (the value of the expression in the parentheses immediately following the **switch** keyword) from the stack. The key is compared with all the case values. If a match is found, the branch offset associated with the case value is taken. If no match is found, the default branch offset is taken.

The difference between **tableswitch** and **lookupswitch** is in how they indicate the case values. The **lookupswitch** instruction is more general purpose than **tableswitch**, but **tableswitch** is usually more efficient.

**Table 16-6.**

Unconditional branch

| Opcode | Operand(s) | Description |
|--------|------------|-------------|
| **goto** | branchbyte1, branchbyte2 | branch to offset |
| **goto_w** | branchbyte1, branchbyte2, branchbyte3, branchbyte4 | branch to offset |

Both instructions are followed by zero to three bytes of padding—enough so that the byte immediately following the padding starts at an address that is a multiple of four bytes from the beginning of the method. (These two instructions, by the way, are the only ones in the entire Java Virtual Machine instruction set that involve alignment on a greater than one-byte boundary.) For both instructions, the next four bytes after the padding make up the default branch offset.

After the zero- to three-byte padding and the four-byte default branch offset, the **lookupswitch** opcode is followed by a four-byte value, npairs, which indicates the number of case value/branch offset pairs that will follow. The case value is an **int**, which highlights the fact that switch statements in Java require a key expression that is an **int**, **short**, **char**, or **byte**. If you attempt to use a **long**, **float**, or **double** as a switch key, your program won't compile. The branch offset associated with each case value is another four-byte offset. The value/branch offset pairs must appear in increasing numerical order of case value.

In the **tableswitch** instruction, the zero- to three-byte padding and the four-byte default branch offset are followed by low and high **int** values. The low and high values indicate the endpoints of a range of case values included in this **tableswitch** instruction. Following the low and high values are high – low + 1 branch offsets—one branch offset for high, one for low, and one for each integer case value in between high and low. The branch offset for low immediately follows the high value.

Thus, when the Java Virtual Machine encounters a **lookupswitch** instruction, it must check the key against each case value until it finds a match, encounters a case value greater than the key (the value/branch offset pairs are sorted in increasing numerical order of case value), or runs out of case values. If the virtual machine doesn't find a match, it uses the

**Table 16-7.**

Table jumping

| Opcode | Operand(s) | Description |
|---|---|---|
| **lookupswitch** | <0-3 byte pad>defaultbyte1, defaultbyte2, defaultbyte3, defaultbyte4, npairs1, npairs2, npairs3, npairs4, case value/branch offset pairs . . . | pop key, match key with case values, if match found jump to associated branch offset, else jump to default branch offset |
| **tableswitch** | <0-3 byte pad>defaultbyte1, defaultbyte2, defaultbyte3, defaultbyte4, lowbyte1, lowbyte2, lowbyte3, lowbyte4, highbyte1, highbyte2, highbyte3, highbyte4, branch offsets . . . | pop key, if not in low/high range jump to default branch offset, else get the (key – low) branch offset and jump |

default branch offset. On the other hand, when the Java Virtual Machine encounters a **tableswitch** instruction, it can simply check to see whether the key is within the range defined by low and high. If not, it takes the default branch offset. If so, it just subtracts low from key to get an offset into the list of branch offsets. This way, it can determine the appropriate branch offset without having to check each case value.

Other than the opcodes described in the preceding table, the only Java Virtual Machine instructions that affect control flow are those that deal with throwing and catching exceptions, finally clauses, and invoking and returning from methods. These opcodes are discussed in later chapters.

# Saying Tomato: A Simulation

The *Saying Tomato* applet, shown in Figure 16-1, demonstrates a Java Virtual Machine executing a sequence of bytecodes. The applet is part of a web page on the CD-ROM in the file **applets/SayingTomato.html**. The bytecode sequence in the simulation was generated by the **javac** compiler for the **argue()** method of the following class:

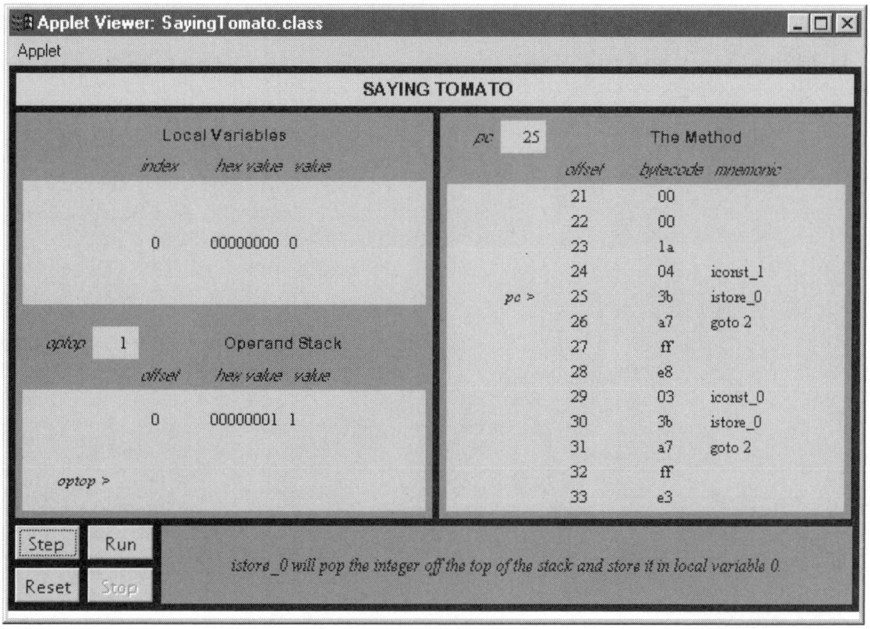

**Figure 16-1.**
The **Saying Tomato**
applet.

```
// On CD-ROM in file opcodes/ex1/Struggle.java
class Struggle {

    public final static int TOMAYTO = 0;
    public final static int TOMAHTO = 1;

    static void argue() {

        int say = TOMAYTO;

        for (;;) {

            switch (say) {

            case TOMAYTO:

                say = TOMAHTO;
                break;

            case TOMAHTO:

                say = TOMAYTO;
                break;
            }
        }
    }
}
```

The bytecodes generated by **javac** for the **argue()** method are as follow:

```
 0 iconst_0          // Push constant 0 (TOMAYTO)
                     // Pop into local var 0:
 1 istore_0          // int say = TOMAYTO;
 2 iload_0           // Push key for switch from local var 0
                     // Perform switch statement:
                     // switch (say) {...
                     // Low case value is 0, high case value 1
                     // Default branch offset will goto 2
 3 tableswitch 0 to 1: default=2
           0: 24 // case 0 (TOMAYTO): goto 24
           1: 29 // case 1 (TOMAHTO): goto 29
                     // Note that the next instruction starts
                     // at address 24, which means the
                     // tableswitch took up 21 bytes
24 iconst_1          // Push constant 1 (TOMAHTO)
25 istore_0          // Pop into local var 0: say = TOMAHTO
                     // Branch unconditionally to 2, top of
26 goto 2            // while loop
29 iconst_0          // Push constant 1 (TOMAYTO)
30 istore_0          // Pop into local var 0: say = TOMAYTO
                     // Branch unconditionally to 2, top of
31 goto 2            // while loop
```

The **argue()** method merely switches the value of **say** back and forth between **TOMAYTO** and **TOMAHTO**. Because the values of **TOMAYTO** and **TOMAHTO** were consecutive (**TOMAYTO** was a 0 and **TOMAHTO** was a 1), the **javac** compiler used a **tableswitch**. The **tableswitch** is a more efficient instruction than a **lookupswitch**, and the equivalent **lookupswitch** instruction would occupy 28 bytes—4 bytes more than **tableswitch**.

It turns out that even if **TOMAYTO** were a 0 and **TOMAHTO** were a 2, the **javac** compiler still would have used a **tableswitch**, because even with the extra default branch offset in there for a 1, the **tableswitch** instruction would occupy only 28 bytes—the same number of bytes as the equivalent **lookupswitch**. Both instructions occupy the same number of bytes, but **tableswitch** is more efficient, so it is used. As soon as you make **TOMAHTO** a 3, however, **javac** starts using a **lookupswitch** because a **tableswitch** would now need two default branch offsets in its list (for 1 and 2), which would push its size up to 32 bytes. Thus, a **lookupswitch** now would require fewer bytes than a **tableswitch**, so **javac** chooses the **lookupswitch**.

The branch offsets for the case values cause the Java Virtual Machine to hop down to code that will change the value of the **say** local variable. The value of **say** will alternate between **TOMAYTO** and **TOMAHTO** indefinitely, until the user aborts the program, thereby calling the whole thing off.

To drive the *Saying Tomato* simulation, use the Step, Reset, Run, and Stop buttons. Each time you click the Step button, the simulator will execute the instruction pointed to by the pc register. If you click the Run button, the simulation will continue with no further coaxing on your part until you click the Stop button. To start the simulation over, click the Reset button. For each step of the simulation, a panel at the bottom of the applet contains an explanation of what the next instruction will do. Happy clicking.

# On the CD-ROM

The CD-ROM contains the source code examples from this chapter in the **opcodes** directory. The *Saying Tomato* applet is contained in a web page on the CD-ROM in the file **applets/SayingTomato.html**. The source code for this applet is found alongside its class files, in the **applets/JVMSimulators** and **applets/JVMSimulators/COM/artima/jvmsim** directories.

# The Resources Page

For more information about the material presented in this chapter, visit the resources page: `http://www.artima.com/insidejvm/flow.html`.

# 17

# Exceptions

This chapter shows how exceptions are implemented in bytecodes. It describes the instruction for throwing an exception explicitly, explains exception tables, and shows how catch clauses work.

Accompanying this chapter on the CD-ROM is an applet that interactively illustrates the material presented in the chapter. The applet, named *Play Ball!*, simulates the Java Virtual Machine executing a method that throws and catches exceptions. At the end of this chapter, you will find a description of this applet and the bytecodes it executes.

# Throwing and Catching Exceptions

Exceptions allow you to smoothly handle unexpected conditions that occur as your programs run. To demonstrate the way the Java Virtual Machine handles exceptions, consider a class named **NitPickyMath** that provides methods that perform addition, subtraction, multiplication, division, and remainder on integers. **NitPickyMath** performs these mathematical operations the same as the normal operations offered by Java's **+**, **-**, **\***, **/**, and **%** operators, except the methods in **NitPickyMath** throw checked exceptions on overflow, underflow, and divide-by-zero conditions. The Java Virtual Machine will throw an **ArithmeticException** on an integer divide-by-zero but will not throw any exceptions on overflow and underflow. The exceptions thrown by the methods of **NitPickyMath** are defined as follows:

```
// On CD-ROM in file except/ex1/OverflowException.java
class OverflowException extends Exception {
}

// On CD-ROM in file except/ex1/UnderflowException.java
class UnderflowException extends Exception {
}

// On CD-ROM in file except/ex1/DivideByZeroException.java
class DivideByZeroException extends Exception {
}
```

A simple method that catches and throws exceptions is the **remainder()** method of class **NitPickyMath**:

```
// On CD-ROM in file except/ex1/NitpickyMath.java
class NitpickyMath {

    static int add(int a, int b)
        throws OverflowException, UnderflowException {

        long longA = (long) a;
        long longB = (long) b;
        long result = a + b;
        if (result > Integer.MAX_VALUE) {
            throw new OverflowException();
        }
        if (result < Integer.MIN_VALUE) {
            throw new UnderflowException();
        }
        return (int) result;
    }
```

```
static int subtract(int minuend, int subtrahend)
    throws OverflowException, UnderflowException {

    long longMinuend = (long) minuend;
    long longSubtrahend = (long) subtrahend;
    long result = longMinuend - longSubtrahend;
    if (result > Integer.MAX_VALUE) {
        throw new OverflowException();
    }
    if (result < Integer.MIN_VALUE) {
        throw new UnderflowException();
    }
    return (int) result;
}

static int multiply(int a, int b)
    throws OverflowException, UnderflowException {

    long longA = (long) a;
    long longB = (long) b;
    long result = a * b;
    if (result > Integer.MAX_VALUE) {
        throw new OverflowException();
    }
    if (result < Integer.MIN_VALUE) {
        throw new UnderflowException();
    }
    return (int) result;
}

static int divide(int dividend, int divisor)
    throws OverflowException, DivideByZeroException {

    // Overflow can occur in division when dividing
    // the negative integer of the largest possible
    // magnitude (Integer.MIN_VALUE) by -1, because
    // this would just flip the sign, but there is no
    // way to represent that number in an int.
    if ((dividend == Integer.MIN_VALUE) &&
        (divisor == -1)) {
        throw new OverflowException();
    }
    try {
        return dividend / divisor;
    }
    catch (ArithmeticException e) {
        throw new DivideByZeroException();
    }
}

static int remainder(int dividend, int divisor)
    throws OverflowException, DivideByZeroException {
```

```
        // Overflow can occur in division when dividing
        // the negative integer of the largest possible
        // magnitude (Integer.MIN_VALUE) by -1, because
        // this would just flip the sign, but there is no
        // way to represent that number in an int.
        if ((dividend == Integer.MIN_VALUE) &&
            (divisor == -1)) {
            throw new OverflowException();
        }
        try {
            return dividend % divisor;
        }
        catch (ArithmeticException e) {
            throw new DivideByZeroException();
        }
    }
}
```

The `remainder()` method simply performs the remainder operation (%) on the two `int`s passed as arguments. The remainder operation throws an `ArithmeticException` if the divisor of the remainder operation is a zero. This method catches this `ArithmeticException` and throws a `DivideByZeroException`.

The difference between these two exceptions is that `DivideByZeroException` is checked and `ArithmeticException` is unchecked. Because the `ArithmeticException` is unchecked, a method need not declare this exception in a `throws` clause even though it might throw it. Any exceptions that are subclasses of either `Error` or `RuntimeException` are unchecked. (`ArithmeticException` is a subclass of `RuntimeException`.) By catching `ArithmeticException` and then throwing `DivideByZeroException`, the `remainder()` method forces its clients to deal with the possibility of a divide-by-zero exception, either by catching it or declaring `DivideByZeroException` in their own `throws` clauses.

`javac` generates the following bytecode sequence for the `remainder` method:

```
// The main bytecode sequence for remainder():

              // Push local variable 0 (arg passed as
  0 iload_0   // dividend)
              // Push the minimum integer value
  1 ldc #1 <Integer -2147483648>
              // If the dividend isn't equal to the minimum
              // integer, jump to the remainder calculation
  3 if_icmpne 19

              // Push local variable 1 (arg passed as
```

```
 6 iload_1   // divisor)
             // Push -1
 7 iconst_m1
             // If the divisor isn't equal to -1, jump
             // to the remainder calculation
 8 if_icmpne 19
             // This is an overflow case, so throw an
             // exception. Create a new OverflowException,
             // push reference to it onto the stack
11 new #4 <Class OverflowException>
14 dup       // Make a copy of the reference
             // Pop one copy of the reference and invoke
             // the <init> method of new OverflowException
             // object
15 invokespecial #10 <Method OverflowException()>
             // Pop the other reference to the
             // OverflowException and throw it
18 athrow

// Calculate the remainder

             // Push local variable 0 (arg passed as
19 iload_0   // dividend)
             // Push local variable 1 (arg passed as
20 iload_1   // divisor)
             // Pop divisor; pop dividend; calculate, push
21 irem      // remainder
22 ireturn   // Return int on top of stack (the remainder)


// The bytecode sequence for the
// catch (ArithmeticException) clause:

             // Pop the reference to the
             // ArithmeticException because it isn't used
23 pop       // by this catch clause.
24 new #2 <Class DivideByZeroException>
             // Create and push reference to new object of
             // class DivideByZeroException.
             // Duplicate the reference to the new object
             // on the top of the stack because it must be
             // both initialized and thrown. The
             // initialization will consume the copy of the
27 dup       // reference created by the dup.
             // Call the no-arg <init> method for the
             // DivideByZeroException to initialize it.
             // This instruction will pop the top reference
             // to the object.
28 invokespecial #9 <Method DivideByZeroException()>
             // Pop the reference to a Throwable object, in
             // this case the DivideByZeroException,
31 athrow    // and throw the exception.
```

The bytecode sequence of the **remainder()** method has two separate parts. The first part is the normal path of execution for the method. This part goes from pc offset zero through 22. The second part is the catch clause, which goes from pc offset 23 through 31.

# The Exception Table

The *irem* instruction in the main bytecode sequence might throw an **ArithmeticException**. If this situation occurs, the Java Virtual Machine knows to jump to the bytecode sequence that implements the catch clause by looking up and finding the exception in a table. Each method that catches exceptions is associated with an *exception table* that is delivered in the class file along with the bytecode sequence of the method. The exception table has one entry for each exception that is caught by each try block. Each entry has four pieces of information:

- the start point
- the end point
- the pc offset within the bytecode sequence to jump to
- a constant pool index of the exception class that is being caught

The exception table for the **remainder()** method of class **NitPickyMath** is as follows:

```
Exception table:
   from    to   target  type
    19     23     23    <Class java.lang.ArithmeticException>
```

The preceding exception table indicates that from pc offset 19 through 22, inclusive, **ArithmeticException** is caught. The try block's endpoint value, listed in the table under the label "to," is always one more than the last pc offset for which the exception is caught. In this case the endpoint value is listed as 23, but the last pc offset for which the exception is caught is 22. This range, 19 to 22 inclusive, corresponds to the bytecode sequence that implements the code inside the try block of **remainder()**. The target listed in the table is the pc offset to jump to if an **ArithmeticException** is thrown between the pc offsets 19 and 22, inclusive.

If an exception is thrown during the execution of a method, the Java Virtual Machine searches through the exception table for a matching entry. An exception table entry matches if the current program counter is

**Table 17-1.**

Throwing
exceptions

| Opcode | Operand(s) | Description |
|--------|-----------|-------------|
| **athrow** | (none) | pops Throwable object reference, throws the exception |

within the range specified by the entry, and if the exception class thrown is the exception class specified by the entry (or is a subclass of the specified exception class). The Java Virtual Machine searches through the exception table in the order in which the entries appear in the table. When the first match is found, the virtual machine sets the program counter to the new pc offset location and continues execution there. If no match is found, the virtual machine pops the current stack frame and rethrows the same exception. When the Java Virtual Machine pops the current stack frame, it effectively aborts execution of the current method and returns to the method that called this method. But instead of continuing execution normally in the previous method, it throws the same exception in that method, which causes the virtual machine to go through the same process of searching through the exception table of that method.

A Java programmer can throw an exception with a throw statement such as the one in the catch (**ArithmeticException**) clause of **remainder()**, where a **DivideByZeroException** is created and thrown. The bytecode that does the throwing is shown in Table 17-1.

The **athrow** instruction pops the top word from the stack and expects it to be a reference to an object that is a subclass of **Throwable** (or **Throwable** itself). The exception thrown is of the type defined by the popped object reference.

# Play Ball!: A Simulation

The *Play Ball!* applet, shown in Figure 17-1, demonstrates a Java Virtual Machine executing a sequence of bytecodes. This applet is embedded in a web page on the CD-ROM in the file **applets/PlayBall.html**. The bytecode sequence in the simulation was generated by **javac** for the **playBall** method of the following class:

```
// On CD-ROM in file except/ex2/Ball.java
class Ball extends Exception {
}

// On CD-ROM in file except/ex2/Pitcher.java
class Pitcher {
```

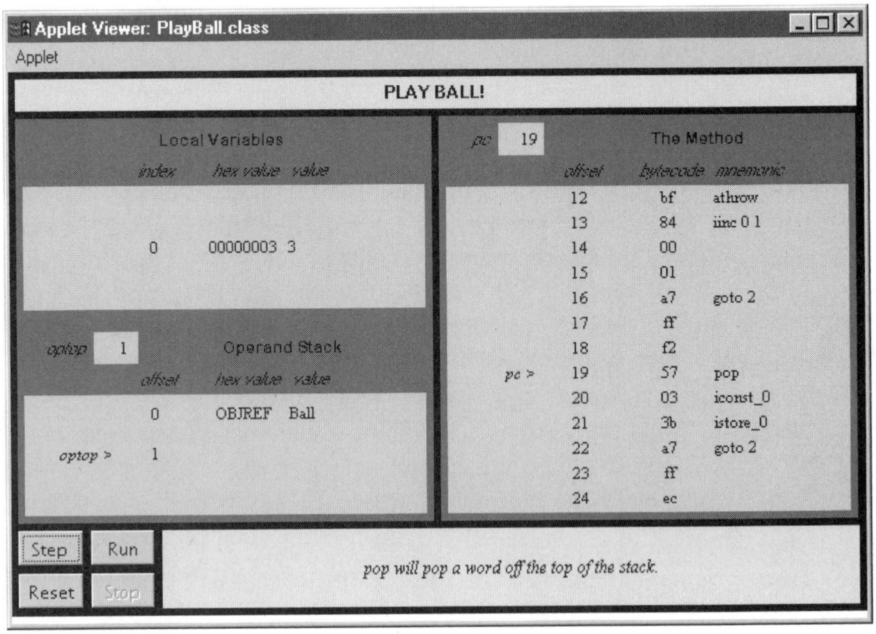

**Figure 17-1.**
The **Play Ball!**
applet.

```
private static Ball ball = new Ball();

static void playBall() {
    int i = 0;
    for (;;) {
        try {
            if (i % 4 == 3) {
                throw ball;
            }
            ++i;
        }
        catch (Ball b) {
            i = 0;
        }
    }
}
```

The bytecodes generated by **javac** for the **playBall** method are as follow:

```
// The main bytecode sequence for playBall():

0 iconst_0        // Push constant 0
1 istore_0        // Pop into local var 0: int i = 0;
                  // The try block starts here (see the
                  // exception table, below).
2 iload_0         // Push local var 0
3 iconst_4        // Push constant 4
```

```
 4 irem              // Calc remainder of top two operands
 5 iconst_3          // Push constant 3
                     // Jump if remainder not equal to 3:
 6 if_icmpne 13      // if (i % 4 == 3) {
                     // Push the static field at constant pool
                     // location #6, which is the Ball
                     // exception eager to be thrown
 9 getstatic #6 <Field Ball ball>
12 athrow            // Heave it home: throw ball;
                     // Increment the int at local var 0 by 1:
13 iinc 0 1          // ++i;
                     // The try block ends here (see the
                     // exception table, below).
16 goto 2            // jump always back to 2: for (;;) {}

// The bytecode sequence for the catch (Ball) clause:

                     // Pop the exception reference because it
19 pop               // is unused
20 iconst_0          // Push constant 0
21 istore_0          // Pop into local var 0: i = 0;
22 goto 2            // Jump always back to 2: for (;;) {}

Exception table:
   from    to  target type
     2     16    19   <Class Ball>
```

The playball() method loops forever. Every fourth pass through the loop, playball() throws a Ball and catches it, just because it's fun. Because the try block and the catch clause are both within the endless while loop, the fun never stops. The local variable i starts at 0 and increments each pass through the loop. When the if statement is true, which happens every time i is equal to 3, the Ball exception is thrown.

The Java Virtual Machine checks the exception table and discovers that an applicable entry is indeed available. The entry's valid range is from 2 to 15, inclusive, and the exception is thrown at pc offset 12. The exception caught by the entry is of class Ball, and the exception thrown is of class Ball. Given this perfect match, the virtual machine pushes the thrown exception object onto the stack and continues execution at pc offset 19. The catch clause, which starts at offset 19, merely resets int i to 0, and the loop starts over.

To drive the *Play Ball!* simulation, use the Step, Reset, Run, and Stop buttons. Each time you click the Step button, the simulator will execute the instruction pointed to by the pc register. If you click the Run button, the simulation will continue with no further coaxing on your part until you click the Stop button. To start the simulation over, click the Reset button. For each step of the simulation, a panel at the bottom of the applet contains an explanation of what the next instruction will do. Happy clicking.

## On the CD-ROM

The CD-ROM contains the source code examples from this chapter in the **except** directory. The *Play Ball!* applet is contained in a web page on the CD-ROM in the file **applets/PlayBall.html**. The source code for this applet is found alongside its class files, in the **applets/JVMSimulators** and **applets/JVMSimulators/COM/artima/jvmsim** directories.

## The Resources Page

For more information about the material presented in this chapter, visit the resources page: **http://www.artima.com/insidejvm/except.html**.

# 18

# Finally Clauses

This chapter describes the way **finally** clauses are implemented in bytecodes. It describes the relevant instructions and shows how they are used. The chapter also describes some surprising behaviors exhibited by **finally** clauses in Java source code and explains this behavior at the bytecode level.

Accompanying this chapter on the CD-ROM is an applet that interactively illustrates the material presented in the chapter. The applet, named *Hop Around*, simulates the Java Virtual Machine executing a method that includes **finally** clauses. At the end of this chapter, you will find a description of this applet and the bytecodes it executes.

# Miniature Subroutines

In bytecodes, **finally** clauses act as "miniature subroutines" within a method. The subroutine for a **finally** clause is "invoked" at each exit point inside a **try** block and its associated **catch**. After the **finally** clause completes—as long as it completes by executing past the last statement in the **finally** clause, not by throwing an exception or executing a **return**, **continue**, or **break**—the miniature subroutine itself "returns." Execution continues just past the point where the miniature subroutine was called in the first place.

The opcode that causes a Java Virtual Machine to jump to a miniature subroutine is the **jsr** instruction. The **jsr** opcode takes a two-byte operand, the 16-bit signed offset from the location of the **jsr** instruction where the miniature subroutine begins. A second variant of the **jsr** instruction is **jsr_w**, which performs the same function as **jsr** but takes a wide (four-byte) operand. When the Java Virtual Machine encounters a **jsr** or **jsr_w** instruction, it pushes a return address onto the stack and then continues execution at the start of the miniature subroutine. The return address is the address (an offset or native pointer) of the bytecode immediately following the **jsr** or **jsr_w** opcode and its operands. The type of the address is **returnAddress**.

After a miniature subroutine completes, it invokes the **ret** instruction, which returns from the subroutine. The **ret** instruction takes one operand, an index into the local variables where the return address is stored. The opcodes that deal with **finally** clauses are summarized in Table 18-1.

Don't confuse a miniature subroutine with a Java method. Java methods use a different set of instructions. Instructions such as **invokevirtual** or **invokespecial** cause a Java method to be invoked, and instructions such as **return**, **areturn**, or **ireturn** cause a Java method to return. The

**Table 18-1.**

**Finally** clauses

| Opcode | Operand(s) | Description |
|--------|-----------|-------------|
| jsr | branchbyte1, branchbyte2 | pushes the return address, branches to offset |
| jsr_w | branchbyte1, branchbyte2, branchbyte3, branchbyte4 | pushes the return address, branches to wide offset |
| ret | index | returns to the address stored in local variable index |
| wide | ret, indexbyte1, indexbyte2 | returns to the address stored in local variable index |

jsr instruction does not cause a Java method to be invoked. It merely causes a jump to a different opcode within the same method. Likewise, the **ret** instruction doesn't return from a method. It just causes the virtual machine to jump back to the opcode in the same method that immediately follows the calling **jsr** opcode and its operands. In this book, the bytecodes that implement a **finally** clause are called a "miniature subroutine" because they act like a small subroutine within the bytecode stream of a single method.

# Asymmetrical Invocation and Return

You might think that the **ret** instruction should pop the return address off the stack because that is the place where it was pushed by the **jsr** instruction. But it doesn't. At the start of each subroutine, the return address is popped off the top of the stack and stored in a local variable—the same local variable from which the **ret** instruction later gets it. This asymmetrical manner of working with the return address is necessary because **finally** clauses (and therefore, miniature subroutines) themselves can throw exceptions or include **return**, **break**, or **continue** statements. Because of this possibility, the extra return address that was pushed onto the stack by the **jsr** instruction must be removed from the stack right away, so it won't still be there if the **finally** clause exits with a **break**, **continue**, **return**, or thrown exception.

As an illustration, consider the following code, which includes a **finally** clause that exits with a break statement. The result of this code is that, irrespective of the parameter **bVal** passed to method **surpriseTheProgrammer()**, the method returns **false**:

```
// On CD-ROM in file opcodes/ex3/Surprise.java
class Surprise {

    static boolean surpriseTheProgrammer(boolean bVal) {
        while (bVal) {
            try {
                return true;
            }
            finally {
                break;
            }
        }
    }
```

```
        return false;
    }
}
```

The preceding example shows the reason that the return address must be stored into a local variable at the beginning of the **finally** clause. Because the **finally** clause exits with a break, it never executes the **ret** instruction. As a result, the Java Virtual Machine never goes back to finish up the **return true** statement. Instead, it just goes ahead with the **break** and drops down past the closing curly brace of the **while** statement. The next statement is **return false**, which is precisely what the Java Virtual Machine does.

The behavior shown by this **finally** clause, which exits with a **break,** is also shown by **finally** clauses that exit with a **return** or **continue**, or by throwing an exception. In any of these cases, the **ret** instruction at the end of the **finally** clause is never executed. Because the **ret** instruction is not guaranteed to be executed, it can't be relied on to remove the return address from the stack. Therefore, the return address is stored into a local variable at the beginning of the **finally** clause's miniature subroutine.

For a complete example of a **finally** clause, consider the following method, which contains a **try** block with two exit points. In this example, both exit points are **return** statements:

```
// On CD-ROM in file opcodes/ex1/Nostalgia.java
class Nostalgia {

    static int giveMeThatOldFashionedBoolean(
        boolean bVal) {
        try {
            if (bVal) {
                return 1;
            }
            return 0;
        }
        finally {
            System.out.println("Got old fashioned.");
        }
    }
}
```

The **giveMeThatOldFashionedBoolean()** method compiles to the following bytecodes:

```
// The bytecode sequence for the try block:
 0 iload_0    // Push local variable 0 (bval parameter)
 1 ifeq 11    // Pop int, if equal to 0, jump to 11 (just
```

```
                     // past the if statement): if (bval) {}
  4 iconst_1  // Push int 1
                     // Pop an int (the 1), store into local
  5 istore_1  // variable 1
                     // Jump to the mini-subroutine for the
  6 jsr 24    // finally clause
  9 iload_1   // Push local variable 1 (the 1)
                     // Return int on top of the stack (the 1):
 10 ireturn   // return 1;
 11 iconst_0  // Push int 0
                     // Pop an int (the 0), store into local
 12 istore_1  // variable 1
                     // Jump to the mini-subroutine for the
 13 jsr 24    // finally clause
 16 iload_1   // Push local variable 1 (the 0)
                     // Return int on top of the stack (the 0):
 17 ireturn   // return 0;

 // The bytecode sequence for a catch clause that catches
 // any kind of exception thrown from within the try block.
                     // Pop the reference to the thrown exception,
 18 astore_2  // store into local variable 2
                     // Jump to the mini-subroutine for the
 19 jsr 24    // finally clause
                     // Push the reference (to the thrown
 22 aload_2   // exception) from local variable 2
 23 athrow    // Rethrow the same exception

 // The miniature subroutine that implements the finally
 // block.
                     // Pop the return address, store it in local
 24 astore_3  // variable 3
                     // Get a reference to java.lang.System.out
 25 getstatic #7 <Field java.io.PrintStream out>
                     // Push reference to "Got old fashioned."
                     // String from the constant pool
 28 ldc #1 <String "Got old fashioned.">
                     // Invoke System.out.println()
 30 invokevirtual #8
    <Method void println(java.lang.String)>
                     // Return to return address stored in local
 33 ret 3     // variable 3
```

The bytecodes for the **try** block include two **jsr** instructions. Another **jsr** instruction is contained in the **catch** clause. The **catch** clause is added by the compiler because, if an exception is thrown during the execution of the **try** block, the finally block must still be executed. Therefore, the **catch** clause merely invokes the miniature subroutine that represents the **finally** clause and then throws the same exception again. The exception table for the **giveMeThatOldFashionedBoolean()** method, which follows, indicates that any exception thrown between and including addresses 0 and 17 (all the bytecodes that implement the **try** block) are handled by the **catch** clause that starts at address 18:

```
Exception table:
    from     to   target type
       0     18       18  any
```

The bytecodes of the **finally** clause begin by popping the return address off the stack and storing it into local variable three. At the end of the **finally** clause, the **ret** instruction takes its return address from the proper place, local variable three.

# Hop Around: A Simulation

The *Hop Around* applet, shown in Figure 18-1, demonstrates a Java Virtual Machine executing a sequence of bytecodes. The applet is embedded in a web page on the CD-ROM in the file **applets/HopAround.html**. The bytecode sequence in the simulation was generated by the **javac** compiler for the **hopAround()** method of the following class:

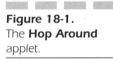

**Figure 18-1.**
The **Hop Around**
applet.

| Applet Viewer: HopAround.class |
|---|

**HOP AROUND**

Local Variables                     pc   21          The Method

| index | hex value | value |  |  | offset | bytecode | mnemonic |
|---|---|---|---|---|---|---|---|
| 0 | 00000001 | 1 |  |  | 18 | 3a | astore 5 |
| 1 | 00000003 | 3 |  |  | 19 | 05 |  |
| 2 |  |  |  |  | 20 | 05 | iconst_2 |
| 3 | 0000001f | RET ADDR |  | pc > | 21 | 3b | istore_0 |
| 4 |  |  |  |  | 22 | a9 | ret 5 |
| 5 | 00000007 | RET ADDR |  |  | 23 | 05 |  |
|  |  |  |  |  | 24 | 06 | iconst_3 |

optop   1          Operand Stack          25   3b   istore_0
                                          26   1a   iload_0
| offset | hex value | value |            27   3c   istore_1
|---|---|---|                             28   a8   jsr 39
| 0 | 00000002 | 2 |                       29   00
                                          30   0b
optop > 1

| Step | Run |
|---|---|
| Reset | Stop |

*istore_0 will pop the integer off the top of the stack and store it in local variable 0.*

```
// On CD-ROM in file opcodes/ex1/Clown.java
class Clown {

    static int hopAround() {
        int i = 0;
        while (true) {
            try {
                try {
                    i = 1;
                }
                finally {  // The first finally clause
                    i = 2;
                }
                i = 3;
                // This return never completes, because of
                // the continue in the second finally
                // clause
                return i;
            }
            finally {        // The second finally clause
                if (i == 3) {
                    // This continue overrides the return
                    // statement
                    continue;
                }
            }
        }
    }
}
```

The bytecodes generated by `javac` for the `hopAround()` method are as follow:

```
  0 iconst_0     // Push constant 0
  1 istore_0     // Pop into local var 0: int i = 0;

// Both try blocks start here (see exception table, below):
  2 iconst_1     // Push constant 1
  3 istore_0     // Pop into local var 0: i = 1;
               // Jump to mini-subroutine at offset 18
  4 jsr 18       // (the first finally clause)
               // Jump to offset 24 (to just below first
  7 goto 24      // finally clause)

// Catch clause for the first finally clause:
               // Pop the reference to thrown exception,
 10 astore 4     // store in local variable 4
               // Jump to mini-subroutine at offset 18
 12 jsr 18       // (the first finally clause)
               // Push the reference (to thrown
```

```
15 aload 4        // exception) from local variable 4
17 athrow         // Rethrow the same exception

// The first finally clause:
                  // Store the return address in local
18 astore 5       // variable 5
20 iconst_2       // Push constant 2
21 istore_0       // Pop into local var 0: i = 2;
                  // Jump to return address stored in local
22 ret 5          // variable 5

// Bytecodes for the code just after the first finally
// clause:
24 iconst_3       // Push constant 3
25 istore_0       // Pop into local var 0: int i = 3;

// Bytecodes for the return statement:
                  // Push the int from local
26 iload_0        // variable 0 (i, which is 3)
                  // Pop and store the int into local
27 istore_1       // variable 1 (the return value, i)
                  // Jump to mini-subroutine at offset 39
28 jsr 39         // (the second finally clause)
                  // Push the int from local variable 1
31 iload_1        // (the return value)
32 ireturn        // Return the int on the top of the stack

// Catch clause for the second finally clause:
                  // Pop the reference to thrown exception,
33 astore_2       // store in local variable 2
                  // Jump to mini-subroutine at offset 39
34 jsr 39         // (the second finally clause)
                  // Push the reference (to thrown
37 aload_2        // exception) from local variable 2
38 athrow         // Rethrow the same exception

// The second finally clause:
                  // Store the return address in local
39 astore_3       // variable 3
40 iload_0        // Push the int from local variable 0 (i)
41 iconst_3       // Push constant 3
                  // If the top two ints on the stack are
                  // equal, jump to offset 47:
42 if_icmpeq 47   // if (i == 3) {
                  // Jump to return address stored in local
45 ret 3          // variable 3
                  // Jump to offset 2 (the top of the while
47 goto 2         // block): continue;

Exception table:
    from    to   target  type
       2     4      10   any
       2    31      31   any
```

The **hopAround()** method returns from the first **finally** clause by executing past the closing curly brace but returns from the second **finally** clause by executing a **continue** statement. The first **finally** clause, therefore, exits via its **ret** instruction. But because the second **finally** clause exits via a **continue**, its **ret** instruction is never executed. The **continue** statement causes the Java Virtual Machine to jump to the top of the **while** loop again. The result is an endless loop, even though it is a **return** statement that originally causes the second **finally** clause to be executed in the first place. The continue statement in the **finally** clause supersedes the **return** statement, so the method never returns.

Note that the bytecodes that implement the **return** statement store a copy of the return value into local variable one before jumping to the miniature subroutine that represents the second **finally** clause. Then, after the miniature subroutine returns (in this case it never does because the continue is always executed), the return value is retrieved from local variable one and returned.

This process highlights the way the Java Virtual Machine returns values when **finally** clauses are also executed. Rather than returning the value of **i** after the **finally** clause is executed, the Java Virtual Machine will return the value that **i** had just *before* the **finally** clause was executed. Therefore, even if the **finally** clause changes the value of **i**, the method will still return the value that **i** had when the **return** statement was first reached before the **finally** clause was invoked. If you wanted the **finally** clause to be able to change the return value of the method, you would have to put an actual **return** statement with the new return value into the **finally** clause itself.

To drive the *Hop Around* simulation, use the Step, Reset, Run, and Stop buttons. Each time you click the Step button, the simulator will execute the instruction pointed to by the pc register. If you click the Run button, the simulation will continue with no further coaxing on your part until you click the Stop button. To start the simulation over, click the Reset button. For each step of the simulation, a panel at the bottom of the applet contains an explanation of what the next instruction will do. Happy clicking.

# On the CD-ROM

The CD-ROM contains the source code examples from this chapter in the **opcodes** directory. The *Hop Around* applet is contained in a web page on the CD-ROM in the file `applets/HopAround.html`. The source code for this applet is found alongside its class files, in the `applets/JVMSimulators` and `applets/JVMSimulators/COM/artima/jvmsim` directories.

# The Resources Page

For more information about the material presented in this chapter, visit the resources page: `http://www.artima.com/insidejvm/finally.html`.

# 19

# Method Invocation
## and Return

The Java Virtual Machine's instruction set has four different instructions that invoke methods. This chapter describes these four instructions and the situations in which each is used.

# Method Invocation

The Java programming language provides two basic kinds of methods: instance methods and class (or static) methods. The difference between these two kinds of methods are as follow:

1. Instance methods require an instance before they can be invoked; class methods do not.

2. Instance methods use dynamic (late) binding; class methods use static (early) binding.

When the Java Virtual Machine invokes a class method, it selects the method to invoke based on the type of the object reference, which is always known at compile-time. When the virtual machine invokes an instance method, by contrast, it selects the method to invoke based on the actual class of the object, which may be known only at runtime.

The Java Virtual Machine uses two different instructions to invoke these two different kinds of methods: **invokevirtual** for example methods and **invokestatic** for class methods. These instructions are shown in Table 19-1.

As mentioned in earlier chapters, references to methods are initially symbolic. All invoke instructions, such as **invokevirtual** and **invokestatic**, refer to a constant pool entry that initially contains a symbolic reference. When the Java Virtual Machine encounters an invoke instruction, if the symbolic reference has not yet been resolved, the virtual machine resolves it as part of the execution of the invoke instruction.

To resolve a symbolic reference, the Java Virtual Machine locates the method being referred to symbolically and replaces the symbolic reference with a direct reference. A direct reference, such as a pointer or offset, allows the virtual machine to invoke the method more quickly if the reference is ever used again in the future.

For example, upon encountering an **invokevirtual** instruction, the Java Virtual Machine forms an unsigned 16-bit index into the constant pool of the current class from the indexbyte1 and indexbyte2 operands

**Table 19-1.**

Method invocation

| Opcode | Operand(s) | Description |
|---|---|---|
| **invokevirtual** | indexbyte1, indexbyte2 | pop objectref and args, invoke instance method at constant pool index |
| **invokestatic** | indexbyte1, indexbyte2 | pop args, invoke class method at constant pool index |

that follow the **invokevirtual** opcode. The constant pool entry contains a symbolic reference to the method to invoke.

During resolution, the Java Virtual Machine also performs several verification checks. These checks ensure that Java language rules are followed and that the invoke instruction is safe to execute. For example, the virtual machine first makes sure the symbolically referenced method even exists. If it exists, it checks to make sure the current class can legally access the method. For example, if the method is private, it must be a member of the current class. If any of these checks fail, the Java Virtual Machine throws an exception. Chapter 5, "The Java Virtual Machine," gives an overview of the resolution process. Chapter 8, "The Linking Model," describes the process in detail.

After a method has been resolved, the Java Virtual Machine is ready to invoke it. If the method is an instance method, it must be invoked on an object. For every instance method invocation, the virtual machine expects a reference to the object (objectref) to be on the stack. In addition to objectref, the virtual machine expects the arguments (args) required by the method, if any, to be on the stack. If the method is a class method, which doesn't require an objectref because class methods aren't invoked on an object, only the args are on the stack.

The objectref and args (or just args, in the case of a class method) must be pushed onto the calling method's operand stack by the instructions that precede the invoke instruction.

## Invoking a Java Method

As mentioned in Chapter 5, the virtual machine creates a new stack frame for each Java (not native) method it invokes. The stack frame contains space for the method's local variables, its operand stack, and any other information required by a particular virtual machine implementation. The size of the local variables and operand stack are calculated at compile-time and placed into the class file, so the virtual machine knows just how much memory will be needed by the method's stack frame. When it invokes a method, it creates a stack frame of the proper size for that method. The virtual machine pushes the new stack frame onto the Java stack.

For an instance method, the virtual machine pops the objectref and args from the operand stack of the calling method's stack frame. It places the objectref on the new stack frame as local variable 0, and all the args as local variable 1, 2, and so on. The objectref is the implicit **this** reference that is passed to any instance method.

For a class method, the virtual machine just pops the args from the operand stack of the calling method's frame and places them onto the new stack frame as local variable 0, 1, 2, and so on.

After the objectref and args (or just the args, for a class method) have been placed into the local variables of the new frame, the virtual machine makes the new stack frame current and sets the program counter to point to the first instruction in the new method.

## Invoking a Native Method

As mentioned in Chapter 5, the virtual machine invokes native methods in an implementation-dependent manner. When invoking a native method, the virtual machine does not push a new stack frame onto the Java stack for the native method. At the point in which the thread enters the native method, it leaves the Java stack behind. When the native method returns, the Java stack will once again be used.

# Other Forms of Method Invocation

Although instance methods are normally invoked with **invokevirtual**, in certain situations, two other opcodes can be used: **invokespecial** and **invokeinterface**. These opcodes are shown in Table 19-2.

The **invokespecial** instruction is used for three situations in which an instance method must be invoked based on the type of the reference, not on the class of the object. The three situations are

1. instance initialization (**<init>()**) methods

2. private methods

3. methods invoked with the **super** keyword

**Table 19-2.**

Method invocation

| Opcode | Operand(s) | Description |
|---|---|---|
| **invokespecial** | indexbyte1, indexbyte2 | pop objectref and args, invoke instance method at constant pool index |
| **invokeinterface** | indexbyte1, indexbyte2 | pop objectref and args, invoke instance method at constant pool index |

**Invokeinterface** is used to invoke an instance method given a reference to an interface.

As mentioned in Chapter 7, "The Lifetime of a Class," class initialization (or **<clinit>()**) methods are always invoked directly by the Java Virtual Machine itself, never by any bytecodes. No instruction in the Java Virtual Machine's instruction set will invoke a method named **<clinit>()**. If some class file attempts to invoke a **<clinit>()** method with any of the four instructions described in this chapter, the virtual machine will throw an exception.

# The **invokespecial** Instruction

**Invokespecial** differs from **invokevirtual** primarily in that **invokespecial** normally (with one special exception) selects a method based on the type of the reference rather than the class of the object. In other words, it does static binding instead of dynamic binding. In each of the three situations in which **invokespecial** is used, dynamic binding wouldn't yield the desired result.

## invokespecial **and** <init>()

As mentioned in Chapter 7, the compiler places code for constructors and instance variable initializers in the **<init>()** method, or instance initialization method. A class gets one **<init>()** method in the class file for each constructor in the source. If you don't explicitly declare a constructor in the source, the compiler will generate a default no-arg constructor for you. This default constructor also ends up as an **<init>()** method in the class file. So just as every class will have at least one constructor, every class will have at least one **<init>()** method. These methods are always invoked with **invokespecial**.

The **<init>()** methods are called only when a new instance is created. At least one **<init>()** method will be invoked for each class along the inheritance path of the newly created object, and multiple **<init>()** methods could be invoked for any one class along that path.

The reason **invokespecial** is used to invoke **<init>()** methods is that subclass **<init>()** methods need to be able to invoke superclass **<init>()** methods. Multiple **<init>()** methods get invoked this way when an object is instantiated. The virtual machine invokes an **<init>()** method de-

clared in the object's class. That `<init>()` method first invokes either another `<init>()` method in the same class, or an `<init>()` method in its
superclass. This process continues all the way up to `Object`.

For example, consider this code:

```
// On CD-ROM in file invoke/ex1/Dog.java
class Dog {
}

// On CD-ROM in file invoke/ex1/CockerSpaniel.java
class CockerSpaniel extends Dog {

    public static void main(String args[]) {
        CockerSpaniel bootsie = new CockerSpaniel();
    }
}
```

When you invoke `main()`, the virtual machine will allocate space for a
new `CockerSpaniel` object and then invoke `CockerSpaniel`'s default no-
arg `<init>()` method to initialize that space. That method will invoke
`Dog`'s `<init>()` method, which will invoke `Object`'s `<init>()` method.
Here are the bytecodes for the `main()` method of class `CockerSpaniel`:

```
0 new #1 <Class CockerSpaniel>
3 invokespecial #3 <Method <init>() of class CockerSpaniel>
6 return
```

`CockerSpaniel`'s `main()` method allocates memory for the new
`CockerSpaniel` object and initializes that memory to default initial values with the `new` instruction. (The `#1` specifies the constant pool entry that
refers to the class to instantiate, in this case, class `CockerSpaniel`.) The
`new` instruction pushes a reference to the newly created `CockerSpaniel`
object onto the stack. The `main()` method then calls the `<init>()` method
of class `CockerSpaniel` using `invokespecial` on that object reference.
(The `#3` specifies the constant pool entry that contains the reference to
`CockerSpaniel`'s `<init>()` method.) The Java Virtual Machine pushes a
new frame onto the Java Stack and places the object reference into local
variable 0 of the new frame. Here are the bytecodes for the `<init>()`
method of class `CockerSpaniel`:

```
0 aload_0
1 invokespecial #4 <Method <init>() of class Dog>
4 return
```

As mentioned earlier, this `<init>()` method corresponds to the default
no-arg constructor generated automatically by the compiler for class

**CockerSpaniel**. It first pushes the reference to the object being initialized onto the stack from local variable 0, and then it invokes the **Dog**'s `<init>()` method on that reference. (The **#4** specifies the constant pool entry that contains the reference to **Dog**'s `<init>()` method.) Here are the bytecodes for **Dog**'s `<init>()` method:

```
0 aload_0
1 invokespecial #3 <Method <init>() of class
      java.lang.Object>
4 return
```

This `<init>()` method corresponds to the default no-arg constructor generated automatically by the compiler for class **Dog**. It first pushes the reference to the object being initialized onto the stack from local variable 0, and then it invokes the **Object**'s `<init>()` method on that reference. (The **#3** specifies the constant pool entry that contains the reference to **Object**'s `<init>()` method. Remember that this constant pool is not the same one as that referred to by the methods of class **CockerSpaniel**. Each class has its own constant pool.) When all three of these `<init>()` methods have returned, the new **CockerSpaniel** object created by **main()** is fully initialized and ready for use.

Because every class has at least one `<init>()` method, classes commonly have `<init>()` methods with the same signature. (A method's *signature* is its name and the number and types of its arguments.) The `<init>()` methods for the three classes in the inheritance path for **CockerSpaniel**, for example, all have the same signature. **CockerSpaniel**, **Dog**, and **Object** all contain a method named `<init>()` that takes no arguments.

Invoking a **Dog**'s `<init>()` method from **CockerSpaniel**'s `<init>()` method using **invokevirtual** would be impossible because **invokevirtual** would perform dynamic binding and invoke **CockerSpaniel**'s `<init>()` method. With **invokespecial**, however, **Dog**'s `<init>` method can be invoked from **CockerSpaniel**'s `<init>()` method because the type of the reference placed in **CockerSpaniel**'s class file (in constant pool entry **#4**) is **Dog**.

## invokespecial and Private Methods

In the case of private instance methods, it must be possible for a subclass to declare an instance method with the same signature as a private instance method in a superclass. (**invokespecial** is not used to invoke private class methods, just private instance methods. Private class methods are invoked with `invokestatic`.) For example, consider the following code in which `interestingMethod()` is declared as `private` in a superclass and with package access in a subclass:

```
// On CD-ROM in file invoke/ex2/Superclass.java
class Superclass {

    private void interestingMethod() {
        System.out.println(
            "Superclass's interesting method.");
    }

    void exampleMethod() {
        interestingMethod();
    }
}

// On CD-ROM in file invoke/ex2/Subclass.java
class Subclass extends Superclass {

    void interestingMethod() {
        System.out.println(
            "Subclass's interesting method.");
    }

    public static void main(String args[]) {
        Subclass me = new Subclass();
        me.exampleMethod();
    }
}
```

When you invoke `main()` in `Subclass` as defined here, it instantiates a new `Subclass` object and invokes `exampleMethod()` on it. Here are the bytecodes for the `main()` method of class `Subclass`:

```
 0 new #2 <Class Subclass>
 3 dup
 4 invokespecial #6 <Method <init>() of class Subclass>
 7 astore_1
 8 aload_1
 9 invokevirtual #8 <Method void exampleMethod() of class
      Superclass>
12 return
```

Subclass inherits `exampleMethod()` from `Superclass`. When `main()` invokes `exampleMethod()` on a `Subclass` object, it uses `invokevirtual`. The Java Virtual Machine will create and push a new frame onto the stack and begin executing the bytecodes of `exampleMethod()` as defined in class `Superclass`. Here are the bytecodes for `exampleMethod()`:

```
0 aload_0
1 invokespecial #7 <Method void interestingMethod() of
      Superclass>
4 return
```

Note that **exampleMethod()** first pushes the reference passed in local variable 0 (the hidden **this** passed to all instance methods) onto the stack. It then invokes **interestingMethod()** on that reference with the **invokespecial** instruction. The class identified in the constant pool entry specified by the **invokespecial** instruction, entry **#7**, is **Superclass**. The Java Virtual Machine invokes the **interestingMethod()** defined in **Superclass** *even though* the object is an instance of class **Subclass** and an accessible **interestingMethod()** is defined in **Subclass**.

The program correctly prints **"Superclass's interesting method"**. If **interestingMethod()** had been invoked with an **invokevirtual** instruction instead of **invokespecial**, the program would have printed **"Subclass's interesting method"**. Why? Because the virtual machine would choose the **interestingMethod()** to call based on the actual class of the object, which is **Subclass**. So it would use **Subclass**'s **interestingMethod()**. With **invokespecial** however, the virtual machine selects the method based on the type of the reference, so **Superclass**'s version of **interestingMethod()** is invoked.

## invokespecial **and** super

In the case of invocation of a method with the **super** keyword, as in **super.someMethod()**, you want the superclass's version of a method to be invoked, even if the current class overrides the method. Once again, **invokevirtual** would invoke the current class's version, so it can't be used. For example, consider this code:

```
// On CD-ROM in file invoke/ex3/Cat.java
class Cat {

    void someMethod() {
    }
}

// On CD-ROM in file invoke/ex3/TabbyCat.java
class TabbyCat extends Cat{

    void someMethod() {
```

```
        super.someMethod();
    }
}
```

Here are the bytecodes for **TabbyCat**'s **someMethod()**:

```
0 aload_0
1 invokespecial #4 <Method void someMethod() of class Cat>
4 return
```

Had **invokevirtual** been used in this case, the **someMethod()** defined in class **TabbyCat** would have been invoked. Because **invokespecial** is used and the constant pool entry (**#4**, in this case) indicates the **someMethod()** declared in class **Cat** should be invoked, the Java Virtual Machine correctly invokes the superclass's (**Cat**'s) version of **someMethod()**.

Whether the Java Virtual Machine actually uses static binding to execute an **invokespecial** instruction or instead uses a special kind of dynamic binding depends on whether the referring class's **ACC_SUPER** flag is set. Prior to JDK version 1.0.2, the **invokespecial** instruction was called **invokenonvirtual** and always resulted in static binding. It turned out, however, that **invokenonvirtual**'s stubborn insistence on static binding did not yield a correct implementation of the semantics of the Java language in all cases. (In other words, the instruction set had a "bug.") In JDK 1.0.2, the **invokenonvirtual** instruction was renamed **invokespecial**, and its semantics were changed. In addition, a new flag, **ACC_SUPER**, was added to the **access_flags** item of the Java class file.

The **ACC_SUPER** flag item of a class file indicates to the Java Virtual Machine which semantics it should use to execute **invokespecial** instructions it encounters in the bytecodes of that class file. If the **ACC_SUPER** flag is not set, the virtual machine uses the old (**invokenonvirtual**) semantics. Else, if the **ACC_SUPER** flag is set, the virtual machine uses the new semantics. All new Java compilers are supposed to set the **ACC_SUPER** flag in every class file they generate.

According to the old semantics, the virtual machine will perform static binding in all cases when executing **invokespecial**. By contrast, the new semantics requires static binding in all cases except one: the invocation of superclass methods.

According to the new semantics, when the Java Virtual Machine resolves an **invokespecial** instruction's symbolic reference to a superclass method, it dynamically searches the current class's superclasses to find the nearest superclass implementation of the method. (As used here, the word *nearest* means the implementation of the method declared in the superclass that is closest to the current class in its inheritance hierarchy.)

In most cases, the virtual machine will likely discover that the nearest implementation of the method is in the superclass listed in the symbolic reference. But the virtual machine possibly could find the nearest implementation in a different superclass.

For example, imagine you created an inheritance hierarchy of three classes: `Animal`, `Dog`, and `CockerSpaniel`. Assume class `Dog` extends class `Animal`, class `CockerSpaniel` extends class `Dog`, and that a method defined in `CockerSpaniel` uses `invokespecial` to invoke a nonprivate superclass method named `walk()`. Assume also that when you compiled `CockerSpaniel`, the compiler set the `ACC_SUPER` flag. In addition, assume that when you compiled `CockerSpaniel`, class `Animal` defined a `walk()` method, but `Dog` didn't. In that case, the symbolic reference from `CockerSpaniel` to the `walk()` method would give `Animal` as its class. When the `invokespecial` instruction in `CockerSpaniel`'s method is executed, the virtual machine would dynamically select and invoke `Animal`'s `walk()` method.

Now imagine that later you added a `walk()` method to `Dog` and recompiled `Dog` but didn't recompile `CockerSpaniel`. `CockerSpaniel`'s symbolic reference to the superclass `walk()` method still claims `Animal` as its class, even though now an implementation of `walk()` appears in `Dog`'s class file. Nevertheless, when the `invokespecial` instruction in `CockerSpaniel`'s method is executed, the virtual machine would dynamically select and invoke `Dog`'s implementation of the `walk()` method.

# The `invokeinterface` Instruction

The `invokeinterface` opcode performs the same function as `invokevirtual`: it invokes instance methods and uses dynamic binding. The difference between these two instructions is that `invokevirtual` is used when the type of the reference is a *class*, whereas `invokeinterface` is used when the type of the reference is an *interface*.

The Java Virtual Machine uses a different opcode to invoke a method on an interface reference because it can't make as many assumptions about the method table offset given an interface reference as it can given a class reference. (Method tables are described in Chapter 8.) Given a class reference, a method will always occupy the same position in the method table, independent of the actual class of the object. This is not true given an interface reference. The method could occupy different locations for different classes that implement the same interface.

For examples of the use of **invokeinterface** in bytecodes, see the "Examples of Method Invocation" section later in this chapter.

# Invocation Instructions and Speed

As you might imagine, invoking a method given an interface reference is likely slower than invoking a method given a class reference. When the Java Virtual Machine encounters an **invokevirtual** instruction and resolves the symbolic reference to a direct reference to an instance method, that direct reference is likely an offset into a method table. From that point forward, the same offset can be used. For an **invokeinterface** instruction, however, the virtual machine will have to search through the method table every single time the instruction is encountered because it can't assume the offset is the same as the previous time.

The fastest instructions will likely be **invokespecial** and **invokestatic** because methods invoked by these instructions are statically bound. When the Java Virtual Machine resolves the symbolic reference for these instructions and replaces it with a direct reference, that direct reference will likely include a pointer to the actual bytecodes.

# Examples of Method Invocation

The following code illustrates the various ways the Java Virtual Machine invokes methods and shows which invocation opcode is used in each situation:

```
// On CD-ROM in file invoke/ex4/InYourFace.java
interface InYourFace {
    void interfaceMethod ();
}

// On CD-ROM in file
// invoke/ex4/ItsABirdItsAPlaneItsSuperclass.java
class ItsABirdItsAPlaneItsSuperclass
    implements InYourFace {

    ItsABirdItsAPlaneItsSuperclass(int i) {
        super();        // invokespecial (of an <init>)
    }
```

```
        static void classMethod() {
        }

        void instanceMethod() {
        }

        final void finalInstanceMethod() {
        }

        public void interfaceMethod() {
        }
    }

// On CD-ROM in file invoke/ex4/Subclass.java
class Subclass extends ItsABirdItsAPlaneItsSuperclass {

        Subclass() {
            this(0);         // invokespecial (of an <init>)
        }

        Subclass(int i) {
            super(i);        // invokespecial (of an <init>)
        }

        private void privateMethod() {
        }

        void instanceMethod() {
        }

        final void anotherFinalInstanceMethod() {
        }

        void exampleInstanceMethod() {

            instanceMethod();                   // invokevirtual
            super.instanceMethod();             // invokespecial

            privateMethod();                    // invokespecial

            finalInstanceMethod();              // invokevirtual
            anotherFinalInstanceMethod();       // invokevirtual

            interfaceMethod();                  // invokevirtual

            classMethod();                      // invokestatic
        }
    }

// On CD-ROM in file invoke/ex4/UnrelatedClass.java
class UnrelatedClass {

        public static void main(String args[]) {
```

```
                                    // invokespecial (of an <init>)
          Subclass sc = new Subclass();
          Subclass.classMethod();            // invokestatic
          sc.classMethod();                  // invokestatic
          sc.instanceMethod();               // invokevirtual
          sc.finalInstanceMethod();          // invokevirtual
          sc.interfaceMethod();              // invokevirtual

          InYourFace iyf = sc;
          iyf.interfaceMethod();             // invokeinterface
      }
}
```

(The compiler generates no bytecodes for the **InYourFace** interface.)

```
// Methods of class ItsABirdItsAPlaneItsSuperclass

// Method <init>(int)
 0 aload_0
 1 invokespecial #4
   <Method <init>() of class java.lang.Object>
 4 return

// Method void classMethod()
 0 return

// Method void instanceMethod()
 0 return

// Method void finalInstanceMethod()
 0 return

// Method void interfaceMethod()
 0 return

// ------------------------------
// Methods of class Subclass

// Method <init>()
 0 aload_0
 1 iconst_0
 2 invokespecial #4 <Method <init>(int) of class Subclass>
 5 return

// Method <init>(int)
 0 aload_0
 1 iload_1
 2 invokespecial #3 <Method <init>(int) of class
   ItsABirdItsAPlaneItsSuperclass>
 5 return

// Method void privateMethod()
 0 return
```

```
// Method void instanceMethod()
 0 return

// Method void anotherFinalInstanceMethod()
 0 return

// Method void exampleInstanceMethod()
 0 aload_0
 1 invokevirtual #9
    <Method void instanceMethod() of class Subclass>
 4 aload_0
 5 invokespecial #8 <Method void instanceMethod() of class
    ItsABirdItsAPlaneItsSuperclass>
 8 aload_0
 9 invokespecial #11
    <Method void privateMethod() of class Subclass>
12 aload_0
13 invokevirtual #7 <Method void finalInstanceMethod() of
    class ItsABirdItsAPlaneItsSuperclass>
16 aload_0
17 invokevirtual #5 <Method void
    anotherFinalInstanceMethod()of class Subclass>
20 aload_0
21 invokevirtual #10 <Method void interfaceMethod() of
    class ItsABirdItsAPlaneItsSuperclass>
24 invokestatic #6 <Method void classMethod() of class
    ItsABirdItsAPlaneItsSuperclass>
27 return

// -------------------------------
// Methods of class UnrelatedClass

// Method <init>()
 0 aload_0
 1 invokespecial #7 <Method java.lang.Object()>
 4 return

// Method void main(java.lang.String[])
 0 new #3 <Class Subclass>
 3 dup
 4 invokespecial #6 <Method <init>() of class Subclass>
 7 astore_1
 8 invokestatic #8 <Method void classMethod() of class
    ItsABirdItsAPlaneItsSuperclass>
11 invokestatic #8 <Method void classMethod() of class
    ItsABirdItsAPlaneItsSuperclass>
14 aload_1
15 invokevirtual #10 <Method void instanceMethod() of
    class Subclass>
18 aload_1
19 invokevirtual #9 <Method void finalInstanceMethod() of
    class ItsABirdItsAPlaneItsSuperclass>
22 aload_1
```

```
23 invokevirtual #12 <Method void interfaceMethod() of
   class ItsABirdItsAPlaneItsSuperclass>
26 aload_1
27 astore_2
28 aload_2
29 invokeinterface (args 1) #11 <Method void
   interfaceMethod() of interface InYourFace>
34 return
```

# Returning from Methods

Several opcodes return from a method, one for each type of return value. These opcodes, which are shown in Table 19-3, take no operands. If a return value does exist, it must be on the operand stack. The return value is popped off the operand stack and pushed onto the operand stack of the calling method's stack frame. The current stack frame is popped, and the calling method's stack frame becomes current. The program counter is reset to the instruction in the calling method just following the instruction that invoked the returning method.

The **ireturn** instruction is used for methods that return **int**, **char**, **byte**, or **short**.

# On the CD-ROM

The CD-ROM contains the source code examples from this chapter in sub-directories of the **invoke** directory.

**Table 19-3.**

Returning from methods

| Opcode | Operand(s) | Description |
|--------|-----------|-------------|
| **ireturn** | none | pop **int**, push onto stack of calling method and return |
| **lreturn** | none | pop **long**, push onto stack of calling method and return |
| **freturn** | none | pop **float**, push onto stack of calling method and return |
| **dreturn** | none | pop **double**, push onto stack of calling method and return |
| **areturn** | none | pop object reference, push onto stack of calling method and return |
| **return** | none | return void |

# The Resources Page

For more information about the material presented in this chapter, visit the resources page: `http://www.artima.com/insidejvm/invoke.html`.

# 20

# Thread Synchronization

One of the strengths of the Java programming language is its support for multithreading at the language level. Much of this support centers on *synchronization*: coordinating activities and data access among multiple threads. The mechanism that Java uses to support synchronization is the *monitor*. This chapter describes monitors and shows how they are used by the Java Virtual Machine. It describes how one aspect of monitors, the locking and unlocking of data, is supported in the instruction set.

# Monitors

A monitor supports two kinds of thread synchronization: *mutual exclusion* and *cooperation*. Mutual exclusion, which is supported in the Java Virtual Machine via object locks, enables multiple threads to work on shared data independently without interfering with each other. Cooperation, which is supported in the Java Virtual Machine via the wait and notify methods of class `Object`, enables threads to work together toward a common goal.

A monitor is like a building that contains one special room that can be occupied by only one thread at a time. The room usually contains some data. From the time a thread enters this room to the time it leaves, it has exclusive access to any data in the room. Entering the monitor building is called *entering the monitor*. Entering the special room inside the building is called *acquiring the monitor*. Occupying the room is called *owning the monitor*, and leaving the room is called *releasing the monitor*. Leaving the entire building is called *exiting the monitor*.

In addition to being associated with a bit of data, a monitor is associated with one or more bits of code called *critical sections*. A critical section is code that needs to be executed as one indivisible operation. In other words, one thread must be able to execute a critical section from beginning to end without another thread concurrently executing a critical section of the same monitor. A monitor enforces this one-thread-at-a-time execution of its critical sections. The only way a thread can enter a monitor is by arriving at the beginning of one of the critical sections associated with that monitor. The only way a thread can move forward and execute the critical section is by acquiring the monitor.

When a thread arrives at the beginning of a critical section, it is placed into an *entry set* for the associated monitor. The entry set is like the front hallway of the monitor building. If no other thread is waiting in the entry set and no other thread currently owns the monitor, the thread acquires the monitor and continues executing the critical section. When the thread finishes executing the critical section, it exits (and releases) the monitor.

If a thread arrives at the beginning of a critical section of a monitor that is already owned by another thread, the newly arrived thread must wait in the entry set. When the current owner exits the monitor, the newly arrived thread must compete with any other threads also waiting in the entry set. Only one thread will win the competition and acquire the monitor.

The first kind of synchronization listed here, mutual exclusion, refers to the mutually exclusive execution of critical sections by multiple threads. At any one time, only one thread can be executing a critical section of a particular monitor. In general, mutual exclusion is important only when multiple threads are sharing data. If two threads are not working with any common data, they usually can't interfere with each other and needn't execute in a mutually exclusive way. On a Java Virtual Machine implementation that doesn't time slice, however, a higher priority thread that is never blocked will interfere with any lower priority threads, even if none of the threads share data. The higher priority thread will monopolize the CPU at the expense of the lower priority threads. Lower priority threads will never get any CPU time. In such a case, a monitor that protects no data can be used to orchestrate these threads to ensure all threads get some CPU time. Nevertheless, in most cases a monitor protects data that is accessed through the critical section code. In cases in which the data can be accessed only through the critical sections, the monitor enforces mutually exclusive access to that data.

The other kind of synchronization listed previously as supported by monitors is cooperation. Whereas mutual exclusion helps keep threads from interfering with one another while sharing data, cooperation helps threads to work together toward some common goal.

Cooperation is important when one thread needs some data to be in a particular state and another thread is responsible for getting the data into that state. For example, one thread, a "read thread," may be reading data from a buffer that another thread, a "write thread," is filling. The read thread needs the buffer to be in a "not empty" state before it can read any data out of the buffer. If the read thread discovers that the buffer is empty, it must wait. The write thread is responsible for filling the buffer with data. After the write thread has done some more writing, the read thread can do some more reading.

The form of monitor used by the Java Virtual Machine is called a *Wait and Notify* monitor. (It is also sometimes called a *Signal and Continue* monitor.) In this kind of monitor, a thread that currently owns the monitor can suspend itself inside the monitor by executing a *wait command*. When a thread executes a wait, it releases the monitor and enters a *wait set*. The thread will stay suspended in the wait set until some time after another thread executes a *notify command* inside the monitor. When a thread executes a notify, it continues to own the monitor until it releases the monitor of its own accord, either by executing a wait or by completing the critical section. After the notifying thread has released the monitor, the waiting thread will be resurrected and will reacquire the monitor.

The kind of monitor used in the Java Virtual Machine is sometimes called a Signal and Continue monitor because after a thread does a notify (the signal) it retains ownership of the monitor and continues executing the critical section (the continue). At some later time, the notifying thread releases the monitor and a waiting thread is resurrected. Presumably, the waiting thread suspended itself because the data protected by the monitor wasn't in a state that would allow the thread to continue doing useful work. Also, the notifying thread presumably executed the notify command after it had placed the data protected by the monitor into the state desired by the waiting thread. But because the notifying thread continued, it may have altered the state after the notify such that the waiting thread still can't do useful work. Alternatively, a third thread may have acquired the monitor after the notifying thread released it but before the waiting thread acquired it, and the third thread may have changed the state of the protected data. As a result, a notify must often be considered by waiting threads merely as a hint that the desired state *may* exist. Each time a waiting thread is resurrected, it may need to check the state again to determine whether it can move forward and do useful work. If it finds the data still isn't in the desired state, the thread could execute another wait or give up and exit the monitor.

As an example, consider once again the previously described scenario that involves a buffer, a read thread, and a write thread. Assume the buffer is protected by a monitor. When a read thread enters the monitor that protects the buffer, it checks to see whether the buffer is empty. If the buffer is not empty, the read thread reads (and removes) some data from the buffer. Satisfied, it exits the monitor. On the other hand, if the buffer is empty, the read thread executes a wait command. As soon as it executes the wait, the read thread is suspended and placed into the monitor's wait set. In the process, the read thread releases the monitor, which becomes available to other threads. At some later time, the write thread enters the monitor, writes some data into the buffer, executes a notify, and exits the monitor. When the write thread executes the notify, the read thread is marked for eventual resurrection. After the write thread has exited the monitor, the read thread is resurrected as the owner of the monitor. If there is any chance that some other thread has come along and consumed the data left by the write thread, the read thread must explicitly check to make sure the buffer is not empty. If there is no chance that any other thread has consumed the data, then the read thread can just assume the data exists. The read thread reads some data from the buffer and exits the monitor.

A graphical depiction of the kind of monitor used by a Java Virtual Machine is shown in Figure 20-1. This figure shows the monitor as three rectangles. In the center, a large rectangle contains a single thread, the monitor's owner. On the left, a small rectangle contains the entry set. On the right, another small rectangle contains the wait set. Active threads are shown as dark gray circles. Suspended threads are shown as light gray circles.

**Figure 20-1.**
A Java monitor.

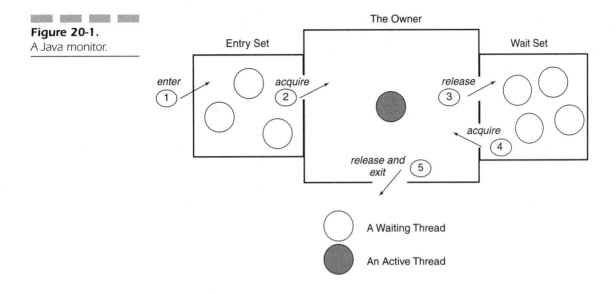

Figure 20-1 also shows several numbered doors that threads must "pass through" to interact with the monitor. When a thread arrives at the start of a critical section, it enters the monitor via the leftmost door, door number one, and finds itself in the rectangle that houses the entry set. If no thread currently owns the monitor and no other threads are waiting in the entry set, the thread passes immediately through the next door, door number two, and becomes the owner of the monitor. As the monitor owner, the thread continues executing the critical section. If, on the other hand, another thread is currently claiming ownership of the monitor, the newly arrived thread must wait in the entry set, possibly along with other threads already waiting there. The newly arrived thread is blocked and therefore doesn't execute any further into the critical section.

Figure 20-1 shows three threads suspended in the entry set and four threads suspended in the wait set. These threads will remain where they are until the current owner of the monitor—the active thread—releases the monitor. The active thread can release the monitor in either of two ways: it can complete the critical section it is executing, or it can execute a wait command. If it completes the critical section, it exits the monitor via the door at the bottom of the central rectangle, door number five. If it executes a wait command, it releases the monitor as it travels through door number three, the door to the wait set.

If the former owner did not execute a notify before it released the monitor (and none of the waiting threads had previously been notified and were waiting to be resurrected), then only the threads in the entry set will compete to acquire the monitor. If the former owner did execute a notify, then the entry set threads will have to compete with one or more threads from the wait set. If a thread from the entry set wins the competition, it passes through the door number two and becomes the new owner of the monitor. If a thread from the wait set wins the competition, it exits the wait set and reacquires the monitor as it passes through door number four. Note that doors three and four are the only ways a thread can enter or exit the wait set. A thread can execute a wait command only if it currently owns the monitor, and it can't leave the wait set without automatically becoming again the owner of the monitor.

In the Java Virtual Machine, threads can optionally specify a time-out when they execute a wait command. If a thread does specify a time-out, and no other thread executes a notify before the time-out expires, the waiting thread in effect receives an automatic notify from the virtual machine. After the time-out expires, the waiting thread will be resurrected even if no other thread has executed an explicit notify.

The Java Virtual Machine offers two kinds of notify commands: "notify" and "notify all." A notify command selects one thread arbitrarily from the wait set and marks it for eventual resurrection. A notify all command marks all threads currently in the wait set for eventual resurrection.

To a great extent, the manner in which a Java Virtual Machine implementation selects the next thread from the wait or entry sets is a decision made by individual implementation designers. For example, implementation designers can decide how to select

- a thread from the wait set given a notify command
- the order to resurrect threads from the wait set given a notify all command
- the order to allow threads from the entry set to acquire the monitor
- how to choose between threads suspended in the wait set versus the entry set after a notify command

You might think it would make sense to implement entry set and wait sets as first-in, first-out (FIFO) queues so that the thread that waits the longest will be the first chosen to acquire the monitor. Alternatively, having 10 FIFO queues, one for each priority a thread can have inside the Java Virtual Machine, might make sense. The virtual machine could then choose the thread that has been waiting the longest in the highest priority queue that contains any waiting threads. Implementations may take such approaches, but you can't depend on it. Implementations are free to implement the entry and wait sets as last-in, first-out (LIFO) queues to select lower priority threads before higher priority threads or to do anything else that may not seem to make sense. Implementations are free to select threads in an arbitrary manner that defies analysis and yields surprising orderings.

As a programmer, you must not rely on any particular selection algorithm or treatment of priorities, at least if you are trying to write a Java program that is platform independent. For example, because you don't know what order threads in the wait set will be chosen for resurrection by the notify command, you should use notify (as opposed to notify all) only when you are absolutely certain only one thread will be suspended in the wait set. If there is a chance more than one thread will be suspended in the wait set at any one time, you should probably use notify all. Otherwise, on some Java Virtual Machine implementations, a particular thread may be stuck in the wait set for a very long time. If a notify always selects the most recent arrival from the wait set and the wait set always contains multiple threads, some threads that have been waiting the longest may never be resurrected.

# Object Locking

As mentioned in earlier chapters, some of the Java Virtual Machine's runtime data areas are shared by all threads, others are private to individual threads. Because the heap and method area are shared by all threads, Java programs need to coordinate multithreaded access to two kinds of data:

- instance variables, which are stored on the heap
- class variables, which are stored in the method area

Programs never need to coordinate access to local variables, which reside on Java stacks, because data on the Java stack is private to the thread to which the Java stack belongs.

In the Java Virtual Machine, every object and class is logically associated with a monitor. For objects, the associated monitor protects the object's instance variables. For classes, the monitor protects the class's class variables. If an object has no instance variables, or a class has no class variables, the associated monitor protects no data.

To implement the mutual exclusion capability of monitors, the Java Virtual Machine associates a *lock* (sometimes called a *mutex*) with each object and class. A lock is like a privilege that only one thread can "own" at any one time. Threads need not obtain a lock to access instance or class variables. If a thread does obtain a lock, however, no other thread can access the locked data until the thread that owns the lock releases it. (To "lock an object" is to acquire the monitor associated with that object.)

Class locks are actually implemented as object locks. As mentioned in earlier chapters, when the Java Virtual Machine loads a class file, it creates an instance of class `java.lang.Class`. When you lock a class, you are actually locking that class's `Class` object.

A single thread is allowed to lock the same object multiple times. For each object, the Java Virtual Machine maintains a count of the number of times the object has been locked. An unlocked object has a count of zero. When a thread acquires the lock for the first time, the count is again incremented to one. Each time the thread acquires a lock on the same object, the count is again incremented. (Only the thread that already owns an object's lock is allowed to lock it again. No other thread can lock the object until the owning thread releases the lock.) Each time the thread releases the lock, the count is decremented. When the count reaches zero, the lock is released and made available to other threads.

A thread in the Java Virtual Machine requests a lock when it arrives at the beginning of a critical section. Java has two kinds of critical sections: synchronized statements and synchronized methods. (They are described in detail later in this chapter.) Each critical section in a Java program is associated with an object reference. When a thread arrives at the first instruction in a critical section, the thread must obtain a lock on the referenced object. The thread is not allowed to execute the code until it obtains the lock. After it has obtained the lock, the thread enters the block of protected code. When the thread leaves the block, no matter how it leaves the block, it releases the lock on the associated object.

Note that, as a Java programmer, you never explicitly lock an object. Object locks are internal to the Java Virtual Machine. In your Java programs, you identify the critical sections of your program by writing synchronized statements and methods. As the Java Virtual Machine runs your program, it automatically locks an object or class every time it encounters a critical section.

# Synchronization Support in the Instruction Set

As mentioned above, the Java language provides two built-in ways to identify critical sections in your programs: synchronized statements and synchronized methods. These two mechanisms, which implement the mutual exclusion aspect of synchronization, are supported by the Java Virtual Machine's instruction set.

## Synchronized Statements

To create a synchronized statement, you use the synchronized keyword with an expression that evaluates to an object reference, as in the following `reverseOrder()` method:

```
// On CD-ROM in file threads/ex1/KitchenSync.java
class KitchenSync {

    private int[] intArray = new int[10];

    void reverseOrder() {
        synchronized (this) {
            int halfWay = intArray.length / 2;
            for (int i = 0; i < halfWay; ++i) {
                int upperIndex = intArray.length - 1 - i;
                int save = intArray[upperIndex];
                intArray[upperIndex] = intArray[i];
                intArray[i] = save;
            }
        }
    }
    // ...
}
```

In the preceding case, the statements contained within the synchronized block will not be executed until a lock is acquired on the current object (**this**). If instead of a **this** reference, the expression yielded a reference to another object, the lock associated with that object would be acquired before the thread continued. If the expression yields a reference to an instance of class **Class**, the lock associated with the class is acquired.

Two opcodes, **monitorenter** and **monitorexit**, are used for synchronization blocks within methods. These opcodes are shown in Table 20-1.

When **monitorenter** is encountered by the Java Virtual Machine, it acquires the lock for the object referred to by objectref on the stack. If the thread already owns the lock for that object, the count that is associated with the lock is incremented. Each time **monitorexit** is executed for the thread on the object, the count is decremented. When the count reaches zero, the monitor is released.

**Table 20-1.**

Monitors

| Opcode | Operand(s) | Description |
| --- | --- | --- |
| monitorenter | none | pop objectref, acquire the lock associated with objectref |
| monitorexit | none | pop objectref, release the lock associated with objectref |

Here is the bytecode sequence generated by the **reverseOrder()** method of the **KitchenSync** class:

```
// First place the reference to the object to lock into
// local variable 1. This local variable will be used by
// both the monitorenter and monitorexit instructions.
 0 aload_0        // Push local var 0 (the this reference)
 1 astore_1       // Store into local var 1

// Now acquire the lock on the referenced object
                  // Push local var 1 (the this reference;
 2 aload_1        // the object to lock)
                  // Pop reference, acquire the lock
 3 monitorenter   // on referenced object

// The code of the synchronized block begins here. A
// thread will not execute the next instruction, aload_0,
// until a lock has been successfully acquired on the this
// reference above.
                  // Push the object ref at loc var 0 (the
 4 aload_0        // this ref)
                  // Pop object ref, push ref to instance
                  // variable intArray
 5 getfield #4 <Field int intArray[]>
 8 arraylength    // Pop array ref, push int array length
 9 iconst_2       // Push constant int 2
10 idiv           // Pop two ints, divide, push int result
                  // Pop int into local var 3:
11 istore_3       // int halfway = intArray.length/2;

// This is the start of the code for the for loop
12 iconst_0       // Push constant int 0
13 istore 4       // Pop into local var 2: int i = 0;
15 goto 65        // Jump to for loop condition check

// This is the start of the body of the for loop
                  // Push the object ref at loc var 0 (the
18 aload_0        // this ref)
                  // Pop object ref, push ref to instance
                  // variable intArray
19 getfield #4 <Field int intArray[]>
22 arraylength    // Pop array ref, push int array length
23 iconst_1       // Push constant int 1
```

```
                        // Pop two ints, subtract, push int
24 isub                 // result
25 iload 4              // Push int at local var 4 (i)
                        // Pop two ints, subtract, push int
27 isub                 // result
                        // Pop int into local var 5: int
28 istore 5             // upperindex = intArray.length - 1 - i;
                        // Push the object ref at loc var 0 (the
30 aload_0              // this ref)
                        // Pop object ref, push ref to instance
                        // variable intArray
31 getfield #4 <Field int intArray[]>
34 iload 5              // Push int at local var 5 (upperIndex)
                        // Pop index, arrayref, push int at
36 iaload              // arrayref[index]
                        // Pop into local var 6:
37 istore 6             // int save = intArray[upperIndex];
                        // Push the object ref at loc var 0 (the
39 aload_0              // this ref)
                        // Pop object ref, push ref to instance
                        // variable intArray
40 getfield #4 <Field int intArray[]>
43 iload 5              // Push int at local var 5 (upperIndex)
                        // Push the object ref at loc var 0 (the
45 aload_0              // this ref)
                        // Pop object ref, push ref to instance
                        // variable intArray
46 getfield #4 <Field int intArray[]>
49 iload 4              // Push int at local var 4 (i)
                        // Pop index, arrayref, push int at
51 iaload              // arrayref[index]
                        // Set arrayref[index] = value:
52 iastore             // intArray[upperIndex] = intArray[i];
                        // Push the object ref at loc var 0 (the
53 aload_0              // this ref)
                        // Pop object ref, push ref to instance
                        // variable intArray
54 getfield #4 <Field int intArray[]>
57 iload 4              // Push int at local var 4 (i)
59 iload 6              // Push int at local var 6 (save)
                        // Set arrayref[index] = value:
61 iastore             // intArray[i] = save;

// The body of the for loop is now done, this instruction
// does the incrementing of the loop variable i
                        // Increment by 1 int at local var 4:
62 iinc 4 1             // ++i;

// This is the for loop condition check:
65 iload 4              // Push int at local var 4 (i)
67 iload_3              // Push int at local var 3 (halfway)
                        // Pop two ints, compare, jump if less
                        // than to top of for loop body:
68 if_icmplt 18         // for (; i < halfway;)
```

```
// The code of the synchronized block ends here

// The next two instructions unlock the object, making it
// available for other threads. The reference to the
// locked object was stored in local variable 1 above.
71 aload_1        // Push local var 1 (the this reference)
72 monitorexit    // Pop ref, unlock object
73 return         // return normally from method

// This is a catch clause for any exception thrown (and
// not caught from within the synchronized block. If an
// exception is thrown, the locked object is unlocked,
// making it available for other threads.
74 aload_1        // Push local var 1 (the this reference)
75 monitorexit    // Pop ref, unlock object
76 athrow         // rethrow the same exception

// The exception table shows the "catch all" clause covers
// the entire synchronized block, from just after the lock
// is acquired to just before the lock is released.
Exception table:
from to target type
   4  71   74    any
```

Note that a catch clause ensures the locked object will be unlocked even if an exception is thrown from within the synchronized block. No matter how the synchronized block is exited, the object lock acquired when the thread entered the block will definitely be released.

## Synchronized Methods

To synchronize an entire method, you just include the synchronized keyword as one of the method qualifiers, as follows:

```java
// On CD-ROM in file threads/ex1/HeatSync.java
class HeatSync {

    private int[] intArray = new int[10];

    synchronized void reverseOrder() {
        int halfWay = intArray.length / 2;
        for (int i = 0; i < halfWay; ++i) {
            int upperIndex = intArray.length - 1 - i;
            int save = intArray[upperIndex];
            intArray[upperIndex] = intArray[i];
            intArray[i] = save;
        }
    }
    // ...
}
```

The Java Virtual Machine does not use any special opcodes to invoke or return from synchronized methods. When the virtual machine resolves the symbolic reference to a method, it determines whether the method is synchronized. If so, the virtual machine acquires a lock before invoking the method. For an instance method, the virtual machine acquires the lock associated with the object upon which the method is being invoked. For a class method, it acquires the lock associated with the class to which the method belongs (it locks a **Class** object). After a synchronized method completes, whether it completes by returning or by throwing an exception, the virtual machine releases the lock.

Here are the bytecodes that **javac** generates for **HeatSync**'s **reverseOrder()** method:

```
                      // Push the object ref at loc var 0 (the
   0 aload_0          // this ref)
                      // Pop object ref, push ref to instance
                      // variable intArray
   1 getfield #4 <Field int intArray[]>
   4 arraylength      // Pop array ref, push int array length
   5 iconst_2         // Push constant int 2
   6 idiv             // Pop two ints, divide, push int result
                      // Pop int into local var 1:
   7 istore_1         // int halfway = intArray.length/2;

// This is the start of the code for the for loop
   8 iconst_0         // Push int constant 0
   9 istore_2         // Pop into local var 2: int i = 0;
  10 goto 54          // Jump to for loop condition check

// This is the start of the body of the for loop
                      // Push the object ref at loc var 0 (the
  13 aload_0          // this ref)
                      // Pop object ref, push ref to instance
                      // variable intArray
  14 getfield #4 <Field int intArray[]>
  17 arraylength      // Pop array ref, push int array length
  18 iconst_1         // Push constant int 1
                      // Pop two ints, subtract, push int
  19 isub             // result
  20 iload_2          // Push int at local var 2 (i)
                      // Pop two ints, subtract, push int
  21 isub             // result
                      // Pop int into local var 3: int
  22 istore_3         // upperindex = intArray.length - 1 - i;
                      // Push the object ref at loc var 0 (the
  23 aload_0          // this ref)
                      // Pop object ref, push ref to instance
                      // variable intArray
  24 getfield #4 <Field int intArray[]>
  27 iload_3          // Push int at local var 3 (upperIndex)
                      // Pop index, arrayref, push int at
```

```
28 iaload          // arrayref[index]
                   // Pop into local var 4:
29 istore 4        // int save = intArray[upperIndex];
                   // Push the object ref at loc var 0 (the
31 aload_0         // this ref)
                   // Pop object ref, push ref to instance
                   // variable intArray
32 getfield #4 <Field int intArray[]>
35 iload_3         // Push int at local var 3 (upperIndex)
                   // Push the object ref at loc var 0 (the
36 aload_0         // this ref)
                   // Pop object ref, push ref to instance
                   // variable intArray
37 getfield #4 <Field int intArray[]>
40 iload_2         // Push int at local var 2 (i)
                   // Pop index, arrayref, push int at
41 iaload          // arrayref[index]
                   // Pop value, index, and arrayref,
                   // Set arrayref[index] = value:
42 iastore         // intArray[upperIndex] = intArray[i];
                   // Push the object ref at loc var 0 (the
43 aload_0         // this ref)
                   // Pop object ref, push ref to instance
                   // variable intArray
44 getfield #4 <Field int intArray[]>
47 iload_2         // Push int at local var 2 (i)
48 iload 4         // Push int at local var 4 (save)
                   // Pop value, index, and arrayref,
                   // Set arrayref[index] = value:
50 iastore         // intArray[i] = save;

// The body of the for loop is now done, this instruction
// does the incrementing of the loop variable i
                   // Increment by 1 int at local var 2:
51 iinc 2 1        // ++i;

// This is the for loop condition check:
54 iload_2         // Push int at local var 2 (i)
55 iload_1         // Push int at local var 1 (halfway)
                   // Pop two ints, compare, jump if less
                   // than to top of for loop body:
56 if_icmplt 13    // for (; i < halfway;)

59 return          // return (void) from method
```

If you compare these bytecodes with the ones shown earlier for **KitchenSync**'s **reverseOrder()** method, you will see that these bytecodes are in effect those of **KitchenSync** with the support for entering and exiting the monitor removed. Instructions at offset 0 through 56 of **HeatSync**'s bytecodes correspond to instructions at offset 4 through 68 of **KitchenSync**'s bytecodes. Because **HeatSync**'s **reverseOrder()** method doesn't need a local variable slot to store the reference to the locked object, the local variable positions used by each method are different. The function of the instructions themselves, however, match up exactly.

Another difference between the two **reverseOrder()** methods is that the compiler doesn't create an exception table for **HeatSync**'s **reverseOrder()** method. In **HeatSync**'s case, an exception table isn't necessary. When this method is invoked, the Java Virtual Machine automatically acquires the lock on the **this** object. If this method completes abruptly, just as if it completes normally, the virtual machine will release the lock on the **this** object automatically.

A synchronized class (static) method operates in the same way as the synchronized instance method shown in the preceding example. The one difference is that instead of acquiring a lock on **this** (as no **this** exists in a class method), the thread must acquire a lock on the appropriate **Class** instance.

# Coordination Support in Class Object

Class **Object** declares five methods that enable programmers to access the Java Virtual Machine's support for the coordination aspect of synchronization. These methods are declared public and final, so they are inherited by all classes. They can be invoked only from within a synchronized method or statement. In other words, the lock associated with an object must already be acquired before any of these methods are invoked. The methods are listed in Table 20-2.

**Table 20-2.**

The wait and notify methods of class **Object**

| Method | Description |
| --- | --- |
| void wait(); | Enter a monitor's wait set until notified by another thread |
| void wait(long timeout); | Enter a monitor's wait set until notified by another thread or **timeout** milliseconds elapses |
| void wait(long timeout, int nanos); | Enter a monitor's wait set until notified by another thread or **timeout** milliseconds plus **nanos** nanoseconds elapses |
| void notify(); | Wake up one thread waiting in the monitor's wait set (If no threads are waiting, do nothing.) |
| void notifyAll(); | Wake up all threads waiting in the monitor's wait set (If no threads are waiting, do nothing.) |

## On the CD-ROM

The CD-ROM contains the source code examples from this chapter in a subdirectory of the **threads** directory.

## The Resources Page

For more information about the material presented in this chapter, visit the resources page: **http://www.artima.com/insidejvm/threads.html**.

# Appendix A

## Instruction Set by Opcode Mnemonic

This appendix lists Java Virtual Machine instructions in alphabetical order by opcode mnemonic. All 200 instructions that may legally appear in the bytecode streams stored in Java class files are described in detail in this appendix.

Besides the opcodes for the 200 instructions that may appear in class files, the Java Virtual Machine specification describes two other families of opcodes: the reserved opcodes and the "**quick**" opcodes. None of these opcodes can legally appear in the bytecode streams of Java class files.

The Java Virtual Machine specification lists three reserved opcodes, which are shown in Table A-1. These opcodes are reserved for internal use by Java Virtual Machine implementations and tools. The specification guarantees that these three opcodes will not be part of any future extension of the Java Virtual Machine's instruction set. As you may have guessed, the intended purpose of the **breakpoint** opcode is to provide a way for debuggers to implement breakpoints. The intended purpose of the other two reserved opcodes, **impdep1** and **impdep2**, is to serve as "back doors" to implementation-dependent software functionality or "traps" to implementation-dependent hardware functionality.

The Java Virtual Machine specification also lists 25 "**_quick**" opcodes, which Sun's virtual machine implementation uses internally to speed up the interpreted execution of bytecodes. This optimization technique is described in general in this book in Chapter 8, "The Linking Model," but the individual "**_quick**" instructions are not described in detail in this appendix. (The "**_quick**" opcodes do appear in Appendix C, which lists their mnemonics and corresponding opcode byte values.) Like the reserved opcodes, the "**_quick**" opcodes may not legally appear in Java class files. But unlike the reserved opcodes, the Java Virtual Machine specification leaves open the possibility that these opcodes will take on new meanings in future extensions of the instruction set.

**Table A-1**

The reserved opcodes

| Mnemonic | Byte Value |
| --- | --- |
| **breakpoint** | 202 (0xca) |
| **impdep1** | 254 (0xfe) |
| **impdep2** | 255 (0xff) |

For each instruction listed in this appendix, you will find the following information:

- The mnemonic
- A short description
- The opcode's byte value in decimal and hex
- The format of the instruction
- The operand stack before and after the instruction is executed
- A description of any constraints associated with the instruction
- A description of the execution of the instruction
- A description of any exceptions or errors that may be thrown by the instruction

The format of each instruction appears as a list of comma-separated items next to the label "Instruction Format," with each item representing one byte in the bytecode stream. The opcode mnemonic appears first (in fixed-width font), followed by any operands (shown in italics).

For each instruction, this appendix shows two snapshots of the operand stack. One snapshot, labeled "Before," shows the contents of the current method's operand stack just before the instruction is executed. The other snapshot, labeled "After," shows the operand stack immediately after execution of the instruction. In both snapshots, the operand stack appears as a list of comma-separated items, with each item representing one word. Although everywhere else in this book the operand stack is shown growing downward (the top of the stack appears at the bottom of the picture), in this appendix the operand stack is shown growing sideways, from left to right. In each snapshot, the top of the stack is the rightmost item shown. Unaffected portions of the operand stack are shown as an ellipsis ( . . . ).

For each instruction, the section labeled "Description" combines three kinds of information: constraints, the process of execution, and exceptions and errors. As mentioned in Chapter 3, "Security," Java Virtual Machine implementations are required to enforce at runtime certain constraints on the bytecodes of every method they execute. Whenever you see the word *must* in an instruction's description in this appendix, you are reading about a constraint every implementation must enforce when executing the instruction. For example, the `goto` instruction, which causes an unconditional jump, may cause only a jump to another opcode of the same method. In this appendix's description for `goto`, this constraint is stated as "The target address *must* be the address of an opcode within the same method as the `goto` opcode."

The designers of each individual Java Virtual Machine implementation can decide how and when to detect violations of the bytecode constraints. If any implementation detects a constraint violation, it must report the violation by throwing a **VerifyError** when (and if) the running program attempts to execute the instruction.

In addition to describing the constraints placed on each instruction, this appendix describes the process of executing each instruction and lists any errors or exceptions that may be thrown during the course of executing the instruction. Besides the errors and exceptions explicitly listed in the instruction descriptions, one other family of errors, subclasses of **VirtualMachineError**, can be thrown at any time as the result of executing any instruction. Four subclasses of **VirtualMachineError**, and the circumstances under which they will be thrown, are:

- **OutOfMemoryError**: The virtual machine has run out of real or virtual memory, and the garbage collector can't reclaim enough space to enable the thread to continue.

- **StackOverflowError**: A thread has exhausted its supply of memory for stack space (usually because the application has an unbounded recursion).

- **InternalError**: The virtual machine has encountered a bug in its own implementation that prevents it from properly implementing the semantics of the Java language.

- **UnknownError**: The virtual machine has encountered some error condition but is unable to report the actual condition by throwing the appropriate exception or error.

# aaload

Load **reference** from array

**OPCODE:**   50 (0x32)

**INSTRUCTION FORMAT:**   `aaload`

**STACK:**
Before:   . . . , *arrayref, index*
After:   . . . , *value*

**DESCRIPTION:** To execute the **aaload** instruction, the Java Virtual Machine first pops two words from the operand stack. The *arrayref* word must be a **reference** that refers to an array of **reference**s. The *index* word must be an **int**. The virtual machine retrieves from the *arrayref* array the **reference** *value* specified by *index* and pushes it onto the operand stack.

If *arrayref* is **null**, the Java Virtual Machine throws **NullPointerException**. Otherwise, if *index* is not a legal index into the *arrayref* array, the virtual machine throws **ArrayIndexOutOfBoundsException**.

For more information about the **aaload** instruction, see Chapter 15, "Objects and Arrays."

# aastore

Store **reference** into array

**OPCODE:** 83 (0x53)

**INSTRUCTION FORMAT:** aastore

**STACK:**
Before:   . . . , *arrayref, index, value*
After:   . . .

**DESCRIPTION:** To execute the **aastore** instruction, the Java Virtual Machine first pops three words from the operand stack. The *arrayref* word must be a **reference** that refers to an array of **float**s. The *index* word must be an **int**, and the *value* word must be a **reference**. The type of *value* must be assignment compatible with the component type of the *arrayref* array. The virtual machine stores **reference** *value* into the *arrayref* array location specified by *index*.

If *arrayref* is **null**, the Java Virtual Machine throws **NullPointerException**. Else, if *index* is not a legal index into the *arrayref* array, the virtual machine throws **ArrayIndexOutOfBoundsException**. Otherwise, if the actual type of *value* is not assignment compatible with the actual type of the components of the *arrayref* array, the virtual machine throws **ArrayStoreException**.

For more information about the **aastore** instruction, see Chapter 15, "Objects and Arrays."

# aconst_null

Push **null** object reference

**OPCODE:** 1 (0x1)

**INSTRUCTION FORMAT:** **aconst_null**

**STACK:**
Before:   . . .
After:   . . . , *null*

**DESCRIPTION:** To execute the **aconst_null** instruction, the Java Virtual Machine pushes a **null** object reference onto the operand stack. (Note that the Java Virtual Machine specification does not dictate any actual value for **null**. The specification leaves that decision to the designers of each individual implementation.)

For more information about the **aconst_null** instruction, see Chapter 10, "Stack and Local Variable Operations."

# aload

Load **reference** from local variable

**OPCODE:** 25 (0x19)

**INSTRUCTION FORMAT:**   **aload**, *index*

**STACK:**
Before:   . . .
After:   . . . , *value*

**DESCRIPTION:** The *index* operand, which serves as an 8-bit unsigned index into the local variables of the current frame, must specify a local variable word that contains a **reference**. To execute the **aload** instruction, the Java Virtual Machine pushes onto the operand stack the **reference** contained in the local variable word specified by *index*.

Note that the **wide** instruction can precede the **aload** instruction, to allow a local variable to be accessed with a 16-bit unsigned offset.

Note also that even though the **astore** instruction may be used to pop a **returnAddress** value off the operand stack and into a local variable, the **aload** instruction cannot be used to push a **returnAddress** value back onto the operand stack. For more information about the use of **returnAddress**, see Chapter 18, "Finally Clauses."

For more information about the **aload** instruction, see Chapter 10, "Stack and Local Variable Operations."

## aload_0

Load **reference** from local variable 0

**OPCODE:**   42 (0x2a)

**INSTRUCTION FORMAT:**   aload_0

**STACK:**
Before:   . . .
After:   . . . , *value*

**DESCRIPTION:**   The local variable word at index zero must contain a **reference**. To execute the **aload_0** instruction, the Java Virtual Machine pushes onto the operand stack the **reference** *value* contained in the local variable word zero.

Note that even though the **astore_0** instruction may be used to pop a **returnAddress** value off the operand stack and into a local variable, the **aload_0** instruction cannot be used to push a **returnAddress** value back onto the operand stack. For more information about the use of **returnAddress**, see Chapter 18, "Finally Clauses."

For more information about the **aload_0** instruction, see Chapter 10, "Stack and Local Variable Operations."

## aload_1

Load **reference** from local variable 1

**OPCODE:** 43 (0x2b)

**INSTRUCTION FORMAT:** `aload_1`

**STACK:**
Before: ...
After: ..., *value*

**DESCRIPTION:** The local variable word at index one must contain a **reference**. To execute the `aload_1` instruction, the Java Virtual Machine pushes onto the operand stack the **reference** *value* contained in the local variable word one.

Note that even though the `astore_1` instruction may be used to pop a **returnAddress** value off the operand stack and into a local variable, the `aload_1` instruction cannot be used to push a **returnAddress** value back onto the operand stack. For more information about the use of **returnAddress**, see Chapter 18, "Finally Clauses."

For more information about the `aload_1` instruction, see Chapter 10, "Stack and Local Variable Operations."

# aload_2

Load **reference** from local variable 2

**OPCODE:** 44 (0x2c)

**INSTRUCTION FORMAT:** `aload_2`

**STACK:**
Before: ...
After: ..., *value*

**DESCRIPTION:** The local variable word at index two must contain a **reference**. To execute the `aload_2` instruction, the Java Virtual Machine pushes onto the operand stack the **reference** *value* contained in the local variable word two.

Note that even though the `astore_2` instruction may be used to pop a **returnAddress** value off the operand stack and into a local variable, the `aload_2` instruction cannot be used to push a **returnAddress** value back onto the operand stack. For more information about the use of **returnAddress**, see Chapter 18, "Finally Clauses."

For more information about the **aload_2** instruction, see Chapter 10, "Stack and Local Variable Operations."

# aload_3

Load **reference** from local variable 3

**OPCODE:**   45 (0x2d)

**INSTRUCTION FORMAT:**   **aload_3**

**STACK:**
Before:   . . .
After:   . . . , *value*

**DESCRIPTION:**   The local variable word at index three must contain a **reference**. To execute the **aload_3** instruction, the Java Virtual Machine pushes onto the operand stack the **reference** *value* contained in the local variable word three.

Note that even though the **astore_3** instruction may be used to pop a **returnAddress** value off the operand stack and into a local variable, the **aload_3** instruction cannot be used to push a **returnAddress** value back onto the operand stack. For more information about the use of **returnAddress**, see Chapter 18, "Finally Clauses."

. For more information about the **aload_3** instruction, see Chapter 10, "Stack and Local Variable Operations."

# anewarray

Allocate new array of reference type components

**OPCODE:**   189 (0xbd)

**INSTRUCTION FORMAT:**   **anewarray**, *indexbyte1*, *indexbyte2*

**STACK:**
Before: ..., *count*
After: *arrayref*

**DESCRIPTION:** The top word of the operand stack, *count*, must be an **int**. To execute the **anewarray** instruction, the Java Virtual Machine first forms an unsigned 16-bit index into the constant pool by calculating *(indexbyte1 << 8) | indexbyte2*. The virtual machine then looks up the constant pool entry specified by the calculated index. The constant pool entry at that index must be a **CONSTANT_Class_info** entry. If it hasn't already, the virtual machine resolves the entry. The entry may be a class, interface, or array type.

If the resolution is successful, the Java Virtual Machine pops *count* and creates on the heap an array of size *count* of the reference type specified by the resolved **CONSTANT_Class_info** entry. The virtual machine initializes each array element to its default initial value (**null**) and pushes *arrayref*, a reference to the new array, onto the operand stack.

As a result of executing this instruction, the Java Virtual Machine may throw any of the linking errors listed in Chapter 8, "The Linking Model," as possible during resolution of a **CONSTANT_Class_info** entry. If resolution succeeds, but *count* is less than zero, the virtual machine throws **NegativeArraySizeException**.

For more information about the **anewarray** instruction, see Chapter 15, "Objects and Arrays."

## areturn

Return **reference** from method

**OPCODE:** 176 (0xb0)

**INSTRUCTION FORMAT:** **areturn**

**STACK:**
Before: ..., *objectref*
After: *[empty]*

**DESCRIPTION:** The return type of the returning method must be **reference**. The top word of the operand stack, *objectref*, must be a

**reference** that is assignment compatible with the type represented by the returning method's descriptor. To execute the **areturn** instruction, the Java Virtual Machine pops *objectref* from the operand stack of the current frame and pushes it onto the operand stack of the invoking method's frame. The virtual machine discards any other words that may still be on the returning method's frame. If the returning method is synchronized, the monitor that was acquired when the method was invoked is released. The invoking method's frame is made current, and the virtual machine continues execution in the invoking method.

For more information about monitors, see Chapter 20, "Thread Synchronization." For more information about the **areturn** instruction, see Chapter 19, "Method Invocation and Return."

## arraylength

Get length of array

**OPCODE:** 190 (0xbe)

**INSTRUCTION FORMAT:** `arraylength`

**STACK:**
Before:   . . . , *arrayref*
After:   . . . , *length*

**DESCRIPTION:** The top word of the operand stack, *arrayref*, must be a **reference** that points to an array. To execute the **arraylength** instruction, the Java Virtual Machine pops *arrayref* and pushes the length of the array pointed to by *arrayref*.

If *arrayref* is **null**, the Java Virtual Machine throws **NullPointerException**.

For more information about the **arraylength** instruction, see Chapter 15, "Objects and Arrays."

## astore

Store **reference** or **returnAddress** into local variable

**OPCODE:** 58 (0x3a)

**INSTRUCTION FORMAT:** astore, *index*

**STACK:**
Before: ..., *value*
After: ...

**DESCRIPTION:** The *index* operand must specify a valid 8-bit unsigned index into the local variables of the current frame. The *value* on the top of the operand stack must be a **reference** or a **returnAddress**. To execute the **astore** instruction, the Java Virtual Machine pops the **reference** or **returnAddress** *value* from the top of the operand stack and stores it into the local variable word specified by *index*.

Note that the **wide** instruction can precede the **astore** instruction, to enable a *value* to be stored into a local variable specified by a 16-bit unsigned offset.

For more information about the **astore** instruction, see Chapter 10, "Stack and Local Variable Operations."

# astore_0

Store **reference** or **returnAddress** into local variable 0

**OPCODE:** 75 (0x4b)

**INSTRUCTION FORMAT:** astore_0

**STACK:**
Before: ..., *value*
After: ...

**DESCRIPTION:** The index zero must be a valid index into the local variables of the current stack frame, and the *value* word on the top of the operand stack must be a **reference** or a **returnAddress**. To execute the **astore_0** instruction, the Java Virtual Machine pops the **reference** or **returnAddress** *value* from the top of the operand stack and stores it into the local variable word at index zero.

For more information about the `astore_0` instruction, see Chapter 10, "Stack and Local Variable Operations."

## astore_1

Store **reference** or **returnAddress** into local variable 1

**OPCODE:**   76 (0x4c)

**INSTRUCTION FORMAT:**   astore_1

**STACK:**
Before:   . . . , *value*
After:   . . .

**DESCRIPTION:**   The index one must be a valid index into the local variables of the current stack frame, and the *value* word on the top of the operand stack must be a **reference** or a **returnAddress**. To execute the `astore_1` instruction, the Java Virtual Machine pops the **reference** or **returnAddress** *value* from the top of the operand stack and stores it into the local variable word at index one.

For more information about the `astore_1` instruction, see Chapter 10, "Stack and Local Variable Operations."

## astore_2

Store **reference** or **returnAddress** into local variable 2

**OPCODE:**   77 (0x4d)

**INSTRUCTION FORMAT:**   astore_2

**STACK:**
Before:   . . . , *value*
After:   . . .

**DESCRIPTION:**  The index two must be a valid index into the local variables of the current stack frame, and the *value* word on the top of the operand stack must be a **reference** or a **returnAddress**. To execute the **astore_2** instruction, the Java Virtual Machine pops the **reference** or **returnAddress** *value* from the top of the operand stack and stores it into the local variable word at index two.

For more information about the **astore_2** instruction, see Chapter 10, "Stack and Local Variable Operations."

## astore_3

Store **reference** or **returnAddress** into local variable 3

**OPCODE:**  78 (0x4e)

**INSTRUCTION FORMAT:**  astore_3

**STACK:**
Before:  . . . , *value*
After:  . . .

**DESCRIPTION:**  The index three must be a valid index into the local variables of the current stack frame, and the *value* word on the top of the operand stack must be a **reference** or a **returnAddress**. To execute the **astore_3** instruction, the Java Virtual Machine pops the **reference** or **returnAddress** *value* from the top of the operand stack and stores it into the local variable word at index three.

For more information about the **astore_3** instruction, see Chapter 10, "Stack and Local Variable Operations."

## athrow

Throw exception or error

**OPCODE:**  191 (0xbf)

**INSTRUCTION FORMAT:** athrow

**STACK:**
Before:    . . . , *objectref*
After:   *objectref*

Note that "Before" shows the operand stack of the frame belonging to the method containing the athrow instruction being executed. "After" shows the operand stack of the frame belonging to the method in which the catch clause is found, *if* a catch clause is found. If no catch clause is found, the thread exits, and no more operand stacks exist for that thread.

**DESCRIPTION:**    The top word of the operand stack, *objectref*, must be a reference that points either to an instance of class java.lang.Throwable or to an instance of some subclass of java.lang.Throwable. To execute the athrow instruction, the Java Virtual Machine pops *objectref* from the operand stack. The virtual machine "throws" the exception by searching through the current method's exception table for the most recent catch clause that catches either the class of the throwable object pointed to by *objectref*, or a subclass of the throwable object's class. If the current method's exception table contains a matching entry, the virtual machine extracts the address of the handler to jump to from the matching exception table entry. The virtual machine pops any words remaining on the operand stack, pushes the *objectref*, sets the program counter to the handler address, and continues execution there. If the current method's exception table doesn't have a matching catch clause, the virtual machine pops the current method's entire frame and rethrows the exception in the previous method. This process repeats until either a matching catch clause is found or the stack frames for all the methods along the current thread's call stack have been popped. If no catch clause is found by this process, the current thread exits.

If the *objectref* word is null, the virtual machine throws NullPointerException.

For more information about the athrow instruction, see Chapter 17, "Exceptions."

# baload

Load byte or boolean from array

**OPCODE:**   51 (0x33)

**INSTRUCTION FORMAT:** `baload`

**STACK:**
Before: ..., *arrayref, index*
After: ..., *value*

**DESCRIPTION:** To execute the `baload` instruction, the Java Virtual Machine first pops two words from the operand stack. The *arrayref* word must be a `reference` that refers to an array of `byte`s or `boolean`s. The *index* word must be an `int`. The virtual machine retrieves from the *arrayref* array the `byte` or `boolean` *value* specified by *index*, sign-extends it to an `int`, and pushes it onto the operand stack.

If *arrayref* is `null`, the Java Virtual Machine throws `NullPointerException`. Otherwise, if *index* is not a legal index into the *arrayref* array, the virtual machine throws `ArrayIndexOutOfBoundsException`.

For more information about the `baload` instruction, see Chapter 15, "Objects and Arrays."

# bastore

Store into `byte` or `boolean` array

**OPCODE:** 84 (0x54)

**INSTRUCTION FORMAT:** `bastore`

**STACK:**
Before: ..., *arrayref, index, value*
After: ...

**DESCRIPTION:** To execute the `bastore` instruction, the Java Virtual Machine first pops three words from the operand stack. The *arrayref* word must be a `reference` that refers to an array of `byte`s or `boolean`s. The *index* and *value* words must be `int`s. The virtual machine truncates the `int` *value* to a `byte` and stores it into the *arrayref* array location specified by *index*.

If *arrayref* is `null`, the Java Virtual Machine throws `NullPointerException`. Otherwise, if *index* is not a legal index into the *arrayref* array, the virtual machine throws `ArrayIndexOutOfBoundsException`.

For more information about the **bastore** instruction, see Chapter 15, "Objects and Arrays."

# bipush

Push 8-bit signed integer

**OPCODE:**   16 (0x10)

**INSTRUCTION FORMAT:**   **bipush**, *byte*

**STACK:**
Before:   . . .
After:   . . . , *value*

**DESCRIPTION:**   To execute the **bipush** instruction, the Java Virtual Machine first sign-extends operand *byte*, an 8-bit signed integer, to an **int**. The virtual machine then pushes the resulting **int** *value* onto the operand stack.

For more information about the **bipush** instruction, see Chapter 10, "Stack and Local Variable Operations."

# caload

Load **char** from array

**OPCODE:**   52 (0x34)

**INSTRUCTION FORMAT:**   **caload**

**STACK:**
Before:   . . . , *arrayref, index*
After:   . . . , *value*

**DESCRIPTION:**   To execute the **caload** instruction, the Java Virtual Machine first pops two words from the operand stack. The *arrayref* word

must be a **reference** that refers to an array of **char**s. The *index* word
must be an **int**. The virtual machine retrieves from the *arrayref* array the
**char** *value* specified by *index*, zero-extends it to an **int**, and pushes it onto
the operand stack.

If *arrayref* is **null**, the Java Virtual Machine throws
**NullPointerException**. Otherwise, if *index* is not a legal index into the *arrayref* array, the virtual machine throws **ArrayIndexOutOfBoundsException**.

For more information about the **caload** instruction, see Chapter 15,
"Objects and Arrays."

## castore

Store into **char** array

**OPCODE:**   85 (0x55)

**INSTRUCTION FORMAT:**   castore

**STACK:**
Before:   . . . , *arrayref, index, value*
After:   . . .

**DESCRIPTION:**   To execute the **castore** instruction, the Java Virtual
Machine first pops three words from the operand stack. The *arrayref* word
must be a **reference** that refers to an array of **char**s. The *index* and *value*
words must be **int**s. The virtual machine truncates the **int** *value* to a
**char** and stores it into the *arrayref* array location specified by *index*.

If *arrayref* is **null**, the Java Virtual Machine throws
**NullPointerException**. Otherwise, if *index* is not a legal index into the *arrayref* array, the virtual machine throws **ArrayIndexOutOfBoundsException**.

For more information about the **castore** instruction, see Chapter 15,
"Objects and Arrays."

## checkcast

Make sure object is of given type

**OPCODE:** 192 (0xc0)

**INSTRUCTION FORMAT:** `checkcast`, *indexbyte1*, *indexbyte2*

**STACK:**
Before: ... , *objectref*
After: ... , *objectref*

**DESCRIPTION:** The top word of the stack, *objectref*, must be a **reference**. To execute the `checkcast` instruction, the Java Virtual Machine first forms an unsigned 16-bit index into the constant pool by calculating *(indexbyte1 << 8) | indexbyte2*. The virtual machine then looks up the constant pool entry specified by the calculated index. The constant pool entry at that index must be a `CONSTANT_Class_info` entry. If it hasn't already, the virtual machine resolves the entry. The entry may be a class, interface, or array type. If *objectref* is `null` or if *objectref* can be cast to the resolved type, the stack remains unchanged. Otherwise, the virtual machine throws `ClassCastException`.

To determine whether the object pointed to by *objectref* can be cast to the resolved type, the virtual machine first determines whether the object is a class instance or array. (It can't be an interface instance because interfaces can't be instantiated.) If it is a class instance, and the resolved type is a class, not an interface, the object can be cast to the resolved class if the object's class is the resolved class or a subclass of the resolved class. Else, if it is a class instance, and the resolved type is an interface, not a class, the object can be cast to the resolved interface if the object's class implements the resolved interface. Otherwise, the object is an array. If the resolved type is a class, it must be `java.lang.Object`. Else, if the resolved type is an array of primitive types, the object must be an array of the same primitive type. Otherwise, the resolved type must be an array with a component type of some reference type, and the object must be an array with a component type that can be cast to the component type of the resolved array type. (Note that the dimension of an array doesn't enter into the `checkcast` check, only the component type of the array.)

As a result of executing this instruction, the virtual machine may throw any of the linking errors listed in Chapter 8, "The Linking Model," as possible during resolution of a `CONSTANT_Class_info` entry. If resolution succeeds, but the resolved type cannot be cast to the resolved type, the virtual machine throws `ClassCastException`.

For more information about the **checkcast** instruction, see Chapter 15, "Objects and Arrays."

## d2f

Convert **double** to **float**

**OPCODE:** 144 (0x90)

**INSTRUCTION FORMAT:** d2f

**STACK:**
Before:  . . . , *value.word1, value.word2*
After:  . . . , *result*

**DESCRIPTION:** The top two words of the operand stack must be a **double**. To execute the **d2f** instruction, the Java Virtual Machine pops the **double** *value* from the operand stack, converts the **double** to a **float**, and pushes the **float** *result*.

To convert the **double** *value* to **float**, the Java Virtual Machine first checks to see whether the *value* equals NaN (Not a Number). If so, the **float** *result* is also NaN. Else, if the magnitude of the **double** *value* is too small to be represented by a **float**, the **float** *result* is a zero of the same sign. Else, if the magnitude of the **double** *value* is too large to be represented by a **float**, the **float** *result* is an infinity of the same sign. Otherwise, the virtual machine converts the **double** *value* to **float** zero using IEEE 754 round-to-nearest mode.

Note that this instruction performs a narrowing primitive conversion. Because not all **double** values can be represented by a **float**, the conversion may result in a loss of magnitude and precision.

For more information about the **d2f** instruction, see Chapter 11, "Type Conversion."

## d2i

Convert **double** to **int**

**OPCODE:** 142 (0x8e)

**INSTRUCTION FORMAT:** `d2i`

**STACK:**
Before:   . . . , *value.word1, value.word2*
After:   . . . , *result*

**DESCRIPTION:** The top two words of the operand stack must be a `double`. To execute the `d2i` instruction, the Java Virtual Machine pops the `double` *value* from the operand stack, converts the `double` to an `int`, and pushes the `int` *result*.

To convert the `double` *value* to `int`, the Java Virtual Machine first checks to see whether the *value* equals NaN (Not a Number). If so, the `int` *result* is zero. Else, if the `double` *value* is not a positive or negative infinity, the virtual machine rounds the *value* toward zero using IEEE 754 round-toward-zero mode. If the resulting integral value can be exactly represented by an `int`, the `int` *result* is that integral value. Otherwise, the magnitude of the `double` *value* is too great be represented in an `int`. If *value* is positive, the `int` *result* is the largest positive integer that can be represented in an `int`. If *value* is negative, the `int` *result* is the smallest negative integer that can be represented in an `int`.

Note that this instruction performs a narrowing primitive conversion. Because not all `double` values can be represented by an `int`, the conversion may result in a loss of magnitude and precision.

For more information about the `d2i` instruction, see Chapter 11, "Type Conversion."

# d2l

Convert `double` to `long`

**OPCODE:** 143 (0x8f)

**INSTRUCTION FORMAT:** `d2l`

**STACK:**
Before:   . . . , *value.word1, value.word2*
After:   . . . , *result.word1, result.word2*

**DESCRIPTION:** The top two words of the operand stack must be a **double**. To execute the **d2l** instruction, the Java Virtual Machine pops the **double** *value* from the operand stack, converts the **double** to a **long**, and pushes the **long** *result*.

To convert the **double** *value* to **long**, the Java Virtual Machine first checks to see whether the *value* equals NaN (Not a Number). If so, the **long** *result* is zero. Else, if the **double** *value* is not a positive or negative infinity, the virtual machine rounds the *value* toward zero using IEEE 754 round-toward-zero mode. If the resulting integral value can be exactly represented by a **long**, the **long** *result* is that integral value. Otherwise, the magnitude of the **double** *value* is too great be represented in a **long**. If *value* is positive, the **long** *result* is the largest positive integer that can be represented in a **long**. If *value* is negative, the **long** *result* is the smallest negative integer that can be represented in a **long**.

Note that this instruction performs a narrowing primitive conversion. Because not all **double** values can be represented by a **long**, the conversion may result in a loss of magnitude and precision.

For more information about the **d2l** instruction, see Chapter 11, "Type Conversion."

# dadd

Add **double**s

**OPCODE:** 99 (0x63)

**INSTRUCTION FORMAT:** dadd

**STACK:**
Before:   ... , *value1.word1, value1.word2, value2.word1, value2.word2*
After:   ... , *result.word1, result.word2*

**DESCRIPTION:** The top four words of the operand stack must be two **double**s, *value1* and *value2*. To execute the **dadd** instruction, the Java Virtual Machine pops *value1* and *value2*, adds them, and pushes the **double** *result*. The *result* produced by the **dadd** instruction is governed by the rules of IEEE 754 floating-point arithmetic.

For more information about the **dadd** instruction, see Chapter 14, "Floating-Point Arithmetic."

# daload

Load **double** from array

**OPCODE:**   49 (0x31)

**INSTRUCTION FORMAT:**   daload

**STACK:**
Before:   . . . , *arrayref, index*
After:    . . . , *value.word1, value.word2*

**DESCRIPTION:**   To execute the **daload** instruction, the Java Virtual Machine first pops two words from the operand stack. The *arrayref* word must be a **reference** that refers to an array of **double**s. The *index* word must be an **int**. The virtual machine retrieves from the *arrayref* array the **double** *value* specified by *index* and pushes it onto the operand stack.

If *arrayref* is **null**, the Java Virtual Machine throws **NullPointerException**. Otherwise, if *index* is not a legal index into the *arrayref* array, the virtual machine throws **ArrayIndexOutOfBoundsException**.

For more information about the **daload** instruction, see Chapter 15, "Objects and Arrays."

# dastore

Store into **double** array

**OPCODE:**   82 (0x52)

**INSTRUCTION FORMAT:**   dastore

**STACK:**
Before:   . . . , *arrayref, index, value.word1, value.word2*
After:    . . .

**DESCRIPTION:**   To execute the **dastore** instruction, the Java Virtual Machine first pops four words from the operand stack. The *arrayref* word must be a **reference** that refers to an array of **double**s. The *index* word must be an **int**, and the *value* words must be a **double**. The virtual machine stores **double** *value* into the *arrayref* array location specified by *index*.

If *arrayref* is **null**, the Java Virtual Machine throws **NullPointerException**. Otherwise, if *index* is not a legal index into the *arrayref* array, the virtual machine throws **ArrayIndexOutOfBoundsException**.

For more information about the **dastore** instruction, see Chapter 15, "Objects and Arrays."

# dcmpg

Compare **double**s (1 on NaN)

**OPCODE:**   152 (0x98)

**INSTRUCTION FORMAT:**   dcmpg

**STACK:**
Before:   . . . , *value1.word1, value1.word2, value2.word1, value2.word2*
After:   . . . , *result*

**DESCRIPTION:**   The top four words of the operand stack must be two **double**s, *value1* and *value2*. To execute the **dcmpg** instruction, the Java Virtual Machine pops *value1* and *value2* off the operand stack and compares one against the other. If *value1* equals *value2*, the virtual machine pushes onto the operand stack **int** *result* zero. Else, if *value1* is greater than *value2*, the virtual machine pushes onto the operand stack **int** *result* one. Otherwise, if *value1* is less than *value2*, the virtual machine pushes onto the operand stack **int** *result* negative one. If either *value1* or *value2* equals NaN (Not a Number), the virtual machine pushes onto the operand stack **int** *result* one.

The *result* produced by the **dcmpg** instruction is governed by the rules of IEEE 754 floating-point arithmetic. Note that the **dcmpg** instruction differs from the **dcmpl** instruction only in its treatment of NaN. For more information about the **dcmpg** instruction, see Chapter 16, "Control Flow."

# dcmpl

Compare **double**s (–1 on NaN)

**OPCODE:**   151 (0x97)

**INSTRUCTION FORMAT:**   dcmpl

**STACK:**
Before:   . . . , *value1.word1, value1.word2, value2.word1, value2.word2*
After:   . . . , *result*

**DESCRIPTION:**   The top four words of the operand stack must be two **double**s, *value1* and *value2*. To execute the **dcmpg** instruction, the Java Virtual Machine pops *value1* and *value2* off the operand stack and compares one against the other. If *value1* equals *value2*, the virtual machine pushes onto the operand stack **int** *result* zero. Else, if *value1* is greater than *value2*, the virtual machine pushes onto the operand stack **int** *result* one. Otherwise, if *value1* is less than *value2*, the virtual machine pushes onto the operand stack **int** *result* negative one. If either *value1* or *value2* equals NaN (Not a Number), the virtual machine pushes onto the operand stack **int** *result* negative one.

The *result* produced by the **fcmpl** instruction is governed by the rules of IEEE 754 floating-point arithmetic. Note that the **dcmpl** instruction differs from the **dcmpg** instruction only in its treatment of NaN. For more information about the **dcmpl** instruction, see Chapter 16, "Control Flow."

# dconst_0

Push **double** constant 0.0

**OPCODE:**   14 (0xe)

**INSTRUCTION FORMAT:**   dconst_0

**STACK:**
Before:   . . .
After:   . . . , *<0.0>-word1, <0.0>-word2*

**DESCRIPTION:**   To execute the **dconst_0** instruction, the Java Virtual Machine pushes the **double** constant 0.0 onto the operand stack.

For more information about the **dconst_0** instruction, see Chapter 10, "Stack and Local Variable Operations."

# dconst_1

Push **double** constant 1.0

**OPCODE:** 15 (0xf)

**INSTRUCTION FORMAT:** dconst_1

**STACK:**
Before:  . . .
After:  . . . , *<1.0>-word1, <1.0>-word2*

**DESCRIPTION:**  To execute the **dconst_1** instruction, the Java Virtual Machine pushes the **double** constant 1.0 onto the operand stack.

For more information about the **dconst_1** instruction, see Chapter 10, "Stack and Local Variable Operations."

# ddiv

Divide **double**s

**OPCODE:** 111 (0x6f)

**INSTRUCTION FORMAT:** ddiv

**STACK:**
Before:  . . . , *value1.word1, value1.word2, value2.word1, value2.word2*
After:  . . . , *result.word1, result.word2*

**DESCRIPTION:**  The top four words of the operand stack must be two **double**s, *value1* and *value2*. To execute the **ddiv** instruction, the Java Virtual Machine pops *value1* and *value2*, divides *value1* by *value2* ( *value1* / *value2*), and pushes the **double** *result*. The *result* produced by the **ddiv** instruction is governed by the rules of IEEE 754 floating-point arithmetic.

For more information about the **ddiv** instruction, see Chapter 14, "Floating-Point Arithmetic."

# dload

Load **double** from local variable

**OPCODE:**   24 (0x18)

**INSTRUCTION FORMAT:**   **dload**, *index*

**STACK:**
Before:   . . .
After:   . . . , *value.word1, value.word2*

**DESCRIPTION:**   The *index* operand, which serves as an 8-bit unsigned index into the local variables of the current frame, must specify the first of two consecutive local variable words that contain a **double**. To execute the **dload** instruction, the Java Virtual Machine pushes onto the operand stack the **double** contained in the two consecutive local variable words specified by *index* and *index + 1*.

Note that the **wide** instruction can precede the **lload** instruction, to allow a local variable to be accessed with a 16-bit unsigned offset.

For more information about the **dload** instruction, see Chapter 10, "Stack and Local Variable Operations."

# dload_0

Load **double** from local variable 0

**OPCODE:**   38 (0x26)

**INSTRUCTION FORMAT:**   **dload_0**

**STACK:**
Before:   . . .
After:   . . . , *value.word1, value.word2*

**DESCRIPTION:**   The two consecutive local variable words at indexes zero and one must contain a **double**. To execute the **dload_0** instruction, the Java Virtual Machine pushes onto the operand stack the **double** *value* contained in local variable words zero and one.

For more information about the **dload_0** instruction, see Chapter 10, "Stack and Local Variable Operations."

# dload_1

Load **double** from local variable 1

**OPCODE:**  39 (0x27)

**INSTRUCTION FORMAT:**  dload_1

**STACK:**
Before:  . . .
After:  . . . , *value.word1, value.word2*

**DESCRIPTION:**  The two consecutive local variable words at indexes one and two must contain a **double**. To execute the **dload_1** instruction, the Java Virtual Machine pushes onto the operand stack the **double** *value* contained in local variable words one and two.

For more information about the **dload_1** instruction, see Chapter 10, "Stack and Local Variable Operations."

# dload_2

Load **double** from local variable 2

**OPCODE:**  40 (0x28)

**INSTRUCTION FORMAT:**  dload_2

**STACK:**
Before:  . . .
After:  . . . , *value.word1, value.word2*

**DESCRIPTION:**  The two consecutive local variable words at indexes two and three must contain a **double**. To execute the **dload_2** instruction, the Java Virtual Machine pushes onto the operand stack the **double** *value* contained in local variable words two and three.

For more information about the **dload_2** instruction, see Chapter 10, "Stack and Local Variable Operations."

## dload_3

Load **double** from local variable 3

**OPCODE:**   41 (0x29)

**INSTRUCTION FORMAT:**   dload_3

**STACK:**
Before:   . . .
After:   . . . , *value.word1, value.word2*

**DESCRIPTION:**   The two consecutive local variable words at indexes three and four must contain a **double**. To execute the **dload_3** instruction, the Java Virtual Machine pushes onto the operand stack the **double** *value* contained in local variable words three and four.

For more information about the **dload_3** instruction, see Chapter 10, "Stack and Local Variable Operations."

## dmul

Multiply **double**s

**OPCODE:**   107 (0x6b)

**INSTRUCTION FORMAT:**   dmul

**STACK:**
Before:   . . . , *value1.word1, value1.word2, value2.word1, value2.word2*
After:   . . . , *result.word1, result.word2*

**DESCRIPTION:**   The top four words of the operand stack must be two **double**s, *value1* and *value2*. To execute the **dmul** instruction, the Java Virtual Machine pops *value1* and *value2*, multiplies them, and pushes the double *result*. The *result* produced by the **dmul** instruction is governed by the rules of IEEE 754 floating-point arithmetic.

For more information about the **dmul** instruction, see Chapter 14, "Floating-Point Arithmetic."

## dneg

Negate **double**

**OPCODE:** 119 (0x77)

**INSTRUCTION FORMAT:** dneg

**STACK:**
Before: ..., *value.word1, value.word2*
After: ..., *result.word1, result.word2*

**DESCRIPTION:** The top two words of the operand stack must be a **double**. To execute the **dneg** instruction, the Java Virtual Machine pops *value*, negates it, and pushes the **double** *result*. The *result* produced by the **dneg** instruction is governed by the rules of IEEE 754 floating-point arithmetic.

Note that the *result* produced by a **dneg** instruction is not always the same as the number that would be produced by subtracting *value* from zero with the **dsub** instruction. The range of IEEE 754 floating-point numbers includes two zeros, a positive zero and a negative zero. When *value* is +0.0, the *result* of the **dneg** instruction is –0.0. By contrast, when subtracting +0.0 from +0.0, the **dsub** instruction yields +0.0.

For more information about the **dneg** instruction, see Chapter 14, "Floating-Point Arithmetic."

## drem

Calculate remainder of division of **double**s

**OPCODE:** 115 (0x73)

**INSTRUCTION FORMAT:** drem

**STACK:**

Before:  *. . . , value1.word1, value1.word2, value2.word1, value2.word2*
After:   *. . . , result.word1, result.word2*

**DESCRIPTION:**   The top four words of the operand stack must be two **double**s, *value1* and *value2*. To execute the **drem** instruction, the Java Virtual Machine pops *value1* and *value2*, calculates the remainder, and pushes the **double** *result*. The remainder equals *value1 – (value1 / value2) * value2*, where *value1 / value2* is a truncating division, rather than the rounding division required by IEEE 754.

The behavior of **drem** is comparable to that of the C library function **fmod()**. The remainder of two **double**s can be calculated according to IEEE 754 floating-point standard via the **IEEERemainder()** method of class **java.lang.Math**.

For more information about the **drem** instruction, see Chapter 14, "Floating-Point Arithmetic."

# dreturn

Return **double** from method

**OPCODE:**   175 (0xaf)

**INSTRUCTION FORMAT:**   **dreturn**

**STACK:**

Before:  *. . . , value.word1, value.word2*
After:   *[empty]*

**DESCRIPTION:**   The return type of the returning method must be **double**. The top two words of the operand stack must be a **double**. To execute the **dreturn** instruction, the Java Virtual Machine pops **double** *value* from the operand stack of the current frame and pushes it onto the operand stack of the invoking method's frame. The virtual machine discards any other words that may still be on the returning method's frame. If the returning method is synchronized, the monitor that was acquired when the method was invoked is released. The invoking method's frame is made current, and the virtual machine continues execution in the invoking method.

For more information about monitors, see Chapter 20, "Thread Synchronization." For more information about the **dreturn** instruction, see Chapter 19, "Method Invocation and Return."

## dstore

Store **double** into local variable

**OPCODE:** 57 (0x39)

**INSTRUCTION FORMAT:** **dstore**, *index*

**STACK:**
Before: ..., *value.word1, value.word2*
After: ...

**DESCRIPTION:** The *index* operand must specify a valid 8-bit unsigned index into the local variables of the current frame. The top two words of the operand stack must be a **double**. To execute the **dstore** instruction, the Java Virtual Machine pops the **double** *value* from the top of the operand stack and stores it into the two consecutive local variable words at indexes *index* and *index + 1*.

Note that the **wide** instruction can precede the **dstore** instruction, to enable a *value* to be stored into a local variable specified by a 16-bit unsigned offset.

For more information about the **dstore** instruction, see Chapter 10, "Stack and Local Variable Operations."

## dstore_0

Store **double** into local variable 0

**OPCODE:** 71 (0x47)

**INSTRUCTION FORMAT:** **dstore_0**

**STACK:**
Before:   . . . , *value.word1, value.word2*
After:   . . .

**DESCRIPTION:**   The indexes zero and one must be valid indexes into the local variables of the current stack frame. The top two words on the operand stack must be a **double**. To execute the **dstore_0** instruction, the Java Virtual Machine pops the **double** *value* from the top of the operand stack and stores it into the two consecutive local variable words at indexes zero and one.

For more information about the **dstore_0** instruction, see Chapter 10, "Stack and Local Variable Operations."

# dstore_1

Store **double** into local variable 1

**OPCODE:**   72 (0x48)

**INSTRUCTION FORMAT:**   dstore_1

**STACK:**
Before:   . . . , *value.word1, value.word2*
After:   . . .

**DESCRIPTION:**   The indexes one and two must be valid indexes into the local variables of the current stack frame. The top two words on the operand stack must be a **double**. To execute the **dstore_1** instruction, the Java Virtual Machine pops the **double** *value* from the top of the operand stack and stores it into the two consecutive local variable words at indexes one and two.

For more information about the **dstore_1** instruction, see Chapter 10, "Stack and Local Variable Operations."

# dstore_2

Store **double** into local variable 2

**OPCODE:**   73 (0x49)

**INSTRUCTION FORMAT:**   `dstore_2`

**STACK:**
Before:   . . . , *value.word1, value.word2*
After:   . . .

**DESCRIPTION:**   The indexes two and three must be valid indexes into the local variables of the current stack frame. The top two words on the operand stack must be a **double**. To execute the **dstore_2** instruction, the Java Virtual Machine pops the **double** *value* from the top of the operand stack and stores it into the two consecutive local variable words at indexes two and three.

For more information about the **dstore_2** instruction, see Chapter 10, "Stack and Local Variable Operations."

# dstore_3

Store **double** into local variable 3

**OPCODE:**   74 (0x4a)

**INSTRUCTION FORMAT:**   `dstore_3`

**STACK:**
Before:   . . . , *value.word1, value.word2*
After:   . . .

**DESCRIPTION:**   The indexes three and four must be valid indexes into the local variables of the current stack frame. The top two words on the operand stack must be a **double**. To execute the **dstore_3** instruction, the Java Virtual Machine pops the **double** *value* from the top of the operand stack and stores it into the two consecutive local variable words at indexes three and four.

For more information about the **dstore_3** instruction, see Chapter 10, "Stack and Local Variable Operations."

# dsub

Subtract **double**s

**OPCODE:** 103 (0x67)

**INSTRUCTION FORMAT:** dsub

**STACK:**
Before:  ..., *value1.word1, value1.word2, value2.word1, value2.word2*
After:  ..., *result.word1, result.word2*

**DESCRIPTION:** The top four words of the operand stack must be two **double**s, *value1* and *value2*. To execute the **dsub** instruction, the Java Virtual Machine pops *value1* and *value2*, subtracts *value2* from *value1* (*value1 – value2*), and pushes the **double** *result*. The *result* produced by the **dsub** instruction is governed by the rules of IEEE 754 floating-point arithmetic.

For more information about the **dsub** instruction, see Chapter 14, "Floating-Point Arithmetic."

# dup

Duplicate top stack word

**OPCODE:** 89 (0x59)

**INSTRUCTION FORMAT:** dup

**STACK:**
Before:  ..., *word*
After:  ..., *word, word*

**DESCRIPTION:** To execute the **dup** instruction, the Java Virtual Machine duplicates the top word of the operand stack and pushes the duplicate. This instruction can be used to duplicate any single-word value from the top of the operand stack. It must not be used to duplicate half of a dual word value (**long** or **double**) that occupies the top of the operand stack.

For more information about the **dup** instruction, see Chapter 10, "Stack and Local Variable Operations."

## dup_x1

Duplicate top stack word and put two down

**OPCODE:**   90 (0x5a)

**INSTRUCTION FORMAT:**   dup_x1

**STACK:**
Before:   ... , *word2, word1*
After:   ... , *word1, word2, word1*

**DESCRIPTION:**   To execute the **dup_x1** instruction, the Java Virtual Machine duplicates the top word of the operand stack and inserts the duplicate two words down. Both *word1* and *word2* must be single-word values.

   For more information about the **dup_x1** instruction, see Chapter 10, "Stack and Local Variable Operations."

## dup_x2

Duplicate top stack word and put three down

**OPCODE:**   91 (0x5b)

**INSTRUCTION FORMAT:**   dup_x2

**STACK:**
Before:   ... , *word3, word2, word1*
After:   ... , *word1, word3, word2, word1*

**DESCRIPTION:**   To execute the **dup_x2** instruction, the Java Virtual Machine duplicates the top word of the operand stack and inserts the duplicate three words down. *word1* must be a single-word value. Both *word2* and *word3* must be single-word values or together constitute one dual-word value (a `long` or `double`).

For more information about the `dup_x2` instruction, see Chapter 10, "Stack and Local Variable Operations."


# dup2

Duplicate top two stack words

**OPCODE:**   92 (0x5c)

**INSTRUCTION FORMAT:**   `dup2`

**STACK:**
Before:   . . . , *word2, word1*
After:   . . . , *word2, word1, word2, word1*

**DESCRIPTION:**   To execute the `dup2` instruction, the Java Virtual Machine duplicates the top two words of the operand stack and pushes the duplicate. This instruction can be used to duplicate any dual-word value or any two single-word values that occupy the top of the operand stack. It must not be used if one single-word value and half of a dual-word value (`long` or `double`) occupy the top of the operand stack.

For more information about the `dup2` instruction, see Chapter 10, "Stack and Local Variable Operations."


# dup2_x1

Duplicate top two stack words and put three down

**OPCODE:**   93 (0x5d)

**INSTRUCTION FORMAT:**   `dup2_x1`

**STACK:**
Before:   . . . , *word3, word2, word1*
After:   . . . , *word2, word1, word3, word2, word1*

**DESCRIPTION:** To execute the `dup2_x1` instruction, the Java Virtual Machine duplicates the top two words of the operand stack and inserts the duplicate three words down. *word3* must be a single-word value. Both *word1* and *word2* must be single-word values or together constitute one dual-word value (a `long` or `double`).

For more information about the `dup2_x1` instruction, see Chapter 10, "Stack and Local Variable Operations."

# dup2_x2

Duplicate top two stack words and put four down

**OPCODE:** 94 (0x5e)

**INSTRUCTION FORMAT:** `dup2_x2`

**STACK:**
Before: . . . , *word4, word3, word2, word1*
After: . . . , *word2, word1, word4, word3, word2, word1*

**DESCRIPTION:** To execute the `dup2_x2` instruction, the Java Virtual Machine duplicates the top two words of the operand stack and inserts the duplicate four words down. *word3* must be a single-word value. Both *word1* and *word2* must be single-word values or together constitute one dual-word value (a `long` or `double`). Likewise, both *word3* and *word4* must be single-word values or together constitute one dual-word value.

For more information about the `dup2_x2` instruction, see Chapter 10, "Stack and Local Variable Operations."

# f2d

Convert `float` to `double`

**OPCODE:** 141 (0x8d)

**INSTRUCTION FORMAT:** `f2d`

**STACK:**
Before:   . . . , *value*
After:   . . . , *result.word1, result.word2*

**DESCRIPTION:**   The top word of the operand stack, *value*, must be a
**float**. To execute the **f2d** instruction, the Java Virtual Machine pops
**float** *value* from the operand stack, converts the **float** to a **double**, and
pushes the **double** *result*.

Note that this instruction performs a widening primitive conversion.
Because all **float** values can be represented by a **double**, the conversion
is exact.

For more information about the **f2d** instruction, see Chapter 11, "Type
Conversion."

## f2i

Convert **float** to **int**

**OPCODE:**   139 (0x8b)

**INSTRUCTION FORMAT:**   **f2i**

**STACK:**
Before:   . . . , *value*
After:   . . . , *result*

**DESCRIPTION:**   The top word of the operand stack, *value*, must be a
**float**. To execute the **f2i** instruction, the Java Virtual Machine pops the
**float** *value* from the operand stack, converts the **float** to an **int**, and
pushes the **int** *result*.

To convert the **float** *value* to **int**, the Java Virtual Machine first
checks to see whether the *value* equals NaN (Not a Number). If so, the
**int** *result* is zero. Else, if the **float** *value* is not a positive or negative infinity, the virtual machine rounds the *value* toward zero using IEEE 754
round-toward-zero mode. If the resulting integral value can be exactly
represented by an **int**, the **int** *result* is that integral value. Otherwise,
the magnitude of the **float** *value* is too great be represented in an **int**. If
*value* is positive, the **int** *result* is the largest positive integer that can be

represented in an **int**. If *value* is negative, the **int** *result* is the smallest negative integer that can be represented in an **int**.

Note that this instruction performs a narrowing primitive conversion. Because not all **float** values can be represented by an **int**, the conversion may result in a loss of magnitude and precision.

For more information about the **f2i** instruction, see Chapter 11, "Type Conversion."

# f2l

Convert **float** to **long**

**OPCODE:** 140 (0x8c)

**INSTRUCTION FORMAT:** f2l

**STACK:**
Before:   . . . , *value*
After:   . . . , *result.word1, result.word2*

**DESCRIPTION:** The top word of the operand stack, *value*, must be a **float**. To execute the **f2l** instruction, the Java Virtual Machine pops the **float** *value* from the operand stack, converts the **float** to a **long**, and pushes the **long** *result*.

To convert the **float** *value* to **long**, the Java Virtual Machine first checks to see whether the *value* equals NaN (Not a Number). If so, the **long** *result* is zero. Else, if the **float** *value* is not a positive or negative infinity, the virtual machine rounds the *value* toward zero using IEEE 754 round-toward-zero mode. If the resulting integral value can be exactly represented by a **long**, the **long** *result* is that integral value. Otherwise, the magnitude of the **float** *value* is too great to be represented in a **long**. If *value* is positive, the **long** *result* is the largest positive integer that can be represented in a **long**. If *value* is negative, the **int** *result* is the smallest negative integer that can be represented in a **long**.

Note that this instruction performs a narrowing primitive conversion. Because not all **float** values can be represented by a **long**, the conversion may result in a loss of magnitude and precision.

For more information about the **f2l** instruction, see Chapter 11, "Type Conversion."

# fadd

Add `float`s

**OPCODE:** 98 (0x62)

**INSTRUCTION FORMAT:** `fadd`

**STACK:**
Before:   . . . , *value1, value2*
After:    . . . , *result*

**DESCRIPTION:**   The top two words of the operand stack, *value1* and *value2*, must be `float`s. To execute the `fadd` instruction, the Java Virtual Machine pops *value1* and *value2*, adds them, and pushes the `float` *result*. The *result* produced by the `fadd` instruction is governed by the rules of IEEE 754 floating-point arithmetic.

For more information about the `fadd` instruction, see Chapter 14, "Floating-Point Arithmetic."

# faload

Load `float` from array

**OPCODE:** 48 (0x30)

**INSTRUCTION FORMAT:** `faload`

**STACK:**
Before:   . . . , *arrayref, index*
After:    . . . , *value*

**DESCRIPTION:**   To execute the `faload` instruction, the Java Virtual Machine first pops two words from the operand stack. The *arrayref* word must be a `reference` that refers to an array of `float`s. The *index* word must be an `int`. The virtual machine retrieves from the *arrayref* array the `float` *value* specified by *index* and pushes it onto the operand stack.

If *arrayref* is `null`, the Java Virtual Machine throws `NullPointerException`. Otherwise, if *index* is not a legal index into the *arrayref* array, the virtual machine throws `ArrayIndexOutOfBoundsException`.

For more information about the `faload` instruction, see Chapter 15, "Objects and Arrays."

# fastore

Store into `float` array

**OPCODE:**   81 (0x51)

**INSTRUCTION FORMAT:**   `fastore`

**STACK:**
Before:   . . . , *arrayref, index, value*
After:   . . .

**DESCRIPTION:**   To execute the `faload` instruction, the Java Virtual Machine first pops three words from the operand stack. The *arrayref* word must be a `reference` that refers to an array of `float`s. The *index* word must be an `int`, and the *value* word must be a `float`. The virtual machine stores `float` *value* into the *arrayref* array location specified by *index*.

If   *arrayref*   is   `null`,   the   Java   Virtual   Machine   throws `NullPointerException`. Otherwise, if *index* is not a legal index into the *arrayref* array, the virtual machine throws `ArrayIndexOutOfBoundsException`.

For more information about the `fastore` instruction, see Chapter 15, "Objects and Arrays."

# fcmpg

Compare `float`s (1 on NaN)

**OPCODE:**   150 (0x96)

**INSTRUCTION FORMAT:**   `fcmpg`

**STACK:**
Before:   . . . , *value1, value2*
After:   . . . , *result*

**DESCRIPTION:** The top two words of the operand stack, *value1* and *value2*, must be two **float**s. To execute the **fcmpg** instruction, the Java Virtual Machine pops *value1* and *value2* off the operand stack and compares one against the other. If *value1* equals *value2*, the virtual machine pushes onto the operand stack **int** *result* zero. Else, if *value1* is greater than *value2*, the virtual machine pushes onto the operand stack **int** *result* one. Otherwise, if *value1* is less than *value2*, the virtual machine pushes onto the operand stack **int** *result* negative one. If either *value1* or *value2* equals NaN (Not a Number), the virtual machine pushes onto the operand stack **int** *result* one.

The *result* produced by the **fcmpg** instruction is governed by the rules of IEEE 754 floating-point arithmetic. Note that the **fcmpg** instruction differs from the **fcmpl** instruction only in its treatment of NaN. For more information about the **fcmpg** instruction, see Chapter 16, "Control Flow."

# fcmpl

Compare **float**s (–1 on NaN)

**OPCODE:** 149 (0x95)

**INSTRUCTION FORMAT:**   fcmpl

**STACK:**
Before:   ... , *value1, value2*
After:   ... , *result*

**DESCRIPTION:** The top two words of the operand stack, *value1* and *value2*, must be two **float**s. To execute the **fcmpl** instruction, the Java Virtual Machine pops *value1* and *value2* off the operand stack and compares one against the other. If *value1* equals *value2*, the virtual machine pushes onto the operand stack **int** *result* zero. Else, if *value1* is greater than *value2*, the virtual machine pushes onto the operand stack **int** *result* one. Otherwise, if *value1* is less than *value2*, the virtual machine pushes onto the operand stack **int** *result* negative one. If either *value1* or *value2* equals NaN (Not a Number), the virtual machine pushes onto the operand stack **int** *result* negative one.

The *result* produced by the **fcmpl** instruction is governed by the rules of IEEE 754 floating-point arithmetic. Note that the **fcmpl** instruction differs from the **fcmpg** instruction only in its treatment of NaN. For more information about the **fcmpl** instruction, see Chapter 16, "Control Flow."

## fconst_0

Push **float** constant 0.0

**OPCODE:** 11 (0xb)

**INSTRUCTION FORMAT:** fconst_0

**STACK:**
Before: . . .
After: . . . , *<0.0>*

**DESCRIPTION:** To execute the **fconst_0** instruction, the Java Virtual Machine pushes the **float** constant 0.0 onto the operand stack.

For more information about the **fconst_0** instruction, see Chapter 10, "Stack and Local Variable Operations."

## fconst_1

Push **float** constant 1.0

**OPCODE:** 12 (0xc)

**INSTRUCTION FORMAT:** fconst_1

**STACK:**
Before: . . .
After: . . . , *<1.0>*

**DESCRIPTION:** To execute the **fconst_1** instruction, the Java Virtual Machine pushes the **float** constant 1.0 onto the operand stack.

For more information about the **fconst_1** instruction, see Chapter 10, "Stack and Local Variable Operations."

# fconst_2

Push **float** constant 2.0

**OPCODE:** 13 (0xd)

**INSTRUCTION FORMAT:** fconst_2

**STACK:**
Before: . . .
After: . . . , *<2.0>*

**DESCRIPTION:** To execute the **fconst_2** instruction, the Java Virtual Machine pushes the **float** constant 2.0 onto the operand stack.

For more information about the **fconst_2** instruction, see Chapter 10, "Stack and Local Variable Operations."

# fdiv

Divide **float**s

**OPCODE:** 110 (0x6e)

**INSTRUCTION FORMAT:** fdiv

**STACK:**
Before: . . . , *value1, value2*
After: . . . , *result*

**DESCRIPTION:** The top two words of the operand stack, *value1* and *value2*, must be **float**s. To execute the **fdiv** instruction, the Java Virtual Machine pops *value1* and *value2*, divides *value1* by *value2* (*value1 / value2*), and pushes the **float** *result*. The *result* produced by the **fdiv** instruction is governed by the rules of IEEE 754 floating-point arithmetic.

For more information about the **fdiv** instruction, see Chapter 14, "Floating-Point Arithmetic."

# fload

Load **float** from local variable

**OPCODE:** 23 (0x17)

**INSTRUCTION FORMAT:** **fload**, *index*

**STACK:**
Before: . . .
After: . . . , *value*

**DESCRIPTION:** The *index* operand, which serves as an 8-bit unsigned index into the local variables of the current frame, must specify a local variable word that contains a **float**. To execute the **fload** instruction, the Java Virtual Machine pushes onto the operand stack the **float** contained in the local variable word specified by *index*.

Note that the **wide** instruction can precede the **fload** instruction, to allow a local variable to be accessed with a 16-bit unsigned offset.

For more information about the **fload** instruction, see Chapter 10, "Stack and Local Variable Operations."

# fload_0

Load **float** from local variable 0

**OPCODE:** 34 (0x22)

**INSTRUCTION FORMAT:** **fload_0**

**STACK:**
Before: . . .
After: . . . , *value*

**DESCRIPTION:** The local variable word at index zero must contain a **float**. To execute the **fload_0** instruction, the Java Virtual Machine pushes onto the operand stack the **float** *value* contained in local variable word zero.

For more information about the **fload_0** instruction, see Chapter 10, "Stack and Local Variable Operations."

# fload_1

Load **float** from local variable 1

**OPCODE:**  35 (0x23)

**INSTRUCTION FORMAT:**  fload_1

**STACK:**
Before:  . . .
After:  . . . , *value*

**DESCRIPTION:**  The local variable word at index one must contain a **float**. To execute the **fload_1** instruction, the Java Virtual Machine pushes onto the operand stack the **float** *value* contained in local variable word one.

For more information about the **fload_1** instruction, see Chapter 10, "Stack and Local Variable Operations."

# fload_2

Load **float** from local variable 2

**OPCODE:**  36 (0x24)

**INSTRUCTION FORMAT:**  fload_2

**STACK:**
Before:  . . .
After:  . . . , *value*

**DESCRIPTION:**  The local variable word at index two must contain a **float**. To execute the **fload_2** instruction, the Java Virtual Machine pushes onto the operand stack the **float** *value* contained in local variable word two.

For more information about the `fload_2` instruction, see Chapter 10, "Stack and Local Variable Operations."

# fload_3

Load **float** from local variable 3

**OPCODE:**   37 (0x25)

**INSTRUCTION FORMAT:**   `fload_3`

**STACK:**
Before:   . . .
After:   . . . , *value*

**DESCRIPTION:**   The local variable word at index three must contain a **float**. To execute the `fload_3` instruction, the Java Virtual Machine pushes onto the operand stack the **float** *value* contained in local variable word three.

For more information about the `fload_3` instruction, see Chapter 10, "Stack and Local Variable Operations."

# fmul

Multiply **float**s

**OPCODE:**   106 (0x6a)

**INSTRUCTION FORMAT:**   `fmul`

**STACK:**
Before:   . . . , *value1, value2*
After:   . . . , *result*

**DESCRIPTION:**   The top two words of the operand stack, *value1* and *value2*, must be **float**s. To execute the `fmul` instruction, the Java Virtual Machine pops *value1* and *value2*, multiplies them, and pushes the **float**

*result*. The *result* produced by the `fmul` instruction is governed by the rules of IEEE 754 floating-point arithmetic.

For more information about the `fmul` instruction, see Chapter 14, "Floating-Point Arithmetic."

## fneg

Negate `float`

**OPCODE:**  118 (0x76)

**INSTRUCTION FORMAT:**  `fneg`

**STACK:**
Before:  *. . . , value*
After:  *. . . , result*

**DESCRIPTION:**  The top word of the operand stack, *value*, must be a `float`. To execute the `fneg` instruction, the Java Virtual Machine pops *value*, negates it, and pushes the `float` *result*. The *result* produced by the `fneg` instruction is governed by the rules of IEEE 754 floating-point arithmetic.

Note that the *result* produced by an `fneg` instruction is not always the same as the number that would be produced by subtracting *value* from zero with the `fsub` instruction. The range of IEEE 754 floating-point numbers includes two zeros, a positive zero and a negative zero. When *value* is +0.0, the *result* of the `fneg` instruction is –0.0. By contrast, when subtracting +0.0 from +0.0, the `fsub` instruction yields +0.0.

For more information about the `fneg` instruction, see Chapter 14, "Floating-Point Arithmetic."

## frem

Calculate remainder of division of `float`s

**OPCODE:**  114 (0x72)

**INSTRUCTION FORMAT:**  `frem`

**STACK:**
Before: ..., *value1, value2*
After: ..., *result*

**DESCRIPTION:** The top two words of the operand stack, *value1* and *value2*, must be **float**s. To execute the **frem** instruction, the Java Virtual Machine pops *value1* and *value2*, calculates the remainder, and pushes the **float** *result*. The remainder equals *value1 – (value1 / value2) \* value2*, where *value1 / value2* is a truncating division rather than the rounding division required by IEEE 754.

The behavior of **frem** is comparable to that of the C library function **fmod()**. The remainder of two **float**s can be calculated according to IEEE 754 floating-point standard via the **IEEERemainder()** method of class **java.lang.Math**.

For more information about the **frem** instruction, see Chapter 14, "Floating-Point Arithmetic."

# freturn

Return **float** from method

**OPCODE:** 174 (0xae)

**INSTRUCTION FORMAT:** freturn

**STACK:**
Before: ..., *value*
After: *[empty]*

**DESCRIPTION:** The return type of the returning method must be **float**. The top word of the operand stack, *value*, must be a **float**. To execute the **freturn** instruction, the Java Virtual Machine pops **float** *value* from the operand stack of the current frame and pushes it onto the operand stack of the invoking method's frame. The virtual machine discards any other words that may still be on the returning method's frame. If the returning method is synchronized, the monitor that was acquired when the method was invoked is released. The invoking method's frame is made current, and the virtual machine continues execution in the invoking method.

For more information about monitors, see Chapter 20, "Thread Synchronization." For more information about the `freturn` instruction, see Chapter 19, "Method Invocation and Return."

## fstore

Store `float` into local variable

**OPCODE:**   56 (0x38)

**INSTRUCTION FORMAT:**   `fstore`, *index*

**STACK:**
Before:   ..., *value*
After:   ...

**DESCRIPTION:**   The *index* operand must specify a valid 8-bit unsigned index into the local variables of the current frame. The *value* on the top of the operand stack must be a `float`. To execute the `fstore` instruction, the Java Virtual Machine pops the `float` *value* from the top of the operand stack and stores it into the local variable word specified by *index*.

Note that the `wide` instruction can precede the `fstore` instruction, to enable a *value* to be stored into a local variable specified by a 16-bit unsigned offset.

For more information about the `fstore` instruction, see Chapter 10, "Stack and Local Variable Operations."

## fstore_0

Store `float` into local variable 0

**OPCODE:**   67 (0x43)

**INSTRUCTION FORMAT:**   `fstore_0`

**STACK:**
Before:  . . . , *value*
After:  . . .

**DESCRIPTION:**   The index zero must be a valid index into the local variables of the current stack frame, and the *value* word on the top of the operand stack must be a **float**. To execute the **fstore_0** instruction, the Java Virtual Machine pops the **float** *value* from the top of the operand stack and stores it into the local variable word at index zero.

For more information about the **fstore_0** instruction, see Chapter 10, "Stack and Local Variable Operations."

## fstore_1

Store **float** into local variable 1

**OPCODE:**   68 (0x44)

**INSTRUCTION FORMAT:**   **fstore_1**

**STACK:**
Before:  . . . , *value*
After:  . . .

**DESCRIPTION:**   The index one must be a valid index into the local variables of the current stack frame, and the *value* word on the top of the operand stack must be a **float**. To execute the **fstore_1** instruction, the Java Virtual Machine pops the **float** *value* from the top of the operand stack and stores it into the local variable word at index one.

For more information about the **fstore_1** instruction, see Chapter 10, "Stack and Local Variable Operations."

## fstore_2

Store **float** into local variable 2

**OPCODE:**   69 (0x45)

**INSTRUCTION FORMAT:** `fstore_2`

**STACK:**
Before:    . . . , *value*
After:    . . .

**DESCRIPTION:**   The index two must be a valid index into the local variables of the current stack frame, and the *value* word on the top of the operand stack must be a `float`. To execute the `fstore_2` instruction, the Java Virtual Machine pops the `float` *value* from the top of the operand stack and stores it into the local variable word at index two.

For more information about the `fstore_2` instruction, see Chapter 10, "Stack and Local Variable Operations."


# `fstore_3`

Store `float` into local variable 3

**OPCODE:**   70 (0x46)

**INSTRUCTION FORMAT:**   `fstore_3`

**STACK:**
Before:    . . . , *value*
After:    . . .

**DESCRIPTION:**   The index three must be a valid index into the local variables of the current stack frame, and the *value* word on the top of the operand stack must be a `float`. To execute the `fstore_3` instruction, the Java Virtual Machine pops the `float` *value* from the top of the operand stack and stores it into the local variable word at index three.

For more information about the `fstore_3` instruction, see Chapter 10, "Stack and Local Variable Operations."


# `fsub`

Subtract `float`s

**OPCODE:**   102 (0x66)

**INSTRUCTION FORMAT:**   `fsub`

**STACK:**
Before:   ... , *value1*, *value2*
After:   ... , *result*

**DESCRIPTION:**   The top two words of the operand stack, *value1* and *value2*, must be `float`s. To execute the `fsub` instruction, the Java Virtual Machine pops *value1* and *value2*, subtracts *value2* from *value1* (*value1* – *value2*), and pushes the `float` *result*. The *result* produced by the `fsub` instruction is governed by the rules of IEEE 754 floating-point arithmetic.

For more information about the `fsub` instruction, see Chapter 14, "Floating-Point Arithmetic."

# `getfield`

Fetch field from object

**OPCODE:**   180 (0xb4)

**INSTRUCTION FORMAT:**   `getfield`, *indexbyte1*, *indexbyte2*

**STACK:**
Before:   ... , *objectref*
After:   ... , *value*
   or
Before:   ... , *objectref*
After:   ... , *value.word1*, *value.word2*

**DESCRIPTION:**   The top word of the stack, *objectref*, must be a `reference`. To execute the `getfield` instruction, the Java Virtual Machine first forms an unsigned 16-bit index into the constant pool by calculating *(indexbyte1 << 8) | indexbyte2*. The virtual machine then looks up the constant pool entry specified by the calculated index. The constant pool entry at that index must be a `CONSTANT_Fieldref_info` entry. If it hasn't already, the virtual machine resolves the entry, which yields the field's width and the field's offset from the beginning of the object image. If the resolution is successful, the virtual machine pops the *objectref* and fetches the field from the object pointed to by *objectref*. If the type of the field is **byte**, **short**, or **char**, the virtual machine sign-extends the field's value to an **int** and pushes the single-word **int** *value* onto the operand stack. Else, if the type is **int**, **boolean**, **float**, or **reference**, the virtual machine pushes the single-word *value* onto the operand stack. Otherwise, the type is **long** or **double**, and the virtual machine pushes the dual-word *value* onto the operand stack.

As a result of executing this instruction, the virtual machine may throw any of the linking errors listed in Chapter 8, "The Linking Model," as possible during resolution of a **CONSTANT_Fieldref_info** entry. As part of the process of resolving the **CONSTANT_Fieldref_info** entry, the virtual machine checks whether the field's access permission enables the current class to access the field. If the field is protected, the virtual machine makes certain the field is a member either of the current class or a superclass of the current class, and that the class of the object pointed to by *objectref* is either the current class or a subclass of the current class. If not (or if any other access permission problem occurs), the virtual machine throws **IllegalAccessError**. Else, if the field exists and is accessible from the current class, but the field is static, the virtual machine throws **IncompatibleClassChangeError**. Otherwise, if *objectref* is **null**, the virtual machine throws **NullPointerException**.

For more information about the **getfield** instruction, see Chapter 15, "Objects and Arrays."

## getstatic

Fetch static field from class

**OPCODE:**   178 (0xb2)

**INSTRUCTION FORMAT:**   **getstatic**, *indexbyte1*, *indexbyte2*

**STACK:**
Before:   . . .
After:    . . . , *value*
  or
Before:   . . .
After:    . . . , *value.word1*, *value.word2*

**DESCRIPTION:** To execute the `getstatic` instruction, the Java Virtual Machine first forms an unsigned 16-bit index into the constant pool by calculating *(indexbyte1 << 8) | indexbyte2*. The virtual machine then looks up the constant pool entry specified by the calculated index. The constant pool entry at that index must be a `CONSTANT_Fieldref_info` entry. If it hasn't already, the virtual machine resolves the entry. If the resolution is successful, the virtual machine fetches the value of the static field. If the type of the field is `byte`, `short`, or `char`, the virtual machine sign-extends the field's value to `int` and pushes the single-word `int` *value* onto the operand stack. Else, if the type is `int`, `boolean`, `float`, or `reference`, the virtual machine pushes the single-word *value* onto the operand stack. Otherwise, the type is `long` or `double`, and the virtual machine pushes the dual-word *value* onto the operand stack.

As a result of executing this instruction, the virtual machine may throw any of the linking errors listed in Chapter 8, "The Linking Model," as possible during resolution of a `CONSTANT_Fieldref_info` entry. As part of the process of resolving the `CONSTANT_Fieldref_info` entry, the virtual machine checks whether the field's access permission enables the current class to access the field. If the field is protected, the virtual machine makes certain the field is a member either of the current class or a superclass of the current class. If not (or if any other access permission problem occurs), the virtual machine throws `IllegalAccessError`. Else, if the field exists and is accessible from the current class, but the field is not static, the virtual machine throws `IncompatibleClassChangeError`.

For more information about the `getstatic` instruction, see Chapter 15, "Objects and Arrays."

## goto

Branch always

**OPCODE:** 167 (0xa7)

**INSTRUCTION FORMAT:** `goto`, *branchbyte1, branchbyte2*

**STACK:** No change

**DESCRIPTION:** To execute the `goto` instruction, the Java Virtual Machine forms a signed 16-bit offset by calculating *(branchbyte1 << 8) | branchbyte2*. The virtual machine then calculates a target (program counter) address by adding the calculated offset to the address of the **goto** opcode. The target address must be the address of an opcode within the same method as the **goto** opcode. The virtual machine jumps to the target address and continues execution there.

For more information about the **goto** instruction, see Chapter 16, "Control Flow."

## goto_w

Branch always (wide index)

**OPCODE:** 200 (0xc8)

**INSTRUCTION FORMAT:** **goto_w = 200**, *branchbyte1*, *branchbyte2*, *branchbyte3*, *branchbyte4*

**STACK:** No change

**DESCRIPTION:** To execute the **goto_w** instruction, the Java Virtual Machine forms a signed 32-bit offset by calculating *(branchbyte1 << 24) | (branchbyte2 << 16) | (branchbyte3 << 8) | branchbyte4*. The virtual machine then calculates a target (program counter) address by adding the calculated offset to the address of the **goto_w** opcode. The target address must be the address of an opcode within the same method as the **goto_w** opcode. The virtual machine jumps to the target address and continues execution there.

Note that despite the 32-bit offset of the **goto_w** instruction, Java methods are currently (in both the 1.0 and 1.1 releases) limited to 65,535 bytes by three items in the Java class file format: the sizes of the indexes in the **LineNumberTable** attribute, the **LocalVariableTable** attribute, and the **Code** attribute's **exception_table** item. According to the Java Virtual Machine specification, the 65,536-byte limit to Java methods may be raised in a future release. For more information about the **goto_w** instruction, see Chapter 16, "Control Flow."

## i2b

Convert **int** to **byte**

**OPCODE:**   145 (0x91)

**INSTRUCTION FORMAT:**   i2b

**STACK:**
Before:   . . . , *value*
After:   . . . , *result*

**DESCRIPTION:**   The top word of the operand stack, *value*, must be an
**int**. To execute the **i2b** instruction, the Java Virtual Machine pops **int**
*value* from the operand stack, truncates the **int** to a **byte**, sign-extends
the result back to an **int**, and pushes the **int** *result*.

Note that this instruction performs a narrowing primitive conversion.
As a result of this conversion, magnitude information may be lost and the
sign bit may change.

For more information about the **i2b** instruction, see Chapter 11, "Type
Conversion."

# i2c

Convert **int** to **char**

**OPCODE:**   146 (0x92)

**INSTRUCTION FORMAT:**   i2c

**STACK:**
Before:   . . . , *value*
After:   . . . , *result*

**DESCRIPTION:**   The top word of the operand stack, *value*, must be an
**int**. To execute the **i2c** instruction, the Java Virtual Machine pops **int**
*value* from the operand stack, truncates the **int** to a **char**, zero-extends
the result back to an **int**, and pushes the **int** *result*.

Note that this instruction performs a narrowing primitive conversion.
As a result of this conversion, magnitude information may be lost and, as
the *result* is always positive, the sign may change.

For more information about the **i2c** instruction, see Chapter 11, "Type
Conversion."

# i2d

Convert **int** to **double**

**OPCODE:** 135 (0x87)

**INSTRUCTION FORMAT:** i2d

**STACK:**
Before:    ... , *value*
After:    ... , *result.word1, result.word2*

**DESCRIPTION:**   The top word of the operand stack, *value*, must be an **int**. To execute the **i2d** instruction, the Java Virtual Machine pops **int** *value* from the operand stack, sign-extends the **int** to a **double**, and pushes the **double** *result*.

Note that this instruction performs a widening primitive conversion. Because all **int** values can be represented by a **double**, the conversion is exact.

For more information about the **i2d** instruction, see Chapter 11, "Type Conversion."

# i2f

Convert **int** to **float**

**OPCODE:** 134 (0x86)

**INSTRUCTION FORMAT:** i2f

**STACK:**
Before:    ... , *value*
After:    ... , *result*

**DESCRIPTION:**   The top word of the operand stack, *value*, must be an **int**. To execute the **i2f** instruction, the Java Virtual Machine pops **int** *value* from the operand stack, converts the **int** to a **float** using the IEEE round-to-nearest mode, and pushes the **float** *result*.

Note that this instruction performs a widening primitive conversion. Because not all **int** values can be exactly represented by a **float**, the conversion may result in a loss of precision.

For more information about the **i2f** instruction, see Chapter 11, "Type Conversion."

# i2l

Convert **int** to **long**

**OPCODE:**   133 (0x85)

**INSTRUCTION FORMAT:**   i2l

**STACK:**
Before:   . . . , *value*
After:   . . . , *result.word1, result.word2*

**DESCRIPTION:**   The top word of the operand stack, *value*, must be an **int**. To execute the **i2l** instruction, the Java Virtual Machine pops **int** *value* from the operand stack, sign-extends the **int** to a **long**, and pushes the **long** *result*.

Note that this instruction performs a widening primitive conversion. Because all **int** values can be represented by a **long**, the conversion is exact.

For more information about the **i2l** instruction, see Chapter 11, "Type Conversion."

# i2s

Convert **int** to **short**

**OPCODE:**   147 (0x93)

**INSTRUCTION FORMAT:**   i2s

**STACK:**
Before:   . . . , *value*
After:   . . . , *result*

**DESCRIPTION:** The top word of the operand stack, *value*, must be an `int`. To execute the `i2s` instruction, the Java Virtual Machine pops `int` *value* from the operand stack, truncates the `int` to a `short`, sign-extends the result back to an `int`, and pushes the `int` *result*.

Note that this instruction performs a narrowing primitive conversion. As a result of this conversion, magnitude information may be lost and the sign bit may change.

For more information about the `i2s` instruction, see Chapter 11, "Type Conversion."

## iadd

Add `int`s

**OPCODE:** 96 (0x60)

**INSTRUCTION FORMAT:** `iadd`

**STACK:**
Before:  . . . , *value1, value2*
After:  . . . , *result*

**DESCRIPTION:** The top two words of the operand stack, *value1* and *value2*, must be `int`s. To execute the `iadd` instruction, the Java Virtual Machine pops *value1* and *value2*, adds them, and pushes the `int` *result*. If overflow occurs, *result* is the 32 lowest order bits of the true mathematical result represented in a sufficiently wide two's-complement format, and the sign of *result* is different from that of the true mathematical result.

For more information about the `iadd` instruction, see Chapter 12, "Integer Arithmetic."

## iaload

Load `int` from array

**OPCODE:** 46 (0x2e)

**INSTRUCTION FORMAT:** `iaload`

**STACK:**
Before: . . . , *arrayref, index*
After: . . . , *value*

**DESCRIPTION:** To execute the `iaload` instruction, the Java Virtual Machine first pops two words from the operand stack. The *arrayref* word must be a `reference` that refers to an array of `int`s. The *index* word must be an `int`. The virtual machine retrieves from the *arrayref* array the `int` *value* specified by *index* and pushes it onto the operand stack.

If *arrayref* is `null`, the Java Virtual Machine throws `NullPointerException`. Otherwise, if *index* is not a legal index into the *arrayref* array, the virtual machine throws `ArrayIndexOutOfBoundsException`.

For more information about the `iaload` instruction, see Chapter 15, "Objects and Arrays."

## iand

Perform boolean AND on `int`s

**OPCODE:** 126 (0x7e)

**INSTRUCTION FORMAT:** `iand`

**STACK:**
Before: . . . , *value1, value2*
After: . . . , *result*

**DESCRIPTION:** The top two words of the operand stack, *value1* and *value2*, must be `int`s. To execute the `iand` instruction, the Java Virtual Machine pops *value1* and *value2*, bitwise ANDs them, and pushes the `int` *result*.

For more information about the `iand` instruction, see Chapter 13, "Logic."

## iastore

Store into `int` array

**OPCODE:** 79 (0x4f)

**INSTRUCTION FORMAT:** `iastore`

**STACK:**
Before: ..., *arrayref, index, value*
After: ...

**DESCRIPTION:** To execute the `iastore` instruction, the Java Virtual Machine first pops three words from the operand stack. The *arrayref* word must be a `reference` that refers to an array of `int`s. The *index* and *value* words must be `int`s. The virtual machine stores `int` *value* into the *arrayref* array location specified by *index*.

If *arrayref* is `null`, the Java Virtual Machine throws `NullPointerException`. Otherwise, if *index* is not a legal index into the *arrayref* array, the virtual machine throws `ArrayIndexOutOfBoundsException`.

For more information about the `iastore` instruction, see Chapter 15, "Objects and Arrays."

# iconst_0

Push `int` constant 0

**OPCODE:** 3 (0x3)

**INSTRUCTION FORMAT:** `iconst_0`

**STACK:**
Before: ...
After: ..., *0*

**DESCRIPTION:** To execute the `iconst_0` instruction, the Java Virtual Machine pushes the `int` constant 0 onto the operand stack.

For more information about the `iconst_0` instruction, see Chapter 10, "Stack and Local Variable Operations."

# iconst_1

Push `int` constant 1

**OPCODE:**   4 (0x4)

**INSTRUCTION FORMAT:**   `iconst_1`

**STACK:**
Before:   . . .
After:   . . . , *1*

**DESCRIPTION:**   To execute the `iconst_1` instruction, the Java Virtual Machine pushes the `int` constant 1 onto the operand stack.

For more information about the `iconst_1` instruction, see Chapter 10, "Stack and Local Variable Operations."

# `iconst_2`

Push `int` constant 2

**OPCODE:**   5 (0x5)

**INSTRUCTION FORMAT:**   `iconst_2`

**STACK:**
Before:   . . .
After:   . . . , *2*

**DESCRIPTION:**   To execute the `iconst_2` instruction, the Java Virtual Machine pushes the `int` constant 2 onto the operand stack.

For more information about the `iconst_2` instruction, see Chapter 10, "Stack and Local Variable Operations."

# `iconst_3`

Push `int` constant 3

**OPCODE:**   6 (0x6)

**INSTRUCTION FORMAT:**   `iconst_3`

**STACK:**
Before:   ...
After:   ..., *3*

**DESCRIPTION:**   To execute the `iconst_3` instruction, the Java Virtual Machine pushes the `int` constant 3 onto the operand stack.

For more information about the `iconst_3` instruction, see Chapter 10, "Stack and Local Variable Operations."

# iconst_4

Push `int` constant 4

**OPCODE:**   7 (0x7)

**INSTRUCTION FORMAT:**   `iconst_4`

**STACK:**
Before:   ...
After:   ..., *4*

**DESCRIPTION:**   To execute the `iconst_4` instruction, the Java Virtual Machine pushes the `int` constant 4 onto the operand stack.

For more information about the `iconst_4` instruction, see Chapter 10, "Stack and Local Variable Operations."

# iconst_5

Push `int` constant 5

**OPCODE:**   8 (0x8)

**INSTRUCTION FORMAT:**   `iconst_5`

**STACK:**
Before:   ...
After:   ..., *5*

**DESCRIPTION:** To execute the `iconst_5` instruction, the Java Virtual Machine pushes the `int` constant 5 onto the operand stack.

For more information about the `iconst_5` instruction, see Chapter 10, "Stack and Local Variable Operations."

# iconst_m1

Push `int` constant –1

**OPCODE:** 2 (0x2)

**INSTRUCTION FORMAT:** `iconst_m1`

**STACK:**
Before: . . .
After: . . . , *–1*

**DESCRIPTION:** To execute the `iconst_m1` instruction, the Java Virtual Machine pushes the `int` constant –1 onto the operand stack.

For more information about the `iconst_m1` instruction, see Chapter 10, "Stack and Local Variable Operations."

# idiv

Divide `ints`

**OPCODE:** 108 (0x6c)

**INSTRUCTION FORMAT:** `idiv`

**STACK:**
Before: . . . , *value1, value2*
After: . . . , *result*

**DESCRIPTION:** The top two words of the operand stack, *value1* and *value2*, must be `ints`. To execute the `idiv` instruction, the Java Virtual

Machine pops *value1* and *value2*, integer divides *value1* by *value2* (*value1 / value2*), and pushes the `int` *result*.

Integer division rounds the magnitude of the true mathematical quotient toward zero to the nearest integer. If the magnitude of the denominator is greater than that of the numerator, the `int` *result* is zero. Else, with one special exception, the sign of *result* is positive if the signs of the numerator and denominator are the same, negative if they are different. The exception to this rule occurs when the numerator is the smallest negative integer that can be represented by an `int` and the denominator is –1. For this division, the true mathematical result is one greater than the largest positive integer that can be represented by an `int`. As a consequence, the division overflows and the result is equal to the numerator.

If *value2* (the denominator) is zero, the Java Virtual Machine throws `ArithmeticException`.

For more information about the `idiv` instruction, see Chapter 12, "Integer Arithmetic."

## ifeq

Branch if equal to 0

**OPCODE:**   153 (0x99)

**INSTRUCTION FORMAT:**   `ifeq`, *branchbyte1, branchbyte2*

**STACK:**
Before:   . . . , *value*
After:   . . .

**DESCRIPTION:**   The top word of the operand stack, *value*, must be an `int`. To execute the `ifeq` instruction, the Java Virtual Machine pops *value* off the operand stack and compares it against zero. If *value* equals zero, the virtual machine forms a signed 16-bit offset by calculating *(branchbyte1 << 8) | branchbyte2*. The virtual machine then calculates a target (program counter) address by adding the calculated offset to the address of the `ifeq` opcode. The target address must be the address of an opcode within the same method as the `ifeq` opcode. The virtual machine jumps to the target address and continues execution there. Otherwise, if *value* does not equal zero, the virtual machine does not take the jump. It simply continues execution at the instruction immediately following the **ifeq** instruction.

For more information about the **ifeq** instruction, see Chapter 16, "Control Flow."

## ifge

Branch if greater than or equal to 0

**OPCODE:**   156 (0x9c)

**INSTRUCTION FORMAT:**   **ifge**, *branchbyte1*, *branchbyte2*

**STACK:**
Before:   . . . , *value*
After:   . . .

**DESCRIPTION:**   The top word of the operand stack, *value*, must be an **int**. To execute the **ifge** instruction, the Java Virtual Machine pops *value* off the operand stack and compares it against zero. If *value* is greater than or equal to zero, the virtual machine forms a signed 16-bit offset by calculating *(branchbyte1 << 8) | branchbyte2*. The virtual machine then calculates a target (program counter) address by adding the calculated offset to the address of the **ifge** opcode. The target address must be the address of an opcode within the same method as the **ifge** opcode. The virtual machine jumps to the target address and continues execution there. Otherwise, if *value* is not greater than or equal to zero, the virtual machine does not take the jump. It simply continues execution at the instruction immediately following the **ifge** instruction.

For more information about the **ifge** instruction, see Chapter 16, "Control Flow."

## ifgt

Branch if greater than 0

**OPCODE:**   157 (0x9d)

**INSTRUCTION FORMAT:**   **ifgt**, *branchbyte1*, *branchbyte2*

**STACK:**
Before:   . . . , *value*
After:   . . .

**DESCRIPTION:**   The top word of the operand stack, *value*, must be an **int**. To execute the **ifgt** instruction, the Java Virtual Machine pops *value* off the operand stack and compares it against zero. If *value* is greater than zero, the virtual machine forms a signed 16-bit offset by calculating *(branchbyte1 << 8) | branchbyte2*. The virtual machine then calculates a target (program counter) address by adding the calculated offset to the address of the **ifgt** opcode. The target address must be the address of an opcode within the same method as the **ifgt** opcode. The virtual machine jumps to the target address and continues execution there. Otherwise, if *value* is not greater than zero, the virtual machine does not take the jump. It simply continues execution at the instruction immediately following the **ifgt** instruction.

For more information about the **ifgt** instruction, see Chapter 16, "Control Flow."

# ifle

Branch if less than or equal to 0

**OPCODE:**   158 (0x9e)

**INSTRUCTION FORMAT:**   **ifle**, *branchbyte1*, *branchbyte2*

**STACK:**
Before:   . . . , *value*
After:   . . .

**DESCRIPTION:**   The top word of the operand stack, *value*, must be an **int**. To execute the **ifle** instruction, the Java Virtual Machine pops *value* off the operand stack and compares it against zero. If *value* is less than or equal to zero, the virtual machine forms a signed 16-bit offset by calculating *(branchbyte1 << 8) | branchbyte2*. The virtual machine then calculates a target (program counter) address by adding the calculated offset to the address of the **ifle** opcode. The target address must be the address of an opcode within the same method as the `ifle` opcode. The virtual machine jumps to the target address and continues execution there. Otherwise, if *value* is not less than or equal to zero, the virtual machine does not take the jump. It simply continues execution at the instruction immediately following the `ifle` instruction.

For more information about the `ifle` instruction, see Chapter 16, "Control Flow."

## `iflt`

Branch if less than 0

**OPCODE:** 155 (0x9b)

**INSTRUCTION FORMAT:** `iflt`, *branchbyte1*, *branchbyte2*

**STACK:**
Before:    . . . , *value*
After:    . . .

**DESCRIPTION:** The top word of the operand stack, *value*, must be an `int`. To execute the `iflt` instruction, the Java Virtual Machine pops *value* off the operand stack and compares it against zero. If *value* is less than zero, the virtual machine forms a signed 16-bit offset by calculating *(branchbyte1 << 8) | branchbyte2*. The virtual machine then calculates a target (program counter) address by adding the calculated offset to the address of the `iflt` opcode. The target address must be the address of an opcode within the same method as the `iflt` opcode. The virtual machine jumps to the target address and continues execution there. Otherwise, if *value* is not less than zero, the virtual machine does not take the jump. It simply continues execution at the instruction immediately following the `iflt` instruction.

For more information about the `iflt` instruction, see Chapter 16, "Control Flow."

## `ifne`

Branch if not equal to 0

**OPCODE:**   154 (0x9a)

**INSTRUCTION FORMAT:**   `ifne`, *branchbyte1*, *branchbyte2*

**STACK:**
Before:   . . . , *value*
After:   . . .

**DESCRIPTION:**   The top word of the operand stack, *value*, must be an
`int`. To execute the `ifne` instruction, the Java Virtual Machine pops *value*
off the operand stack and compares it against zero. If *value* does not equal
zero, the virtual machine forms a signed 16-bit offset by calculating
*(branchbyte1 << 8) | branchbyte2*. The virtual machine then calculates a
target (program counter) address by adding the calculated offset to the
address of the `ifne` opcode. The target address must be the address of an
opcode within the same method as the `ifne` opcode. The virtual machine
jumps to the target address and continues execution there. Otherwise, if
*value* does equal zero, the virtual machine does not take the jump. It simply continues execution at the instruction immediately following the `ifne`
instruction.

For more information about the `ifne` instruction, see Chapter 16, "Control Flow."

# ifnonnull

Branch if not null

**OPCODE:**   199 (0xc7)

**INSTRUCTION FORMAT:**   `ifnonnull`, *branchbyte1*, *branchbyte2*

**STACK:**
Before:   . . . , *value*
After:   . . .

**DESCRIPTION:**   The top word of the operand stack, *value*, must be a
`reference`. To execute the `ifnonnull` instruction, the Java Virtual Machine pops *value* off the operand stack and compares it against `null`. If

*value* is not **null**, the virtual machine forms a signed 16-bit offset by calculating *(branchbyte1 << 8) | branchbyte2*. The virtual machine then calculates a target (program counter) address by adding the calculated offset to the address of the **ifnonnull** opcode. The target address must be the address of an opcode within the same method as the **ifnonnull** opcode. The virtual machine jumps to the target address and continues execution there. Otherwise, if *value* is **null**, the virtual machine does not take the jump. It simply continues execution at the instruction immediately following the **ifnonnull** instruction.

For more information about the **ifnonnull** instruction, see Chapter 16, "Control Flow."

## ifnull

Branch if null

**OPCODE:**  198 (0xc6)

**INSTRUCTION FORMAT:**  **ifnull**, *branchbyte1*, *branchbyte2*

**STACK:**
Before:  . . . , *value*
After:  . . .

**DESCRIPTION:**  The top word of the operand stack, *value*, must be a **reference**. To execute the **ifnull** instruction, the Java Virtual Machine pops *value* off the operand stack and compares it against **null**. If *value* is **null**, the virtual machine forms a signed 16-bit offset by calculating *(branchbyte1 << 8) | branchbyte2*. The virtual machine then calculates a target (program counter) address by adding the calculated offset to the address of the **ifnull** opcode. The target address must be the address of an opcode within the same method as the **ifnull** opcode. The virtual machine jumps to the target address and continues execution there. Otherwise, if *value* is not **null**, the virtual machine does not take the jump. It simply continues execution at the instruction immediately following the **ifnull** instruction.

For more information about the **ifnull** instruction, see Chapter 16, "Control Flow."

# if_acmpeq

Branch if object references are equal

**OPCODE:**   165 (0xa5)

**INSTRUCTION FORMAT:**   if_acmpeq, *branchbyte1, branchbyte2*

**STACK:**
Before:   . . . , *value1, value2*
After:   . . .

**DESCRIPTION:**   The top two words of the operand stack, *value1* and *value2*, must be **reference**s. To execute the if_acmpeq instruction, the Java Virtual Machine pops *value1* and *value2* off the operand stack and compares one against the other. If *value1* equals *value2* (in other words, if they both point to exactly the same object or are both **null**), the virtual machine forms a signed 16-bit offset by calculating *(branchbyte1 << 8) | branchbyte2*. The virtual machine then calculates a target (program counter) address by adding the calculated offset to the address of the if_acmpeq opcode. The target address must be the address of an opcode within the same method as the if_acmpeq opcode. The virtual machine jumps to the target address and continues execution there. Otherwise, if *value1* does not equal *value2*, the virtual machine does not take the jump. It simply continues execution at the instruction immediately following the if_acmpeq instruction.

For more information about the if_acmpeq instruction, see Chapter 16, "Control Flow."

# if_acmpne

Branch if object references not equal

**OPCODE:**   166 (0xa6)

**INSTRUCTION FORMAT:**   if_acmpne, *branchbyte1, branchbyte2*

**STACK:**
Before:   . . . , *value1, value2*
After:   . . .

**DESCRIPTION:**   The top two words of the operand stack, *value1* and *value2*, must be **reference**s. To execute the **if_acmpne** instruction, the Java Virtual Machine pops *value1* and *value2* off the operand stack and compares one against the other. If *value1* does not equal *value2* (in other words, if they don't both point to exactly the same object and they aren't both **null**), the virtual machine forms a signed 16-bit offset by calculating *(branchbyte1 << 8) | branchbyte2*. The virtual machine then calculates a target (program counter) address by adding the calculated offset to the address of the **if_acmpne** opcode. The target address must be the address of an opcode within the same method as the **if_acmpne** opcode. The virtual machine jumps to the target address and continues execution there. Otherwise, if *value1* equals *value2*, the virtual machine does not take the jump. It simply continues execution at the instruction immediately following the **if_acmpne** instruction.

For more information about the **if_acmpne** instruction, see Chapter 16, "Control Flow."

# if_icmpeq

Branch if **int**s equal

**OPCODE:**   159 (0x9f)

**INSTRUCTION FORMAT:**   **if_icmpeq**, *branchbyte1, branchbyte2*

**STACK:**
Before:   . . . , *value1, value2*
After:   . . .

**DESCRIPTION:**   The top two words of the operand stack, *value1* and *value2*, must be **int**s. To execute the **if_icmpeq** instruction, the Java Virtual Machine pops *value1* and *value2* off the operand stack and compares one against the other. If *value1* equals *value2*, the virtual machine forms a signed 16-bit offset by calculating *(branchbyte1 << 8) | branchbyte2*. The virtual machine then calculates a target (program counter) address by adding the calculated offset to the address of the **if_icmpeq** opcode. The target address must be the address of an opcode within the same method as the **if_icmpeq** opcode. The virtual machine jumps to the target address and continues execution there. Otherwise, if *value1* does not equal *value2*, the virtual machine does not take the jump. It simply continues execution at the instruction immediately following the `if_icmpeq` instruction.

For more information about the `if_icmpeq` instruction, see Chapter 16, "Control Flow."

# `if_icmpge`

Branch if **int** greater than or equal to other **int**

**OPCODE:**    162 (0xa2)

**INSTRUCTION FORMAT:**    `if_icmpge`, *branchbyte1, branchbyte2*

**STACK:**
Before:    . . . , *value1, value2*
After:    . . .

**DESCRIPTION:**    The top two words of the operand stack, *value1* and *value2*, must be **int**s. To execute the `if_icmpge` instruction, the Java Virtual Machine pops *value1* and *value2* off the operand stack and compares one against the other. If *value1* is greater than or equal to *value2*, the virtual machine forms a signed 16-bit offset by calculating *(branchbyte1 << 8) | branchbyte2*. The virtual machine then calculates a target (program counter) address by adding the calculated offset to the address of the `if_icmpge` opcode. The target address must be the address of an opcode within the same method as the `if_icmpge` opcode. The virtual machine jumps to the target address and continues execution there. Otherwise, if *value1* is not greater than or equal to *value2*, the virtual machine does not take the jump. It simply continues execution at the instruction immediately following the `if_icmpge` instruction.

For more information about the `if_icmpge` instruction, see Chapter 16, "Control Flow."

# `if_icmpgt`

Branch if **int** greater than other **int**

**OPCODE:** 163 (0xa3)

**INSTRUCTION FORMAT:** `if_icmpgt`, *branchbyte1*, *branchbyte2*

**STACK:**
Before: ..., *value1, value2*
After: ...

**DESCRIPTION:** The top two words of the operand stack, *value1* and *value2*, must be `int`s. To execute the `if_icmpgt` instruction, the Java Virtual Machine pops *value1* and *value2* off the operand stack and compares one against the other. If *value1* is greater than *value2*, the virtual machine forms a signed 16-bit offset by calculating *(branchbyte1 << 8) | branchbyte2*. The virtual machine then calculates a target (program counter) address by adding the calculated offset to the address of the `if_icmpgt` opcode. The target address must be the address of an opcode within the same method as the `if_icmpgt` opcode. The virtual machine jumps to the target address and continues execution there. Otherwise, if *value1* is not greater than *value2*, the virtual machine does not take the jump. It simply continues execution at the instruction immediately following the `if_icmpgt` instruction.

For more information about the `if_icmpgt` instruction, see Chapter 16, "Control Flow."

## if_icmple

Branch if `int` less than or equal to other `int`

**OPCODE:** 164 (0xa4)

**INSTRUCTION FORMAT:** `if_icmple`, *branchbyte1*, *branchbyte2*

**STACK:**
Before: ..., *value1, value2*
After: ...

**DESCRIPTION:** The top two words of the operand stack, *value1* and *value2*, must be `int`s. To execute the `if_icmple` instruction, the Java Virtual Machine pops *value1* and *value2* off the operand stack and compares one against the other. If *value1* is less than or equal to *value2*, the virtual machine forms a signed 16-bit offset by calculating *(branchbyte1 << 8) | branchbyte2*. The virtual machine then calculates a target (program counter) address by adding the calculated offset to the address of the **if_icmple** opcode. The target address must be the address of an opcode within the same method as the **if_icmple** opcode. The virtual machine jumps to the target address and continues execution there. Otherwise, if *value1* is not less than or equal to *value2*, the virtual machine does not take the jump. It simply continues execution at the instruction immediately following the **if_icmple** instruction.

For more information about the **if_icmple** instruction, see Chapter 16, "Control Flow."

## if_icmplt

Branch if **int** less than other **int**

**OPCODE:**   161 (0xa1)

**INSTRUCTION FORMAT:**   **if_icmplt**, *branchbyte1, branchbyte2*

**STACK:**
Before:   . . . , *value1, value2*
After:   . . .

**DESCRIPTION:**   The top two words of the operand stack, *value1* and *value2*, must be **int**s. To execute the **if_icmplt** instruction, the Java Virtual Machine pops *value1* and *value2* off the operand stack and compares one against the other. If *value1* is less than *value2*, the virtual machine forms a signed 16-bit offset by calculating *(branchbyte1 << 8) | branchbyte2*. The virtual machine then calculates a target (program counter) address by adding the calculated offset to the address of the **if_icmplt** opcode. The target address must be the address of an opcode within the same method as the **if_icmplt** opcode. The virtual machine jumps to the target address and continues execution there. Otherwise, if *value1* is not less than *value2*, the virtual machine does not take the jump. It simply continues execution at the instruction immediately following the **if_icmplt** instruction.

For more information about the `if_icmplt` instruction, see Chapter 16, "Control Flow."

## if_icmpne

Branch if **int**s not equal

**OPCODE:**  160 (0xa0)

**INSTRUCTION FORMAT:**  `if_icmpne`, *branchbyte1*, *branchbyte2*

**STACK:**
Before:  . . . , *value1, value2*
After:  . . .

**DESCRIPTION:**  The top two words of the operand stack, *value1* and *value2*, must be **int**s. To execute the `if_icmpne` instruction, the Java Virtual Machine pops *value1* and *value2* off the operand stack and compares one against the other. If *value1* does not equal *value2*, the virtual machine forms a signed 16-bit offset by calculating *(branchbyte1 << 8) | branchbyte2*. The virtual machine then calculates a target (program counter) address by adding the calculated offset to the address of the `if_icmpne` opcode. The target address must be the address of an opcode within the same method as the `if_icmpne` opcode. The virtual machine jumps to the target address and continues execution there. Otherwise, if *value1* equals *value2*, the virtual machine does not take the jump. It simply continues execution at the instruction immediately following the `if_icmpne` instruction.

For more information about the `if_icmpne` instruction, see Chapter 16, "Control Flow."

## iinc

Increment **int** local variable by constant

**OPCODE:**  132 (0x84)

**INSTRUCTION FORMAT:**  `iinc`, *index*, *const*

**STACK:**   No change

**DESCRIPTION:**   The *index* operand must specify a valid 8-bit unsigned index into the local variables of the current frame. To execute the `iinc` instruction, the Java Virtual Machine adds the 8-bit signed increment *const* to the local variable word specified by *index*.

Note that the `wide` instruction can precede the `iinc` instruction, to enable a local variable specified by a 16-bit unsigned offset to be incremented by a signed 16-bit constant.

For more information about the `iinc` instruction, see Chapter 12, "Integer Arithmetic."


# `iload`

Load `int` from local variable

**OPCODE:**   21 (0x15)

**INSTRUCTION FORMAT:**   `iload`, *index*

**STACK:**
Before:   . . .
After:   . . . , *value*

**DESCRIPTION:**   The *index* operand, which serves as an 8-bit unsigned index into the local variables of the current frame, must specify a local variable word that contains an `int`. To execute the `iload` instruction, the Java Virtual Machine pushes onto the operand stack the `int` *value* contained in the local variable word specified by *index*.

Note that the `wide` instruction can precede the `iload` instruction, to allow a local variable to be accessed with a 16-bit unsigned offset.

For more information about the `iload` instruction, see Chapter 10, "Stack and Local Variable Operations."


# `iload_0`

Load `int` from local variable 0

**OPCODE:** 26 (0x1a)

**INSTRUCTION FORMAT:** `iload_0`

**STACK:**
Before: ...
After: ..., *value*

**DESCRIPTION:** The local variable word at index zero must contain an `int`. To execute the `iload_0` instruction, the Java Virtual Machine pushes onto the operand stack the `int` *value* contained in the local variable word zero.

For more information about the `iload_0` instruction, see Chapter 10, "Stack and Local Variable Operations."

# iload_1

Load `int` from local variable 1

**OPCODE:** 27 (0x1b)

**INSTRUCTION FORMAT:** `iload_1`

**STACK:**
Before: ...
After: ..., *value*

**DESCRIPTION:** The local variable word at index one must contain an `int`. To execute the `iload_1` instruction, the Java Virtual Machine pushes onto the operand stack the `int` contained in the local variable word one.

For more information about the `iload_1` instruction, see Chapter 10, "Stack and Local Variable Operations."

# iload_2

Load `int` from local variable 2

**OPCODE:**   28 (0x1c)

**INSTRUCTION FORMAT:**   `iload_2`

**STACK:**
Before:   . . .
After:   . . . , *value*

**DESCRIPTION:**   The local variable word at index two must contain an `int`. To execute the `iload_2` instruction, the Java Virtual Machine pushes onto the operand stack the `int` *value* contained in the local variable word two.

For more information about the `iload_2` instruction, see Chapter 10, "Stack and Local Variable Operations."

## iload_3

Load `int` from local variable 3

**OPCODE:**   29 (0x1d)

**INSTRUCTION FORMAT:**   `iload_3`

**STACK:**
Before:   . . .
After:   . . . , *value*

**DESCRIPTION:**   The local variable word at index three must contain an `int`. To execute the `iload_3` instruction, the Java Virtual Machine pushes onto the operand stack the `int` *value* contained in the local variable word three.

For more information about the `iload_3` instruction, see Chapter 10, "Stack and Local Variable Operations."

## imul

Multiply `int`s

**OPCODE:** 104 (0x68)

**INSTRUCTION FORMAT:** `imul`

**STACK:**
Before: . . . , *value1, value2*
After: . . . , *result*

**DESCRIPTION:** The top two words of the operand stack, *value1* and *value2*, must be `int`s. To execute the `imul` instruction, the Java Virtual Machine pops *value1* and *value2*, multiplies them, and pushes the `int` *result*. If overflow occurs, *result* is the 32 lowest order bits of the true mathematical result represented in a sufficiently wide two's-complement format, and the sign of *result* may be different from that of the true mathematical result.

For more information about the `imul` instruction, see Chapter 12, "Integer Arithmetic."

# `ineg`

Negate `int`

**OPCODE:** 116 (0x74)

**INSTRUCTION FORMAT:** `ineg`

**STACK:**
Before: . . . , *value*
After: . . . , *result*

**DESCRIPTION:** The top word of the operand stack, *value*, must be an `int`. To execute the `ineg` instruction, the Java Virtual Machine pops *value*, negates it, and pushes the `int` *result*.

The *result* produced by an `ineg` instruction is the same number that would be produced by subtracting *value* from zero with the `isub` instruction. As a consequence, when *value* is the smallest negative integer that can be represented by an `int`, the negation overflows. For this negation, the true mathematical result is one greater than the largest positive integer that can be represented by an **int**, and the actual *result* is equal to *value* with no change in sign.

For more information about the **ineg** instruction, see Chapter 12, "Integer Arithmetic."

## instanceof

Determine whether an object is of a given type

**OPCODE:** 193 (0xc1)

**INSTRUCTION FORMAT:** **instanceof**, *indexbyte1*, *indexbyte2*

**STACK:**
Before:   . . . , *objectref*
After:   . . . , *result*

**DESCRIPTION:** The top word of the stack, *objectref*, must be a **reference**. To execute the **instanceof** instruction, the Java Virtual Machine first forms an unsigned 16-bit index into the constant pool by calculating *(indexbyte1 << 8) | indexbyte2*. The virtual machine then looks up the constant pool entry specified by the calculated index. The constant pool entry at that index must be a **CONSTANT_Class_info** entry. If it hasn't already, the virtual machine resolves the entry. The entry may be a class, interface, or array type. If *objectref* is not **null** and the object pointed to by *objectref* is an "instance of" the resolved type, the virtual machine pushes an **int** one *result* onto the operand stack. Otherwise, the virtual machine pushes an **int** zero *result* onto the operand stack.

To determine whether the object pointed to by *objectref* is an "instance of" the resolved type, the virtual machine first determines whether the object is a class instance or array. (It can't be an interface instance because interfaces can't be instantiated.) If it is a class instance, and the resolved type is a class, not an interface, the object is "an instance" of the resolved class if the object's class is the resolved class or a subclass of the resolved class. Else, if it is a class instance, and the resolved type is an interface, not a class, the object is "an instance" of the resolved interface if the object's class implements the resolved interface. Otherwise, the object is an array. If the resolved type is a class, it must be **java.lang.Object**. Else, if the resolved type is an array of primitive types, the object must be an array of the same primitive type. Otherwise, the resolved type must be an array with a component type of some reference type, and the object must be an array with a component type that is an "instance of" the component type of the resolved array type. (Note that the dimension of an array doesn't enter into the **instanceof** check, only the component type of the array.)

As a result of executing this instruction, the virtual machine may throw any of the linking errors listed in Chapter 8, "The Linking Model," as possible during resolution of a **CONSTANT_Class_info** entry.

For more information about the **instanceof** instruction, see Chapter 15, "Objects and Arrays."

# invokeinterface

Invoke interface method

**OPCODE:**    185 (0xb9)

**INSTRUCTION FORMAT:**    **invokeinterface**, *indexbyte1*, *indexbyte2*, *nargs*, *0*

**STACK:**
Before:    . . . , *objectref, [arg1, [arg2 . . . ]]*
After:    . . .

**DESCRIPTION:**    To execute the **invokeinterface** instruction, the Java Virtual Machine first forms an unsigned 16-bit index into the constant pool by calculating *(indexbyte1 << 8) | indexbyte2*. The virtual machine then looks up the constant pool entry specified by the calculated index. The constant pool entry at that index must be a **CONSTANT_InterfaceMethodref_info** entry. If it hasn't already, the virtual machine resolves the entry. The resolved method's descriptor must exactly match the descriptor of one of the methods declared in the resolved interface. The method must not be an instance initialization method, "**<init>**", or a class initialization method, "**<clinit>**."

The *nargs* operand is an unsigned byte that indicates the number of words of parameters required by the method being invoked (including the hidden **this** reference). The operand stack must contain *nargs – 1* words of parameters and the *objectref* word. The parameter words must match the order and type of parameters required by the resolved method. The *objectref* word, the reference to the object upon which to invoke the instance method, must be a **reference**. If the resolution is successful, the virtual machine pops *nargs – 1* parameter words and *objectref*.

To invoke the method, the virtual machine retrieves the direct reference to the instance method to invoke from a method table. It locates the method table for the class of object pointed to by *objectref* and searches through it for a method with a name and descriptor that matches exactly the name and descriptor of the resolved method. (If the object's class is an array type, the virtual machine uses the method table for class **java.lang.Object**. An array type, of course, can implement an interface only if **Object** itself implements the interface.)

If the method is synchronized, the Java Virtual Machine, on behalf of the current thread, acquires the monitor associated with *objectref*.

If the method to invoke is not native, the virtual machine creates a new stack frame for the method and pushes the new stack frame onto the current thread's Java stack. The virtual machine then places the *objectref* word and *nargs – 1* parameter words that it popped from the operand stack of the calling method's frame into the local variables of the new stack frame. It places *objectref* into local variable position zero, *arg1* into local variable position one, and so on. (*objectref* is the hidden **this** reference passed to all instance methods.) The virtual machine makes the new stack frame current, sets the program counter to the address of the first instruction in the new method, and continues execution there.

If the method to invoke is native, the virtual machine invokes the native method in an implementation-dependent manner.

As a result of executing this instruction, the virtual machine may throw any of the linking errors listed in Chapter 8, "The Linking Model," as possible during resolution of a **CONSTANT_InterfaceMethodref_info** entry. If no method exists in the object's class with the required name and descriptor, the virtual machine throws **IncompatibleClassChangeError**. Else, if the method exists but is static, the virtual machine throws **IncompatibleClassChangeError**. Else, if the method exists but is not public, the virtual machine throws **IllegalAccessError**. Else, if the method is abstract, the virtual machine throws **AbstractMethodError**. Else, if the method is native, and the native implementation of the method can't be loaded or linked, the virtual machine throws **UnsatisfiedLinkError**. Otherwise, if *objectref* is **null**, the virtual machine throws **NullPointerException**.

For more information about the **invokeinterface** instruction, see Chapter 19, "Method Invocation and Return."

# invokespecial

Invoke instance method with special handling for private, superclass, and instance initialization methods

**OPCODE:** 183 (0xb7)

**INSTRUCTION FORMAT:** **invokespecial**, *indexbyte1*, *indexbyte2*

**STACK:**
Before: ... , *objectref, [arg1, [arg2 ... ]]*
After: ...

**DESCRIPTION:** To execute the **invokespecial** instruction, the Java Virtual Machine first forms an unsigned 16-bit index into the constant pool by calculating *(indexbyte1 << 8) | indexbyte2*. The virtual machine then looks up the constant pool entry specified by the calculated index. The constant pool entry at that index must be a **CONSTANT_Methodref_info** entry. If it hasn't already, the virtual machine resolves the entry, which yields a direct reference to the method's data, including the number of words of parameters to the method, *nargs*. The resolved method's descriptor must exactly match the descriptor of one of the methods declared in the resolved class. The method must not be a class initialization method, "**<clinit>**."

The **invokespecial** instruction is used to invoke three special kinds of instance methods: superclass methods, private methods, and instance initialization methods. **invokespecial** contrasts with **invokevirtual** in the way it invokes an instance method. Whereas **invokevirtual** always selects the method to invoke at runtime based on the class of the object (dynamic binding), **invokespecial** normally (with one exception) selects the method to invoke at compile-time based on the type of the reference (static binding).

The one exception to **invokespecial**'s pure static binding behavior occurs if

- the resolved method is not private and is not an instance initialization method,

- the resolved method's class is a superclass of the current method's class, and

- the **ACC_SUPER** flag is set in the current method's class.

In this situation, the Java Virtual Machine dynamically selects at run-time the method to invoke by finding the method in the closest superclass that has a descriptor that exactly matches the resolved method's descriptor, irrespective of the class of the resolved method. In the majority of cases, the class of the selected method will most likely be the class of the resolved method anyway, but it possibly could be some other class.

For example, imagine you create an inheritance hierarchy of three classes: `Animal`, `Dog`, and `CockerSpaniel`. Assume class `Dog` extends class `Animal`, class `CockerSpaniel` extends class `Dog`, and that a method defined in `CockerSpaniel` uses `invokespecial` to invoke a nonprivate superclass method named `walk()`. Assume also that when you compiled `CockerSpaniel`, the compiler set the `ACC_SUPER` flag. In addition, assume that when you compiled `CockerSpaniel`, class `Animal` defined a `walk()` method, but `Dog` didn't. In that case, the symbolic reference from `CockerSpaniel` to the `walk()` method would give `Animal` as its class. When the `invokespecial` instruction in `CockerSpaniel`'s method is executed, the virtual machine would dynamically select and invoke `Animal`'s `walk()` method.

Now imagine that, later, you added a `walk()` method to `Dog` and recompiled `Dog`, but you didn't recompile `CockerSpaniel`. `CockerSpaniel`'s symbolic reference to the superclass `walk()` method still claims `Animal` as its class, even though an implementation of `walk()` now appears in `Dog`'s class file. Nevertheless, when the `invokespecial` instruction in `CockerSpaniel`'s method is executed, the virtual machine would dynamically select and invoke `Dog`'s implementation of the `walk()` method.

This special (not static binding) treatment of superclass invocations was the motivation for adding the `ACC_SUPER` flag to the class `access_flags` item of class files, and for changing the name of this opcode from its original name, `invokenonvirtual`, to its current name, `invokespecial`. If the `CockerSpaniel` class of the preceding example had been compiled by an old compiler that didn't set the `ACC_SUPER` flag, the virtual machine would invoke `Animal`'s implementation of `walk()` regardless of whether `Dog` declared a `walk()`. As mentioned in Chapter 6, "The Java Class File," all new Java compilers should set the `ACC_SUPER` flag in every class file they generate.

If the resolved method is an instance initialization method, "`<init>`," the method must be invoked only once on each uninitialized (except to default initial values) object. In addition, an instance initialization method must be invoked on each uninitialized object before the first backward branch. In other words, the bytecodes of a method need not call an `<init>` method with `invokespecial` right after a `new` instruction. Other instructions could intervene between the **new** and the **invokespecial** for the **<init>**, but none of those instructions can branch backward (such as a **goto** to the beginning of the method).

The operand stack must contain *nargs – 1* words of parameters and the *objectref* word. The parameter words must match the order and type of parameters required by the resolved method. The *objectref* word, the reference to the object upon which to invoke the instance method, must be a **reference**. If the resolution is successful, the virtual machine pops *nargs – 1* parameter words and *objectref*.

If the method is synchronized, the Java Virtual Machine, on behalf of the current thread, acquires the monitor associated with *objectref*.

If the method to invoke is not native, the virtual machine creates a new stack frame for the method and pushes the new stack frame onto the current thread's Java stack. The virtual machine then places the *objectref* word and *nargs – 1* parameter words that it popped from the operand stack of the calling method's frame into the local variables of the new stack frame. It places *objectref* into local variable position zero, *arg1* into local variable position one, and so on. (*objectref* is the hidden **this** reference passed to all instance methods.) The virtual machine makes the new stack frame current, sets the program counter to the address of the first instruction in the new method, and continues execution there.

If the method to invoke is native, the virtual machine invokes the native method in an implementation-dependent manner.

As a result of executing this instruction, the virtual machine may throw any of the linking errors listed in Chapter 8, "The Linking Model," as possible during resolution of a **CONSTANT_Methodref_info** entry. As part of the process of resolving the **CONSTANT_Methodref_info** entry, the virtual machine checks whether the method's access permission enables the current class to access the method. If the method is protected, the virtual machine makes certain the method is a member either of the current class or a superclass of the current class, and that the class of the object pointed to by *objectref* is either the current class or a subclass of the current class. If not (or if any other access permission problem occurs), the virtual machine throws **IllegalAccessError**. Else, if the method exists and is accessible from the current class, but the method is static, the virtual machine throws **IncompatibleClassChangeError**. Else, if the method is abstract, the virtual machine throws **AbstractMethodError**. Else, if the method is native and the native implementation of the method can't be loaded or linked, the virtual machine throws **UnsatisfiedLinkError**. Otherwise, if *objectref* is **null**, the virtual machine throws **NullPointerException**.

For more information about the `invokespecial` instruction, see Chapter 19, "Method Invocation and Return."

# `invokestatic`

Invoke a class (static) method

**OPCODE:**   184 (0xb8)

**INSTRUCTION FORMAT:**   `invokestatic`, *indexbyte1*, *indexbyte2*

**STACK:**
Before:   . . . , *[arg1, [arg2 . . . ]]*
After:   . . .

**DESCRIPTION:**   To execute the `invokestatic` instruction, the Java Virtual Machine first forms an unsigned 16-bit index into the constant pool by calculating *(indexbyte1 << 8) | indexbyte2*. The virtual machine then looks up the constant pool entry specified by the calculated index. The constant pool entry at that index must be a `CONSTANT_Methodref_info` entry. If it hasn't already, the virtual machine resolves the entry, which yields a direct reference to the method's data, including the number of words of parameters to the method, *nargs*. The resolved method's descriptor must exactly match the descriptor of one of the methods declared in the resolved class. The method must not be an instance initialization method, "`<init>`", or a class initialization method, "`<clinit>`."

The operand stack must contain *nargs* words of parameters. The parameter words must match the order and type of parameters required by the resolved method. If the resolution is successful, the virtual machine pops the *nargs* parameter words.

If the method is synchronized, the Java Virtual Machine, on behalf of the current thread, acquires the monitor associated with the `Class` instance that represents the resolved method's class.

If the method to invoke is not native, the virtual machine creates a new stack frame for the method and pushes the new stack frame onto the current thread's Java stack. The virtual machine then places the *nargs* parameter words that it popped from the operand stack of the calling method's frame into the local variables of the new stack frame. It places *arg1* into local variable position zero, *arg2* into local variable position one, and so on. The virtual machine makes the new stack frame current, sets the program counter to the address of the first instruction in the new method, and continues execution there.

If the method to invoke is native, the virtual machine invokes the native method in an implementation-dependent manner.

As a result of executing this instruction, the virtual machine may throw any of the linking errors listed in Chapter 8, "The Linking Model," as possible during resolution of a **CONSTANT_Methodref_info** entry. As part of the process of resolving the **CONSTANT_Methodref_info** entry, the virtual machine checks whether the method's access permission enables the current class to access the method. If the method is protected, the virtual machine makes certain the method is a member either of the current class or a superclass of the current class. If not (or if any other access permission problem occurs), the virtual machine throws **IllegalAccessError**. Else, if the method exists and is accessible from the current class, but the method is not static, the virtual machine throws **IncompatibleClassChangeError**. Else, if the method is abstract, the virtual machine throws **AbstractMethodError**. Otherwise, if the method is native, and the native implementation of the method can't be loaded or linked, the virtual machine throws **UnsatisfiedLinkError**.

For more information about the **invokestatic** instruction, see Chapter 19, "Method Invocation and Return."

## invokevirtual

Invoke instance method, dispatch based on an object's class at runtime

**OPCODE:**   182 (0xb6)

**INSTRUCTION FORMAT:**   **invokevirtual**, *indexbyte1*, *indexbyte2*

**STACK:**
Before:   ... , *objectref, [arg1, [arg2 ... ]]*
After:   ...

**DESCRIPTION:**   To execute the **invokevirtual** instruction, the Java Virtual Machine first forms an unsigned 16-bit index into the constant pool by calculating *(indexbyte1 << 8) | indexbyte2*. The virtual machine then looks up the constant pool entry specified by the calculated index. The constant pool entry at that index must be a `CONSTANT_Methodref_info` entry. If it hasn't already, the virtual machine resolves the entry, which yields the method's method table index, *index*, and the number of words of parameters to the method, *nargs*. The resolved method's descriptor must exactly match the descriptor of one of the methods declared in the resolved class. The method must not be an instance initialization method, "`<init>`", or a class initialization method, "`<clinit>`."

The operand stack must contain *nargs – 1* words of parameters and the *objectref* word. The parameter words must match the order and type of parameters required by the resolved method. The *objectref* word, the reference to the object upon which to invoke the instance method, must be a `reference`. If the resolution is successful, the virtual machine pops *nargs – 1* parameter words and *objectref*.

To invoke the method, the virtual machine retrieves the direct reference to the instance method to invoke from a method table. It locates the method table for the class of object pointed to by *objectref* and looks up the direct reference that occupies method table position *index*. (If the object's class is an array type, the virtual machine uses the method table for class `java.lang.Object`.)

If the method is synchronized, the Java Virtual Machine, on behalf of the current thread, acquires the monitor associated with *objectref*.

If the method to invoke is not native, the virtual machine creates a new stack frame for the method and pushes the new stack frame onto the current thread's Java stack. The virtual machine then places the *objectref* word and *nargs – 1* parameter words that it popped from the operand stack of the calling method's frame into the local variables of the new stack frame. It places *objectref* into local variable position zero, *arg1* into local variable position one, and so on. (*objectref* is the hidden `this` reference passed to all instance methods.) The virtual machine makes the new stack frame current, sets the program counter to the address of the first instruction in the new method, and continues execution there.

If the method to invoke is native, the virtual machine invokes the native method in an implementation-dependent manner.

As a result of executing this instruction, the virtual machine may throw any of the linking errors listed in Chapter 8, "The Linking Model," as possible during resolution of a `CONSTANT_Methodref_info` entry. As part of the process of resolving the `CONSTANT_Methodref_info` entry, the virtual machine checks whether the method's access permission enables the current class to access the method. If the method is protected, the virtual machine makes certain the method is a member either of the current class or a superclass of the current class, and that the class of the object pointed to by *objectref* is either the current class or a subclass of the current class. If not (or if any other access permission problem occurs), the virtual machine throws **IllegalAccessError**. Else, if the method exists and is accessible from the current class, but the method is static, the virtual machine throws **IncompatibleClassChangeError**. Else, if the method is abstract, the virtual machine throws **AbstractMethodError**. Else, if the method is native, and the native implementation of the method can't be loaded or linked, the virtual machine throws **UnsatisfiedLinkError**. Otherwise, if *objectref* is **null**, the virtual machine throws **NullPointerException**.

For more information about the **invokevirtual** instruction, see Chapter 19, "Method Invocation and Return."

## ior

Perform boolean OR on **int**s

**OPCODE:**   128 (0x80)

**INSTRUCTION FORMAT:**   ior

**STACK:**
Before:   ... , *value1, value2*
After:   ... , *result*

**DESCRIPTION:**   The top two words of the operand stack, *value1* and *value2*, must be **int**s. To execute the **ior** instruction, the Java Virtual Machine pops *value1* and *value2*, bitwise ORs them, and pushes the **int** *result*.

For more information about the **ior** instruction, see Chapter 13, "Logic."

## irem

Calculate remainder of division of **int**s

**OPCODE:**   112 (0x70)

**INSTRUCTION FORMAT:** `irem`

**STACK:**
Before: ..., *value1, value2*
After: ..., *result*

**DESCRIPTION:** The top two words of the operand stack, *value1* and *value2*, must be `int`s. To execute the `irem` instruction, the Java Virtual Machine pops *value1* and *value2*, calculates the integer remainder, and pushes the `int` *result*. The integer remainder equals *value1 – (value1 / value2) * value2*.

The `irem` instruction implements Java's remainder operator: `%`. The `irem` behaves such that the following Java expression is always `true`, where `n` and `d` are any two `int`s:

```
(n/d)*d + (n%d) == n
```

This behavior means that the *result* of an `irem` instruction always takes the same sign as the numerator, which is popped off the operand stack as *value1*.

If *value2* (the denominator) is zero, the Java Virtual Machine throws `ArithmeticException`.

For more information about the `irem` instruction, see Chapter 12, "Integer Arithmetic."

# `ireturn`

Return `int` from method

**OPCODE:** 172 (0xac)

**INSTRUCTION FORMAT:** `ireturn`

**STACK:**
Before: ..., *value*
After: *[empty]*

**DESCRIPTION:** The return type of the returning method must be `byte`, `short`, `int`, or `char`. The top word of the operand stack, *value*, must be an **int**. To execute the **ireturn** instruction, the Java Virtual Machine pops **int** *value* from the operand stack of the current frame and pushes it onto the operand stack of the invoking method's frame. The virtual machine discards any other words that may still be on the returning method's frame. If the returning method is synchronized, the monitor that was acquired when the method was invoked is released. The invoking method's frame is made current, and the virtual machine continues execution in the invoking method.

For more information about the **ireturn** instruction, see Chapter 19, "Method Invocation and Return." For more information about monitors, see Chapter 20, "Thread Synchronization."

## ishl

Perform left shift on **int**

**OPCODE:** 120 (0x78)

**INSTRUCTION FORMAT:** ishl

**STACK:**
Before:   . . . , *value1, value2*
After:   . . . , *result*

**DESCRIPTION:** The top two words of the operand stack, *value1* and *value2*, must be **int**s. To execute the **ishl** instruction, the Java Virtual Machine pops *value1* and *value2*, shifts *value1* left by the number of bits specified in the five lowest order bits of *value2* (from 0 to 31 bit positions), and pushes the **int** *result*.

For more information about the **ishl** instruction, see Chapter 13, "Logic."

## ishr

Perform arithmetic right shift on **int**

**OPCODE:**   122 (0x7a)

**INSTRUCTION FORMAT:**   `ishr`

**STACK:**
Before:   . . . , *value1, value2*
After:   . . . , *result*

**DESCRIPTION:**   The top two words of the operand stack, *value1* and *value2*, must be `int`s. To execute the `ishr` instruction, the Java Virtual Machine pops *value1* and *value2*, shifts *value1* right with sign extension by the number of bits specified in the five lowest order bits of *value2* (from 0 to 31 bit positions), and pushes the `int` *result*.

For more information about the `ishr` instruction, see Chapter 13, "Logic."


# istore

Store `int` into local variable

**OPCODE:**   54 (0x36)

**INSTRUCTION FORMAT:**   `istore`, *index*

**STACK:**
Before:   . . . , *value*
After:   . . .

**DESCRIPTION:**   The *index* operand must specify a valid 8-bit unsigned index into the local variables of the current frame. The *value* word on the top of the operand stack must be an `int`. To execute the `istore` instruction, the Java Virtual Machine pops the `int` *value* from the top of the operand stack and stores it into the local variable word specified by *index*.

Note that the `wide` instruction can precede the `istore` instruction, to enable a *value* to be stored into a local variable specified by a 16-bit unsigned offset.

For more information about the `istore` instruction, see Chapter 10, "Stack and Local Variable Operations."

## istore_0

Store **int** into local variable 0

**OPCODE:**   59 (0x3b)

**INSTRUCTION FORMAT:**   `istore_0`

**STACK:**
Before:   ... , *value*
After:   ...

**DESCRIPTION:**   The index zero must be a valid index into the local variables of the current stack frame, and the *value* word on the top of the operand stack must be an **int**. To execute the **istore_0** instruction, the Java Virtual Machine pops the **int** *value* from the top of the operand stack and stores it into the local variable word at index zero.

For more information about the **istore_0** instruction, see Chapter 10, "Stack and Local Variable Operations."

## istore_1

Store **int** into local variable 1

**OPCODE:**   60 (0x3c)

**INSTRUCTION FORMAT:**   `istore_1`

**STACK:**
Before:   ... , *value*
After:   ...

**DESCRIPTION:**   The index one must be a valid index into the local variables of the current stack frame, and the *value* word on the top of the operand stack must be an **int**. To execute the **istore_1** instruction, the Java Virtual Machine pops the **int** *value* from the top of the operand stack and stores it into the local variable word at index one.

For more information about the **istore_1** instruction, see Chapter 10, "Stack and Local Variable Operations."

# istore_2

Store **int** into local variable 2

**OPCODE:** 61 (0x3d)

**INSTRUCTION FORMAT:** `istore_2`

**STACK:**
Before:  . . . , *value*
After:  . . .

**DESCRIPTION:** The index two must be a valid index into the local variables of the current stack frame, and the *value* word on the top of the operand stack must be an **int**. To execute the `istore_2` instruction, the Java Virtual Machine pops the **int** *value* from the top of the operand stack and stores it into the local variable word at index two.

For more information about the `istore_2` instruction, see Chapter 10, "Stack and Local Variable Operations."

# istore_3

Store **int** into local variable 3

**OPCODE:** 62 (0x3e)

**INSTRUCTION FORMAT:** `istore_3`

**STACK:**
Before:  . . . , *value*
After:  . . .

**DESCRIPTION:** The index three must be a valid index into the local variables of the current stack frame, and the *value* word on the top of the operand stack must be an **int**. To execute the `istore_3` instruction, the Java Virtual Machine pops the **int** *value* from the top of the operand stack and stores it into the local variable word at index three.

For more information about the `istore_3` instruction, see Chapter 10, "Stack and Local Variable Operations."

## isub

Subtract `ints`

**OPCODE:** 100 (0x64)

**INSTRUCTION FORMAT:** isub

**STACK:**
Before:   . . . , *value1, value2*
After:   . . . , *result*

**DESCRIPTION:** The top two words of the operand stack, *value1* and *value2*, must be `int`s. To execute the `isub` instruction, the Java Virtual Machine pops *value1* and *value2*, subtracts *value2* from *value1* (*value1 – value2*), and pushes the `int` *result*. If overflow occurs, *result* is the 32 lowest order bits of the true mathematical result represented in a sufficiently wide two's-complement format, and the sign bit of *result* may be different from the true mathematical result.

For more information about the `isub` instruction, see Chapter 12, "Integer Arithmetic."

## iushr

Perform logical right shift on `int`

**OPCODE:** 124 (0x7c)

**INSTRUCTION FORMAT:** iushr

**STACK:**
Before:   . . . , *value1, value2*
After:   . . . , *result*

**DESCRIPTION:** The top two words of the operand stack, *value1* and *value2*, must be `int`s. To execute the `iushr` instruction, the Java Virtual Machine pops *value1* and *value2*, shifts *value1* right with zero extension by the number of bits specified in the five lowest order bits of *value2* (from 0 to 31 bit positions), and pushes the `int` *result*.

For more information about the `iushr` instruction, see Chapter 13, "Logic."

## ixor

Perform boolean XOR on `int`s

**OPCODE:**   130 (0x82)

**INSTRUCTION FORMAT:**   `ixor`

**STACK:**
Before:   *. . . , value1, value2*
After:   *. . . , result*

**DESCRIPTION:**   The top two words of the operand stack, *value1* and *value2*, must be `int`s. To execute the `ixor` instruction, the Java Virtual Machine pops *value1* and *value2*, bitwise exclusive ORs them, and pushes the `int` *result*.

For more information about the `ixor` instruction, see Chapter 13, "Logic."

## jsr

Jump to subroutine

**OPCODE:**   168 (0xa8)

**INSTRUCTION FORMAT:**   `jsr`, *branchbyte1, branchbyte2*

**STACK:**
Before:   *. . .*
After:   *. . . , address*

**DESCRIPTION:**   To execute the `jsr` instruction, the Java Virtual Machine pushes the (program counter) address of the opcode immediately following the `jsr` instruction, the *address* word, onto the operand stack. The virtual machine then forms a signed 16-bit offset by calculating *(branchbyte1 << 8) | branchbyte2*. It calculates a target (program counter) address by adding the calculated offset to the address of the **jsr** opcode. The target address must be the address of an opcode within the same method as the **jsr** opcode. The virtual machine jumps to the target address and continues execution there.

For more information about the **jsr** instruction, see Chapter 18, "Finally Clauses."

## jsr_w

Jump to subroutine (wide index)

**OPCODE:**   201 (0xc9)

**INSTRUCTION FORMAT:**   **jsr_w**, *branchbyte1, branchbyte2, branchbyte3, branchbyte4*

**STACK:**
Before:   . . .
After:   . . . , *address*

**DESCRIPTION:**   To execute the **jsr_w** instruction, the Java Virtual Machine pushes the (program counter) address of the opcode immediately following the **jsr_w** instruction, the *address* word, onto the operand stack. The virtual machine then forms a signed 32-bit offset by calculating *(branchbyte1 << 24) | (branchbyte2 << 16) | (branchbyte3 << 8) | branchbyte4*. The virtual machine then calculates a target (program counter) address by adding the calculated offset to the address of the **jsr_w** opcode. The target address must be the address of an opcode within the same method as the **jsr_w** opcode. The virtual machine jumps to the target address and continues execution there.

Note that despite the 32-bit offset of the **jsr_w** instruction, Java methods are currently (in both the 1.0 and 1.1 releases) limited to 65,535 bytes by three items in the Java class file format: the sizes of the indexes in the **LineNumberTable** attribute, the **LocalVariableTable** attribute, and the **Code** attribute's **exception_table** item. According to the Java Virtual Machine specification, the 65,536-byte limit to Java methods may be raised in a future release. For more information about the **jsr_w** instruction, see Chapter 18, "Finally Clauses."

# l2d

Convert **long** to **double**

**OPCODE:**  138 (0x8a)

**INSTRUCTION FORMAT:**  l2d

**STACK:**
Before:  *. . . , value.word1, value.word2*
After:   *. . . , result.word1, result.word2*

**DESCRIPTION:**  The top two words of the operand stack must be a **long**. To execute the **l2d** instruction, the Java Virtual Machine pops the **long** *value* from the operand stack, converts the **long** to a **double** using the IEEE round-to-nearest mode, and pushes the **double** *result*.

Note that this instruction performs a widening primitive conversion. Because not all **long** values can be exactly represented by a **double**, the conversion may result in a loss of precision.

For more information about the **l2d** instruction, see Chapter 11, "Type Conversion."

# l2f

Convert **long** to **float**

**OPCODE:**  137 (0x89)

**INSTRUCTION FORMAT:**  l2f

**STACK:**
Before:  *. . . , value.word1, value.word2*
After:   *. . . , result*

**DESCRIPTION:**  The top two words of the operand stack must be a **long**. To execute the **l2f** instruction, the Java Virtual Machine pops the long *value* from the operand stack, converts the **long** to a **float** using the IEEE round-to-nearest mode, and pushes the **float** *result*.

Note that this instruction performs a widening primitive conversion. Because not all **long** values can be exactly represented by a **float**, the conversion may result in a loss of precision.

For more information about the **l2f** instruction, see Chapter 11, "Type Conversion."

# l2i

Convert **long** to **int**

**OPCODE:** 136 (0x88)

**INSTRUCTION FORMAT:** l2i

**STACK:**
Before:   . . . , *value.word1, value.word2*
After:    . . . , *result*

**DESCRIPTION:**   The top two words of the operand stack must be a **long**. To execute the **l2i** instruction, the Java Virtual Machine pops **long** *value* from the operand stack, truncates the **long** to an **int**, and pushes the **int** *result*.

Note that this instruction performs a narrowing primitive conversion. As a result of this conversion, magnitude information may be lost and the sign bit may change.

For more information about the **l2i** instruction, see Chapter 11, "Type Conversion."

# ladd

Add **long**s

**OPCODE:** 97 (0x61)

**INSTRUCTION FORMAT:** `ladd`

**STACK:**

Before: . . . , *value1.word1, value1.word2, value2.word1, value2.word2*
After: . . . , *result.word1, result.word2*

**DESCRIPTION:** The top four words of the operand stack must be two `long`s, *value1* and *value2*. To execute the `ladd` instruction, the Java Virtual Machine pops *value1* and *value2*, adds them, and pushes the `long` *result*. If overflow occurs, *result* is the 64 lowest order bits of the true mathematical result represented in a sufficiently wide two's-complement format, and the sign of *result* is different from that of the true mathematical result.

For more information about the `ladd` instruction, see Chapter 12, "Integer Arithmetic."

# laload

Load `long` from array

**OPCODE:** 47 (0x2f)

**INSTRUCTION FORMAT:** `laload`

**STACK:**

Before: . . . , *arrayref, index*
After: . . . , *value.word1, value.word2*

**DESCRIPTION:** To execute the `laload` instruction, the Java Virtual Machine first pops two words from the operand stack. The *arrayref* word must be a `reference` that refers to an array of `long`s. The *index* word must be an `int`. The virtual machine retrieves from the *arrayref* array the `long` *value* specified by *index* and pushes it onto the operand stack.

If *arrayref* is `null`, the Java Virtual Machine throws `NullPointerException`. Otherwise, if *index* is not a legal index into the *arrayref* array, the virtual machine throws `ArrayIndexOutOfBoundsException`.

For more information about the `laload` instruction, see Chapter 15, "Objects and Arrays."

# land

Perform boolean AND on **long**s

**OPCODE:**   127 (0x7f)

**INSTRUCTION FORMAT:**   **land**

**STACK:**
Before:   ..., *value1.word1, value1.word2, value2.word1, value2.word2*
After:   ..., *result.word1, result.word2*

**DESCRIPTION:**   The top four words of the operand stack must be two **long**s, *value1* and *value2*. To execute the **land** instruction, the Java Virtual Machine pops *value1* and *value2*, bitwise ANDs them, and pushes the **long** *result*.

For more information about the **land** instruction, see Chapter 13, "Logic."

# lastore

Store into **long** array

**OPCODE:**   80 (0x50)

**INSTRUCTION FORMAT:**   **lastore**

**STACK:**
Before:   ..., *arrayref, index, value.word1, value.word2*
After:   ...

**DESCRIPTION:**   To execute the **lastore** instruction, the Java Virtual Machine first pops four words from the operand stack. The *arrayref* word must be a **reference** that refers to an array of **long**s. The *index* word must be an **int**, and the *value* words must be a **long**. The virtual machine stores **long** *value* into the *arrayref* array location specified by *index*.

If *arrayref* is **null**, the Java Virtual Machine throws **NullPointerException**. Otherwise, if *index* is not a legal index into the *arrayref* array, the virtual machine throws **ArrayIndexOutOfBoundsException**.

For more information about the **lastore** instruction, see Chapter 15, "Objects and Arrays."

## lcmp

Compare **long**s

**OPCODE:**   148 (0x94)

**INSTRUCTION FORMAT:**   lcmp

**STACK:**
Before:   ... , *value1.word1, value1.word2, value2.word1, value2.word2*
After:   ... , *result*

**DESCRIPTION:**   The top four words of the operand stack must be two **long**s, *value1* and *value2*. To execute the **lcmp** instruction, the Java Virtual Machine pops *value1* and *value2* off the operand stack and compares one against the other. If *value1* equals *value2*, the virtual machine pushes onto the operand stack **int** *result* zero. Else, if *value1* is greater than *value2*, the virtual machine pushes onto the operand stack **int** *result* one. Otherwise, if *value1* is less than *value2*, the virtual machine pushes onto the operand stack **int** *result* negative one.

For more information about the **lcmp** instruction, see Chapter 16, "Control Flow."

## lconst_0

Push **long** constant 0

**OPCODE:**   9 (0x9)

**INSTRUCTION FORMAT:**   lconst_0

**STACK:**
Before:   ...
After:   ... , *<0>-word1, <0>-word2*

**DESCRIPTION:** To execute the `lconst_0` instruction, the Java Virtual Machine pushes the `long` constant 0 onto the operand stack.

For more information about the `lconst_0` instruction, see Chapter 10, "Stack and Local Variable Operations."

## lconst_1

Push `long` constant 1

**OPCODE:** 10 (0xa)

**INSTRUCTION FORMAT:** `lconst_1`

**STACK:**
Before: . . .
After: . . . , *<1>-word1, <1>-word2*

**DESCRIPTION:** To execute the `lconst_1` instruction, the Java Virtual Machine pushes the `long` constant 1 onto the operand stack.

For more information about the `lconst_1` instruction, see Chapter 10, "Stack and Local Variable Operations."

## ldc

Push item from constant pool

**OPCODE:** 18 (0x12)

**INSTRUCTION FORMAT:** `ldc`, *index*

**STACK:**
Before: . . .
After: . . . , *item*

**DESCRIPTION:** The *index* operand must be a valid unsigned 8-bit index into the current constant pool. To execute the `ldc` instruction, the Java Virtual Machine first looks up the constant pool entry specified by the *index*

operand. At constant pool entry *index*, the virtual machine must find either a
`CONSTANT_Integer_info`, `CONSTANT_Float_info`, or `CONSTANT_String_info`
entry. If it hasn't already, the virtual machine resolves the entry. If the
entry is a `CONSTANT_Integer_info`, the virtual machine pushes the **int**
value represented by the entry onto the operand stack. Else, if the entry
is a `CONSTANT_Float_info`, the virtual machine pushes the **float** value
represented by the entry onto the operand stack. Otherwise, the entry is
a `CONSTANT_String_info` entry, and the virtual machine pushes a reference to the interned **string** object that was produced by the process of resolving the entry onto the operand stack.

Note that the `ldc_w` instruction performs the same function but offers
a wide (16-bit) constant pool index.

For more information about the `ldc` instruction, see Chapter 10, "Stack
and Local Variable Operations."

## ldc_w

Push item from constant pool (wide index)

**OPCODE:**  19 (0x13)

**INSTRUCTION FORMAT:**  `ldc_w`, *indexbyte1*, *indexbyte2*

**STACK:**
Before:  . . .
After:  . . . , *item*

**DESCRIPTION:**  To execute the `ldc_w` instruction, the Java Virtual
Machine first forms an unsigned 16-bit index into the constant pool by
calculating *(indexbyte1 << 8) | indexbyte2*. The virtual machine then looks
up the constant pool entry specified by the calculated index. The constant
pool entry at that index must be either a `CONSTANT_Integer_info`, a
`CONSTANT_Float_info`, or a `CONSTANT_String_info` entry. If it hasn't already, the virtual machine resolves the entry. If the entry is a `CONSTANT_`
`Integer_info`, the virtual machine pushes the **int** value represented by
the entry onto the operand stack. Else, if the entry is a `CONSTANT_Float_`
`info`, the virtual machine pushes the **float** value it represents onto the
operand stack. Otherwise, the entry is a `CONSTANT_String_info`, and the
virtual machine pushes a reference to the interned **string** object that was
produced by the process of resolving the entry onto the operand stack.

Note that the `ldc_w` instruction performs the same function as `ldc` but offers a wide (16-bit) constant pool index as opposed to `ldc`'s 8-bit constant pool index.

For more information about the `ldc_w` instruction, see Chapter 10, "Stack and Local Variable Operations."

## ldc2_w

Push **long** or **double** from constant pool (wide index)

**OPCODE:**   20 (0x14)

**INSTRUCTION FORMAT:**   `ldc2_w`, *indexbyte1*, *indexbyte2*

**STACK:**
Before:   . . .
After:   . . . , *item.word1, item.word2*

**DESCRIPTION:**   To execute the `ldc2_w` instruction, the Java Virtual Machine first forms an unsigned 16-bit index into the constant pool by calculating *(indexbyte1 << 8) | indexbyte2*. The virtual machine then looks up the constant pool entry specified by the calculated index. The constant pool entry at that index must be either a **CONSTANT_Long_info** or **CONSTANT_Double_info** entry. The virtual machine resolves the entry. If the entry is a **CONSTANT_Long_info**, the virtual machine pushes the **long** value represented by the entry onto the operand stack. Otherwise, it is a **CONSTANT_Double_info** entry, and the virtual machine pushes the **double** value represented by the entry onto the operand stack.

Note that there is no "`ldc2`" instruction that performs the same function as `ldc2_w` but with an 8-bit constant pool index. All two-word constants must be retrieved from the constant pool with an `ldc2_w` instruction, which has a wide (16-bit) constant pool index.

For more information about the `ldc2_w` instruction, see Chapter 10, "Stack and Local Variable Operations."

## ldiv

Divide **long**s

**OPCODE:** 109 (0x6d)

**INSTRUCTION FORMAT:** `ldiv`

**STACK:**

Before: . . . , *value1.word1, value1.word2, value2.word1, value2.word2*
After: . . . , *result.word1, result.word2*

**DESCRIPTION:** The top four words of the operand stack must be two `long`s, *value1* and *value2*. To execute the `ldiv` instruction, the Java Virtual Machine pops *value1* and *value2*, integer divides *value1* by *value2* (*value1* / *value2*), and pushes the `long` *result*.

Integer division rounds the magnitude of the true mathematical quotient toward zero to the nearest integer. If the magnitude of the denominator is greater than that of the numerator, the `long` *result* is zero. Else, with one special exception, the sign of *result* is positive if the signs of the numerator and denominator are the same, negative if they are different. The exception to this rule occurs when the numerator is the smallest negative integer that can be represented by a `long` and the denominator is – 1. For this division, the true mathematical result is one greater than the largest positive integer that can be represented by a `long`. As a consequence, the division overflows and the result is equal to the numerator.

If *value2* (the denominator) is zero, the Java Virtual Machine throws `ArithmeticException`.

For more information about the `ldiv` instruction, see Chapter 12, "Integer Arithmetic."

# `lload`

Load `long` from local variable

**OPCODE:** 22 (0x16)

**INSTRUCTION FORMAT:** `lload`, *index*

**STACK:**
Before: . . .
After: . . . , *value.word1, value.word2*

**DESCRIPTION:** The *index* operand, which serves as an 8-bit unsigned index into the local variables of the current frame, must specify the first of two consecutive local variable words that contain a **long**. To execute the **lload** instruction, the Java Virtual Machine pushes onto the operand stack the **long** contained in the two consecutive local variable words specified by *index* and *index + 1*.

Note that the **wide** instruction can precede the **lload** instruction, to allow a local variable to be accessed with a 16-bit unsigned offset.

For more information about the **lload** instruction, see Chapter 10, "Stack and Local Variable Operations."

# lload_0

Load **long** from local variable 0

**OPCODE:** 30 (0x1e)

**INSTRUCTION FORMAT:** lload_0

**STACK:**
Before: ...
After: ..., *value.word1, value.word2*

**DESCRIPTION:** The two consecutive local variable words at indexes zero and one must contain a **long**. To execute the **lload_0** instruction, the Java Virtual Machine pushes onto the operand stack the **long** *value* contained in local variable words zero and one.

For more information about the **lload_0** instruction, see Chapter 10, "Stack and Local Variable Operations."

# lload_1

Load **long** from local variable 1

**OPCODE:** 31 (0x1f)

**INSTRUCTION FORMAT:** lload_1

**STACK:**
Before:   . . .
After:    . . . , *value.word1, value.word2*

**DESCRIPTION:**   The two consecutive local variable words at indexes one and two must contain a **long**. To execute the **lload_1** instruction, the Java Virtual Machine pushes onto the operand stack the **long** *value* contained in local variable words one and two.

For more information about the **lload_1** instruction, see Chapter 10, "Stack and Local Variable Operations."

## lload_2

Load **long** from local variable 2

**OPCODE:**   32 (0x20)

**INSTRUCTION FORMAT:**   lload_2

**STACK:**
Before:   . . .
After:    . . . , *value.word1, value.word2*

**DESCRIPTION:**   The two consecutive local variable words at indexes two and three must contain a **long**. To execute the **lload_2** instruction, the Java Virtual Machine pushes onto the operand stack the **long** *value* contained in local variable words two and three.

For more information about the **lload_2** instruction, see Chapter 10, "Stack and Local Variable Operations."

## lload_3

Load **long** from local variable 3

**OPCODE:**   33 (0x21)

**INSTRUCTION FORMAT:**   lload_3

**STACK:**
Before:  . . .
After:  . . . , *value.word1, value.word2*

**DESCRIPTION:**  The two consecutive local variable words at indexes three and four must contain a `long`. To execute the `lload_3` instruction, the Java Virtual Machine pushes onto the operand stack the `long` *value* contained in local variable words three and four.

For more information about the `lload_3` instruction, see Chapter 10, "Stack and Local Variable Operations."

# lmul

Multiply `long`s

**OPCODE:**  105 (0x69)

**INSTRUCTION FORMAT:**  `lmul`

**STACK:**
Before:  . . . , *value1.word1, value1.word2, value2.word1, value2.word2*
After:  . . . , *result.word1, result.word2*

**DESCRIPTION:**  The top four words of the operand stack must be two `long`s, *value1* and *value2*. To execute the `lmul` instruction, the Java Virtual Machine pops *value1* and *value2*, multiplies them, and pushes the `long` *result*. If overflow occurs, *result* is the 64 lowest order bits of the true mathematical result represented in a sufficiently wide two's-complement format, and the sign of *result* may be different from that of the true mathematical result.

For more information about the `lmul` instruction, see Chapter 12, "Integer Arithmetic."

# lneg

Negate `long`

**OPCODE:**   117 (0x75)

**INSTRUCTION FORMAT:**   `lneg`

**STACK:**
Before:   . . . , *value.word1, value.word2*
After:   . . . , *result.word1, result.word2*

**DESCRIPTION:**   The top two words of the operand stack must be a `long`, *value*. To execute the `lneg` instruction, the Java Virtual Machine pops *value*, negates it, and pushes the `long` *result*.

The *result* produced by an `lneg` instruction is the same number that would be produced by subtracting *value* from zero with the `lsub` instruction. As a consequence, when *value* is the smallest negative integer that can be represented by a `long`, the negation overflows. For this negation, the true mathematical result is one greater than the largest positive integer that can be represented by a `long`, and the actual *result* is equal to *value* with no change in sign.

For more information about the `lneg` instruction, see Chapter 12, "Integer Arithmetic."


# lookupswitch

Access jump table by key match and jump

**OPCODE:**   171 (0xab)

**INSTRUCTION FORMAT:**   `lookupswitch`, . . . *0-3 byte pad . . . , defaultbyte1, defaultbyte2, defaultbyte3, defaultbyte4, npairs1, npairs2, npairs3, npairs4,* . . . *match-offset pairs . . .*

**STACK:**
Before:   . . . , *key*
After:   . . .

**DESCRIPTION:**   The `lookupswitch` opcode is followed by zero to three bytes of padding—enough so that the byte immediately following the padding starts at an address that is a multiple of four bytes from the beginning of the method. Each padding byte is a zero. Immediately following the padding is a signed 32-bit default branch offset, *default*. Following *default* is *npairs*, a signed count of the number of case value/branch offset pairs embedded in this **lookupswitch** instruction. The value of *npairs* must be greater than or equal to zero. Following *npairs* are the case value/branch offset pairs themselves. For each pair, the signed 32-bit case value, *match*, precedes the signed 32-bit branch offset, *offset*. The virtual machine calculates all these signed 32-bit values from the four individual bytes as *(byte1 << 24) | (byte2 << 16) | (byte3 << 8) | byte4*.

The top word of the operand stack, *key*, must be an **int**. To execute the **lookupswitch** instruction, the Java Virtual Machine pops *key* off the operand stack and compares it to the *match* values. If the key is equal to one of the *match* values, the virtual machine calculates a target (program counter) address by adding the signed *offset* that corresponds to the matching *match* value to the address of the **lookupswitch** opcode. The target address must be the address of an opcode within the same method as the **lookupswitch** opcode. The virtual machine jumps to the target address and continues execution there.

For more information about the **lookupswitch** instruction, see Chapter 16, "Control Flow."

# lor

Perform boolean OR on **long**s

**OPCODE:**   129 (0x81)

**INSTRUCTION FORMAT:**   lor

**STACK:**
Before:   . . . , *value1.word1, value1.word2, value2.word1, value2.word2*
After:   . . . , *result.word1, result.word2*

**DESCRIPTION:**   The top four words of the operand stack must be two **long**s, *value1* and *value2*. To execute the **lor** instruction, the Java Virtual Machine pops *value1* and *value2*, bitwise ORs them, and pushes the **long** *result*.

For more information about the **lor** instruction, see Chapter 13, "Logic."

# lrem

Calculate remainder of division of **long**s

**OPCODE:** 113 (0x71)

**INSTRUCTION FORMAT:** lrem

**STACK:**
Before: ..., *value1.word1, value1.word2, value2.word1, value2.word2*
After: ..., *result.word1, result.word2*

**DESCRIPTION:** The top four words of the operand stack must be two **long**s, *value1* and *value2*. To execute the **lrem** instruction, the Java Virtual Machine pops *value1* and *value2*, calculates the integer remainder, and pushes the **long** *result*. The integer remainder equals *value1 – (value1 / value2) * value2*.

The **lrem** instruction implements Java's remainder operator, **%**, on **long**s. The **lrem** behaves such that the following Java expression is always **true**, where **n** and **d** are any two **long**s:

```
(n/d)*d + (n%d) == n
```

This behavior means that the *result* of an **lrem** instruction always takes the same sign as the numerator, which is popped off the operand stack as *value1*.

If *value2* (the denominator) is zero, the Java Virtual Machine throws **ArithmeticException**.

For more information about the **lrem** instruction, see Chapter 12, "Integer Arithmetic."

# lreturn

Return **long** from method

**OPCODE:** 173 (0xad)

**INSTRUCTION FORMAT:** lreturn

**STACK:**
Before:   . . . , *value.word1, value.word2*
After:   *[empty]*

**DESCRIPTION:**   The return type of the returning method must be
**long**. The top two words of the operand stack must be a **long**. To execute
the **lreturn** instruction, the Java Virtual Machine pops the **long** *value*
from the operand stack of the current frame and pushes it onto the
operand stack of the invoking method's frame. The virtual machine discards any other words that may still be on the returning method's frame.
If the returning method is synchronized, the monitor that was acquired
when the method was invoked is released. The invoking method's frame
is made current, and the virtual machine continues execution in the invoking method.

For more information about monitors, see Chapter 20, "Thread Synchronization." For more information about the **lreturn** instruction, see
Chapter 19, "Method Invocation and Return."

# lshl

Perform left shift on **long**

**OPCODE:**   121 (0x79)

**INSTRUCTION FORMAT:** lshl

**STACK:**
Before:   . . . , *value1.word1, value1.word2, value2*
After:   . . . , *result.word1, result.word2*

**DESCRIPTION:**   The top word of the operand stack, *value2*, must be an
**int**. The next two words down must be a **long**, *value1*. To execute the **lshl**
instruction, the Java Virtual Machine pops *value1* and *value2*, shifts
*value1* left by the number of bits specified in the six lowest order bits of
*value2* (from 0 to 63 bit positions), and pushes the **long** *result*.

For more information about the **lshl** instruction, see Chapter 13,
"Logic."

# lshr

Perform arithmetic right shift on **long**

**OPCODE:**   123 (0x7b)

**INSTRUCTION FORMAT:** lshr

**STACK:**
Before:   . . . , *value1.word1, value1.word2, value2*
After:   . . . , *result.word1, result.word2*

**DESCRIPTION:**   The top word of the operand stack, *value2*, must be an **int**. The next two words down must be a **long**, *value1*. To execute the **lshr** instruction, the Java Virtual Machine pops *value1* and *value2*, shifts *value1* right with sign extension by the number of bits specified in the six lowest order bits of *value2* (from 0 to 63 bit positions), and pushes the **long** *result*.

For more information about the **lshr** instruction, see Chapter 13, "Logic."

# lstore

Store **long** into local variable

**OPCODE:**   55 (0x37)

**INSTRUCTION FORMAT:** lstore, *index*

**STACK:**
Before:   . . . , *value.word1, value.word2*
After:   . . .

**DESCRIPTION:**   The *index* operand must specify a valid 8-bit unsigned index into the local variables of the current frame. The top two words of the operand stack must be a **long**. To execute the **lstore** instruction, the Java Virtual Machine pops the **long** *value* from the top of the operand stack and stores it into the two consecutive local variable words at indexes *index* and *index + 1*.

Note that the **wide** instruction can precede the **lstore** instruction, to enable a *value* to be stored into a local variable specified by a 16-bit unsigned offset.

For more information about the **lstore** instruction, see Chapter 10, "Stack and Local Variable Operations."

# lstore_0

Store **long** into local variable 0

**OPCODE:**   63 (0x3f)

**INSTRUCTION FORMAT:**   lstore_0

**STACK:**
Before:   . . . , *value.word1, value.word2*
After:   . . .

**DESCRIPTION:**   The indexes zero and one must be valid indexes into the local variables of the current stack frame. The top two words on the operand stack must be a **long**. To execute the **lstore_0** instruction, the Java Virtual Machine pops the **long** *value* from the top of the operand stack and stores it into the two consecutive local variable words at indexes zero and one.

For more information about the **lstore_0** instruction, see Chapter 10, "Stack and Local Variable Operations."

# lstore_1

Store **long** into local variable 1

**OPCODE:**   64 (0x40)

**INSTRUCTION FORMAT:**   lstore_1

**STACK:**
Before:   . . . , *value.word1, value.word2*
After:   . . .

**DESCRIPTION:** The indexes one and two must be valid indexes into the local variables of the current stack frame. The top two words on the operand stack must be a **long**. To execute the **lstore_1** instruction, the Java Virtual Machine pops the **long** *value* from the top of the operand stack and stores it into the two consecutive local variable words at indexes one and two.

For more information about the **lstore_1** instruction, see Chapter 10, "Stack and Local Variable Operations."

# lstore_2

Store **long** into local variable 2

**OPCODE:** 65 (0x41)

**INSTRUCTION FORMAT:** lstore_2

**STACK:**
Before: . . . , *value.word1, value.word2*
After: . . .

**DESCRIPTION:** The indexes two and three must be valid indexes into the local variables of the current stack frame. The top two words on the operand stack must be a **long**. To execute the **lstore_2** instruction, the Java Virtual Machine pops the **long** *value* from the top of the operand stack and stores it into the two consecutive local variable words at indexes two and three.

For more information about the **lstore_2** instruction, see Chapter 10, "Stack and Local Variable Operations."

# lstore_3

Store **long** into local variable 3

**OPCODE:** 66 (0x42)

**INSTRUCTION FORMAT:** lstore_3

**STACK:**
Before:   . . . , *value.word1, value.word2*
After:   . . .

**DESCRIPTION:**   The indexes three and four must be valid indexes into the local variables of the current stack frame. The top two words on the operand stack must be a **long**. To execute the **lstore_3** instruction, the Java Virtual Machine pops the **long** *value* from the top of the operand stack and stores it into the two consecutive local variable words at indexes three and four.

For more information about the **lstore_3** instruction, see Chapter 10, "Stack and Local Variable Operations."

## lsub

Subtract **long**s

**OPCODE:**   101 (0x65)

**INSTRUCTION FORMAT:**   lsub

**STACK:**
Before:   . . . , *value1.word1, value1.word2, value2.word1, value2.word2*
After:   . . . , *result.word1, result.word2*

**DESCRIPTION:**   The top four words of the operand stack must be two **long**s, *value1* and *value2*. To execute the **lsub** instruction, the Java Virtual Machine pops *value1* and *value2*, subtracts *value2* from *value1* (*value1 – value2*), and pushes the **long** *result*. If overflow occurs, *result* is the 64 lowest order bits of the true mathematical result represented in a sufficiently wide two's-complement format, and the sign bit of *result* is different from the true mathematical result.

For more information about the **lsub** instruction, see Chapter 12, "Integer Arithmetic."

## lushr

Perform logical right shift on **long**

**OPCODE:**   125 (0x7d)

**INSTRUCTION FORMAT:** `lushr`

**STACK:**
Before:   . . . , *value1.word1, value1.word2, value2.word1, value2.word2*
After:   . . . , *result.word1, result.word2*

**DESCRIPTION:**   The top word of the operand stack, *value2*, must be an `int`. The next two words down must be a `long`, *value1*. To execute the `lushr` instruction, the Java Virtual Machine pops *value1* and *value2*, shifts *value1* right with zero extension by the number of bits specified in the six lowest order bits of *value2* (from 0 to 63 bit positions), and pushes the `long` *result*.

For more information about the `lushr` instruction, see Chapter 13, "Logic."


# lxor

Perform boolean XOR on `long`s

**OPCODE:**   131 (0x83)

**INSTRUCTION FORMAT:** `lxor`

**STACK:**
Before:   . . . , *value1.word1, value1.word2, value2.word1, value2.word2*
After:   . . . , *result.word1, result.word2*

**DESCRIPTION:**   The top four words of the operand stack must be two `long`s, *value1* and *value2*. To execute the `lxor` instruction, the Java Virtual Machine pops *value1* and *value2*, bitwise exclusive ORs them, and pushes the `long` *result*.

For more information about the `lxor` instruction, see Chapter 13, "Logic."


# monitorenter

Enter and acquire object monitor

**OPCODE:**   194 (0xc2)

**INSTRUCTION FORMAT:**   `monitorenter`

**STACK:**
Before:   . . . , *objectref*
After:   . . .

**DESCRIPTION:**   The top word of the operand stack, *objectref*, must be a `reference`. To execute the `monitorenter` instruction, the Java Virtual Machine pops *objectref* and, on behalf of the current thread, acquires the monitor associated with *objectref*.

If the *objectref* word is `null`, the virtual machine throws `NullPointerException`.

For more information about the `monitorenter` instruction, see Chapter 20, "Thread Synchronization."

# monitorexit

Release and exit object monitor

**OPCODE:**   195 (0xc3)

**INSTRUCTION FORMAT:**   `monitorexit`

**STACK:**
Before:   . . . , *objectref*
After:   . . .

**DESCRIPTION:**   The top word of the operand stack, *objectref*, must be a `reference`. To execute the `monitorenter` instruction, the Java Virtual Machine pops *objectref* and, on behalf of the current thread, releases and exits the monitor associated with *objectref*.

If the *objectref* word is `null`, the virtual machine throws `NullPointerException`.

For more information about the `monitorexit` instruction, see Chapter 20, "Thread Synchronization."

# multianewarray

Allocate new multidimensional array

**OPCODE:** 197 (0xc5)

**INSTRUCTION FORMAT:** multianewarray, *indexbyte1, indexbyte2, dimensions*

**STACK:**
Before:  . . . , *count1, [count2, . . . ]*
After: *arrayref*

**DESCRIPTION:** The *dimensions* operand, an unsigned byte that indicates the number of dimensions in the array to create, must be greater than or equal to one. The top *dimensions* words of the operand stack, *count1, [count2, . . . ]*, must contain ints that have nonnegative values. Each of these words gives the number of elements in one dimension of the array. For example, consider an array declared as follows:

```
int[][][] example = new int[3][4][5];
```

For this array, *dimensions* would be equal to three, and the operand stack would contain three "count" words. The *count1* word would be three; *count2,* four; and *count3,* five.

To execute the multianewarray instruction, the Java Virtual Machine first forms an unsigned 16-bit index into the constant pool by calculating *(indexbyte1 << 8) | indexbyte2.* The virtual machine then looks up the constant pool entry specified by the calculated index. The constant pool entry at that index must be a CONSTANT_Class_info entry. If it hasn't already, the virtual machine resolves the entry. The entry must be an array type of dimensionality greater than or equal to *dimensions.*

If the resolution is successful, the Java Virtual Machine creates the *dimensions*-dimensional array on the heap. The virtual machine initializes the elements of the first-dimension array with references to the second-dimension arrays; it initializes the elements of each of the second-dimension arrays with references to the third-dimension arrays, and so on. The virtual machine initializes the elements of the last-dimension arrays with their default initial values. Lastly, the Java Virtual Machine pushes a reference to the new *dimensions*-dimensional array onto the operand stack.

As a result of executing this instruction, the virtual machine may throw any of the linking errors listed in Chapter 8, "The Linking Model," as possible during resolution of a **CONSTANT_Class_info** entry. If resolution succeeds and the array's component type is a reference type, but the current class does not have permission to access that reference type, the virtual machine throws **IllegalAccessError**. Otherwise, if any of the counts popped off the operand stack have a negative value, the Java Virtual Machine throws **NegativeArraySizeException**.

Note that the dimensionality of the array type specified in the resolved **CONSTANT_Class_info** entry need not be equal to the *dimensions* operand —it can also be greater than *dimensions*. For example, the name of the array class for a three-dimensional array of **int**s is "[[[I." The actual constant pool entry referenced by a **multianewarray** instruction that creates a three-dimensional array of **int**s must have at least three dimensions but can have more. For example, resolved array types of "[[[I," "[[[[I," and "[[[[[[I" would all yield three-dimensional arrays of **int** as long as the *dimensions* operand is three. This flexibility in specifying multidimensional array types to the **multianewarray** instruction can reduce the number of entries required in the constant pool of some classes.

For more information about the **multianewarray** instruction, see Chapter 15, "Objects and Arrays."

## new

Create a new object

**OPCODE:** 187 (0xbb)

**INSTRUCTION FORMAT:** **new**, *indexbyte1*, *indexbyte2*

**STACK:**
Before: . . .
After: . . . , *objectref*

**DESCRIPTION:** To execute the **new** instruction, the Java Virtual Machine first forms an unsigned 16-bit index into the constant pool by calculating *(indexbyte1 << 8) | indexbyte2*. The virtual machine then looks up the constant pool entry specified by the calculated index. The constant pool entry at that index must be a **CONSTANT_Class_info** entry. If it hasn't already, the virtual machine resolves the entry. The entry must be a class type, not an interface or array type. The virtual machine allocates sufficient memory from the heap for the new object's image and sets the object's instance variables to their default initial values. Lastly, the virtual machine pushes *objectref*, a reference to the new object, onto the operand stack.

As a result of executing this instruction, the virtual machine may throw any of the linking errors listed in Chapter 8, "The Linking Model," as possible during resolution of a **CONSTANT_Class_info** entry. If resolution succeeds, but the resolved type is an interface, abstract class, or array, the virtual machine throws an **InstantiationError**. Else, if the current class doesn't have permission to access the resolved class, the virtual machine throws an **IllegalAccessError**.

For more information about the **new** instruction, see Chapter 15, "Objects and Arrays."

## newarray

Allocate new array of primitive type components

**OPCODE:**   188 (0xbc)

**INSTRUCTION FORMAT:**   **newarray**, *atype*

**STACK:**
Before:   . . . , *count*
After:   *arrayref*

**DESCRIPTION:**   The top word of the operand stack, *count*, must be an **int**. The *atype* operand, which is used to indicate the array type, must take one of the values shown in Table A-2. To execute the **newarray** instruction, the Java Virtual Machine pops *count* and creates on the heap an array of size *count* of the primitive type specified by *atype*. The virtual machine initializes each array element to its default initial value and pushes *arrayref*, a reference to the new array, onto the operand stack.

If *count* is less than zero, the Java Virtual Machine throws **NegativeArraySizeException**.

For more information about the **newarray** instruction, see Chapter 15, "Objects and Arrays."

**Table A-2**

Values for **atype**

| Array Type | atype |
|------------|-------|
| T_BOOLEAN | 4 |
| T_CHAR | 5 |
| T_FLOAT | 6 |
| T_DOUBLE | 7 |
| T_BYTE | 8 |
| T_SHORT | 9 |
| T_INT | 10 |
| T_LONG | 11 |

## nop

Do nothing

**OPCODE:** 0 (0x0)

**INSTRUCTION FORMAT:** nop

**STACK:** No change

**DESCRIPTION:** To execute the nop instruction, the Java Virtual Machine takes a coffee break.

For more information about the nop instruction, see Chapter 10, "Stack and Local Variable Operations."

## pop

Pop top stack word

**OPCODE:** 87 (0x57)

**INSTRUCTION FORMAT:** pop

**STACK:**
Before:   . . . , *word*
After:    . . .

**DESCRIPTION:**   To execute the **pop** instruction, the Java Virtual Machine pops the top word from the operand stack. This instruction can be used to pop any single-word value from the top of the operand stack. It must not be used to remove half of a dual word value (**long** or **double**) from the top of the operand stack.

For more information about the **pop** instruction, see Chapter 10, "Stack and Local Variable Operations."

## pop2

Pop top two stack words

**OPCODE:**   88 (0x58)

**INSTRUCTION FORMAT:**   **pop2**

**STACK:**
Before:   . . . , *word2, word1*
After:    . . .

**DESCRIPTION:**   To execute the **pop2** instruction, the Java Virtual Machine pops the top two words from the operand stack. This instruction can be used to pop any dual-word value from the top of the operand stack, or any two single-word values. It must not be used to remove one single-word value and half of a dual word value (**long** or **double**) from the top of the operand stack.

For more information about the **pop2** instruction, see Chapter 10, "Stack and Local Variable Operations."

## putfield

Set field in object

**OPCODE:**   181 (0xb5)

**INSTRUCTION FORMAT:**   `putfield`, *indexbyte1, indexbyte2*

**STACK:**
Before:   ..., *objectref, value*
After:   ...
   or
Before:   ..., *objectref, value.word1, value.word2*
After:   ...

**DESCRIPTION:**   To execute the `putfield` instruction, the Java Virtual Machine first forms an unsigned 16-bit index into the constant pool by calculating *(indexbyte1 << 8) | indexbyte2*. The virtual machine then looks up the constant pool entry specified by the calculated index. The constant pool entry at that index must be a `CONSTANT_Fieldref_info` entry. If it hasn't already, the virtual machine resolves the entry, which yields the field's width and the field's offset from the beginning of the object image.

The type of the single or double-word *value* occupying the top of the stack must be compatible with the descriptor of the resolved field. If the resolved field's descriptor is `byte`, `short`, `char`, `boolean`, or `int`, the type of *value* must be `int`. If the resolved field's descriptor is `long`, the type of *value* must be `long`. If the resolved field's descriptor is `float`, the type of *value* must be `float`. If the resolved field's descriptor is `double`, the type of *value* must be `double`. If the resolved field's descriptor is a reference type, the type of *value* must be `reference` and must be assignment-compatible with the resolved descriptor type. The *objectref* word must be a `reference`.

The virtual machine pops *value* and *objectref* and assigns *value* to the appropriate field in the object pointed to by *objectref*.

As a result of executing this instruction, the virtual machine may throw any of the linking errors listed in Chapter 8, "The Linking Model," as possible during resolution of a `CONSTANT_Fieldref_info` entry. As part of the process of resolving the `CONSTANT_Fieldref_info` entry, the virtual machine checks whether the field's access permission enables the current class to access the field. If the field is protected, the virtual machine makes certain the field is a member either of the current class or a superclass of the current class, and that the class of the object pointed to by *objectref* is either the current class or a subclass of the current class. If not (or if any other access permission problem occurs), the virtual machine throws `IllegalAccessError`. Else, if the field exists and is accessible from the current class, but the field is static, the virtual machine throws **IncompatibleClassChangeError**. Otherwise, if *objectref* is **null**, the virtual machine throws **NullPointerException**.

For more information about the **putfield** instruction, see Chapter 15, "Objects and Arrays."

## putstatic

Set static field in class

**OPCODE:** 179 (0xb3)

**INSTRUCTION FORMAT:** **putstatic**, *indexbyte1*, *indexbyte2*

**STACK:**
Before: . . . , *value*
After: . . .
or
Before: . . . , *value.word1, value.word2*
After: . . .

**DESCRIPTION:** To execute the **putstatic** instruction, the Java Virtual Machine first forms an unsigned 16-bit index into the constant pool by calculating *(indexbyte1 << 8) | indexbyte2*. The virtual machine then looks up the constant pool entry specified by the calculated index. The constant pool entry at that index must be a **CONSTANT_Fieldref_info** entry. If it hasn't already, the virtual machine resolves the entry.

The type of the single or double-word *value* occupying the top of the stack must be compatible with the descriptor of the resolved field. If the resolved field's descriptor is **byte**, **short**, **char**, **boolean**, or **int**, the type of *value* must be **int**. If the resolved field's descriptor is **long**, the type of *value* must be **long**. If the resolved field's descriptor is **float**, the type of *value* must be **float**. If the resolved field's descriptor is **double**, the type of *value* must be **double**. If the resolved field's descriptor is a reference type, the type of *value* must be **reference** and must be assignment-compatible with the resolved descriptor type.

The virtual machine pops and assigns *value* to the appropriate static field.

As a result of executing this instruction, the virtual machine may throw any of the linking errors listed in Chapter 8, "The Linking Model," as possible during resolution of a **CONSTANT_Fieldref_info** entry. As part of the process of resolving the **CONSTANT_Fieldref_info** entry, the virtual machine checks whether the field's access permission enables the current class to access the field. If the field is protected, the virtual machine makes certain the field is a member either of the current class or a superclass of the current class. If not (or if any other access permission problem occurs), the virtual machine throws **IllegalAccessError**. Else, if the field exists and is accessible from the current class, but the field is not static, the virtual machine throws **IncompatibleClassChangeError**.

For more information about the **putstatic** instruction, see Chapter 15, "Objects and Arrays."

## ret

Return from subroutine

**OPCODE:** 169 (0xa9)

**INSTRUCTION FORMAT:** **ret**, *index*

**STACK:** No change

**DESCRIPTION:** The *index* operand is an 8-bit unsigned offset into the local variables. The local variable word specified by *index* must be a **returnAddress**. To execute the **ret** instruction, the Java Virtual Machine sets the program counter to the **returnAddress** value stored in local variable *index*, and continues execution there. (In other words, the virtual machine jumps to the **returnAddress**.)

Note that the **wide** instruction can precede the **ret** instruction, to allow a local variable to be accessed with a 16-bit unsigned offset.

For more information about the **ret** instruction, see Chapter 18, "Finally Clauses."

## return

Return (**void**) from method

**OPCODE:** 177 (0xb1)

**INSTRUCTION FORMAT:** `return`

**STACK:**
Before:  ...
After:  *[empty]*

**DESCRIPTION:** The return type of the returning method must be `void`. To execute the `return` instruction, the Java Virtual Machine discards any words that may still be on the returning method's frame. If the returning method is synchronized, the monitor that was acquired when the method was invoked is released. The invoking method's frame is made current, and the virtual machine continues execution in the invoking method.

For more information about monitors, see Chapter 20, "Thread Synchronization." For more information about the `return` instruction, see Chapter 19, "Method Invocation and Return."


# saload

Load `short` from array

**OPCODE:** 53 (0x35)

**INSTRUCTION FORMAT:** `saload`

**STACK:**
Before:  ... , *arrayref, index*
After:  ... , *value*

**DESCRIPTION:** To execute the `saload` instruction, the Java Virtual Machine first pops two words from the operand stack. The *arrayref* word must be a `reference` that refers to an array of `shorts`. The *index* word must be an `int`. The virtual machine retrieves from the *arrayref* array the `short` *value* specified by *index*, sign-extends it to an `int`, and pushes it onto the operand stack.

If *arrayref* is `null`, the Java Virtual Machine throws `NullPointerException`. Otherwise, if *index* is not a legal index into the *arrayref* array, the virtual machine throws `ArrayIndexOutOfBoundsException`.

For more information about the **saload** instruction, see Chapter 15, "Objects and Arrays."

## sastore

Store into **short** array

**OPCODE:** 86 (0x56)

**INSTRUCTION FORMAT:** sastore

**STACK:**
Before: *. . . , array, index, value*
After: *. . .*

**DESCRIPTION:** To execute the **sastore** instruction, the Java Virtual Machine first pops three words from the operand stack. The *arrayref* word must be a **reference** that refers to an array of **short**s. The *index* and *value* words must be **int**s. The virtual machine truncates the **int** *value* to a **short** and stores it into the *arrayref* array location specified by *index*.

If *arrayref* is **null**, the Java Virtual Machine throws **NullPointerException**. Otherwise, if *index* is not a legal index into the *arrayref* array, the virtual machine throws **ArrayIndexOutOfBoundsException**.

For more information about the **sastore** instruction, see Chapter 15, "Objects and Arrays."

## sipush

Push 16-bit signed integer

**OPCODE:** 17 (0x11)

**INSTRUCTION FORMAT:** sipush, *byte1*, *byte2*

**STACK:**
Before: *. . .*
After: *. . . , value*

**DESCRIPTION:** To execute the **sipush** instruction, the Java Virtual Machine first forms an intermediate 16-bit signed integer from *byte1* and *byte2* by calculating *(byte1 << 8) | byte2*. The virtual machine then sign-extends the intermediate 16-bit signed integer to an **int** and pushes the resulting **int** *value* onto the operand stack.

For more information about the **sipush** instruction, see Chapter 10, "Stack and Local Variable Operations."

## swap

Swap top two stack words

**OPCODE:** 95 (0x5f)

**INSTRUCTION FORMAT:** swap

**STACK:**
Before:   . . . , *word2, word1*
After:   . . . , *word1, word2*

**DESCRIPTION:** To execute the **swap** instruction, the Java Virtual Machine swaps the top two words of the operand stack. Both *word1* and *word2* must be single-word values.

For more information about the **swap** instruction, see Chapter 10, "Stack and Local Variable Operations."

## tableswitch

Access jump table by index and jump

**OPCODE:** 170 (0xaa)

**INSTRUCTION FORMAT:** tableswitch, *. . . 0-3 byte pad . . . , defaultbyte1, defaultbyte2, defaultbyte3, defaultbyte4, lowbyte1, lowbyte2, lowbyte3, lowbyte4, highbyte1, highbyte2, highbyte3, highbyte4, . . . jump offsets . . .*

**STACK:**
Before:   ... , *index*
After:    ...

**DESCRIPTION:**   The `tableswitch` opcode is followed by zero to three bytes of padding—enough so that the byte immediately following the padding starts at an address that is a multiple of four bytes from the beginning of the method. Each padding byte is a zero. Immediately following the padding is a signed 32-bit default branch offset, *default*. Following *default* are two signed 32-bit endpoints of the range of case values embedded in this `tableswitch` instruction: *low*, the low endpoint, and *high*, the high endpoint. The value of *low* must be less than or equal to the value of *high*. Following *low* and *high* are *high – low + 1* signed 32-bit branch offsets—one branch offset for high, one for low, and one for each integer case value in between high and low. These offsets serve as a zero-based jump table. The branch offset for *low*, the first entry in the jump table, immediately follows the *high* endpoint value. The virtual machine calculates all these signed 32-bit values from the four individual bytes as *(byte1 << 24) | (byte2 << 16) | (byte3 << 8) | byte4*.

The top word of the operand stack, *index*, must be an `int`. To execute the `tableswitch` instruction, the Java Virtual Machine pops *index* off the operand stack, compares it to *low* and *high*, and selects a branch offset. If *index* is less than *low* and greater than *high*, the virtual machine selects *default* as the branch offset. Else, the virtual machine selects the branch offset at position *index – low* in the jump table. After it has selected a branch offset, the virtual machine calculates a target (program counter) address by adding the signed branch offset to the address of the `tableswitch` opcode. The target address must be the address of an opcode within the same method as the `tableswitch` opcode. The virtual machine jumps to the target address and continues execution there.

For more information about the `tableswitch` instruction, see Chapter 16, "Control Flow."

# wide

Extend a local variable index with additional bytes

**OPCODE:**   196 (0xc4)

**INSTRUCTION FORMAT:**
**wide**, *<opcode>*, *indexbyte1*, *indexbyte2*
   or
**wide**, **iinc**, *indexbyte1*, *indexbyte2*, *constbyte1*, *constbyte2*

**STACK:**   To see how the stack changes when an instruction is modified by **wide**, see the entry for the unmodified instruction. The stack change for an instruction modified by **wide** is identical to the stack change for that same instruction unmodified.

**DESCRIPTION:**   The **wide** opcode modifies instructions that reference the local variables, extending the modified instruction's unsigned 8-bit local variable index to an unsigned 16-bit index. As shown under "Instruction Format," a **wide** instruction comes in two formats. When the **wide** opcode modifies **iload**, **fload**, **aload**, **lload**, **dload**, **istore**, **fstore**, **astore**, **lstore**, **dstore**, or **ret**, the instruction has the first format. When the **wide** opcode modifies **iinc**, the instruction has the second format.

To execute any **wide** instruction, the Java Virtual Machine first forms an unsigned 16-bit index into the local variables by calculating *(indexbyte1 << 8) | indexbyte2*. Irrespective of the opcode that **wide** modifies, the calculated index must be a valid index into the local variables of the current frame. If the **wide** opcode modifies **lload**, **dload**, **lstore**, or **dstore**, then one more than the calculated index must also be a valid index into the local variables. Given a valid unsigned 16-bit (wide) local variable index, the virtual machine executes the modified instruction using the wide index.

When a **wide** opcode modifies an **iinc** instruction, the format of the **iinc** instruction changes. An unmodified **iinc** instruction has two operands, an 8-bit unsigned local variable *index* and an 8-bit signed increment *const*. When modified by **wide**, however, both the **iinc** instruction's local variable index and its increment are extended by an extra byte. To execute this instruction, the virtual machine forms a signed 16-bit increment by calculating *(constbyte1 << 8) | constbyte2*.

Note that from the perspective of the bytecode verifier, the opcode modified by **wide** is seen as an operand to the **wide** opcode. The bytecodes are not allowed to treat opcodes modified by **wide** independently. For example, it is illegal for a **goto** instruction to jump directly to an opcode modified by **wide**.

For more information about the **wide** instruction, see Chapter 10, "Stack and Local Variable Operations."

# Appendix B

Opcode Mnemonic by Function Group

## Stack and Local Variable Operations (Chapter 10)

### Instructions That Push a Constant onto the Stack

| | |
|---|---|
| aconst_null | Push null object reference |
| iconst_m1 | Push int constant –1 |
| iconst_0 | Push int constant 0 |
| iconst_1 | Push int constant 1 |
| iconst_2 | Push int constant 2 |
| iconst_3 | Push int constant 3 |
| iconst_4 | Push int constant 4 |
| iconst_5 | Push int constant 5 |
| lconst_0 | Push long constant 0 |
| lconst_1 | Push long constant 1 |
| fconst_0 | Push float constant 0.0 |
| fconst_1 | Push float constant 1.0 |
| fconst_2 | Push float constant 2.0 |
| dconst_0 | Push double constant 0.0 |
| dconst_1 | Push double constant 1.0 |
| bipush | Push 8-bit signed integer |
| sipush | Push 16-bit signed integer |
| ldc | Push item from constant pool |
| ldcw | Push item from constant pool (wide index) |
| ldc2_w | Push long or double from constant pool (wide index) |

# Instructions That Load a Local Variable onto the Stack

| | |
|---|---|
| iload | Load **int** from local variable |
| lload | Load **long** from local variable |
| fload | Load **float** from local variable |
| dload | Load **double** from local variable |
| aload | Load **reference** from local variable |
| iload_0 | Load **int** from local variable 0 |
| iload_1 | Load **int** from local variable 1 |
| iload_2 | Load **int** from local variable 2 |
| iload_3 | Load **int** from local variable 3 |
| lload_0 | Load **long** from local variable 0 |
| lload_1 | Load **long** from local variable 1 |
| lload_2 | Load **long** from local variable 2 |
| lload_3 | Load **long** from local variable 3 |
| fload_0 | Load **float** from local variable 0 |
| fload_1 | Load **float** from local variable 1 |
| fload_2 | Load **float** from local variable 2 |
| fload_3 | Load **float** from local variable 3 |
| dload_0 | Load **double** from local variable 0 |
| dload_1 | Load **double** from local variable 1 |
| dload_2 | Load **double** from local variable 2 |
| dload_3 | Load **double** from local variable 3 |
| aload_0 | Load **reference** from local variable 0 |
| aload_1 | Load **reference** from local variable 1 |
| aload_2 | Load **reference** from local variable 2 |
| aload_3 | Load **reference** from local variable 3 |
| iaload | Load **int** from array |
| laload | Load **long** from array |
| faload | Load **float** from array |
| daload | Load **double** from array |
| aaload | Load **reference** from array |

| baload | Load **byte** or **boolean** from array |
| caload | Load **char** from array |
| saload | Load **short** from array |

# Instructions That Store a Value from the Stack into a Local Variable

| istore | Store **int** into local variable |
| lstore | Store **long** into local variable |
| fstore | Store **float** into local variable |
| dstore | Store **double** into local variable |
| astore | Store **reference** or **returnAddress** into local variable |
| istore_0 | Store **int** into local variable 0 |
| istore_1 | Store **int** into local variable 1 |
| istore_2 | Store **int** into local variable 2 |
| istore_3 | Store **int** into local variable 3 |
| lstore_0 | Store **long** into local variable 0 |
| lstore_1 | Store **long** into local variable 1 |
| lstore_2 | Store **long** into local variable 2 |
| lstore_3 | Store **long** into local variable 3 |
| fstore_0 | Store **float** into local variable 0 |
| fstore_1 | Store **float** into local variable 1 |
| fstore_2 | Store **float** into local variable 2 |
| fstore_3 | Store **float** into local variable 3 |
| dstore_0 | Store **double** into local variable 0 |
| dstore_1 | Store **double** into local variable 1 |
| dstore_2 | Store **double** into local variable 2 |
| dstore_3 | Store **double** into local variable 3 |
| astore_0 | Store **reference** or **returnAddress** into local variable 0 |
| astore_1 | Store **reference** or **returnAddress** into local variable 1 |

| | |
|---|---|
| astore_2 | Store **reference** or **returnAddress** into local variable 2 |
| astore_3 | Store **reference** or **returnAddress** into local variable 3 |
| iastore | Store into **int** array |
| lastore | Store into **long** array |
| fastore | Store into **float** array |
| dastore | Store into **double** array |
| aastore | Store into **reference** array |
| bastore | Store into **byte** or **boolean** array |
| castore | Store into **char** array |
| sastore | Store into **short** array |

## The **wide** Instruction

| | |
|---|---|
| wide | Extend a local variable index with additional bytes |

## Generic (Typeless) Stack Operations

| | |
|---|---|
| **nop** | Do nothing |
| **pop** | Pop top stack word |
| **pop2** | Pop top two stack words |
| **dup** | Duplicate top stack word |
| **dup_x1** | Duplicate top stack word and put two down |
| **dup_x2** | Duplicate top stack word and put three down |
| **dup2** | Duplicate top two stack words |
| **dup2_x1** | Duplicate top two stack words and put two down |
| **dup2_x2** | Duplicate top two stack words and put three down |
| **swap** | Swap top two stack words |

## Type Conversion (Chapter 11)

| | |
|---|---|
| `i2l` | Convert `int` to `long` |
| `i2f` | Convert `int` to `float` |
| `i2d` | Convert `int` to `double` |
| `l2i` | Convert `long` to `int` |
| `l2f` | Convert `long` to `float` |
| `l2d` | Convert `long` to `double` |
| `f2i` | Convert `float` to `int` |
| `f2l` | Convert `float` to `long` |
| `f2d` | Convert `float` to `double` |
| `d2i` | Convert `double` to `int` |
| `d2l` | Convert `double` to `long` |
| `d2f` | Convert `double` to `float` |
| `i2b` | Convert `int` to `byte` |
| `i2c` | Convert `int` to `char` |
| `i2s` | Convert `int` to `short` |

## Integer Arithmetic (Chapter 12)

| | |
|---|---|
| `iadd` | Add `int`s |
| `ladd` | Add `long`s |
| `isub` | Subtract `int`s |
| `lsub` | Subtract `long`s |
| `imul` | Multiply `int`s |
| `lmul` | Multiply `long`s |
| `idiv` | Divide `int`s |
| `ldiv` | Divide `long`s |
| `irem` | Calculate remainder of division of `int`s |
| `lrem` | Calculate remainder of division of `long`s |
| `ineg` | Negate `int` |

| `lneg` | Negate `long` |
| `iinc` | Increment `int` local variable by constant |

# Logic (Chapter 13)

## Shift Operations

| `ishl` | Perform left shift on `int` |
| `lshl` | Perform left shift on `long` |
| `ishr` | Perform arithmetic right shift on `int` |
| `lshr` | Perform arithmetic right shift on `long` |
| `iushr` | Perform logical right shift on `int` |
| `lushr` | Perform logical right shift on `long` |

## Bitwise Boolean Operations

| `iand` | Perform boolean AND on `int`s |
| `land` | Perform boolean AND on `long`s |
| `ior` | Perform boolean OR on `int`s |
| `lor` | Perform boolean OR on `long`s |
| `ixor` | Perform boolean XOR on `int`s |
| `lxor` | Perform boolean XOR on `long`s |

# Floating-Point Arithmetic (Chapter 14)

| `fadd` | Add `float`s |
| `dadd` | Add `double`s |
| `fsub` | Subtract `float`s |
| `dsub` | Subtract `double`s |
| `fmul` | Multiply `float`s |

| | |
|---|---|
| `dmul` | Multiply **double**s |
| `fdiv` | Divide **float**s |
| `ddiv` | Divide **double**s |
| `frem` | Calculate remainder of division of **float**s |
| `drem` | Calculate remainder of division of **double**s |
| `fneg` | Negate **float** |
| `dneg` | Negate **double** |

# Objects and Arrays (Chapter 15)

## Instructions That Deal with Objects

| | |
|---|---|
| `new` | Create a new object |
| `checkcast` | Make sure object is of a given type |
| `getfield` | Fetch field from object |
| `putfield` | Set field in object |
| `getstatic` | Fetch static field from class |
| `putstatic` | Set static field in class |
| `instanceof` | Determine whether an object is of a given type |

## Instructions That Deal with Arrays

| | |
|---|---|
| `newarray` | Allocate new array of primitive type components |
| `anewarray` | Allocate new array of reference type components |
| `arraylength` | Get length of an array |
| `multianewarray` | Allocate a new multidimensional array |

# Control Flow (Chapter 16)

## Conditional Branch Instructions

| | |
|---|---|
| `ifeq` | Branch if equal to 0 |

| | |
|---|---|
| `ifne` | Branch if not equal to 0 |
| `iflt` | Branch if less than 0 |
| `ifge` | Branch if greater than or equal to 0 |
| `ifgt` | Branch if greater than 0 |
| `ifle` | Branch if less than or equal to 0 |
| `if_icmpeq` | Branch if `int`s equal |
| `if_icmpne` | Branch if `int`s not equal |
| `if_icmplt` | Branch if `int` less than other `int` |
| `if_icmpge` | Branch if `int` greater than or equal to other `int` |
| `if_icmpgt` | Branch if `int` greater than other `int` |
| `if_icmple` | Branch if `int` less than or equal to other `int` |
| `ifnull` | Branch if `null` |
| `ifnonnull` | Branch if not `null` |
| `if_acmpeq` | Branch if object references are equal |
| `if_acmpne` | Branch if object references not equal |

# Comparison Instructions

| | |
|---|---|
| `lcmp` | Compare `long`s |
| `fcmpl` | Compare `float`s (−1 on NaN) |
| `fcmpg` | Compare `float`s (1 on NaN) |
| `dcmpl` | Compare `double`s (-1 on NaN) |
| `dcmpg` | Compare `double`s (1 on NaN) |

# Unconditional Branch Instructions

| | |
|---|---|
| `goto` | Branch always |
| `goto_w` | Branch always (wide index) |

# Table Jumping Instructions

| | |
|---|---|
| `tableswitch` | Access jump table by index and jump |
| `lookupswitch` | Access jump table by key match and jump |

# Exceptions (Chapter 17)

athrow                 Throw exception or error

# Finally Clauses (Chapter 18)

jsr                    Jump to subroutine

jsr_w                  Jump to subroutine (wide index)

ret                    Return from subroutine

# Method Invocation and Return (Chapter 19)

## Method Invocation Instructions

invokevirtual          Invoke instance method, dispatch based on an
                       object's class at runtime

invokespecial          Invoke instance method, dispatch based on
                       compile-time type

invokestatic           Invoke a class (static) method

invokeinterface        Invoke interface method

## Method Return Instructions

ireturn                Return **int** from method

lreturn                Return **long** from method

freturn                Return **float** from method

dreturn                Return **double** from method

areturn                Return **reference** from method

return                 Return (**void**) from method

# Thread Synchronization (Chapter 20)

| | |
|---|---|
| `monitorenter` | Enter and acquire object monitor |
| `monitorexit` | Release and exit object monitor |

# Appendix C

Opcode Mnemonic by Opcode

## Standard Opcodes

| 0 | 0x00 | nop |
|----|------|------------|
| 1 | 0x01 | aconst_null |
| 2 | 0x02 | iconst_m1 |
| 3 | 0x03 | iconst_0 |
| 4 | 0x04 | iconst_1 |
| 5 | 0x05 | iconst_2 |
| 6 | 0x06 | iconst_3 |
| 7 | 0x07 | iconst_4 |
| 8 | 0x08 | iconst_5 |
| 9 | 0x09 | lconst_0 |
| 10 | 0x0a | lconst_1 |
| 11 | 0x0b | fconst_0 |
| 12 | 0x0c | fconst_1 |
| 13 | 0x0d | fconst_2 |
| 14 | 0x0e | dconst_0 |
| 15 | 0x0f | dconst_1 |
| 16 | 0x10 | bipush |
| 17 | 0x11 | sipush |
| 18 | 0x12 | ldc |
| 19 | 0x13 | ldc_w |
| 20 | 0x14 | ldc2_w |
| 21 | 0x15 | iload |
| 22 | 0x16 | lload |
| 23 | 0x17 | fload |
| 24 | 0x18 | dload |
| 25 | 0x19 | aload |
| 26 | 0x1a | iload_0 |

| | | |
|---|---|---|
| 27 | 0x1b | `iload_1` |
| 28 | 0x1c | `iload_2` |
| 29 | 0x1d | `iload_3` |
| 30 | 0x1e | `lload_0` |
| 31 | 0x1f | `lload_1` |
| 32 | 0x20 | `lload_2` |
| 33 | 0x21 | `lload_3` |
| 34 | 0x22 | `fload_0` |
| 35 | 0x23 | `fload_1` |
| 36 | 0x24 | `fload_2` |
| 37 | 0x25 | `fload_3` |
| 38 | 0x26 | `dload_0` |
| 39 | 0x27 | `dload_1` |
| 40 | 0x28 | `dload_2` |
| 41 | 0x29 | `dload_3` |
| 42 | 0x2a | `aload_0` |
| 43 | 0x2b | `aload_1` |
| 44 | 0x2c | `aload_2` |
| 45 | 0x2d | `aload_3` |
| 46 | 0x2e | `iaload` |
| 47 | 0x2f | `laload` |
| 48 | 0x30 | `faload` |
| 49 | 0x31 | `daload` |
| 50 | 0x32 | `aaload` |
| 51 | 0x33 | `baload` |
| 52 | 0x34 | `caload` |
| 53 | 0x35 | `saload` |
| 54 | 0x36 | `istore` |
| 55 | 0x37 | `lstore` |
| 56 | 0x38 | `fstore` |
| 57 | 0x39 | `dstore` |
| 58 | 0x3a | `astore` |
| 59 | 0x3b | `istore_0` |

| | | |
|---|---|---|
| 60 | 0x3c | `istore_1` |
| 61 | 0x3d | `istore_2` |
| 62 | 0x3e | `istore_3` |
| 63 | 0x3f | `lstore_0` |
| 64 | 0x40 | `lstore_1` |
| 65 | 0x41 | `lstore_2` |
| 66 | 0x42 | `lstore_3` |
| 67 | 0x43 | `fstore_0` |
| 68 | 0x44 | `fstore_1` |
| 69 | 0x45 | `fstore_2` |
| 70 | 0x46 | `fstore_3` |
| 71 | 0x47 | `dstore_0` |
| 72 | 0x48 | `dstore_1` |
| 73 | 0x49 | `dstore_2` |
| 74 | 0x4a | `dstore_3` |
| 75 | 0x4b | `astore_0` |
| 76 | 0x4c | `astore_1` |
| 77 | 0x4d | `astore_2` |
| 78 | 0x4e | `astore_3` |
| 79 | 0x4f | `iastore` |
| 80 | 0x50 | `lastore` |
| 81 | 0x51 | `fastore` |
| 82 | 0x52 | `dastore` |
| 83 | 0x53 | `aastore` |
| 84 | 0x54 | `bastore` |
| 85 | 0x55 | `castore` |
| 86 | 0x56 | `sastore` |
| 87 | 0x57 | `pop` |
| 88 | 0x58 | `pop2` |
| 89 | 0x59 | `dup` |
| 90 | 0x5a | `dup_x1` |
| 91 | 0x5b | `dup_x2` |
| 92 | 0x5c | `dup2` |

| 93  | 0x5d | **dup2_x1** |
| 94  | 0x5e | **dup2_x2** |
| 95  | 0x5f | **swap** |
| 96  | 0x60 | **iadd** |
| 97  | 0x61 | **ladd** |
| 98  | 0x62 | **fadd** |
| 99  | 0x63 | **dadd** |
| 100 | 0x64 | **isub** |
| 101 | 0x65 | **lsub** |
| 102 | 0x66 | **fsub** |
| 103 | 0x67 | **dsub** |
| 104 | 0x68 | **imul** |
| 105 | 0x69 | **lmul** |
| 106 | 0x6a | **fmul** |
| 107 | 0x6b | **dmul** |
| 108 | 0x6c | **idiv** |
| 109 | 0x6d | **ldiv** |
| 110 | 0x6e | **fdiv** |
| 111 | 0x6f | **ddiv** |
| 112 | 0x70 | **irem** |
| 113 | 0x71 | **lrem** |
| 114 | 0x72 | **frem** |
| 115 | 0x73 | **drem** |
| 116 | 0x74 | **ineg** |
| 117 | 0x75 | **lneg** |
| 118 | 0x76 | **fneg** |
| 119 | 0x77 | **dneg** |
| 120 | 0x78 | **ishl** |
| 121 | 0x79 | **lshl** |
| 122 | 0x7a | **ishr** |
| 123 | 0x7b | **lshr** |
| 124 | 0x7c | **iushr** |
| 125 | 0x7d | **lushr** |

| 126 | 0x7e | iand  |
|-----|------|-------|
| 127 | 0x7f | land  |
| 128 | 0x80 | ior   |
| 129 | 0x81 | lor   |
| 130 | 0x82 | ixor  |
| 131 | 0x83 | lxor  |
| 132 | 0x84 | iinc  |
| 133 | 0x85 | i2l   |
| 134 | 0x86 | i2f   |
| 135 | 0x87 | i2d   |
| 136 | 0x88 | l2i   |
| 137 | 0x89 | l2f   |
| 138 | 0x8a | l2d   |
| 139 | 0x8b | f2i   |
| 140 | 0x8c | f2l   |
| 141 | 0x8d | f2d   |
| 142 | 0x8e | d2i   |
| 143 | 0x8f | d2l   |
| 144 | 0x90 | d2f   |
| 145 | 0x91 | i2b   |
| 146 | 0x92 | i2c   |
| 147 | 0x93 | i2s   |
| 148 | 0x94 | lcmp  |
| 149 | 0x95 | fcmpl |
| 150 | 0x96 | fcmpg |
| 151 | 0x97 | dcmpl |
| 152 | 0x98 | dcmpg |
| 153 | 0x99 | ifeq  |
| 154 | 0x9a | ifne  |
| 155 | 0x9b | iflt  |
| 156 | 0x9c | ifge  |
| 157 | 0x9d | ifgt  |
| 158 | 0x9e | ifle  |

| 159 | 0x9f | `if_icmpeq` |
| 160 | 0xa0 | `if_icmpne` |
| 161 | 0xa1 | `if_icmplt` |
| 162 | 0xa2 | `if_icmpge` |
| 163 | 0xa3 | `if_icmpgt` |
| 164 | 0xa4 | `if_icmple` |
| 165 | 0xa5 | `if_acmpeq` |
| 166 | 0xa6 | `if_acmpne` |
| 167 | 0xa7 | `goto` |
| 168 | 0xa8 | `jsr` |
| 169 | 0xa9 | `ret` |
| 170 | 0xaa | `tableswitch` |
| 171 | 0xab | `lookupswitch` |
| 172 | 0xac | `ireturn` |
| 173 | 0xad | `lreturn` |
| 174 | 0xae | `freturn` |
| 175 | 0xaf | `dreturn` |
| 176 | 0xb0 | `areturn` |
| 177 | 0xb1 | `return` |
| 178 | 0xb2 | `getstatic` |
| 179 | 0xb3 | `putstatic` |
| 180 | 0xb4 | `getfield` |
| 181 | 0xb5 | `putfield` |
| 182 | 0xb6 | `invokevirtual` |
| 183 | 0xb7 | `invokespecial` |
| 184 | 0xb8 | `invokestatic` |
| 185 | 0xb9 | `invokeinterface` |
| 187 | 0xbb | `new` |
| 188 | 0xbc | `newarray` |
| 189 | 0xbd | `anewarray` |
| 190 | 0xbe | `arraylength` |
| 191 | 0xbf | `athrow` |
| 192 | 0xc0 | `checkcast` |

| 193 | 0xc1 | `instanceof` |
| 194 | 0xc2 | `monitorenter` |
| 195 | 0xc3 | `monitorexit` |
| 196 | 0xc4 | `wide` |
| 197 | 0xc5 | `multianewarray` |
| 198 | 0xc6 | `ifnull` |
| 199 | 0xc7 | `ifnonnull` |
| 200 | 0xc8 | `goto_w` |
| 201 | 0xc9 | `jsr_w` |

# Quick Opcodes

| 203 | 0xcb | `ldc_quick` |
| 204 | 0xcc | `ldc_w_quick` |
| 205 | 0xcd | `ldc2_w_quick` |
| 206 | 0xce | `getfield_quick` |
| 207 | 0xcf | `putfield_quick` |
| 208 | 0xd0 | `getfield2_quick` |
| 209 | 0xd1 | `putfield2_quick` |
| 210 | 0xd2 | `getstatic_quick` |
| 211 | 0xd3 | `putstatic_quick` |
| 212 | 0xd4 | `getstatic2_quick` |
| 213 | 0xd5 | `putstatic2_quick` |
| 214 | 0xd6 | `invokevirtual_quick` |
| 215 | 0xd7 | `invokenonvirtual_quick` |
| 216 | 0xd8 | `invokesuper_quick` |
| 217 | 0xd9 | `invokestatic_quick` |
| 218 | 0xda | `invokeinterface_quick` |
| 219 | 0xdb | `invokevirtualobject_quick` |
| 221 | 0xdd | `new_quick` |
| 222 | 0xde | `anewarray_quick` |
| 223 | 0xdf | `multianewarray_quick` |

| 224 | 0xe0 | `checkcast_quick` |
| 225 | 0xe1 | `instanceof_quick` |
| 226 | 0xe2 | `invokevirtual_quick_w` |
| 227 | 0xe3 | `getfield_quick_w` |
| 228 | 0xe4 | `putfield_quick_w` |

# Reserved Opcodes

| 202 | 0xca | `breakpoint` |
| 254 | 0xfe | `impdep1` |
| 255 | 0xff | `impdep2` |

# Appendix D

## Slices of Pi: A Simulation of the Java Virtual Machine

This appendix describes one final interactive illustration that's included on the CD-ROM that accompanies this book. The *Slices of Pi* applet, shown in Figure D-4, demonstrates a Java Virtual Machine executing a sequence of bytecodes that calculates pi. This applet is embedded in a web page on the CD-ROM in file called `applets/SlicesOfPi.html`.

## The `PiCalculator` Class

The bytecode sequence in the simulation was generated by `javac` for the `calculatePi()` method of the `PiCalculator` class as follows:

```
// On CD-ROM in file pi/ex1/PiCalculator.java
class PiCalculator {

    static void calculatePi() {

        double pi = 4.0;
        double sliceWidth = 0.5;
        double y;

        int iterations = 1;

        for (;;) {

            double x = 0.0;
            while (x < 1.0) {

                y = Math.sqrt(1 - (x * x));
                pi -= 4 * (sliceWidth * y);
                x += sliceWidth;

                y = Math.sqrt(1 - (x * x));
                pi += 4 * (sliceWidth * y);
                x += sliceWidth;
            }

            ++iterations;

            sliceWidth /= 2;
        }
    }
}
```

# The Algorithm

The `calculatePi()` method loops forever in an attempt to find and capture the elusive pi, the ratio of the circumference of a circle to its diameter. To calculate pi, the `calculatePi()` method tries to determine the area of a circle that has a radius of one. Because the circle has a radius of one, the circle's area is pi itself.

To determine the area of the circle with radius one, the `calculatePi()` method works to find the area of one fourth of the circle and then multiplies that area by four to get pi. Figure D-1 shows a circle with the area on which `calculatePi()` focuses shaded in gray.

To find the area of the portion of the circle shown in gray in Figure D-1, the `calculatePi()` method slices the area into progressively smaller rectangular segments, as shown in Figure D-2.

**Figure D-1.**
One fourth the area of a circle of radius one.

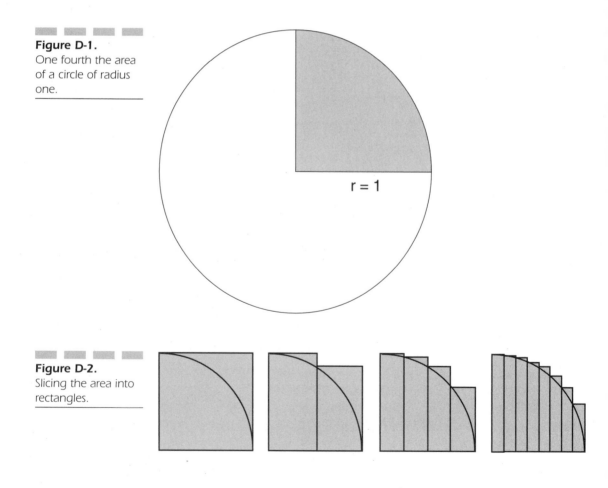

**Figure D-2.**
Slicing the area into rectangles.

Because calculating the area of a rectangle is a piece of cake (or in this case, a slice of pi), the `calculatePi()` method can approximate pi by calculating and summing the areas of the rectangles and then multiplying the result by four. As you can see from the diagram, this approach to calculating pi will always yield an approximation of pi that is too large. As the rectangles get thinner and more numerous, the approximation will get closer and closer to the real pi.

The `calculatePi()` method works by making repeated passes at calculating the area of the quarter circle, with each subsequent pass using a smaller slice width. Each iteration of `calculatePi()`'s for loop represents one attempt to calculate the area of the quarter circle. For any particular iteration of the for loop, the `slicewidth` variable gives the $x$ (horizontal) width of the slice, which remains constant during the entire iteration of the for loop. At the end of each for loop iteration, the slice width is halved.

The value of the `pi` variable keeps a running record of the current approximation of pi. Each pass of `calculatePi()`'s for loop starts by initializing the `x` local variable to 0.0 and then incrementing `x` by `slicewidth` until `x` reaches the end of the circle's radius at 1.0.

The while loop that is contained inside the for loop iterates once for every two slice widths. In effect, each iteration of the while loop takes a large rectangle from the previous iteration of the for loop, discards half of the large rectangle's area, and calculates a new value for the discarded portion. Because the slice width is halved at the end of each iteration of the for loop, the width of the rectangles calculated by the previous iteration of the for loop is always twice as wide as the slice width of the current iteration. Figure D-3 shows the steps the `calculatePi()` method takes to divide two rectangles into four.

**Figure D-3.**
Dividing two rectangles into four.

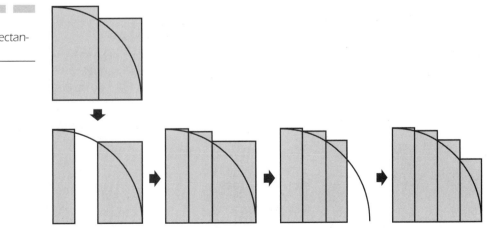

# The Results of the Algorithm

For a better idea of what kind of results you can expect from the `calculatePi()` method, consider this close cousin to the `PiCalculator` class:

```java
// On CD-ROM in file pi/ex1/PiCalculatorPrinter.java
class PiCalculatorPrinter {

    static void calculateAndPrintPi() {

        double pi = 4.0;
        double sliceWidth = 0.5;
        double y;

        int iterations = 1;

        for (;;) {

            double x = 0.0;
            while (x < 1.0) {

                y = Math.sqrt(1 - (x * x));
                pi -= 4 * (sliceWidth * y);
                x += sliceWidth;

                y = Math.sqrt(1 - (x * x));
                pi += 4 * (sliceWidth * y);
                x += sliceWidth;
            }

            System.out.println(iterations + ": " + pi);
            ++iterations;

            sliceWidth /= 2;
        }
    }

    public static void main(String[] args) {
        calculateAndPrintPi();
    }
}
```

The `PiCalculatorPrinter.calculateAndPrintPi()` method uses the same algorithm to calculate pi as the `PiCalculator.calculatePi()` method, but along the way `calculateAndPrintPi()` reports its progress to the standard output. Here is the output of `PiCalculatorPrinter`, when it is run as a Java application and left to work for a while:

```
1: 3.732050807568877
2: 3.4957090681024408
3: 3.339819144357174
4: 3.248253037827741
```

```
 5: 3.1976024228771323
 6: 3.170546912779685
 7: 3.156405792396616
 8: 3.1491180829572345
 9: 3.145397402719659
10: 3.143509891539023
11: 3.1425565279114656
12: 3.1420764488577837
13: 3.1418352081747196
14: 3.1417141631514287
15: 3.141653490490536
16: 3.141623101073998
17: 3.1416078875969236
18: 3.1416002742226636
19: 3.141596465189377
20: 3.1415945598432646
21: 3.141593606876806
22: 3.1415931302901634
23: 3.1415928919598097
24: 3.1415927727818502
25: 3.1415927131888464
26: 3.1415926833899084
27: 3.141592668491482
28: 3.141592661041216
29: 3.141592657315469
```

The value of the static final **PI** field of class **java.lang.Math**, which is the **double** value that is closer than any other to the real value of pi, is 3.14159265358979323846. As you can see from the preceding output, after 29 iterations of the for loop, the algorithm has generated the first nine significant decimal digits of pi: 3.14159265. As expected, all the approximations of pi are greater than the real value. The algorithm is approaching the real value of pi from above.

# The Bytecodes

The bytecodes generated by **javac** for the **calculatePi()** method are shown here:

```
// Push dual-byte value from constant pool entry
                // In this case, a double 4.0
 0 ldc2_w #10 <Double 4.0>
                // Pop double, store into local
 3 dstore_0     // variables 0 and 1: double pi = 4;
                // Push dual-byte value from constant
                // pool entry. In this case, a
                // double 0.5
 4 ldc2_w #6 <Double 0.5>
```

```
                                 // Pop double, store into local
                                 // variables 2 and 3:
       7 dstore_2                // double slicewidth = 0.5;
       8 iconst_1                // Push int constant 1
                                 // Pop int, store into local
       9 istore 6                // variable 6: int iterations = 1;
      11 dconst_0                // Push double constant 0.0
                                 // Pop double, store into local
      12 dstore 7                // variables 7 and 8: double x = 0.0;
      14 goto 75                 // Jump to offset 75
      17 dconst_1                // Push double constant 1.0
                                 // Push double from local variables 7
      18 dload 7                 // and 8 (x)
                                 // Push double from local variables 7
      20 dload 7                 // and 8 (x)
                                 // Pop two doubles, multiply them, push
      22 dmul                    // double result
                                 // Pop two doubles, subtract them, push
      23 dsub                    // double result
                                 // Invoke the static method indicated
                                 // by the constant entry, in this case
                                 // Math.sqrt(double), which pops a
                                 // double parameter and pushes a double
                                 // return value
      24 invokestatic #5 <Method double sqrt(double)>
                                 // Pop double, store into local
                                 // variables 4 and 5:
      27 dstore 4                // y = Math.sqrt(1 - (x * x));
                                 // Push double from local variables 0
      29 dload_0                 // and 1 (pi)
                                 // Push dual-byte value from constant
                                 // pool entry. In this case, a
                                 // double 4.0
      30 ldc2_w #10 <Double 4.0>
                                 // Push double from local variables 2
      33 dload_2                 // and 3 (slicewidth)
                                 // Push double from local variables 4
      34 dload 4                 // and 5 (y)
                                 // Pop two doubles, multiply them, push
      36 dmul                    // double result
                                 // Pop two doubles, multiply them, push
      37 dmul                    // double result
                                 // Pop two doubles, subtract them, push
      38 dsub                    // result double
                                 // Pop double, store into local
                                 // variables 0 and 1:
      39 dstore_0                // pi -= 4 * (slicewidth * y);
                                 // Push double from local variables 7
      40 dload 7                 // and 8 (x)
                                 // Push double from local variables 2
      42 dload_2                 // and 3 (slicewidth)
                                 // Pop two doubles, add them, push
      43 dadd                    // double result
```

```
                          // Pop double, store into local
44 dstore 7               // variables 7 and 8: x += slicewidth;
46 dconst_1               // Push double constant 1.0
                          // Push double from local variables 7
47 dload 7                // and 8 (x)
                          // Push double from local variables 7
49 dload 7                // and 8 (x)
                          // Pop two doubles, multiply them, push
51 dmul                   // double result
                          // Pop two doubles, subtract them, push
52 dsub                   // double result
                          // Invoke the static method indicated
                          // by the constant entry, in this case
                          // Math.sqrt(double), which pops a
                          // double parameter and pushes a double
                          // return value
53 invokestatic #5 <Method double sqrt(double)>
                          // Pop double, store into local
                          // variables 4 and 5:
56 dstore 4               // y = Math.sqrt(1 - (x * x));
                          // Push double from local variables 0
58 dload_0                // and 1 (pi)
                          // Push dual-byte value from constant
                          // pool entry. In this case, a
                          // double 4.0
59 ldc2_w #10 <Double 4.0>
                          // Push double from local variables 2
62 dload_2                // and 3 (slicewidth)
                          // Push double from local variables 4
63 dload 4                // and 5 (y)
                          // Pop two doubles, multiply them, push
65 dmul                   // double result
                          // Pop two doubles, multiply them, push
66 dmul                   // double result
                          // Pop two doubles, add them, push
67 dadd                   // double result
                          // Pop double, store into local
                          // variables 0 and 1:
68 dstore_0               // pi += 4 * (slicewidth * y);
                          // Push double from local variables 7
69 dload 7                // and 8 (x)
                          // Push double from local variables 2
71 dload_2                // and 3 (slicewidth)
                          // Pop two doubles, add them, push
72 dadd                   // double result
                          // Pop double, store into local
73 dstore 7               // variables 7 and 8: x += slicewidth;
                          // Push double from local variables 7
75 dload 7                // and 8 (x)
77 dconst_1               // Push double constant 1.0
                          // Pop two doubles, compare them, push
78 dcmpg                  // int result
                          // Pop int, branch if less than zero to
```

```
79 iflt 17          // offset 17: while (x < 1.0) {}
                    // Increment local variable 6 by 1:
82 iinc 6 1         // ++iterations;
                    // Push double from local variables 2
85 dload_2          // and 3 (slicewidth)
                    // Push dual-byte value from constant
                    // pool entry. In this case, a
                    // double 2.0
86 ldc2_w #8 <Double 2.0>
                    // Pop two doubles, divide them, push
89 ddiv             // double result
                    // Pop double, store into local
90 dstore_2         // variables 2 and 3: slicewidth /= 2;
                    // Jump unconditionally to offset 11:
91 goto 11          // for(;;) {}
```

Note that the `calculatePi()` method includes a few good demonstrations of the way in which the Java Virtual Machine calculates larger expressions using the operand stack. To calculate the "`pi -= 4 * (slicewidth * y);`" expression, for example, the Java Virtual Machine pushes all four values (`pi`, 4.0, `slicewidth`, and `y`) onto the operand stack; then it performs two multiply instructions and a subtract, finally storing the result into the `pi` local variable. In addition, to calculate "`(1 - (x * x))`," the Java Virtual Machine pushes all three values (1, `x`, and `x`) onto the operand stack and then performs a multiply and a subtract.

# The Trouble with `double`

The `calculatePi()` method has two major problems. First, it takes a long time to get even a few significant digits of pi. Its inherent slowness is compounded by the fact that it is running in a simulated Java Virtual Machine that executes only about two instructions a second.

The other major problem with the `calculatePi()` method is that it doesn't deal with rounding errors. Although the `calculatePi()` method will indeed execute forever, eventually the `sliceWidth /= 2;` statement will cause the value of `sliceWidth` to underflow to zero. After that, the value of the `pi` variable will never change, but its value won't be equal to `Math.PI` because of rounding errors that accumulate prior to the `pi` variable reaching its final value.

Despite these problems, the `calculatePi()` method does serve as a good example of the Java Virtual Machine operating on `double`s and calculating larger expressions.

# Running the Applet

As you run the simulation, you can monitor the progress of the **calculatePi()** method by watching the local variables portion of the stack frame. The local variables of **calculatePi()** were arranged by the **javac** compiler into the local variable slots of the stack frame as shown in Table D-1.

To drive the *Slices of Pi* simulation, which is shown in Figure D-4, use the Step, Reset, Run, and Stop buttons. Each time you press the Step but-

**Table D-1**

The local variables of **calculatePi()**

| Local Variable | Slot(s) |
| --- | --- |
| pi | 0 and 1 |
| slicewidth | 2 and 3 |
| y | 4 and 5 |
| iterations | 6 |
| x | 7 and 8 |

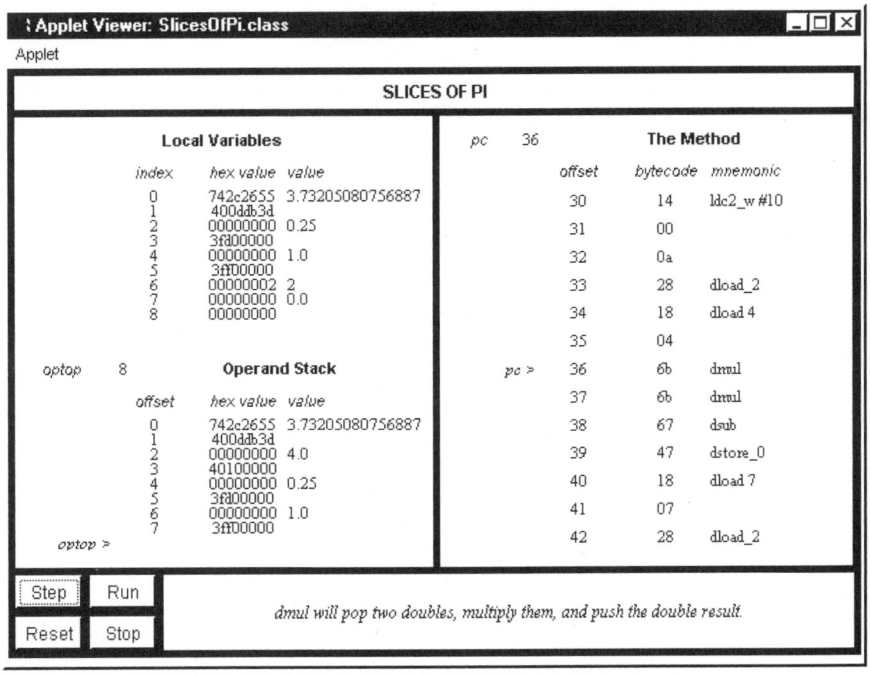

**Figure D-4.**
The **Slices of Pi** applet.

ton, the simulator will execute the instruction pointed to by the pc register. If you press the Run button, the simulation will continue with no further coaxing on your part until you press the Stop button. To start the simulation over, press the Reset button. Happy clicking.

# On the CD-ROM

The CD-ROM contains the source code examples from this appendix in the **pi** directory. The *Slices of Pi* applet is part of a web page on the CD-ROM in file **applets/SlicesOfPi.html**. The source code for this applet is found alongside its class files, in the **applets/JVMSimulators** and **applets/JVMSimulators/COM/artima/jvmsim** directories.

# INDEX

# ABOUT THE AUTHOR

Bill Venners provides software consulting services to Silicon Valley and the world under the name Artima Software Company (`http://www.artima.com`). You can reach him at `bv@artima.com`.

This binary code license ("License") contains rights and restrictions associated with use of the accompanying software and documentation ("Software"). Read the License carefully before installing the Software. By installing the Software you agree to the terms and conditions of this License.

**1. Limited License Grant.** Sun grants to you ("Licensee") a non-exclusive, non-transferable limited license to use the Software without fee for evaluation of the Software and for development of Java symbol 228 \f "Symbol" \s 12 ‰ compatible applets and applications. Licensee may make one archival copy of the Software. Licensee may not re-distribute the Software in whole or in part, either separately or included with a product. Refer to the Java Runtime Environment Version 1.1.4 binary code license (http://www.javasoft.com/ products/JDK/1.1.4/index.html) for the availability of runtime code which may be distributed with Java compatible applets and applications.

**2. Java Platform Interface.** Licensee may not modify the Java Platform Interface ("JPI", identified as classes contained within the "java" package or any subpackages of the "java" package), by creating additional classes within the JPI or otherwise causing the addition to or modification of the classes in the JPI. In the event that Licensee creates any Java-related API and distributes such API to others for applet or application development, Licensee must promptly publish an accurate specification for such API for free use by all developers of Java-based software.

**3. Restrictions.** Software is confidential copyrighted information of Sun and title to all copies is retained by Sun and/or its licensors. Licensee shall not modify, decompile, disassemble, decrypt, extract, or otherwise reverse engineer Software. Software may not be leased, assigned, or sublicensed, in whole or in part. **Software is not designed or intended for use in on-line control of aircraft, air traffic, aircraft navigation or aircraft communications; or in the design, construction, operation or maintenance of any nuclear facility. Licensee warrants that it will not use or redistribute the Software for such purposes.**

**4. Trademarks and Logos.** This License does not authorize Licensee to use any Sun name, trademark or logo. Licensee acknowledges that Sun owns the Java trademark and all Java-related trademarks, logos and icons including the Coffee Cup and Duke ("Java Marks") and agrees to: (i) to comply with the Java Trademark Guidelines at http://java.com/trademarks.html; (ii) not do anything harmful to or inconsistent with Sun's rights in the Java Marks; and (iii) assist Sun in protecting those rights, including assigning to Sun any rights acquired by Licensee in any Java Mark.

**5. Disclaimer of Warranty.** Software is provided "AS IS," without a warranty of any kind. ALL EXPRESS OR IMPLIED REPRESENTATIONS AND WARRANTIES, INCLUDING ANY IMPLIED WARRANTY OF MERCHANTABILITY, FITNESS FOR A PARTICULAR PURPOSE OR NON-INFRINGEMENT, ARE HEREBY EXCLUDED.

**6. Limitation of Liability.** SUN AND ITS LICENSORS SHALL NOT BE LIABLE FOR ANY DAMAGES SUFFERED BY LICENSEE OR ANY THIRD PARTY AS A RESULT OF USING OR DISTRIBUTING SOFTWARE. IN NO EVENT WILL SUN OR ITS LICENSORS BE LIABLE FOR ANY LOST REVENUE, PROFIT OR DATA, OR FOR DIRECT, INDIRECT, SPECIAL, CONSEQUENTIAL, INCIDENTAL OR PUNITIVE DAMAGES, HOWEVER CAUSED AND REGARDLESS OF THE THEORY OF LIABILITY, ARISING OUT OF THE USE OF OR INABILITY TO USE SOFTWARE, EVEN IF SUN HAS BEEN ADVISED OF THE POSSIBILITY OF SUCH DAMAGES.

**7. Termination.** Licensee may terminate this License at any time by destroying all copies of Software. This License will terminate immediately without notice from Sun if Licensee fails to comply with any provision of this License. Upon such termination, Licensee must destroy all copies of Software.

**8. Export Regulation.** Software, including technical data, is subject to U.S. export control laws, including the U.S. Export Administration Act and its associated regulations, and may be subject to export or import regulations in other countries. Licensee agrees to comply strictly with all such regulations and acknowledges that it has the responsibility to obtain licenses to export, re-export, or import Software. Software may not be downloaded, or otherwise exported or re-exported (i) into, or to a national or resident of, Cuba, Iraq, Iran, North Korea, Libya, Sudan, Syria or any country to which the U.S. has embargoed goods; or (ii) to anyone on the U.S. Treasury Department's list of Specially Designated Nations or the U.S. Commerce Department's Table of Denial Orders.

**9. Restricted Rights.** Use, duplication or disclosure by the United States government is subject to the restrictions as set forth in the Rights in Technical Data and Computer Software Clauses in DFARS 252.227-7013(c)(1)(ii) and FAR 52.227-19(c)(2) as applicable.

**10. Governing Law.** Any action related to this License will be governed by California law and controlling U.S. federal law. No choice of law rules of any jurisdiction will apply.

**11. Severability.** If any of the above provisions are held to be in violation of applicable law, void, or unenforceable in any jurisdiction, then such provisions are herewith waived to the extent necessary for the License to be otherwise enforceable in such jurisdiction. However, if in Sun's opinion deletion of any provisions of the License by operation of this paragraph unreasonably compromises the rights or increase the liabilities of Sun or its licensors, Sun reserves the right to terminate the License and refund the fee paid by Licensee, if any, as Licensee's sole and exclusive remedy.